Advanced Financial Accounting

Sixth Edition

JOHN C.C. MACINTOSH, Ph.D., C.A. (SA)
York University

with a contribution by

Ian P.N. Hague, B.Sc., C.A.
Principal, Accounting Standards Board

Captus Press

ADVANCED FINANCIAL ACCOUNTING, Sixth Edition

Copyright © 1991–2005 by John C.C. Macintosh and Captus Press Inc.

First Published 1991; Fifth Edition 2001; Sixth Edition 2005

Captus Press Inc.
Units 14 & 15
1600 Steeles Avenue West
Concord, Ontario   L4K 4M2   Canada
Phone: (416) 736–5537
Fax: (416) 736–5793
Email: info@captus.com
Internet: http://www.captus.com

Excerpts from and references to the CICA *Handbook* and case material referenced CICA FQE are reprinted with the permission of the Canadian Institute of Chartered Accountants, Toronto.

The names given to companies, institutions, and individuals in the cases, exercises, and problems included in this text are fictitious. Any resemblance to living or deceased persons or to existing companies is co-incidental.

Canada We acknowledge the financial support of the Government of Canada through the Book Publishing Industry Development Program (BPIDP) for our publishing activities.

The National Library of Canada has catalogued this publication as follows:

Advanced financial accounting (North York, Ont.)
  Advanced financial accounting

Every 2 or 3 years.
[1st ed.] –
Prepared by John C.C. Macintosh, 1st ed.-   .
ISSN 1205–2965
ISBN 1–55322–090–0 (6th edition)

1. Accounting.   I. Macintosh, John C.C.   II. Title.

HF5635.M135   657'.046   C97–300637–4

0 9 8 7 6 5 4 3 2
Printed in Canada

Table of Contents

APPENDICES

Preface to Sixth Edition

The preparation of this edition has provided me with the opportunity to revise and review the text in accordance with the overall philosophy of the text of being "lean and mean" and "straight to the point". Consequently, unnecessary material has been eliminated from the text wherever possible. As with the previous editions, it continues to use the "analysis of equity" approach to the consolidation of financial statements.

The case material has all been re-examined and a considerable number of new exercises and problems have been added. The text has also been extensively updated. Specifically, Chapter One on the nature of financial reporting has been revised to take the effects of the accounting scandals of 2001–2002 into account and the changes in the requirements for compliance with the CICA *Handbook*. Chapters 18, 19, and 20 have also been widely reviewed to clarify the application of the accounting and control requirements for nonprofit organizations and entities of the public sector. Chapter 17 on financial instruments and the hedging of currency risk has been completely rewritten by Ian P.N. Hague, principal with the Canadian Accounting Standards Board, who is acknowledged both nationally and internationally as an expert in this field.

I also wish to acknowledge the constructive criticisms of the fifth edition of the text by Dominique Lecocq and Sandra Scott, whose names have, consequently, been added to the long list of those who have provided such helpful information and constructive criticisms on the previous editions. I also wish, once again, to place on record my sincere thanks to Peter Martin of the Canadian Institute of Chartered Accountants for answering my many questions relating to the recent changes in accounting requirements. The responsibility of the text remains, of course, entirely mine.

John C.C. Macintosh
Toronto
June 15, 2004

The Nature of Financial Reporting 1

LEARNING OBJECTIVES

After studying this chapter you should be able to:

1. Understand the nature of financial reporting and the environment in which it takes place in Canada;
2. Appreciate the need for a theoretical framework on which to base the development of accounting; and
3. Understand what is meant by the term "generally accepted accounting principles" and their application and enforcement in Canada.

THE MEANING OF THE TERM "FINANCIAL REPORTING"

The term "financial reporting" covers a wide and complex area of accounting. It is normally used to refer to the provision of information on the financial activities and operations of a business corporation to those **persons external** to the reporting entity who have no other means of obtaining the information they need. It is affected by the social, economic, legal and political environment in which it operates and, to further complicate the issue, the various approaches to financial reporting have different objectives. There are also different theories on which the reporting is based. As a result, no definition of the term is completely acceptable to all accountants.

Notwithstanding its description, financial reporting is not restricted to the provision of financial information. Certain other information of a non-financial nature may be provided to satisfy either statutory or professional reporting requirements or management's perceptions of the users' informational needs. It is recognized, however, that the non-financial information included in financial reports should only be provided to make the financial statements more meaningful or to meet specific informational needs.

Originally, financial reports were mainly concerned with reporting the results of past operations and activities. Today, with a greater public interest in the role of corporations in society and the increased complexity of corporate activities, financial reporting has become more standardized and financial reports include considerable future and socially oriented information. As a result, there has been a significant increase in both the provision of quantitative and narrative information in financial reports.

No matter how the approach to financial reporting and the information provided in financial reports may have changed over the years, its basic purpose has remained the same. It was originally conceived as the means of communicating information on the operations and activities of the reporting entity to interested parties, and this has not changed.

What has, however, occurred is that two different approaches to financial reporting have emerged. In the USA, the provision of information for economic decision-making has been accepted as the basis for financial reporting while, elsewhere, an approach based on accountability enjoys considerable support amongst accountants.[1]

THE TWO APPROACHES TO FINANCIAL REPORTING

The Investment Decision Approach to Financial Reporting

The investment decision approach to financial reporting enjoys widespread acceptance amongst contemporary accountants and it has been accepted in the USA for many years as the basic purpose of financial statements. It is based on the premise that the main objective of accounting (and, consequently, financial reporting) is to provide information useful for making economic decisions.

This approach to financial reporting is attributable to an almost general acceptance by American accounting academics and accounting associations of the neo-classical theory of investment on which much of the study of corporate finance is based. It is, therefore, mainly concerned with the provision of information considered necessary for the making of investment decisions and the efficient operation of capital markets. In this respect, the objective of economic decision-making is to facilitate "buy, hold or sell" decisions by investors and to evaluate alternative investments through the prediction of future cash flows to them from dividends and the estimated selling price of their securities.

The investment-decision approach is justified on the grounds that it satisfies the needs of existing and potential shareholders and loan creditors who are the most prominent group of users of financial information. It also satisfies the needs of those financial intermediaries, like stockbrokers and financial analysts, who are actively involved in the trading of corporate securities.

It also reflects the influence of those concerned with corporate finance on present day accounting thought. Today, accounting is viewed as being primarily concerned with the presentation of information on activities and financial position, while corporate finance uses the information provided by accountants for decision-making purposes. However, the distinction between accounting and corporate finance is, at times, somewhat blurred, and it is often difficult to see exactly where the one function ends and the other begins.

It is also understandable why the investment decision approach to financial reporting is supported by the proponents of the **efficient markets hypothesis** (EMH). The EMH is based on the assumption that security markets are free and competitive, and that share prices reflect the equilibrium price for that security (i.e., where supply equals demand at the prevailing price). **The efficiency of the market is measured by the speed at which it reacts to**

---

[1]   In a survey carried out in 1977 by the Financial Accounting Standards Board, only 37% of the respondents supported the contention that the main objective of financial statements was to provide information useful for making economic decisions whilst, those who disagreed (i.e., 63%) generally took the position that the most important objective of financial reporting was to report on management's stewardship over corporate assets (Marshall S. Armstrong, "The Politics of Establishing Accounting Standards", *The Journal of Accountancy*, February 1977). In 1980, a survey carried out for the Financial Accounting Foundation found that 52% of all respondents felt that the stewardship function should either receive priority in financial reporting or was at least equal in importance to meeting the "decision usefulness" (or investment decision) objective (Louis Harris and Associates, *A Study of the Attitudes Toward and an Assessment of the Financial Accounting Standards Board*, Prepared for the Financial Accounting Foundation, 1980).

the information provided. The assumption is that financial reports are only used by sophisticated financial intermediaries and market analysts who participate in the market either for themselves or on behalf of their investors and, therefore, the reports should only be directed at highly sophisticated users.

This approach supports the use of general purpose financial statements. It is based on the belief that since it is impossible to provide financial information that will satisfy the needs of all users, a single set of financial statements is produced which, hopefully, meets all their informational needs. In this respect, it is generally believed that the information of interest to investors and creditors also satisfies the informational needs of other users.

The Accountability Approach to Financial Reporting

The accountability (or stewardship) approach to financial reporting is based on the principle of accountability, which presumes a relationship between two parties; an accountor is accountable for his actions to an accountee.[2] Where this situation exists, the accountor is both morally and legally bound to give an account of his actions to the accountee.

Even though the concept of accountability still applies to present day financial reporting, it is usually viewed in its traditional connotation. This is because accountability developed from the English Manorial system from the need for the Lord of the Manor to obtain from his stewards (i.e., managers), to whom the use of and custodianship over the assets and resources had been entrusted, an account of their actions.

With the development of the corporate form of business organization in Britain in the 19th century, accountability became the basis of financial reporting. The officers of companies were entrusted with the control and use of investors' capital, and were held accountable to them for their actions. Where companies were large enough for a division between ownership and management to exist, management was looked upon as a group of persons running a business for the benefit of the shareholders, to whom they were strictly accountable.[3] In 1844, the principle of accountability was enshrined in British corporate law by the *Joint Stock Companies Act* which, for the first time, required companies to issue audited balance sheets to their shareholders.

Over the years, this accountability requirement has been extended in corporate law in Britain, Canada and many other countries to cover all financial reporting requirements. Shareholders are looked upon as joint owners of companies to which management is strictly accountable. In view of the British influence on the development of Canada, this aspect underlies the reporting philosophy of the *Canada Business Corporations Act* and Canadian provincial corporate law.

It should be noted that in the USA, corporate reporting is based on British corporate law in operation at the time of the American War of Independence (i.e., 1775–1783). At that time the requirement to provide shareholders with audited financial statements was not in operation, and the present requirements apparently stem from the listing requirements the New York Stock Exchange.[4]

---

[2] For a full analysis of the modern accountability approach to financial reporting, see Yuji Ijiri, *Theory of Accounting Measurement*, Studies in Accounting Research No. 10, American Accounting Association, 1975.

[3] See Michael Chatfield, *A History of Accounting Thought* (Hinsdale, IL: Dryden, 1974) for an excellent and comprehensive review of the situation.

[4] See *The Journal of Accountancy* (May 1933, p. 31), where, as part of the editorial comment, it was reported that the New York Stock Exchange would require audited financial statements from all companies applying for listing after July 1, 1933.

The Effects of These Two Approaches on Financial Reporting

The emphasis placed on the investment decision approach to financial reporting in contemporary accounting literature has, unfortunately, led to a situation where the objective of accountability is frequently overlooked and, at times, even ignored. The main criterion is the provision of information for the efficient operation of security markets, and financial reporting is seen as applying almost entirely to those companies whose securities are publicly traded. In these conditions, there is little need to be concerned with the communication of information to users because they are expected to be sufficiently knowledgeable in financial matters to understand the information provided; if not, they are expected to seek expert advice. And, because the direction of the reporting is specified as applying to investors and loan creditors, there is little need to consider the needs of other users or potential users of financial reports.[5]

On the other hand, financial reporting based on the traditional accountability or stewardship approach[6] enjoys considerable support. This is probably because in Canada, like the USA and many other countries, the majority of businesses are small and it is accepted that the reporting system should provide information on the use of resources to those persons who have invested in these businesses.

The question of whether or not accountability still forms the basis of reporting by those large companies whose securities are publicly traded on a stock exchange is, however, a matter for debate. This is because the wide dispersion of ownership of the large public companies has resulted in a position that, where shareholders are dissatisfied with the performance of the company, they are more likely to sell their investments in the company than demand from management an account of their actions. However, today, from a purely social point of view, it is recognized that the large, publicly-owned corporations are increasingly being held accountable by society for their actions relating to the protection of the environment, their hiring practices and their place in the community in which they operate.

The incredible growth in the investment in the shares of public companies by the institutional investors (i.e., insurance companies, mutual funds and pension funds) over the past three decades **indicates** that some type of shareholder control may re-emerge in the future, albeit among major shareholders. This will occur as these institutional investors reach the position where they will have an effect on the election of directors of the large public companies in which they have invested.

What is important is that, no matter how they are viewed, both approaches to financial reporting are still fully accepted by accountants and, consequently, there is no consensus amongst them.

---

[5] The entire field of financial reporting is in a state of change as we enter the "information age". For example, the Ontario Securities Commission has formulated rules for the implementation of the *System for Electronic Document Analysis and Retrieval* for the electronic filing of information by companies. In the USA, the similar *Electronic Data Gathering and Retrieval System* (EDGAR) of the Securities and Exchange Commission has been in operation for many years.

[6] This approach has, since the early 1980s, been rationalized in terms of agency theory. However, as far as Robert N. Anthony (*Tell It Like It Was: A Conceptual Framework for Financial Accounting*, Homewood, IL: Irwin, 1983, p. 224) is concerned, there is no difference between agency theory and stewardship for financial reporting purposes.

THE ENVIRONMENT IN WHICH FINANCIAL REPORTING TAKES PLACE

The Financial Reporting Environment

The environment in which financial reporting takes place is highly regulated. This is because reporting systems are heavily influenced by the political, social and economic conditions in which they operate. For example, the financial reporting system in operation in Brazil or France, where the majority of businesses are privately owned, differs considerably from that found in Canada, the USA, the Netherlands, Britain and the rest of the English-speaking world, where there is a public ownership of companies. These conditions are reflected by the legal and professional requirements covering financial reporting, which specify what information is to be provided and how it should be presented.

This regulation is justified on the grounds that, without such control, financial reports would be based purely on management's perceptions of users' needs, and would fail to provide investors with all the information considered necessary for investment decision-making or their other informational needs. It is also likely that without any control, financial reports would reflect management's self interests in presenting the company's affairs in the best possible light. This regulation reduces what is referred to as the "**conflict between preparers and users**" by specifying the minimum level of disclosure of information in financial reports.

Additional strict reporting requirements also apply to financial reporting by companies whose securities are publicly traded on a recognized stock exchange. These requirements are necessary to facilitate the marketing of securities and to ensure that the interests of investors are not prejudiced through the selective disclosure of information. Without such regulation, the operation of the capital markets system (i.e., the utilization of the financial resources of individuals to provide the capital for commercial and industrial development) would be virtually impossible.

To fully understand the position as it applies in Canada, it is necessary to examine the development of the financial reporting environment in both Britain and the USA.

Historical Background of Regulation

It is generally recognized that accounting developed as the needs for record keeping and the control of resources arose. What is not always appreciated is that it was the development of the modern publicly-owned corporation that led to the regulation of financial reporting.

This first occurred in Britain through the passing of a series of Acts of the British Parliament to control and regulate the activities of companies and to ensure that they were accountable to investors. Of these, the *Joint Stock Companies Act of 1844* was the most important because it allowed companies to be formed by registration rather than by Royal Charter, required companies to keep proper books of account and, as outlined earlier, to provide shareholders with audited balance sheets of the companies in which they had invested.

The need for audited financial statements led, in turn, to the development of the accounting profession and its organization into professional associations. These associations were initially concerned with the regulation of professional activities but, as they became more organized, they began to issue recommendations to their members on various accounting matters, including those relating to their responsibilities as auditors. At the same time, a series of important British legal cases provided accountants with a clearer picture of their responsibilities to the public. Many of these were incorporated into British corporate law, which now includes relatively detailed financial reporting requirements.

At this stage, many British accountants had emigrated to the USA and were instrumental in the organization of the American accounting profession. Conditions differed considerably because most businesses in the USA at that time were relatively small, and American corporate law was based on that in operation at the time of the American War of Independence (i.e., 1775–1783).

Even though attempts were made to regulate financial reporting in the USA, very little was achieved until after the crash of the New York Stock Exchange in 1929. What occurred was that, following a period of unprecedented economic growth and speculation, the American investing public lost confidence in corporate securities and the banking sector that led to the virtual collapse of the entire American capital market system. In 1933, the Senate Committee investigating the reasons for this collapse exposed a sordid picture of how bankers and stock market dealers had manipulated stock prices through cleverly designed marketing schemes and insider trading.[7]

It was recognized that something had to be done to restore the confidence of the American investing public. This led, first, to passing of the *Securities Act* of 1933, which required the full disclosure of information by the sellers of new securities and imposed severe penalties on those responsible for the omission or misstatement of any material fact in prospectuses. This was followed by the *Securities and Exchange Act* of 1934, which created the **Securities and Exchange Commission** (SEC) to administer the *Securities Act* and to regulate the various securities markets in the USA, the marketing of securities, and the "full and fair" disclosure of information by those companies whose securities were traded on those markets. As far as financial reporting was concerned, the effect of this was that an authoritative body was established with the primary responsibility of satisfying investor and loan creditor needs. The responsibility for setting the actual accounting standards was delegated by the SEC to, first, the American Institute of Certified Public Accountants, and then to the FASB in 1973.

Financial reporting in the USA is, therefore, closely monitored by the SEC to ensure that it meets the needs of the investing public and to take action when required (e.g., following the accounting scandals of 2001–2003 covered later). Its reporting requirements are also directed at a sophisticated audience of financial analysts, investment dealers and other financial intermediaries like stockbrokers, etc.

The Position in Canada

The environment in which financial reporting takes place in Canada is the result of both the British and American requirements. Canadian corporate law is based on British corporate law applying immediately before Confederation in 1867. As a result, the financial reporting requirements of Canadian corporate law are based largely on the principle of accountability and, except where companies are exempt from these requirements on account of their nature,[8] there is an audit requirement. It also follows the American model because financial reporting by companies whose securities are publicly traded is strictly controlled and monitored by the Securities Commissions of Alberta, British Columbia, Ontario, Saskatchewan, and Quebec which operate in much the same manner as the SEC in the USA.

In Canada accounting standards are set by the Accounting Standards Board (AcSB) of the CICA. They are given the "force of law" because the *Canada Business Corporations Act* (and all provincial corporate law) requires that the financial statements issued to shareholders must "be prepared in accordance with the standards, as they exist from time to time, of the Canadian Institute of Chartered Accountants set out in the C.I.C.A. Handbook."[9]

The overall objective of this regulation is, first, to ensure that, within the limitations of historical cost accounting, financial reports reasonably reflect the results of operations and financial position of the reporting entity. Second, it is necessary to facilitate the operation of capital markets. In this respect, financial reports should allow for the comparison of results of

---

[7] See M.P. Mayer, Extract from *Wall Street: Men and Money*, New York: Harper, 1955, for a detailed explanation of what took place.

[8] In 1994, Parliament amended the *Canada Business Corporations Act*, eliminating the requirement for privately-held corporations to file audited financial statements with the director of the Corporations Branch of Industry Canada. As a result, these companies will now be able to decide for themselves if they wish to be audited.

[9] Section 44 of the *Regulations Under the Canada Business Corporations Act*.

operations and financial position of companies within the same industry. To do so, the minimum amount of information to be disclosed in financial reports is strictly prescribed.

Accounting standards for nonprofit organizations (NPOs) are also set by the AcSB of the CICA. Financial reporting by NPOs has not been as strictly controlled as that of the private sector and the objective of the CICA has been to set standards designed to standardize reporting by these entities.

Since 1981, the Public Sector Accounting Board (PSAB) of the CICA has also been entrusted with setting standards for the federal, provincial, territorial and local governments and their various agencies and corporations. As a result of their efforts, considerable progress has been made in improving and standardizing the financial reporting practices of these bodies.

RECENT DEVELOPMENTS IN CORPORATE FINANCIAL REPORTING

The Effects of the Accounting Scandals of 2001–2002

During 2001 and 2002, investors in the USA and elsewhere were shocked to learn that a number of large and ostensibly successful companies had inflated their profits through incorrect revenue recognition and through the use of complicated and highly innovative schemes to misrepresent their financial position. In the case of Enron, a Houston, Texas-based energy trader, the company entered into partnerships with outsiders that were, in effect, nothing more than cleverly designed schemes to convert investments or loans into revenue flows.[10,11]

Since these revelations were made public, additional scandals have rocked the financial analyst community, the mutual fund industry, and the bond markets. Certain financial analysts were found to have issued favourable reports on companies that they themselves knew to be false in order to secure lucrative investment banking fees. More recently, preferential trading activities by mutual fund managers for their own benefit and the charging of excessive fees have come to light. This has led to a general lack of confidence in both the accounting profession and the integrity of the securities markets themselves.

The Failure of the Audit Function

The most disturbing of all was the fact that the audit function, considered the shareholders' last safeguard against improper actions by management, failed to expose the inflation of profits by Enron and others. In an investigation by the SEC in the USA that commenced in October 2001, the accounting firm of Arthur Andersen & Company (Enron's auditors), that had received massive consulting fees (about US $500-million which was roughly twice the annual audit fee) from Enron during the period under review, was found to have destroyed thousands of documents and e-mail messages sought by the investigating committee. This deliberate destruction of evidence, together with other revelations about the cozy relationship between the auditors and the management of Enron, led to the demise of the accounting firm

---

10 The type of scheme carried out was that the company invested, say, $10-million in a partnership made up of itself and a senior executive of the company acting in his personal capacity. The partnership then purchased a licence to trade in the goods and services of the lender from the lender for $10-million. The loan of $10-million was, therefore, converted from an investment or loan into a revenue flow to the investor. The loan to the partnership was then treated as an account receivable.

11 The manipulation of earnings, together with other questionable accounting practices, allowed Enron to deliberately overstate its earnings by US $580-million over the four-year period 1997–2001. When the facts became known, the company filed for bankruptcy protection and its share prices plummeted from US $83 in January 2001 to US 67 cents by January 2002. Some of its senior executives have been charged with securities fraud but, as this text went to press, none had been convicted.

following the cancellation of its licence to practice. It also led to a general scepticism relating to the independence of auditors and what reliance could be placed on the audit function in both Canada and the USA.[12]

The failure of the audit function, once again, raised the question of whether accounting firms having consulting arms can operate independently in their dealings with their audit clients? In responding to the concerns by the investing public and the regulatory authorities, virtually all of the major accounting firms in Canada and the USA have now divested themselves of their consulting divisions.

Part of the problem is that the amount paid to auditors is not a disclosable expense in terms of the CICA *Handbook*. For many years companies in other countries, like Australia and the United Kingdom of Great Britain, have been required to disclose the amounts paid to auditors in the notes to their financial statements distinguishing between the amounts paid for audit services and those for "other services" (which must be detailed) so that the amounts paid to the auditors can be questioned by shareholders and the financial press. In 2000, the SEC in the USA changed the position by requiring companies to disclose the amounts paid to their auditors in their proxy statements.[13] No such requirement applies in Canada and the practice is entirely voluntary. A large percentage of Canadian companies whose securities are publicly traded do, however, disclose the amounts paid to their auditors in their financial statements.

To ensure that there is no repeat of the accounting scandals, the Public Company Accounting Oversight Board was established in the USA. This board, under the control of the SEC, is to oversee accountants acting as auditors of US companies traded on the NYSE and NASDAQ. Its powers also extend to those foreign accounting firms that audit companies whose shares are traded on the US securities markets. And, as one of its first actions, the Board voted to strip the AICPA of its authority to issue auditing standards after concluding that the accounting profession could no longer regulate itself effectively.[14]

Following the US lead, the Canadian Public Accountability Board was formed in 2002 with the mission of contributing to the public confidence in financial reporting and to promote high-quality and independent auditing. The CPAB is to inspect firms that audit public companies to ensure that they comply with professional standards, rules and regulatory requirements. It will also serve to satisfy the requirements of the SEC relating to the audit of Canadian companies whose shares are traded on the US security markets.[15]

The formation of the CPAB is unlikely to satisfy its critics, because its independence is jeopardized by drawing part of its financing from the CICA. The problem is that both accounting and auditing standards in Canada are set by the accounting profession, and not an independent body as in the USA. Accounting standards in the USA are set by the FASB, and those relating to auditing have, as outlined above, been taken away from the American Institute of Certified Public Accountants by the Public Company Accounting Oversight Board. It is a case of **the setting of standards by accountants for other accountants to follow**. As ex-Professor of Accounting Al Rosen contends, auditors are still pretty close to management because they are appointed by operating management, whose appointments are then rubber stamped by the directors and shareholders.[16]

The Ontario government also formed a Public Accounts Council in August 2003 to enforce new rules relating to the qualification and professional conduct of the auditors of

---

[12]   For example, in 2003 and 2004 serious accounting problems were also reported by Nortel Networks, Canada's high-tech flagship. Of the greatest concern was that the company reported that it was going to restate its financial statements for the second time in three years (*The Globe and Mail*, May 3, 2004). Revelations of this nature make one wonder what the auditors were doing.

[13]   See *The Wall Street Journal* as reported by *The Globe and Mail* of April 10, 2001.

[14]   *The Wall Street Journal* as reprinted in *The Globe and Mail* of April 18, 2003.

[15]   *The Globe and Mail*, July 9, 2003.

[16]   *The Globe and Mail*, October 9, 2003.

companies.[17] Of great importance are the requirements of the Ontario Securities Commission (OSC) that will, first, require the chief executive officer and chief financial officers of public companies to certify that the financial statements of their companies accurately portray the firm's financial position, and, second, that their audit committees are made up entirely of independent directors. As far as the other requirements are concerned, companies will be able to decide whether they will follow the OSC guidelines. The OSC guidelines are expected to be followed by the securities commissions in all provinces except British Columbia and Quebec, which have stated that they intend to draft their own recommendations.[18]

Whether these moves will be able to restore confidence in the accounting profession, the financial statements of public companies, the financial analyst community, and the mutual fund industry remains to be seen.

CHANGES IN THE ROLE OF CORPORATE MANAGEMENT AND CORPORATE GOVERNANCE STANDARDS

As the accounting and financial scandals emerged, a disturbing change in the philosophy of corporate management became apparent. The traditional role of corporate management to **maximize shareholder wealth** (i.e., the running of corporations for the benefit of the shareholders) seems to have been replaced with that of **maximizing management's wealth**. The amounts earned by top executives, whether in the form of executive pay, benefits (i.e., pensions and severance packets), the issue of stock options have reached staggering amounts. Many of the accounting and financial irregularities of those companies that have had to restate their financial results appear to have been due to the deliberate inflation of profits to increase the value of the company's stock to provide executives, who exercised their stock options at that time, to reap enormous profits. As a result, the SEC and the FASB have made numerous changes to corporate governance practices in the USA. And, moves to make mandatory the disclosure of the cost of stock options in the income statements of companies are well under way.

Corporate governance refers to how the board of directors oversees the management of a company. Essentially, it attempts to ensure that a company will be well run and that the shareholders are kept fully informed on matters affecting them and their investments. Changes made, or envisaged, are designed to rectify the position where the board of directors claimed that they had no idea of what the senior executives, particularly those involved with the accounting function, were doing. The objective of these changes is to provide a system of basic checks and balances over top management.

In the USA, this led to the passing of the *Sarbanes-Oxley Act* by the American Congress in 2002 which, together with changes to the regulations of the SEC covering companies whose securities are traded on US security markets (e.g., the NYSE and NASDAQ), requires the separation of the positions of chief executive officer of the company and chairman of the board of directors, and the appointment of more independent directors (i.e., those not having business ties to the company). The changes are far-reaching, and require fully independent audit committees (to handle the annual audit), independent compensation committees (to oversee management compensation), independent nominating committees (to suggest and recruit independent directors), and limits on the amounts paid to directors by companies for any services other than serving on the board of directors.[19] The Act also forbids companies from making loans to company insiders (i.e., directors and senior executives) unless those loans are

---

17 See *The Globe and Mail*, August 30, 2003.
18 *The Globe and Mail*, January 17, 2004.
19 For those serving on the boards of companies traded on NASDAQ, the limit is US $60,000. For those traded on the NYSE, the limit is US $100,000 (*The Wall Street Journal*, as reprinted in *The Globe and Mail*, November 5, 2003).

also available to the general public.[20] This was in response to the extent of loans made to senior executives of such companies as Worldcom, Tyco and Adelphia.

The Canadian position is that the formation of the CPAB and the OSC's Public Accounts Council will have the effect of increasing the pressure on companies to improve their governance procedures. However, **there is little evidence that effective changes will be made,** despite the number of pronouncements by the regulatory bodies to change the present position, because **compliance with these requirements in Canada is voluntary**. For example, in the case of executive loans, the general viewpoint is that in view of the predominance of family-owned businesses in Canada, the prohibition of these loans would be unrealistic. Whether these requirements will be sufficient to restore investor confidence remains to be seen. However, some progress has been made because a survey of the 2002 financial reports of 319 Canadian public companies found that 80% of the companies had corporate governance committees (up from 69% a year earlier), and 49% reported how much they paid their auditors for non-audit work (up from 24% in 2001).[21]

The Future of Canadian Accounting Standards

The entire Canadian accounting standards setting system is under threat as more and more Canadian companies are using the FASB's accounting standards or are seriously considering doing so. The CICA's position on the adoption of FASB's accounting standards is that Canadian accounting standards have been designed to provide the basis of financial reporting by all Canadian companies and, as such, they continue to be relevant to Canadian investors. If, however, the position were to change, the position would be re-examined by the securities regulators (e.g., the Ontario Securities Commission) and the CICA.

There are two main reasons for the current position. First, a considerable number of Canadian companies have raised capital through issuing their shares on American security markets. These Canadian companies must provide a reconciliation of their Canadian reported profits and those using US GAAP. Second, the development of an internationally accepted accounting system under the auspices of the International Accounting Standards Board has, as yet, not occurred. The USA has, therefore, not relaxed its reporting requirements for foreign companies to any appreciable extent, and any company listing its securities on US security markets must comply with their reporting requirements. Some companies have responded fully to the situation and now prepare their financial statements for distribution to their American shareholders using US GAAP. These companies are, however, still required to report to the Canada Revenue Agency and the Securities Commissions using Canadian GAAP.

Pressure for change will also increase as a result of the North American Free Trade Agreement. If one looks to the European Union as an indication of future developments, the economic interdependence of the two countries will increase. The EU started as an economic union and is now a political union, having its own parliament and its own currency, the Euro, for transactions between countries in the EU that have agreed to adopt it (i.e., largely all except the United Kingdom and Denmark). Similar economic integration is bound to occur between Canada and the USA[22] (and, in time, Mexico), and to continue using different accounting standards just does not make sense.

---

[20] Banning loans to insiders has not emerged as a priority for the OSC. The policy of making loans to company executives has been defended on the grounds that it allows senior executives to buy shares in their employer companies as a means of attracting experienced executives to a company that could not offer the same salaries as their executives' previous employers (*The Globe and Mail*, October 10, 2002).

[21] As reported by *The Globe and Mail* of January 13, 2004, the survey was carried out jointly by Patrick O'Callaghan and Associates and Korn/Ferry International.

[22] At present, roughly 87% of Canada's foreign trade is with the USA.

In order to assist the move to harmonize accounting standards on a worldwide basis, the FASB is relaxing its position on the use of certain International Accounting Standards (IASs) by foreign companies. However, there is considerable resistance to the move in the USA because many accounting firms feel that the detailed FASB accounting standards, as opposed to the standards of the IASB (and the CICA) that are based on broad principles, allow them to avoid malpractice liability by arguing that they have certified financial statements in accordance with generally accepted accounting principles.

THE NEED FOR A THEORETICAL FRAMEWORK OF ACCOUNTING

For many years it has been accepted that the proper development of accounting and financial reporting was only possible if it was based on a theoretical framework. This was because many different methods of handling similar transactions were being used and, in the absence of a theoretical framework against which the various accounting practices could be evaluated, it was difficult to justify the use of one practice over another. Where accounting standards existed, they had been developed on an "issue by issue" basis as the needs arose rather than in response to the general improvement of financial reporting. Of the most importance was that the alternative methods of handling similar transactions had led to a situation where the results of operations and the financial positions of companies in the same industry could not be readily compared with one another.

A series of attempts was made in the USA and elsewhere to formulate an acceptable theory of accounting. None of these were successful, and it was only after the formation of the FASB in 1973 in the USA that some progress was made on the issue. This occurred when the FASB commenced work on its "conceptual framework" of accounting, which it described as "... a coherent system of interrelated objectives and fundamentals that can lead to consistent standards and that prescribes the nature, function, and limits of financial accounting and financial statements."[23]

The FASB's "conceptual framework" consisted of what was essentially a three-tiered hierarchical structure having, at its highest level, conceptual considerations (i.e., the objectives of accounting, the elements of financial statements, their measurement and the qualitative characteristics of accounting information), from which accounting standards and practices would flow. This hierarchy is diagrammatically presented as Illustration 1–1.

In 1988, the CICA issued its version of the "conceptual framework" as section 1000 of the CICA *Handbook*. This section drew heavily on the FASB's "conceptual framework", but did not present its "financial accounting concepts" in the form of a hierarchical structure. What it did do was formulate objectives of financial statements that differed from those of the FASB, and clarified certain aspects of the Canadian financial reporting system.

These frameworks are referred to as "conceptual frameworks" because they have been established by accounting associations on concepts (which are nothing more than ideas or notions formulated by them) **to guide and improve accounting practice**. In this respect, accounting is a man-made discipline that does not follow the laws of nature, but rather the rules or objectives laid down by those who formulated them. The problem is that these "conceptual frameworks" tend to be regarded as theoretical structures (which should be expressions of truth about accounting) and not merely a framework of ideas designed to give the discipline direction.

---

[23] *Conceptual Framework for Accounting and Reporting: Consideration of the Report of the Study Group on the Objectives of Financial Reporting*, Discussion Memorandum, Financial Accounting Standards Board, 1974.

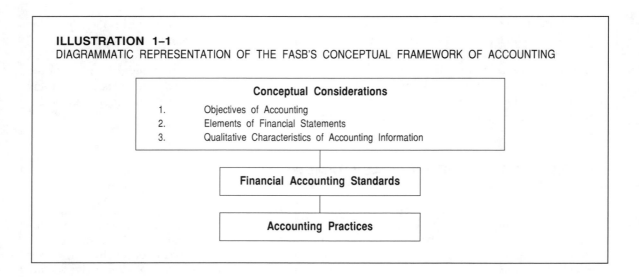

ILLUSTRATION 1–1
DIAGRAMMATIC REPRESENTATION OF THE FASB'S CONCEPTUAL FRAMEWORK OF ACCOUNTING

What is interesting is that, to date, only very few countries have moved towards adopting theoretical, "conceptual" or other structures of accounting. The International Accounting Standards Board and the Australian Accounting Standards Board have adopted "conceptual frameworks" similar to those of the FASB and the CICA. The New Zealand Society of Accountants has also developed its own "conceptual framework" of accounting.

Those aspects of the FASB's "conceptual framework" and the CICA's "financial statement concepts" affecting and influencing financial reporting for profit-oriented enterprises are examined hereunder; those relating to nonprofit organizations and the public sector are examined in a later chapter.

AT WHOM ARE FINANCIAL REPORTS DIRECTED?

Ownership Theories as They Apply to Financial Reporting

In any examination of financial reporting, it is necessary to establish the audience at whom the financial reports are directed to ensure that the information provided in these reports satisfies users' needs.

If the reporting is directed purely at the shareholders of the parent company, the reporting would take on a proprietary perspective because it is mainly concerned with the informational needs of its owners or shareholders. On the other hand, if the reporting entity is viewed as an entity existing in its own right and in which all interested parties (i.e., owners, contributors of loan capital, etc.) have a direct or indirect interest, the reporting would be based on a **wider** entity basis to meet the informational needs of all these parties. From an accounting theory viewpoint, these two alternative reporting approaches are referred to as the **proprietary or entity ownership theories**, respectively.

The Proprietary Ownership Theory

With the proprietary ownership theory, the reporting is concerned with the position of the owner. The balance sheet with this theory is, therefore, presented in accordance with the accounting equation **Assets – Liabilities = Owners' Equity**. Net income is seen as a residual balance, and represents the amount accruing to the owners after all expenses and other claims to income (i.e., like income taxes and the interests of the minority) have been deducted from revenues.[24] Expressed in equation form, it is **Revenues – Expenses = Net Income**.

With current financial reporting, the proprietary theory is normally applied to the balance sheets of proprietorship businesses (i.e., one-man businesses) and partnerships where the direction of the reporting is to present the financial position of the owner or owners. This also applies to the income statement which, irrespective of whether it is used for proprietorships or companies, is based on the proprietorship ownership theory because it is designed to reflect the net income for the period concerned attributable to the owners or shareholders.

The Entity Ownership Theory

The entity ownership theory, on the other hand, looks upon the corporate entity as an entity that exists independently of its shareholders. It is, therefore, the business entity that is of interest rather than the interests of its owners. The assets of the business are represented by the claims of the company to both the owners and loan creditors, and the balance sheet is drawn up using the accounting equation of **Assets = Liabilities + Shareholders' Equity or, more correctly, Assets = Liabilities + Equities**. This situation is, to some extent, reflected by current corporate reporting, where the balance sheet tends to be presented in this manner.

This position exists because, with the entity ownership theory, the shareholdings and loan conditions are considered to differ from one another only insofar as to the degree of risk they take in investing in the company. Net income belongs to the company until such time as it is distributed and, as a result, the income statement drawn up using this ownership theory should reflect the total earnings of the reporting entity. This means that it should give an earnings figure before any distributions to shareholders, loan creditors and other providers of capital. The distributions or apportionments of income are, therefore, represented by the amounts paid as interest on mortgages and bonds as well as dividends on preferred and common shares.

Reporting in this manner appears to be gaining greater acceptance, particularly in Europe, as the broader role of companies is recognized. In this respect, it is accepted that companies have a responsibility to the communities in which they operate and, consequently, there are a considerable number of persons other than investors, like employees and suppliers, who have an interest (or a stake) in the continued existence of the reporting entity. As a result, it is suggested that the emphasis of the financial reporting system should be broadened, and directed at the entity as a whole, and not merely at the contributors of its capital.

The Proprietary and Entity Theories as Bases for Reporting

Neither the proprietary nor the entity theories are fully accepted by accountants as the basis for financial reporting. Accounting literature and accounting practice show that accountants have tended to use whatever ownership theory suits their immediate needs. In fact, as far back as 1929, Canning[25] wrote: "While the accountant subscribes fundamentally to the entity theory, he appears to shift to the representative [i.e., proprietary] theory when it suits his convenience." Evidence of this situation was also provided by Paton and Littleton in 1940, where they stated that as "... the corporate balance sheet is a statement of the business entity and not of the shareholders ... [it] requires the treatment of business earnings as

---

[24] Alternatives to the historical cost accounting model look upon net income as a change in owners' wealth.
[25] John B. Canning, *The Economics of Accountancy*, New York: Ronald Press, 1929, p. 252.

income of the enterprise itself until such time as transfer to the individual participants [i.e., shareholders] has been effected by dividend declaration."[26] There are many other examples in current accounting literature of this interchange between ownership theories.

THE OBJECTIVES OF FINANCIAL REPORTING

The Objectives That Have Been Formulated

As outlined above, both the FASB and the CICA have formulated objectives of accounting for business enterprises.

The objectives of the FASB were those contained in its *Statement of Financial Accounting Concepts No. 1: Objectives of Financial Reporting by Business Enterprises*, issued in 1978. The main objective was that financial reporting "... should **provide** information that is useful to present and potential investors and creditors and other users in making rational investment, credit and similar decisions" (emphasis added).

To meet this main objective, financial reporting should **provide** information to help present and potential investors in assessing the amounts, timing and uncertainty of their prospective cash flows; information on the enterprise's economic resources, obligations and owners' equity; and its financial performance during the period. It also stated that financial reporting should provide information on how the management of the enterprise had discharged its stewardship responsibilities to shareholders in its use of the resources entrusted to it.

In section 1000 of the CICA *Handbook* it was stated that the objectives of financial statements, as the primary means of financial reporting, were "... to **communicate** information that is useful to investors, members, contributors, creditors and other users ... in making their resource allocation decisions **and/or** assessing management stewardship" (emphasis added).[27] It also stated that to satisfy these objectives, financial statements should also provide information about the reporting entity's resources, obligations and equities and its economic performance.

These two sets of financial reporting objectives are important because, even though they are relatively similar, they show that there are two significant differences between the financial reporting philosophies adopted in the USA and Canada. First, the objectives of the CICA recognized stewardship (or accountability) as a major objective of financial reporting in addition to resource allocation/economic decision-making. Second, that financial reports should **communicate** with, and not merely **provide** information to users.

The Analysis of These Objectives

The importance of the objectives of financial reporting is that they define the audience at which the financial reports are directed. And, once the audience at whom the reports are directed has been established, it should be possible to determine what information should be provided. However, no matter how simple this analysis appears to be, this is not necessarily the case.

The problem is that even though accounting literature contains considerable material on the perceived informational needs of the users of financial reports, **no one really knows what information users need**. This is because financial reporting is essentially a one-way communication system. Information is provided by the reporting entity to those persons who either have a right to receive that information or have an interest in it, without any real feedback to the reporting entity.

---

[26] W.A. Paton, and A.C. Littleton, *An Introduction to Corporate Accounting Standards*, Monograph No. 3, American Accounting Association, 1940, p. 8.
[27] CICA *Handbook*, section 1000.

The position is further complicated by the problem that the shareholding in large companies is usually widely dispersed, whereas in small companies it is normally restricted to relatively few shareholders. In this respect, the holding of shares in large companies is normally for investment purposes while, in small companies, that is often carried out for other reasons, like the restriction of personal liability, income tax considerations and convenience.

However, it is accepted that those persons who have either invested in or loaned money to companies find the information contained in financial reports of interest. This also applies to those persons who depend upon the use of financial information for their livelihood or occupation. There are also the various customers, suppliers, and employees of the company who all, in their different ways, have an interest in the operations and continued existence of the company. These latter groups of interested parties are referred to as **stakeholders** because they have a stake in the continued existence of the company.

What information these interested parties **actually use or need** is based largely on conjecture. To overcome these difficulties, financial reports are directed at those investors and loan creditors who provide the capital.

There are two reasons for this. First, **as our free market-oriented economy is characterized by the public ownership of companies, there must be an efficient capital markets system**. Financial reports should, therefore, assist investors in making "buy, hold or sell" decisions. Second, **they should be able to use the financial reports to assess how the management of the companies in which they have invested have used the resources provided**. Today, this would also include such matters as the safety of the company's products and the effect of their operations on the environment.

It should be noted that, like the position with the entity ownership theory, the only difference between investors and loan creditors is the amount of risk they are prepared to take. This is reflected in Illustration 1–2 by the spectrum of risk as it applies to the providers of capital. On this spectrum, the mortgage holders take the least risk of losing their money because it is secured over the immovable property of the business, whereas the common shareholders take the greatest risk because they stand to lose their entire investment if the company fails. And, for anyone to invest in a company, the return on the investment must be commensurate with the risks taken.

The problem of defining the objectives of financial reporting is compounded because investors in large companies are usually concerned with their investments, whereas the investors in small companies often do so as the means of carrying out their occupations and the earning of a living. In situations such as these, differences in informational needs must be expected.

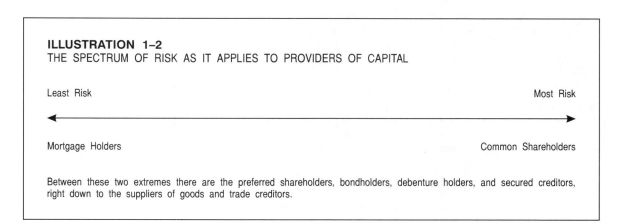

ILLUSTRATION 1–2
THE SPECTRUM OF RISK AS IT APPLIES TO PROVIDERS OF CAPITAL

Least Risk   Most Risk

Mortgage Holders   Common Shareholders

Between these two extremes there are the preferred shareholders, bondholders, debenture holders, and secured creditors, right down to the suppliers of goods and trade creditors.

It is also doubtful whether the objective of the CICA that financial reports should communicate information to users can be achieved. This is because accounting is highly technical in nature and to be able to understand the information provided, users of financial reports should be relatively well informed on accounting and business matters. As a result, accountants have in the past paid little more than lip service to the communication of information in financial reports and any change in current practice is doubtful.

As far as the management of companies is concerned, financial reports provide the means of reporting on the discharge of their stewardship responsibilities to shareholders or to convey information on the company's activities to investors. In this respect, **the amount of net income is normally taken as a measure of the reporting enterprise's performance or the effectiveness of its management**. Financial reports may also allow management to show that it has carried out its commitments relating to contractual agreements (or covenants) like those relating to loans where, for example, the payment of dividends may be restricted while the loan is outstanding.

The objectives of financial reporting as they apply to both users and preparers are as follows:

The **common objectives** are to provide (or communicate) information on:
(a) The results of operations.
(b) The financial position of the reporting entity.
(c) Information on the inflows and outflows of cash to the enterprise.
(d) Its stewardship over the resources provided by investors.
(e) The discharge of its accountability responsibilities to the community in which it operates.

The **investor specific objective** is to provide information to allow investors to predict their return on investment (ROI) or potential ROI which, in accordance with the FASB objectives, is expressed as the cash flows or potential cash flows to investors.

The **preparer specific objective** is the demonstration by management of the discharge of any specific contractual requirements.

Although these objectives appear straightforward, some confusion has occurred with the reference to estimated cash flows. This is because, for investors, **cash flows are, in reality, merely surrogates for the projected return on investment**, which is based on the projected net income or the selling price of the securities. It may also be used for economic measurement purposes, because the value of assets may be taken as the discounted value of future cash flows. It can also be argued that investors, like management, require cash flow information to assess the economic viability and continued existence and solvency of the company concerned.

It should also be borne in mind that the objectives of financial reporting are interrelated because they cover both the needs of investors and management. It is, therefore, difficult to specifically segregate them into definite categories. They also differ from user to user, because not all objectives apply to the same group of users or to each company. The objectives must, therefore, be looked at from the point of view of each user. For example, an investor in a company will look at a financial report in a somewhat different manner from an environmental activist.

It should also be borne in mind that financial reports are normally prepared to cater for the needs of investors and creditors, and the needs of other users like employees, consumers, government agencies, and other interested parties have not been properly formulated. However, there are numerous examples of where special purpose reports have been produced to meet the informational needs of these users.[28]

---

[28] Guidelines for the preparation of special purpose reports were provided by the American Accounting Association in *A Statement of Basic Accounting Theory*, 1966.

THE ELEMENTS OF FINANCIAL STATEMENTS

Both the FASB and the CICA have defined the elements that make up the financial statements. These are the assets, liabilities, equities, revenues, expenses, gains, and losses of the enterprise concerned. The importance of doing so is that they provide the guidelines on where the various items should be included in the financial statements, and how they should be recognized and measured. For example, assets and liabilities are defined, respectively, as economic resources and obligations: revenues are increases in economic resources, while expenses are decreases in economic resources.[29] Recognition is by inclusion in the financial statements, while measurement represents the amount at which they are reflected in the financial statements.

The defining of these elements is an essential part of any conceptual framework of accounting because, even though they are normally fully understood by accountants, there are times when unusual items occur on which an accountant may find it necessary to seek guidance. These definitions, recognition criteria, and measurement rules provide that guidance.

THE QUALITATIVE CHARACTERISTICS OF
ACCOUNTING INFORMATION

The qualitative characteristics of accounting information was the third conceptual consideration of the FASB's "conceptual framework" of accounting and was concerned with those attributes of the information provided by the accounting system that makes the information useful. The CICA and the FASB agree on the nature of these qualitative characteristics that are, for convenience, presented in Illustration 1–3 in the form of the FASB's hierarchical structure of accounting qualities.[30]

Illustration 1–3 shows that these qualitative characteristics operate between the constraints of "benefits exceed costs" and "materiality". Information should only be provided if the benefits of doing so exceed the costs, and only significant items of information are provided. As far as the actual qualitative characteristics are concerned, the information must be understandable, relevant, reliable and comparable.

To be **relevant, the information must relate to or have a bearing on the matter under consideration**. To do so it must have predictive and feedback value, and be received in time to influence decisions. **Reliability, on the other hand, refers to the extent to which users can depend upon the information** to represent the economic conditions under review, be verifiable, neutral and faithfully represent the issues under consideration. And, finally, the financial statements should be comparable with those of other entities by being prepared in a consistent manner from year to year. **Comparability refers to the use of the same accounting policies by reporting entities so that their activities and financial position can be compared with one another. Consistency, on the other hand, refers to the use of the same accounting policies and practices from year to year.**

There is a trade-off between relevance and reliability and between comparability and consistency. Some reliability may be sacrificed in favour of making the information more relevant. For example, the inclusion of a forecast would increase the relevance of the information but it would not necessarily improve its reliability. Similarly, some consistency could be foregone in order to increase comparability.

---

[29] Section 1000 of the CICA *Handbook*.
[30] Financial Accounting Standards Board, *Statement of Financial Accounting Concepts No. 2: Qualitative Characteristics of Accounting Information*, 1980.

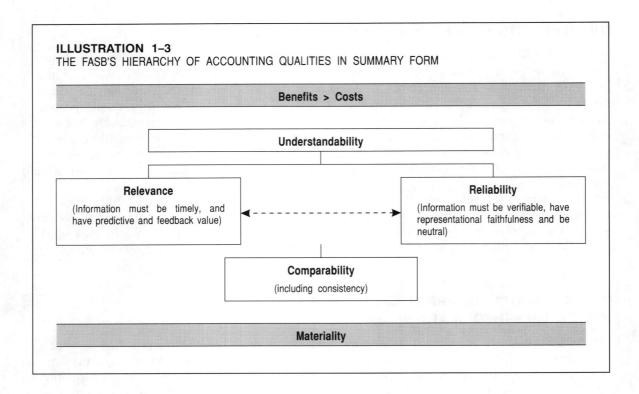

ILLUSTRATION 1–3
THE FASB'S HIERARCHY OF ACCOUNTING QUALITIES IN SUMMARY FORM

GENERALLY ACCEPTED ACCOUNTING PRINCIPLES

Up to this point, the nature and environment in which financial reporting operates has been examined. It is now necessary to examine that body of accounting knowledge that is referred to as "generally accepted accounting principles" (GAAP), and how it applies to financial reporting.

What Is Meant by GAAP?

Over the years, the term "generally accepted accounting principles" has meant different things to different people. To some it referred to the entire body of accounting knowledge, while to others it referred specifically to the rules relating to the information provided in financial reports.

It is, therefore, understandable why the CICA followed the lead of the American Institute of Certified Public Accountants[31] to clarify the issue. It did so by defining GAAP as encompassing broad principles and conventions of general application as well as the rules and procedures that determine accepted accounting practices at a particular time.[32] GAAP in Canada, therefore, covers all aspects of the reporting system that enjoy acceptance amongst

---

[31]   GAAP was defined in para. 137 of its Accounting Principles Board's *Statement No. 4: Basic Concepts and Accounting Principles Underlying Financial Statements of Business Enterprises* as "... the consensus at a particular time as to which economic resources and obligations should be recorded as assets and liabilities by financial accounting, which changes in assets and liabilities should be recorded, when these changes should be recorded, how the assets and liabilities and changes in them should be measured, what information should be disclosed and how it should be disclosed, and which financial statements should be prepared."

[32]   Section 1100.

accountants. It may also include specific accounting or reporting requirements included in the law governing the operations of specialized industry segments, like banks, or the operation of investment companies.

The term GAAP is often used by accountants in a specific sense to refer to those rules and regulations covering the recording of transactions and the preparation of financial reports. This is because a business enterprise can virtually follow any accounting procedures or practices in recording its various transactions, but as soon as it prepares financial statements for reporting to outside parties, it must follow GAAP.

The recommendations contained in the CICA *Handbook* represent the most important primary source of GAAP in Canada. Other primary sources of GAAP in descending order of importance are accounting guidelines, abstracts of issues discussed by the Emerging Issues Committee (i.e., EIC Abstracts), the background information and bases for conclusions accompanying pronouncements in the CICA *Handbook* and accounting guidelines, any illustrative material and implementation guides authorized by the AcSB.

The contents of the CICA *Handbook* tend to be phrased in general, rather than specific terms. This is to overcome the potential problem of stifling the development of accounting practice by imposing too rigid a reporting system because, where the accounting procedures to be followed are prescribed in detail, there is little room for change. The philosophy is, therefore, to provide a broad explanation of what is required and leave its implementation to those who are applying it.

The Application of GAAP to Financial Reporting

The GAAP contained in the CICA *Handbook* must be followed in the preparation of financial statements and financial reports in Canada. In fact, section 5400 of the CICA *Handbook* makes it quite clear that it is Canadian "generally accepted accounting principles" that must be used. It also suggests that where the reporting entity is operating in an international environment, it may be desirable to specify that Canadian GAAP has been used in the preparation of the financial statements.

Many Canadian companies have listed their shares on one or other of the three American security markets (i.e., the New York Stock Exchange, the American Stock Exchange and NASDAQ[33,34]) to raise capital and improve their corporate image. These companies often prepare additional financial statements for their American shareholders using US GAAP. These are special purpose financial statements and they must, therefore, be described as such and include a reconciliation of the net income reflected by the Canadian financial statements with that using US GAAP.[35]

Even though the CICA *Handbook* is specific in detailing its reporting requirements, **there are a considerable number of areas where GAAP allows the use of alternative methods**. For example, there are at least four acceptable methods of amortizing capital assets. There are also different ways in which revenues can be recognized, and accounting practices that are peculiar to specific industries. In those cases where the issue is not specifically covered by the CICA *Handbook*, any method may be used. And here, the choice of which method to use is purely a matter of professional judgment.

From time to time, the financial statements of Canadian companies must be submitted to or filed with the SEC and, in these cases, they must comply with certain American financial reporting requirements. These additional reporting requirements should be provided in a form

---

[33] The National Association of Security Dealers Automated Quotation System.

[34] On November 3, 1998, *The Globe and Mail* reported that the NASDAQ-American Stock Exchange merger had been completed. The two exchanges will, however, continue to operate as separate entities for the next few years. This position continues at the present time.

[35] For example, Hummingbird Communications Ltd. of Toronto announced that from April 1, 1997, it would be preparing its financial statements for distribution to its American shareholders using US GAAP.

that makes it quite clear that the information is provided for that purpose and does not form part of the financial statements prepared in accordance with Canadian reporting requirements.

In certain cases, specific industries report in a manner that is not recognized by the CICA *Handbook*. For example, investment companies often value their investments at market value and recognize holding gains or losses on these investments in the income statement. These reporting practices are known as "industry standards" and are generally accepted by the industry concerned. The use of these "industry standards" is, again, a matter of professional judgment.

It is necessary to clarify what is meant by the term "generally accepted" when referring to accounting principles. Although "generally accepted" has not been specifically defined by professional accounting associations, it is accepted that for a particular practice to be considered "generally accepted", (a) the practice must be in general use, and (b) its use must be supported in the pronouncements of professional accounting associations or standard setting bodies. This latter aspect applies, no matter how unpopular the practice may be.

The Role of International Accounting Standards

The International Accounting Standards Committee (IASC) was formed in 1973 by the professional accounting bodies of Australia, Canada, France, Germany, Japan, Mexico, the Netherlands, the United Kingdom of Great Britain, and the USA.

The objective of the IASC was to improve and harmonize accounting standards on a worldwide basis. It also provided countries that did not have the resources to develop their own accounting on their own with a ready-made set of accounting standards. In 2001 the IASC was reconstituted as the International Accounting Standards Board (IASB) with responsibilities similar to those of the FASB in the USA. Its objective was to develop IAS that would apply across international borders to cater for the increasing importance of international trade and the operation of multinational corporations in the global economy. As one of its major achievements, the European Community will start using IAS developed by the IASB in 2005 for financial reporting purposes.[36]

Canada was a founding member of the IASC. Therefore, the CICA, the Certified General Accountants' Society of Canada, and the Society of Management Accountants of Canada are all obliged to support the work of the IASB. The CICA, as the body responsible for setting local accounting standards, has reaffirmed its support of the IASB's objective of harmonizing accounting standards by stating that on the issue of an IAS, it will compare the IAS with present Canadian accounting practice. Where an IAS varies significantly from Canadian practice, the matter will be examined and unless there are specific Canadian circumstances that require a different position, the CICA *Handbook* will be amended to incorporate the IAS. In cases where there are no recommendations covering the topic, the CICA's AcSB will decide whether to initiate a project to develop local standards covering the topic.

The CICA has amended its accounting recommendations for joint ventures and financial instruments to bring them in line with those of the IAS. With the pressure on Canada to adopt US GAAP, the position may change.

Until such time as high-quality IAS emerges, however, the FASB will continue to set its own accounting standards. It will, however, contribute to the acceptability of the IAS by accepting the use of certain IAS in the reporting by foreign companies whose securities are traded on US security markets. When high quality international accounting standards emerge, these will be accepted by the FASB. On this issue, the current chairman of the FASB, Robert

---

[36] The attempt to introduce a global set of International Accounting Standards is not progressing well. *The Wall Street Journal* (as reprinted in *The Globe and Mail* of February 9, 2004) reported that Japan is upset because the EU wants Japanese companies to use IAS and not Japanese accounting standards if they wish to list their securities on EU securities markets in 2005. The EU itself, under pressure from EU banking institutions, is still arguing with the IASB over its proposed derivatives (i.e., financial instruments) reporting requirements.

Herz, stated that the adoption of global accounting standards was "doable" within five to seven years.[37] The comments came as members of the CICA, the FASB and the IASB met in Toronto in October 2003 in an attempt to go ahead with a single set of accounting standards by 2007 despite a strong movement in the USA to preserve the detailed FASB accounting standards.

THE DISCLOSURE OF INFORMATION

Disclosure in financial reporting refers to the provision of financial information to the users of financial reports. It applies essentially to those companies whose securities are publicly traded on securities markets because the definition of financial reporting is the provision of information to those users who have no other means of obtaining the information they need. Consequently, from a decision-usefulness approach to financial reporting, the objective of disclosure is to provide investors with the information considered necessary for the making of investment decisions and the efficient operation of capital markets.

The means of disclosing information by companies is through interim (i.e., quarterly) and annual financial reports, and press releases. The objective is that companies should release information in such a manner that all investors, large and small, have an equal chance of receiving that information. Regrettably, this has not always been the case because a number of companies have released information to a select group of financial analysts and institutionalized investors (e.g., mutual funds and insurance companies) in advance of the information being made public. This "selective disclosure of information" in Canada came to the forefront when Air Canada advised a select group of financial analysts on October 5, 2000, that they should lower their earnings expectations for the company without issuing a public statement to that effect. Analysts revised their estimates downwards, leading to large scale selling of the stock by the institutionalized investors before the public was informed.

Understandably, individual investors were incensed, and both the Ontario Securities Commission (OSC) and the Toronto Stock Exchange (TSE) indicated that steps would be taken to rectify the position. The practice has already been **outlawed in the USA**, where the SEC issued a "Fair Disclosure" rule on October 23, 2000, which required that companies whose securities are publicly traded on US security markets must reveal the same information to all investors at virtually the same time through public announcements, by access to any conference calls via **webcasts** (i.e., simultaneous announcements on the Internet) and by attendance at private investor meetings. The objective was to create a "level playing field" for small and large investors. Unfortunately, to date neither the OSC nor the TSE has followed the lead of the US SEC in introducing a similar reporting requirement in Canada.

THE APPLICATION OF PROFESSIONAL JUDGMENT

In the carrying out of any professional occupation, there are always numerous cases where it is necessary to exercise judgment. It occurs so often that few professionally qualified persons are even conscious of having made a decision to follow this or that course of action. In accounting, the need to exercise judgment is often an integral part of the application of many accounting standards.

This situation is particularly valid in the case of the recommendations contained in the CICA *Handbook* which, as outlined earlier, tend to be phrased in general rather than specific terms. This is recognized by paragraph 1100.06 of the CICA *Handbook*, which makes it quite clear that:

---

[37] *The Globe and Mail* of October 22, 2003.

No rule of general application can be phrased to suit all circumstances or combination of circumstances that may arise. As a result, matters may arise that are not specifically addressed in the primary sources of GAAP. It is necessary to refer to other sources when the primary sources do not deal with the accounting and reporting issues, or transactions or events encountered by the entity.

The selection of appropriate accounting policies and disclosures requires the exercise of professional judgment. In doing so, an entity would take the primary sources of GAAP into account, as well as the concepts described in section 1000 of the CICA *Handbook* dealing with financial statement concepts. The AcSB considers a source to be consistent with financial reporting concepts when it is compatible with the qualitative characteristics of financial information, the elements of financial statements, and the recognition and measurement criteria in section 1000. The ability to exercise such judgment depends upon a person's professional competence, experience and knowledge of accounting. This would include a full knowledge and understanding of the objectives of financial reporting, accounting measurement and disclosure requirements, the qualitative characteristics of accounting information, and generally accepted accounting principles.

THE ACTUAL FINANCIAL REPORTS

The Present Position

Public companies normally report to their shareholders and other interested parties through an annual report including the financial statements and other information. These documents are issued voluntarily by companies because other than in Quebec, there is no specific statutory requirement for companies in Canada to issue annual reports to their shareholders.

The financial statements of holding companies (i.e., companies that control the operations of other companies) are presented as consolidated financial statements that report on the "group of companies" as if it were a single economic entity. Each company in the group of companies must also prepare their own financial statements for income tax purposes and be able to issue them to their shareholders, loan creditors, and other interested parties.

The securities commissions of Ontario, Quebec and Saskatchewan also require companies to include information on the financial condition and results of operations as part of the annual report. All companies whose securities are publicly traded are also required by the various provincial securities commissions to include additional information, like the "ten-year financial review" of their activities. In addition, all public companies are encouraged to include "**a statement of management's responsibility for financial reporting**" in their financial statements.

The **management's discussion and analysis** statement is also required. This is a narrative statement explaining the operations and activities of the company for the financial year under review. It covers such topics as its results of operations, extraordinary items, special charges, liquidity, capital expenditures, and future prospects. Future-oriented information in the form of forecasts and projections is included in this statement. Where these forecasts and projections are included, they must be based on stated assumptions and specify the audience at which they are directed.

The inclusion of a statement of "management's responsibility for financial statements" in the annual report has also been encouraged by the CICA since 1992. Its purpose is to acknowledge management's responsibility for the financial statements of the company. It should also include a statement detailing the role of the board of directors in overseeing the preparation, and subsequent review and approval, of the financial statements.

Jointly, these statements are designed to satisfy the informational needs of users and to ensure that management and the board of directors fully recognize their reporting responsibilities. It also recognizes the accountability responsibilities of those who control the operations and activities of companies.

Reporting Comprehensive Income

In June 1997, the FASB issued *SFAS No. 130: Reporting Comprehensive Income* in response to the worldwide trend of moving towards an all-inclusive income concept.[38] The purpose was to require companies to report, as an integral part of their financial statements, all changes in the equity of an enterprise that result from recognized transactions and other economic events of the period other than capital transactions. Prior to the issue of *SFAS No. 130*, some of these changes in equity were reflected in the income statement, while others were reflected as adjustments to individual components of the equity in the balance sheet.[39] By reflecting all these changes, it is believed that investors, creditors, and others would be better able to assess the entity's activities and the timing and magnitude of the enterprise's future cash flows.

In 2003, the CICA issued, as part of the revision of the CICA *Handbook*, requirements on financial instruments, an *Exposure Draft* in which it was proposed that companies should present comprehensive income and its components in a financial statement that was to be displayed with the same prominence as other financial statements as part of the annual financial statements. The statement of comprehensive income was to show net income for the period, as well as each component of revenue, expense, or gain or loss that is now required to be recognized as comprehensive income by the various sections of the CICA *Handbook*. An illustration of such a statement is provided as Illustration 1–4.

ENFORCING COMPLIANCE WITH FINANCIAL REPORTING REQUIREMENTS

As outlined above, the body having the primary responsibility of developing and implementing accounting standards in Canada is the CICA even though additional reporting requirements for public companies are imposed by the various provincial securities commissions. There is, therefore, a distinction between the reporting requirements of private or closely held companies and those public companies whose securities are publicly traded.

Compliance with the reporting requirements of the various securities commissions for companies whose securities are publicly traded is easy to obtain because those commissions have the right to impose sanctions on delinquent companies and, if everything else fails, to suspend trading of the concerned company's securities through the issue of "cease-trading orders".

This position has taken on greater prominence since the formation of the Canadian Public Accountability Board in 2002 with the mission to contribute to the public confidence in financial reporting by ensuring compliance with Canadian reporting requirements, and to promote high-quality and independent auditing. As pointed out earlier, the CPAB will inspect firms that audit public companies to ensure that they are complying with professional standards, rules and regulatory requirements. Rules announced by the CPAB in July 2002 include the requirement that audit firms will have to rotate the lead partners on specific accounts to ensure that an individual does not serve as the engagement partner for more than seven consecutive years.[40] Additional rules to limit the amount of non-audit services an auditor can perform for a client are also envisaged.

---

[38] The concept is not new because in 1992, the United Kingdom Accounting Standards Board (ASB) issued its *Financial Reporting Standard No. 3: Reporting Financial Performance* ,which introduced *a statement of total recognized gains and losses* as a supplement to the profit and loss account (i.e., the income statement). The issue of a similar statement has also been considered by the International Accounting Standards Board.

[39] There are a number of cases where the FASB's accounting standards allow the adjustments to by-pass the income statement. These include certain transactions relating to foreign currency translation, changes in the value of futures contracts that qualify as hedges, and the unrealized gains or losses on certain securities.

[40] *The Globe and Mail*, July 18, 2002.

ILLUSTRATION 1–4
THE STATEMENT OF COMPREHENSIVE INCOME

The following proposed statement of comprehensive income was included in the *Exposure Draft: Comprehensive Income* issued by the CICA in March 2003:

Statement of Comprehensive income

	20X2	20X1
	(in $000's)	
Net income	$ 651	$22
Other comprehensive Income, net of tax:		
Unrealized gains and losses on translating financial statements of self-sustaining foreign operations	547	627
Gains and losses on hedges of unrealized foreign currency translation losses and gains	(545)	(618)
Unrealized foreign currency translation gains and losses	2	9
Unrealized gains and losses on available-for-sale financial assets arising during the period	1,689	277
Reclassification adjustment for gains and losses included in net income	(317)	62
Change in unrealized gains and losses on available-for-sale financial assets	1,372	339
Gains or losses on derivatives designated as cash flow hedges	1,723	687
Gains or losses on derivatives designated as cash flow hedges in prior periods transferred to net income in the current period	(995)	(333)
Changes in gains and losses on derivatives designated as cash flow hedges	728	354
Other comprehensive income	$2,102	$702
Comprehensive income	$2,753	$724

Note: Gains and losses on self-sustaining foreign operations and foreign currency translation are covered in Chapter 16. The balance of the items included above relates to financial instruments that are covered in Chapter 17.

The Public Accounts Council formed by the Ontario government in August 2003 will also enforce new rules relating to the qualification and professional conduct of persons acting as auditors of companies. Of these, the most important is the requirement of the OSC that will require the chief executive officer and chief financial officers of public companies to certify that the financial statements of their companies accurately portray the firm's financial position. Similar proposals will apply in other provinces.

The position relating to reporting by private or closely held companies is somewhat more difficult. The public accounting profession is self-regulating, and members are required to comply with the "rules of professional conduct" of their provincial institutes. For example, keeping up to date with accounting standards and complying with the CICA *Handbook* are two of these requirements for members of the Institute of Chartered Accountants of Ontario.

All full-time or part-time practitioners who are members of the ICAO are also subject to **practice review** or, as it is often referred to, peer review. For example, in Ontario[41], practitioners must make their working paper files and any books, documents or other materials relating to work carried out on behalf of clients available for inspection by a member of the ICAO, acting on behalf of its Practice Inspection Committee. Any failure to maintain proper professional standards brought to light by the inspection is referred to the ICAO, which then takes appropriate action.

The accounting profession, therefore, relies mainly on the ethical standards of its members in carrying out their duties but with oversight by the CPAB and the various provincial securities commissions. In cases where members do not meet these standards of behaviour or

---

[41] *Bylaw 58* of the Institute of Chartered Accountants of Ontario *Member's Handbook*.

do not comply with the rules and regulations of their institutes, they may be disciplined and have their right to practice suspended. If necessary, the institutes may cancel their membership. Generally speaking, this self-regulation works well, but there are, unfortunately, cases where the actions of certain members are not always in the best interests of the profession and the public. Compliance with the reporting requirements of the CICA *Handbook* is, therefore, largely in the hands of individual accountants in the carrying on of their duties as either accountants or auditors.

SUMMARY

This chapter examines financial reporting as the means of providing users external to the reporting entity with the information they need. It traces the development of the accountability and investment decision approaches to the reporting system. And, through an historical examination of the development of the environment in which financial reporting takes place, it shows how the influence of British corporate law and the close association with the USA have shaped the Canadian reporting system.

The effects of the accounting and reporting scandals of 2001–2002 on both the accounting profession and financial reporting are examined. Of the most importance was the failure of the audit function and the change in the role of corporate management. In order to restore confidence in the accounting profession and the financial reports of companies, considerable changes to the regulation of the accounting profession and the governance of corporations have been made.

The need for an acceptable theory on which to base the development of the reporting system is then examined. No such theory has been developed, and the only progress that has been made is the development of "conceptual frameworks of accounting" by the FASB, the IASC, and the Australian Accounting Standards Board and the statement on "financial accounting concepts" by the CICA. Here it is shown that differences in the formulation of the objectives of financial reporting are due to historical differences in the application of corporate law in the two countries. There is, however, no difference between these two conceptual frameworks insofar as the elements of financial statements and the qualitative characteristics of accounting information are concerned. Finally, the nature of generally accepted accounting principles is examined together with the exercising of professional judgment and the reporting of comprehensive income.

REVIEW QUESTIONS

1. What is the basic purpose of financial reporting?
2. Explain what is meant by the investment decision and accountability approaches to financial reporting.
3. Why, and in what way, does the investment decision approach to financial reporting enjoy such acceptance in the USA?
4. How did the accountability approach to financial reporting develop?
5. What effect has the emphasis on the investment decision approach to financial reporting had on the way financial reporting is viewed?
6. Why is it debatable whether the accountability approach to financial reporting applies to large publicly traded companies?
7. What is meant by the "conflict between the preparers and users of financial reports"?
8. Why was the passing by the British Parliament of the *Joint Stock Companies Act* of 1844 so important for the development of financial reporting in Britain?
9. What led to the creation of the Securities and Exchange Commission in the USA?
10. Which provinces have Securities Commissions? What is their purpose?

11. What effect did the accounting scandals of 2001–2002 have on the regulation of the accounting profession and corporate governance in the USA?
12. What was the Canadian response to the accounting scandals?
13. Why is a proper theory of accounting on which to base the development of the discipline considered important?
14. Why is the FASB's "conceptual framework of accounting" not a theory?
15. Explain what is meant by the proprietary and entity ownership theories. Which one has been adopted by the FASB?
16. In which ways do the objectives of financial reporting formulated by the FASB differ from those of the Accounting Standards Board of the CICA?
17. Why is the defining of the elements of financial statements considered an important part of the "conceptual framework of accounting"?
18. Why are the qualitative characteristics of accounting information of importance?
19. What interpretation has the Accounting Standards Board of the CICA placed on the term "generally accepted accounting principles"?
20. What is the role of the International Accounting Standards Board?

CASES

CASE 1–1   **The Accounting Students CA Finalists Program**

You are a senior manager with the firm of Greene, Cicconi and Ayling, Chartered Accountants of Toronto. At seven o'clock that morning, you had received a telephone call from Bruce, the partner to whom you were responsible, asking you to stand in for him and present a lecture and lead a discussion group that evening for the Accounting Students CA Finalists Program on certain aspects of financial reporting. The material required for the presentation would be delivered to the office later that morning.

On examining the material you discover that the lecture involved a presentation on the financial reporting objectives of four companies, the details of which are provided below.

(a)   Latham Financial Enterprises Inc., a closely held private company, carries on business of investment consultants in Toronto. The shares in the company are held equally by Brian Evans, his wife Cathy, and his father-in-law, Bert Latham. Brian Evans is the president and chief executive officer of the company. Bert Latham, who acted as vice-president finance, has recently retired and moved to Victoria on Vancouver Island. Besides attending board meetings, Cathy takes little active interest in the company.

(b)   Forbes Brothers Inc. is a closely held construction company in which the shares are owned jointly by Peter and Bill Forbes, who were responsible for the day-to-day management of the company. Three years ago, the company had found itself in financial difficulties. To avoid the company declaring bankruptcy, the major creditor of the company, Ajax Finance Corporation Ltd., had assumed the company's liabilities of $400,000 in return for an interest payment of 15% per year on the amounts outstanding and two seats on the board of directors: one that carried the chair of the board of directors and the other as an additional casting vote in the event of an equality of votes. This agreement was to continue until the outstanding amount had been repaid in full. The company had returned to profitable trading conditions and, at the end of the last financial year, the amount owing to the Ajax Finance Corporation had been reduced to $360,000.

(c)   The ITS Purchasing Company Inc., a public company having 40 shareholders, had been formed some eight years ago as the central purchasing company by the owners of 40 independent ladies' clothing shops in Metropolitan Toronto to take advantage of bulk buying. The chief executive officer of the company was

Albert Bozzo, who was responsible for his actions to the company's board of directors, which consisted of five members.

(d)   Rice-Davidson Inc. is a public company involved in the manufacture and supply of paper products whose shares were publicly traded on the Toronto Stock Exchange. The shareholding in the company was widely dispersed, and no single shareholder owned more than 1% of the shares in the company. Even though the company had earned good profits over the past few years, shareholder apathy had been so great that the present board of directors of the company had been re-elected every year for the past four years by less than 2% of the votes being cast in person or by proxy.

REQUIRED

Analyze and list, with suitable reasons and in a form that could be distributed to the CA finalists at the conclusion of your lecture, the objectives of financial reporting as they would apply (or be of importance) to (1) the shareholders, and (2) the management of the four companies given above.

CASE 1–2   ### Babinski's Hams and Bacon Ltd.

In June of the current year, Chicago Meat Packers Inc. announced that it had acquired a controlling interest in Babinski's Hams and Bacon Ltd. of Edmonton, Alberta.

The purchase of the controlling interest in Babinski's had been strongly contested by a group of shareholders but, eventually, the holders of 54% of the shares had agreed to sell their shares to Chicago Meat Packers. The senior executives of Babinski's took early retirement, and a new management team from Chicago took over with effect from October 1.

The purchase of Babinski's was considered a good buy because it had developed a good name for its products over the years and, to ensure itself of a ready supply of meat, it operated a large cattle ranch and pig farm on the outskirts of Edmonton. Most important, however, was that it also held the following investments:

(a)   A 75% interest in Allison's Feeds Inc., a well-established and local livestock feed company operating in and around Edmonton. The 25% interest in the company was widely dispersed amongst the local farming community.

(b)   A 49% interest in Wolpe's Delis Ltd., a chain of delicatessen stores operating throughout the western provinces. The other 51% interest was owned by Manfred Wolpe and his two sons in equal shares.

REQUIRED

Prepare a report on the statutory and other financial reporting responsibilities of Babinski's and its associated companies for the new management of the company.

CASE 1–3   ### The Delaney Drug Company Inc.

The Delaney Drug Company Inc. enjoyed a market share of roughly one-third of the entire Canadian market for veterinary products. It had been formed in the 1920s by Philip Delaney and, in 1952, the company had gone public. Even though the shares of the company were listed on the Toronto Stock Exchange, Philip Delaney had owned a 55% interest in the company. In March of the current year, he sold his entire holding in the company to Alpha-Rotor Chemicals PLC, a major British pharmaceutical company, for an undisclosed sum with effect from April 1.

Alpha-Rotor was a multinational company that had for many years carried on business in Australia, New Zealand, Hong Kong, India, Malaysia and Singapore, as well as in the European Union. The purchase of the controlling interest in Delaney Drugs was its first venture into the North American market.

Shortly after the formalities relating to the take-over had been completed, the accountant of Delaney Drugs received a letter from the group accountant in Britain advising him that, in order to comply as far as possible with the parent company's accounting and other policies, the following matters required attention:

(a) The financial year end of the company was to be June 30. Where this was not the case, application must be made immediately to the Canada Revenue Agency to give effect to this requirement.

(b) Supplies of those pharmaceutical products not manufactured by Delaney Drugs but purchased locally would now be supplied by either the British holding company or its Australian subsidiary at cost plus 15%.

(c) All packaging requirements would henceforth be supplied directly from its British packaging division.

(d) A management fee of two and one-half percent of gross sales was to be charged against revenues and remitted quarterly to the holding company. The first such payment was to be made on June 30 and cover sales for the six-month period ending on that date.

(e) To standardize, as far as possible, accounting procedures and to facilitate the presentation of the consolidated financial statements of the group, the following procedures were to be followed:
    i. All inventory was to be valued at FIFO;
    ii. Any receivables outstanding for more than 120 days were to be treated as irrecoverable and written off as bad.
    iii. Amortization of capital assets was to be charged using the straight-line method and standardized at 10% per year on plant and equipment excluding buildings and 20% per year on motor vehicles. **No amortization** was to be charged on buildings.
    iv. All land and buildings were to be revalued by a qualified appraiser every five years and the adjustments credited or debited, as the case may be, against a capital reserve/surplus account.
    v. Future (or deferred) income taxes were to be calculated on a partial allocation basis in which only those timing differences that would reverse within three years were to be recognized.
    vi. All intangible assets, including goodwill, were to be amortized over three years.

The letter from the group accountant recognized that certain of these requirements may have to be modified to take local conditions into account, but all accountants were expected to implement these policies to the fullest possible extent.

REQUIRED

1. Prepare a reply to the group accountant on the extent to which these requirements could be carried out by the Delaney Drug Company; and
2. Consider the effects, if any, of these requirements on the balance of the shareholders in the Delaney Drug Company.

CASE 1–4 **Ralph, Sarah and Theresa**

Ralph, Sarah and Theresa, three accounting students, were discussing the nature of section 1000 of the CICA *Handbook*.

Ralph had this to say: "I don't really see the importance of this section. We are told that a 'conceptual framework' is necessary for the proper development of accounting because it provides a framework against which all accounting standards are judged. However, virtually the whole of the CICA *Handbook* was written before section 1000 was issued and even before the Financial Accounting Standards Board issued their 'conceptual framework of accounting.'"

"That's not the real purpose of section 1000," said Sarah. "It's there to tell us to whom we should direct our reports."

"Nonsense," Theresa stated, "it was issued to tell us what information to include in financial reports."

"That is why they included the four qualitative characteristics of accounting information in section 1000 because the information provided should be understandable, relevant, reliable and comparable," Ralph commented.

"That's garbage! How can anyone suggest that the inclusion of assets at their historical cost on the balance sheet provides relevant information when the assets are often worth considerably more than that?" said Sarah.

"It's no use questioning something as sacred to accountants as historical cost accounting," Theresa interjected. "You know as well as I do, accountants have been telling us for years that the balance sheet is not supposed to be a statement reflecting the financial position of an entity at a point in time — it's just a record of historical balances."

There was a brief silence until Ralph stated: "I'm not so sure that is not just an excuse for continuing to use historical cost accounting. I have serious misgivings on whether accountants have all the right answers."

REQUIRED

Explain and comment on the correctness or otherwise of the views expressed in relation to:

1. Section 1000 of the CICA *Handbook*; and
2. The validity of the four qualitative characteristics of accounting information as they apply to: (a) the valuation of assets at historical cost, and (b) assets valued at market value.

2

A Re-examination of the Historical Cost Accounting Model

LEARNING OBJECTIVES

After studying this chapter you should be able to:

1. Understand the development of the historical cost accounting model and its application to financial reporting in Canada and the USA;
2. Detail the characteristics and shortcomings of the historical cost accounting model and its effects on present-day financial reporting; and
3. Understand why the historical cost accounting model still enjoys widespread popularity.

THE NATURE AND USE OF HISTORICAL COST ACCOUNTING

The historical cost accounting model is an accounting system in which the recording and reporting of an enterprise's operations and their financial effects are measured using historical (or actual) costs. Assets and liabilities are retained in the books of enterprises at their transaction or cost prices until amortized or sold, irrespective of changes in their values arising from changes in the purchasing power of money.

Historical cost accounting is widely used even though it has been subjected to severe criticism. For example, in 1966 the American Accounting Association[1] concluded that though it found historical cost information relevant, it was not adequate as a basis of predicting future earnings, solvency and management effectiveness. Alternative accounting systems have been proposed in many countries and actually implemented in the Netherlands and Great Britain. However, in virtually every case, accountants have returned to the historical cost model.

There is also considerable resistance by accountants to change. The CICA *Handbook*[2] has, for example, taken the position that there should be no departure from historical cost accounting except in two cases. The one involves the valuation of assets arising from the

---

[1] American Accounting Association, *A Statement of Basic Accounting Theory*, 1966.
[2] Section 3060.

reorganization of a business, and the other relates to the revaluation of the assets of an acquired company in certain circumstances.[3]

This chapter re-examines the historical cost accounting model as it applies to financial reporting in Canada and the USA and how much reliance can be placed on the financial statements of reporting entities prepared using this model. It also examines why it continues to enjoy such widespread support.

THE DEVELOPMENT OF THE PRESENT ACCOUNTING MODEL

The historical cost accounting model is based on the system of double-entry bookkeeping developed in the city states of Italy during the mercantile period (from about 1080 to 1500 A.D.). This system of bookkeeping was first described in 1494 by a Franciscan monk, Luca Pacioli, in his book on mathematics entitled *Summa de Arithmetica, Geometria, Proportioni et Proportionalita*, which may be translated as "All about Arithmetic, Geometry, and Proportions."

No one knows when the system of double entry bookkeeping was developed. What is known is that it had been used for many years in different forms before 1494 by Italian merchants, bankers, and by governmental officials. The oldest record of such a system is the "Massari accounts" of the City (or Commune) of Genoa, by which the city accounted for its operations.[4] At that time, the criterion for deciding whether an accounting system satisfied the requirement of double entry bookkeeping was that the debit entries had to equal the credit entries.

There are a number of excellent translations of Pacioli's book.[5] Those who read them are usually surprised to see that, except for procedural matters relating to the initial transactions, the extraction of the trial balance, the annual closing of the books, and the adjustments required by accrual accounting, the system of double entry bookkeeping has remained almost unchanged since that time. The major differences are that, in those early times, there was no set reporting period and the accounting for commercial activities was usually on a venture basis. The closing off the books only occurred on the completion of the venture and, at that time, the balances of assets, liabilities and capital accounts were transferred to a new ledger.

Financial statements were developed considerably later as statements of assets and liabilities for various purposes: for example, their use for taxation purposes in France in the late 1600s. They were also developed to assist the managers of the major British corporate trading ventures of the 18th century to keep investors informed of the state of their investments because, in view of the size of these ventures, it was impossible for all interested parties to have access to the ledger.

With the onset of the Industrial Revolution in Britain in the mid-1700s, a different form of entity was required to cope with the growth in size and nature of business ventures. This led to considerable legislation affecting the formation and control of companies and the protection of investors. Of this legislation, the *Joint Stock Companies Act* in 1844 was, as outlined in Chapter One, the most important because it made the formation of companies considerably easier and introduced the requirement that audited balance sheets must be presented to shareholders.[6]

---

[3] See section 1625 on the use of "push down" accounting as a means of accounting for wholly-owned or virtually wholly-owned subsidiaries.

[4] See Michael Chatfield, *A History of Accounting Thought*, Hinsdale, Ill.: Dryden, 1974, for an excellent account of the development of the system.

[5] For example, *Ancient Double-Entry Bookkeeping* by John B. van Geijsbeek (1914), which was reprinted in 1974 by the Scholars Book Company of Houston, Texas.

[6] It was only in terms of the British *Companies Act* of 1928 that the presentation of an audited income statement became mandatory in that country.

The balance sheet, which was until relatively recent times considered the most important statement, was developed from the "balance statement" or forerunner of the post closing trial balance. Originally, as Pacioli described the system,[7] the various revenue and expense accounts in the ledger were closed off to the "increase and deficit", account in the ledger (i.e., the equivalent of the present income summary account), and the profit or loss transferred to the capital account. At this stage, a "balance statement" was prepared by extracting the balances from the ledger. This statement served two purposes. First, it established the accuracy of the bookkeeping and, second, it provided a convenient list of debit and credit balances to be used to open the new ledger. When an income statement was required, it was merely extracted from the "increase and deficit" account in the ledger. In the late 19th century, the cash flow statement was developed as a summary of the cash journals.

The *Joint Stock Companies Act* of 1844 also provided the impetus for the development of accounting associations in Britain.[8] They were established to control and regulate entry into the accounting profession and, as they developed, they did much to improve accounting and financial reporting requirements. A series of important legal decisions also helped to shape the form and content of financial statements in that country, so that towards the end of the 19th century, the British reporting system was relatively well developed. Considerable immigration of British accountants to North America occurred and, even though accounting and reporting requirements trailed well behind those in Britain, the accounting profession was well established in North America by the late 1890s.[9]

As accounting and reporting requirements became more complex, the model was adjusted to take accrual accounting, estimates, and allowances into account. However, little improvement in financial reporting occurred in North America until after the US Senate investigation into the reasons for the crash of the New York Stock Exchange in 1929. This occurred in 1933 when the Securities and Exchange Commission was formed and, for the first time, companies whose securities were traded on the New York Stock Exchange were required by the NYSE to have their financial statements audited. It also led to the beginnings of the development of accounting standards in the USA.

At about the same time, the viewpoint emerged in the USA that accounting was essentially concerned with the determination of net income and that the valuation of assets and liabilities was only of secondary importance.[10] This had an important effect on the development of accounting in the USA, because American accounting academics and professional associations started to direct their attention towards the measurement of earnings and to look upon the income statement as the most important financial statement. This viewpoint still **dominates American accounting thought**. In fact, when the Financial Accounting Standards Board tried to move towards a more "balance sheet" approach in its Discussion Memorandum on the objectives of financial reporting in 1976, this move was vehemently opposed by the business community.[11]

The "income statement" approach was, however, **not accepted** in Britain and in those countries following a similar reporting model, and the balance sheet continued to enjoy widespread support. The position has remained relatively unchanged, and that is why the

---

[7] van Geijsbeek, 1914, *op cit.*

[8] The first such body was the Edinburgh Society of Accountants formed in 1854 by royal charter giving us the term "Chartered Accountant". This Society, together with the Institute of Accountants and Actuaries of Glasgow, and the Society of Accountants in Aberdeen eventually united to become the Institute of Chartered Accountants of Scotland.

[9] See John L. Carey, *The Rise and Fall of the Accounting Profession: From Technician to Professional 1896–1936*, New York: American Institute of Certified Public Accountants, 1969, for an excellent review of the development of the accounting profession in the USA.

[10] For example, in 1936 the American Accounting Association stated in its "Tentative Statement of Accounting Principles" that "Accounting is thus not essentially a process of valuation, but the allocation of historical costs and revenues to the current and succeeding fiscal periods."

[11] See Eugene H. Flegm, "The Limitations of Accounting", *Accounting Horizons*, September 1989, pp. 90–97, for a full discussion of the topic.

revaluation of assets appearing on the balance sheets of companies in these countries is an acceptable accounting practice in what is referred to as the "modified historical cost accounting" model. It is also the reason why the International Accounting Standards Committee recognizes that companies may want to record their property, plant and equipment at revalued amounts.

From the 1930s onwards, accounting practices continued to be developed in accordance with the reporting philosophies and legislation of the individual countries. Today, despite similarities in the reporting environment in many countries, financial reporting still reflects local conditions. The only real common denominator is that, other than in the Netherlands, where a system of replacement value accounting may be used, accounting systems are all **still based** on historical cost accounting.

THE CHARACTERISTICS OF THE MODEL

The major characteristic of the historical cost accounting model is that transactions are **initially recorded** at their transaction values using the monetary unit as the measure of value. In this respect, transactions are identified as those events that affect the accounting equation (i.e., assets – liabilities = equities; or, for companies, assets = liabilities + shareholders' equity). The cost is measured in terms of the monetary exchange price at the time the transaction is completed.

This method of recording transactions is believed to provide an **objective measurement of the value** of an asset or item of expenditure because it is based on the **exchange price** established at the point of purchase or sale by persons dealing at arm's length. Furthermore, because the price at which the transaction took place is easily verifiable, it is thought to eliminate the use of **subjective or arbitrary values**.

The operation of the model is that expenditures are deferred as assets (i.e., as probable future benefits) if income flows or future benefits are expected to flow from them. If not, the amounts are written off as expenses. On the other hand, liabilities are recognized as probable future sacrifices of economic benefits arising from present obligations, and revenues are inflows of resources. Equities are considered to be the differences between assets and liabilities.

Net income is based on a residual concept and is the balance remaining after deducting expenses from revenues over a set period in accordance with the **matching principle**. It is important to note that the matching principle requires the matching of revenues and expenses **over a period of time**, and is **not** the matching of actual revenues and expenses against one another. This is because expenditures, like the insurance of property against fire damage, apply to the period under review, and cannot be identified with any specific revenues. As a result, we recognize the revenues for a specific period, and deduct from that amount, the expenses for that same period to arrive at the net income.

The **flow of resources** in and out of the entity is presented by reconciling and summarizing the differences between the opening and closing cash (or cash equivalent) balances. Where financing activities have occurred in forms other than in cash, these transactions are presented as adjustments to the cash flows.

It should be noted that the model is only concerned with **past transactions**. It is also based on the **assumption that the monetary unit is stable** and it is, therefore, assumed that the values at which assets are recorded on the balance sheet are not affected by changes in the purchasing power of money.

The information provided by this model is presented in three main financial statements: the **balance sheet**, the **income statement** and the **cash flow statement**. Additional statements are also required by companies. Besides the report of the auditors, a **statement of retained earnings** is required to reconcile the opening and closing balances of undistributed net income earned in prior periods. In Canada and the USA, a **management report and**

analysis explaining significant aspects of the financial statements and acknowledging management's responsibilities for the financial information is also required to be included as part of the annual report of companies whose securities are publicly traded.

THE THREE MAJOR FACTORS THAT HAVE INFLUENCED THE MODEL

An examination of the current historical cost accounting model shows that three major factors were influential in its development. These three factors are examined in this section.

Setting Accounting Standards Without a Proper Theoretical Framework

Up until the issue by the FASB of its "conceptual framework", accounting standards in the USA had been developed on an issue-by-issue basis without any agreement on the objectives of accounting and reporting. As the now defunct accounting firm Arthur Andersen & Co.[12] pointed out, this led to a situation where the rules and methods of accounting were **substituted for the objectives** of the accounting system. This was also the position in Canada, where accounting and reporting practices have been heavily influenced by those in the USA.

The most important example is where **historical cost**, which is only a method of recording value, has been treated as a **major objective of the accounting system**. In describing what occurred, Arthur Andersen & Co.[13] had this to say:

> ... the means to an end have become more controlling than the end itself. As a consequence, value reporting has been for the most part rejected. Accounting principles and accounting rules have been devised to create a substitute for valuation, and accountants even say that financial statements do not purport to present values but rather purport to present cost. Some accountants contend that "accounting does not try to reflect values," but that the balance sheet is merely a "repository for costs on their way to the income statement."

The problem is largely the result of the **American emphasis** on the **measurement of earnings** and the importance of the income statement in financial reporting. It stems from the long held viewpoint that the purpose of accounting is to provide information to allow investors and loan creditors to assess the amounts, timing and uncertainty of cash flows to them. As a result, the **balance sheet** is considered of **relatively little importance** and, consequently, assets and liabilities have been valued at cost and treated in a way that facilitates the determination of net income.

For example, depreciation (also now referred to as amortization) is no longer considered the amount by which the service potential of an asset has declined during the reporting period, but merely an allocation of costs to different accounting periods. The CICA *Handbook*[14] is quite clear on this point where it states that as far as it is concerned, "Amortization [or depreciation and depletion] is the charge to income which recognizes that life is finite and the cost less salvage value or residual value of an item of property, plant and equipment is allocated to periods of service provided by the asset."

Past pension costs also provide a typical example of this position. The outstanding liability is not recorded on the balance sheet, even though a proportionate share of these costs is charged against revenues in the income statement as part of the annual pension expense.

---

[12]   See Arthur Andersen & Co., *Objectives of Financial Statements for Business Enterprises*, 1972, for a full discussion of this point.

[13]   *Ibid.*

[14]   Section 3060.

It also applies to intangible assets that are required to be amortized over their expected useful lives. As a result, perpetual franchises, trademarks, brand names, and other intangible assets that can be separately identified (i.e., other than goodwill which applies to the entity as a whole), may be carried on the balance sheet at a fraction of their actual value.

The problem goes even deeper. Accounting standards setters, in having to tackle pressing accounting issues, have often approved accounting standards that resolve the immediate issue without sufficient regard for its theoretical correctness. For example, both the amortization of past pension costs and the carryback of income tax losses, which are adjustments relating to prior periods, violate the matching principle, because they are brought into account in periods different from those in which they arose.

The position has changed, to some extent, since the acceptance by the FASB of its "conceptual framework" of accounting. It has subsequently approved the use of the liability basis of income tax allocation, where the emphasis is on the valuation of the future liability for income taxes on the balance sheet. It has also stated that it is moving towards a full market valuation of securities.

Any suggestion that a change in emphasis may be at hand is premature. As outlined in Chapter One, the FASB's "conceptual framework" of accounting is not a theoretical structure, but a framework of ideas designed to improve accounting practice. Accounting standards are, therefore, based on **accounting doctrine**[15] and depend for their acceptance on what the standard setters see as the goals and objectives of the accounting system. At present, there is little evidence to indicate that any real change has occurred.

The Principle of Conservatism

The second major issue affecting the historical cost accounting model is the **principle of conservatism**. It holds that where an **alternative exists** in the valuation of an asset or liability, or the recognition of revenues and expenses, **the one giving the least favourable effect should always be chosen**.

The principle of conservatism, which still enjoys considerable acceptance amongst practising accountants, was, up until the early 1960s, considered an acceptable accounting principle. It was considered so important by Sterling[16] that he described it as the dominant principle in accounting and the premise on which the "historical cost-realization rule" was derived. In making his point, Sterling even went as far as to imply that the justification for using the historical cost accounting model falls away if the principle of conservatism no longer applies.

The reality of the situation is that **conservatism pervades** virtually every aspect of an accountant's life. For years accountants have been on the receiving end of jokes regarding their dress, behaviour and attitude. Even though accusations of conservatism in dress can often be easily dismissed, those of conservatism in behaviour and attitude are **usually correct**. To see how true this is, one has to look no further than the CICA *Handbook*.

The lower of cost and market rule in valuing inventories is blatant conservatism. So is the requirement that any write-down of the carrying value of investments and foreign assets cannot be reversed if there is a recovery in their value.

Recessionary conditions have also provided a different slant to the application of conservatism. In many cases, accountants in the USA and Canada have been conservative in not

---

15   The distinction between theory and doctrine was explained by Louis Goldberg ("Varieties of Accounting Theories", in *Foundations of Accounting Theory*, Willard E. Stone (Ed.), Gainsville, Fl: University of Florida Press, 1971), where he pointed out that accounting theory is concerned with discovering propositions of a generalized nature about accounting phenomena, while accounting doctrine is concerned with propounding or laying down standards that govern the activities of accountants.

16   Robert R. Sterling, "Conservatism: The Fundamental Principle of Valuation in Traditional Accounting", *Abacus*, December 1967, pp. 109–32.

insisting that investments in real estate be revalued downwards by lending institutions because they believed that the decline in value was only temporary in nature.

Attempts are being made to eliminate some of the most glaring applications of conservatism. For example, intermediate accounting textbooks now promote the use of valuing inventory at the lower-of-cost-or-market on a "major category" or group basis rather than by every individual item. Similarly, the use of deferrals or allowances to account for the decline in value of portfolios of temporary investments is being encouraged rather than the individual write-down of each investment.

There can be no doubt that conservatism is a major problem in accounting. Unfortunately, accountants are conservative by nature, and the historical cost accounting model provides little incentive to act otherwise.

The Proprietorship Emphasis of the Reporting System

The third major factor that has influenced the development of the model is the original emphasis on the interests of the owner or owners of the business. This emphasis remains the cornerstone of the present accounting and reporting system and, as far as the FASB is concerned, it will continue to be the position for the foreseeable future.

As outlined in the previous chapter, this emphasis is referred to as the proprietary ownership theory. With this theory, the emphasis of the reporting system is on the owners, and the accounting equation is Assets – Liabilities = Owners' Equity. This focus of attention is also reflected by the income statement, which is drawn up on the basis of Revenues – Expenses = Net Income attributable to Owners.

The more recent innovation is the entity ownership theory, which developed with the increased use of companies for business ventures. Its formulation is attributable to Paton,[17] who argued that, as a company was an entity that existed in its own right and for the benefit of the equity owners, the accounting equation should be presented as Assets = Liabilities + Shareholders' Equity. The argument was based on the contention that the contributors of capital, whether they are shareholders or loan creditors, have a claim against the assets of the entity according to their contracts.[18] As a result, the presentation of the income statement under this theory, which has never been properly presented in accounting literature, implies that interest on loans should be treated as a distribution of income and not an expense.

Today, even though the balance sheets of companies tend to be presented along the lines applicable to the entity ownership accounting equation, the shareholders' equity section continues to present information based on the proprietary ownership theory. In this respect, the equity is described as the "shareholders' equity", and the balance of retained earnings represents the amount available to be distributed to shareholders.[19] As far as the income statement is concerned, the net income (or loss) is presented as the amount available for distribution to shareholders in the form of a dividend.

VALUATION AT HISTORICAL COST

How Objective Is Historical Cost?

Historical costs are believed to be objective and unbiased because they are based on exchange prices. An examination of the recording of assets and expenditures shows that this

---

[17]   William A. Paton, *Accounting Theory*, New York: The Ronald Press, 1922.

[18]   W.A. Paton and A.C. Littleton, *An Introduction to Corporate Accounting Standards*, Chicago: American Accounting Association, 1940.

[19]   It is for this reason that the interests of minority shareholders are not reflected as part of the equity of the consolidated entity on the consolidated balance sheet.

is not necessarily the case because the amount expended is not a conclusive measure of value or an expense. The question lies in what is recorded as the historic cost depends upon **market conditions** and the **subjective judgment** of the person concerned.

Historical costs can also only provide an objective measurement of value or price in **conditions of perfect competition and market efficiency**. In this respect, the amount paid by a large organization for an asset would, in all probability, be considerably less than that paid by a relatively small company. Therefore, the prices at which assets or expenses are recorded only relate to the exchange prices of the reporting entity.

Using exchange prices is also only the first step in the valuation process because the historical cost of an item only represents its historical exchange price at the time of purchase. From that time onwards, the exchange price seldom, if ever, provides the correct value at which the asset is recorded. For example, the actual cost of inventory depends upon the inclusion or exclusion of freight charges, discounts, and overhead. It also depends upon whether the inventory is valued at FIFO, LIFO, average or standard cost. With assets like land, buildings and equipment, the inclusion of many expenses depends entirely upon the judgment of the person recording the asset.

Where assets are not acquired by purchase, the issue of cost is even more subjective. This is because the cost of self-created assets depends upon the policy relating to the charging of overhead, supervision, administration, and interest on borrowed moneys. Moreover, the cost of a building can differ substantially depending upon whether it was financed from borrowings with the capitalization of interest or from existing cash resources.

The Assumption That the Monetary Unit Is Stable

The historical cost accounting model is based on the assumption that the monetary unit is stable. As a result, it fails to consider changes in the purchasing power of money over time and, as a result, items expressed in terms of historical cost become less useful and less comparable over time.

To rectify the position, an adjustment in their values is required. Where such an adjustment is made to recognize the amount by which the purchasing power of money has affected the value of an asset, the restated amount is referred to as being at its **real value**. Consequently, we call such an adjustment a restatement of value in **real terms**.

The problem applies mainly to fixed assets because they are normally held for periods of more than of one year. Current assets, on the other hand, are held for only relatively short periods of time, and changes in their values are not as marked as with fixed assets. The position is similar with liabilities. As the purchasing power of money declines, the amount outstanding for longterm liabilities decreases in real terms providing, at times, considerable advantages to borrowers. Current liabilities are normally of a monetary nature and are, like current assets, only outstanding for relatively short periods of time.

Amortization and Depreciation

As historical cost accounting fails to recognize changes in the purchasing power of money, it results in the carrying of capital assets on the balance sheet at unrealistic amounts. The effect of this is that the amounts by which these assets are expensed (or amortized) are also incorrect in terms of their current values.

For example, assume that an item of equipment was purchased for $100,000 on January 1, 20X1 and was being amortized on the straight-line basis over 10 years with no residual value. Assume also that the rate of decline in the purchasing power of the dollar (or rate of inflation) for 20X1 was 12%, and that prices increased in proportion to the decline in the purchasing power of the dollar. On December 31, 20X1, an amount of $112,000 would have been required to purchase an identical item of equipment. In effect, this means that the equipment would be undervalued by $12,000 and the amortization for 20X1 of $10,000 (i.e., $100,000/10) would have been understated by $1,200 (i.e., $112,000/10 – $100,000/10).

The problem is that the decline in the real value of assets in times of rising prices **is cumulative and compounded**. Assume, using the above example, that the decline in the purchasing power of money was 11% in 20X2 and 20X3. If so, the purchase price of the equipment in real terms at December 31, 20X2 and 20X3 would have been $124,320 (i.e., $112,000 + [11% × $112,000]) and $137,995 (i.e., $124,320 + [11% × $124,320]) respectively. The corresponding depreciation expense for 20X2 and 20X3 in real terms would have been $12,432 (i.e., $124,320/10) and $13,799 (i.e., $137,995/10).

The Asymmetric Valuation of Assets and Liabilities

The valuation of assets and liabilities at their historical cost without any regard for changes in the purchasing power of the money also results in what is called the asymmetrical valuation of assets and liabilities.

For example, assume that the balance sheet of a company reflects land at the value of $120,000. An examination of this item shows that it consists of two pieces of land each costing $60,000, one in Toronto and the other in suburban Mississauga. The Toronto property was purchased in 1902, is situated in the heart the financial district and has been cleared pending the construction of a new building; a conservative estimate of its current value is $12-million. As far as the other is concerned, the land is an undeveloped plot of land purchased some two months earlier at what was considered a fair price. However, in terms of the historical cost accounting, these assets are both properly valued.

No matter how unrealistic the above situation may appear, the valuation of assets in this manner is exactly what is required by the CICA *Handbook*, which recommends in section 3061 that "[t]he cost of a capital asset should be recorded at cost." Assets must, therefore, be valued and recorded at their cost on the balance sheet, irrespective of the date on which they were purchased.

The problem is that the values of assets is not only unrealistic but it could also result in identical assets being carried on the balance sheet at different values. It may, therefore, be said that with historical cost accounting the assets do not represent a basket of apples or pears, but rather a basket of vastly different fruits — a pineapple, some apples, apricots, pears and an orange. As outlined earlier, the amortization of assets depends upon the value at which the assets are recorded, and the longer they are held, the greater the difference between the actual decline in service potential and the amount charged against revenues in the income statement.

ITS FAILURE TO RECOGNIZE HOLDING GAINS AND LOSSES

The Position with Inventories

The "all inclusive" concept of income required by the CICA *Handbook* requires that gains and losses arising from the sale of capital assets and investments must be disclosed as separate items in the income statement in the year in which they occur. The reason for this is that they are considered to be non-recurring items arising from transactions that are not typical of the normal operations of the entity.

With the sale of goods and services, however, gains or losses arising from changes in the value of inventory need not be disclosed at all. As a result, these changes in value are merely treated as part of the cost of goods sold. The difference in treatment is justified because changes in the value of inventory occur relatively often, and these gains or losses are part of the normal operations of the reporting entity.

This difference in treatment has concerned accountants for many years.[20] The concern is that the net income figure is distorted by the inclusion of gains or losses arising from changes in the value of inventory between the time of acquisition and sale. These changes may arise through the purchase of goods in anticipation of an increase in price or from other factors over which the entity has no control. They are called "**realized holding gains or losses**" if they apply to goods that have been sold, and as "**unrealized holding gains or losses**" if the items to which they relate have not been sold.

These holding gains or losses are not considered part of the normal trading operations of the entity unless they were acquired and held in anticipation of an increase in price. They should, therefore, be recorded separately from the calculation of net income.

The historical cost income statement is easily adjusted to reflect these holding gains. All that is required is to split the historical cost net income into its two components: the actual net income from the sale of goods, and the gain or loss arising from holding the inventory. The unrealized gain or loss is then brought into account as a separate item. It is also necessary to adjust the value at which the inventory is carried on the balance sheet.

An illustration of how the income statement may be restated to reflect the operational net income excluding holding gains is provided in Illustration 2–1. In this illustration, the adjusted income statement reflects both the actual profit on the sale of $30,000 and the realized gain of $20,000 to equal the historical cost net income of $50,000. The unrealized gain of $15,000 on the remaining item of equipment is brought into account as additional capital surplus and as an increase in the value of the inventory.

The need to recognize these holding gains is to ensure that the net income of the reporting entity is not overstated by the inclusion of amounts arising from changes in the value of inventory. In the case of a company, this could lead to the overpayment of dividends and the erosion of its capital to the extent that it may no longer be able to operate effectively. Accountants normally only recognize income after providing for the maintenance of the capital and, if the income has not been properly determined, this cannot be carried out.

To illustrate this point, assume that immediately after the sale of the equipment on October 31, 20X4 in Illustration 2–1, the company paid out the entire historical cost net income of $50,000 as a dividend. When the company purchased the additional item of equipment on November 1, 20X4 for $120,000, it would have been short of cash by $20,000. This is because it should have retained the holding gain of $20,000 in the business as the capital required to restore the business to its previous position of holding one item of equipment for resale.

Other Holding Gains and Losses

Unrealized gains or losses also occur from changes in the value of fixed assets and investments held by the reporting entity. In fact, the revaluation of investments at their market value by taking holding gains and losses into account is an **accepted industry practice** with mutual funds.

As outlined earlier, the CICA *Handbook* does not allow companies to recognize unrealized gains on fixed or other capital assets. The treatment is inconsistent and ultra-conservative because it requires that a decline in the value of an asset must be recognized and written down when it is considered permanent in nature. However, no allowance is made for any increases in the value of assets.

Unrealized gains or losses also arise with other assets, but changes in their values are **rarely considered important**. Accounts receivables, for example, are not discounted to their

---

[20] It was considered in relation to the cost of goods sold in *Accounting and Reporting Standards for Corporate Financial Statements*, 1957 Revision, American Accounting Association; in *The Realization Concept*, Report of the 1964 Concepts and Standards Research Study Committee, American Accounting Association, 1965; and by F.E.P. Sandilands, *Inflation Accounting — Report of the Inflation Accounting Committee* (i.e., "The Sandilands Report"), London: Her Majesty's Stationery Office, Cmnd. 6225, 1975.

ILLUSTRATION 2–1
ACCOUNTING FOR UNREALIZED GAINS AND LOSSES USING THE CONCEPT OF PRODUCTIVE CAPACITY CAPITAL MAINTENANCE

Trader Inc., a company having a December 31 year end, was formed on July 31, 20X4 with a capital of $100,000 in cash. On August 1, 20X4, the company purchased an item of equipment for cash for resale at a cost of $100,000 On October 31, 20X4 it sold the equipment for $150,000. On November 1, 20X4, it purchased an identical item of equipment for $120,000, which was also the replacement cost of the equipment sold on October 31, 20X4. On December 31, 20X4, the unsold equipment had a replacement cost of $135,000. To simplify the illustration, administrative and selling expenses are ignored.

The determination of the net income for the five-month period ended December 31, 20X4 using, first, a conventional historical cost basis and then, second, by comparing it with the recognition of holding gains and losses is provided below:

	Historical Cost	Recognition of Holding Gains
Sales	$150,000	$150,000
Cost of Goods Sold:		
At Historical Cost	100,000	—
At Replacement Cost	—	120,000
Net Income	$ 50,000	$ 30,000
Realized Holding Gain ($120,000 − $100,000)		$ 20,000
Unrealized Holding Gain ($135,000 − $120,000)		$ 15,000

The entries recording the realized and unrealized holding gains would be as follows:

Retained Earnings	20,000	
Capital Surplus — Realized Holding Gains		20,000
Adjustment to record realized holding gain.		
Inventory	15,000	
Capital Surplus — Unrealized Holding Gains		15,000
Revaluation of inventory (i.e., equipment) to record unrealized holding gain.		

present value because the collection period is normally too short to affect the balance sheet or net income. However, where the changes in value are material in amount, they should always be recognized and brought into account.

THE ALLOCATION PROBLEM

A cost allocation approach is used by the historical cost accounting model to recognize the amortization of all capital assets other than land. With this method, the cost less any residual value is written off systematically over a set number of years. The amortization must be recognized in a rational and systematic manner that is appropriate to the nature of the item of property, plant and equipment.[21] The amount of amortization that should be charged against income should be the greater of the cost of the asset less salvage value or residual value over the life of the asset. Any one of the generally accepted amortization methods (i.e., straight-line, declining balance, sum-of-years-digits, etc.) may be used.

The amortization of capital assets is carried out to recognize, as an expense, the amount by which the value of the asset has declined during the period under review. These amounts are, at best, only estimates, and accountants acknowledge that the various methods of amortizing capital assets give rise to different amounts. As a result, the net income and the values at

---

[21] CICA *Handbook*, section 3061.

which the assets are carried on the balance sheet can vary considerably depending upon which method has been used. In deciding which method to use, an accountant should select the method that will best represent economic reality.

In the late 1960s and mid-1970s, Arthur L. Thomas[22] examined the entire issue of accounting allocations.[23,24] In his first study, completed in 1969, he concluded that these allocations were almost **all arbitrary in nature,** and that there was "... no theoretically justified way to support most of the figures now appearing on financial statements." In his second study published in 1974, he further concluded that these allocations were also **incorrigible,** and that no legitimate purpose was being advanced by making these allocations. Therefore, the **making of financial allocations should cease.**

Thomas was not only concerned with the allocation of the service costs associated with any asset, but also other items like the allocation of past service pension benefits. His concern was to determine how much of the estimated service value of an asset should be associated with any period and which method, if any, should be used.

He reached the conclusion that all allocation methods were **arbitrary** because they could not be theoretically justified. To be theoretically justifiable, an allocation method must clearly be the appropriate method. This, in turn, requires that the method should explain how the allocation should be made, be defensible against all other methods, and divide up what is to be allocated exactly. Here, Thomas argued that as all methods were justifiable to some extent, no single method could be considered the only appropriate one.

To be **incorrigible,** the issue must be one that is impossible to prove correct or incorrect. Thomas concluded that accounting allocations are incorrigible because they cannot be verified by reference to any real world phenomena or values. For example, cost less accumulated depreciation does not give the correct value of a fixed asset or the extent to which its service potential has declined over a period of time. There is, therefore, no way to establish the correctness of the allocation.

The **overall conclusion** reached by Thomas was that accountants should find an allocation-free method of determining net income or abandon the effort completely. This was, as far as he was concerned, only possible using a current exit value basis where depreciation, for example, is the difference between the realizable value at the beginning and end of the accounting period.[25]

To what extent it is possible to achieve an entirely allocation-free accounting system is a matter for debate. There can, however, be no doubt the cost allocation methods presently used by accountants are subjective and, consequently, unsatisfactory. If nothing else, Thomas's research has made accountants aware of some of these shortcomings.

SUPPORT FOR THE MODEL

Over the years, the historical cost accounting model has continued to enjoy considerable support and, even in times of severe inflation, any suggestions of adopting an alternative reporting model have been resisted. The main reason for this, as expressed by Ijiri[26] and others, is that historical costs are objective and form the basis for all accounting figures. The major area of

---

[22] Arthur L. Thomas, *The Allocation Problem in Financial Accounting Theory*, Studies in Accounting Research No. 3, American Accounting Association, 1969; and, *The Allocation Problem: Part Two*, Studies in Accounting Research No. 9, American Accounting Association, 1974.

[23] Much of this and subsequent paragraphs are based on the excellent review of this research by Leonard G. Eckel, "Can Financial Accounting Allocations be Justified?" *CA Magazine*, May 1978, pp. 49–53.

[24] This work was considered so important that he received a gold medal from the American Institute of Certified Public Accountants for making such an outstanding contribution to accounting literature.

[25] See Jayne Godfrey, Allan Hodgson and Scott Holmes, *Accounting Theory*, Third Edition (Brisbane: John Wiley & Sons, 1997) for an excellent review of exit value accounting.

[26] For example, see Yuji Ijiri, *op cit.*, 1981, where this is the underlying theme throughout the research study.

concern to accountants is that any change in the model would require the **subjective valuation** of assets. Experience has shown that this attitude is unlikely to change because assets recorded at their actual cost are considered by them to be unbiased, objective and easily verifiable. They also believe that **any adoption of value accounting would increase the likelihood of legal action against them**.

The belief that the subjective valuation of assets would lead to the overvaluation of assets is, however, subject to debate. This is because one of the major areas of interest to investors is the return on investment (ROI), and any overvaluation of assets would result in a lower ROI, something that a publicly traded company would try to avoid. The ongoing revaluation of assets would, in all probability, lead to more realistic asset values because any overvaluation in one period would be rectified in the following period.

It also appears that much of the support for historical cost accounting is due to **familiarity with the existing model**. Irrespective of the reason, the inclusion of figures adjusted for changes in the purchasing power of money in financial statements or the notes thereto have been rejected by practising accountants in Britain, Canada and the USA.[27]

Support from the **financial analyst community** is, however, somewhat different. This is because much of the theory on which the study of corporate finance is based was developed in times of relative price stability and when the rates of inflation were low. As a result, their theoretical models are based on the assumption that inflation does not apply. They also look upon the maintenance of capital from the financial point of view that holds that the capital invested in a business is the amount contributed by the owners plus any retained earnings re-invested in the business. As a result, there is no need to calculate the capital employed in real terms.

This group has also successfully argued that there is **no evidence** that financial statements prepared using historical costs are **less useful** than those prepared using alternative methods. They also point out that financial statements no longer enjoy their former importance in investment decision making because more reliance is being placed on other aspects of financial reporting, including financial forecasts, macro-economic indicators, and information relating to the supply and demand for goods and services.

There is also considerable support for the model from those who look to **agency theory** to resolve (or explain) certain current reporting problems. Supporters of this theory point out that managers (as the agents of the shareholders) often enter into contracts with the reporting entity that have objectives that differ from those of the shareholders, and that these contracts are all based on the information provided by the historical cost accounting model.

In addition, research related to the **efficient markets hypothesis** (EMH) suggests that investors seem to understand financial information whether acting on their own or through intermediaries. Securities markets also react to those accounting changes affecting economic events and not necessarily to those accounting adjustments arising from changes in reporting requirements. It, therefore, makes little difference how the information is presented.

Accounting literature also contains additional arguments supporting **specific aspects of historical cost accounting**. These all fall into one or other of the following areas:

1. All economic decisions, and particularly those predicting the future, are based on past events. Historical cost provides undisputed evidence of those transactions.
2. Historical cost accounting provides irrefutable evidence of the existence and value of assets for managerial control and the demonstration of stewardship. The chance of manipulating balances are, therefore, reduced.

---

[27] *Statement of Standard Accounting Practice No. 16: Current Cost Accounting*, issued in Britain in 1980; section 4510 of the CICA *Handbook*, issued in 1982; and, *Statement of Financial Accounting Standards No. 33: Financial Reporting and Changing Prices*, issued in 1979 by the FASB and replaced in 1986 by *SFAS No. 89* under the same title.

3. Historical costs provide a more equitable means of distributing income to shareholders, loan creditors and others than their alternatives because they are not based on the hypothetical opportunity costs used by alternative models.
4. The results of business transactions can really only be measured on completion of the venture, disposal of assets or the discharge of liabilities. Any determinations of gains or losses in the interim are merely estimates.
5. Historical cost accounting is based on the going concern concept and, as the firm is not going to sell its fixed assets, there is little need to revalue them. Where changes in the values at which assets are recorded have been made, these changes can easily be presented as supplementary data.

ANALYSIS OF THE SHORTCOMINGS OF THE MODEL

It is necessary to assess the shortcomings of financial statements prepared using historical costs and their effects on financial reporting.

The **balance sheet**, when prepared on this basis, has serious limitations in providing a statement of the financial position of the reporting entity. The problem is largely one of valuation because the assets are recorded at their historical costs, which seldom provide an indication of their true value. This situation arises from two issues: First, the failure to recognize changes in the purchasing power of money; second, the refusal of the standard setting bodies in the USA and Canada to recognize the effects of economic factors on the value of assets and invested capital. Historical cost accounting also restricts the concept of capital maintenance to the amounts originally contributed. As a result, it is also doubtful whether the balance sheet can be used to predict the continued solvency of the business with any accuracy. From a conceptual point of view, this also places in doubt the issue of "representational faithfulness" in relation to the reliability of the information provided.

The **income statement**, likewise, does not provide a proper measure of the performance of an entity over a period of time. This is because the combined effects of conservatism, arbitrary cost allocations, and the systematic and arbitrary write-off of intangible assets all point to the fact that reported net income is not an accurate measure of performance. It is also doubtful whether it provides the means of predicting future earnings. Differences in the valuation of inventories also place doubts in the extent to which the results of operations (and the value of assets) are comparable.

In addition, **in times of rising prices**, income is also overstated. This is because the amounts charged against revenues for depreciation (or amortization) depend upon the value at which the assets have been recorded. The longer assets are held, the greater the effects of the changes in the purchasing power of money. The failure to recognize holding gains also leads to the overstatement of operating net income which could, depending upon the dividend policy of the company concerned, also lead to a reduction in real capital.

There are certain other important general financial reporting issues that have **not been covered** in this examination of the historical cost accounting model. The reason for this is that they apply to financial reporting in general and are not specific to historical cost accounting. For example, certain other assets, like "self-created" goodwill, the expertise developed from research and development expenditures, and human resources, are not recognized even though they may be extremely valuable assets of the firm. Increases in value from discovery and accretion are usually also ignored.

When viewed objectively, there can be no doubt that the **relevance** of the information provided by the historical cost accounting model has been **sacrificed in favour of its reliability**. Taken together, the situation is so serious that the balance sheet can no longer be considered a statement reflecting the financial position of an entity at a point in time. It is also questionable whether the income statement really provides a realistic measure of the performance of the entity for the period under review. As a result, it appears that **analyses of performance** of an entity using historical costs can really only be determined by comparing the changes in reported performance from one year to another.

Finally, it should be borne in mind that these are **not merely limitations** of the reporting system, but **serious flaws** in the accounting model. They can be rectified, but only through the acceptance that change is necessary. And, as the present low levels of inflation cannot be expected to continue indefinitely, the reporting system will again be subject to further substantial inaccuracies. Evidence also suggests that accountants and the financial analyst community will not be prepared to voluntarily accept changes to the model. The only solution may be for the authorities to mandate change. Unfortunately, there is little likelihood of this occurring until such time as the authorities are prepared to assess income taxes on inflation adjusted figures.

SOME POPULAR MISCONCEPTIONS

There are a number of misconceptions regarding historical cost accounting that are sometimes used to justify its continued use. The two most important are:

1. Historical cost accounting has **stood the test of time**. Certainly, it has been around for about 600 years, but it is only in the last 80–100 years that the change in the purchasing power of money (or inflation) has become a major factor in distorting reported figures.
2. **The demonstration of stewardship or accountability requires** the use of historical cost figures. Stewardship is essentially concerned with the control over physical assets, and it makes little difference how they are recorded because stewardship can be demonstrated equally well (if not better) with other accounting models. Furthermore, the absence of information on the real amortization of capital assets (i.e., the amount by which the service potential of the assets has declined) and holding gains or losses in figures provided by historical cost accounting makes it doubtful whether these figures can be used to assess accountability for the efficient and effective use of resources.

SUMMARY

This chapter re-examines the historical cost accounting model and the reasons it still enjoys widespread acceptance. It points out that the model was developed from the system of accounting used in the Italian city states in the mercantile period, and was adjusted to cater for more complex reporting requirements as the needs arose. In the 1930s, the income statement and the determination of net income became the primary area of attention of the model in the USA.

The chapter continues by drawing attention to the fact that the emphasis on the determination of net income in the USA and the setting of accounting standards without a proper theoretical framework led to the rejection of value accounting in favour of recording them at historical cost. As a result, the balance sheet was regarded as a repository for costs awaiting amortization in the determination of net income. The principle of conservatism also played an important role in development of the historical cost accounting model. The current financial reporting model is also based on the original emphasis on the owner or owners of the business entity.

The valuation of assets and liabilities was then examined to establish the objectivity of historical costs. It also examined the effect of basing the valuation of assets and liabilities on the assumption that the monetary unit was stable. This has led to the undervaluation of assets and the amounts by which they are amortized. It has also led to the asymmetrical valuation of assets. The difference in treatment of gains or losses on disposal of assets also results in the failure of the historical cost accounting model to recognize holding gains and losses on inventory. The allocation of costs was then examined in relation to the amortization of capital assets. Here, research has shown that all cost allocations are arbitrary and cannot be theoretically justified.

The support for the historical cost accounting model and its shortcomings was then examined. Here, it was explained that accountants perceive historical cost information as unbiased, objective, and easily verifiable. The financial analyst community supports the use of the model because there is no real evidence to show that the information provided by the model is less useful than that provided by other reporting models. Taken together, the shortcomings of the model are so severe that the balance sheet does not reflect the financial position of the reporting entity and the income statement does not provide a proper measure of the performance for the period under review. From an examination of the support for the model, it concludes that the support for the historical cost accounting model is so strong that it would probably be necessary to mandate any change to another reporting model.

REVIEW QUESTIONS

1. Besides the fact that Luca Pacioli described the system of bookkeeping that was being used, how do we know that it was in use before 1494?
2. In what major areas does the present double entry bookkeeping system differ from that described by Pacioli?
3. How did the present balance sheet evolve? The statement of cash flows?
4. How did the American emphasis on the determination of net income and the income statement influence the development of the present historical cost accounting model?
5. Was the American emphasis on the determination of net income universally accepted?
6. What role does conservatism play in historical cost accounting?
7. How objective is historical cost?
8. In which ways has the assumption that the monetary unit is stable affected the recording of assets on the balance sheet?
9. What is meant by the asymmetrical valuation of assets and liabilities?
10. How do unrealized holding gains or losses arise?
11. Why gains and losses on fixed assets are disclosed in the income statement, but those that relate to inventories are not?
12. Will the failure to recognize holding gains have any effect on the capital of a company if the total net income is paid out as a dividend?
13. Describe what is meant by the "allocation problem" in accounting. Why is it important?
14. What solution to the allocation problem did Arthur L. Thomas suggest?
15. Why do accountants support the continued use of the historical cost accounting model?
16. Why does the financial analyst community support historical cost accounting?
17. What general accounting issues were not examined in this chapter? How important are they?
18. Do you agree that a change in the present accounting system will only come about as a result of mandated changes? If not, why not?

CASES

CASE 2–1   **MacKinnon Chemicals Inc.**

In March of the current year, MacKinnon Chemicals Inc. had acquired a controlling interest in Pristine Soaps and Detergents Ltd., through a share exchange of one share in MacKinnon for four shares in Pristine. In making the offer, MacKinnon had hoped to obtain all Pristine's issued shares. However, only 82% of the shareholders agreed to the share exchange. Formalities relating to the acquisition were completed by April 30, and MacKinnon took control of the company on May 1.

EXHIBIT C2–1
VALUE OF THE NET ASSETS OF PRISTINE SOAPS AND DETERGENTS LTD.
AT DATE OF ACQUISITION

	Book Value	Market Value
Land	$ 1,802,000	$ 2,850,000
Plant and Equipment	16,700,500	21,900,650
Office Furniture and Equipment	456,325	864,000
Accounts Receivable	3,507,065	3,500,000
Inventories	4,100,700	4,130,765
	26,566,590	33,245,415
Liabilities	14,310,550	14,337,550
Net Assets/Equity	$12,256,040	$18,907,865

Pristine was a well-established company having been formed in 1946. It was the producer of the Zap brand of household detergents which accounted for some 70% of its turnover and 9% of the Canadian market. The balance of its business came from the sale of its range of Madelaine Soaps and Goliath Industrial Cleansers. MacKinnon's main reason for making the offer was to acquire the Zap trademark. It was also felt that the Goliath detergents and degreasers were highly regarded, and would complement its range of industrial chemical products. Furthermore, its factories were well situated for the possible future expansion into the US market.

Pre-acquisition research had indicated that Pristine was worth about $18-million. At the close of business on the day prior to the announcement of its intention to make the offer, MacKinnon's shares had been traded at $8 each on the Toronto Stock Exchange. Immediately following the success of its offer, MacKinnon had the assets and liabilities of Pristine appraised in order to establish the true cost of the acquisition.

In the course of this appraisal, MacKinnon found that Pristine owned considerably more plant assets than it had expected. The major surprise was that the land on which two fully depreciated warehouses were situated had been overlooked in the original estimation of its value because, in 1946, the land on which the warehouses had been erected had been included with that of Pristine's main plant. The book and appraised values of Pristine's assets and liabilities **excluding** the Zap trademark, which was worth at least another $1-million, are reflected in Exhibit C2–1.

On your arrival to commence the annual audit of the company, Angus MacKinnon, chairman and chief executive officer, had asked to see you regarding the value of Pristine's assets. On being ushered into his office, he told you that he knew that the CICA *Handbook* required that the value of Pristine's assets were to be reflected in the consolidated financial statements at their fair market values. However, this would give negative goodwill of $2,384,448, calculated as follows.

Purchase Consideration (1,640,000 shares at $8 each)		$13,120,000
Net Equity Acquired (82% $12,256,040)	$10,049,952	
Add: Fair Market Value Adjustments (82% $18,907,865 – $12,256,040])	5,454,496	15,504,448
Negative Goodwill		$ 2,384,448

He understood that in Canada, the negative goodwill should be written off proportionately against the assets acquired unless this would result in unrealistic values. In which case, the negative goodwill could be deferred and written off to income over six years which was the period MacKinnon was expected to be benefited from the acquisition of Pristine.

Mr. MacKinnon also whether that, in view of the fact that the company was considering a share issue, it would be possible to revalue all the company's net assets so that the financial statements of the company would reflect their current values. He had recently read that in Australia, Britain, and New Zealand, the revaluation of capital assets upwards or downwards to reflect them at their fair market values was considered fully acceptable. This, he understood, was called the modified historical cost accounting system.

REQUIRED

1. Evaluate the position taken by the CICA on its adherence to historical cost accounting and, in particular, its position relating to the revaluation of capital assets and the treatment of negative goodwill in the case of MacKinnon Chemicals;

2. Further consider whether, in terms of the CICA's stand on the operation of historical cost accounting, a value could be allocated to the Zap trademark and reflect it as a separate asset on the balance sheet of the company; and

3. Explain how the requirements of paragraph 1400.03 of the CICA *Handbook*, given below, may be satisfied in the above situation. Paragraph 1400.03 reads as follows:

> "Financial statements should present fairly in accordance with Canadian generally accepted accounting principles the financial position, results of operations and cash flows of an entity (that is, represent faithfully the substance of transactions and other events in accordance with the elements of financial statements, and the recognition and measurement criteria set out in financial statement concepts, Section 1000)."

CASE 2–2 **Standard Setting and Asset Values**

The economic downturn of the economies of Canada and the USA experienced during the late 1980s and 1990s brought attention to certain shortcomings in the historical cost accounting model that were not obvious in former times of relative affluence. These arose from the refusal by the CICA's Accounting Standards Board and the Financial Accounting Standards Board to accept its shortcomings. These applied to the valuation of capital assets contributing to the failure of certain financial institutions through lending money against overvalued immovable property. In many cases, these failures led to charges of negligence being brought against the auditors of these institutions. In fact, the position became so serious in the USA that the US Congress was called on to pass legislation to limit the liability of auditors for company failures relating to the overvaluation of fixed property.

The situation stemmed from the reluctance of accountants to write down the value of fixed assets unless there was irrefutable evidence that the decline in value was permanent in nature. Of particular importance was the 1992 statement by Mr. Walter P. Schuetze,[28] Chief Accountant of the Securities and Exchange Commission in the USA at that time and a former KPMG Peat Marwick partner, that US auditors should not look to the government to protect them against liability suits until they operated under more realistic accounting and auditing regulations. In particular, he deplored the resistance to valuing assets at their current cost. He also stated that "historical cost has lulled auditors to sleep." Mr. Schuetze also expressed the hope that the SEC would not have to take over the responsibility of standard setting in the USA from the FASB and call for the rotation of auditors. To make his point, he posed the question of whether, following the collapse of a major corporation from overstated asset values, the SEC would "mandate [the] rotation of auditing firms so as to make it more likely that auditors, who know they will be replaced, will not allow clients to report assets in excess of market values." He also called on the accounting profession to face the "issues of relevance and credibility in financial reporting, so as to maintain their own relevance and credibility."

---

[28] In an address to the Annual General Meeting of the American Accounting Association held in Washington, D.C., August 19–22, 1992.

The position in Canada is that section 3061 of the CICA *Handbook* requires that all capital assets must be recorded at historical cost, and that the value of capital assets should be written down in value when the amount at which they are recorded on the balance sheet exceeds their net recoverable amount. A write-down may not be reversed if the net recoverable amount subsequently increases. This gives rise to the problem that companies put off write-downs for as long as possible.

The Canadian and US position is interesting because the revaluation of fixed assets, either upwards or downwards, is fully acceptable in countries like Australia, Britain and New Zealand. The principle applied to the revaluation of fixed assets in these three countries is that the revaluation should be carried out systematically, preferably on an annual basis, and applied to all assets in the same class of assets. The valuations must, however, be carried out by an independent valuer or reviewed by such a person. The name of the valuer concerned must also be disclosed in the financial statements.

REQUIRED

Consider and discuss to what extent:

1. The reversal of write-downs of capital assets would improve the historical cost accounting model; and
2. The adoption of a current value approach would eliminate the problems of the overvaluation of capital assets.

Feasible Alternative Accounting Models 3

LEARNING OBJECTIVES

After studying this chapter you should be able to:

1. Appreciate that the adoption of an alternative accounting model is perfectly feasible;
2. Understand the nature of inflationary conditions and their effects on determining income and the maintenance of capital;
3. Apply and understand the price-level adjusted and current cost accounting models; and
4. Evaluate price-level adjusted accounting and current cost accounting in relation to the historical cost accounting model.

THE OBJECTIVE AND SCOPE OF THE CHAPTER

In the previous chapter, the historical cost accounting model was re-examined. It was concluded that the model was seriously flawed as a means of presenting the financial position of an entity and its performance over a period of time. The current low levels of inflation in North America and Europe have reduced the perceived need for an alternative reporting model but the shortcomings of historical cost accounting cannot be ignored indefinitely. Furthermore, inflation also continues to be a major problem in many countries and it is essential that accountants are aware of the nature and operation of the alternative accounting models.[1]

The use of an alternative accounting model is quite feasible. The multinational corporation, *N.V. Philips Electronics* of Eindhoven, in Holland (from now on called *Philips*), has used a system of replacement value accounting based on the work of Theodore Limperg[2] since 1951. This system also enjoys fairly widespread support in the Netherlands.

---

[1] For example, *The Globe and Mail* of December 20, 1995, reported that the current annual rate of inflation in Mexico was about 50%. The 2003 rate of inflation in Zimbabwe exceeded 500%.

[2] The work of Theodore Limperg (1879–1961), founder of the Commerce Faculty of the University of Amsterdam, was published posthumously by three of his former students, namely, A. Mey, J.L. Meij, and H.J. van der Schroeff, in six books entitled *Bedrijfseconomie: Verzameld Werk van Prof. Dr. Th. Limperg Jnr.*, Deventer: A.E. Kluwer, 1964–1968. But, because these books were written in Dutch, Limperg's work received little attention in Canada and the USA.

Price-level adjusted accounting and an integrated current cost accounting system have also been used in Britain. In the late 1970s and 1980s, supplementary price level and current cost data was also included in notes to the financial statements of certain public companies in the USA, Canada and elsewhere. There was, however, little support for these changes and, other than in the Netherlands, where replacement value accounting continues to be used, these reporting requirements are now voluntary or have been withdrawn.

Accountants have three choices. First, they can continue to use the historical cost accounting model with all its flaws. Second, they could adopt a system of price level-adjusted accountings that would provide more realistic information. Third, they could use a form of value accounting on a supplementary or fully integrated basis that would resolve most of the problems facing accountants.

Although other value accounting models exist, like current realizable value accounting[3], they have little practical significance. This chapter, therefore, only examines and evaluates two alternative accounting models — price-level adjusted accounting and current (replacement) cost accounting — which have proved to be feasible alternatives to historical cost accounting.

PRELIMINARY MATTERS OF IMPORTANCE

Measuring the Change in the Purchasing Power of Money

Economists, accountants and others find it difficult to define inflation. What they do agree upon is that **in inflationary conditions, the general purchasing power of the dollar declines and there is a general increase in the level of prices**. The opposite occurs in deflationary conditions.

The most common method of measuring changes in the purchasing power of the dollar is to use the Consumer Price Index (CPI) produced by Statistics Canada.[4] The CPI represents a measure of the amount by which a "basket of goods" and other costs, like housing and transportation, have increased in price across the country over a set period. The initial cost of the goods and services is given an index value of 100, and is adjusted monthly to reflect the general increase (or decrease) in prices.

For example, assume that at the end of June 20X1, Statistics Canada valued a "basket of goods" and the cost of housing and transportation at $912.78. At that date, the CPI stood at 127.33. If the value of these goods and services at the end of July 20X1 had increased by $6.39 to $919.17, the CPI at the end of July 20X1 would have been adjusted to 128.22. The rate of inflation for the month of July 20X1 would, therefore, have been 0.70% (i.e., [$128.22/ $127.33 × 100] − 100).

The problem with the CPI is that it only measures the general increase in prices, and not the actual increase in prices experienced by an individual or a business enterprise. Furthermore, the longer it is used, the more inaccurate it becomes, as eating and other habits change. Improved technology could also affect the amounts included in the CPI. It is, therefore, necessary to revise the "basket of goods" and services every few years.

---

3 This model was originally proposed by Kenneth MacNeal (*Truth in Accounting*, Philadelphia: University of Pennsylvania Press, 1939) and subsequently developed by Raymond Chambers (*Accounting, Evaluation and Economic Behavior*, Englewood Cliffs, NJ: Prentice-Hall, 1966). Assets are valued at their net realizable value as soon as they are acquired and, although it is of considerable theoretical interest, it represents too great a departure from current accounting thought to be considered a viable alternative to historical cost accounting.

4 Other measures are available like the Wholesale Price Index, the Industrial Selling Price Index and the Gross National Expenditure Deflator, all of which are produced by Statistics Canada.

The Use of Money as a Measure of Value

For many years accountants have used money as a measure of value and as the means of reducing values to a common denomination. In doing so, accountants have managed to express the value of many diverse assets and liabilities in simple and understandable amounts. Unfortunately, this has led to the position where **money** is often looked upon as the **only measure of value**. And, as outlined in the previous chapter, the major problem with historical cost accounting is that it is based on the assumption that the value of the monetary unit is stable.

Nonmonetary assets can be restated by using a different measure of value, like **purchasing power units (PPUs)** or **common dollars**. The CPI or some similar index may also be used to reflect the value of nonmonetary assets **either** at the **average value** for the period under review or at their **value at the end of the period**.

Monetary and Nonmonetary Assets and Liabilities

Assets and liabilities may be either monetary or nonmonetary assets in nature. **Monetary assets and liabilities** are those that are fixed by contract or are otherwise fixed in terms of money irrespective of changes in the value of the assets or liabilities. For example, a fixed mortgage of $100,000 repayable in 10 years will be settled by the payment of $100,000. Cash, accounts receivable, accounts payable, loans, mortgages, and bonds all fall into this group. **Nonmonetary assets and liabilities**, on the other hand, are those that are not fixed in terms of the monetary unit. They comprise such items as inventories, marketable securities, land, plant and equipment. Unlike monetary assets, the values of nonmonetary assets change considerably over time.

The classification into monetary or nonmonetary items is, at times, difficult. For example, items like allowances for warranties pose certain problems. The criterion is whether these amounts are fixed in monetary terms or not. If they are, they are monetary; if not, they are nonmonetary.[5]

Persons holding **monetary assets** like loans or mortgages during times of rising prices incur **monetary holding losses** because the amounts due to them will be repaid in money that would have decreased in purchasing power. On the other hand, holding **monetary liabilities** gives rise to **monetary holding gains**. As a result, it is often said that in times of rising prices, people should borrow as much money as they can.

The effects of holding monetary assets or liabilities may be calculated as the difference between the actual and restated net monetary assets or liabilities at the beginning and end of the period under review. The calculation can also be in either **average common dollars** for the year or **year-end common dollars**. This is outlined in Illustration 3–1 which shows that all that is required is to restate the inflows and outflows of cash in **common dollars**, and to deduct from these amounts the corresponding unadjusted monetary amounts.

Income and the Maintenance of Capital

The alternative accounting models are all based on the concept of income put forward by Hicks[6] where he stated that "... we ought to define a man's income as the maximum value he can consume in a week and still expect to be as well off at the end of the week as he was at the beginning." This means that income should only be recognized after maintaining the capital of the entity at an amount at which it is as "well off" at the end of the period as it was at the beginning of the period. The recognition of income only after the capital of the entity has been maintained is generally called the "maintenance of capital".

---

[5] Paragraphs 96–100 of the Financial Accounting Standards Board's *Statement of Financial Accounting Standard No. 89* provide a detailed guide to be used in times of difficulties.

[6] John R. Hicks, *Value and Capital*, Oxford: Clarendon Press, 1939.

ILLUSTRATION 3–1
CALCULATION OF MONETARY GAINS OR LOSSES

The net current monetary assets (i.e., cash and accounts receivables less accounts payables) of Jezebel Inc. were $40,000 and $45,000 at January 1 and December 31, 20X6 respectively. During the year ended December 31, 20X6, cash inflows from sales had amounted to $100,000 for the year. Cash outflows for 20X6 had amounted to $95,000, made up of purchases and administrative expenses of $80,000, including interest payments, and a dividend of $15,000 declared on October 1, 20X6 and paid on October 31. Jezebel Inc. also had $100,000 10-year 10% debentures, which were repayable on December 31, 20X9. The CPI was 120 at January 1, 20X6 and increased evenly to 128 at the end of the year. Sales, purchases and administration expenses also accrued evenly throughout the year.

The net monetary gain for 20X6 is calculated in year-end common dollars as follows:

	Monetary Balance	Conversion	Restated Balance	Gain/(Loss)
NET MONETARY ASSETS:				
Beginning Balance	$ 40,000	128/120	$ 42,667	
Add Net Cash Inflows from Sales	100,000	128/124	103,226	
Less: Cash Outflows				
Purchases and Administration	(80,000)	128/124	(82,581)	
Dividends (October 1)	(15,000)	128/126	(15,238)	
Ending Balance	$ 45,000		48,074	
Less: Monetary Balance			45,000	$(3,074)
LONGTERM MONETARY LIABILITY:				
Beginning Balance	$100,000	128/120	$106,667	
Ending Balance	$100,000		100,000	6,667
Net Monetary Gain for Year				$ 3,593

Notes:
[1] The restatement in this illustration is in year-end common dollars.
[2] Interest payments are normally treated like administration expenses. However, restatement could be on the actual payment dates, and either method is acceptable provided it is applied consistently from year to year.
[3] The operative date for dividends is the date of declaration and not the date of payment.
[4] Monetary gains or losses arising from current and longterm monetary holdings are normally calculated and presented separately for disclosure purposes. However, there is no need to do so.

The Hicksian concept of income **raises two important issues**. First, **net income is regarded as a change in wealth** that is, in turn, dependent upon the value of the net assets at the beginning and end of the period. The second issue, which is not readily apparent, is that **the amount of net income also depends upon the amounts set aside to maintain the capital of the enterprise** which, once again, depends upon the concept of capital maintenance used.

Concepts of Capital Maintenance

The Hicksian concept of income is conditional upon the maintenance of the enterprise's capital at the end of the reporting period. This means that any distribution of profits to investors must be limited to an amount that does not impair the reporting entity's ability to continue to operate (i.e., by leaving the capital intact).

The three main approaches to calculating the amount at which the capital of an entity must be maintained are outlined below.

1. Financial Capital Maintenance: Financial capital maintenance is based on the assumption that the monetary unit is stable and, therefore, income and the amount required to maintain capital can be measured in **monetary terms**. It follows the original **proprietary emphasis** of historical cost accounting in which the emphasis is on the owner or owners of the business and the capital contributed by them. If, for example, the owner had commenced business with $20,000 in cash, financial capital maintenance would only be concerned with maintaining the original investment of $20,000.

2. Price-Level Adjusted Capital Maintenance: In times of inflation, net income and the maintenance of capital can be measured by restating the historical cost figures in a way that eliminates the effects of changes in the purchasing power of the monetary unit. For example, assume that the owner of a business commenced business on January 1, 20X1 with $30,000. If the consumer price index increased from 110 at the beginning of the year (i.e., January 1, 20X1) to 120 at the end of the year (i.e., December 31, 20X1), the capital would have to be maintained at, at least, $32,727 (i.e., $30,000 × 120/110).

3. Productive Capacity Capital Maintenance: This approach to maintaining capital, which is also known as **operating capacity capital maintenance**, measures net income and the maintenance of capital using current replacement costs. It differs from the two previous approaches in that the emphasis of the reporting is on the entity as a whole. Consequently, capital includes capital from all sources (i.e., including capital from loan creditors). All gains and losses resulting from the holding of inventory or assets are **excluded** from net income and treated as amounts required to maintain the entity's productive capacity at at least its present level.

For example, assume that a was company formed and commenced business on January 1, 20X1 with a share capital of $100,000 that was immediately invested in inventory. The inventory was all sold on December 31, 20X1, when its replacement cost was $120,000. Here, its capital would have to be maintained at $120,000 to maintain its productive capacity at its previous level, which is the original investment of $100,000 plus the holding gain of $20,000 required to repurchase the same quantity of inventory at a cost of $120,000.

The Valuation of Assets

The determination of net income and the amount required for capital maintenance purposes depends upon the value at which the assets are valued. The four ways in which assets may be valued are historical cost, economic value, current (replacement) cost, or realizable value.

Historical cost is considered objective and easily verifiable because it represents the exchange price involved in the contract of purchase and sale between two parties dealing at arms' length (i.e., a sale conducted in the normal course of business between two independent parties). It is also readily understood, and provides a convenient method of valuing assets.

In times of rising or falling prices, however, historical cost provides asset values that are virtually useless for comparative purposes. As outlined earlier, to overcome this problem, these assets may be restated in terms of **units of purchasing power** or **common dollars**. This means that the asset values are adjusted to reflect their value in relation to the general increase (or decrease) in the purchasing power of the dollar using the CPI.

The **economic value** (or capitalization) method of valuing assets operates by discounting the expected cash flows from an asset over its remaining useful life. It is widely used for capital budgeting purposes and for comparative purposes in investment decision making. Its use in other areas of accounting is, however, usually limited to the valuation of mortgages, bonds, leases, etc. where the cash flows, the time period involved, and the interest or discount rates are either known or can be estimated with a reasonable degree of accuracy.

Assets can also be restated at their **current costs**. This means the assets are restated at the value the firm would have to pay, for a similar asset, in a similar condition. The way in which this is carried out is examined in detail later in the chapter.

THE BASIS OF EVALUATION

In this chapter, the evaluation of the alternative accounting models is based on the following three criteria:

1. Does the balance sheet provide a better statement of the financial position of the reporting entity?
2. Does the income statement provide a realistic measure of performance?
3. Does the alternative model provide the necessary information to establish whether the reporting entity has maintained its capital?

PRICE-LEVEL ADJUSTED ACCOUNTING

The Objective and Acceptance of the Model

The objective of price level accounting is to reflect the financial position of an entity and its performance in terms of units of purchasing power (or constant dollars) and not money. It is nothing new, and suggestions for its use go at least as far back as 1918.[7]

Considerable research into the use of the model was carried out in both Britain and the USA. However, it was only in the 1970s that the first steps were taken to implement the model. This occurred in May 1974 when the Institute of Chartered Accountants in England and Wales issued *Provisional Statement of Standard Accounting Practice No. 7*,[8] which required companies whose securities were publicly traded to present supplementary financial statements drawn up in terms of "current purchasing power" accounting. In 1976, *PSSAP No. 7* was withdrawn following the release of *The Sandilands Report*,[9] which recommended the adoption of current cost accounting. In 1979, a form of supplementary price-level adjusted information was also introduced in the USA by the FASB's *SFAS No. 33*.[10] However, *SFAS No. 33* was withdrawn and re-issued in 1986 as *SFAS No. 89* in which the disclosure of inflation adjusted information was made voluntary.[11] At this point, the official support for price-level adjusted accounting information came to an end.

Even though price-level adjusted accounting is no longer supported by accounting standard setting bodies, it does not mean that it is not useful or is not used. For example, it remains the only way in which historical cost figures, like the 10-year summary of financial information included in the financial statements of companies whose securities are publicly traded, can be restated in real terms or almost real terms.

The Presentation of Price-Level Adjusted Information

Price-level adjusted accounting does not represent a fundamental departure from historical cost accounting because it is merely a reformulation of the historical cost financial statements in terms of units of purchasing power. The restatement process only applies to the

---

[7] I.L. Middleditch, "Should Accounts Reflect the Changing Value of the Dollar?" *The Journal of Accountancy*, February 1918, pp. 114–20.

[8] *PSSAP No. 7: Accounting for Changes in the Purchasing Power of Money*, Institute of Chartered Accountants in England and Wales, May 1974.

[9] F.E.P. Sandilands, *Inflation Accounting: Report of the Inflation Accounting Committee* ("The Sandilands Report"), London: HMSO, Cmnd 6225, 1975.

[10] Financial Accounting Standards Board, *Statement of Financial Accounting Standards No. 33: Financial Reporting and Changing Prices*, September 1979.

[11] It is interesting to note that the change from mandatory to voluntary disclosure of inflation adjusted information in *SFAS No. 89* was passed by the FASB by a 4:3 vote. With effect from January 1, 1991, the FASB required a vote of 5:2 or greater for changes of this nature.

balance sheet and **income statement,** because the **statement of cash flows**, being concerned with monetary flows, does not require restatement.

The price-level restatement may be in terms of "**average for the year**" common dollars or "**end of year**" common dollars.[12] To illustrate the difference between them, assume that the CPI for the year increased evenly from 110 to 116. If an item having a value of $2,000 at the beginning of the year is to be restated in "**average for the year**" common dollars, it would amount to $2,054 (i.e., $2,000 × {[110 + 116]/2]/110} = $2,000 × [113/110]). If, however, the restatement was in "**end of year**" common dollars, it would amount to $2,109 (i.e., $2,000 × 116/110]).

Restatement in "average for the year" figures eliminates the need to adjust sales, purchases and other items that accrue evenly throughout the year. For example, assume that the total cost of a recurring item of expenditure of $120,000 had increased evenly throughout the year because the CPI had increased from 110 to 120. The average CPI for the year would, therefore, have been 115 (i.e., [110 + 120]/2). To express the $120,000 in "average-for-the-year" dollars would not require any change, because it would be expressed as $120,000 × 115/115 = $120,000.

On the other hand, "end of year" figures reflect the restated financial position at the reporting date and its performance for the period ending on that date which, it is submitted, is correct for financial reporting purposes. Using the example in the previous paragraph, this is reflected by the adjusted amount of $120,000 in "end-of-year" dollars of $120,000 × 120/115 = $125,217. The restatement process is, therefore, presented and illustrated in this chapter using "end of year" figures.

The Restatement of the Balance Sheet

The restatement of the balance sheet with its comparative figures for the previous year is a three-step procedure. First, the balance sheet at the end of the previous year is updated and then used, as the second step, to provide the comparative figures for the current year. Third, the balance sheet for the current year is restated. Steps two and three are carried out at the same time.

Step One: Updating the Opening Balance Sheet The first step is to restate the balance sheet at the end of the year immediately preceding the year in which the restatement is to be carried out. This step is required to provide the starting point for the restatement procedure. It is important to note that it is only carried out once because, from that point onwards, the current year's restated balance sheet provides the unadjusted comparative figures for each successive year.

The mechanics of the procedure are as follows:

(a) All nonmonetary items are adjusted by the change in the CPI from the date of acquisition to the end of the previous year.

(b) No adjustments are made to the monetary items.

(c) The common stock and any preferred stock are restated by the change in the CPI from the date on which it was contributed to the company because these two items are **not** considered monetary in nature.

(d) The restated retained earnings figure is the "plug" figure, or the amount required to balance the two sides of the balance sheet.

---

[12] *PSSAP No. 7* required the use of "end of year figures", while the FASB's *SFAS Nos. 33 and 89*, which only presented selected price-level adjusted figures, required the use of "average for the year figures".

This procedure is outlined in Illustration 3–2 using the historical cost balance sheet figures for 20X5 and 20X6. At this stage, we are only interested in the restatement of the 20X5 balance sheet into common dollars at December 31, 20X5.

ILLUSTRATION 3–2
THE RESTATEMENT OF FINANCIAL STATEMENTS IN TERMS OF
PRICE-LEVEL ADJUSTED ACCOUNTING — STEP ONE

The abbreviated balance sheets given below apply to Kanga Inc. for the financial years ended December 31, 20X5 and 20X6:

BALANCE SHEETS

		20X5		20X6
CURRENT ASSETS:		$178,000		$185,000
Cash	$ 18,000		$ 15,000	
Accounts Receivable	75,000		80,000	
Inventories (Note 2)	85,000		90,000	
CAPITAL ASSETS: (Note 3)		162,000		172,000
Plant and Equipment, at cost	230,000		300,000	
Less: Accumulated Amortization	68,000		128,000	
		$340,000		$357,000
CURRENT LIABILITIES:				
Accounts Payable		$ 64,000		$ 62,000
LONGTERM LIABILITIES:				
Ten-year 8% Bonds		100,000		100,000
SHAREHOLDERS' EQUITY:		176,000		195,000
Common Stock	150,000		150,000	
Retained Earnings	26,000		45,000	
		$340,000		$357,000

Notes:

[1] The company had commenced business on January 1, 20X4.

[2] The inventory had all been purchased evenly over the last three months of the year.

[3] The plant and equipment consisted entirely of plant and equipment that was being amortized on the straight-line basis at 20% per annum with no residual value. The detailed breakdown of this amount is as follows:

			Amortization	
Purchases	Cost	20X4	20X5	20X6
January 1, 20X4	$150,000	$30,000	$30,000	$30,000
June 30, 20X5	80,000	—	8,000	16,000
Balance at December 31, 20X5	230,000	30,000	38,000	46,000
January 1, 20X6	70,000	—	—	14,000
Balance at December 31, 20X6	$300,000	$30,000	$38,000	$60,000

[4] The Consumer Price Index for 20X5 and 20X6 was as follows:

	20X4	20X5	20X6
January 1	108	116	124
April 1	110	118	126
June 30	112	120	128
October 1	114	122	130
December 31	116	124	132

ILLUSTRATION 3–2 (Continued)

Step One restates the **20X5 balance sheet** into common dollars at the **end** of 20X5 as follows:

BALANCE SHEET

	Historic Figures	Conversion	Restated	Figures
CURRENT ASSETS:	(178,000)			$178,691
Cash	$ 18,000	—	$ 18,000	
Accounts Receivable	75,000	—	75,000	
Inventories (Note 2)	85,000	124/123*	85,691	
FIXED ASSETS:	(162,000)			177,734
Plant and Equipment (see workings)	230,000	Calc.	254,889	
Accumulated Amortization	68,000	Calc.	77,155	
	$ 340,000			$356,425
CURRENT LIABILITIES:				
Accounts Payable	$ 64,000	—		$ 64,000
LONGTERM LIABILITIES:				
Ten-year 8% Bonds	100,000	—		100,000
SHAREHOLDERS' EQUITY:	(176,000)			192,425
Common Stock	150,000	124/108	172,222	
Retained Earnings	26,000	Plug	20,203	
	$ 340,000			$356,425

* (122 + 124)/2 = 123

WORKINGS

Plant and Equipment and Amortization:	Restated Cost	Amortization — 20% 20X4	20X5	Balance
January 1, 20X4 — $150,000 × 124/108	$172,222	$34,444	$34,444	$68,888
June 30, 20X5 — $80,000 × 124/120 × 6/12	82,667	—	8,267	8,267
Balance at December 31, 20X5	$254,889	$34,444	$42,711	$77,155

Step Two: Establishing the Comparative Figures for 20X6 The second step is to convert the figures appearing on the restated balance sheet established in step one (i.e., 20X5 in Illustration 3–2) into common dollars at the end of the current year (i.e., 20X6) and enter them as the comparative figures. This step requires the restatement of **both** monetary and nonmonetary assets and liabilities into common dollars at the end of the year.

This step, with step three, is outlined in Illustration 3–3. This illustration shows that all assets and liabilities on the balance sheet at December 20X5 are restated as comparative figures in common dollars at the end of 20X6.

Step Three: Restating the Current Balance Sheet Step three is the restatement of the current balance sheet. This is carried out in the same manner as that applying in step one outlined in Illustration 3–3.

It is important to note that Illustration 3–3 provides a balance sheet that is **fully comparable** with that of the previous year because both the 20X6 and 20X5 figures are stated in

ILLUSTRATION 3–3
THE RESTATEMENT OF FINANCIAL STATEMENTS IN TERMS OF
PRICE-LEVEL ADJUSTED ACCOUNTING — STEPS TWO AND THREE

This Illustration is a continuation of Illustration 3–2, in which the balance sheet of Kanga Inc. for 20X5 was restated into common dollars at December 31, 20X5.

Step Two restates the "restated 20X5 balance sheet" as the comparative figures for 20X6 in "end of the year dollars" at December 31, 20X6 irrespective of whether the balance sheet items are monetary or nonmonetary. With Step Three, the 20X6 figures are restated in the same manner as that outlined in Illustration 3–2.

BALANCE SHEETS

	Conversion 20X6	Conversion 20X5	Balance Sheets 20X6	Balance Sheets 20X5
CURRENT ASSETS:			(185,687)	(190,219)
Cash	—	132/124	$ 15,000	$ 19,161
Accounts Receivable	—	132/124	80,000	79,839
Inventories	132/131*	132/124	90,687	91,219
FIXED ASSETS:			(194,547)	(189,200)
Plant and Equipment, at cost (Note 1)	Calc.	132/124	345,850	271,333
Less: Accumulated Amortization	Calc.	132/124	151,303	82,133
TOTAL ASSETS			$ 380,234	$ 379,419
CURRENT LIABILITIES:				
Accounts Payable	—	132/124	$ 62,000	$ 68,128
LONGTERM LIABILITIES:				
Ten-year 8% Bonds (Note 2)	—	132/124	100,000	106,452
SHAREHOLDER'S EQUITY:			(218,234)	(204,839)
Common Stock (Note 3)	132/124	132/124	183,333	183,333
Retained Earnings	Plug	132/124	34,901	21,506
TOTAL LIABILITIES AND EQUITIES			$ 380,234	$ 379,419

* (130 + 132)/2 = 131

Notes:

[1] The plant and equipment and accumulated amortization were calculated as follows:

	20X5	Conver.	20X6
Restated Balance at December 31, 20X5	$254,889	132/124	$ 271,333
Purchases January 1, 20X6	70,000	132/124	74,517
	$324,889		$ 345,850
Accumulated Amortization at December 31, 20X5	$ 77,155	132/124	$ 82,133
Depreciation Expense for 20X6 — 20% × $345,850			69,170
Accumulated Amortization at December 31, 20X6			$ 151,303

[2] The differences between the 20X6 and 20X5 restated figures show that the indebtedness of the bonds has decreased in real terms during the year by $6,452.

[3] The common stock remains unchanged for the two years in restated figures. In this case, the calculation is based on the beginning of the year balance and adjusted to year end figures. If the price level at the date of acquisition had been used, the figure would have been exactly the same (i.e., $150,000 × 132/108 = $183,333).

terms of December 31, 20X6 common dollars. Here, the most important aspects are that the indebtedness for the bonds of $100,000 has decreased by $6,452 in real terms from 20X5 to 20X6, and that the common stock has remained unchanged in real terms at $183,333.

Restatement of the Income and Retained Earnings Statements

The restatement of the **income statement** in comparative form follows a similar three-step procedure. Step one updates the opening income statement; step two provides the comparative figures; and step three gives the restated income statement for the current year. The only complication is that the calculation of the gain or loss arising from the holding of monetary assets and liabilities is required.

The mechanics of the restatement procedure for both the prior and current year **using year-end common dollars** are as follows:

(a) Revenues and those expenses that accrue evenly throughout the year are restated in common dollars at the end of the year by the change in the CPI.

(b) The cost of goods sold must be established using restated beginning and ending restated inventory at the end of the year.

(c) The amounts for the amortization of capital assets and intangibles (that are nonmonetary assets) are calculated on the year-end restated balances.

(d) Amounts received or paid in cash, like interest, are normally treated in the same way as expenses that accrue evenly throughout the year. However, where necessary, these amounts may be restated in common dollars using the CPI on the date on which they are received or paid. All that is required is that the treatment be applied consistently from year to year.

(e) Income taxes are treated like any other item of expense because they are considered to accrue evenly throughout the year.

(f) Dividends are normally restated using the CPI at the date of declaration. However, they may also be considered monetary items and included at their nominal amounts. As with interest, either treatment is acceptable provided the method is disclosed in the notes to the financial statements and it is applied consistently from year to year.

(g) The gain or loss arising from holding monetary assets and liabilities is calculated as outlined in Illustration 3–1 and included in net income.

(h) The price-level adjusted net income or loss for the year **before adjustment** for monetary gains and losses is established by deducting the restated expenses from the restated revenues. The monetary gains or losses are then brought into account to give the net income or loss for the period.

It is important to note that the **statement of retained earnings** must be restated and agreed with the "plug" figure for retained earnings at the end of the year. The only adjustments relate to the retained earnings at the beginning of the year and the dividends paid. Here, the retained earnings at the beginning of the year is the adjusted figure brought forward from the comparative balance sheet at the end of the previous year. And, as explained above, the dividends are included at either the restated or monetary amounts depending upon the policy of the firm.

As with the conversion of the balance sheet, the **comparative figures** for the prior year are obtained by restating all the revenues and expenses from the previous year into common dollars at the end of the current year irrespective of how they arose. Once again, the figures are fully comparable with those of the previous year.

An illustration of the restatement of the income statement is provided as Illustration 3–4 which is a continuation of Illustrations 3–2 and 3–3. It shows that the restated net income of $38,586 is arrived at after the inclusion of net monetary gains of $6,194 and is still $6,414 less than the historical cost net income of $44,000. It should also be noted that in this illustration, the dividends were also restated in year-end dollars.

Some Practical Considerations

The example provided in Illustrations 3–2, 3–3 and 3–4 is a theoretical model designed to outline price-level adjusted accounting. However, revenues and expenses do not accrue evenly throughout the year because every type of commercial activity is to some extent cyclical in nature. Therefore, sales and other administration figures (like sales commissions, etc.) must be calculated and restated by applying changes in the CPI on a more realistic quarterly or monthly basis. This is outlined in Illustration 3–5.

Similarly, the calculations of the net monetary gains or losses provided in Illustrations 3–1 and 3–4 are theoretical calculations based on the simplistic assumption that accruals of revenues and expenses take place evenly throughout the year. This is seldom the case and the calculation of the net monetary gain or loss arising from holding monetary current assets or liabilities may be treated, in practice, as a "plug" or balancing figure. The restatement of assets using the CPI may also give totally unrealistic asset values. Therefore, the values at which assets are restated should be carefully examined and adjusted downwards if it appears that they are overvalued.[13]

Evaluation of Price-Level Accounting

There can be no doubt that the **restated balance sheet** provides a better indication of the entity's financial position at a point in time than historical cost accounting. Assets are restated at figures that reflect the changes in the original purchase prices which, after deducting the liabilities, provide a more realistic equity figure. Provided the three-step restatement procedure is followed, it gives figures that are fully comparable with those of the previous year.

However, it should be borne in mind that the restated balance sheet figures are only restated historical costs that may not have been recorded at their true cost. They are also subject to the shortcomings of the CPI in that all assets do not increase in value according to the decline in purchasing power of the monetary unit.

As far as the measurement of performance is concerned, the **price-level adjusted income statement** provides a more realistic portrayal of its revenues and expenses. They are also fully comparable with those of the previous year. However, considerable care must be exercised in interpreting the price-level adjusted net income figure because:

(a) The revenues and expense figures are subject to the limitations of the CPI.
(b) It includes the net gains and losses from holding monetary assets and liabilities that are really nothing more than a reflection of the financing activities of the entity.
(c) It does not eliminate the shortcomings of historical cost accounting in relation to the inclusion of holding gains or losses and arbitrary cost allocations.

Compared with historical cost accounting, price-level adjusted accounting also provides a more effective assessment of the amounts required to **maintain capital**. In this respect, the amount available for distribution to owners is limited to that amount above the amount required to maintain the contributed capital in real terms.

It should also be borne in mind that the price-level adjusted model does not attempt to restate the financial statements in a way that eliminates the effects of changes in the purchasing power of the monetary unit. All it does is restate the financial statements in relatively realistic terms in relation to the current purchasing power of the monetary unit. In this respect, it does not involve a major departure from current reporting practices.

---

[13] This treatment was required by para. 21 of *PSSAP No. 7.*

ILLUSTRATION 3–4
THE PRICE-LEVEL RESTATEMENT OF THE INCOME AND RETAINED EARNINGS STATEMENT

Kanga Inc.'s abbreviated historical cost combined income and retained earnings statement for 20X6 and its restatement into common dollars at the end of the year is given hereunder. This illustration represents a continuation of Illustration 3–3 in which the **restated equity** at December 31, 20X5 and 20X6 was as follows:

	20X6	20X5
Common Stock	$183,333	$ 183,333
Retained Earnings	34,901	21,506
	$218,234	$ 204,839

The restatement for 20X6 into year-end common dollars is carried out as follows:

	Historical Cost		Conversion	Restated	
Sales		$1,160,000	132/128		$1,196,250
Cost of Goods Sold:					
Beginning Inventory (Note 2)	85,000		132/123	91,219	
Purchases	793,000		132/128	817,781	
	878,000			909,000	
Ending Inventory (Note 2)	90,000	788,000	132/131	90,687	818,313
Gross Profit		372,000			377,937
Less: Administration Expenses	224,000		132/128	231,000	
Amortization (Note 5)	60,000		Calc.	69,170	
Income Taxes (50%)	44,000	328,000	132/128	45,375	345,545
Income before Monetary Gains		44,000			32,392
Net Monetary Gains:					
On Longterm Loans		—	Calc.	6,452	
Less Other Losses		—	Calc.	258	6,194
Net Income for Year		44,000			38,586
Retained Earnings at January 1		26,000	20X5		21,506
		70,000			60,092
Dividends (November 15)		25,000	132/131		25,191
Retained Earnings at December 31		$ 45,000	Bal./Sh.		$ 34,901

Calculation of Monetary Gain or Loss:

	Monetary Balance	Conversion	Restated Balance	Gain/ Loss
NET MONETARY ASSETS:				
CURRENT ASSETS AND LIABILITIES:				
Beginning Balance ($18,000 + $75,000 − $64,000)	$ 29,000	132/124	$ 30,871	
Add: Increase in Cash*	99,000	132/128	102,094	
Less: Purchase Equipment (Note 3)	(70,000)	132/124	(74,516)	
Less: Dividends (Note 4)	(25,000)	132/131	(25,191)	
Ending Balance ($15,000 + $80,000 − $62,000)	$ 33,000		33,258	
Less: Monetary Balance			33,000	$ (258)
LONGTERM LIABILITIES:				
8% Bonds	$100,000	132/124	$106,542	
Less: Monetary Balance			100,000	6,452
Net Monetary Gain				$ 6,194

Notes:

[1] All expenses, purchases and revenues accrued evenly throughout the period 20X4–20X6.

[2] In both years, the ending inventory had all been purchased evenly over the last three months of the year.

[3] The equipment costing $70,000 was paid for in full on January 1, 20X6.

[4] The dividends were declared and paid on November 15.

[5] Details relating to the depreciation expense are provided in Illustration 3–3.

* The difference between the beginning and ending balances of $29,000 and $33,000 is made up of the cash inflows less the outflows for the purchase of equipment and the dividend paid. The $99,000 is, therefore, a "plug" figure because details of the actual cash flows other than dividends and the purchase of equipment have not been provided.

ILLUSTRATION 3–5
RESTATEMENT OF CYCLICAL SALES

If the sales for Kanga Inc. for 20X6 of $1,160,000 were cyclical in nature and amounted to $160,000, $240,000, $280,000 and $480,000 in the four quarters of the year, and the CPI rose evenly from 124 to 132 at the end of the year, the sales would have been restated at $1,188,585 as follows:

First Quarter:	132/125* × $ 160,000	=	$ 168,960
Second Quarter:	132/127* × $ 240,000	=	249,449
Third Quarter:	132/129* × $ 280,000	=	286,512
Fourth Quarter:	132/131* × $ 480,000	=	483,664
	$1,160,000	=	$1,188,585

* The restatement is in end of year CPI over the average for each quarter (i.e., 132/[124 + 126] ÷ 2) = 132/125

There are, however, two **major disadvantages** of the model.

1. The most important of these is that **price-level adjusted figures only provide supplementary information** to the main historical cost accounting figure. As such, these figures will always be looked upon as additional information.
2. Equally important is that **the restatement of figures in terms of PPU's or common dollars is not readily understood by non-accountants**. Readers of price-level adjusted financial statements tend to be confused by two sets of figures both prefaced by the "$" or other monetary symbols. Proposals to refer to restated figures as "Common $'s", "PPU's", etc. have met with little success.

A Final Note on Price-Level Adjusted Accounting

There is also the constant cry from its opponents that the cost of producing price-level adjusted financial statements is not justified by the benefits derived from them. When compared with the current cost model, this may be true. However, it appears that the **main reason for its unpopularity** with the preparers of financial statements stems from the fact that in virtually every case the restatement gives a decrease in reported net income.

CURRENT COST ACCOUNTING

The Nature of the Model

Current cost accounting is also known as replacement value accounting in reference to the fact that the net assets are valued at their current replacement values. The only difference between them is one of semantics because the one refers to the current cost of purchasing assets while the other refers to the cost at which the assets could be replaced.[14] The model has been called "current cost accounting" since its use by "The Sandilands Report"[15] in 1975 to describe its proposed system of inflation accounting. The term "current cost" was used

---

[14] See W.D. Hamman, W.A. Joubert and H.F. Redelinghuys, *Income Determination*, Cape Town: Juta, 1977, for a complete description of Limperg's replacement value accounting and its application to *N.V. Philips Gloeilampenfabrieken* (now *N.V. Philips Electronics*) in Holland. In their analysis of the model, Hamman *et al.* point out that the choice of the description "replacement value" was unfortunate because it really referred to what is currently described as "current cost". See also H.J. van der Schroef, *Bedrijfseconomische Grondslagen van de Winstbepaling*, Amsterdam: Kosmos, 1975, p. 43.
[15] See F.E.P. Sandilands, *op cit.*

because the accounting model was viewed as a progression from the use of historical costs to current costs.

Suggestions for the use of an accounting model based on the "market values" of assets dated back many years. In 1939, Kenneth MacNeal[16] argued that because financial statements were supposed to reflect "present economic values", they were only useful to the extent that they did so and, consequently, some "truth in accounting" was required. In the late 1940s and 1950s similar suggestions were made in the USA, but they gave way to the more popular price-level adjusted model. It was only after Theodore Limperg[17] developed his replacement value theory that these proposals gained acceptance, and then it was only in the Netherlands.

Limperg's theory held that an enterprise will continue to produce goods and services for as long as the direct realizable values of assets exceed their current costs. To be able to do so, management must always know the values of the inputs into the production process and the effects of changing values on the capital of the firm. As a result, assets and expenses must be recorded and reported at their current costs.

Today, the position is no different. The basis of the current cost model is to adjust the carrying value of assets to reflect their current costs and, where the assets are consumed in the production process, to amortize the revalued assets over their expected useful lives. For example, assume that plant that cost $100,000 is being amortized over five years on the straight-line basis. If the current cost of that plant increased from $110,000 at the beginning of the year to $120,000 at the end of the year, the amortization expense for the year would be calculated at $23,000 (i.e., {[20% of $110,000 to give $22,000] + [20% of $120,000 to give $24,000]}/2).

Acceptance of the model was fairly widespread and, besides its use in the Netherlands, current cost accounting was required by *Statement of Standard Accounting Practice No. 16: Current Cost Accounting* issued in Britain in 1980,[18] and on a supplementary reporting basis by the ill-fated section 4510 of the CICA *Handbook*[19] in 1982. Similar proposals were also introduced in Australia and New Zealand. Of these, only the British *SSAP No. 16* required the presentation of a current cost balance sheet and income statement, while the others only required the supplementary disclosure of current cost figures. Certain current cost figures were also required to be disclosed by large public companies by the FASB's *SFAS No. 33* in 1975 and its successor, *SFAS No. 89* in 1986. Today, these requirements have all been withdrawn except *SFAS No. 89* in which the disclosure of inflation adjusted figures is voluntary.

In this section, current cost accounting is explained and outlined using a fully integrated model. This is because the presentation of supplementary current cost data in the form

---

[16] Kenneth MacNeal, *Truth in Accounting*, *op cit.*

[17] The importance of the work of Theodore Limperg (1879–1961) tended to be overlooked in the English speaking world because he did not publish widely and, as outlined earlier, when he did, it was in Dutch. As a result, it was left to people like A. Goudeket ("An Application of Replacement Value Theory", *The Journal of Accountancy*, July 1960, pp. 37–47), Reg S. Gynther (*Accounting for Price-Level Changes: Theory and Procedures*, Oxford: Pergamon Press, 1966), and Hamman *et al.* (*op cit.*) to draw attention to his work. Unfortunately, these authors did not receive the attention their writings deserved because, to this very day, Limperg's work has received little or no attention.

[18] *SSAP No. 16* was issued to apply from January 1, 1980, to those large companies satisfying at least two of the three criteria of having a turnover of more than £5-million, total assets of £2.5-million, and more than 250 employees. It was withdrawn in 1985 following a lack of support for the standard.

[19] Section 4510 of the CICA *Handbook* was doomed from the moment it was issued because it attempted to introduce an overcomplicated supplementary reporting system. For example, *Domtar Inc.*, a Toronto-based public company, detailed its reasons for not complying with the standard in its 1984 Annual Report as follows: "Based on its experience in 1983, the Corporation concluded that the CICA standard is far too complex to be meaningful. Also, the new CICA standard requires techniques and approaches that strive for a high degree of precision and theoretical refinement and yet are subjective in their application. Consequently, the results from company to company, even within our industry, will not be easily comparable. Therefore, Domtar does not believe that the supplementary information recommended by the CICA is useful to the readers of its financial statements and has accordingly not included it in this Annual Report."

required by *SFAS No. 33* and *SFAS No. 89* and section 4510 of the CICA *Handbook* all give an incomplete picture of the model.

Establishing the Current Cost of Assets

The **current cost** of an asset is the amount that the firm would have to expend to obtain a similar asset in a similar condition. The determination should also be made in perfect market conditions (i.e., that the supply of assets exactly satisfies demand) to establish the correct replacement cost. The problem is that perfect market conditions rarely prevail, and firms seldom replace existing assets with identical assets because of advances in technology.

As a result, current costs are usually established by applying the following recommendations of the American Accounting Association, which apply in descending order:[20]

1. Quoted market prices provide the most objective evaluation of current cost;
2. The purchase price (less amortization) of similar assets providing similar service capacities provides the next best method of valuation if a second hand market for the assets does not exist;
3. The historical cost of the assets may then be adjusted using specific price indices;
4. The asset values may be established by appraisals; and
5. If none of the above methods are suitable, management's estimates may be used.

As a working rule, *The Sandilands Report*[21] proposed the use of the **"value to the business"** as a method to be used by management to estimate the value of assets. This represents the opportunity cost to the firm of holding that asset, and its value is taken as **the amount the firm would lose if deprived of that asset completely**.

With a fully integrated current cost accounting model, the assets and liabilities of an enterprise are revalued and **recorded in the ledger** at their current costs, with the increase in value being recorded as a capital surplus or revenue surplus, depending upon the model used.[22] For example, if the net assets of an enterprise are revalued upwards by $50,000, the adjustment in journal entry form would be:

Assets	50,000	
Capital Surplus arising from Asset Revaluations		50,000

The "Backlog" Amortization Problem

The revaluation of depreciable assets brings with it what is known as the "backlog" amortization problem. What occurs is that in times of rising (or falling) prices, the amounts charged against revenues as amortization of capital assets do not equal the required amount of accumulated amortization at the end of the year. As a result, a further adjustment is required, which is known as the "backlog" amortization (or depreciation) adjustment.

The problem is outlined in Illustration 3–6 where, according to normal accounting practice, the accumulated amortization at the year end is based on the **end-of-year value** of the assets to which it applies. Amortization expense, on the other hand, is based on the average replacement cost of the asset.

Illustration 3–6 shows that in years 20X1 through 20X4, the accumulated amortization arising on the revalued asset must be adjusted upwards to give the correct carrying value on

---

[20] American Accounting Association, "Accounting for Land, Buildings and Equipment — Supplementary Statement No. 1", *The Accounting Review*, July 1964, pp. 693–99 and, in particular, p. 696.

[21] F.E.P. Sandilands, *Inflation Accounting: Report of the Inflation Accounting Committee* ("The Sandilands Report"), London: HMSO, Cmnd. 6225, 1975.

[22] Such an accounting system was envisaged by *SSAP No. 16* in Britain.

ILLUSTRATION 3–6
THE "BACKLOG" AMORTIZATION ADJUSTMENTS

Logger Inc. accounts for its activities using a fully integrated current cost accounting system. On January 1, 20X1, it purchased equipment for $100,000 that was to be amortized using the straight-line method over four years with no residual value. If the replacement cost of the same equipment increased evenly every year by $20,000 per year, this would give rise to the following valuation, amortization expense, and "backlog" amortization adjustments:

	20X1	20X2	20X3	20X4
Replacement Value at December 31	$120,000	$140,000	$160,000	$180,000
Amortization Expense at 25% on Average Cost				
25% × ([$100,000 + $120,000]/2)	27,500			
25% × ([$120,000 + $140,000]/2)		32,500		
25% × ([$140,000 + $160,000]/2)			37,500	
25% × ([$160,000 + $180,000]/2)				42,500
Accumulated Amortization at December 31:				
From Amortization Expense	$ 27,500	$ 60,000	$ 97,500	$140,000
Accumulated "Backlog" Amortization	—	2,500	10,000	22,500
Backlog Amortization Adjustment	2,500	7,500	12,500	17,500
Accumulated Amortization on Year End Balance	$ 30,000	$ 70,000	$120,000	$180,000

the balance sheet. For example, this occurred in 20X1, where the accumulated amortization at the end of the year should have been 25% of $120,000 or $30,000. However, the amortization expense for 20X1 was only $27,500, which required a "backlog" amortization adjustment of $2,500 to bring it up to the required $30,000.

A further problem arises from the need to recognize the "backlog" amortization in the financial statements. As it is not a current expense, it cannot be expensed in the current period. It is also not a prior period adjustment because it did not arise until the current revaluation of the asset. **The only solution to the problem is to treat it as a reduction of the amount by which the assets are revalued.** The revaluation adjustment and the "backlog" amortization adjustments in journal entry form for the four years ended December 31, 20X4 are as follows:

20X1:

Equipment	20,000	
Accumulated Amortization (Backlog Adjustment)		2,500
Capital Surplus arising on Revaluation of Equipment		17,500

20X2:

Equipment	20,000	
Accumulated Amortization (Backlog Adjustment)		7,500
Capital Surplus arising on Revaluation of Equipment		12,500

20X3:

Equipment	20,000	
Accumulated Amortization (Backlog Adjustment)		12,500
Capital Surplus arising on Revaluation of Equipment		7,500

20X4:

Equipment	20,000	
Accumulated Amortization (Backlog Adjustment)		17,500
Capital Surplus arising on Revaluation of Equipment		2,500

The Simple Current Cost Accounting Model

A simplest form of current cost accounting is where the assets are revalued and the increases in value are treated as realized and unrealized holding gains. The cost of goods sold is based on the replacement costs of the goods actually sold, and amortization is based on the revalued cost of the assets.

Such a simple illustration of current cost accounting is presented as Illustration 3–7 using both the financial capital maintenance (FCM) concept and the productive capacity capital maintenance concept (PCCM). As far as the income statement items are concerned, the cost of goods sold is restated to reflect the current costs of the inventory at the date of sale and the amortization expense, as outlined above, is based on the average replacement costs of the fixed assets. The other expense items remain unchanged.

A comparison of the income statements using FCM and PCCM in Illustration 3–7 shows that the only difference between them is that with FCM all realized and unrealized holding gains are treated as revenue items whereas with PCCM, these amounts are set aside to maintain the capital of the reporting entity. The increase in the capital surplus arising from the revaluation of assets is presented in the manner recommended by *The Sandilands Report*.[23]

Establishing Current Cost Expenses

It should be noted that the current cost income statement adjustments are limited to an adjustment to the cost of goods sold and the amortization expense. In Illustration 3–7, these expenses are either given or established from the information provided. In practice, however, the establishment of these items is somewhat more difficult.

The Cost of Goods Sold Adjustment The method of calculating the cost of goods sold in Illustration 3–7 is only possible with items that are specifically identifiable like motor vehicles, items of equipment and the like. A different treatment is required with items of relatively low value that are not specifically identifiable.

This can be carried out in two ways using a "cost of goods sold adjustment". These are the **internal index method** and the **averaging method**.

The **internal index method** is used by *Philips*[24] together with a fully integrated standard costing system. The changes in the cost of the individual items are monitored closely so that an internal index of changes in the current costs of its inventory items can be determined from the price variances. Obviously, indices are not calculated for every item, but for classes of items that are known to display similar changes in value. Once the indices have been determined, they are used to calculate the cost of goods sold adjustment as the increase (or decrease) in the actual cost of items sold.

These internal indices are easy to calculate, and may also be applied to labour costs and the like. For example, if the cost of some item of equipment increased from $58 to $62 in one month, the cost of all similar items would be increased by the internal index of 1.06896 calculated at $62/$58. Similarly, if labour costs had increased in a specific month by, say 2%, all labour costs would be increased by the same amount.

The alternative method is the **averaging method** proposed by *The Sandilands Report* and subsequently adopted by the CICA and others. This method is presented as Appendix 3A to this chapter, and is based on the two assumptions that any increase (or decrease) in the amount of inventory occurs evenly throughout the year, and that price changes occur evenly throughout the year.

Irrespective of which method is used, the cost of goods sold adjustment is brought into account as an adjustment to the cost of goods sold and the capital surplus. For example, if the

---

23 *Op cit.*
24 See Hamman *et al., op cit.*, pp. 71–72.

cost of goods sold adjustment amounted to $57,000, the entry recording this amount would be as follows:

Cost of Goods Sold	57,000	
Capital Surplus		57,000

Amortization Expense As outlined in Illustration 3–7, the amortization expense is based on the value of assets at the beginning and end of the year established through the valuation process outlined earlier. The actual calculation of the amortization expense requires no explanation other than the fact that it is based on the average value of the assets for the period involved.

ILLUSTRATION 3–7
A COMPARISON OF THE USE OF CURRENT COST ACCOUNTING USING BOTH THE FINANCIAL AND PRODUCTIVE CAPACITY CAPITAL MAINTENANCE CONCEPTS

The historical cost financial statements of Mace Inc. for the year ended December 31, 20X5 were as follows:

INCOME STATEMENT

Sales (18,000 units at $18 each)		$324,000
Cost of Goods Sold (3,000 units at $8 + 15,000 units at $10)		174,000
Gross Profit		150,000
Less: Administration Expenses	$46,000	
Amortization Expense (20% of $60,000)	12,000	
Interest Expense	2,000	
Income Tax Expense (40%)	36,000	96,000
Net Income for Year		$ 54,000

BALANCE SHEET

Cash	$ 36,000
Inventory (5,000 units at $10 each)	50,000
Land	40,000
Plant and Equipment, at cost	60,000
Less: Accumulated Amortization	(12,000)
	$174,000
10% Mortgage Loan	$ 20,000
Common Stock (50,000 Shares of no par value)	100,000
Retained Earnings	54,000
	$174,000

You are also informed that:

1. Mace uses the FIFO method of accounting for its inventory.
2. The inventory was purchased in two transactions: 3,000 units for $8 each in January, and 20,000 units in June at $10 each. Sales took place when their replacement costs were $12 each.
3. At December 31, 20X5, the replacement cost of the inventory was $15 per unit.
4. The replacement cost of the land and equipment increased by 40% during the year.
5. The equipment is amortized using the straight-line method at the rate of 20% per year with no residual value.
6. Interest was paid on the mortgage on June 30 and December 31.
7. Income tax was payable at the rate of 40%.
8. All expenses were paid in cash when incurred.

ILLUSTRATION 3–7 (CONTINUED)

The presentation of the financial statements in terms of current cost accounting using both the financial and productive capacity capital maintenance concepts is as follows:

	Financial Capital Maintenance		Productive Capacity Capital Maintenance	
INCOME STATEMENT				
Sales (18,000 units at $18 each)		$324,000		$324,000
Cost of Goods Sold (18,000 units at $12)		216,000		216,000
Gross Profit		108,000		108,000
Less: Administration Expenses	$46,000		$46,000	
Amortization Expense (20% of [$60,000 + $84,000] ÷ 2)	14,400		14,400	
Interest Expense	2,000		2,000	
Income Tax Expense (40%)	36,000	98,400	36,000	98,400
Net Operating Income for Year		9,600		$ 9,600
Realized Holding Gains:				
Inventory ([3,000 × ($12 − $8)] + [15,000 × ($12 − $10)])	42,000			
Amortization ($14,400 − $12,000) — Note 1	2,400	44,400		
Unrealized Holding Gains:				
Inventory (5,000 × [$15 − $10])	25,000			
Land (40% × $40,000) or ($56,000 − $40,000)	16,000			
Plant and Equipment — Note 2	19,200	60,200		
Net Income for Year		$114,200		
Capital Surplus Arising from Revaluation of Assets (Note 3)				
Inventory ($42,000 + $25,000)				$ 67,000
Land				16,000
Equipment ($2,400 + $19,200)				21,600
				$104,600
BALANCE SHEETS				
Cash		$ 36,000		$ 36,000
Inventory (5,000 units at $15 each)		75,000		75,000
Land (140% × $40,000)		56,000		56,000
Plant and Equipment (140% × $60,000)		84,000		84,000
Less: Accumulated Amortization (20%)		(16,800)		(16,800)
		$234,200		$234,200
10% Mortgage Loan		$ 20,000		$ 20,000
Common Stock (50,000 shares of no par value)		100,000		100,000
Capital Surplus arising from Revaluation of Assets		—		104,600
Retained Earnings		114,200		9,600
		$234,200		$234,200

Notes:

[1] The realized holding gain of $2,400 is the difference between the historical cost and current cost amortization expense. This amount must be taken into account to agree historical cost net income with the current cost net income and realized gains using the financial capital maintenance concept.

[2] This amount represents the difference between the historical cost and current cost carrying value on the balance sheet at December 31, 20X5.

[3] The items making up the capital surplus are reflected as a separate schedule immediately below the income statement, as recommended by *The Sandilands Report* (*op cit.*).

Unrealized Gains on Capital Assets This calculation is relatively straightforward because it represents the change in the net current cost of the capital assets for the year. This is outlined in Illustration 3–7, where it is pointed out that for 20X5, it represents the increase in the current cost of the equipment of $24,000 (i.e., $84,000 – $60,000) less the realized holding gain on current cost amortization for the current year plus any backlog adjustments for the current and previous years. In Illustration 3–7, there is only the backlog adjustment for 20X5 of $2,400. However, in 20X6, this would include the backlog adjustment for 20X5 and 20X6 to bring the total accumulated amortization to the required total based on the current cost value of the equipment.

Productive Capacity or Financial Capital Maintenance?

Should a PCCM or FCM method of presentation be used? The answer to this question depends upon the way in which the reporting entity is viewed.

As outlined earlier, with FCM the focus of attention is on the owners of the entity in what is called the proprietary entity concept. The emphasis is on the interest of the owners or proprietors and net income is taken as the return on the investment which, in turn, had been maintained in monetary terms. In Illustration 3–7, the net income of $114,200 established using FCM is considered the return to the investors on their original investment of $100,000.

With PCCM, however, the focus of attention is on the entity itself rather than on its owners and, therefore, what is important is its ability to continue to operate. As a result, the total holding gains are transferred to the capital surplus account to maintain the capital (or productive capacity) of the reporting entity at, at least, its previous level. As a result, in Illustration 3–7 the net income was only $9,600.

FCM and PCCM serve different users. As the CICA[25] has pointed out, some users may be concerned with the use of financial information as the basis for assessing sustainable income, and would attach particular significance to the measurement of income after maintaining the productive capacity of the reporting entity. Others may be more concerned with the evaluation of the general performance of the entity and would attach greater significance to the measurement of income after the maintenance of financial capital.

The Financing Adjustment

The simple current cost accounting model using PCCM is ideally suited to small, closely-held companies in which the objective is to maintain the productive capacity of the entity. However, where the company has been financed by both shareholders and loan creditors, the transfer of all holding gains and losses to the capital surplus account is seen as placing the burden of maintaining productive capacity entirely on the shoulders of the shareholders. To meet this criticism, a **financing adjustment** was introduced[26] to limit the transfer of holding gains to the capital surplus account to an amount based on the equity ÷ (debt + equity) ratio.

The way in which the financing adjustment operates is to calculate the ratio that the **average outstanding debt** for the year bears to the **average outstanding debt calculated on a current cost basis plus the average shareholders' equity from all sources**. This debt ÷ (debt + equity) ratio is then applied to the **total current cost adjustments for the year** (i.e., amortization, cost of goods sold, and the realized and unrealized holding gains). The resulting amount is then included as a **revenue item** in the current cost income statement prepared using PCCM as a "financing adjustment".

---

[25] CICA *Handbook*, section 4510 para. A.8.
[26] By both *SSAP No. 16* and by section 4510 of the CICA *Handbook*.

For example, assume that the average equity and average debt of a company for the year were $120,000 and $80,000, respectively. Net income for the year was $50,000. If the current cost adjustments were $20,000, the financing adjustment would be calculated as follows:

Financing Adjustment	=	(Debt/[Debt + Equity] Ratio) × Current Cost Adjustments
	=	($80,000/[$80,000 + $120,000]) × $20,000
	=	($80,000/$200,000) × $20,000
	=	$8,000

The journal entry recording the financing adjustment would be:

Capital Surplus Account arising from Asset Revaluation	8,000	
Financing Adjustment/Retained Earnings		8,000
Financing Adjustment for Year		

The current cost net income for the year would, therefore, be restated as follows:

Current Cost Net Income before the Financing Adjustment	$50,000
Add: Financing Adjustment	8,000
Current Cost Net Income for Year	$58,000

Evaluation of Current Cost Accounting

The presentation of a current cost income statement rectifies, to a large extent, the shortcomings of historical cost accounting. In this respect, it is undoubtedly an improvement on that presented using historical cost accounting because it recognizes holding gains or losses, and the amortization expense is based on realistic asset values. As far as the balance sheet is concerned, the reflection of assets at their current values provides an indication of the actual capital employed on either an FCM or a PCCM basis.

There are, however, two common criticisms of the model:

1. The most common objection to the model is that **the valuation of assets is subjective** and could lead to the overstatement of asset values. It stems mainly from the concern of the accounting profession that it would increase the responsibility of auditors and could lead to negligence charges being brought against them.

   Even though much of this concern may be valid, the case is overstated and is largely the result of familiarity with the historical cost accounting model. This is because any overvaluation of asset values will show up in **decreased returns on capital invested** and the annual reassessment of asset values will provide a **continuous re-appraisal** of the value of the reporting entity.[27] It also ignores the theoretical consideration of relevance versus reliability in financial reporting. And, is it not better to be **almost correct** than **always precisely wrong?**

   What is often overlooked is that the valuation of certain assets is already on a current cost basis. For example, the requirements of section 1650 of the CICA *Handbook* for reporting the value of self-sustaining foreign operations are based on the current value of the investment at balance sheet date. Similarly, with mutual funds, investments are recorded and reported at their current market values, and the FASB is moving towards the accounting for temporary investments at their market value.

---

[27] Considerable concern is being expressed on the failure of accountants to insist on the revaluation downwards of assets. In fact, Mr. Walter Schuetze, Chief Accountant of the Securities and Exchange Commission in the USA, has stated that the American Congress is unlikely to consider protecting auditors against negligence claims until such time as they operate under more realistic accounting and auditing regulations including, the valuation of assets at their current costs. As far as he is concerned, "historical cost has lulled auditors to sleep." See *The Bottom Line*, November 1992, for a full report on his views.

2. The current cost accounting model presented in this section does not recognize changes in the purchasing power of the monetary unit but rather **changes in asset values**.[28] As a result, the income statement reflects figures, like sales and operating expenses, that are assumed to reflect the current costs of the business. It also fails to provide fully comparable figures unless they are restated in terms of current units of purchasing power.

A Final Note on Current Cost Accounting

As with price-level adjusted accounting, the major objection to current cost accounting is that inflation adjusted net income is, in virtually every case, considerably less than that reflected using historical cost accounting. It is, therefore, unpopular with corporate management. It is also unpopular with the financial analyst community because the theory of corporate finance does not take inflation into account. And, as far as the accounting profession is concerned, any extension of their responsibilities is also rejected.

SUMMARY

The chapter examines two feasible alternative accounting models. These are price-level adjusted accounting and current (or replacement) cost accounting.

It commences with an examination of money as a unit of measure, the effects of changes in the purchasing power of money, and the distinction between monetary and nonmonetary assets. This latter aspect is important because it provides the means of establishing the gains or losses arising from the holding of monetary assets and liabilities in times of changes in the purchasing power of the monetary unit.

The chapter then examines the Hicksian concept of income and its effect on capital maintenance. The three major methods of establishing whether capital has been maintained are presented with the methods of valuing assets and liabilities.

The price-level adjusted accounting model is then presented. It points out that the restatement consists of a three-step procedure for both the balance sheet and income statement. When evaluated in relation to presentation of information on financial position, the performance of the entity and its maintenance of capital, it provides more realistic figures than historical cost accounting.

The current (or replacement) cost accounting model is then examined using both financial capital maintenance and productive capacity capital maintenance. Once again, when the model is evaluated using the same criteria as with price-level adjusted accounting, it also provides more relevant information than historical cost accounting.

APPENDIX 3A: THE AVERAGING METHOD OF CALCULATING THE COST OF GOODS SOLD ADJUSTMENT

The average method of calculating the cost of goods sold adjustment follows the five steps outlined below:

---

[28] This aspect of current cost accounting has been recognized for many years. See, for example, Edgar Edwards and Philip Bell, *The Theory and Measurement of Business Income*, Berkeley: University of California Press, 1961, for a full discussion of this topic. Essentially, the problem can be rectified by restating the current cost figures in price-level rather than monetary figures.

Step 1. Restate the ending inventory figure by taking the average unit cost (or CPI) and dividing it by the ending unit cost (or CPI).

Step 2. Restate the beginning inventory figure by taking the average unit cost (or CPI) and dividing it by the beginning unit cost (or CPI).

Step 3. Deduct the amount calculated in Step 2 from the amount arrived at in Step 1.

Step 4. Deduct the beginning inventory at historical cost from the ending inventory at historical cost.

Step 5. Deduct the amount from Step 4 from that arrived at in Step 3 to give the cost of goods sold adjustment.

For example, assume that in 20X2, Norris Inc. purchased goods for $960,000 and had beginning and ending inventories of $160,000 and $200,000 respectively to give a cost of goods sold of $920,000. If the CPI (or indices) increased evenly from 100 to 120 throughout the year, the cost of goods sold would be increased by $32,667 calculated using the five steps as follows:

Step 1:	$200,000 × 110/120	=	$183,333
Step 2:	$160,000 × 110/100	=	176,000
Step 3:	(Step 1 − Step 2)	=	7,333
Step 4:	$200,000 − $160,000	=	40,000
Step 5:	Cost of Goods Sold Adjustment	=	$ 32,667

In this case, the journal entry recording the adjustment would have been:

Cost of Goods Sold Adjustment	32,667	
Realized Holding Gain		32,667

SELF-STUDY PROBLEMS

PROBLEM 3A† The historical cost financial statements of Weston Industries Inc. for the year ended December 31, 20X7 were as follows:

INCOME STATEMENT

Sales:	February 28	— 50,000 units at $6 each	$300,000	
	April 30	— 20,000 units at $7 each	140,000	
	November 30	— 75,000 units at $8 each	600,000	$1,040,000
Cost of Goods Sold:				
Opening Inventory — 12,500 units at $4 each			50,000	
Purchases:	January 31	— 60,000 units at $5 each	300,000	
	March 31	— 50,000 units at $4 each	200,000	
	October 31	— 32,500 units at $6 each	195,000	
			745,000	
Less:	Closing Inventory — 10,000 units at $4 each		40,000	705,000
Gross Profit				335,000
Less:	Administration Expenses		175,000	
	Amortization of Capital Assets		10,000	
	Income Tax Expense		80,000	265,000
Net Income				70,000
Retained Earnings at January 1, 20X7				30,000
				100,000
Dividends Declared and Paid (November 30, 20X7)				10,000
Retained Earnings at December 31, 20X7				$ 90,000

† The solution is provided in Appendix B to this text.

BALANCE SHEET

Cash	$ 35,000
Accounts Receivable	95,000
Inventory	40,000
Equipment	100,000
Accumulated Amortization	(30,000)
	$ 240,000
Accounts Payable	$ 25,000
Bank Loan Payable	40,000
Common Stock (8,500 shares of no par value)	85,000
Retained Earnings	90,000
	$ 240,000

You are further informed that:

(a) The company was formed on January 1, 20X5, and all outstanding shares were issued on that date.

(b) The equipment was all purchased on January 1, 20X5 and is being amortized on a straight-line basis over 10 years.

(c) The inventory was purchased evenly throughout both 20X6 and 20X7.

(d) Administration and income tax expenses accrued evenly throughout the year.

(e) All transactions were in cash.

(f) Changes in the CPI for 20X5 through 20X7 were as follows:

Date	CPI
January 1, 20X5	80
20X6 average	96
December 31, 20X6	100
January 31, 20X7	101
February 28, 20X7	104
March 31, 20X7	103
April 30, 20X7	102
October 31, 20X7	109
November 30, 20X7	112
December 31, 20X7	115
20X7 average	108

REQUIRED

On the assumption that the opening retained earnings was $26,334 in common dollars, prepare the price-level adjusted income statement and balance sheet of Weston Industries for 20X7 using year-end common dollars. A calculation of the net monetary gain or loss is not required.

PROBLEM 3B† You are provided with the following information relating to Maximillan Enterprises Inc.:

(a) The company was formed on January 1, 20X6, and all outstanding shares were issued on that date.

(b) The replacement values of the inventory sold were as follows:

---

† The solution is provided in Appendix B to this text.

The first 8,000 units at $260 each to give	$2,080,000
The next 2,000 units at $280 each to give	560,000
The next 8,000 units at $300 each to give	2,400,000
The last 9,000 units at $330 each to give	2,970,000
Total sales of 27,000 units at replacement values of	$8,010,000

(c)   The replacement value of the inventory on hand at December 31, 20X8 was $340 per unit.

(d)   The equipment had been purchased for $10-million on January 1, 20X6. Its replacement value had increased to $10½-million at the end of 20X6, $11-million at the end of 20X7, and $12-million at the end of 20X8. This equipment was being amortized at 10% per year using the straight-line method.

The historical cost financial statements of Maximillan Enterprises Inc. for the year ended December 31, 20X8 were as follows:

INCOME STATEMENT

Sales: 15,000 units at $500 each			$ 7,500,000
12,000 units at $525 each			6,300,000
			13,800,000
Cost of Goods Sold:			
Opening Inventory (3,000 units at $220 each)		660,000	
Purchases: March 31 — 13,000 units at $250		3,250,000	
September 30 — 15,000 units at $280 each		4,200,000	
		8,110,000	
Less: Closing Inventory (4,000 units at $280 each)		1,120,000	6,990,000
Gross Profit			6,810,000
Less: Administration and Selling Expenses		2,870,000	
Amortization of Capital Assets		1,000,000	3,870,000
Net Income			2,940,000
Retained Earnings at January 1, 20X8			1,120,000
			4,060,000
Dividends Declared and Paid (October 15, 20X8)			1,800,000
Retained Earnings at December 31, 20X8			$ 2,260,000

BALANCE SHEET

Cash	$ 1,125,000
Accounts Receivable	5,360,000
Inventory (4,000 units at $280 each)	1,120,000
Equipment	10,000,000
Accumulated Amortization	(3,000,000)
	$14,605,000
Accounts Payable	$ 2,345,000
Common Stock (20,000,000 shares of no par value)	10,000,000
Retained Earnings	2,260,000
	$14,605,000

REQUIRED

1.   Prepare the income statement and balance sheet of Maximillan Enterprises for 20X8 on a current cost basis using the financial capital maintenance concept on the assumption that the current cost retained earnings at December 31, 20X7 was $1,920,000.

2.   Give the shareholder's equity section of the balance sheet at December 31, 20X8 on a current cost basis using the productive capacity capital maintenance concept on the assumption that at December 31, 20X7, Maximillan Enterprises had a capital surplus of $1.2-million and retained earnings of $720,000.

REVIEW QUESTIONS

1. What is the problem with the most common method of measuring the general increase in prices?
2. Why is it necessary to revise the "basket of goods" that is used to establish the changes in the consumer price index?
3. Accountants have traditionally used money as a measure of value. Why?
4. Define monetary and nonmonetary assets and liabilities. Why is it necessary to distinguish between them?
5. How did Hicks define income? What two issues are raised by this definition?
6. Explain what you understand by the term "capital maintenance".
7. Distinguish between financial capital maintenance, price-level adjusted capital maintenance and productive capacity capital maintenance.
8. Do assets restated in terms of increases in the price-level give realistic asset values? If not, why not?
9. Why does the economic valuation of assets and liabilities have only limited use in accounting?
10. What is the objective of price-level adjusted accounting?
11. In what way do price-level adjusted financial statements differ from the historical cost financial statements on which they are based?
12. Price-level adjusted financial statements can be restated in terms of "average for the year" or "year-end" dollars. What advantages are seen as flowing from the use of either method?
13. List and explain the three-step price-level restatement procedure.
14. How is the price-level adjusted retained earnings figure established?
15. What overriding consideration applies to the restatement of asset values in terms of common dollars?
16. Why must care be exercised in interpreting price-level adjusted figures?
17. What are the two major disadvantages of the price-level adjusted accounting model?
18. Explain what you understand by the term "current cost accounting".
19. How are the current costs of assets determined?
20. What is the "backlog amortization problem", and how is it resolved in integrated current cost accounting systems?
21. What is the difference between the current cost income statements prepared using financial capital maintenance and productive capacity maintenance? The balance sheets?
22. Two methods are used to calculate the "cost of goods sold adjustment". What are they and how are they calculated?
23. What is the purpose of the financing adjustment? How does it operate?
24. What are the two major criticisms of the current cost accounting model?
25. What is believed to be the main reason for the rejection of the current cost accounting model?

CASE

CASE 3–1   **Notice 201 of the Public Accounting Standards Board**

On October 1 of the current year, the quasi-governmental Public Accounting Standards Board announced by Notice 201 that with effect from January 1, companies would no longer be permitted to value and report to their shareholders using the current values of their assets and liabilities. No matter how inaccurate the figures would be, companies would now have to revert to valuing their assets on the balance sheet at their original or historical cost.

Mr. Sam Jones, spokesman for the PASB, stated that following repeated requests from the financial analyst community, the PASB had agreed to consider the issue of changing the manner of reporting to make it easier to predict movements in the value of securities and to analyze financial statements by excluding changes in values brought about by changes in the purchasing power of the dollar. Similar requests had been made by the Canadian Association of Mutual Fund Managers and the Canadian Life Assurance Association, who had expressed concern regarding the low rate of return reflected by the financial statements of companies that excluded holding gains from their profit figure and based the amortization of capital assets on the current values of assets.

Reactions to the move differed. The Association of Mutual Fund Managers and the Life Assurance Association both welcomed the move. "We can now move forward in valuing our portfolios without having to concern ourselves with changes in the value of the dollar," stated Mr. Alexander Perry, Chairman of the Canadian Investment Analysts Society. Ms. Alice Kahn, Director of Lending Services of the Bank of Ontario, was more guarded in pointing out that the banking community would now have to revalue all assets of companies seeking loans, and this would involve considerable expense that would, in turn, be passed on to the public. Spokespersons for the professional accounting bodies were against the move, stating that the audit opinion would now be valueless, little trust would be placed in financial statements certified by them and in the words of Ms. Michelle Soon, Director of the Canadian Institute of Public Accountants, "The public is going to ask us whether the figures we produce are worth the paper they are printed on. The lay public will continue thinking that the values reflected on the balance sheet are realistic, whereas they may be way out. It is a very serious situation."

In commenting on the fear that the move would lead to a loss in faith in financial figures, Mr. Sam Jones of the PASB said that, although tradition dies hard, he was sure that the public would soon see that reported financial information had never been intended to provide accurate information. "Do you think that the financial statements of companies were ever intended to give an accurate picture of their results of operations and financial position?" he asked.

REQUIRED

Consider, to what extent, support of the historical cost accounting model is based on familiarity with the existing model.

EXERCISES

(* denotes that it applies to the Appendix)

EXERCISE 3–1   You have been requested by the Board of Directors of your employer company to produce a schedule indicating what the results of operations of the company had been in real terms (i.e., excluding the effects of inflation) for the last five years. The figures are to be presented in terms of 20X6 year-end common dollars.

Information relating to the cash flows of the company was unavailable, and the only relevant information is given below:

	20X6	20X5	20X4	20X3	20X2
Net Income (000s)	$3,329	$3,193	$3,050	$2,963	$2,666
Consumer Price Index at December 31	144	134	126	118	110

REQUIRED

From the information given above, prepare a schedule giving the results of operations for the five years 20X2 through 20X6 in real terms. The consumer price index at December 31, 20X1 was 100, and you may assume that the net income was earned evenly throughout the five years.

EXERCISE 3–2 The following abbreviated comparative financial statements apply to Nicholson Inc. at December 31, 20X3:

	20X3	20X2
Monetary Assets	$ 60,000	$ 20,000
Inventory	42,000	36,000
Plant and Equipment	160,000	160,000
Less: Accumulated Amortization	(32,000)	(16,000)
	$230,000	$200,000
Monetary Liabilities	$ 85,000	$ 75,000
Common Stock	100,000	100,000
Retained Earnings	45,000	25,000
	$230,000	$200,000

Additional Information:

(a) The company had been formed and had commenced business on January 1, 20X1.

(b) The plant and equipment, which was being amortized on the straight-line basis at 10% per year, was purchased for cash on January 1, 20X2.

(c) The inventory was purchased on June 30 in each year.

(d) The consumer price index for the three years ended December 31, 20X3 was as follows:

	20X1	20X2	20X3
January 1	116	120	124
June 30	118	122	126
December 31	120	124	128

(e) All revenues and expenses accrued evenly throughout the years.

REQUIRED

Restate the balance sheet in comparative form in "year-end" dollars at December 31, 20X3 using the "three-step" conversion procedure.

EXERCISE 3–3 The abbreviated combined income and retained earnings statement of Odell Inc. for the year ended December 31, 20X6 was as follows:

		20X6
Sales		$1,800,000
Cost of Goods Sold	$ 900,000	
Administration Expenses	400,000	
Amortization of Capital Assets	130,000	
Income Tax Expense	170,000	1,600,000
Net Income for Year		200,000
Dividends Paid (October 1)		60,000
		140,000
Retained Earnings at January 1		220,000
Retained Earnings at December 31		$ 360,000

You are also provided with the following information relating to Odell Inc.:

(a) The company had been formed and had commenced business on January 1, 20X3, when the consumer price index was 105. On that date plant and equipment were purchased for $500,000, and were being amortized on the straight-line basis at the rate of 20% per year. On April 1, 20X6, additional plant and equipment, that was being amortized on the same basis as before, was purchased for $200,000.

(b) The consumer price index for 20X6 was 126 on January 1, and increased evenly throughout the year, to end at 130.

(c) All revenues and expenses (including income taxes) accrued evenly throughout the year.

(d) Net monetary assets other than cash were $70,000 at January 1, 20X6, and $210,000 at December 31, 20X6.

(e) Details of the cash inflows and outflows for the year were as follows:

Cash and Bank Balances at January 1, 20X6		$ 240,000
Inflows from Sales and Receivables		1,820,000
Outflows:		2,060,000
For Plant and Equipment	$ 200,000	
Sundry Operating Expenses	1,660,000	
Dividends Paid	60,000	1,920,000
Cash and Bank Balances at December 31, 20X6		$ 140,000

REQUIRED

Restate the combined income and retained earnings statement for the year ended December 31, 20X6 in "year-end" common dollars.

EXERCISE 3–4

REQUIRED

Using the information provided in Exercise 3–3, restate the combined income and retained earnings statement for the year ended December 31, 20X6 in "average-for-the-year" common dollars.

EXERCISE 3–5

You are provided with the following abbreviated balance sheet of Sellem Inc. for the year ended December 31, 20X4:

Cash	$14,000
Inventory (1,000 units at $6 each)	6,000
Plant and Equipment	80,000
Less Accumulated Amortization (at 10% per year)	(8,000)
	$92,000
Accounts Payable	$ 8,000
8% Bonds	20,000
Common Stock	50,000
Retained Earnings	14,000
	$92,000

You are also informed that:

(a) The company was formed and commenced trading operations on January 1, 20X4.

(b) During the year the company purchased 5,000 items for resale at $6 each, and sold 4,000 items for $16 each, when their replacement cost was $8 each.

(c) Administrative and Selling Expenses for the year amounted to $18,000, and the amortization on the plant and equipment was $8,000.

(d) At December 31, 20X4, the replacement cost of the inventory was $10 each, the current replacement cost of the plant and equipment was $88,000, and the market value of the 8% bonds was $18,000.

REQUIRED

1. Prepare the current cost income statement and balance sheet for 20X4 using the financial capital maintenance concept; and

2. Explain what differences would have occurred if the productive capacity capital maintenance concept had been used.

EXERCISE 3–6 KNM Motor Parts Ltd. was a major supplier of replacement parts to the automobile trade. In order to be able to fix the selling prices of parts, the company carefully monitored the price of its purchases from suppliers.

During the month of March 20X6, the increase in price of its inventory purchases and the unadjusted cost of goods sold were as given below.

INCREASES IN PRICES OF INVENTORY — March 20X6

Category	Increase/(Decrease) in Price	Cost of Goods Sold
A	1.45%	$ 54,076
B	0.58%	687,851
C	3.60%	543,841
D	5.12%	148,882
E	(4.62%)	459,506
F	0.76%	432,875
G	5.42%	176,229

REQUIRED

Calculate the cost of goods sold adjustment for March using the internal index method.

EXERCISE 3–7* On April 1 and April 30, 20X5, the value of the opening and closing inventory of NOP Inc. was $853,335 and $876,234, respectively.

REQUIRED

Calculate the cost of goods sold adjustment for April 20X5 using the averaging method if the consumer price index rose from 117.46 on April 1 to 119.98 on April 30.

EXERCISE 3–8 The following information was extracted from the current cost adjusted books and records of Prose Inc., a company having a December 31 year-end, **before** taking the "financing adjustment" into account:

	20X3	20X4
Current Cost Adjustments for Year	$ 62,000	$ 58,000
Longterm Liabilities at December 31 (10% Bonds)	100,000	100,000
Net Current Monetary Liabilities at December 31	68,000	76,000
Common Stock (100,000 shares of no par value)	300,000	300,000
Capital Surplus Arising from Asset Revaluation	148,000	210,000
Retained Earnings at January 1	42,000	70,000
Current Cost Net Income for Year	28,000	46,000

REQUIRED

1. Calculate the "financing adjustment" for 20X4; and
2. Explain how the "financing adjustment" would be taken into account/adjusted on both the income statement and balance sheet for 20X4.

PROBLEMS

PROBLEM 3–1 The following information relates to Marshall Inc. for the year ended December 31, 20X6:

(a) The company had commenced business on January 1, 20X6. On that date, the cash on hand had amounted to $150,000 arising from the issue of the common stock and the 10% bonds.

(b) All revenues and expenses (including the cost of goods sold) accrued evenly throughout the years.

(c) The inventory was all purchased on June 30, 20X6.

(d) The consumer price index for 20X6 increased evenly from 140 on January 1 to 160 at December 31.

(e) The purchase of plant was in cash.

(f) The plant and equipment is amortized using the straight-line method at the rate of 20% per year with no residual value. Details of these items at December 31, 20X6 were as follows:

	Cost	Accumulated Amortization
Purchases — January 1, 20X6	$100,000	$20,000
Purchases — June 30, 20X6	40,000	4,000
	$140,000	$24,000

(g) The abbreviated balance sheet at December 31, 20X6 and the combined income and retained earnings statement of Marshall for the year ended on that date were as follows:

COMBINED INCOME AND RETAINED EARNINGS STATEMENT

Sales		$255,000
Cost of Goods Sold	$130,000	
Amortization of Capital Assets	24,000	
Other Expenses	35,000	
Total Expenses		$189,000
Net Income for Year		$ 66,000
Dividend Declared and Paid (October 1)		20,000
Retained Earnings at December 31		$ 46,000

BALANCE SHEET

Cash	$ 40,000
Accounts Receivable	145,000
Inventory	35,000
Plant and Equipment	140,000
Less: Accumulated Amortization	(24,000)
	$336,000
Accounts Payable	$140,000
Ten-year 10% Bonds	50,000
Common Stock	100,000
Retained Earnings	46,000
	$336,000

REQUIRED

Restate the balance sheet and income statement for 20X6 in terms of price-level adjusted accounting in "year-end" dollars.

PROBLEM 3–2   **REQUIRED**

Using the information provided in Problem 3–1, restate the balance sheet and income statement for 20X6 in terms of price-level adjusted accounting in "average-for-the-year" dollars.

PROBLEM 3–3   **REQUIRED**

Prepare a balance sheet and income and retained earnings statement for Wilbur for 20X7 using a price-level adjusted accounting model in year-end common dollars on the assumption that the opening retained earnings in common dollars was $22,000. Include the monetary gain or loss as a "plug figure".

You are provided with the following information relating to Wilbur Inc.:

(a) The company was formed on January 1, 20X5. All outstanding shares were issued at that time.
(b) The equipment was purchased on January 1, 20X5 and is being amortized on a straight-line basis over its useful life of 10 years.
(c) Wilbur uses the LIFO method of accounting for its inventory.
(d) The opening inventory was purchased evenly throughout 20X6.
(e) On January 1, 20X7, all assets and liabilities had replacement costs equal to their historical cost.
(f) Administration and income tax expense occurred evenly throughout the year.
(g) CPI information is as follows:

Date	CPI
January 1, 20X5	70
January 1, 20X6	80
20X6 Average	95
December 31, 20X6	100
January 31, 20X7	101
February 28, 20X7	104
March 31, 20X7	103
April 30, 20X7	102
October 31, 20X7	109
November 30, 20X7	112
December 31, 20X7	115
20X7 Average	108

The historical cost accounting financial statements of Wilbur Inc. for the year ended December 31, 20X7 were as follows:

INCOME AND RETAINED EARNINGS STATEMENT

Sales on the following dates:

February 28	— 50,000 units at $6.00 each		$ 300,000
April 30	— 20,000 units at $5.00 each		100,000
November 30	— 75,000 units at $8.00 each		600,000
Total Sales			$1,000,000

Cost of Goods Sold:

Opening Inventory	— 12,500 units at $4.00 each		$ 50,000
Purchases on the following dates:			
January 31	— 60,000 units at $5.00 each	$300,000	
March 31	— 50,000 units at $4.00 each	200,000	
October 31	— 32,500 units at $6.00 each	195,000	695,000
			745,000
Ending Inventory	— 10,000 units at $4.00 each		40,000
			$ 705,000

Gross Profit			$ 295,000
Less: Expenses			
Administration		175,000	
Depreciation		10,000	
Taxes		80,000	265,000
Net Income for Year			30,000
Retained Earnings, January 1, 20X7			20,000
			50,000
Dividends (November 30)			10,000
Retained Earnings, December 31, 20X7			$ 40,000

BALANCE SHEET

Cash on Hand	$ 30,000
Accounts Receivable	20,000
Inventory	40,000
Equipment	100,000
Accumulated Amortization	(30,000)
	$ 160,000
Accounts Payable	$ 20,000
Bank Loan Payable	90,000
Common Stock (1,000 shares of no par value)	10,000
Retained Earnings	40,000
	$ 160,000

PROBLEM 3–4 Della Inc. was incorporated on January 1, 20X8, and its entire capital stock was issued on that date for $100,000 in cash. Transactions relating to its activities for the two months ended February 28, 20X8 were as follows:

BANK ACCOUNT

20X8					
Jan.	1	Share capital	100,000		100,000
	1	Equipment		40,000	
	1	Purchases Inventory — 800 items at $60 each		48,000	
	31	Administration Expenses		10,000	2,000
	31	Sales — 700 items at $90 each	63,000		65,000
Feb.	1	Purchases Inventory — 700 items at $70 each		49,000	
	28	Administration Expenses		11,000	
	28	Sales — 500 items at $100 each	50,000		55,000

You are also informed that:

(a) The plant and equipment purchased for $40,000 was expected to have a five-year life with no residual value. It was to be amortized using the straight-line method. On February 28, 20X8, the replacement value of the equipment was $42,000.

(b) All sales were for cash and took place on the last day of each month.

(c) The consumer price index increased evenly throughout the two months from 102 at January 1, 20X8 to 104 at February 28, 20X8.

(d) The company uses the FIFO method of recording its inventory.

REQUIRED

Given the above information relating to Della, prepare an income statement for the two months ended February 28, 20X8 and a balance sheet on that date, using:

1. Price-level adjusted accounting in "year-end" common dollars on the assumption that all revenues and expenses accrued evenly throughout the period;

2. Current cost accounting using the financial capital maintenance concept, and on the assumption that the replacement cost of the inventory at February 28 was $80 each.

PROBLEM 3–5 You are provided with the following information relating to Belcourt Industries Inc.:

(a) The increases in the prices of inventory between the date of purchase and sale, monitored through a fully integrated standard costing system, amounted to 10% (i.e., an internal index of 10%). The same percentage increase applied to the ending inventory at balance sheet date.

(b) The replacement cost of the plant and equipment at December 31, 20X9 that was being amortized at 20% per year on the straight-line basis with no residual value was $720,000. At December 31, 20X8, it was $680,000.

(c) The 10% bonds had a market price of $85,000 at December 31, 20X9.

(d) The current cost retained earnings at December 31, 20X8, using financial capital maintenance was $49,000.

At December 31, 20X9, the abbreviated historical cost accounting financial statements of Belcourt Industries were as follows:

BALANCE SHEET

Cash	$ 30,000
Accounts Receivable	160,000
Inventory	140,000
Plant and Equipment	600,000
Less Accumulated Amortization	(240,000)
	$ 690,000
Accounts Payable	$ 200,000
10% Bonds	100,000
Common Stock	300,000
Retained Earnings	90,000
	$ 690,000

COMBINED INCOME AND RETAINED EARNINGS STATEMENT

Sales		$1,200,000
Beginning Inventory	100,000	
Purchases	670,000	
	770,000	
Ending Inventory	140,000	630,000
Gross Profit		570,000
Less: Expenses		
Administrative Expenses	200,000	
Amortization of Capital Assets	120,000	
Income Tax	125,000	445,000
Net Income for Year		125,000
Less Dividends		40,000
		85,000
Retained Earnings at January 1, 20X9		5,000
Retained Earnings at December 31, 20X9		$ 90,000

REQUIRED

Using the above information:

1. Restate the balance sheet and combined income and retained earnings statement of Belcourt Industries in terms of current cost accounting using financial capital maintenance; and

2. Give the net income and shareholders' equity of Belcourt Industries if the productive capacity capital maintenance concept had been used and if the $49,000 retained earnings given in point (d) above included a capital surplus arising from the revaluation of assets in 20X8 of $38,000. (**Ignore** the financing adjustment.)

PROBLEM 3–6 You are provided with the following information relating to Johnson Inc.:

(a) The company was formed on January 1, 20X5.

(b) At December 31, 20X5, the current cost balance sheets of Johnson disclosed the following balances:

	Financial Capital Maintenance	Productive Capacity Capital Maintenance
Equipment	$600,000	$600,000
Accumulated Depreciation	(60,000)	(60,000)
Capital Surplus Arising from Revaluation of Assets	—	65,000
Retained Earnings	105,000	40,000

(c)   The inventory on hand at January 1, 20X6 was all sold when the replacement cost was $5.00/unit. Of the sales of 180,000 units, 100,000 units were sold when the replacement cost was $7.00/unit and the balance when the replacement cost was $8.00/unit. At December 31, 20X6, the replacement cost of the inventory was $9.00/unit.

(d)   The replacement costs of the equipment at December 31, 20X6 were $700,000.

(e)   The equipment was being amortized on the straight-line basis with no residual value over 10 years.

The historical cost accounting combined income and retained earnings statement of Johnson for the year ended December 31, 20X6 was as follows:

INCOME AND RETAINED EARNINGS STATEMENT

Sales (180,000 units at $10.00 each)			$1,800,000
Cost of Goods Sold:			$1,010,000
Opening Inventory (35,000 units at $4.00 each)		140,000	
Purchases (170,000 units at $6.00 each):		1,020,000	
		1,160,000	
Ending Inventory (25,000 units at $6.00 each)		150,000	
Administration Expenses			335,000
Amortization of Capital Assets			60,000
Income Taxes			80,000
			$1,485,000
Net Income for Year			$ 315,000
Retained Earnings, January 1, 20X6			60,000
			375,000
Dividends (November 30)			20,000
Retained Earnings, December 31, 20X6			$ 355,000

REQUIRED

From the information provided above, prepare a current cost combined income and retained earnings statement for Johnson for 20X6 using

1.   The financial capital maintenance concept; and
2.   The productive capacity capital maintenance concept.

Business Combinations 4

LEARNING OBJECTIVES

After studying this chapter you should be able to:

1. Understand what is meant by the term "business combination" and recognize the various forms of business combinations;
2. Compare and evaluate the different methods of combining businesses; and
3. Account for business combinations effected as a purchase by either an existing business or a new entity.

THE NATURE OF BUSINESS COMBINATIONS[1]

In accounting, the term business combination is used to describe the combining of two or more business enterprises into **a single economic entity**. The CICA defines the term in a more general way by stating that a business combination occurs when an enterprise acquires net assets that constitute a business, or acquires equity interests of one or more other enterprises and obtains control over that enterprise or enterprises.[2]

Business combinations may vary in nature from the acquisition of a small, unincorporated business to gaining control of a multinational corporation.[3] From an accounting point of view, however, the important aspect is that the combined enterprises represent a single economic or accounting entity from the date on which the combination took effect. From that point onwards, the single economic entity carries on the activities of the previous separate, independent enterprises.

The legal form of the combination is of little consequence because it is the continuing or new economic entity formed by the combination that is the focus of attention for

---

[1] CICA *Handbook*, section 1581.
[2] CICA *Handbook*, section 1600.
[3] The significance of corporate mergers and acquisitions in the business world is reflected by the report of the *The Globe and Mail* {October 26, 1999} that in the first nine months of 1999, Corporate America alone spent a staggering US $24.1-billion to complete 181 mergers and acquisitions of Canadian companies.

financial reporting purposes. This is because it is the accounting entity that defines the area of economic interest of the combined business, and the combination is accounted for on the basis of the continuing accounting entity from the date on which the combination took place.

THE DIFFERENCE BETWEEN THE PURCHASE OF ASSETS AND A BUSINESS COMBINATION

In any examination of business combinations, it is necessary to distinguish between the mere purchase of assets by a company and the combination of two or more businesses. This is because the purchase of certain assets of a business cannot be considered to be a combination unless the transaction covers all, or virtually all, of the assets of the acquired business. And, to establish whether a combination has occurred, **the deciding factor** is whether control of the business has been transferred to another party. At times the distinction between the two may be difficult to establish but it is usually the **inability of the acquired business to continue to operate independently of its new owner that indicates that a business combination has occurred**.

THE FORMS OF BUSINESS COMBINATIONS

There are three ways businesses may be combined. These are:

1. Where one business acquires another
2. When a new entity is formed
3. Where one company gains control over another

Where One Business Acquires Another

Where one business enterprise purchases another business, the acquired business becomes part of the acquiring business. This is referred to as a **merger** because, in these cases, the interests of one business are merged with those of another business. However, to be considered a merger, the acquisition must involve all or a substantial portion of the assets of the acquired business because, after the acquisition, the acquired business must cease to exist as a separate entity.

In practice, the acquiring company usually only purchases the assets of the acquired business, and the selling company discharges its own liabilities before liquidating the company. In certain cases, however, the liabilities of the acquired business are also taken over together with the assets. However, this latter form of combination is somewhat rare, because the new owners are seldom prepared to assume the liabilities of the acquired business, particularly where they may consist of substantial unrecorded liabilities like unfunded pension benefits or other, similar commitments.

When a New Entity Is Formed

In those cases where a new company is formed to carry on the operations of two previously independent businesses, the combination is considered to be a purchase by the new entity of those two previously independent businesses, and it is accounted for in the same manner as the acquisition of one business by another.

Where One Company Gains Control over Another

A business combination occurs when one company acquires control over another company. This normally occurs when the acquiring company, has **the right to elect a majority of**

members to its board of directors.[4] This right usually arises from the ownership, either directly or indirectly, of the majority of shares having voting rights in the other company and the combination is, therefore, recorded as an investment in the shares of the investee company.

With this form of business combination, the acquiring company is usually referred to as a parent company, and the company over which control is exercised is known as a subsidiary company. The relationship between the two companies is usually referred to as an affiliation of companies in a "parent company — subsidiary company relationship".

The advantage of this form of business combination is that the investing company gains control over an existing business from the date on which control may be exercised. And, provided that the acquisition did not involve the purchase of the subsidiary's entire issued common stock, the investing company also gains control over the acquired company at a considerably lower price than that which would have been required for an outright purchase of the business.

Where Two Businesses Combine with One Another

Any two businesses, including a parent company and its subsidiary, may combine with one another. The formations of these new entities is sometimes referred to as "statutory amalgamation" because the combination is carried out in terms of some or other statutory provision.[5]

Reverse Takeovers

A "**reverse takeover**" is said to have taken place if the owners of all the shares in a company sell all their shares to another company in exchange for sufficient shares to control the acquiring company. For example, assume that Companies A and B have issued 20,000 and 10,000 voting shares respectively. If all the voting shares in Company B are acquired by Company A in exchange for 25,000 additional voting shares in Company A, control of Company B passes to Company A, but Company A is now controlled by the former shareholders in Company B.[6]

ACCOUNTING FOR BUSINESS COMBINATIONS EFFECTED AS A PURCHASE

Recording of Assets and Liabilities

Where a business combination arises as the result of an outright purchase by one business of the assets (or assets and liabilities) of another business, the accounting treatment is based on the rule that the acquisition must be treated in the same manner as that applying to the purchase of any other assets.

This means that the assets (and liabilities, where applicable) acquired are, therefore, recorded by the purchasing company at their fair market values at the date of acquisition and any earnings from those assets accrue to the acquiring company from the date of acquisition.

---

[4] This is the legal definition of control. Control in the accounting sense is somewhat different and is outlined in Chapter 6.

[5] For example, in terms of section 181 of the *Canada Business Corporations Act*, any two companies may amalgamate and continue to operate as a single corporation.

[6] For example, in March 1993 it was reported that international Epitek Inc. of Kanata, Ontario, a manufacturer of printed circuit boards, had agreed to a reverse takeover of Computer Assembly Systems Ltd., a subsidiary of Compas Inc. of Brockville, Ontario. The takeover was to be effected through a swap by Compas shareholders of $1.4-million in equity in Computer Assembly Systems Ltd. and its American subsidiary, American Computer Assembly Inc. of Ogdensburg, N.Y., for 7.3-million Epitek shares giving Compas control of 83% of Epitek's outstanding common stock.

Any accumulated amortization of capital assets acquired is, therefore, ignored and the **purchase consideration** is established either by the amount actually paid in cash or, in the case of a purchase effected by a share issue, by the market value of the shares issued on the date on which the acquisition took place.

The amount paid in cash requires no explanation. However, where the **purchase consideration** is settled by **the issue of shares**, the amount to be paid is established from the **market value** of the shares at the date of acquisition. In those cases where the purchase consideration **cannot be established by using either the cash paid or market value of the shares issued**, the purchase consideration may be established by using the fair market value of the net assets acquired. In those cases where the acquisition of an interest in another business is through **an exchange of assets** unrelated to its trading operations, the purchase consideration is the fair market value of the assets acquired through the exchange.

It must be noted that **expenses relating to the combination must also be included as part of the purchase price**. Direct costs of the combination would include accounting, legal, consulting, and finder's fees, and are added to the purchase consideration. Indirect expenses are items like share issue expenses, where the combination was effected by a share issue, and managerial salaries and travelling expenses incurred during the merger. Share issue expenses are usually written off immediately against the share capital, while other indirect costs are written off as expenses when incurred.

The way the accounting for the assets of the acquisition is normally handled is to debit the purchase consideration and any direct expenses to an **investment account**. The balance on this account is drawn down as the assets acquired are valued and transferred to their respective asset accounts, as outlined in the following sub-section.

The Allocation of the Purchase Consideration between the Net Assets and Goodwill

On the acquisition of a business, the purchase consideration must first be allocated to the net assets acquired by valuing the assets and liabilities at their fair market value. In allocating the purchase price to the acquired assets and liabilities, suitable values should also be assigned to those intangible assets that can be separately identified (e.g., franchises, patents, trademarks, etc.). Any balance remaining is treated as the amount paid for goodwill.

For example, if the sum of $600,000 was paid by the purchasing company for the net assets of a business having a fair market value of $700,000 and monetary liabilities of $200,000, the purchase consideration would be allotted as to $500,000 to the net assets (i.e., $700,000 − $200,000) and $100,000 to goodwill.

The valuation of assets and liabilities acquired follows the normal valuation rules. The fair market value of nonmonetary assets and identifiable intangible assets is established from their current realizable values or replacement costs using quoted market prices where these are available. Where these market prices are unavailable, the purchase price of similar assets less amortization should be used. Where market prices or the values of similar assets are not available, estimates of the fair value should be made using the best information available and the results of valuation techniques like the present value of expected future cash flows, option pricing models, etc. As far as monetary assets and liabilities are concerned, these are valued at their monetary values less any necessary adjustments. For example, accounts receivable would be valued at their face value less any adjustment for uncollectible accounts and collection expenses.

The goodwill arising on the acquisition of a business is no different from any other form of purchased goodwill and must be reflected as a separate item on the balance sheet and accounted for using the impairment method.

The Impairment Method of Accounting for Goodwill

An impairment method of accounting for goodwill has been adopted by the CICA. It requires that goodwill should be **initially recorded at cost but written down for impairment** whenever an event or series of events indicates that its value has been impaired. This replaces the former method, where purchased goodwill was recorded at cost on acquisition and then amortized on a straight-line basis over a period not exceeding 40 years unless the goodwill had been impaired, in which case it was to be written down accordingly. The change in approach recognizes that in a growing or well run business, goodwill is likely to increase in value and its systematic write-off does not reflect economic reality. It also recognized that the value of goodwill of companies can fluctuate dramatically.[7]

The CICA's accounting requirements specify that the acquiring company must carry out an **initial assessment** of the value of goodwill. At this point, if the goodwill appears to be properly valued, no further action is required. If, however, the goodwill appears to be overvalued, then a **second assessment** must be carried out by the financial year end to establish the value of goodwill by carrying out a complete revaluation of the net assets.

To simplify the assessment of the value of goodwill, the amount allocated to goodwill on acquisition should be allocated to the various reporting units of the acquired business expected to be benefited by the acquisition. In this respect, a **reporting unit** is defined as a unit of the business entity that can be distinguished physically, operationally and for internal reporting purposes from the other activities, operations and assets of the entity.

The goodwill allocation is, therefore, to the various reporting units. Such an allocation makes it **easier to identify the portion of the goodwill that has become impaired** or, in the case of **the disposal** of part of the interest in the acquired business, **the amount of goodwill sold**. This allocation to the various reporting units should be on a *pro rata* basis unless there is evidence to suggest that another method is more appropriate.

In the years following the initial or second assessment, the value of the goodwill should be **reviewed for impairment** on an annual basis. This annual review must also take place **at the same time** each year (e.g., on September 1 each year) The **extent to which the goodwill has been impaired** is established by comparing the fair value of the goodwill with its carrying value based on the difference between the fair value of the net assets and their book value. If the fair value of the goodwill is less than its carrying value, difference would be considered **an impairment loss** and written off against revenues in the year in which it is recognized. If, however, the carrying value of the goodwill is less than its fair value, the goodwill is left unchanged. There is no provision for the upward valuation of goodwill, and the goodwill appearing on the balance sheet is reflected at the original amount less any write-downs for impairment.

At anytime between the annual reviews, if an event or a series of events occurs that indicates the value of the goodwill may have been impaired, **an additional review** should be carried out. Events that would trigger such a review would include an actual or forecasted change in the cash flows or profitability of the entity, reduced market share of its products, loss of key personnel, reduced credit rating, and significant legal challenges to its existence and/or profitability. Once the decision has been reached that the goodwill has been impaired, then the extent of the write-down must be decided upon.

The **annual test** for impairment need not be carried out if **all** of the following three criteria are met:

1. There has been no significant change in the composition of the assets and the liabilities of the reporting unit since the last annual review;

---

[7] For example, JDS Uniphase wrote down goodwill by US $45-billion in 2002 arising from various takeovers of businesses at the peak of the "high-tech boom" (as reported by the *The Globe and Mail*, July 27, 2002).

2. The most recent review has indicated that the fair value of the net assets is substantially greater than their book value; and

3. There is no reason to believe that the goodwill may be impaired during the current reporting period.

The impairment method **does not apply retroactively**. As a result, the unamortized balance of goodwill existing at the date of change in method is no longer amortized but is carried forward on the balance sheet and reviewed for impairment when necessary from that time onwards.

Establishing Whether the Goodwill Has Been Impaired

Goodwill is a residual asset. This means that, on acquisition, it represents the amount by which the purchase price of a business entity exceeds the fair value of the net assets acquired. It exists because the reporting entity is expected to earn a higher than normal rate of return on capital invested. This situation exists because of imperfect market conditions; the entity possessing goodwill may have superior products, a good management team, good reputation, good location, etc. At any one time, therefore, the value of goodwill may be considered the present value of the expected excess profits for the period over which the excess earnings are expected to continue.

No matter how well this describes the nature of goodwill, the valuation of goodwill is, in practice, the amount remaining after writing off any amounts for impairment. This situation will prevail for as long as historical cost accounting continues to be used and there is no recognition of internally generated goodwill.

Presentation of Goodwill Charges on the Income Statement

Any impairment losses, which are referred to as **goodwill charges**, must be written off as soon as they are recognized through the income statement as **a separate line item**. This line item must appear after a subtotal described as "net income before goodwill charges and extraordinary items" (and, if applicable, discontinued operations). If the goodwill impairment is associated with a discontinued operation, it should be included as part of the gain or loss on the discontinued operations.

A full description of the facts and circumstances leading to the impairment must be disclosed. In those cases where the extent of the impairment is only an estimate that has not been finalized, this must be made clear, together with the details of any subsequent adjustments. An example of how goodwill charges must be presented is given as Illustration 4–1.

The Elimination of Negative Goodwill

If, on the allocation of the purchase consideration, it is found that the fair value of the identifiable assets exceeds the purchase consideration, the shortfall represents negative goodwill. This amount must be allocated on a *pro rata* basis to the identifiable assets **other than inventory, monetary assets (i.e., cash, cash equivalents, and trade receivables), financial assets that are carried on the balance sheet at fair value (e.g., mortgage loans), assets that are to be sold, and those relating to discontinued operations**. For example, if negative goodwill of $60,000 is to be allocated over the plant and equipment having a fair value of $750,000 and identifiable intangible assets having a fair value of $150,000, the adjustments would be as follows:

Plant and Equipment	$750,000 − ($750,000/$900,000 × $60,000)	=	$700,000
Identifiable Intangible Assets	$150,000 − ($150,000/$900,000 × $60,000)	=	$140,000
Total Adjustable Assets less Negative Goodwill (i.e., $900,000 − $60,000)			$840,000

ILLUSTRATION 4–1
DISCLOSURE OF GOODWILL CHARGES IN THE INCOME STATEMENT

The following abbreviated income statement reflects the manner in which goodwill charges are to be disclosed:

ABC Communications, Inc.
Income and Retained Earnings Statement

	Years Ended December 31	
	(000s)	
	20X4	**20X3**
Communication service revenues	$171,000	$147,000
Operating expenses (details as required)	146,000	130,000
Net income from operations	25,000	17,000
Interest revenue	800	300
Earnings before income taxes	25,800	17,300
Income tax expense	8,700	7,900
Net income before goodwill charges and extraordinary items	17,100	9,400
Goodwill charges — note 9	2,800	—
Net income before extraordinary items	14,300	9,400
Extraordinary loss arising from flood damage — note 10	1,700	—
Net income for year	$ 12,600	$ 8,600

The note to the goodwill charges would be presented along the following lines:

9. The value of the goodwill is reviewed for impairment at the end of each financial year or whenever considered necessary. Following such an assessment carried out in December 20X4, the company concluded that goodwill relating to the cable networking system was overvalued, and that it should be revalued accordingly.

On completion of the revaluation, the values allocated to the assets should be re-examined to ensure that the values allocated to the assets are realistic. If not, they should be revalued accordingly. After such a reassessment, if negative goodwill still remains, this amount should be treated as **an extraordinary revenue item** in the income statement.

Contingent Consideration

A contingent consideration occurs where the contract of sale contains a clause adjusting the acquisition price on the happening of some event or the fulfillment of some or other condition.[8] It is normally **recognized when the contingency is resolved** and the amount is settled or becomes payable. The contingent consideration is treated as part of the purchase consideration or as an expense, depending upon the nature of the contingency and how it is paid.

The CICA *Handbook*[9] requires that if the amount can be reasonably estimated at the date of acquisition and the outcome of the contingency can be determined **without a reasonable doubt**, the amount should be recognized at the date of acquisition as part of the purchase price. However, if the amount or outcome of the contingency cannot be so determined,

---

[8] For example, the acquisition of Promotory Communications by Nortel Networks where the initial payment was $705-million in stock with the proviso that if Promotory met certain financial targets, Nortel would increase its purchase price by an additional $73-million in stock (*The Globe and Mail*, January 7, 2000).

[9] Section 1581.

then the contingency should be disclosed by way of a note. When, if ever, the contingency is resolved and the amount becomes payable, it must be treated as an additional cost of the purchase.

Where the contingency becomes payable on **achieving or maintaining certain earnings levels**, the amount must also be recorded at its fair market value at that date as an additional cost of purchase. Up until that stage, details of the contingency should be disclosed by way of a note.

The contingency may also be based on the **future market price** of the shares. In these cases, if the value of the shares issued to effect the acquisition does not equal a specified amount, the acquiring company may have to issue additional shares or other securities or pay an additional amount to the seller. However, the original issue of shares represents the cost of acquisition and the issue of additional shares does not affect this cost.[10] Therefore, the current fair value of the additional shares issued or amounts payable should be offset by an equivalent deduction in the original cost of acquisition. For example, if A Inc. issued 400,000 Class B shares of no par value at $1.20 each to acquire all the shares in BC Traders Inc. on January 1, 20X1, the acquisition cost would be recorded as $480,000. Assume that the value of the shares issued by A Inc. declined to 90 cents by August 31, 20X3. To fulfill a contingency, the loss in the value of the shares was to be made good by the payment of $120,000 in cash. In this case, the purchase consideration would still be recorded as $480,000, but the $120,000 would be debited to share capital to adjust the value of the shares originally issued to acquire the investment.

ACCOUNTING FOR ACQUISITIONS INVOLVING A NEW ENTITY

Where a new entity is formed to acquire two or more existing businesses, the acquisition must be treated in exactly the same manner as that applying to the purchase of one business by another. For example, if Peanut Inc. and Butter Inc. combine with one another by transferring all their assets and liabilities to Peanut Butter Inc., a new company, Peanut Butter Inc., would be considered the purchasing company.

WHERE ONE COMPANY GAINS CONTROL OVER ANOTHER COMPANY

Where one company gains control over another company, the purchasing company, also known as the investor, **records its investment** in the shares of the company over which it now exercises control (i.e., the investee or subsidiary company) **as a longterm investment**. In consolidation terminology, **the investor company is referred to as the parent or holding company**.[11]

The existence of such a "parent company-subsidiary company" relationship requires the preparation of what are referred to as consolidated financial statements for external financial reporting purposes in all but a few exceptional cases. However, as the preparation of these consolidated financial statements forms the subject matter of a considerable part of this book, our discussion on this type of combination is, at this stage, limited to the recording of the interest in the subsidiary company as an investment.

---

[10] *Ibid.*

[11] Even though section 1 of the *Canada Business Corporations Act* refers to holding companies, the term "parent company" is more widely used and has been adopted in this text.

It should be noted that from time to time companies owning controlling interests in other companies rearrange or re-organize their investments for various purposes by transferring investments from one company to another within the affiliated group. It is, therefore, important to note that the term "business combination" does not cover the **internal reorganization** of affiliated companies or between companies associated with one another in some other form. This is because to be considered a business combination, there must be a change in the ownership of the assets or control of the businesses concerned. A reorganization, on the other hand, is concerned with a **change** in the relationships between the assets and liabilities of a company that may also affect the rights and obligations of the shareholders in that company: for example, where there has been a re-organization of a company resulting from the restructuring of its debt or capital.

The term, **associated company**, merely means that the companies are associated with one another in some way. This may occur where, for example, the shares of two companies are owned by the same persons.

COMPARING THE DIFFERENT FORMS OF BUSINESS COMBINATIONS

The three ways businesses may be combined with one another give different amounts for assets and liabilities. This is because, with the exception of the acquisition of a controlling interest in a company, the assets and liabilities of the companies are combined using different values.

With a **purchase** of an existing business, the purchased assets are brought into account at their fair market values at the date of purchase. These are added to those of the acquiring company, which have been recorded at cost in the normal manner. Using the new entity approach, all items are brought into account at their fair market values. The purchase of a **controlling interest** in a company is, however, merely reflected as an investment on the balance sheet of the parent company.

An example of the differences in the values at which the assets and liabilities are carried on the balance sheets of the purchasing or continuing companies immediately after an acquisition or combination is provided in Illustration 4–2, which shows the effects on the balance sheets of the three different methods of combining business entities.

IDENTIFYING THE ACQUIRING PARTY

In most business combinations, the acquiring party can be easily identified. However, in certain cases the acquisition is **contingent** upon the happening of some or other event. In these cases, the transaction is only recognized once the event in question has taken place. At other times, however, it may be difficult to determine which company is the acquiring party. In these circumstances, an examination of the transaction in the following light may assist in providing the necessary answer:

(a) Which company issued shares or paid cash for the net assets of the other party to the transaction?
(b) Which is the company whose members hold more than 50% of the shares in the continuing entity?
(c) Where the shareholders in the continuing company each hold 50% of the voting shares of the continuing entity, other factors may indicate which company was the acquiring party. These factors may involve the composition of the board of directors, the participation in the management of the company, etc.

ILLUSTRATION 4–2
COMPARISON OF A BUSINESS COMBINATION EFFECTED THROUGH A PURCHASE, THE CREATION OF A NEW ENTITY, AND BY ACQUIRING A CONTROLLING INTEREST THROUGH A SHARE PURCHASE

The abbreviated balance sheets of Lisa Inc. and Mark Inc. at December 31, 20X2 were as follows:

	Lisa		Mark	
	Cost	Fair Market Value	Cost	Fair Market Value
Cash	$ 20,000	$ 20,000	$ 4,000	$ 4,000
Inventory	90,000	80,000	16,000	18,000
Accounts Receivable	150,000	145,000	80,000	72,000
Plant and Equipment	320,000	400,000	160,000	190,000
	$580,000		$260,000	
Accounts Payable	$ 60,000	55,000	$ 20,000	16,000
Common Stock	400,000		200,000	
Retained Earnings	120,000		40,000	
	$580,000		$260,000	

Assume that on January 1, 20X3:

(a) Lisa purchased the assets and liabilities of Mark for $268,000, which was the fair market value of the net assets of Mark.

(b) Nora Inc. took over the assets and liabilities of Lisa and Mark by issuing its common stock to the shareholders of both Lisa and Mark in proportion to the fair market value of their net assets (i.e., $590,000 and $268,000).

(c) Lisa acquired the entire issued common stock of Mark by issuing common stock worth $268,000 to the shareholders of Mark.

The resultant balance sheets at January 1, 20X3 were as follows:

	Purchase	New Entity	Controlling Interest
Cash	—	$ 24,000	$ 20,000
Inventory	$108,000	98,000	90,000
Accounts Receivable	222,000	217,000	150,000
Investment in Mark	—	—	268,000
Plant and Equipment	510,000	590,000	320,000
	$840,000	$929,000	$848,000
Bank Overdraft — see note below	$244,000	$ —	$ —
Accounts Payable	76,000	71,000	60,000
Common Stock	400,000	858,000	668,000
Retained Earnings	120,000	—	120,000
	$840,000	$929,000	$848,000

These differences arose because the combination of assets and liabilities of the two companies were as follows:

(a) With the purchase method, the assets and liabilities of Mark were valued at their fair market value and combined with the assets and liabilities of Lisa, which were at cost.

(b) With the new entity approach, the assets and liabilities of both Lisa and Mark were transferred to the new entity (i.e., Nora) at their fair market values with a corresponding issue of common stock.

(c) With the acquisition of a controlling interest, the investment in Mark was recorded at the cost to the acquiring company.

Note: The bank overdraft arose from the purchase consideration of $268,000 less the cash on hand of $24,000 (i.e., $20,000 from Lisa and $4,000 from Mark).

DISCLOSURE OF INFORMATION RELATING TO ACQUISITIONS OR MERGERS

Full disclosure of the particulars relating to an acquisition or merger is required in the financial statements of the acquiring company in the year in which it occurs. The basic information required covers: the name and description of the business acquired when shares were acquired, the percentage of voting shares acquired, the period for which the earnings of the acquired enterprise are included in the income statement of the combined enterprise, the cost of the purchase and the number of any equity instruments issued or issuable, the value assigned to those equity instruments, and the basis for determining that value. Additional detailed disclosures are required including a condensed balance sheet disclosing the amount assigned to each major class of asset and liability of the acquired enterprise at the date of acquisition must be included together with details of any contingent payments, options, or commitments specified in the acquisition agreement and the accounting treatment that will be followed should any such contingency occur.[12]

It is also considered advisable to include supplementary *pro forma* information showing the results of operations of the combined companies for the entire year in which the combination took place, as if the combination had occurred at the beginning of that year, to provide users with information on the potential effect of the acquisition on earnings.

Securities legislation also requires the disclosure of certain information relating to the acquisition of interests in companies. These requirements are covered in later chapters.

THE POSITION RELATING TO THE SELLING OR LIQUIDATING PARTY

Where a company sells part or the whole of its business to another company, the sale must be treated by the selling company either as a sale of part of the business or as a liquidation of the business. The accounting for the sale of part of the business is merely to establish the profit or loss on the transaction after allowing for expenses. This would be accounted for as a discontinued operation in the income statement of the selling company.

Where the sale is of the whole of the business, the company is liquidated. In these cases, the remaining assets are realized, any liabilities not taken over as part of the purchase are discharged, any expenses incurred are paid, and any remaining balance is paid out to shareholders. In these cases, the balance on the retained earnings account is paid out as a dividend and the capital account is closed with the repayment of capital to shareholders. Certain legal formalities must, of course, be carried out to have the company's name cancelled and to complete the liquidation.

For convenience, the accounting for the liquidation of a company is carried out using a liquidation account in the ledger. All assets and liabilities are transferred to this account and, as they are realized or discharged in cash, the liquidation account is debited or credited accordingly until such time as only a gain or loss on liquidation remains. This amount is then transferred to the retained earnings account to give the final balance of retained earnings or accumulated loss. If the retained earnings account is in credit, this amount is paid out to shareholders as a liquidating dividend together with the repayment of capital. If, however, the retained earnings account reflects a debit balance, this amount must be written off as a capital loss prior to any repayment of capital. In these cases, the loss is treated as a loss of capital. An illustration of the liquidation of a company is given in Illustration 4–3.

---

[12] CICA *Handbook*, section 1581.55.

ILLUSTRATION 4–3
LIQUIDATION OF A COMPANY

On October 31, 20X0, Micrometer Inc. sold its microchip manufacturing business, excluding the cash of $2,280 at the bank, to New Age Components Inc. for $16,000 in cash. After the sale of assets and the discharge of its liabilities, Micrometer was to be liquidated. The costs of liquidation amounted to $2,200, and the balance of retained earnings and common stocks were paid out to the shareholders on November 30, 20X0.

The abbreviated balance sheet of Micrometer at October 31, 20X0, and the amounts at which the assets and liabilities were realized in cash during the month of November 20X0, would have been as follows:

Cash at Bank	$ 2,280	Accounts Payable	$ 8,380
Accounts Receivable	13,500	10% Debentures	5,000
Inventory	2,400	Common Shares	15,000
Capital Assets	12,650	Retained Earnings	6,450
Goodwill	4,000		
	$34,830		$34,830

Liquidation Account

		Dr.	Cr.	Balance
Nov. 1	Selling Price		16,000	(16,000)
	Transfer Accounts Receivable	13,500		
	Transfer Inventory	2,400		
	Transfer Capital Assets	12,650		
	Transfer Goodwill	4,000		
	Transfer Accounts Payable		8,380	
Nov. ?	Transfer 10% Debentures		5,000	3,170
?	Costs of Liquidation	2,200		5,370
30	Loss on Liquidation		5,370	Nil

Cash

Oct. 31	Balance	2,280		2,280
Nov. 1	Selling Price	16,000		18,280
Nov. ?	Costs of Liquidation		2,200	16,080
30	Liquidation Dividend		1,080	15,000
	Repayment of Capital		15,000	Nil

Common Stock

Nov. 1	Balance		15000	(15,000)
30	Cash — Repayment of Capital	15,000	Nil	

Retained Earnings

Nov. 1	Balance		6,450	(6,450)
?	Loss on Liquidation	5,370		(1,080)
30	Cash — Liquidation Dividend		Nil	

SUMMARY

This chapter examines business combinations and the way they occur. In this respect, a business combination takes place when one company combines with another company or when one company obtains control over another company. The criterion for distinguishing between a business combination and the mere sale of part of a business or a group of assets is that after a business combination has taken place, the selling company is unable to continue to operate on its own.

Business combinations may be effected in three different ways. First, one business may acquire another business. Second, a new entity may be formed to acquire two or more businesses. Third, a company may acquire control over another company by purchasing a controlling interest in that company.

In all cases other than where control over the company is obtained, the amount paid to acquire a business is first treated as representing the fair market value of the net assets acquired, and the balance is treated as goodwill. Where control exists, the purchase consideration is treated as the cost of the investment. The ways in which goodwill and negative goodwill arising on acquisition are treated is also presented, and the results of using the different methods of combining businesses are compared with one another.

SELF-STUDY PROBLEM
(covering purchase of interests)

PROBLEM 4A† On January 1, 20X4, Andrew Inc. and Beatrice Inc. merged their interests. The merger was effected by the issue by Andrew of common shares in exchange for the entire 1,200,000 no par value common shares of Beatrice that had been issued for $4 each. Prior to the merger, Andrew had 3,000,000 shares outstanding. The shares of both Andrew and Beatrice were listed on the Toronto Stock Exchange and immediately prior to the announcement of the merger, the shares were trading at $5.20 and $6.10 each.

The abbreviated balance sheets of the two companies at December 31, 20X3 were as follows:

	Andrew		Beatrice	
	Book Value	Fair Market Value	Book Value	Fair Market Value
Current Assets	$ 4,200,000	$ 5,075,000	$ 3,200,000	$ 3,875,000
Property, Plant and Equipment (net)	12,050,000	21,780,000	8,120,000	14,115,000
Intangible Assets	1,600,000	1,400,000	88,000	80,000
	$17,850,000		$11,408,000	
Current Liabilities	$ 2,740,000	$ 2,655,000	$ 1,490,000	$ 1,970,000
6% Bonds	5,000,000	4,000,000	2,000,000	1,700,000
Common Shares (of no par value)	6,000,000		4,800,000	
Capital Surplus	1,200,000		—	
Retained Earnings	2,910,000		3,118,000	
	$17,850,000		$11,408,000	

REQUIRED

Prepare the balance sheet of Andrew at January 1, 20X4, immediately after the merger on the assumption that the merger was treated as a purchase by the issue of 3-million shares by Andrew to the former shareholders of Beatrice.

---

† The solution is provided in Appendix B to this text.

REVIEW QUESTIONS

1. Describe what is meant by a business combination and explain what you understand by:
   (a) A merger of interests;
   (b) An associated company;
   (c) A statutory amalgamation; and
   (d) A parent company-subsidiary company relationship.

2. Describe the three ways a business combination may be effected.

3. How does one company become a subsidiary of another company?

4. Explain what is meant by a "reverse take-over".

5. Outline the way assets and liabilities acquired as a result of a purchase of a business are valued by the purchasing company. Why are they valued in this manner?

6. How does goodwill arise in a business combination, and how must it be treated in terms of the CICA *Handbook*?

7. What do you understand by the term "goodwill charges", and how are they disclosed in the income statement?

8. In what way is negative goodwill arising from the purchase of assets eliminated by the acquiring business?

9. How are the expenses of a business combination accounted for if the combination is treated as a purchase?

10. What is a contingent consideration? How are contingent considerations treated?

11. What information is required to be disclosed in terms of the CICA *Handbook* in the financial statements of a company relating to the acquisition of another business during the financial year in question?

12. Describe, from an accounting point of view, how a company is liquidated.

CASES

CASE 4–1   **Warren and Company Inc.**

Warren and Company Inc. carried on the business of wholesale fruit and vegetable suppliers to the hotel and restaurant business in Toronto. It also held a contract to supply two major supermarket chains in Metropolitan Toronto with fresh produce.

The success of the business was its buying and distribution system, which relied heavily on the services of Maken's Transport Services Inc., also of Toronto, to transport its purchases of fresh produce from the southern USA to Toronto and to distribute the produce locally.

Fred Maken was approaching retirement age and had indicated that, provided he could continue to be actively involved in the administration of the business until his seventieth birthday, he was prepared to sell his 60% interest in the business. The balance of the shares was held equally by his two senior managers, David Jones and Mario Rossi. The transfer of shares in the company was restricted in terms of its articles of incorporation.

The most recent audited balance sheet of the company reflected net assets of $9-million. The shares in the company had recently been valued at $40 each, which translated into an approximate net asset value of the company of $20-million.

As Maken's Transport Services had been such an integral part of its operations for many years, Warren and Company was considering either to purchase the transport business or entering into some arrangement whereby the two businesses could be combined.

REQUIRED

Advise the management of Warren and Company which of the following three proposals would best meet the company's needs:

1. The purchase of Fred Maken's 60% interest in Maken's Transport Services for the sum of $12.5-million. In this case, Fred Maken would be retained as the director of the transport division of Warren and Company for the five years until his retirement at age seventy at an annual salary of $150,000 plus reasonable expenses. The sale would only be agreed upon by David Jones and Mario Rossi, aged 46 and 41 years respectively, provided they were guaranteed continued employment in their current capacities until age sixty-five.

2. The purchase of the net assets of Maken's Transport Services for $20-million. Fred Maken, David Jones and Mario Rossi would all retire from the business as soon as suitable replacements had been trained to take over the running of the business.

3. The issue of 500,000 additional shares in Warren and Company. The shares would be issued to Fred Maken, Mario Rossi and David Jones so that after the issue, the shares in Warren and Company would be held as to 40% by the existing shareholders, 36 percent by Fred Maken and 12% each by Mario Rossi and David Jones.

CASE 4–2   **A.L. Jones Inc.**

A.L. Jones Inc. had been closely associated with Magna Services Inc. for many years. The association had commenced when A.L. Jones Inc. (ALJ) had negotiated a five-year contract to supply Magna with hydrated magnesium silicate from its mine in southern Manitoba. The contract had proved beneficial to both companies, and it had led to additional contracts between the two whereby Magna would supply ALJ with various mining supplies. Trade between the two companies was running at about $20-million a year.

In December of the previous year, Magna had signed a contract worth approximately $15-million to supply one of the major US oil companies with hydrated magnesium silicate to be used in absorbing oil spills. In negotiating the contract with the management of ALJ, it became obvious that the relationship between the two companies was such that the present and future success of both companies depended largely on their continued association. In this respect, reciprocal trade between the two companies covered a whole range of products. It was, therefore, understandable why the management of the two companies entered into discussions on the possibility of merging their interests in June 20X0.

In the course of their discussions, the following information became available:

(a) With the exception of a 10% interest in Magna held by Jim Carter and a 20% interest in ALJ held by Albert Jones, the shareholding in the two companies was relatively widespread.

(b) The net assets of Magna and ALJ at appraised values were $50-million and $35-million respectively.

(c) The cash position of Magna was relatively good. However, it was going to have to borrow money to execute the $15-million contract.

(d) The issued shares of Magna and ALJ were one million in each case.

REQUIRED

Evaluate the two following proposals from the viewpoint of both Magna and ALJ:

1. An outright purchase by Magna of the entire shareholding in ALJ for $40-million to be settled by a share exchange in which the existing shareholders of ALJ would receive one share in Magna for every two shares in ALJ previously held. This would involve the issue of an additional 500,000 common shares in Magna at $80 each.

2. A purchase by Magna of the 20% shareholding by Albert Jones and sufficient additional shares from the other shareholders at $25 per share to give Magna a

controlling interest in the company. An assessment of the situation had indicated that the holders of approximately 50% of the remaining issued shares would offer their shares for sale. This, together with the 20% interest of Albert Jones, would give Magna an interest of about 70% in the combined company.

EXERCISES

EXERCISE 4–1

REQUIRED

In each of the following questions, indicate which alternative you consider to be correct:

1. At December 31, 20X2, the assets and liabilities of Abel Inc. and Barry Inc. were as follows:

		Book Value	Fair Market Value
Abel:	Assets	$2,700,000	$3,150,000
	Liabilities	1,000,000	900,000
Barry:	Assets	1,250,000	1,400,000
	Liabilities	900,000	950,000

If Abel purchased the net assets of Barry on January 1, 20X3 for $600,000 in cash, the net assets of Abel immediately after the acquisition would have amounted to:

   (a) $1,700,000   (b) $2,050,000
   (c) $2,250,000   (d) $2,700,000

2. If Abel and Barry had decided to form a new company, Charlie Inc., to acquire their net assets as reflected above with effect from January 1, 20X3, the net assets of Charlie on January 1, 20X3, immediately after the merger, would have amounted to:

   (a) $1,700,000   (b) $2,150,000
   (c) $2,250,000   (d) $2,700,000

3. Negative goodwill of $200,000 arose on the acquisition by David Inc. of the net assets of Eric Inc., which have a fair market value of $2.4-million on January 1, 20X3. The liabilities of Eric were all properly valued, and the fair market value of its nonmonetary assets consisted of plant of $3.2-million and inventory of $800,000.

   If the relocation expenses of the plant amounted to $60,000, at what value would the net assets acquired be recorded on the balance sheet of David immediately after the acquisition?

   (a) $2,060,000   (b) $2,140,000
   (c) $2,260,000   (d) $2,460,000
   (e) $2,200,000

4. The liabilities side of the balance sheet of Frank Inc. at December 31, 20X3 reflected the following position:

Liabilities		$ 800,000
Common Stock of no par value	1,000,000	
Less: Accumulated Loss	400,000	600,000
		$1,400,000

On January 1, 20X4, George Inc. purchased the assets of Frank for $1.5-million. On receipt of the purchase consideration, Frank was liquidated; costs of liquidation amounted to $200,000.

The total dividends and capital repaid to the stockholders of Frank on completion of the liquidation amounted to:

(a)	$500,000	(b)	$700,000
(c)	$800,000	(d)	$900,000

EXERCISE 4–2   On January 1, 20X4, Bee Inc. and Honey Inc. merged their interests. Expenses of the merger amounted to $170,000 made up as follows:

Appraisal Fees — Plant and Equipment	$60,000
Share Issue Expenses	40,000
Legal Fees Relating to Merger	70,000

The abbreviated balance sheets of the two companies at December 31, 20X3 were as follows:

	Bee	Honey	
	Book Value	Book Value	Fair Market Value
Cash	$ 400,000	$ 200,000	$200,000
Inventory	600,000	250,000	240,000
Plant and Equipment (net)	2,200,000	700,000	840,000
	$3,200,000	$1,150,000	
Liabilities	$ 500,000	$ 200,000	180,000
Common Stock	2,000,000	600,000	
Retained Earnings	700,000	350,000	
	$3,200,000	$1,150,000	

REQUIRED

Give the journal entries to record the above transactions on the assumption that the combination was effected by Bee by the purchase of the assets and liabilities of Honey by issuing 50,000 of its own shares having a market value of $20 each.

EXERCISE 4–3   The abbreviated balance sheets of Dick Inc. and Harry Inc. at December 31, 20X1, together with the fair market value of the assets and liabilities of the two companies, are presented below.

	Dick		Harry	
	Cost	Fair Market Value	Cost	Fair Market Value
Accounts Payable	$ 300,000	$300,000	$ 500,000	$500,000
10% Bonds Payable	400,000	400,000	—	—
Common Stock — Note	1,000,000		800,000	
Retained Earnings	600,000		500,000	
	$2,300,000		$1,800,000	
Cash	$ 80,000	80,000	$ 100,000	100,000
Accounts Receivable	700,000	650,000	900,000	800,000
Inventory	400,000	400,000	300,000	240,000
Plant and Equipment	1,120,000	980,000	400,000	700,000
Goodwill	—		100,000	Nil
	$2,300,000		$1,800,000	

Note: The common shares consisted of 100,000 shares of no par value for both companies.

On November 30, 20X1, Tom Inc. was formed with an authorized capital of 500,000 common shares of no par value with the express purpose of taking over the businesses of Dick and Harry on January 1, 20X2. The merger was to be effected by Tom by the issue of shares at an agreed value of $20 per share based on the equity of the companies at December 31, 20X1, calculated on the fair market value of the assets and liabilities.

REQUIRED

1. Calculate the number of shares in Tom that have to be issued to the shareholders of both Dick and Harry to effect the merger; and
2. Prepare the balance sheet of Tom immediately after the acquisition of Dick and Harry.

EXERCISE 4–4 On July 1, 20X1, Optics Inc. paid $2.4-million for goodwill on the acquisition of the net assets of the software division of Zano Inc. The allocation of the goodwill to the assets acquired was as follows:

Communications Software Division	$ 300,000
Production Software Division	1,600,000
Depreciable assets used in production	500,000
Total goodwill	$2,400,000

You are also informed that:

(a) The financial year end of Optics is December 31.
(b) Optics carried out an assessment of the value of its goodwill on December 31, 20X1 and left the goodwill unchanged.
(c) At December 31, 20X2, following an assessment of the goodwill for impairment, Optics decided to write down the assets of the communications software division to zero and to discontinue the production of the Zaptics software that had accounted for 25% of the goodwill allocated to the production software division. Impairment of the goodwill relating to the balance of the depreciable assets was estimated to be 20%.
(d) The after tax net operating income of Optics was $6-million before goodwill charges and an extraordinary gain of $675,000 net of applicable income taxes.
(e) The goodwill impairment of the goodwill of Optics, other than that applicable to the goodwill on the assets purchased from Zano, for the year ended December 31, 20X2 was $980,000.

REQUIRED

Give the income statement presentation of the goodwill charges of Optics for the year ended December 31, 20X2.

EXERCISE 4–5 Negative goodwill of $200,000 arose from the purchase by Punch Inc. of the net assets (except cash) of Judy Inc. on January 1, 20X1. Legal costs involved in the acquisition amounted to $110,000. At the date of acquisition, the abbreviated balance sheet of Judy was as follows:

	Book Value	Fair Market Value
Cash	$ 100,000	$100,000
Accounts Receivable	400,000	350,000
Inventory	300,000	250,000
Land	600,000	900,000
Equipment (net)	500,000	600,000
	$1,900,000	
Accounts Payable	$ 500,000	400,000
Common Stock	1,250,000	
Retained Earnings	150,000	
	$1,900,000	

REQUIRED

1. How would the negative goodwill of $200,000 be allocated on a pro rata basis to the net assets acquired by Punch?
2. How much did Punch pay for the net assets of Judy?
3. At what amount would the equipment acquired be recorded by Punch?
4. What amounts would be paid out to the shareholders of Judy as a liquidation dividend and repayment of capital if the costs of liquidation amounted to $75,000?

EXERCISE 4–6

On April 1, 20X2, Gamma Inc. issued 500,000 shares of its common stock at $5 per share in exchange for the entire issue of 100,000 shares of Delta Inc. At the close of business on March 31, 20X2, the abbreviated balance sheets of the two companies were as follows:

	Gamma	Delta
Current assets	$2,500,000	$1,000,000
Capital Assets	4,700,000	1,400,000
	$7,200,000	$2,400,000
Current Liabilities	$ 600,000	$ 800,000
Common Shares of no par value		
450,000 shares	4,500,000	
100,000 shares		800,000
Capital Surplus	300,000	500,000
Retained Earnings	1,800,000	300,000
	$7,200,000	$2,400,000

You are also informed that any negative goodwill arising from acquisitions is to be written off against capital assets in full.

REQUIRED

Prepare the balance sheet of Gamma at April 1, 20X2 on the assumption that at that date the assets and liabilities of Delta were considered to be fairly valued, except for the capital assets, which were considered to be undervalued by:

1. $400,000.
2. $1-million.

EXERCISE 4–7

The balance sheets of Lisa Inc. and Monica Inc. at October 31, 20X1 were as follows:

	Lisa		Monica	
	Book Value	Fair Market Value	Book Value	Fair Market Value
Current Assets	$ 955,000	$ 920,000	$1,290,000	$1,370,000
Investments	1,000,000	1,400,000	—	—
Capital Assets (net)	1,600,000	2,250,000	1,800,000	2,300,000
	$3,555,000		$3,090,000	
Current Liabilities	$ 535,000	570,000	$ 450,000	470,000
Common Stock	1,500,000		2,400,000	
Retained Earnings	1,520,000		240,000	
	$3,555,000		$3,090,000	

You are also informed that the common stock of each company consisted of no par value shares of $1.00 each. On October 31, 20X1, the market value of these shares was $1.50 for Lisa and $1.80 for Monica. Any negative goodwill arising from the acquisition was to be written off in full against capital assets.

REQUIRED

1. Give the journal entry recording the purchase by Lisa of the assets and liabilities of Monica on November 1, 20X1 by the issue of 2-million common shares. Direct expenses relating to the merger amounted to $1,100.
2. Prepare the balance sheet of Nora Inc., a company formed with an authorized share capital of $15-million shares of no par value for the express purpose of acquiring the assets and liabilities of Lisa and Monica, at November 1, 20X1, immediately after the acquisitions. To effect the acquisitions, Nora issued two shares in itself at $5 each for every three shares held by the shareholders of Lisa and three shares for every five held by the shareholders of Monica.

EXERCISE 4–8 Patrick Inc. acquired the net assets of Sally Inc. on January 1, 20X2 for $3-million in cash. The following table shows the balance of Sally and two possible situations relating to the merger at January 1, 20X2:

	Historical Cost	Fair Market Values	
		Situation 1	Situation 2
Current Assets	$ 600,000	$ 900,000	$1,000,000
Land	1,000,000	1,500,000	900,000
Equipment	1,800,000	1,400,000	1,800,000
	$3,400,000		
Liabilities	$ 800,000		700,000
Common Stock	2,000,000	600,000	
Retained Earnings	600,000		
	$3,400,000		

You are also advised that:

(a) Liquidation expenses paid by Sally were $42,000.
(b) Direct costs relating to the merger were legal expenses of $30,000 and the valuation of the land and equipment of $15,000. These expenses were to be pro rated (i.e., allocated on a *pro rata* basis) where applicable.

REQUIRED

1. Give the **amount** of the liquidation dividend and the repayment of capital by Sally to its shareholders.
2. Give the amounts at which the **land and equipment** of Sally would be recorded by Patrick after the merger **using the figures presented as Situation 1**.
3. Give the journal entries recording the merger in the books of Patrick **using the figures presented as Situation 2**.

EXERCISE 4–9 On January 1, 20X1, Olga Inc. purchased the assets and liabilities of Pamela Inc. (except the bank loan) for $2-million in cash. In terms of the purchase agreement, Pamela was to go into liquidation immediately following the purchase of the assets.

The balance sheet of Pamela at December 31, 20X0 was as follows:

Inventory	$ 950,000
Accounts Receivable	900,000
Plant and Equipment (net)	1,300,000
	$3,150,000
Bank Loan	$ 200,000
Accounts Payable	250,000
10% Bonds Payable	800,000
Common Stock — 200,000 shares of no par value	1,500,000
Retained Earnings	400,000
	$3,150,000

REQUIRED

Give the journal entries to record the liquidation of Pamela on the assumption that the costs of liquidation amounted to $55,000.

EXERCISE 4–10   On January 31, 20X5, Penny Inc. entered into an agreement with the shareholders of Silvia Inc. whereby it would acquire the assets of Silvia, excluding the cash, for $1.5-million in cash and the issue of 300,000 of its no par value stock having a market value of $11 per share. After the merger, Silvia was to be liquidated.

The abbreviated balance sheet and net asset values of Silvia at January 31, 20X5 were as follows:

	Book Value	Fair Market Value
Cash	$ 300,000	$ 300,000
Accounts Receivable	1,050,000	1,000,000
Inventory	150,000	100,000
Plant and Equipment	3,000,000	3,800,000
	$4,500,000	
Accounts Payable	$1,300,000	1,300,000
Common Stock (200,000 common shares no par value)	500,000	
Retained Earnings	2,700,000	
	$4,500,000	

REQUIRED

1. Give the journal entry/entries required to record the merger by Penny.
2. Give the journal entries to record the liquidation of Silvia.

PROBLEMS

PROBLEM 4–1   Jay Inc. acquired the assets and liabilities of Kay Inc. on April 1, 20X1. At the date of acquisition, the abbreviated balance sheet of Kay was as follows:

	Book Value	Fair Market Value
Current Assets	$ 60,000	$ 55,000
Capital Assets	180,000	220,000
	$240,000	
Current Liabilities	$ 50,000	50,000
Common Stock	100,000	
Retained Earnings	90,000	
	$240,000	

REQUIRED

1. Give the journal entries required to record the sale of the net assets of Kay for $240,000 in cash and its subsequent liquidation in the books of Kay on the assumption that the costs of liquidation amounted to $400.
2. Give the journal entries to record the acquisition of the net assets of Kay by Jay if the purchase consideration was $240,000 and on the assumption that direct costs involved in the merger amounted to $2,200, all of which related to the capital assets.
3. Rework part (2) above on the assumptions that the purchase consideration was $200,000 and that the direct expenses relating to the capital assets were $3,000. Legal expenses that were not identifiable specifically with any assets or liabilities acquired amounted to $1,100.

PROBLEM 4–2   On October 1, 20X3, Network Six Inc. purchased the net assets of Alliance-Dot-Com Inc. You are informed that:

(a) The goodwill arising from the purchase was to be allocated to the two divisions on a pro rata basis, with 60% of the goodwill allocated to plant and equipment.

(b) The software inventory was made up of networking software that was awaiting shipment to customers.

(c) Twenty-five percent of the plant and equipment relating to the networking division was to be scrapped and written off as worthless following a review of asset values on December 31, 20X3, the end of the financial year. All other assets were to be considered fairly valued.

The net assets acquired valued at their fair market value were as follows:

	Networking	Fibre Optics	Total
Accounts Receivable	$ 380,000	$ 600,000	$ 980,000
Software Inventory	—	400,000	400,000
Plant and Equipment	3,600,000	3,840,000	7,440,000
Trademarks	80,000	100,000	180,000
	4,060,000	4,940,000	9,000,000
Less: Accounts Payable	280,000	420,000	700,000
	$3,780,000	$4,520,000	$8,300,000

REQUIRED

1. Give the allocation of the goodwill arising from the purchase of the net assets of Alliance-Dot-Com for $9-million over the two divisions.
2. Calculate the goodwill charges for 20X3.
3. Give the goodwill appearing on the balance sheet at December 31, 20X3.

Problem 4–3 The following balance sheets at December 31, 20X1 reflect the cost and fair market values of the assets and liabilities of Company A and Company B, both acquired by Purchaser Inc. on January 1, 20X2.

	Company A		Company B	
	Book Value	Fair Market Value	Book Value	Fair Market Value
Cash	$ 50,000	$ 50,000	$ 100,000	$100,000
Accounts Receivable	300,000	200,000	260,000	250,000
Inventory	400,000	450,000	340,000	350,000
Land	150,000	200,000	250,000	450,000
Equipment	500,000	600,000	500,000	550,000
	$1,400,000		$1,450,000	
Accounts Payable	$ 650,000	400,000	$ 300,000	400,000
Common Stock	600,000		1,000,000	
Retained Earnings	150,000		150,000	
	$1,400,000		$1,450,000	

REQUIRED

1. For Company A:
   i. Give the journal entries to record the acquisition in the books of Purchaser if the purchase consideration was $900,000 and the direct costs of the acquisition (paid by Purchaser) amounted to $40,000.
   ii. If, on completion of the valuation of the equipment acquired from Company A, the amount at which the equipment is valued is unrealistic (i.e., too low), what action should be taken to rectify the position?
   iii. Give the liquidation dividend paid to the shareholders of Company A on January 1, 20X2 if the costs of liquidation (Company A) amounted to $15,000.

2. For Company B:
   i. Determine the amounts to be allocated to eliminate the negative goodwill of $120,000 arising on the acquisition by Purchaser of the net assets (except cash on hand).
   ii. Determine the amount paid by Purchaser to acquire the net assets of Company B.
   iii. Give the amount at which the equipment acquired from Company B would have been recorded by Purchaser.
   iv. Give the amounts that would have been paid out to the shareholders of Company B as a liquidation dividend and the repayment of capital if the costs of liquidation (paid by Company B) had amounted to $80,000.

PROBLEM 4-4 At December 31, 20X1, the balance sheets of John Inc. and Ken Inc. were as follows:

	John	Ken
Cash	$ 700,000	$ 60,000
Inventory	900,000	250,000
Accounts Receivable	1,100,000	300,000
Plant and Equipment (net)	1,700,000	650,000
	$4,400,000	$1,260,000
Accounts Payable	$ 360,000	$ 300,000
Dividends Payable	240,000	—
Common Stock:		
300,000 shares of no par value	3,000,000	
100,000 shares of no par value		800,000
Retained Earnings	800,000	160,000
	$4,400,000	$1,260,000

You are also informed that:

(a) Agreement between the two companies was reached in November 20X1 that John would acquire the assets and liabilities of Ken on January 1, 20X2, on the following conditions:

   i. A dividend of 80 cents per share would be declared by John during December 20X1 and paid to its shareholders on January 1, 20X2.
   ii. That John would take over the assets and liabilities of Ken, other than cash, at a valuation made on December 31, 20X1. The amount arrived at was for $960,000 made up as follows:

Inventory	$ 280,000
Accounts Receivable	250,000
Plant and Equipment (net)	750,000
	1,280,000
Accounts Payable	320,000
	$ 960,000

   iii. The purchase consideration would be settled by the issue by John of five shares in John for every four shares in Ken. For the purpose of the merger, the shares in John were to be valued at $12 per share.

(b) Indirect legal expenses incurred by John in effecting the merger amounted to $80,000 and were paid in cash on January 1, 20X2.

REQUIRED

1. Give the journal entries to record the merger in the books of John; and
2. Prepare the balance sheet of John immediately after the merger.

PROBLEM 4–5   The abbreviated financial statements and fair market values of the assets and liabilities of Jason Inc. and Kelly Inc. at December 31, 20X1 were as follows:

	Jason		Kelly	
BALANCE SHEETS	**Book Value**	**Fair Market Value**	**Book Value**	**Fair Market Value**
Cash	$ 25,000	$ 25,000	$ 35,000	$ 35,000
Accounts Receivable	295,000	290,000	355,000	330,000
Inventory	240,000	220,000	340,000	310,000
Land	350,000	185,000	180,000	205,000
Plant Assets (net)	800,000	700,000	640,000	710,000
	$1,710,000		$1,550,000	
Accounts Payable	$ 220,000	220,000	$ 120,000	120,000
10% Bonds Outstanding	240,000	220,000	—	
Common Stock	800,000		1,000,000	
Capital Surplus	—		100,000	
Retained Earnings	450,000		330,000	
	$1,710,000		$1,550,000	

INCOME AND RETAINED EARNINGS STATEMENTS	**Book Value**	**Book Value**
Sales	$3,200,000	$2,600,000
Cost of Goods Sold	$1,200,000	$1,240,000
Operating Expenses	1,730,000	1,180,000
	$2,930,000	$2,420,000
Net Operating Income	$ 270,000	$ 180,000
Extraordinary Gain	40,000	—
Net Income for Year	310,000	180,000
Retained Earnings, January 1, 20X1	260,000	230,000
	570,000	410,000
Dividends	120,000	80,000
Retained Earnings, December 31, 20X1	$ 450,000	$ 330,000

Additional information:
(a)   The common stock of both companies consisted entirely of no par value shares issued at $1.00 each.
(b)   The market values of the shares of Jason and Kelly at December 31, 20X1 were $1.40 and $1.10 respectively.

REQUIRED

Prepare:
1.   The financial statements of Jason at January 1, 20X2 on the assumption that Jason had purchased the assets and liabilities of Kelly, excluding cash at bank on that date, for $2-million and that Kelly had ceased trading on December 31, 20X1. The purchase was financed by the issue of 800,000 shares of no par value and a bank loan for the balance.
2.   The liquidation, bank, share capital, capital surplus, and retained earnings ledger accounts recording the liquidation of Kelly for the month of January 20X2. Assume that the liquidation was effected during January 20X2 and completed by January 31, 20X2. Expenses of the liquidation amounted to $48,000.

Accounting for Longterm Investments 5

LEARNING OBJECTIVES

After studying this chapter you should be able to:

1. Recognize the nature of longterm investments and the classification of these investments for accounting purposes;
2. Understand the nature and application of significant influence over an investee company and how this affects the accounting for longterm investments;
3. Account for longterm investments using the cost and equity methods in cases of both single- and multiple-steps acquisitions of shares; and
4. Understand the nature of non-voting shares and the safeguards accorded to the holders of these shares.

WHAT ARE LONGTERM INVESTMENTS?

From an accounting point of view, longterm investments are usually defined in the negative as those investments made by investors that do not meet the two criteria of, first, being readily marketable and, second, held with the intention of being converted into cash within 12 months. These longterm investments may consist of bonds or shares of common or preferred stock that are usually held for investment purposes. However, they may also be held by the investor company to secure a steady supply of raw materials or to provide a sales outlet for its products through the ability to be able to exert significant influence over the affairs of the investee company.

In the context of business combinations, however, longterm investments are those investments made by an investor company in those companies over which they can exert significant influence or control. Where investments have been made in companies over which the investor company does not exert significant influence, these investments may be **either temporary or portfolio investments,** depending upon their nature and the period for which they are expected to be held. From an investing point of view, temporary investments are those investments that are expected to be held for only a short period of time. If, however, the investments are to be held for the long term, they are referred to as portfolio investments.

SIGNIFICANT INFLUENCE AND CONTROL

Significant Influence

The term, **significant influence**, refers to the influence an investor company may be able to exert over the operations and activities of the company in which it has invested. **This influence usually arises from the voting power conferred by the holding of shares having voting rights, which allows it to elect persons of its choice to the board of directors of the investee company.** Normally, the investor company must hold a substantial number of shares having voting rights to be in this position. The holdings of other types of longterm investments that do not carry voting rights, like non-voting shares, preferred shares and bonds, have little or no effect on the investor company's ability to exert significant influence.

The extent to which voting shares are held is important from an accounting point of view. This is because, as a rough "rule of thumb", the extent of the investor's interest in the voting shares of the company indicates the extent to which it can exert significant influence over the investee company. However, even though this is the normal position, the exercising of significant influence may depend upon other factors, like the ability to participate in policy-making decisions, the existence of material intercompany transactions, the interchange of managerial personnel between the companies or the provision of technical information by one company to another.[1]

Significant influence is also not necessarily confined to one party. In this respect, the existence of a substantial or even a majority interest by another investor would not always preclude an investor from exercising significant influence.[2] For example, a majority shareholder in a company may find it necessary to take note of the wishes of a relatively minor shareholder if that minor shareholder was the provider of technical information or someone who could exert substantial influence over a major customer of the investee company.

With public companies whose shares are publicly traded, it is normally relatively easy to establish whether significant influence exists. The dispersion of shares is normally so great that the existence of major shareholders is relatively uncommon, and it is difficult for minor shareholders, even if they are directors, to obtain sufficient proxy votes to outvote the major shareholders. It is, however, often difficult to establish in small private or closely held companies. Even though there are relatively few shareholders, the relationships between them are not always easy to identify. For example, where there are two major shareholders holding an equal number of, say 25% of the voting shares, it cannot be assumed that they will always act in unison, and the ability to exercise significant influence may depend upon the support they enjoy from the other shareholders. A single shareholder holding more than 50% of the voting shares would also tend to, but would not always, exclude any other shareholders from exercising significant influence. In this case, one would have to look to other issues like the extent to which another relatively major shareholder could exert pressure on the controlling shareholder through the supply of goods or technical information.

The exercising of significant influence also involves the method of voting. Normally, each share having voting rights gives the holder the right to cast one vote for each place to be filled on the board of directors. This means that if there are nine directors, each voting share carries nine votes. However, since the 1950s, a system of **cumulative voting** has been allowed in certain provinces (e.g., Ontario and Manitoba), as well as by the *Canada Business Corporations Act* to provide minority shareholders with a greater say in the running of corporate affairs. Cumulative voting allows each shareholder to cast their votes in a cumulative manner. The shareholder can, therefore, cast all nine votes for a single candidate or, say, six votes for one candidate and one vote each for an additional three positions on the board. Where cumulative voting occurs, it is considerably easier to exert significant influence.

---

[1]   See section 3050 of the CICA *Handbook*.
[2]   *Ibid.*

The importance of all this is that where a company does not exert significant influence over the affairs of an investee company, the investment must be treated, for accounting purposes, as a portfolio investment. On the other hand, where significant influence can be exercised over the investee company, the investment should be accounted for using the equity method. In those cases where control is exercisable by one company over another, consolidated financial statements must be prepared.

For convenience, however, the extent of this influence is normally considered to be based on the extent of the investment by the investor company in the voting shares of the investee company as follows:

Less Than a 20% Interest Where a company holds an investment of less than 20% of the voting shares of another company, it is presumed that, **unless there is strong evidence to the contrary**, the investor company does not have the ability to exert significant influence over the affairs of the investee company. The investment is, therefore, considered to be a portfolio investment.

More Than 20% Interest An investment of more than 20% normally indicates that the investor company has the ability to exercise significant influence over the investee company. However, the holding of 20% or more of shares having voting rights does not by itself provide significance influence. Each case must be examined on its merits. For convenience, the rule that is applied is that more than a 20% interest indicates that significant influence exists, **unless there is evidence to the contrary**.

More Than a 50% Interest Where more than 50% of the shares having voting rights are held by an investor company, the investor has control over the investee company, and the investee company is referred to as a subsidiary company. Where this is the case, the investor company must account for the activities of the investee company in accordance with the requirements relating to the consolidation of financial statements.

It should, however, be borne in mind that the figure of 20% is, in effect, nothing more than an indicator that the equity method of accounting may be appropriate. It provides a figure against which the presumption of significant influence can be examined, because **the further one moves away from the 20% rule, the greater the need for certainty that significant influence actually exists**. The same position applies to the 50% interest, because other factors may determine whether control exists.

Control

For a company to be able to exercise *control* over the affairs of another company, it must have the power to determine the strategic operating, investing and financing policies of an entity without the co-operation of others.[3] The issue of control is fully covered in the following chapter. However, for the purposes of this chapter it is sufficient to know that this situation normally exists when one company has the power to elect the majority of members to the board of directors of the company concerned.[4]

---

[3] *Ibid.*, section 1590.
[4] *Canada Business Corporations Act*, section 2 (3).

RECORDING LONGTERM INVESTMENTS

The Cost Method

The cost method is always used to account for investments where the investor company does not have the ability to exert a significant influence over the investee company. In these cases, the investment is treated as a portfolio investment and classified as a longterm investment. As a portfolio investment, its value is normally not adjusted to bring it down to the lower of cost or market, as with temporary investments, and any material changes in its value are normally disclosed by way of a note.

On purchase, the investor company records its investment in an investee company at the cost of that investment to itself. The balance on the account remains unchanged until there is either an increase or decrease in the number of shares held or the value of the investment is written down to reflect a permanent decline in its value. Dividends received are recorded as revenues in the ledger and included as "dividend income" in the income statement of the investor company in the period to which they relate.

Where the value of the investment declines to an amount below that paid for the shares and the decrease in value appears to be permanent, the investment must be written down to reflect that decrease in value. This occurs, for example, where the cost of the investment included an amount paid for goodwill and the value of that goodwill has declined.

In accordance with the rules applicable to accounting for investments in Canada, once the value of the investment has been adjusted downwards, it may not be adjusted upwards in the event of a subsequent increase in its value and must remain at its written-down value. Where the investment has been purchased in more than one transaction, the weighted average method of valuing the investment must be used to determine any gains or losses arising from the disposal of part of the investment.[5]

The Equity Method

An investment in a company over which an investor exercises significant influence **must be reported** by the investor company using the equity method. Using the rough "rule of thumb" outlined earlier, this is indicated in those cases where the investor company holds between 20 and 50% of the voting shares of the investee company.

The use of this method requires the investor company to include in its income statement its share of the investee company's net income for the year in question and not merely the dividends to which it was entitled. This share of net income is also sometimes referred to as the "equity pick-up".

The actual recording of investments using the equity method operates in basically the following manner. The investment is initially recorded at cost. Thereafter, the value of the investment is adjusted each year by increasing its carrying or book value by the investor's share of the reported net income of the investee company and decreasing its value by the dividends received during the year. A simple example of this is provided in Illustration 5–1.

Illustration 5–1 shows that on receipt of the dividend from Investee, this amount is credited against the cost of the investment and is not treated as a revenue item. However, on the establishment of the net income for the year earned by Investee, Investor recognized its share of this amount by crediting its revenue account and debiting the investment account accordingly. The resulting position is that the investment is reflected at the amount of $209,000, which shows that the interest of Investor has increased by $9,000, being 30% of its share of net income from Investee not yet paid out to Investor.

It should also be noted that where the equity method is used, the increase in the net income of the investor company (and, consequently, its retained earnings) is balanced by the

---

[5] CICA *Handbook*, section 3050.

ILLUSTRATION 5–1
THE EQUITY METHOD OF ACCOUNTING FOR A LONGTERM INVESTMENT

Assume that on January 1, 20X2, Investor Inc. acquired a 30% interest in Investee Inc. on its formation for the sum of $200,000, which allowed it to exert a significant influence over the affairs of Investee. The operations of Investee were successful and, during the financial year ended December 31, 20X2, the net income earned amounted to $50,000, of which $20,000 was paid out as a dividend on December 10, 20X2. In these circumstances, the investment in Investee would have been recorded by Investor using the equity method as follows:

In the Journal of Investor

20X2

Jan. 1	Investment in Investee	200,000	
	Cash		200,000
	Purchase of 30% interest in Investee		
Dec. 10	Cash	6,000	
	Investment in Investee		6,000
	Dividend Received		
Dec. 31	Investment in Investee	15,000	
	Income from Investee		15,000
	Share of Net Income from Investee		

In the Ledger of Investor

INVESTMENT IN INVESTEE

		Dr.	Cr.	Total
20X2				
Jan. 1	Purchase of 30% Interest	200,000		200,000
Dec. 10	Dividends Received		6,000	194,000
Dec. 31	Net Income for Year	15,000		209,000

SHARE OF NET INCOME FROM INVESTEE

20X2				
Dec. 31	Net Income for Year		15,000	15,000
	Closed to Income Summary	15,000		Nil

increase in the carrying value of the investment and the increase in the cash account from the receipt of the dividends. The figures provided in Illustration 5–1 show that the increase in the net income of the investor company of $15,000 is balanced by a net increase in the Investment in Investee of $9,000 and the receipt of the dividend of $6,000. The value of the investment is, therefore, reflected on the balance sheet of the investor company at a more realistic value than its original cost.

WHY DO WE USE THE EQUITY METHOD?

During the late 1960s it became apparent that large multinational companies were manipulating their reported net income by influencing the dividend policy of those companies over which they exerted significant influence. In those years where the investor company's net income was low, an investor company could force its investee companies to declare higher dividends while, in those years where the investor company's net income was high, it could force its investee companies to retain their profits by declaring lower dividends.

The situation was clearly unsatisfactory and, in 1971, the American Institute of Certified Public Accountants issued *Accounting Principles Board Opinion No. 18: The Equity Method of Accounting for Investments in Common Stock* to rectify the situation. *APB Opinion No. 18*, by introducing the requirements for equity accounting, made it impossible for companies to manipulate their net income through influencing the dividend policy of their investee companies because they were now required to recognize their share of net income from the investee company irrespective of the dividends declared. It was not long after the issue of *APB Opinion No. 18* that section 3050 of the CICA *Handbook* was issued to ensure that the same requirements applied in Canada.

The equity method is also important in drawing attention to the wider reporting responsibilities of the investor company. With the cost method, the reporting entity is the investor company that merely receives revenues in the form of dividends from another company. The use of the equity method, however, introduces the concept that the area of economic interest of the reporting entity extends beyond the investor company to embrace that part of the investee company over which it exerts significant influence. The value of the investment in the investee company is, therefore, adjusted to reflect its current value.

GOODWILL ARISING FROM THE PURCHASE OF LONGTERM INVESTMENTS

Any goodwill arising on the acquisition of an investment in a company over which the investor exerts significant influence must, in accordance with the accounting requirements relating to goodwill, be **reviewed for a permanent decline in its value (i.e., impairment)** on an annual basis or when an event or series of events have occurred that indicate that its value has decreased. If the **value of the goodwill has decreased**, the amount by which it has become impaired must be written off against earnings in the period **in which the impairment is recognized**. If there is a subsequent increase in its value, the impairment should not be reversed.

Goodwill represents the amount by which the purchase consideration exceeds the fair market value of its proportionate share of the net assets of the investee company acquired. For example, if $280,000 is paid to acquire a 30% interest in an investee company having net assets with a fair market value of $900,000, goodwill of $10,000 arises, as calculated in the following manner:

Purchase Consideration	$280,000
Less: 30% of the Net Assets of $900,000	270,000
Goodwill Arising on Acquisition	$ 10,000

This goodwill, even though it is not recorded by the investor company and only becomes apparent on an analysis of the investment, is no different from any other form of goodwill because it represents part of the cost of the investment. It must, therefore, be reviewed for impairment and, if necessary, revalued downwards accordingly.

Where the longterm investment is recorded using the equity method, the write-down of any goodwill arising from its impairment is against the cost of the investment. This is because, even though the goodwill arising from the purchase is not reflected separately by the investor company, it still forms part of the purchase consideration. It should also be noted that because the amount paid for goodwill does not appear on the balance sheet of the investor company, its write-down cannot be disclosed as a separate item on the income statement of the investor company. It is, therefore, **deducted from the share of net income from the investee company**.

Up to the coming into effect of the **impairment method of accounting for goodwill**, purchased goodwill was required to be recorded at cost and amortized on a straight-line basis over a period not exceeding 40 years. If, at any time during the amortization period, it became obvious that the goodwill had decreased in value, it was to be immediately written down to reflect its true value. This is important because the present accounting requirements specify that the **impairment method is not to apply in retrospect** to goodwill arising from acquisitions occurring prior to the adoption of the impairment method. The value of the goodwill in these cases is to be recognized at its amortized value and be reviewed for impairment from that point onwards. The effect of this is that with the equity method, the value of an investment in a company over which the investor exercises significant influence entered into before the coming into effect of the impairment method **could reflect both the amortization of goodwill and impairment losses.** Such a situation is reflected in Illustration 5–2, which presents the investment in an investee company recorded using the equity method over a two-year period.

The correctness of reflecting goodwill impairment losses against the net income of the investee company is questionable, because it represents the write-off of part of the cost of an

---

ILLUSTRATION 5–2
THE WRITE-DOWN OF GOODWILL ARISING FROM THE PURCHASE OF AN INTEREST IN AN INVESTEE COMPANY USING THE EQUITY METHOD

An amount of $80,000 was paid by Investor Inc. for a 25% interest in Investee Inc. on January 1, 20X1. At that date, Investee had common stock of $200,000 and retained earnings of $40,000.

The net income earned and dividends paid by Investee during 20X1 and 20X2 were as follows:

	20X1	**20X2**
Net Income for Year	$48,000	$44,000
Dividends Paid (November 30)	20,000	18,000

Goodwill of $20,000 arose on the purchase of a 25% interest of the revalued net equity of Investee (i.e., $80,000 − .25% of $200,000 + $40,000). The policy of Investor up until the coming into effect of the impairment method in 20X2 was to amortize goodwill over a 10-year period. Following a review of the goodwill for impairment at December 31, 20X2, a loss on impairment of $3,000 was recognized by Investor on the goodwill arising from the purchase of its 25% interest in Investee.

The investment account of Investee in the ledger of Investor at December 31, 20X2 using the equity method would, therefore, reflect the following position:

INVESTMENT IN INVESTEE

		Dr.	**Cr.**	**Total**
20X1				
Jan. 1	Purchase of 25% interest	80,000		80,000
Nov. 30	Dividends Received (25% of $20,000)		5,000	75,000
Dec. 31	Share of Net Income (25% of $48,000)	12,000		85,000
	Goodwill Amortization ($20,000/10 years)		2,000	85,000
20X2				
Nov. 30	Dividend Received (25% of $18,000)		4,500	80,500
Dec. 31	Share of Net Income (25% × $44,000)	11,000		
	Impairment of Goodwill		3,000	88,500

The adjustments relating to the amortization of goodwill in 20X1 and its write-down in 20X2 for impairment should be entered as shown above in the investment account. However, neither of these amounts appears in the income statement of Investor as expenses because the goodwill arising from the purchase of the 25% interest is not reflected on the balance sheet of Investor. The only way in which these amounts are recognized is to deduct them from the "Share of Net Income from Investee Company" included by Investor in its income statement. These amounts for 20X1 and 20X2 would, therefore, have been as follows:

20X1 — $10,000 (i.e., $12,000 − $2,000)
20X2 — $$8,000 (i.e., $11,000 − $3,000)

investment in one company (i.e., the investor company) against the net income of another company (i.e., the investee company). This practice is apparently justified on the grounds that the amount paid for goodwill is the discounted value of future excess earnings of the investment and it should, therefore, be written off against the earnings to which it relates. The issue of negative goodwill does not arise because, as outlined earlier, this amount must be eliminated by the revaluation downwards of assets at the date of acquisition.

ADJUSTMENTS TO THE INVESTOR'S SHARE OF THE NET INCOME

Compliance with the Valuation Principles Applicable to the Purchase of Net Assets

As outlined in the previous chapter, the accounting requirements for purchased assets are that the net assets (including identifiable intangible assets) acquired must be valued by the acquiring company at their fair market values, and any balance of the purchase price remaining must be treated as goodwill. This valuation principle also applies to the purchase of longterm investments, even though only a relatively small proportion of the net assets may have been acquired.

From a practical point of view, however, the recognition of the fair market value of the proportion of the net assets acquired and the goodwill arising from the acquisition of longterm investments only applies to those longterm investments over which an investor exerts significant influence. This is because **access by an investor company to the books and records of an investee company to establish the fair market value of the net assets acquired is only possible where it is in a position to exert a substantial degree of influence over the affairs of the company concerned** by, for example, having been elected a member of the board of directors.

These adjustments are fully discussed and analyzed in the chapters that follow but, for a full understanding of the accounting for longterm investments, it is necessary to briefly examine those adjustments relating to the valuation of capital assets at their fair market value, and the effects of these adjustments on the share of net income from the investee company recognized by the investor company.

Adjustments Relating to the Values of Net Assets

As outlined above, the net assets of the investee company should be valued at their fair market values on purchase of the investment to provide the correct value for goodwill arising from the acquisition of the interest in the investee company. This also provides the information required to make the necessary adjustments arising from the differences in the fair market and the carrying values of the net assets.

Where a difference between the carrying value of an asset and its fair market value at the date on which the interest in the investee company is acquired has been recognized, this should be taken into account in establishing the share of net income from the investee company recognized by the investor company. This is because, for example, where depreciable assets have been revalued upwards, additional depreciation (now also called amortization) applies to the amount by which the asset has been revalued. This only applies to depreciable assets because it is only the amortization of the increase (or decrease) in value that affects the share of net income that is recognized.

To illustrate how this adjustment is made, assume that a 30% interest is acquired in a company in which an asset being amortized on a straight-line basis and, having a 10-year remaining life, is undervalued by $20,000 on the date on which the investment is purchased. In these circumstances, the increase in value of $6,000 (i.e., 30% of $20,000) recognized by the investor company must also be amortized over the remaining life of the asset concerned. From the investor company's point of view, this would reduce its share of the net income from the

---

ILLUSTRATION 5–3
APPORTIONMENT OF NET INCOME IN THE CASE OF AN ACQUISITION PART WAY THROUGH
A YEAR WHEN FINANCIAL STATEMENTS ARE NOT PREPARED AT THE DATE OF ACQUISITION

A 40% interest in an investee company is acquired half way through its financial year on July 1, 20X4 for $160,000. Financial statements were not prepared at the date of acquisition, but at December 31, 20X3, the investee company had common stock of $200,000 and retained earnings of $120,000. The net income of the investee company for 20X4 was $100,000.

Analysis of Equity at the Date of Acquisition:

Common Stock		$200,000
Retained Earnings at December 31, 20X3	$120,000	
Net Income for Period January 1 to June 30, 20X4 (i.e., $100,000 × 6/12)	50,000	170,000
		$370,000

Establishment of the Share of Equity Acquired and the Goodwill Arising on Acquisition:

Acquisition of 40% of Total Equity (i.e., 40% of $370,000)	$148,000
Purchase Consideration	160,000
Goodwill Arising on Acquisition	$ 12,000

Recognition of Share of Net Income from Subsidiary:

Net Income for Period July 1 to December 31, 20X4 (i.e., 40% of $100,000 × 6/12)	$ 20,000

---

investee company by $600 per year for the next 10 years (i.e., $6,000/10). This is adjusted by reducing both the investor company's share of the net income in each year by $600 and reducing the cost of the investment by the same amount. Obviously, this adjustment is only made when the amounts involved are material in amount.

RECOGNITION OF EARNINGS FROM THE DATE OF ACQUISITION

In accordance with the rule that earnings from assets only accrue to the purchaser from the date of acquisition, **an investor company may only recognize earnings from an investment in an investee company from the date on which the interest in the investee company is acquired. Earnings prior to the date of acquisition form part of the equity acquired.**

Where financial statements are not prepared at the date on which the acquisition took place, it may be assumed that net income accrues evenly throughout the year. Obviously, where financial statements are prepared at the date of acquisition, those figures must be used.

An example of the apportionment of net income is provided by Illustration 5–3. In this case, the net income recognized from the investee company by the investor company would be $20,000 being 40% of the net income for the last six months of 20X4 of $100,000 (i.e., 40% × 6/12 × $100,000) earned during the period July 1 through December 31, 20X4.

The earnings of all businesses are, to some or other extent, cyclical in nature. However, for simplicity and unless you are informed to the contrary, the earnings of all companies are assumed in this text to accrue evenly throughout the periods under consideration.

THE POSITION WITH NON-VOTING SHARES

The Nature of Non-Voting Shares

As outlined above, the exertion of significant influence and control is largely dependent upon the holding of shares having voting rights. Over the years, however, the issue of shares without voting rights has been relatively commonplace in Canada and the USA. In many cases, the reason for doing so has been to allow the founders of a company to retain control of a company by vesting all voting rights in a relatively small number of shares held by themselves.[6] Today, the issue of non-voting stock is looked upon with disfavour by securities commissions and, unless there are compelling reasons for doing so, it would be difficult to make such an issue.

There are, however, cases where it is necessary to issue non-voting shares **to meet investment levels without giving the investor company a proportionate level of control**: for example, where foreign investment is involved and the Canadian Foreign Investment Review Agency, the federal government agency that monitors foreign investment in Canada, imposes limits on the foreign ownership of companies.[7]

It is, of course, not necessary to issue non-voting stock as part of an investment arrangement because the infusion of additional capital could be achieved by the issue of preferred stock or debentures. However, even though the holding of non-voting stock does not directly contribute towards the exercising of significant influence, it provides the means of increasing the investor's share of equity in the investee company.

The accounting treatment of investments in non-voting stock follows those that are applicable to voting stock. If the holding of voting shares requires that the equity method be used, the equity method is also used for the non-voting stock. This is because, other than voting rights, the non-voting stock normally enjoys exactly the same rights as voting shares in relation to net income, dividends and the share of net assets in the event of liquidation of the company. To treat the investment in non-voting stock differently from that relating to the voting stock would serve no purpose.

An example of the treatment of non-voting stock is provided by Illustration 5–4. In this case, an investor company purchased a 25% interest in the voting shares and 15% of the non-voting shares in an investee company in which all shares shared equally in profits and losses. The analysis of the investment is carried out by apportioning the retained earnings over the two classes of shares. The illustration shows that the investment in the two classes of stock is recorded separately in separate investment accounts in the ledger that reflects the purchase consideration, the proportionate share of net income, and the dividends received on each class of stock.

Coattail Provisions for Non-Voting Shares

Notwithstanding the position outlined above, there are certain circumstances in which non-voting shares do enjoy voting rights. This occurs when a company is subject to **a change in control or is the target of a takeover bid**, and the so-called **coattail provisions** come into operation. These provisions convert all non-voting stock into voting shares. The extent of the use of these provisions varies between jurisdictions, but in Ontario they have been mandatory since the early 1980s for all companies whose securities are traded on the Toronto Stock Exchange. They are designed to safeguard the rights of non-voting shareholders but are also often included as a condition of the offering merely to make the issue of non-voting shares more attractive.

---

[6] For example, William Z. Ripley (*Main Street to Wall Street*, Boston: Little, Brown & Co., 1927) provides the classic example of a manufacturer of root beer that invited the public to subscribe for 180,000 shares of Class A and Class B shares, with the concentration of control in 3,872 "management shares", so that management of the corporation would remain unchanged and continue in the hands of the Hires family.

[7] Such a situation occurred with the 1994 merger between American Airlines and Canadian Airlines where, in return for an investment of US $250-million, AMR Corporation of Fort Worth, Texas (which owns American Airlines) obtained a 25% voting interest and a larger share of the total equity in PWA Corporation (which owned Canadian Airlines International of Calgary, Alberta) through the issue of non-voting shares. The limit of 25% foreign ownership of voting shares was imposed by the federal *Transportation Act* at that time.

ILLUSTRATION 5–4

ACCOUNTING FOR ACQUISITIONS INVOLVING BOTH VOTING AND NON-VOTING STOCK

Pitcher Inc. purchased 25% of the Class A voting shares and 15% of the Class B non-voting shares of Stein Inc. on January 1, 20X2 for $180,000 and $200,000 respectively. The purchase of the 25% interest in the voting stock of Pitcher allowed it to exert significant influence over the affairs of Stein.

At the date of acquisition, the equity of Stein amounted to $1,800,000, made up of 500,000 Class A no par value shares, 1,000,000 Class B no par value non-voting shares, and retained earnings of $300,000. Both classes of stock had been issued at $1 per share. The articles of association of Stein stated that Class A and Class B shares were to share equally in profits and losses. During 20X2, Stein earned net income of $420,000 and paid dividends of $150,000 on December 31, 20X2.

ANALYSIS OF THE INVESTMENT

	Total	Class A Shares (25%)	Class B Shares (15%)
At Acquisition:			
Common Stock:			
Class A Shares	$ 500,000	$125,000	
Class B shares	1,000,000		$150,000
Retained Earnings:	300,000		
To Class A Shares (25% × [500,000/1,500,000 × $300,000])		25,000	
To Class B Shares (15% × [1,000,000/1,500,000 × $300,000])			30,000
		150,000	180,000
Purchase Consideration		180,000	200,000
Goodwill Arising on Acquisition		$ 30,000	$ 20,000
Since Acquisition:			
Net Income	420,000		
To Class A Shares (25% × [500,000/1,500,000 × $420,000])		$ 35,000	
To Class B Shares (15% × 1,000,000/1,500,000 × $420,000])			$ 42,000
Less: Dividends	(150,000)		
To Class A Shares (25% × [500,000/1,500,000 × $150,000])		(12,500)	
To Class B Shares (15% × [1,000,000/1,500,000 × $150,000])			(15,000)

RECORDING THE INVESTMENT

As the investment in the two classes of shares would be kept separate for accounting purposes, the individual investment accounts would be as follows:

Investment in Class A Voting Shares of Stein

20X2					
Jan. 1	Purchase Consideration (125,000 shares)	180,000			180,000
Dec. 31	Share of Net Income	35,000			
	Dividends Received			12,500	202,500

Investment in Class B Non-Voting Shares of Stein

20X2					
Jan. 1	Purchase Consideration (150,000 shares)	200,000			200,000
Dec. 31	Share of Net Income	42,000			
	Dividends Received			15,000	227,000

RECORDING THE SHARE OF NET INCOME

As the two classes of shares share equally in the payment of dividends, the share of net income from the investment is not split between the two investments, but disclosed as a separate item on the income statement for 20X2 as follows:

Share of Net Income from Investee Company $77,000
(i.e., $35,000 + $42,000)

ILLUSTRATION 5–5

DIFFERENCES BETWEEN THE RECORDING OF INVESTMENTS IN AN INVESTEE COMPANY
USING THE EQUITY AND COST BASES

On January 1, 20X1, Investor Inc. purchased a 30% interest in Investee Inc. for $300,000 on the formation of Investee. During 20X1, the net income earned and dividends paid by Investee amounted to $300,000 and $100,000 respectively.

The abbreviated financial statements at December 31, 20X1 given below are those of Investor on the assumption that no investment in Investee had been made, and then those of Investor on the assumption that the 30% investment in Investee had been accounted for, first, using the cost basis and, second, on the equity basis.

		Investment in Investee	
	No Investment	on Cost Basis	on Equity Basis
BALANCE SHEETS			
Current Assets	$1,350,000	$1,080,000	$1,080,000
Investment in Investee Company	—	300,000	360,000
Plant Assets (net of Amortization)	2,500,000	2,500,000	2,500,000
	$3,850,000	$3,880,000	$3,940,000
Current Liabilities	$ 500,000	$ 500,000	$ 500,000
Common Stock	2,400,000	2,400,000	2,400,000
Retained Earnings	950,000	980,000	1,040,000
	$3,850,000	$3,880,000	$3,940,000
COMBINED INCOME AND RETAINED EARNINGS STATEMENTS			
Net Operating Income	$ 800,000	$ 800,000	$ 800,000
Dividends from Investee Company	—	30,000	—
Net Income from Investee Company	—	—	90,000
	800,000	830,000	890,000
Less: Dividends Paid	250,000	250,000	250,000
	550,000	580,000	640,000
Retained Earnings at January 1, 20X1	400,000	400,000	400,000
Retained Earnings at December 31, 20X1	$ 950,000	$ 980,000	$1,040,000

Note: The decrease in the current assets is because the cash on hand would have been reduced by the purchase consideration of $300,000 and increased by the dividend received of $30,000.

THE DIFFERENCES ARISING FROM USING THE COST AND EQUITY METHODS

The differences in recording the investment in an investee company using the cost and equity methods is presented in Illustration 5–5. This illustration provides the abbreviated financial statements of an investor company presented as if no investment in an investee company had been made, and then the financial statements of the investor company on the assumption that it had made an investment in an investee company using, first, the cost method and, second, the equity method.

Illustration 5–5 shows that the two sets of financial statements of Parent Inc. prepared using the cost and equity methods differ considerably from one another in relation to the value of the actual investment in the investee company, the retained earnings, and the net income for the year. It is important that these differences between the two methods are fully understood because they affect much of the material covered in the following nine chapters. These differences are, therefore, detailed hereunder.

The Investment Account As explained earlier, this amount remains unchanged until there is a change in the extent of ownership or the goodwill is adjusted downwards to reflect its current value. With the cost method, the investment in the investee company is merely reflected as the cost of the investment at the date of acquisition. In Illustration 5–5, this is the $300,000 paid for the interest in Investee Inc.

Where the equity method is used, the original cost of the investment is adjusted each year by increasing it by its adjusted share of the net income of the investee company for the year and decreasing it by the dividends received. In Illustration 5–5, this amounted to $360,000 made up of the original investment of $300,000 plus its share of net income of $90,000 less the dividends received of $30,000.

The Income from the Investee Company The differences in income recognized by the investor company are reflected in Illustration 5–5. The amount appearing as income from the investee company of $90,000 using the equity method represents the investor company's share of net income of Investor Inc. With the cost method, however, the income statement reflects the dividends of $30,000 actually received from the investee company.

The Retained Earnings of the Investor Company As outlined earlier, with the equity method, the income statement of the investor company includes its share of the current net income of the investee company. As a result, the investor company's share of net income from the investee company is included in the retained earnings of the parent company carried forward at the end of the year. With the cost method, however, the investor company's share of the earnings of the subsidiary company from the date of acquisition to the date of consolidation is limited to its share of the dividends paid by the subsidiary company.

STEP ACQUISITIONS OF AN INVESTEE COMPANY

Investments in investee companies are often made over a period of time, and it may be only after the second or third purchase of shares that the investor company finds itself in a position where it can exert significant influence over the investee's activities. Where this is the case, the cost method is used to account for the investment until the use of the equity method becomes appropriate. From that point onwards, the equity method is used. **There are no retroactive adjustments**, and the change in the basis of accounting is applied prospectively.[8] Adjustments to the investment are made when they occur. **Numerous purchases of small numbers of shares may be grouped together and treated as a single purchase**.[9]

---

[8] The CICA *Handbook* does not specifically deal with the matter but refers, in the explanatory material of section 1506, that "... the initial adoption or alteration of an accounting policy that are clearly different in substance from those previously occurring ..." is not considered to be a change in accounting policy.

   This differs from the position in the USA, where the share of net income from the investee company is adjusted retroactively. In Canada, unlike the position in the USA, the owning of, say, a 30% interest in an investee company does not mean that the investor is entitled to 30% of the post-acquisition earnings because it depends not upon the degree of ownership, but on what dividends were declared before the investor company was in a position to exert significant influence over the affairs of the investee company. This matter is further discussed with the acquisition and disposals of part interests in subsidiary companies.

   The Canadian position is of interest because APB *Opinion No. 18: The Equity Method of Accounting for Investments in Common Stock* (American Institute of Certified Public Accountants, 1971), on which section 3050 of the CICA *Handbook* is based, states in section 19(m) that where an investment qualifies for the use of the equity method, "[t]he investment, results of operations (current and prior periods presented), and retained earnings of the investor should be adjusted retroactively in a manner consistent with the accounting for step-by-step acquisition of a subsidiary."

[9] CICA *Handbook*, section 1600.

As this position is fully examined in Chapter Twelve, it is considered unnecessary to examine it in detail at this stage. However, for those who wish to familiarize themselves with the position, it is fully explained and illustrated in Appendix 5A to this chapter.

SALE OF PART INTERESTS IN INVESTMENTS

If a part interest in an investment is sold, all that is required is to offset a proportionate share of the balance on the investment account at the date of sale against the selling price. This applies irrespective of whether the investment is **recorded in the books** of the selling company at cost or using the full equity method.

DISCLOSURE OF LONGTERM INVESTMENTS

The disclosure requirements for longterm investments (other than bonds, preferred shares and investments in joint ventures) are covered in section 3050 of the CICA *Handbook*.

The requirements are portfolio investments, investments subject to significant influence, and other investments in affiliated companies should be disclosed separately. In this respect, portfolio investments should be recorded at cost unless their value has declined below their cost and the decline in value is considered permanent in nature, in which case they should be disclosed at their fair market value. Where portfolio investments consist of (or include) marketable securities, the quoted market value of such investments as well as their carrying value should be disclosed.

Investments subject to significant influence should also be disclosed separately. They should give the percentage ownership, the reason for assuming significant influence, any differences between the cost and carrying value of the investee's assets and how such differences have been treated by the investor company.

Where the investor can exercise control over an investee company but, for some reason or other, does not include the investee in its consolidated financial statements, the investment should be accounted for using the equity method. In these cases, the reason for this treatment should be disclosed in addition to the name of the company concerned and the extent of ownership.

WHERE SIGNIFICANT INFLUENCE NO LONGER EXISTS

Where an investment in an investee company drops to a level where significant influence no longer exists and the use of the equity method is no longer appropriate, the investor company no longer accrues its share of income or losses from the investee company.[10] In these cases, **the balance remaining on the investment account becomes the carrying value of the investment and is not adjusted retroactively**. If, in any subsequent period, the dividends received by the investor company exceed its proportionate share of net income from the investee company for those or any other periods, the excess should be treated as a reduction in the carrying value of the investment and not as revenues.

It may also become necessary to determine whether or not an adjustment to the carrying value of the investment is required. This is because the loss of the ability to exert significant influence can substantially affect the valuation of the investment.

---

10 *Ibid.*, section 3050.

SUMMARY

This chapter examines the accounting for longterm investments. It first examines what is meant by the term "significant influence", and how the existence of significant influence affects the way longterm investments are recorded and accounted for in the books of investor companies. It explains that longterm investments are accounted for as portfolio investments until such time as the investor company can exert significant influence or control over the investee company. When this occurs, longterm investments are accounted for using the equity method.

The chapter then examines the application of the equity method. Here, it outlines how the existence of goodwill arising on the acquisition of an interest in an investee company is treated and amortized against, or written down for impairment of, the investor company's share of net income. It also examines the adjustments arising from differences in the value of the assets of the investee company and the position relating to non-voting shares.

It continues by examining how the effect of using the cost and equity methods of reporting interests in investee companies affects the financial statements of the reporting entity. It then looks at the situation arising from step acquisitions of interests in investee companies and the way in which the accounting for longterm investments using the cost method is converted to one, using the equity method, and from an equity to a cost basis.

APPENDIX 5A: STEP ACQUISITIONS OF AN INVESTEE COMPANY

An illustration of a step acquisition of shares is provided by Illustration 5A–1. This shows that it is only from the time the use of the equity method becomes appropriate that the share of net income from the investee company is calculated. It also shows that it is only possible to calculate the goodwill on acquisition from the time when significant influence is exercisable. Furthermore,

(a) The investor company's share of the fair market value of the assets and liabilities and the goodwill arising on acquisition is determined **on the date on which significant influence is exercisable** as if the total interests in the investee company had been acquired on that date. In such a case, the amount of goodwill is determined by offsetting the proportion of net assets from all investments in the investee company against the total purchase price of all the shares acquired. The reason for this is that it is only from the date on which significant influence can be exercised that the investor company would have access to the books and records of the investee company and be able to determine its share of the fair market value of the net assets of the investee company.

(b) The share of net income attributable to the investor from the investee company is determined from the date on which the additional purchase of shares occurred.

REVIEW QUESTIONS

1. Distinguish between portfolio, temporary and longterm investments.
2. List the conditions that are necessary to account for longterm investments using:
   (a) The cost method; and
   (b) The equity method
3. Distinguish between the cost and equity methods of recording an investment in an investee company.
4. What is the objective of using the equity method?
5. In what circumstances would the cost of an investment accounted for using the cost method be adjusted downwards in value?
6. Why are non-voting shares presently issued? What effect do they have on the exercising of significant influence or control?

ILLUSTRATION 5A–1

ACCOUNTING FOR AN INVESTMENT ON A COST AND THEN AN EQUITY BASIS

On January 1, 20X2, Investor Inc., a company having a December 31 year end, purchased a 10% interest in Investee Inc. for $124,000 when Investee had common stock of $800,000 and retained earnings of $220,000. On July 1, 20X2, Investor purchased a further 15% interest in Investee for $173,200, at which date it was established that certain plant of Investee having a five-year remaining life and no residual value, was undervalued by $100,000. Goodwill is accounted for using the impairment method.

The trading results and dividends declared and paid during 20X2 for Investee were:

Net Income for Year	$120,000
Dividends Declared and Paid:	
Interim on June 15	12,000
Final on December 15	20,000

Accounting for this situation would, therefore, be as follows:

(a) The first step is to analyze the equity of Investee to be able to calculate and recognize the revenues from Investee over the two acquisitions and to determine the goodwill arising on acquisition as follows:

	Total	**10%**	**15%**
At January 1, 20X2:			
Common Stock	$800,000	$ 80,000	$120,000
Retained Earnings	220,000	22,000	33,000
Equity Acquired from First Purchase		102,000	
Transfer to Second Purchase		−102,000	+102,000
Goodwill on First Purchase		$ Nil	
At July 1, 20X2:			
Net Income — Six months to June 30	60,000	Nil	9,000
Interim Dividend on June 15	(12,000)	(1,200)	(1,800)
Adjustment for Fair Market Value of Assets (25%)	100,000		25,000
Total Equity Acquired (i.e., 25%)			287,200
Purchase Consideration (i.e., $124,000 + $173,200)			297,200
Goodwill on Acquisition			$ 10,000
At December 31, 20X2:			
Net Income — Six Months to December 31	60,000	6,000	9,000
Final Dividend on December 15	(20,000)	(2,000)	(3,000)

(b) The second step determines the net income from Investee appearing on the income statement of Investor for 20X2. This is made up of two parts. For the first six months, Investor would only recognize the dividends of $1,200 applying to the first acquisition because at that time the investment was merely a portfolio investment and is accounted for using the cost method. For the last six months, however, Investor can exert significant influence over the affairs of Investee and would use the equity method and recognize its "share of the net income" of $12,500 (i.e., net income of $6,000 + $9,000 less fair market value adjustment of $2,500 [i.e., $25,000/5 × 6/12]). Even though no goodwill arose from the first acquisition, Investor's share of the equity purchased must be recognized for the calculation of goodwill on July 1 when significant influence is exercisable. This share of the equity acquired is, therefore, transferred to the 15% acquisition column.

(c) The income statement of Investor would, therefore, reflect both dividend revenue of $1,200 and its share of net income from Investee of $12,500 for the year ended December 31, 20X2. The investment in Investee would be reflected on Investor's balance sheet at December 31, 20X2 at $304,700 (i.e., $297,200 + $12,500 − $5,000) because the dividend of $1,200 would have been credited to revenue when received.

7. How is the share of net income and dividends received by an investor company from its investment in the non-voting shares of an investee company treated by the investor company? Why are they treated in this manner?

8. How are non-voting shares accounted for by the investee company?

9. What do you understand by the term "coattail provision" in relation to non-voting shares?

10. What principle underlies the valuation of the net assets of an investee company over which an investor company exerts significant influence?

11. In which three areas do the financial statements of a company using the equity method of recording investments in investee companies differ from those cases where the cost method is used?

12. Describe what adjustments, if any, would be required to be made to the income statement of an investor company if its interest in an investee company increased from 10 to 20% during the year?

13. Are any adjustments to the statement of retained earnings necessary when a company increases its investment in an investee company so that it now exerts significant influence over the investee company?

CASES

CASE 5–1   **The Adams Investment Company Ltd.**

Barry Adams, of Calgary, Alberta, transferred a substantial portion of his assets to the Adams Investment Company Ltd.

At December 31, 20X3, the financial year end of the company, the assets of the company consisted of:

1. A one-quarter share in Adams Petroleum Resources Ltd. of Calgary transferred to the company at a value of $920,000. The shares of this company were actively traded on the Canadian Venture Exchange. Barry's younger brother, Neil, also held a 25% interest in the company while the balance of the shares was widely held.

2. A one-third interest (i.e., 50,000 shares of no par value) in the Bar Circle Ranch Ltd., which had been valued at $7 per share on transfer to the company. The balance of the shares was held equally by his brother Neil and his sister, Sarah.

3. A 40% interest in Cascade Apartment Holdings Inc. The balance of the shares was held by Barry's wife, Sheila. Barry's 40% interest in the company had been valued on transfer at $180,000.

4. A 100% interest in #34598442 Inc., an Alberta numbered company holding the title to a chalet in Banff, Alberta. The chalet had been transferred to the company at $140,000.

5. Investments consisting of shares in Canadian companies listed on the Toronto Stock and Canadian Venture Exchanges that had cost a little over $125,000. Of these, shares costing $35,000 had been bought as a temporary investment in March 20X3 on the expectation that prices for natural gas would increase. Unfortunately, this had not occurred, and they had decreased in value by some 30%. It was expected that they would have to be held for at least another six months before their prices would increase to a level where they could be realized at a profit.

6. Canada Savings Bonds to the value of $20,000 purchased in November 20X3 from surplus cash.

REQUIRED

Explain, giving reasons, how these investments should be reflected on the balance sheet of the company to satisfy the requirements of the CICA *Handbook*.

CASE 5–2   **Mrs. Aster Muldoon's Investments**

Mrs. Aster Muldoon, a prospective client, has approached you to handle the accounting matters relating to her investments which, on the advice of her previous accountants, are held by Aster Investment's Ltd., a company in which she is the sole shareholder.

She informs you that she understands that where an investor holds 20% or more of the issued share capital in a company, the equity method of accounting for these investments must be used. Her current investments consist of the following:

(a)   Two hundred thousand shares of common stock in Bahadur's Carpet Bazaars Inc. The total issued and outstanding common stock of the company consists of 1,000,000 shares of common stock;

(b)   One hundred thousand shares of $15 cumulative preferred stock in Carter's Development Company Ltd., out of a total issue of 400,000 shares of preferred stock;

(c)   One hundred and fifty thousand shares of common stock in Dodd's Transport Services Ltd., out of a total issue of 1,000,000 common shares (see point (a) above). A further 300,000 of these common shares are held by Bahadur's Carpet Bazaars; and

(d)   Ninety-nine thousand shares of common stock in Eriksen and Eriksen Ltd. This company had issued 500,000 shares of common stock but, as it required shares to issue to its employees in terms of an employee stock option plan, it had purchased 10,000 common shares in itself that were being held as treasury stock at December 31, 20X4.

REQUIRED

In a brief letter, explain to Mrs. Muldoon:

1.   The application of the 20% rule; and
2.   To what extent this rule would apply to Aster Investments Ltd. on the assumption that, with the exception of the investment by Bahadur's Carpet Bazaars in Dodd's Transport Services Ltd., no single investor holds more than 10% of the shares in the companies concerned.

CASE 5–3   **Brendall Investments Inc.**

You are the auditor of Brendall Investments Inc., a Vancouver-based investment company. Mr. Barney Brender, the major shareholder in the company, has asked you to explain to him how the following investments would be disclosed in the financial statements of the company at December 31, 20X4:

(a)   Four hundred thousand shares of common stock in Allen's Motels Ltd. purchased on November 15, 20X4 out of temporary excess cash resources. The investment, which represented a 40% interest in Allen's Motels, was purchased as a means of utilizing Brendall's Investments' excess cash resources and was expected to be realized at a substantial profit in early 20X5. The balance of Allen's Motels' common stock was widely held, with no single investor holding more than 5% of the total share issue.

(b)   Ninety-six thousand shares out of a total issue of 500,000 shares of common stock in Barrymore Suppliers Inc. purchased on February 28, 20X4. As with Allen's Motels, the balance of the common stock in the company was widely held and no other single shareholder held more than five percent of the common stock.

(c)   A 30% interest in Charles Chandler and Company Ltd., consisting of 300,000 shares of common stock purchased in June 20X3. The balance of the common stock was held equally by Charles Chandler and his only daughter, Charleen.

(d)   Six hundred thousand shares of common stock in Dauod Ibrahim and Sons Inc., representing a 60% interest in the company. The shares had been acquired in terms of a stock exchange effected on October 1, 20X4.

(e)   Two hundred and fifty thousand common shares, representing a 25% interest in Enrico's Pastries Inc. The investment was acquired in two purchases; 100,000 shares on January 4, 20X3, and 150,000 shares on June 30, 20X4. The first purchase of shares had represented the entire shareholding of the major shareholder in the company.

REQUIRED

Respond to Mr. Brender's request.

EXERCISES

EXERCISE 5–1   **REQUIRED**

Indicate, in each of the following cases, which is the correct answer:

1. Paul Inc. paid $90,000 for a 25% interest in Sally Inc. on January 1, 20X2, based on the estimated fair market value of Sally's total net assets of $280,000 on that date. Following this purchase, Paul became the second largest single shareholder in Sally, but was unable to exert significant influence over its affairs.

    If, during the financial year ended December 31, 20X2, Sally earned net income of $100,000 and paid a dividend of $40,000, how much income from Sally would be recognized by Paul?

    (a) $10,000 (b) $14,500
    (c) $24,500 (d) $25,000
    (e) None of the above

2. If, in point 1 above, Paul could have exerted significant influence over the affairs of Sally after the purchase of the 25% interest, the income recognized by Paul from Sally for 20X2 would have been:

    (a) $14,000 (b) $14,500
    (c) $24,000 (d) $24,500
    (e) None of the above

3. If Paul became the single largest shareholder in Sally on January 3, 20X2 by acquiring an additional 25% interest in Sally (to give a 50% interest) for another $90,000 (see question above), how much income from Sally would it recognize for the financial year ended December 31, 20X2:

    (a) $29,000 (b) $30,000
    (c) $49,000 (d) $50,000
    (e) None of the above

EXERCISE 5–2   On July 1, 20X3, Pam Inc. acquired a 25% interest in Sam Inc. for the sum of $240,000, which included $40,000 paid for goodwill that was accounted for using the impairment method. The year-end of Sam is December 31, and dividends are declared each year on November 1, payable on December 10. Information relating to the trading activities of Sam and the dividends declared and paid for 20X3 and 20X4 were as follows:

Year	Net Income	Dividends
20X3	$80,000	$30,000
20X4	60,000	30,000

REQUIRED

1. On the assumption that Pam does not exert significant influence over the operations and activities of Sam, give the journal entries to record the purchase and subsequent transactions relating to the interest in Sam in the books of Pam for 20X3 and 20X4.

2. Rework Part (1) above on the assumption that the investment by Pam **did allow it** to exert significant influence over the activities of Sam.

EXERCISE 5–3   On January 1, 20X5, Pillow Inc. acquired a 40% interest in Sleep Inc. for $220,000. On that date Sleep had common stock of $400,000 and retained earnings of $100,000. The net income of Sleep for 20X5 was $240,000, and during the year it declared and paid a dividend of $80,000 on December 5, 20X5. Pillow accounts for its investment in Sleep using the equity method, and reviews goodwill for impairment at the end of every year.

REQUIRED

1. Give the goodwill appearing on the balance sheet of Pillow at December 31, 20X5 relating to the purchase of its interest in Sleep if impairment of 10% had been recognized on December 31, 20X5;
2. Give the net income from Sleep reflected on the income statement of Pillow for 20X5; and
3. Give the balance on the "Investment in Sleep" account as it would appear in the ledger of Pillow at December 31, 20X5.

EXERCISE 5–4   On October 1, 20X3, Pacific Inc., a company having a December 31 year end, purchased a 25% interest in Shoreline Inc. for $120,000 in cash. Financial statements were not prepared on that date. Relevant information relating to the two companies extracted from their ledgers was as follows:

	Pacific	Shoreline
Common stock (shares of no par value issued at $1 each)	$400,000	$220,000
Retained earnings at January 1, 20X3	160,000	48,000
Net income from operations for 20X3	240,000	96,000
Net income from operations for 20X4	220,000	80,000
Dividends declared and Paid on December 10, 20X3	80,000	20,000
Dividends declared and Paid on December 12, 20X4	70,000	—
Impairment of goodwill on December 31, 20X4	20%	—

REQUIRED

Calculate:

1. The share of net income from Shoreline recognized by Pacific for 20X3;
2. The goodwill, if any, reflected on the balance sheet of Pacific at December 31, 20X4; and
3. The balance on the "Investment in Shoreline" account in the ledger of Pacific at December 31, 20X4.

EXERCISE 5–5   On April 1, 20X4, Place Inc. acquired a 40% interest in Serve Inc. for $300,000. On revaluation of the assets of Serve on April 2, 20X4, it was found that the fair market value of the net assets of Serve was $680,000. The excess of the purchase consideration was treated as goodwill.

The net income of Serve for the year ended December 31, 20X4 amounted to $320,000 before the recognition of a 10% impairment of the goodwill on December 31, 20X4. A dividend of $120,000 was declared and paid during November 20X4.

REQUIRED

1. Give the ledger account recording the Investment in Serve as it would appear in the ledger of Place at December 31, 20X4; and
2. Show how the effect of the investment by Place in Serve would be reflected on the income statement of Place for the year ended December 31, 20X4.

EXERCISE 5–6   On July 1, 20X6, Please Inc. acquired a 40% interest in Sir Inc. for $120,000. At January 1, 20X6, Sir had common stock of $200,000 and retained earnings of $40,000.

The net income of Sir for 20X6 was $120,000, and during the year it declared and paid an interim dividend of $40,000 on May 31 and a final dividend of $60,000 on December 15. In 20X7, the net income of Sir was $100,000, and it only paid a final dividend of $40,000 on December 20.

REQUIRED

1. What is the net income from Sir reflected on the income statement of Please for 20X6?
2. What is the net income from Sir reflected on the income statement of Please for 20X7 if the goodwill arising from the acquisition of the interest in Sir was considered to be impaired by 25% at December 31, 20X7?
3. What is the balance on the "Investment in Sir" account in the ledger of Please at December 31, 20X7?

EXERCISE 5–7 Pass Inc. acquired a 20% interest in Shoot Inc. on April 1, 20X2. This purchase did not allow Pass to exercise significant influence over the affairs of Shoot. On July 1, 20X2, Pass acquired a further 20% interest in Shoot. The goodwill arising on acquisition was considered to be fairly valued.

The income statements of the two companies for the year ended December 31, 20X2, prepared without any consideration of intercompany investments, were as follows:

	Pass	Shoot
Sales	$1,400,000	$1,000,000
Cost of Goods Sold	(800,000)	(450,000)
Administration Expenses	(250,000)	(250,000)
Net Income from Operations	350,000	300,000
Retained Earnings at January 1, 20X2	400,000	200,000
	750,000	500,000
Dividends Paid:		
Interim on May 31	(100,000)	(50,000)
Final on November 30	(200,000)	(120,000)
Retained Earnings at December 31, 20X2	$ 450,000	$ 300,000

REQUIRED

Prepare the combined income and retained earnings statement of Pass for the year ended December 31, 20X2.

PROBLEMS

PROBLEM 5–1 At January 1, 20X4, the stockholders' equity section of the balance sheets of Peach Inc. and Stone Inc. were as follows:

	Peach	Stone
Common Stock	$600,000	$ 200,000
Retained Earnings	200,000	100,000
	$800,000	$ 300,000

The trading results of the two companies for the financial years ended December 31, 20X4 and 20X5 were as follows:

	Peach	Stone
20X4:		
Net Operating Income/(Loss)	$200,000	$ (60,000)
Dividends Paid (November 30)	80,000	—
20X5:		
Net Operating Income	250,000	100,000
Dividends Paid (December 4)	100,000	60,000

REQUIRED

1.   On the assumption that Peach purchased a 10% interest in Stone on September 1, 20X4 for $36,000, calculate:

   i.   The balance on the "Investment in Stone" in the ledger of Peach at December 31, 20X4.
   ii. The net loss from Stone reflected on the income statement of Peach for 20X4.
   iii. The retained earnings of Peach at December 31, 20X5.

2.   On the assumption that Peach purchased a 30% interest in Stone for $102,000 on September 1, 20X4, calculate:

   i.   The balance on the "Investment in Stone" in the ledger of Peach at December 31, 20X4.
   ii. The net loss from Stone reflected on the Income Statement of Peach for 20X4.
   iii. The retained earnings of Peach at December 31, 20X5.

PROBLEM 5–2   On January 1, 20X3, Plant Inc. purchased a 40% interest in Seed Inc. for $440,000 when Seed had common stock of $800,000 and retained earnings of $150,000. The purchase price included an amount of $60,000 that was paid for goodwill and that was being accounted for on an impairment basis. During 20X3, the net income earned and dividends paid by Seed amounted to $300,000 and $100,000 respectively. The net income and dividends for 20X4 were $400,000 and $150,000.

   The retained earnings of Plant at January 1, 20X3 was $200,000 and its net income from operations for the two years ended December 31, 20X3 and 20X4 were $1-million and $1.1-million respectively.

REQUIRED

Give the balance of retained earnings of Plant at December 31, 20X4 on the assumption that:

1.   Significant influence could **not** be exercised over the affairs of Seed; and
2.   Significant influence could be exercised over the affairs of Seed and that, on December 31, 20X4, impairment of goodwill of $5,000 was recognized.

PROBLEM 5–3   On January 1, 20X5, Peer Inc. purchased 30% of the Class A no par value voting shares of Stare Inc. for $100,000. At that date, the equity of Stare was made up as follows:

Common Stock:	
Class A — 100,000 no par value voting shares	$ 200,000
Class B — 300,000 no par value non-voting shares	600,000
Retained Earnings	400,000
Total Equity	$1,200,000

On July 1, 20X5, Peer purchased 30,000 Class B shares of Stare for $96,500.

   During the year ended December 31, 20X5, Stare earned net income of $120,000 and paid a dividend of 10 cents per share on both the Class A and Class B shares on December 15, 20X5.

   In terms of the articles of association of Stare, Class A and Class B shares were to share equally in profits and dividends.

REQUIRED

1.   Give the investment accounts in the ledger of Peer recording its investment in Stare at December 31, 20X5; and
2.   Give the "Share of Net Income from Stare" to be reflected on the income statement of Peer for the year ended December 31, 20X5.

PROBLEM 5–4 Plumb Inc. acquired a 40% interest in Stupid Inc. on January 1, 20X2 for $720,000 when the retained earnings of Stupid were $400,000. The balance sheets and combined income and retained earnings statements of the two companies twelve months later were as follows:

	Plumb	Stupid
BALANCE SHEETS		
Current Assets	$1,020,000	$ 800,000
Investment in Stupid	795,000	—
Capital Assets (Net)	1,000,000	1,100,000
	$2,815,000	$1,900,000
Current Liabilities	$ 440,000	$ 300,000
Common Stock	1,500,000	1,000,000
Retained Earnings	875,000	600,000
	$2,815,000	$1,900,000
INCOME AND RETAINED EARNINGS STATEMENTS		
Sales	$2,500,000	$1,200,000
Cost of Goods Sold	$1,250,000	$ 660,000
Operating Expenses	850,000	240,000
	$2,100,000	$ 900,000
Net Operating Income	$ 400,000	$ 300,000
Share of Net Income from Stupid	115,000	—
Net Income	515,000	300,000
Retained Earnings at January 1, 20X2	660,000	400,000
	1,175,000	700,000
Dividends Paid (November 25)	300,000	100,000
Retained Earnings at December 31, 20X2	$ 875,000	$ 600,000

REQUIRED

Prepare the balance sheet and combined income and retained earnings statement for the year ended December 31, 20X2 if goodwill arising on acquisition was written down by $5,000 for impairment in December 20X2.

PROBLEM 5–5 On July 1, 20X5, Peter Inc. announced that it had acquired an interest in Saul Inc. as a result of the purchase of 30% of Saul's voting stock in three purchases as follows:

Date	No. of Shares Purchased	Interest Acquired	Purchase Consideration
March 1, 20X2	100,000	10%	$300,000
September 1, 20X4	50,000	5%	180,000
July 1, 20X5	150,000	15%	400,000

The total goodwill arising from the purchase was $100,000. In each year, the dividends were declared on November 30 and paid on December 10.

Details relating to the net income and dividends declared and paid for the four years ended December 31, 20X5 were as follows:

Year	Net Income	Dividends
20X2	$ 96,000	$30,000
20X3	120,000	50,000
20X4	120,000	60,000
20X5	150,000	70,000

REQUIRED

1. Give the Investment in Saul account as it would appear in the ledger of Peter at December 31, 20X5, on which date an impairment of the goodwill of $5,000 was recognized.

2. Give the journal entry to record the sale by Peter of 50,000 shares in Saul on January 1, 20X6 for $200,000.

The Consolidation of Financial Statements: Introduction 6

LEARNING OBJECTIVES

After studying this chapter you should be able to:

1. Understand the basic philosophy underlying the preparation and presentation of consolidated financial statements;
2. Recognize the issues involved in consolidating financial statements;
3. Understand the consolidation process as it applies to both wholly- and partly-owned subsidiary companies; and
4. Identify and apply the conditions in which consolidated financial statements need not be prepared.

THE NATURE OF CONSOLIDATED FINANCIAL STATEMENTS

In accounting **the term "consolidation" is used in a specific sense to refer to the practice of combining the financial statements of two or more companies affiliated in a "parent company-subsidiary company" relationship into a single set of financial statements**. Consolidated financial statements have been presented by companies in America and the United Kingdom since at least the beginning of the 20th century. The purpose of reporting in this way is to reflect the financial position, results of operations and cash flows of the affiliated group of companies as if it were a single accounting or economic entity regardless of who owns the investments.

Consolidated financial statements consist of four statements: the consolidated balance sheet, the consolidated income statement, the consolidated statement of retained earnings, and the consolidated statement of cash flows. They are the only financial statements presented by the parent company to its shareholders in "parent company-subsidiary company" relationships in Canada and the USA. In other countries, like Britain and Australia, which have similar financial reporting requirements, consolidated financial statements do not enjoy quite the same prominence as they do in North America because they are presented to their shareholders together with the normal financial statements of the parent company. This chapter introduces the topic and examines the consolidated balance sheet and income statement. The consolidated statement of cash flows and other aspects of the consolidation process are explained in the following seven chapters.

THE CASE FOR CONSOLIDATION

The presentation of consolidated financial statements is not without its critics. The issue is whether the information provided by consolidated financial statements is more informative than that provided by using the equity method.

Those favouring consolidated financial statements argue that any company controlling the activities of another company should present a single set of financial statements covering all the assets, liabilities, revenues and expenses controlled by it, as well as the interests of the minority shareholders in the equity of the various controlled companies. This position is supported by the CICA *Handbook*,[1] which states that the parent and its subsidiary companies, even though they may be separate legal entities, constitute a single economic entity and, consequently, the information on its resources and results of operations should be presented in a manner that reflects that position. And, to ensure that the disclosure of information is complete, the consolidated financial statements should also be supplemented by disaggregating the consolidated amounts (see later chapter) to provide more detailed information on the activities of the group of companies.

On the other hand, the presentation of information using the equity method is based on the argument that the inclusion of the parent company's share of net income from its various subsidiaries is simple to apply and provides a clearer picture of the company's investing policies. In this respect, proponents of the equity method point out that the aggregation of revenues, expenses, assets and liabilities in the consolidated financial statements, even though the information may be supplemented with additional information, fails to draw attention to those companies in the group experiencing financial difficulties or adverse trading conditions. It is also felt that the equity method provides more detailed information than consolidation on the success or otherwise of the parent company's investments in subsidiary companies. It is for these reasons that consolidated financial statements are presented to shareholders together with the financial statements of the parent company that reflect their investments using the equity method in countries like the United Kingdom, Australia, New Zealand and South Africa.

The general consensus amongst North American accountants and accounting standard setting bodies is that the consolidation of financial statements is superior to the equity method because it recognizes the existence of the economic entity. The use of the equity method falls down on this count and is, therefore, not as informative as consolidated financial statements. The equity method is also criticized on the grounds that it does not facilitate financial statement analysis because it is impossible to use financial ratios like the current and acid test (or quick) ratios. Similarly, the overall liquidity and solvency of the group of companies cannot be assessed without detailed information on the total cash resources and assets. As a result, consolidated financial statements are the only financial statements presented to shareholders in Canada and the USA.

THE BASIC PRINCIPLE UNDERLYING THE CONSOLIDATION
OF FINANCIAL STATEMENTS

The basic premise of consolidation is that when a company exercises control over another company or companies, the operations and financial position of this affiliated group of companies should be presented in the form of a single set of consolidated financial statements **as if the companies were a single reporting entity**. The accounting for the affiliated group is, therefore, concerned with the area of economic influence or interest of the parent company, and not with the operations and activities of the individual companies making up the group of companies.

---

[1]   Section 1590.

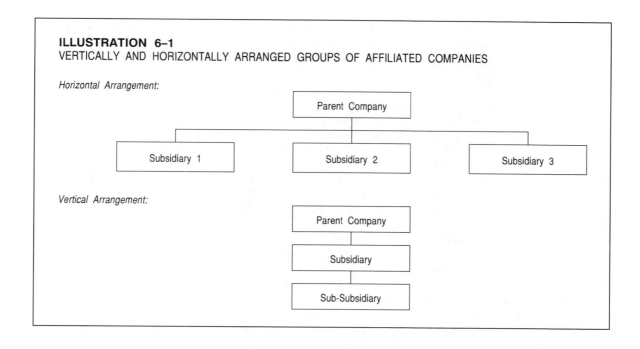

ILLUSTRATION 6–1
VERTICALLY AND HORIZONTALLY ARRANGED GROUPS OF AFFILIATED COMPANIES

Horizontal Arrangement:

Parent Company

Subsidiary 1   Subsidiary 2   Subsidiary 3

Vertical Arrangement:

Parent Company

Subsidiary

Sub-Subsidiary

GROUPS OF AFFILIATED COMPANIES

Groups of affiliated companies come into being when a parent (or holding) company has the ability to exert control, either directly or indirectly, over the operations and activities of two or more companies. These groups of companies may take any form because control may be exercised by the parent company either horizontally or vertically depending upon the nature of the organization structure of the affiliated group.

With horizontal arrangements, the parent company has direct control over a number of companies that have no connection with one another. On the other hand, a vertical arrangement exists where the parent company controls one or more subsidiary companies that, in turn, control other companies. In these latter cases, the companies controlled by the subsidiaries are called sub-subsidiaries or merely subsidiaries. In practice, however, both types of arrangement are common, and a single group of companies will often consist of a complex group of companies made up of companies arranged in both horizontal and vertical patterns. Examples of horizontally and vertically arranged groups of companies are diagrammatically represented in Illustration 6–1.

CONTROL OVER COMPANIES

The Meaning of Control

Control of an enterprise was defined by the CICA[2] in 1992 as **the continuing power to determine the strategic operating, investing and financing policies of an entity without the co-operation of others**. Prior to that date, the holding of more than 50% of the voting shares was considered necessary for control to exist.

---

[2] CICA *Handbook*, section 1590.

The carrying out of the operating, investing and financing policies of a company are the responsibility of the board of directors, who are elected by the shareholders at the annual general meeting of a company to hold office for a specified period of time. For all practical purposes, therefore, a company has control over another company when it has the power to either elect a majority of members to the board of directors or control the majority of votes exercisable by the directors. This is recognized by the definition of control given above because, in the absence of such control, the carrying out of the policies of a company would be impossible.

Legally, control exists where one company (or one person) holds more than 50% of the shares of the company having voting rights **and** the votes attached to those shares are sufficient to elect a majority of the directors to the board of directors of the company concerned.[3] From an accounting point of view, this is not the case because, in terms of the CICA's definition of control, control is concerned with the actual power to exert control, and not its legal aspects. The consolidation of financial statements is, therefore, concerned with the substance of the association between the group of companies, and not the legal form.

It is also **not necessary to actually hold a majority of shares having voting rights to exert control**, because control may also be exercised in other ways: for example, through **a shareholder agreement**, which confers upon one party the right to elect a majority of members to the board of directors. Control may also be conferred upon one company by another in terms of a "**debt covenant**", or condition relating to longterm debt.[4] In addition, there is the extent to which "**dormant shareholdings**" (i.e., the number of shares held by shareholders who are untraceable) may allow control to be exercised by the holding of less than 50% of the voting shares. As far as this latter point is concerned, public companies find that over time a considerable number of their shareholders lose or misplace their share certificates or otherwise fail to keep in contact with the company in which they have invested. After failing to trace the investor, these shares are transferred from the current share register to a "dormant share register" where they remain until the owners are eventually located. As the company continues to operate, the number of untraceable shares increases, and the number of shares required for absolute control falls below the 50% level.[5]

Effective control can also be exercised over **a public company** through the holding of relatively few shares. This is because, as a result of shareholder apathy, few shareholders in companies whose shares are publicly traded ever bother exercising their votes, even by proxy, and control rests with those who command the most votes when the directors are elected to hold office.[6] However, even though effective control may be exercised by one company over another by holding less than 50% of the voting shares, the basis of control may be tenuous and subject to certain conditions. For example, control may be exercised over a publicly owned company for so long as no-one else manages to control sufficient votes to elect a majority of members to the board of directors. Therefore, in practice, some definite evidence of control is necessary. **And, as one moves further away from more than a 50% ownership of voting shares or the command of voting rights, the stronger the evidence that is required to show that control actually exists.**

---

[3] *Canada Business Corporations Act*, section 3; the Ontario *Business Corporations Act*, section 1 (5), and similar provisions in other provincial corporate legislation.

[4] For example, to avoid bankruptcy, a company may confer the right to elect a majority of members to its board of directors to the holder of a mortgage or longterm loan for a specific period of time. An example of the type of arrangement that can be entered into was that by Peoples Jewellers Ltd. of Toronto, which announced on August 26, 1992, that in return for a 9.9% share in its equity, the Bank of Nova Scotia was extending its $87.5-million credit line to the company until the end of April 1993, and making a further $6-million available in short-term financing.

[5] For example, *The Globe and Mail* of November 16, 1995, reported that 6,352 shares in *Petrofina Canada Ltd.* held by 2,505 shareholders in the 1982 takeover of the company by *Petro-Canada Inc.* could not be traced. In an attempt to trace these shareholders, their names had been published in the November 1995 issue of the federal government's *Canada Gazette*.

[6] In certain countries control is at a level far less than 50%. For example, in Japan a holding of 33.4% of the issued shares in a company is all that is required for control.

Direct and Indirect Control

Control may be direct or indirect. Direct control exists where the parent company holds more than 50% of shares having voting rights or has the right to elect a majority of members to the board of directors. A company may also be able to exercise control indirectly by virtue of holding a controlling interest in a company that, in turn, controls another company.

Consider, for example, the following vertical arrangements reflecting direct and indirect control:

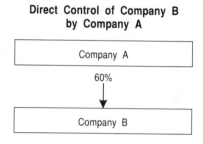

Direct Control of Company B by Company A

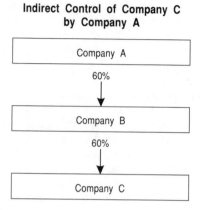

Indirect Control of Company C by Company A

In the above cases, Company A controls Company B by holding a 60% interest in its voting shares. Company A would also control Company C indirectly through its control of Company B. This occurs even though the extent of interest in Company C is only 36% (i.e., 60% of 60%) because control is determined at each level in a vertical arrangement of affiliated companies. For example, if Company B only held 40% of the shares in Company C, the control by Company A would cease with Company B. A would no longer indirectly control C, although it would still control B.

Two subsidiary companies may also jointly control another company. For example, subsidiaries C and D may each own 30% of the voting shares in Company E which, from the group's point of view, represents a 60% interest in Company E.

Control is only exercised over another company (i.e., the investee company) through the holding of common shares having voting rights. In those cases where non-voting common stock has been issued by the investee company, the holding of these shares has no effect on the determination of control. However, **as the issue of non-voting stock now only occurs in special cases**, all references to common stock in this text should be taken as referring to common stock having voting rights, unless you are specifically informed otherwise.

Preferred stock does not form part of the residual equity of a company and, therefore, the holding of this type of stock does not normally affect the exercising of control. This is because preferred shares only have voting rights in certain conditions: such as, for example, where the preferred stock is cumulative in relation to dividends, and the dividends are in arrear. Therefore, for all practical purposes, the voting rights attached to preferred stock may be ignored.

Where the parent company holds the entire voting shares of a subsidiary company, we refer to the subsidiary as a **wholly-owned subsidiary**. In those cases where the parent company does not hold all the shares having voting rights, the subsidiary is called a **partly-owned subsidiary**, and we refer to the shares or interests held by persons other than members of the affiliated group of companies as the **minority interests**, the **interests of the outside shareholders**, or the **noncontrolling interests** in the subsidiary.

As a holding of more than 50% of the voting shares is not necessary for control, the CICA *Handbook* has replaced the term "minority interests" with "noncontrolling interests". However, as the term "minority interests" properly describes the situation prevailing with partly-owned subsidiaries, it is unlikely that it will be replaced by the term "noncontrolling interests" in the foreseeable future. The term "noncontrolling interest" is also unsuitable for describing the shareholding in cases where significant influence is exercisable and, consequently, where this situation exists, this text continues to use the term "outside shareholders' interests".

The Extent of Control

The holding of sufficient shares to be able **to elect the majority of members to the board of directors** is all that is required to control a subsidiary company. However, the extent of control is important for a number of reasons. For example, with wholly-owned subsidiaries, administration is considerably easier, because there are no outside shareholders to consider and, consequently, the appointment of directors and the holding of the annual general meeting can take place at any convenient time. The share capital of the company can also be increased or decreased as required, and there is no need for a set dividend policy because dividends can be declared and paid to meet the cash requirements of the group of companies. It also allows the parent company to carry out internal re-organizations and to interchange personnel within the group without restriction.

It would, therefore, be desirable from an administrative viewpoint for the group of companies to consist of the parent company and only wholly-owned subsidiaries. Unfortunately, the level of control is often dictated by financial reasons. Control of a subsidiary through, say, the purchase of a 51% interest, requires considerably less resources than, say, an 80% interest. The need to raise capital for the expansion of the business from outside sources normally also requires the issue of shares to outside parties. In many cases, the acquisition of a controlling interest in a private or closely held company allows the founder of the company to continue as president of the company until retirement, on which date the balance of the shares is transferred to the parent company. The existence of partly-owned subsidiary companies is, therefore, very common.

SOME PRELIMINARY MATTERS OF IMPORTANCE

The Consolidation Process Is Carried Out from the Beginning to End Each Time

Before examining the way in which financial statements are consolidated, it should be noted that **the consolidation of financial statements is carried out each time as a separate exercise** covering the period from the date of acquiring control of the companies concerned to the end of the current financial year. It is carried out using the financial statements of the various companies making up the group, and consists of a process in which the amounts are entered and adjusted on detailed spreadsheets and working papers. These working papers are used for reference purposes from one year to another to facilitate the consolidation process because they provide, other than the consolidated financial statements themselves, the only record of the consolidated figures. With particularly large and complicated groups of companies, permanent schedules and analyses are, however, kept to assist in the consolidation process from year to year.

The Link between Consolidation and the Equity Method

The consolidated net income determined by the consolidation process is exactly the same as that calculated using the equity method. The only difference is that with the equity method, the "share of net income from investee company" is reflected as a single figure on the income statement of the parent company, whereas the consolidated net income is arrived at after the inclusion of the revenues and expenses of the subsidiary company. This is achieved by, first, including any expenses relating to the subsidiary company with those of the parent company. Second, the share of net income from the subsidiary is recognized by including the total revenues and expenses of the subsidiary with those of the parent company, and then deducting therefrom the share of the net income attributable to the outside shareholders. And, finally, any goodwill charges are then deducted.

The Contents of Consolidated Financial Statements

Consolidated financial statements are similar to the normal financial statements of companies. In this respect, the consolidated balance sheet consists of the combined assets and liabilities of the group of companies adjusted for any goodwill arising on acquisition, the equity of the parent company and any minority (or noncontrolling) interests in the consolidated group of companies. The consolidated statement of cash flows presents the inflows and outflows of resources for the group as a whole.

The consolidated income statement also contains essentially the same information as that provided in the income statement of a parent company that accounts for its interests in subsidiary companies or companies over which it exerts significant influence. In fact, the consolidated net income for the year is exactly the same amount as would have been reported by the parent company had it used the equity method of accounting for its interest in the subsidiary company. The difference is that the share of net income from the subsidiary company appearing on the income statement of the parent company is replaced by the actual revenues and expenses of the subsidiary company and those relating to the valuation of assets and liabilities. The consolidated net income is arrived at by deducting the interests of the minority (or outside shareholders) in the net income of the subsidiary companies from the total net income of the group.

The preparation of consolidated financial statements does not in any way eliminate the need for each company in the group to prepare its own financial statements. In this respect, the companies in the group are separate legal entities which are required to prepare their own financial statements by corporate, securities, and taxation law.

The Presentation of Consolidated Financial Statements Used in This Text

Throughout this section, the emphasis is on the principles of consolidation involved. The terminology used is designed with understandability and clarity in mind and, as far as is possible, unnecessary detail has been eliminated. For example, no income tax or accumulated amortization figures are included in the illustrations or examples unless the effect of these items on the consolidation process is being explained. Parent companies are given names starting with the letter "P", while the names of subsidiaries start with the letter "S". All companies also have December 31 financial year ends.

The use of a statement of cash flows and a separate statement of retained earnings is dispensed with, and the illustrations, exercises and problems are presented using a combined income statement and statement of retained earnings. Any references to the income statement should, therefore, always be construed as including the statement of retained earnings. Balance sheets are also presented in abbreviated and unclassified form.

THE "ANALYSIS OF EQUITY" APPROACH TO CONSOLIDATING FINANCIAL STATEMENTS

There are a number of ways consolidated financial statements can be prepared. The method presented and explained in this text is what is described as the "analysis of equity" approach. It provides a simple, concise and straightforward method of preparing consolidated balance sheets and income statements that is also equally suitable for accounting for those investments in companies over which the investor exerts significant influence.

This method is also particularly suited to the use of computer spreadsheet applications and the consolidation of large groups of affiliated companies consisting of 10, 20 or more companies. For example, if the group of affiliated companies consists of the parent company and four subsidiaries in a horizontal arrangement, the working paper spreadsheet would be presented as follows:

Details of the Balance Sheet or Income Statement Items	Consolidated Amounts	Parent	Sub. 1	Sub. 2	Sub. 3	Sub. 4

In the above illustration, the balances appearing in the consolidation column are those that would be used to prepare the consolidated financial statements in a form suitable for publication. However, in the interests of simplicity, separate consolidated financial statements for publication are not provided in this text.

THE CONSOLIDATION PROCESS

The consolidation process consists essentially of only two steps: the "analysis of the equity" and the adjustment and aggregation of the figures. These two steps are explained and illustrated in the following subsections.

Step One — the Analysis of Equity

The first step in the consolidation process is to analyze the equity of the subsidiary company. This is carried out to establish the proportion of the equity in the subsidiary company that is attributable to the parent company and applicable to the interests of the minority shareholders.

With wholly-owned subsidiaries, the equity is all attributable to the parent company. However, with partly-owned subsidiaries, the analysis of the equity of the subsidiary company involves an apportionment of the equity between the parent company and the minority interests in the subsidiary company.

To illustrate this apportionment, let us assume that on January 1, 20X4, a parent company acquired all the common stock of a subsidiary company for $420,000 when the subsidiary company had total equity of $400,000, made up of common stock of $300,000 and retained earnings of $100,000. In this case, all the equity of the subsidiary is attributable to the parent company, and is apportioned as follows:

	Parent
Common Stock	$300,000
Retained Earnings	100,000
Equity Attributable to the Parent Company	$400,000

As $420,000 was paid for the 100% interest in the subsidiary company, the goodwill arising on acquisition would be $20,000. This is established by deducting the $400,000 of equity acquired from the purchase consideration of $420,000.

If, however, only 60% of the shares of common stock in this subsidiary had been acquired for, say $250,000, the position would be somewhat different. This is because the subsidiary is a partly-owned subsidiary company and, as outlined in Illustration 6–2, the analysis of the equity must take this situation into account.

ILLUSTRATION 6–2
THE ANALYSIS OF THE EQUITY OF A PARTLY OWNED SUBSIDIARY AT
BOTH THE DATE OF ACQUISITION AND ONE YEAR LATER

Parent Inc. acquired a 60% interest in Subsidiary Inc. on January 1, 20X4 for $250,000. On that date, the equity of Subsidiary consisted of shares of common stock of $300,000 and retained earnings of $100,000. During the year ended December 31, 20X4, Subsidiary earned net income of $80,000, and paid a dividend of $30,000.

The "Analysis of the Equity" of Subsidiary is carried out as follows:

	Total	Parent 60%	Minority Interests 40%
At Acquisition:			
Common Stock	$300,000	$180,000	$120,000
Retained Earnings	100,000	60,000	40,000
Apportionment of Equity	400,000	240,000	160,000
Purchase Consideration		250,000	
Goodwill Arising on Acquisition		$ 10,000	
Since Acquisition:			
Net Income — 20X4	80,000	48,000	32,000
Dividends Declared and Paid	(30,000)	(18,000)	(12,000)
Total Equity	$450,000		
Total Minority Interests (40% of $450,000)			$180,000

Illustration 6–2 shows that because the subsidiary is **partly-owned**, the equity at the date of acquisition must be apportioned into the amount attributable to the parent company (i.e., 60% or $240,000) and the amount attributable to the minority interests (i.e., 40% or $160,000). And, by deducting the purchase consideration from the parent company's share of the equity, it shows that goodwill of $10,000 arose on acquisition by the parent company of its 60% interest in the subsidiary.

This illustration also shows that, as the consolidation process is carried out after the date of acquisition of the controlling interest, it is also necessary to analyze the post-acquisition profits and their distribution as dividends between the parent company and the minority interests. In this illustration, Subsidiary earned net income of $80,000 during the year ended December 31, 20X4, and that $30,000 of these profits were distributed as a dividend. These amounts are, therefore, also apportioned between the parent company and the minority interests to give minority interests at December 31, 20X4 of $180,000 (i.e., 40% of the total equity on that date of $450,000).

It is also necessary to apportion the retained earnings of the subsidiary in the "analysis of equity" into pre- and post-acquisition net income because the amount paid for an interest in a subsidiary is based largely on the equity at the date of acquisition and, consequently, the retained earnings existing on that date must be capitalized as part of the equity purchased. As explained later, it is only those amounts earned after the date of acquisition that are treated as part of the consolidated net income of the group in the consolidation process.

It should also be noted that the allocation of the pre-acquisition equity to the parent company in the analysis of equity is necessary to establish exactly what share of the equity has been acquired and capitalized by the parent company as its investment in the subsidiary company at the date of acquisition. As shown in Illustration 6–2, the retained earnings earned up to the date of acquisition forms part of the equity acquired, and **may not be distributed to the parent company as revenue dividends**.

Step Two — the Aggregation of the Amounts

The final step in the consolidation process is to aggregate and adjust the assets and liabilities, and revenues and expenses, of the group of companies in such a manner that the consolidated balance sheet and income statement can be prepared.

All that is required is to, first, list the balances not used to analyze the equity of the subsidiary (i.e., all balances except the equity accounts of the subsidiary and the investment in subsidiary account from the parent company) in the order that they normally appear on the balance sheet. This should be carried out in columnar form so that, after the inclusion of the goodwill arising on consolidation and the minority interests, they can be aggregated to give the consolidated balance sheet. And, second, to list the income statement items in the same manner to give the net income (or adjusted net income) of each company. After deduction of the minority interests share of the net income of the subsidiary, these balances are merely aggregated to give the consolidated income statement. The statement of retained earnings is then drawn up in the normal manner.

Analysis of the Two Steps

At this stage it is necessary to examine the two steps in the consolidation process objectively. Doing so will clarify the entire objective of the consolidation process.

The purpose of **step one** is to show that the equity of a partly owned subsidiary is jointly owned by the parent company and the minority interests. This is reflected by the analysis of equity where the parent company's share is offset against the purchase consideration to give the goodwill, if any, arising on acquisition. The share of the minority is then carried forward on the consolidated balance sheet as a part of the total consolidated equity and is reflected as a separate item immediately above the consolidated shareholders' equity. This is because the minority interests plus the shareholders equity reflected on the consolidated balance sheet represents the total equity of the consolidated group of companies. **Step two** shows that all that remains to be done is to add, after certain adjustments, the assets and liabilities of the subsidiary to those of the parent company to give the consolidated financial statements.

Using the equations of Current Assets + Investment in Subsidiary + Fixed Assets = Liabilities + Shareholders Equity for the parent company and Current Assets + Fixed Assets[7] = Liabilities + Parent Company's Share of Shareholders' Equity + Minority Interests in the subsidiary company, the consolidation process may be expressed mathematically as follows:

Parent: $\qquad CA_1 + \text{Investment} + FA_1 \qquad = L_1 + SE_1$

Subsidiary: $\qquad CA_2 \qquad\qquad + FA_2 \qquad = L_2 + PSE_2$ (i.e., the Parent's Share of SE) + MI

On Consolidation: $\displaystyle\sum_{i=1}^{2} CA_i + (\text{Investment} - PSE_2) + \sum_{i=1}^{2} FA_i = \sum_{i=1}^{2} L_i + SE_1 + MI$

Consolidated: $\displaystyle\sum_{i=1}^{2} CA_i + \text{Goodwill} + \sum_{i=1}^{2} FA_i = \sum_{i=1}^{2} L_i + SE_1 + MI$

The restated accounting equation shows that on consolidation at the date of acquisition, both the current and fixed assets and the liabilities of the consolidated entities remain

---

[7] Even though fixed assets are now referred to as capital assets by the CICA *Handbook*, the term fixed asset is being used for clarity's sake.

unchanged. As outlined above, the equity of the subsidiary is offset against the cost of the investment and included as the minority interests on the consolidated balance sheet.

It should also be noted that as we progress through the various aspects of the consolidation of financial statements, various adjustments to these figures will become necessary but, irrespective of the necessity to make those adjustments, the above equations show exactly what occurs on consolidation.

The Adjustments That Are Necessary

Review of the Goodwill for Impairment Goodwill arising on consolidation must be reviewed for impairment in exactly the same manner as that applying to any other goodwill arising from other forms of business combinations. As explained in Chapter Four, the value of the goodwill should be reviewed for impairment on an annual basis or when an event or series of events occur that indicate that its value has been impaired.

With the equity method, any impairment of goodwill arising on acquisition is deducted from the investor company's share of the net income from the investee company. The same applies to the recording of the parent company's share of net income from subsidiaries. For example, if the parent company's share of net income from a subsidiary is $48,000 and if, at the end of that year, the goodwill was written down for impairment by $2,000, the share of net income from the subsidiary would be shown as $46,000. However, because the consolidated income statement includes the total revenues and expenses of the subsidiary, the amount by which the goodwill is written down for impairment is reflected as a separate line item on the consolidated income statement, before extraordinary items and discontinued operations.

The Elimination of Intercompany Loans and Balances All intercompany loans and balances must be eliminated in the consolidation process. The financial statements of the companies to be consolidated should, therefore, be examined to see if any intercompany loans exist and, if so, they are merely set off against one another in the consolidated workings. The receipts and payments of interest on intercompany loans must also be set off against one another.

In those cases where intercompany loans exist but the balances appearing on the balance sheets of the companies concerned do not agree, this must be corrected before proceeding with the consolidation process. The rule to be followed is that the adjustment must be made in the company that would normally **reciprocate** the entry. For example, if the subsidiary had forwarded goods for resale to the parent company on the last day of the financial year, and the goods had not been received by the parent company until after the year end, the parent company's balance sheet must be adjusted to reflect the position as if the goods had been received before the year end.

Accounting for the Capital Assets of the Subsidiary Company The CICA *Handbook*[8] requires that capital assets of the companies in which a controlling interest has been acquired should be treated as if they had been purchased on the date of acquisition. This means that all capital assets of the subsidiary must be valued at their fair market values on the date of acquisition. This procedure is fully dealt with in a later chapter, but is mentioned at this stage to give a full picture of the adjustments that are required in the consolidation process.

---

[8] Section 1600.

ILLUSTRATION OF THE CONSOLIDATION PROCESS

The Simplest Case — Consolidating Wholly Owned Subsidiaries Acquired on the Date of Their Formation One Year after Acquisition

The simplest case of consolidation is where the **entire** share capital was issued to the parent company on the formation of the subsidiary. As there are no minority interests, the consolidation process is straightforward because the assets, liabilities and earnings of the subsidiary are merely added to those of the parent company. In addition, all dividends declared by the subsidiary company accrue to the parent. An example of the consolidation of such a wholly-owned subsidiary is presented in Illustration 6–3.

This illustration shows that the first step in the consolidation process is to analyze the equity of the subsidiary company and to offset the equity attributable to the parent company against the purchase consideration appearing as part of the "Investment in Subsidiary" account on the balance sheet of the parent company. As the subsidiary is wholly-owned, there is no apportionment of the equity between the parent and subsidiary companies, and all the post-acquisition net income is allocated to the parent company. There is also no goodwill arising on consolidation because the parent company acquired the entire share capital of the subsidiary on the date of its formation.

The second and final step is carried out by merely adjusting and aggregating the figures from the individual balance sheets and income statements to give the relevant consolidated balance sheet and combined income and retained earnings statement. Here, the only

---

ILLUSTRATION 6–3
CONSOLIDATING A WHOLLY-OWNED SUBSIDIARY ACQUIRED ON THE DATE OF
ITS FORMATION, ONE YEAR AFTER ACQUISITION

Parent Inc. acquired the entire issued share capital of Subsidiary Inc. for $100,000 on January 1, 20X4, the date on which Subsidiary was formed. The abbreviated financial statements of the two companies at December 31, 20X4 were as follows:

	Parent	Subsidiary
BALANCE SHEETS		
Assets	$1,195,000	$165,000
Investment in Subsidiary	115,000	—
	$1,310,000	$165,000
Liabilities	$ 200,000	$ 50,000
Common Stock	1,000,000	100,000
Retained Earnings	110,000	15,000
	$1,310,000	$165,000
COMBINED INCOME AND RETAINED EARNINGS STATEMENTS		
Sales	$ 890,000	$300,000
Expenses	810,000	280,000
Net Income	80,000	20,000
Share of Income from Subsidiary	20,000	—
	100,000	20,000
Less: Dividends Declared and Paid	30,000	5,000
	70,000	15,000
Retained Earnings at January 1, 20X4	40,000	—
Retained Earnings at December 31, 20X4	$ 110,000	$ 15,000

ILLUSTRATION 6–3 (Continued)

The consolidation of the financial statements of Parent and its subsidiary company is carried out using the following two steps:

STEP ONE: The "Analysis of Equity"

At Acquisition:

Common Stock	$100,000
Purchase Consideration	100,000
Goodwill	Nil

Since Acquisition:

Net Income for Year	$ 20,000
Less: Dividends	(5,000)

STEP TWO: Adjustment and Aggregation

	Consolidated	Parent	Subsidiary
BALANCE SHEETS			
Assets	$1,360,000	$1,195,000	$165,000
Liabilities	$ 250,000	$ 200,000	$ 50,000
Common Stock	1,000,000	1,000,000	—
Retained Earnings	110,000	110,000	—
	$1,360,000	$1,310,000	$ 50,000
COMBINED INCOME AND RETAINED EARNINGS STATEMENT			
Sales	$1,190,000	$ 890,000	$300,000
Expenses	1,090,000	810,000	280,000
Consolidated Net Income	100,000	$ 80,000	$ 20,000
Retained Earnings at January 1, 20X4	40,000		
	140,000		
Less: Dividends	30,000		
Retained Earnings at December 31, 20X4	$ 110,000		

Note: The "Investment in Subsidiary of $115,000" from Parent has been offset against the equity purchased of $100,000 and the Retained Earnings of Subsidiary of $15,000 (i.e., the $20,000 less the dividend paid of $5,000) at December 31, 20X4.

adjustments are those required to offset the "Investment in Subsidiary Inc." of $115,000 appearing on the balance sheet of the parent company against the common stock of $100,000 and retained earnings of $15,000 appearing on the balance sheet of the subsidiary.

The adjustments to the income statement are merely a re-arrangement of the amounts required to establish the parent company's "Share of Net Income from Subsidiary". Here, instead of including the parent company's share of the net income on the income statement, the net income attributable to it is established by adding the revenues and expenses of the subsidiary company to those of the parent company.

At this stage it should be noted that, other than for the illustrations provided in this chapter, the listing of the balance sheets of companies being consolidated in the columnar form is not used. This is because the illustrations used in this text cover relatively simple situations. The consolidated balance sheet may, therefore, be prepared by merely aggregating and adjusting the parent company's equity and obtaining the remaining consolidated figures by adding the assets, liabilities, goodwill and other amounts from the individual balance sheets and analysis of equity together. With the consolidated income statement, however, the listing and aggregating procedure is used throughout to explain and illustrate the somewhat more complicated adjustments to the net income of the companies concerned.

Consolidation of a Partly-Owned Subsidiary Company One Year after Its Formation

The consolidation process with partly-owned subsidiary companies is somewhat more complicated. This is because the equity must be apportioned between the parent company and the minority interests, and the net income must be adjusted to reflect the share of the minority in the net income for the year. The differences are outlined in Illustration 6–4, in which Subsidiary Inc. is a 60%-owned subsidiary.

The consolidation process, however, still uses the two-step procedure outlined above. In this respect, it is first necessary to analyze the equity of the subsidiary and then to adjust and aggregate the figures to give the consolidated balance sheet and combined income and retained earnings statement.

The analysis of the equity of the subsidiary in Illustration 6–4 shows that the purchase consideration of $130,000 for a 60% holding in the subsidiary gave rise to goodwill of $40,000 and the right to recognize net income of $12,000 in the current year.

The only other aspect relating to the balance sheet is the disclosure of the minority interests at the balance sheet date. This amount is reflected as a separate item, and **should** appear immediately above the equity section on the balance sheet; this is **because it is not a liability** of the consolidated entity, but the ownership of part of the equity of a subsidiary by the outside shareholders or minority interests.

ILLUSTRATION 6–4
CONSOLIDATING A PARTLY-OWNED SUBSIDIARY ONE YEAR AFTER ACQUISITION

Parent Inc. purchased 60% of the issued share capital of Subsidiary Inc. for $130,000 on January 2, 20X4 when Subsidiary had retained earnings of $50,000. The excess of the price paid for the shares over and above the value of the equity purchased was to be treated as goodwill. There was no write-down of goodwill for impairment in 20X4.

The abbreviated financial statements of the two companies at December 31, 20X4 were as follows:

	Parent	Subsidiary
BALANCE SHEETS		
Assets	$1,220,000	$220,000
Investment in Subsidiary — Note 1	142,000	—
	$1,362,000	$220,000
Liabilities	$ 230,000	$ 50,000
Common Stock	1,000,000	100,000
Retained Earnings	132,000	70,000
	$1,362,000	$220,000
COMBINED INCOME AND RETAINED EARNINGS STATEMENTS		
Sales	$ 890,000	$300,000
Expenses	810,000	280,000
Net Income	80,000	20,000
Share of Income from Subsidiary (60%) — Note 2	12,000	—
	92,000	20,000
Retained Earnings, Beginning of Year	40,000	50,000
Retained Earnings, End of Year	$ 132,000	$ 70,000

ILLUSTRATION 6–4 (CONTINUED)

The consolidation of the financial statements of Parent and its subsidiary company is carried out as follows:

STEP ONE: The "Analysis of the Equity"

	Total	Parent 60%	Minority Interests
At Acquisition:			
Common Stock	$100,000	$ 60,000	$ 40,000
Retained Earnings	50,000	30,000	20,000
		90,000	
Purchase Consideration		130,000	
Goodwill		$ 40,000	
Since Acquisition:			
Net Income for Year	20,000	12,000	8,000
Total Minority Interests			$ 68,000

Notes:

[1] The investment in Subsidiary is reflected using the equity method and consists of the $130,000 purchase price of the shares plus 60% of the net income of Subsidiary for the year. The investment account is, therefore, $130,000 + $12,000 = $142,000.
[2] The net income of Parent is $12,000 because Parent's share of the net income is 60% of $20,000.

STEP TWO: Adjustment and Aggregation

The Consolidated Balance Sheet and Combined Income and Retained Earnings Statement are then prepared by adjusting and aggregating the relevant balances as follows:

	Consolidated	Parent	Subsidiary
BALANCE SHEET			
Assets	$1,440,000	$1,220,000	$220,000
Goodwill	40,000	40,000	—
	$1,480,000	$1,260,000	$220,000
Liabilities	$ 280,000	$ 230,000	$ 50,000
Minority Interests	68,000	68,000	—
Common Stock	1,000,000	1,000,000	—
Retained Earnings	132,000	132,000	—
	$1,480,000	$1,430,000	$ 50,000
COMBINED INCOME AND RETAINED EARNINGS STATEMENT			
Sales	$1,190,000	$ 890,000	$300,000
Less: Expenses	1,090,000	810,000	280,000
	100,000	80,000	20,000
Less: Minority Interests (40%)	8,000	—	8,000
Consolidated Net Income	92,000	$ 80,000	$ 12,000
Retained Earnings at January 1, 20X4	40,000		
Retained Earnings at December 31, 20X4	$ 132,000		

As far as the adjustments to the income statement are concerned, the only difference between the consolidated income statement of a wholly- and partly-owned subsidiary is the deduction of the share of net income for the year that is attributable to the minority interests and, where applicable, the reflection of goodwill charges for impairment. Here, as the total revenues and expenses are included in the consolidated income statement, it is necessary to deduct the minority's share of the net income of the subsidiary from the **total net income** to arrive at the amount attributable to the shareholders of the consolidated group. In Illustration 6–4, this amount was $8,000, being 40% of the total net income of Subsidiary Inc.

As outlined in Chapter Four, the disclosure of any impairment of goodwill is reflected as a separate line item on the consolidated income statement. Two aspects of the disclosure are of importance. The first is that if the company is reporting any gains or losses arising from discontinued operations, the net income must be described as **net income before goodwill charges and discontinued operations**. A similar description is required where there are extraordinary items. Second, the CICA *Handbook* requires that the goodwill charges must be reflected on a net-of-tax basis. However, as the amortization of goodwill **rarely attracts income taxes**, the tax considerations of goodwill are not covered in this text.

REVIEW OF THE CONSOLIDATION PROCESS

At this stage, a review of the consolidation process is not out of place. A considerable number of steps, analyses and techniques have been presented that could have masked the basic purpose of the consolidation process.

The objective of consolidation is to combine the financial statements of a group of companies in a manner that reflects the results of operations, financial position, and (as outlined later) the cash flows, as if it were a single economic entity. To do so, the equity of each subsidiary is analyzed to apportion its equity into its two parts (i.e., that part owned by the parent company and that part owned by the minority interests). On consolidation, the equity owned by the parent company is offset against the purchase consideration to give the goodwill arising on consolidation while that owned by the minority shareholders is reflected on the consolidated balance sheet as the amount owned by outside shareholders. Once this has been done, all that remains is to aggregate the net assets and revenues and expenses of all the companies making up the group so that it reflects the consolidated position of the companies making up the group.

The **consolidated financial statements are presented using the proprietary ownership theory** described in Chapter One. This occurs in three areas. First, as outlined in Illustration 6–4, the consolidated net income is the amount attributable to the parent company after deducting the minority interests' share of the net income from the subsidiary company. Second, the goodwill arising on acquisition represents the amount accruing to the parent company from its purchase of its share of the equity of the subsidiary, and any amounts applicable to the minority interests are totally ignored. Third, the minority interests appearing on the consolidated balance sheet are not reflected as part of the total equity of the consolidated entity, but as a separate item appearing immediately above the consolidated shareholders' equity.

WHERE CERTAIN COMPANIES NEED NOT BE CONSOLIDATED

Section 1590 of the CICA *Handbook* requires that companies must consolidate all their subsidiaries[9] irrespective of their nature. Therefore, where a "parent company-subsidiary company" relationship exists, all companies, **other than those that are wholly-owned subsidiaries of another company**, must present consolidated financial statements to their members.

The only exception is where **control over a subsidiary is temporary**. This occurs where the subsidiary is to be disposed of in the foreseeable future, it is in receivership or subject to bankruptcy proceedings, or where restrictions placed on the operations of a subsidiary are so

---

[9]   CICA *Handbook*, section 1590.

severe that they indicate that control is no longer possible.[10] This latter situation may occur where foreign subsidiaries are subject to exchange control regulations, currency export restrictions, or political unrest.

Despite these requirements, there will be cases where the financial statements of subsidiary companies are not consolidated with those of the parent company: for example, in the case of private or closely held companies where the owners of all voting and non-voting securities have unanimously consented to the presentation of non-consolidated financial statements.

Where consolidation of a subsidiary is **not appropriate**, the subsidiary must be accounted for using the equity method unless, as may be the case with foreign subsidiaries, the existence of control is so doubtful that the cost method should be used or, in extreme cases, the investment may be written off as being worthless. And, where neither consolidation nor the use of the equity method would prove the best method of providing information on the activities of these subsidiary companies, disclosure would presumably be supplemented using one of the following:

(a) Separate financial statements of the subsidiary;
(b) Combined financial statements of similar and nonconsolidated subsidiaries; or
(c) Condensed financial statements provided they include all the relevant information relating to the subsidiaries concerned.

Where a subsidiary is not consolidated with its parent company, this must be drawn to the attention of interested parties giving the reasons why this is the position. Details of the nature of the investment must also be disclosed.

Detailed disclosures are also required where a reporting entity has control over a company (and includes it in its consolidated financial statements) but does not own sufficient voting shares to be able to elect a majority of the members to its board of directors. The same thing applies where the parent owns sufficient voting shares to elect the majority of the members of the board of directors of an investee company. Detailing these disclosures is beyond the scope of this text, and interested readers should refer to section 1590 of the CICA *Handbook*.

SUMMARY

In this chapter, the nature of affiliated groups of companies and the conditions under which control is exercised by one company over another were outlined. Attention is drawn to the fact that control is defined by the CICA as the power to determine the operating, investing and financial activities of an entity. This is normally possible through having the ability to appoint a majority of members to the board of directors of the company concerned.

The method of consolidating the results of operations and financial position of companies affiliated in a "parent company-subsidiary company relationship" is then outlined using the "analysis of equity" approach. This approach is essentially a two-step procedure in which the equity of the investee company is analyzed and apportioned into that part attributable to the parent company and that attributable to the minority or outside interests. The portion of the equity attributable to the parent company is offset against the purchase consideration to give the goodwill arising on consolidation while the portion attributable to the minority interests appears on the consolidated balance sheet. Once the equity has been analyzed, all that remains is to adjust and aggregate the amounts to give the consolidated income statement, statement of retained earnings and consolidated balance sheet.

The chapter emphasizes that the consolidation process is carried out using the financial statements of the companies concerned, and that the process is carried out every time from

---

10   CICA *Handbook*, section 1590.

start to finish as a completely separate exercise. Finally, it looks at the position where the financial statements of subsidiaries need not be consolidated with those of the parent company.

REVIEW QUESTIONS

1. What is the basic principle underlying the consolidation of financial statements?
2. How is control defined by the CICA? Why?
3. Is it necessary for a parent company to hold more than 50% of the voting shares of a company before that company can be regarded as being a subsidiary of the parent company?
4. Why is the extent of control important?
5. Explain what is meant by indirect control.
6. How does goodwill arise on consolidation? Is it any different from other amounts reflected as goodwill on the balance sheet?
7. What two steps are necessary in consolidating financial statements using the "analysis of equity approach"?
8. What is the purpose of "analyzing the equity" of a subsidiary company in the consolidation process?
9. Parent Inc. acquired a 100% interest in Subsidiary Inc. on January 1, 20X2; no goodwill arose on the acquisition. During 20X2, Parent reported net income of $75,000 using the equity method. If Subsidiary had reported net income for the same period of $40,000 and paid a dividend of $25,000, what was the consolidated net income of the group for 20X2?
10. If the financial statements of a subsidiary company are not consolidated with those of its parent company, how are the investment and income from that investment reflected by the parent company?

CASE

CASE 6–1   **Commonwealth Preferences**

Before the entry of the United Kingdom of Great Britain into the European Union, it encouraged trade between countries of the British Commonwealth of Nations by imposing preferential rates of import duties on Commonwealth goods. As far as Canada was concerned, this induced a number of American companies like Ford, Chrysler, General Motors, Goodyear Tire, and others to build manufacturing plants in Canada, that were operated through subsidiary companies in Canada. Exports from these companies to Britain and other Commonwealth countries could, therefore, be classified as Canadian-made and enjoy preferential import duties. And, in gestures designed to allow Canadian citizens to share in the profits and to give these foreign companies a local flavour, they issued some of their stock in Canada.

With the entry of Britain into the European Union, the advantages of goods being Canadian-made in the case of exports to Britain fell away. Even though the Commonwealth preferences remained in the case of exports to such countries as Australia, India, Malaysia, Singapore, etc., the importance of being a Commonwealth exporting country was reduced considerably. As a result of this, most of these companies have purchased the shares issued in Canada from their local shareholders.

Corporate law allows a company to acquire the shares from the minority interests if it already owns 90% or more of the issued share capital or by negotiation if the minority interests own more than 10% of the company's shares. However, the acquisition must be at a fair value. This latter aspect has resulted in many cases of protracted legal action between the companies concerned and the minority shareholders:

for example, the case of Goodyear Canada Inc. in 1993[11] and the more recent case of the Ford Motor Company of Canada Inc., which is before the courts at present.[12]

REQUIRED

Consider what advantages would flow to the parent company from enjoying complete ownership of their Canadian subsidiary companies.

EXERCISES

EXERCISE 6–1

On January 1, 20X2, Pam Inc. acquired an 80% interest in Sam Inc. for $200,000 when Sam was formed. The capital of Sam at formation was 100,000 common shares of no par value that were issued at $2.50 per share. Sam started trading immediately and the net income of Sam for the financial year ended December 31, 20X2 amounted to $120,000. At December 31, 20X2, the equity section of the balance sheet of Pam consisted of common stock of $750,000 and retained earnings of $200,000.

REQUIRED

1. Give the "Investment in Sam" account as it would appear in the ledger of Pam at December 31, 20X2.
2. What amount would appear as the minority interests in Sam on the consolidated balance sheet at December 31, 20X2?
3. Give the shareholders' equity section of the consolidated balance sheet of Pam at December 31, 20X2 if Sam was its only subsidiary.

EXERCISE 6–2

Paul Inc. acquired an 80% interest in Saul Inc. on January 1, 20X5 for $148,000 when Saul had common stock of $120,000 and retained earnings of $45,000. No writedown of goodwill for impairment occurred in 20X5.

The abbreviated balance sheets of Paul and its 80%-owned subsidiary, Saul, at December 31, 20X5 were as follows:

	Paul	Saul
Assets	$350,000	$255,000
Investment in Saul	180,000	—
	$530,000	$255,000
Liabilities	$100,000	$ 50,000
Common Stock	200,000	120,000
Retained Earnings	230,000	85,000
	$530,000	$255,000

REQUIRED

1. From the information given above prepare the consolidated balance sheet of Paul and its subsidiary company at December 31, 20X5.
2. Give the reconstruction of the "Investment in Saul" account at December 31, 20X5.

EXERCISE 6–3

Goodwill of $20,000 arose from the purchase of an 80% interest in Starboard Inc. by Port Inc. on January 1, 20X6. Port accounts for any goodwill arising on acquisition using the impairment method.

The abbreviated income statements of the two companies for the year ended December 31, 20X6 were as follows:

---

11   *The Globe and Mail*, April 19, 1993.
12   *The Globe and Mail*, January 24, 2004.

	Port	Starboard
Sales	$ 600,000	$ 400,000
Cost of Goods Sold	(320,000)	(240,000)
Administration and Selling Expenses	(120,000)	(100,000)
Net Income	160,000	60,000
Share of Net Income from Subsidiary	48,000	—
	208,000	60,000
Retained Earnings at January 1, 20X6	40,000	20,000
	248,000	80,000
Dividends Declared and Paid	100,000	10,000
Retained Earnings at December 31, 20X6	$ 148,000	$ 70,000

REQUIRED

Prepare the combined consolidated income and retained earnings statement of Port for the year ended December 31, 20X6.

EXERCISE 6–4   The abbreviated income statements of Pen Inc. and Scribe Inc. for the year ended December 31, 20X4 were as follows:

	Pen	Scribe
Sales	$ 400,000	$ 250,000
Cost of Goods Sold	(220,000)	(160,000)
Administration and Selling Expenses	(120,000)	(100,000)
Net Income (Loss)	60,000	(10,000)
Share of Net Loss from Subsidiary	(7,500)	—
	52,500	(10,000)
Retained Earnings, January 1, 20X4	40,000	—
Retained Earnings/(Accumulated Loss), December 31, 20X4	$ 92,500	$ (10,000)

Goodwill of $15,000 arose from the purchase by Pen on January 1, 20X4 of a 75% interest in Scribe for $200,000. Pen accounts for goodwill on an impairment basis.

REQUIRED

1. Prepare the combined consolidated income and retained earnings statement of Pen for the year ended December 31, 20X4;
2. Give the "Investment in Scribe" account in the ledger of Pen at December 31, 20X4, from the above information.

EXERCISE 6–5   The following information relates to Purse Inc. and Satchel Inc. for the financial year ended December 31, 20X5:

	Purse	Satchel
Net Income from **Trading** Operations	$400,000	$100,000
Retained Earnings at January 1, 20X5	300,000	—
Dividends Declared on December 31, 20X5	160,000	40,000

Additional Information:

(a) Satchel had been formed and had commenced business operations on January 1, 20X5; and
(b) Purse acquired an 80% interest in Satchel on April 1, 20X5.

REQUIRED

In each of the following cases, what amount would appear as:

1. The goodwill relating to the acquisition appearing on the balance sheet of Purse at December 31, 20X5?
2. The consolidated net income for 20X5?
3. The dividends appearing on the consolidated statement of retained earnings for the year ended December 31, 20X5?
4. The consolidated retained earnings at December 31, 20X5?

EXERCISE 6–6   On January 1, 20X4, Pout Inc. purchased a 75% interest in Smile Inc. for $285,000 when Smile had common stock of $200,000 and retained earnings of $100,000.

At December 31, 20X4, the abbreviated financial statements of the two companies were as follows:

INCOME STATEMENTS	Pout	Smile
Fee Income	$1,300,000	$800,000
Less: Administration Expenses	1,000,000	680,000
Net Operating Income	300,000	120,000
Add: Share of Net Income from Smile	90,000	—
Net Income	390,000	120,000
Retained Earnings at January 1, 20X4	700,000	100,000
	1,090,000	220,000
Less: Dividends Declared and Paid	300,000	80,000
Retained Earnings at December 31, 20X4	$ 790,000	$140,000

BALANCE SHEETS		
Current Assets	$ 555,000	$220,000
Investment in Smile	315,000	—
Capital Assets (Net)	677,000	260,000
	$1,547,000	$480,000
Current Liabilities	$ 157,000	$140,000
Common Stock	600,000	200,000
Retained Earnings	790,000	140,000
	$1,547,000	$480,000

REQUIRED

Prepare the consolidated balance sheet and combined income and retained earnings statement of Pout for the year ended December 31, 20X4.

EXERCISE 6–7   On January 1, 20X4, Plunge Inc. purchased a 60% interest in Spill Inc. for $1,900,000. At the date of acquisition, Spill had common stock of $2,000,000 and retained earnings of $800,000. At December 31, 20X4, the goodwill arising on acquisition was considered to be fairly valued.

The abbreviated financial statements of the two companies at December 31, 20X4 were as follows:

INCOME AND RETAINED EARNINGS STATEMENTS	Plunge	Spill
Sales	$10,000,000	$6,000,000
Less Operating Expenses	8,500,000	4,800,000
Net Income from Operations	1,500,000	1,200,000
Share of Net Income from Spill	720,000	—
Net Income	2,220,000	1,200,000
Retained Earnings at January 1, 20X4	1,100,000	800,000
	3,320,000	2,000,000
Dividends Paid (December 5)	500,000	400,000
Retained Earnings at December 31, 20X4	$ 2,820,000	$1,600,000

BALANCE SHEETS	Plunge	Spill
Current Assets	$ 4,420,000	$1,400,000
Investment in Spill	2,380,000	—
Capital Assets (Net)	6,600,000	3,400,000
	$13,400,000	$4,800,000
Current Liabilities	$ 3,080,000	$1,200,000
Common Stock	7,500,000	2,000,000
Retained Earnings	2,820,000	1,600,000
	$13,400,000	$4,800,000

REQUIRED

Prepare the consolidated income and retained earnings statement and consolidated balance sheet of Plunge for 20X4.

EXERCISE 6–8   On January 1, 20X3, Posture Inc. purchased a 75% interest in Stature Inc. for $265,000 when Stature had common stock of $200,000 and retained earnings of $100,000.

At December 31, 20X3, the abbreviated and combined income and retained earnings statements of the two companies were as follows:

	Posture	Stature
Fee Income	$1,200,000	$680,000
Less: Administration Expenses	800,000	560,000
	400,000	120,000
Add: Share of Net Income from Stature	90,000	—
	490,000	120,000
Retained Earnings at January 1, 20X3	710,000	100,000
	1,200,000	220,000
Less: Dividends Declared and Paid	200,000	60,000
Retained Earnings at December 31, 20X3	$1,000,000	$160,000

REQUIRED

Prepare the consolidated and combined income and retained earnings statement of Posture for the year ended December 31, 20X3 from the information given.

PROBLEMS

PROBLEM 6–1   Pill Inc. acquired the entire issued share capital of Swallow Inc. for $1-million on January 1, 20X3, the date on which Swallow Inc. was formed. The abbreviated financial statements of the two companies at December 31, 20X3 were:

COMBINED INCOME AND RETAINED EARNINGS STATEMENTS	Pill	Swallow
Sales	$12,400,000	$7,500,000
Administration and Other Expenses	9,300,000	6,100,000
Net Operating Income	3,100,000	1,400,000
Share of Net Income from Swallow	1,400,000	—
Net Income	4,500,000	1,400,000
Less: Dividends Paid	2,000,000	800,000
	2,500,000	600,000
Retained Earnings at January 1, 20X3	2,500,000	—
Retained Earnings at December 31, 20X3	$ 5,000,000	$ 600,000

BALANCE SHEETS	Pill	Swallow
Cash	$ 800,000	$ 200,000
Accounts Receivable	1,220,000	870,000
Loan to Swallow	900,000	—
Inventory	3,080,000	480,000
Investment in Swallow	1,600,000	—
Plant and Equipment (Net)	3,400,000	1,800,000
	$11,000,000	$3,350,000
Accounts Payable	$ 800,000	$ 850,000
Loan from Pill	—	900,000
Common Stock	5,200,000	1,000,000
Retained Earnings	5,000,000	600,000
	$11,000,000	$3,350,000

REQUIRED

Prepare the consolidated balance sheet and combined income and retained earnings statement for 20X3 from the abbreviated financial statements of the two companies at December 31, 20X3.

PROBLEM 6–2 The financial statements of Pave Inc. and Seal Inc. at December 31, 20X5 were as follows:

COMBINED INCOME AND RETAINED EARNINGS STATEMENTS	Pave	Seal
Sales	$1,700,000	$900,000
Cost of Goods Sold	$1,100,000	$500,000
Administration Expenses	200,000	120,000
Depreciation Expense	120,000	80,000
	$1,420,000	$700,000
Net Income from Operations	$ 280,000	$200,000
Share of Net Income from Seal	147,000	—
Net Income for Year	427,000	200,000
Retained Earnings, January 1, 20X5	400,000	100,000
	827,000	300,000
Dividends Paid	200,000	80,000
Retained Earnings, December 31, 20X5	$ 627,000	$220,000

BALANCE SHEETS		
Cash	$ 40,000	$ 20,000
Accounts Receivable	550,000	190,000
Inventory	280,000	210,000
Investment in Seal	597,000	—
Land	—	80,000
Plant and Equipment (Net)	1,060,000	370,000
	$2,527,000	$870,000
Accounts Payable	$ 400,000	$150,000
Common Stock	1,500,000	500,000
Retained Earnings	627,000	220,000
	$2,527,000	$870,000

You are informed that:

(a) Pave acquired a 75% interest in Seal on January 1, 20X5 for $510,000.
(b) Following a review in 20X5 of the value of goodwill arising on acquisition, an impairment loss of 5% was recognized.

REQUIRED

Prepare the consolidated income and retained earnings statement and consolidated balance sheet of Pave for 20X5.

PROBLEM 6–3

Prepare Inc. had purchased 80% of the issued share capital of Start Inc. for $3-million on January 1, 20X4 when Start had common stock of $2-million and retained earnings of $750,000. Following a review of the value of goodwill carried out in 20X4, an impairment loss of $40,000 was recognized.

The abbreviated financial statements of Prepare and Start at December 31, 20X4 were as follows:

COMBINED INCOME AND RETAINED EARNINGS STATEMENTS	Prepare	Start
Sales	$ 9,800,000	$6,800,000
Administration and Other Expenses	7,940,000	6,350,000
Net Income	1,860,000	450,000
Share of Net Income from Start	320,000	—
	2,180,000	450,000
Less: Dividends Declared and Paid	1,000,000	300,000
	1,180,000	150,000
Retained Earnings at January 1, 20X4	2,000,000	750,000
Retained Earnings at December 31, 20X4	$ 3,180,000	$ 900,000

BALANCE SHEETS	Prepare	Start
Assets	$ 7,460,000	$3,500,000
Investment in Start	3,080,000	—
	$10,540,000	$3,500,000
Liabilities	$ 1,360,000	$ 600,000
Common Stock	6,000,000	2,000,000
Retained Earnings	3,180,000	900,000
	$10,540,000	$3,500,000

REQUIRED

Give the consolidated balance sheet and combined income and retained earnings statement for Prepare for 20X4.

PROBLEM 6–4

The abbreviated financial statements of Penalty Inc. and Sanction Inc. at December 31, 20X4 were as follows:

COMBINED INCOME AND RETAINED EARNINGS STATEMENTS	Penalty	Sanction
Sales	$2,500,000	$ 900,000
Cost of Goods Sold	$1,200,000	$ 330,000
Expenses	400,000	220,000
	$1,600,000	$ 550,000
Net Operating Income	$ 900,000	$ 350,000
Share of Net Income from Sanction	265,000	—
Net Income	1,165,000	350,000
Retained Earnings at January 1, 20X4	800,000	500,000
	1,965,000	850,000
Dividends Declared and Paid	300,000	125,000
Retained Earnings at December 31, 20X4	$1,665,000	$ 725,000

BALANCE SHEETS

	Penalty	Sanction
Current Assets	$ 850,000	$ 800,000
Investment in Sanction	1,065,000	—
Plant and Equipment (Net)	1,250,000	755,000
	$3,165,000	$1,555,000
Current Liabilities	$ 500,000	$ 280,000
Common Stock	1,000,000	550,000
Retained Earnings	1,665,000	725,000
	$3,165,000	$1,555,000

On January 1, 20X4, Penalty had acquired an 80% interest in Sanction for the sum of $900,000 when Sanction had common stock of $550,000. Following a review for impairment carried out during the year, Penalty wrote down goodwill arising on consolidation by 25%.

REQUIRED

Prepare the consolidated financial statements of Penalty at December 31, 20X4.

PROBLEM 6–5   On January 1, 20X5, Pot Inc. had acquired a 75% interest in Skillet Inc. for $550,000 when the issued share capital of Skillet was 60,000 common shares of no par value that had been issued for $10 per share.

The abbreviated balance sheets and combined statements of income and retained earnings of the two companies at December 31, 20X5 were as follows:

COMBINED INCOME AND RETAINED EARNINGS STATEMENTS

	Pot	Skillet
Sales	$ 800,000	$180,000
Cost of Goods Sold	$ 580,000	$110,000
Operating Expenses	40,000	30,000
	$ 620,000	$140,000
Net Operating Income	$ 180,000	$ 40,000
Share of Net Income from Skillet	27,500	—
Net Income	207,500	40,000
Retained Earnings at January 1, 20X5	46,800	100,000
	254,300	140,000
Dividends Paid (December 2)	40,000	8,000
Retained Earnings at December 31, 20X5	$ 214,300	$132,000

BALANCE SHEETS

Cash	$ 60,000	$ 10,000
Accounts Receivable	210,000	590,000
Inventory	133,000	272,000
Investment in Skillet	571,500	—
Plant and Equipment (Net)	590,000	110,000
	$1,564,500	$982,000
Current Liabilities	$ 350,200	$250,000
Common Stock	1,000,000	600,000
Retained Earnings	214,300	132,000
	$1,564,500	$982,000

REQUIRED

Prepare the consolidated financial statements of Pot for 20X5 on the assumption that the goodwill arising on consolidation was written down for impairment by 10%.

PROBLEM 6–6

On January 1, 20X4, Prize Inc. purchased a 75% interest in Special Inc. for $2.35-million when Special had common stock of $3.2-million and an accumulated loss of $200,000.

The following abbreviated income statements and balance sheets of Prize and Special for the year ended December 31, 20X4 were as follows:

INCOME STATEMENTS	Prize	Special
Sales	$ 5,000,000	$ 2,700,000
Cost of Goods Sold	(3,200,000)	(1,800,000)
Administration and Selling Expenses	(1,200,000)	(1,000,000)
Net Income (Loss)	600,000	(100,000)
Share of Net Loss from Special	(85,000)	—
	515,000	(100,000)
Retained Earnings, January 1, 20X4	500,000	(200,000)
Retained Earnings/(Accumulated Loss), December 31, 20X4	$ 1,015,000	$ (300,000)

BALANCE SHEETS		
Current Assets	$ 1,550,000	$ 1,000,000
Investment in Special	2,265,000	—
Capital Assets (Net)	3,000,000	2,850,000
	$ 6,815,000	$ 3,850,000
Current Liabilities	$ 800,000	$ 950,000
Common Stock (no par value shares of $1 each)	5,000,000	3,200,000
Retained Earnings/Accumulated Loss	1,015,000	(300,000)
	$ 6,815,000	$ 3,850,000

During 20X4, Prize recognized an impairment loss of goodwill of $10,000.

REQUIRED

1. Give the "Investment in Special" account in the ledger of Prize.
2. Prepare the consolidated balance sheet and combined income and retained earnings statement of Prize for the year ended December 31, 20X4.

PROBLEM 6–7

You are provided with the following abbreviated financial statements of Preach Inc. and Sermon Inc.:

COMBINED INCOME AND RETAINED EARNINGS STATEMENTS	Preach	Sermon
Sales	$ 4,000,000	$1,600,000
Cost of Goods Sold	$ 2,800,000	$1,100,000
Operating Expenses	400,000	300,000
	$ 3,200,000	$1,400,000
Net Operating Income	$ 800,000	$ 200,000
Share of Net Income from Sermon	148,000	—
Net Income	948,000	200,000
Retained Earnings at January 1, 20X5	468,000	200,000
Retained Earnings at December 31, 20X5	$ 1,416,000	$ 400,000

BALANCE SHEETS		
Current Assets	$ 4,000,000	$ 700,000
Investment in Sermon	1,216,000	—
Plant and Equipment (Net)	8,200,000	1,100,000
	$13,416,000	$1,800,000
Current Liabilities	$ 2,000,000	$ 400,000
Common Stock	10,000,000	1,000,000
Retained Earnings	1,416,000	400,000
	$13,416,000	$1,800,000

Additional Information:

(a) Preach had acquired an 80% interest in Sermon on January 1, 20X4 for $1-million when Sermon had retained earnings of $100,000.

(b) Net income of $100,000 was earned by Sermon in 20X4, which was considered insufficient to pay a dividend.

(c) Goodwill impairment losses of $12,000 were recognized in both 20X4 and 20X5; and

(d) The assets and liabilities of Sermon were fairly valued at the date of acquisition.

REQUIRED

Prepare the consolidated balance sheet and income statement of Preach at December 31, 20X5.

7 Consolidations: The Completion of the Basic Consolidation Process

LEARNING OBJECTIVES

After studying this chapter you should be able to:

1. Understand the nature and division of the earnings and dividends of subsidiary companies into their pre-acquisition and post-acquisition portions on consolidation;
2. Adjust the value of assets to their fair market value at the date of acquisition and their subsequent amortization;
3. Eliminate management fees and intercompany interest between affiliated companies;
4. Recognize the issues relating to the consolidation of foreign subsidiaries and the nature of "push-down" accounting; and
5. Prepare the consolidated statement of cash flows.

THE SCOPE OF THE CHAPTER

In the previous chapter, the consolidation of the financial statements of wholly- and partly-owned subsidiaries was illustrated using examples in which the consolidation process was relatively straightforward. The acquisition of the controlling interest was at the beginning of the year and the assets and liabilities of the investee company were considered to be fairly valued at the date of acquisition. In this chapter, the consolidation process is outlined where the acquisition of the controlling interest in a subsidiary takes place during the financial year, and where fair market values are assigned to the assets and liabilities of the subsidiary at the date of acquisition. And, to complete the basic consolidation process, the preparation of the consolidated statement of cash flows is explained and outlined.

THE TREATMENT OF PRIOR YEARS EARNINGS

The Apportionment into Pre- and Post-Acquisition Earnings

Except in those cases where a controlling interest in a company is acquired as the result of a share issue or on the day the subsidiary is formed, the acquisition of a controlling interest in a company seldom occurs on the first day of a subsidiary's financial year. Where this occurs, it is necessary to apportion the net income of the subsidiary company into pre- and post-acquisition earnings.

ILLUSTRATION 7–1
ACQUISITION OF A SUBSIDIARY COMPANY DURING THE YEAR

On May 1, 20X4, Parent Inc. purchased a 75% interest in Subsidiary Inc. for $400,000. At December 31, 20X3, the balance sheet of Subsidiary reflected common stock of $300,000 and retained earnings of $140,000.

Financial statements of Subsidiary were not prepared to reflect the position at May 1, 20X4. Net income of $180,000 was, however, reflected by the income statement of Subsidiary for the financial year ended December 31, 20X4. No dividends were declared or paid by Subsidiary during 20X4 and the net income accrued evenly over the year.

The Analysis of Equity of Subsidiary at December 31, 20X4 would be as follows:

	Total	Parent (75%)	Minority Interests
At Acquisition:			
Common Stock	$300,000	$225,000	$ 75,000
Retained Earnings at December 31, 20X3	140,000	105,000	35,000
Net Income for 20X4 — 4 months	60,000	45,000	15,000
		375,000	
Purchase Consideration		400,000	
Goodwill		$ 25,000	
Since Acquisition:			
Net Income for 20X4 — 8 months	120,000	$ 90,000	30,000
Total Minority Interests			$155,000

Earnings arising before the date of acquisition form part of the equity purchased and must be reflected as prior earnings in the analysis of equity. This also applies to that portion of the current net income of the subsidiary earned up to the date of acquisition. In these cases, the net income (or loss) earned up to the date of acquisition is capitalized as part of the equity acquired and the balance is treated as post-acquisition net income.

The rule that is applied is that **where financial statements are prepared at the date of acquisition, those financial statements are used to determine the earnings up to the date of acquisition. Where financial statements are not prepared at the date of acquisition, the earnings may be apportioned on a daily or monthly basis provided cyclical trading patterns or other relevant conditions are taken into account.**

The apportionment of the retained earnings and current net income of an investee company where a controlling interest has been acquired during the year is outlined in Illustration 7–1. In this case, the acquisition took place four months after the beginning of the financial year, and the current net income of $180,000 was apportioned into pre- and post-acquisition earnings on a monthly basis in the ratio of 4/12ths to 8/12ths (i.e., $60,000) capitalized as pre-acquisition net income, and $120,000 is treated as post-acquisition net income.

The Treatment of Dividends

Where dividends are declared and paid by a subsidiary company, they are accounted for as a distribution of earnings by the subsidiary company. The rule is that, because **dividends are always considered to have been paid out of current earnings**, the dividends are taken as having been paid out of the net income earned in the period in which they are declared.[1] **Where insufficient net income has been earned to cover the dividends, they are**

---

[1] As soon as a dividend is declared by a company, a contract comes into being between the company and its shareholders and, if the company subsequently fails to pay the dividend, the shareholders can take the company to court to enforce the payment of that dividend. It is, therefore, the date on which the dividend is declared and *not* the date on which the dividend is paid, which is of importance.

ILLUSTRATION 7–2
THE "SINCE ACQUISITION" ANALYSIS OF EQUITY OF A SUBSIDIARY

Parent company acquired an 80% interest in a subsidiary on April 1, 20X2. The net income and dividends paid by the subsidiary for the three years ended December 31, 20X2 through 20X4 were as follows:

	20X2	20X3	20X4
Net Income	$20,000	$40,000	$50,000
Dividends Declared and Paid (In November)	10,000	20,000	25,000

If the financial statements of the subsidiary were to be consolidated with those of the parent company at December 31, 20X4, the **since acquisition** portion of the "Analysis of Equity" of the subsidiary at December 31, 20X4 would have been as follows:

	Total	Parent (80%)	Minority Interests
Since Acquisition:			
Net Income for 20X2 — 9 months	15,000	12,000	3,000
Less Dividends — 20X2	(10,000)	(8,000)	(2,000)
Net Income for 20X3 — 12 months	40,000	32,000	8,000
Less: Dividends — 20X3	(20,000)	(16,000)	(4,000)
Net Income for 20X4 — 12 months	50,000	40,000	10,000
Less: Dividends 20X4	(25,000)	(20,000)	(5,000)
Total Minority Interests			??

taken as having been paid out of the net income of prior periods. This usually means that they are paid out of retained earnings.

This treatment is explained in Illustration 7–2 where the net income earned and dividends paid **since** the date of acquisition are analyzed individually in the "since acquisition" section of the analysis of equity. This shows that, in each case, the dividends are deducted from the net income to which they relate.

The reason for detailing and analyzing the net income and dividends in the manner outlined in the analysis of equity in Illustration 7–2 is to ensure that the parent company's share of the net income and dividends are treated properly in the consolidation process.

The share of net income from the subsidiary reflects the amount of net income that accrues to the parent company from the subsidiary. The dividends received from the subsidiary merely reflect the amount of the subsidiary's net income **actually paid** to the parent company. The difference between the share of net income from the subsidiary recorded by the parent company and the dividends paid (as recorded in the investment account) reflects the share of earnings of the subsidiary that have not **yet** been paid over to the parent company.

To clarify the position, it should be noted that the net increase in retained earnings recorded in the investment account (i.e., the share of net income less dividends received) reflects the parent company's share of the undistributed post-acquisition retained earnings (i.e., since acquisition) of the subsidiary. On the other hand, the parent company's share of net income from the subsidiary, when added to the net income of the parent company, gives the consolidated net income of the group that is available for distribution as a dividend. This is outlined in Illustration 7–2, where the detailed analysis of the net income and dividends paid shows that the increase in the consolidated retained earnings is $84,000 (i.e., $12,000 + $32,000 + $40,000), while the investment account would have been increased by only $40,000 — the net income of $84,000 (i.e., as given above) less the dividends of $44,000 (i.e., $8,000 + $16,000 + $20,000).

If, however, only the post-acquisition retained earnings of the subsidiary of $50,000 (i.e., the total net income since acquisition of $105,000 [i.e., $15,000 + $40,000 + $50,000] less the total dividends paid during this period of $55,000 [i.e., $10,000 + $20,000 + $25,000]) appearing on the income statement of the subsidiary had been analyzed, it would have given the correct increase in the investment account of $40,000 (i.e., 80% of $50,000). However, it would have understated the consolidated retained earnings by the same amount (i.e., $84,000 [80% of $105,000] – $44,000 [80% of $55,000]). It is, therefore, necessary to record and analyze the net income earned and dividends paid by the subsidiary individually from the date of acquisition.

The Treatment of Pre-Acquisition Goodwill and Future Taxes

The CICA *Handbook* requires that any goodwill or future income tax assets and liabilities recognized by a subsidiary prior to the company becoming a subsidiary must be ignored in the preparation of the consolidated financial statements.[2] As a result, a zero balance should be allocated to these items should they appear on the balance sheet of a subsidiary at the date of acquisition.

ACCOUNTING FOR PRE-ACQUISITION DIVIDENDS

In the previous section it was pointed out that **the retained earnings of a subsidiary company were capitalized at the date of acquisition and treated as part of the equity acquired.** It is, therefore, only the net income earned since the date of acquisition that may be recognized by the parent company as income from the subsidiary company.

From time to time, however, dividends are declared and paid out of earnings earned prior to the acquisition by the parent company of an interest in the subsidiary. These dividends are known as **pre-acquisition dividends and represent the repayment of part of the cost of the investment in the subsidiary company**. They represent a repayment of both part of the purchase consideration and part of the pre-acquisition earnings of the subsidiary company. Where all or most of the cash holdings of a subsidiary are paid out as pre-acquisition dividends, the practice is called "dividend stripping".

The accounting treatment in these cases is that the investment in a subsidiary company must be credited with any pre-acquisition dividends received. For example, assume that a parent company acquired a 75% interest in a subsidiary on January 1, 20X4 for $500,000 when the subsidiary had common stock of $300,000 and retained earnings of $100,000. If, on January 2, 20X4, the subsidiary declared a dividend of $80,000 payable on January 10, 20X4 out of its net income earned prior to acquisition, this amount would be treated as a reduction in the purchase price of the investment by the parent company as follows:

Investment in Subsidiary Inc.

20X4					
Jan. 1	Purchase Consideration	500,000			500,000
10	Pre-Acquisition Dividend		60,000		440,000

It is necessary to treat pre-acquisition dividends separately in the analysis of equity and in the investment account. This is because the payment of a pre-acquisition dividend affects any capital gain or loss arising on the sale of part or the entire investment in the subsidiary at some later date. This aspect of pre-acquisition dividends is considered later in Chapter Twelve.

The reduction of the purchase consideration by the receipt of any pre-acquisition dividends applies equally to any investments in companies over which the investor company can

2 CICA *Handbook*, section 1581.

ILLUSTRATION 7–3
THE ABSENCE OF ANY EFFECT ON THE GOODWILL IN CASES WHERE
A PRE-ACQUISITION DIVIDEND IS PAID

An 80% interest in a company having common stock of $100,000 and retained earnings of $40,000 was acquired on January 1, 20X5. If the purchase consideration was $120,000, the goodwill would remain at $8,000 irrespective of whether a pre-acquisition dividend of $30,000 is paid on January 2. This is reflected below in the analysis of the subsidiary company's equity showing the position where there has been a payment of a pre-acquisition dividend and where no such dividend has been paid.

	Payment of a Pre-Acquisition Dividend (80%)		No Payment of a Pre-Acquisition Dividend (80%)
Common Stock		$80,000	$ 80,000
Retained Earnings	$ 32,000		32,000
Less: Pre-Acquisition Dividend	24,000	8,000	—
		88,000	112,000
Purchase Consideration	120,000		120,000
Less: Pre-Acquisition Dividend	24,000	96,000	—
Goodwill		$ 8,000	$ 8,000

exert significant influence. This is because, as outlined above, dividends of this nature represent a repayment of part of the purchase consideration.

The payment of a pre-acquisition dividend does not, however, affect the amount of goodwill arising on acquisition. This is because the reduction in the purchase consideration is offset by a proportionate reduction in the share of the retained earnings attributable to the parent company at acquisition in the analysis of equity, and the amount of goodwill remains unchanged. This situation is reflected in Illustration 7–3.

As far as the payment of a dividend is concerned, the payment of any amount in excess of the net income for the year must be considered as having been paid out of retained earnings earned in prior years. However, where the retained earnings since acquisition have been exhausted by the payment of dividends, or where there are no retained earnings since acquisition out of which the dividend could have been paid, any amount paid out as a dividend in excess of the available since-acquisition earnings must be treated as a pre-acquisition dividend. Once again, this applies equally to investments over which significant influence is exercised.

It is also necessary to distinguish between pre-acquisition dividends and ordinary dividends in the investment account maintained on the equity basis. This is important because on the sale of part of the investment, the proceeds will have to be apportioned between the cost of the investment and the amount included in the retained earnings brought forward and available for distribution as a dividend. This aspect is, however, dealt with in Chapter Twelve in the section dealing with disclosure of transactions involving the acquisition and sale of investments in subsidiary companies.

RECOGNITION OF THE TRADING OPERATIONS IN THE YEAR OF ACQUISITION OR DISPOSAL

Where a controlling interest in a subsidiary is acquired during the year, revenues and expenses relating to that company **can only be recognized by the acquiring company from the date of acquisition.** There is also only a partial recognition of the trading operations of a subsidiary in the year in which a subsidiary is sold. This is because the purchase method of accounting for business acquisitions only recognizes ownership interests from the date of acquisition or, in the case of a disposal of an interest in a subsidiary, up to the date of sale. This is covered by the

ILLUSTRATION 7–4
RECOGNITION OF THE TRADING OPERATIONS OF SUBSIDIARIES ACQUIRED DURING THE YEAR

On July 1, 20X3, Pep Inc. purchased an 80% interest in See Inc. No goodwill arose on acquisition. The abbreviated income statements of the two companies for 20X3 were as follows:

	Pep	See
Sales	$650,000	$290,000
Cost of Goods Sold	$370,000	$180,000
Administration Expenses	65,000	60,000
	$435,000	$240,000
Operating Net Income	$215,000	$ 50,000
Share of Net Income from See ($50,000 × 80% × 6/12)	20,000	—
	235,000	50,000
Retained Earnings at January 1, 20X3	84,000	40,000
	319,000	90,000
Less: Dividends Paid (November 15)	200,000	20,000
Retained Earnings at December 31, 20X3	$119,000	$ 70,000

The income statement drawn up to recognize the trading operations of See acquired during the year would be as follows if revenues and expenses occurred evenly throughout the year:

	Consolidated	Pep	See (6/12)
Sales	$795,000	$650,000	$145,000
Cost of Goods Sold	$460,000	$370,000	$ 90,000
Administration Expenses	95,000	65,000	30,000
	$555,000	$435,000	$120,000
Net Operating Income	$240,000	$215,000	$ 25,000
Less: Minority Interests (20%)	5,000	—	5,000
Consolidated Net Income	235,000	$215,000	$ 20,000
Retained Earnings at January 1, 20X3	84,000		
	319,000		
Less: Dividends Paid (November 15)	200,000		
Retained Earnings at December 31, 20X3	$119,000		

CICA *Handbook*,[3] which states, *inter alia*, that only post-acquisition and pre-disposal income in a subsidiary is included in consolidated net income.

An illustration of the recognition of the post-acquisition trading activities of a subsidiary is provided in Illustration 7–4, which shows that only the trading activities of the subsidiary since acquisition are included in the consolidated income statement.

It should also be noted that in those cases where the net income of a consolidated subsidiary is made up of both operating income and extraordinary items, it is **only that proportion of the extraordinary items applicable to the parent company that is disclosed separately on the consolidated income statement**. The materiality of the proportionate amount of the extraordinary item from the subsidiary is, of course, the deciding factor in deciding whether or not the amount would be disclosed as a separate item. Where any impairment in the value of goodwill has occurred, this write-down is reflected in full in the income statement in the year in which the impairment is recognized.

---

[3] Section 1600.

THE VALUATION OF ASSETS AT THEIR FAIR MARKET VALUE

The purchase method of accounting for longterm investments requires that assets and liabilities must be valued at their fair market value when acquired. To comply with this requirement in the consolidation process, fair market values must be assigned to the assets and liabilities of the subsidiary company at the date of acquisition.

This is necessary for two reasons. First, the assets and liabilities of the subsidiary company should be incorporated into the consolidated financial statements at a realistic figure and, second, the value of the assets and liabilities acquired should be correctly valued on acquisition to establish the correct amount for goodwill. However, it should be noted that these "fair market value adjustments" only apply to the **parent company's interests** in the subsidiary company and not to the minority interests.[4]

This peculiarity is due to the fact that consolidated financial statements are presented using **the proprietary ownership theory**. The situation is that even though assets purchased should be recorded at their purchase price, this principle is modified by only recognizing the parent company's share of the adjustments in value. This is justified on the grounds that the interests of the minority should be ignored because they can exert little or no influence over the affairs of the parent company and the shares held by them should be valued at a lower amount than those held by the majority. No matter how realistic an assessment of the position this may be, it represents **illogical thought** on the topic. It just does not make sense to increase the value of an asset for consolidation purposes by, say 60% of its increase in value, because the company is 60% controlled by another company. However, this is the prevailing position.

Recognition of these adjustments in the consolidation process is carried out by adjusting the equity in the analysis of equity by the differences between the fair market value and the book values of the assets and liabilities acquired. These differences in value are added to or subtracted from, as the case may be, the value of the assets or liabilities to which they apply when being combined with those of the parent company on the consolidated balance sheet. And, if the revalued assets are depreciable assets, the increases in value are amortized, as with any other similar assets.

This treatment is fully explained in Illustration 7–5, which shows that the fair market value adjustment of $10,000 is apportioned to the parent company in proportion to the interest acquired. In this case, as an 80% interest was acquired, only the parent company's share of the increase of $8,000 is added to the asset values on the consolidated balance sheet. This adjustment reduces the amount determined as goodwill by $8,000. And, because the revalued equipment is depreciable, additional amortization at the rate of 20% per year would be recognized on the consolidated income statement and by increasing the accumulated amortization on the consolidated balance sheet. The additional fair market values are, therefore, written off over their expected lives against the income of the parent company.

The adjustments to the fair market values of the net assets acquired apply to all items recognized by the companies concerned. They may, therefore, consist of differences in the value of capital assets, longterm leases, current assets like inventories and accounts receivable, or liabilities like bonds. The adjustments for these amounts become more complicated as we move through the various aspects of the consolidation process. It is, therefore, often difficult to establish whether the over- and under-valuation of assets or liabilities should be added or subtracted from the equity acquired.

---

[4] Section 1600 of the CICA *Handbook* states that the minority interest's share of the subsidiary's assets and liabilities is based on their book or carrying values and not on their fair market values.

ILLUSTRATION 7–5
THE ASSIGNMENT OF FAIR MARKET VALUES TO ASSETS

Parent Inc. purchased an 80% interest in Subsidiary Inc. for $80,000 on January 1, 20X5. At the date of acquisition, Subsidiary had common stock of $50,000 and retained earnings of $20,000. Certain equipment having a five-year additional life was undervalued by $10,000 on the date of acquisition.

The adjustments to take the fair market value adjustment to the value of the equipment into account in the analysis of equity are given below:

	Total	Parent	Minority Interests
Common Stock	$50,000	$40,000	$10,000
Retained Earnings	20,000	16,000	4,000
Fair Market Value Adjustment — Equipment	10,000	8,000	—
		64,000	
Purchase Consideration		80,000	
Goodwill		$16,000	
Minority Interests			$14,000

The adjustments required to recognize this increase in the fair market value of the equipment of $8,000 (i.e., 80% of $10,000) would be, first, to increase the cost of equipment by $8,000. Second would be to charge amortization on the increased value of the equipment in the consolidated income statement by increasing both the amortization expense of Parent by $1,600 (i.e., 20% of $8,000) and increasing the accumulated amortization on equipment by the same amount.

The easiest way to overcome this problem is to **return to basics and use the accounting equation of Assets = Liabilities + Shareholders' Equity to establish the adjustment**. For example, if bonds issued by the subsidiary are undervalued by $40,000, the adjustment is to subtract the $40,000 from shareholders' equity in the analysis of equity and increase the bonds by an equal amount. This would be established by adjusting the accounting equation by adding $40,000 to the liabilities and subtracting $40,000 from the shareholders' equity. Similarly, an increase in the value of inventories of $20,000 would be adjusted by adding $20,000 to the equity acquired to keep the accounting equation in balance.

It is important to note that because all assets must be recorded at their fair market values, **any accumulated amortization on the capital assets of the subsidiary at the date of acquisition must be ignored**. The capital assets of the subsidiary are, therefore, included in the consolidated financial statements at the fair market values assigned to them on the date of acquisition. **Any amortization is calculated on the fair market values from that date onwards**. However, in accordance with the overall philosophy of this text, this complication is ignored in all illustrations, exercises and problems except where they specifically relate to the issues being considered.

ELIMINATION OF MANAGEMENT FEES AND INTERCOMPANY INTEREST

Parent companies often handle certain administrative duties for their subsidiaries for which they charge a management fee. This also applies to interest charged on intercompany loans. These amounts are reflected as revenues on the income statement of the parent company and as expenses by the subsidiaries. On consolidation these amounts are offset against each other to ensure that the operating results of the group of companies are not distorted by the inclusion of these intercompany transfers. This is carried out by entering the amounts received or expensed against the individual companies on a single line in the consolidated workings so that a nil balance is extended into the consolidated column.

EXTRAORDINARY ITEMS AND DISCONTINUED OPERATIONS

In terms of section 1520 of the CICA *Handbook*, extraordinary items[5] and discontinued operations must be reflected separately and net of taxes on the income statement below the net income derived from operations. **Where these items appear on the financial statement of a parent company, they are presented in full** on the consolidated income statement below the consolidated net income derived from operations after the deduction of the minority's interests therein. **If, however, they appear on a subsidiary's income statement, they must be apportioned** in the analysis of equity **between the parent company and the minority interests**, and it is only the parent company's proportionate share that appears on the consolidated income statement.

For example, assume that during the year, a 60%-owned subsidiary company incurred an after tax loss of $292,000 on discontinuing certain operations and had property expropriated at a gain of $228,000 after deduction of applicable taxes (i.e., as a capital gain). In such a case, the consolidated income statement would recognize 60% of the loss and 60% of the extraordinary gain and be presented along the following lines:

Consolidated Net Income before Discontinued Operations and Extraordinary Items	$1,845,000
Less: Loss from Discontinued Operations (60% × $292,000)	175,200
Consolidated Net Income before Extraordinary Items	1,669,800
Add: Extraordinary Item (60% × $228,000)	136,800
Consolidated Net Income for Year	$1,806,600

CONSOLIDATING FOREIGN SUBSIDIARIES

The consolidation of foreign subsidiaries is required except in those cases **where control is expected to be only temporary or where there is doubt regarding the control of the subsidiary.** The extent to which control actually exists over foreign subsidiaries is of the utmost importance because where a foreign subsidiary is subject to currency exchange control regulations and severe restrictions apply to the transfer of funds to Canada, the requirement of control of being able to determine the operating and financing policies of the subsidiary may not apply. Similarly, the future sale of the shares in the foreign subsidiary or the realization of the foreign assets may also be subject to governmental control. Great care should, therefore, be exercised in deciding whether or not these subsidiaries should be consolidated.

As outlined earlier, the position is that where the parent company has the ability to control the strategic operating, investing and financing policies of the foreign subsidiary, consolidation is required. **Where there is doubt that control actually exists but the parent company still exercises significant influence over the foreign subsidiary, the equity method should be used. Where even the ability to exercise significant influence is absent, the investment in the foreign subsidiary should be written down to its realizable value and classified as a portfolio investment. And, where there is doubt that the investment still exists, it should be written off completely.**

Accounting for foreign subsidiaries requires that where the financial statements of foreign subsidiaries are consolidated, or combined using the equity method, with those of the parent company, they must first be converted into Canadian GAAP. This aspect is covered later in Chapter Sixteen on foreign exchange transactions and foreign operations which also explains what other adjustments are necessary on consolidation.

---

[5] In terms of section 3480 of the CICA *Handbook*, only amounts relating to "Acts of God" (i.e., resulting from floods, lightening, tornados, etc.) and expropriations of property qualify as extraordinary items.

PUSH-DOWN ACCOUNTING

Push-down accounting refers to the practice of revaluing the assets and liabilities of a subsidiary to reflect their fair market values on the date of acquisition by recording **these adjusted values in the books of the subsidiary** rather than by merely making the necessary adjustments in the consolidation working papers. These adjustments are made by debiting or crediting the asset concerned with the parent company's share of the difference between the book value of the asset or liability and its fair market value on the date of acquisition and crediting the same amount to a capital surplus account. For example, if the values of the assets of a 90%-owned subsidiary are revalued upwards by $10,000, the increase in value and the adjustment to the capital surplus account by the subsidiary company would be as follows:

Assets (90% of $10,000)	9,000	
Capital Surplus		9,000

Capital surplus arising from the revaluation of assets to reflect the proportionate adjustment for the fair market value.

Where push-down accounting is used, the capital surplus is apportioned in the analysis of equity to the parent company and the minority interests in proportion to their interests in the subsidiary. For example, if push-down accounting had been used in the case of a 90%-owned subsidiary, the analysis of equity **at the date of acquisition** would have appeared as follows:

	Total	Parent Inc.	Minority Interests
Common Stock	$100,000	90,000	10,000
Retained Earnings	40,000	36,000	4,000
Capital Surplus Arising from Fair Market Value Adjustment — Equipment	10,000	9,000	—
		135,000	
Purchase Consideration		150,000	
Goodwill		$ 15,000	
Minority Interests			$14,000

The **revaluation of a subsidiary's assets using push-down accounting** follows the same allocation as that used for the recognition of increases or decreases in the value of assets and liabilities at the date of acquisition.[6] The difference is, as explained above, that the increase in the asset value of $9,000 in the above analysis of equity is recorded in the books of the subsidiary by increasing the asset by $9,000 and crediting the same amount to the subsidiary's capital surplus account.

As this is a major departure from current practice, the CICA *Handbook*[7] only recommends that push-down accounting be used when an acquired subsidiary is wholly-owned or virtually all of the equity interests of an entity have been acquired in order to establish a sufficiently comprehensive basis for revaluing the enterprise's assets and liabilities. An acquirer that holds at least 90% of the equity interests after the acquisition is presumed to have acquired virtually all of the entity's equity interests. The CICA *Handbook* also requires that where push-down accounting has been used, the retained earnings of the subsidiary at the date of acquisition that has not been included in the parent company's retained earnings must be reclassified as either share capital, contributed capital, or as a separately identified account within shareholders' equity.

---

6 CICA *Handbook*, section 1625
7 Ibid.

CONSOLIDATING VARIABLE INTEREST ENTITIES

Variable Interest Entities (VIEs) are entities in which one party (the primary beneficiary) does not hold a controlling interest in the VIE but enjoys a beneficial interest in the entity through a special relationship with the other interest holders. They differ in nature and may be formed as companies, partnerships, joint ventures, trusts, or some other type of venture. **Their common features are that (1) the expected returns or losses for the beneficial owner from the entity are not in proportion to the voting rights held; and (2) that substantially all of the VIE's activities in providing financing or buying assets are conducted on behalf of the beneficial having disproportionately few voting rights.**

These VIEs were used extensively by Enron in the manipulation of its reported earnings and to hide the extent of its borrowings (see Chapter One). The CICA has, therefore, issued an *Exposure Draft* on a new *Accounting Guideline 15* that would require that these entities be consolidated by the beneficial companies. To do so, the CICA's accounting requirements for subsidiaries and joint ventures (see Chapter Fourteen) will be modified to take these requirements into account because up to this point, the VIEs have been accounted for using the equity method. The *Guideline* would also provide guidance for consolidating VIEs and the disclosure of information on the nature of its involvement with the VIE (i.e., when that involvement began; the nature, purpose, size, and activities of the VIE; and the beneficial party's maximum exposure to loss). These provisions are expected to apply to companies having year ends ending after October 31, 2004.

THE CONSOLIDATED STATEMENT OF CASH FLOWS

The consolidated statement of cash flows is essentially the same as that prepared for any other company. Differences exist, however, in relation to the treatment of the interests of the minority in the net income for the year and the dividends paid to the minority interests during the year. The way in which these items are treated depends on whether the direct or indirect method is used. At present, both these methods are allowed by the CICA *Handbook*.[8]

The Direct Method

With the **direct (or income statement) method**, the objective is to show the total inflows of cash into the entity and then to deduct from this amount the amounts paid out in cash to suppliers, employees, to the government as income taxes, and the like to arrive at the net cash inflows from operations. Any amounts attributable to the minority interests are ignored in the preparation of the statement because these amounts **are not cash flows, but merely book entries**. In addition, there is **no inclusion of noncash items** like the share of net income from an investee company using the equity method because, as with the amounts attributable to the minority interests, these are merely book entries.

After the net cash inflows from operations have been established, the amounts arising from the investing and financing activities are included. Here, any dividends received by the investor company from an investee company are treated as **cash inflows from investments**. The only other adjustments to the investing activities are the cash outflows arising from dividends paid by a subsidiary to its minority interests, and these are added to the dividends paid by the parent company to its shareholders. The final result is the increase or decrease in cash resources during the reporting period.

---

[8] Section 1540.

The Indirect Method

The **indirect method** commences with the consolidated net income. The net cash inflows from operations are established by adding to the consolidated net income those items not expended in cash (like the amortization of capital assets, the impairment of goodwill, the share of the minority interest in a subsidiary's net income, the share of the net income of any investment using the equity method) and those adjustments required to convert the net income from an accrual to a cash basis. In other respects, however, the preparation of the cash flow statement is the same as that for the direct method given above.

An example of the preparation of the consolidated statement of cash flows using both the direct and indirect method is provided as Illustration 7–6. In both cases, other than the financing and investment items that are not inflows or outflows of cash but are specifically required to be included in the cash flow statement, the objective is to show the cash inflows and outflows of the consolidated entity.

Adjustments Where the Equity Method Has Been Used

The preparation of the consolidated statement of cash flows is also affected where the equity method has been used to account for the investments over which it exerts significant influence. This also applies where subsidiary companies have not been consolidated with those of the parent company. In these cases, the net income of the parent (or investor) company is increased by its share of the net income for the year, and the investment account is increased accordingly by the same amount.

The inclusion of this share of net income is merely a book entry and is made without a corresponding inflow of cash. It must, therefore, be deducted from the "consolidated net income" on preparation of the statement of cash flows. This position is reflected in Illustration 7–6.

THE AMERICAN METHOD OF ACCOUNTING FOR PRE-ACQUISITION TRADING OPERATIONS OF SUBSIDIARIES ACQUIRED DURING THE YEAR

Where a subsidiary is acquired during the year, American accounting principles allow for the inclusion of the trading results of a subsidiary for the year in which the controlling interest was acquired. Where this choice is made, the trading activities of the subsidiary prior to the date of acquisition are brought into account in the consolidated income statement in the normal manner in the year in which the acquisition took place. However, this amount is excluded from the consolidated net income as "pre-acquisition earnings" as a single figure along the lines of that applying to minority interests.

American accounting requirements also allow companies to include post-acquisition revenues and expenses as in Canada.

SUMMARY

This chapter further explains the consolidation process. First, it examines the apportionment of the earnings of a subsidiary company into pre- and post-acquisition earnings and the treatment of dividends paid by subsidiaries. It stresses that pre-acquisition earnings relate to the cost of the investment while post-acquisition earnings are recognized as current net income. Where dividends are paid by the subsidiary company, they are credited to the investment account. However, care should be exercised to ensure that if they are pre-acquisition dividends, they are applied to reduce the cost of the investment.

ILLUSTRATION 7–6
CONSOLIDATED STATEMENT OF CASH FLOWS

You are provided with the following abbreviated consolidated balance sheets of DCM Inc. at December 31, 20X4 and 20X5 which also owns an interest in a company over which it exerts significant influence:

	20X5	20X4	Difference
BALANCE SHEETS			
Cash	$ 66,000	$ 50,000	$ 16,000
Inventory	98,000	95,000	3,000
Accounts Receivable	160,000	186,000	(26,000)
Plant and Equipment	540,000	460,000	80,000
Less: Accumulated Amortization	(240,000)	(245,000)	5,000
Investment in Investee Company	125,000	100,000	25,000
Goodwill	20,000	24,000	(4,000)
	$ 769,000	$ 670,000	$ 99,000
Accounts Payable	$ 165,000	$ 155,000	$ 10,000
Minority Interests	119,000	110,000	9,000
Common Stock	360,000	300,000	60,000
Retained Earnings	125,000	105,000	20,000
	$ 769,000	$ 670,000	$ 99,000

Additional Information:

1. The abbreviated income statement of DCM Inc. for the year ended December 31, 20X5 was as follows

Sales	$1,340,000
Cost of Goods Sold	$1,110,000
Administrative Expenses	126,000
Total Expenses	$1,236,000
Operating Net Income	$ 104,000
Share of Net Income from Investee Company	35,000
Total Net Income	139,000
Less Minority Interest Net Income	15,000
Net Income before Goodwill Charges	124,000
Goodwill Charges	4,000
Consolidated Net Income	120,000
Retained Earnings at January 1, 20X5	105,000
	225,000
Dividends Paid	100,000
Retained Earnings at December 31, 20X5	$ 125,000

2. The minority interest in net income was $15,000, but the minority interests on the balance sheet had only increased by $9,000 because $6,000 had been distributed to the minority shareholders as a dividend during the year.
3. During the year equipment that originally cost $50,000 was sold for $15,000 on December 31, 20X5. This equipment was replaced with new equipment costing $130,000. The total amortization expense for the year was $30,000.
4. On December 10, 20X5, the company effected a one for six stock issue.
5. DCM holds a 30% interest in the investee company, which allows DCM to exert significant influence over its affairs. During 20X5, DCM's share of net income from the investee company was $35,000, of which $10,000 was received as a dividend.

ILLUSTRATION 7–6 (Continued)

The consolidated statement of cash flows is drawn up in exactly the same manner as that applying to individual companies, except for the adjustments relating to the net income and dividends applicable to the investee company and the minority interests. This is outlined below using the direct method.

DCM Inc.
STATEMENT OF CHANGES IN CASH FLOWS
for the Year Ended December 31, 20X5

Operating Activities:		
Cash Receipts from Customers — see note 1	$1,366,000	
Cash Dividend from Investee company	10,000	$1,376,000
Less: Cash Paid to Suppliers — see note 2	$1,103,000	
Administration Expenses — note 3	96,000	1,199,000
		177,000
Investing Activities:		
Proceeds from the Sale of Capital Assets	$ 15,000	
Less: Purchase of Equipment	130,000	(115,000)
Financing Activities:		
Proceeds from Share Issue	$ 60,000	
Less: Dividends Paid (inclusive of $6,000 paid to Minority Shareholders)	106,000	(46,000)
Increases in Cash		$ 16,000

If, however, the indirect method had been used, the cash flows would have been as follows:

Operating Activities:		
Consolidated Net Income		$ 120,000
Add: Amounts Not Expended in Cash:		
Share of Minority Interests in Net Income	$ 15,000	
Amortization of Capital Assets	30,000	
Goodwill Impairment	4,000	49,000
Less: Share of Net Income in Investee company		(35,000)
Changes in Working Capital Items		
Decrease in Current Assets	23,000	
Increase in Current Liabilities	10,000	33,000
Add: Cash Dividend from Investee company		10,000
		177,000
Investing Activities:		
Proceeds from the Sale of Capital Assets	$ 15,000	
Less: Purchase of Equipment	130,000	(115,000)
Financing Activities:		
Proceeds from Share Issue	$ 60,000	
Less: Dividends Paid (inclusive of $6,000 paid to Minority Shareholders)	106,000	(46,000)
		$ 16,000

Notes:
[1] The cash received from customers is $186,000 + $1,340,000 − $160,000 = $1,366,000.
[2] The cash paid to suppliers can be calculated as the amount paid out to creditors of $1,100,000 (i.e., $155,000 + $1,110,000 − $165,000) plus the difference in inventory of $3,000 (i.e., $98,000 − $95,000) = $1,103,000.
[3] The cash outflows for administration expenses is the $130,000 less the amortization of capital assets and the impairment of the goodwill of $30,000 plus $4,000, to give $96,000.

The extent to which the trading operations of a company over which control was acquired during the year is then presented. In Canada, the trading operations are only recognized and included in the consolidated income statement from the date of acquisition whereas in the USA they could be recognized from the beginning of the year in which control was acquired.

The assignment of fair market values to the assets and liabilities of subsidiary companies at the date of acquisition is necessary to satisfy the requirement that assets and liabilities acquired must be valued at their fair market values. However, only that portion applicable to the parent company is recognized in the consolidation process and depreciated over their useful lives. "Push-down accounting", where assets and liabilities of subsidiaries are adjusted in the books of the subsidiary, is examined in relation to the position taken by the CICA.

Finally, the consolidated statement of cash flows is covered. With companies over which significant influence may be exercised, the adjustments relate to the share of net income from the investee company and dividends received. In both cases, the deciding factor is whether the amounts involved represent inflows or outflows of cash.

SELF-STUDY PROBLEM
(covering Chapters 6 and 7)

PROBLEM 7A†   The abbreviated financial statements of Placid Inc. and Serene Inc. for the two years ended December 31, 20X4 and 20X5 were as follows:

	Placid		Serene	
BALANCE SHEETS	**20X4**	**20X5**	**20X4**	**20X5**
Cash	$ 215,000	$ 192,000	$ 180,000	$ 150,000
Accounts Receivable	1,615,000	1,560,000	690,000	780,000
Inventory	840,000	920,000	390,000	420,000
Investment in Serene	1,722,500	1,942,500	—	—
Plant and Equipment (Net)	1,800,000	2,498,000	800,000	980,000
	$6,192,500	$7,112,500	$2,060,000	$2,330,000
Accounts Payable	850,000	790,000	340,000	250,000
Common Stock	3,000,000	3,000,000	1,000,000	1,000,000
Retained Earnings	2,342,500	3,322,500	720,000	1,080,000
	$6,192,500	$7,112,500	$2,060,000	$2,330,000
COMBINED INCOME AND RETAINED EARNINGS STATEMENTS				
Sales	$4,700,000	$4,900,000	$2,600,000	$3,000,000
Cost of Goods Sold	$1,980,000	$2,040,000	$1,100,000	$1,380,000
Administration Expenses	1,360,000	1,450,000	1,020,000	1,060,000
	$3,340,000	$3,490,000	$2,120,000	$2,440,000
Net Income from Operations	$1,360,000	$1,410,000	$ 480,000	$ 560,000
Net Income from Serene	82,500	370,000	—	—
Net Income	1,442,500	1,780,000	480,000	560,000
Retained Earnings at January 1	1,400,000	2,342,500	400,000	720,000
	2,842,500	4,122,500	880,000	1,280,000
Dividends Paid:				
Interim on March 18	140,000	—	60,000	—
Final on December 15	360,000	800,000	100,000	200,000
Retained Earnings at December 31	$2,342,500	$3,322,500	$ 720,000	$1,080,000

---

† The solution is provided in Appendix B to this text.

Additional Information:

1. Placid acquired a 75% interest in Serene on October 1, 20X4 for $1,715,000.
2. At the date of acquisition, the assets and liabilities of Serene were considered to be fairly valued except for an item of plant that was undervalued by $160,000 and had a remaining useful life of four years with no residual value. Capital assets are amortized on a straight-line basis.
3. Following a review, the value of the goodwill was written down for impairment by $20,000 in 20X5.

REQUIRED

Prepare the consolidated combined income and retained earnings statements and balance sheets of Placid for 20X4 and 20X5.

REVIEW QUESTIONS

1. Explain the way in which post-acquisition earnings are treated in the analysis of equity.
2. What rule applies to the payment of dividends?
3. Why is it necessary to treat dividends paid by a subsidiary separately in the analysis of equity in the year of acquisition? In the current year?
4. Why is it necessary to show pre-acquisition dividends separately in the investment account maintained on an equity basis?
5. Explain why the amount calculated for goodwill is not affected by the payment of a pre-acquisition dividend.
6. Parent Inc. purchased an 80% interest in Subsidiary Inc. for $150,000 on July 1, 20X5 when Subsidiary had common stock of $100,000 and retained earnings of $50,000. If the net income of Subsidiary for 20X5 was $40,000 and it paid a dividend of $15,000 on December 31 in that year, what net income would Parent have included as its share of the net income from Subsidiary on **its** income statement if the value of goodwill remained unchanged?
7. What do you understand by the term, "push-down accounting"? What does it represent?
8. What accounting treatment is recommended where push-down accounting is used?
9. How are the trading operations of a company in which a controlling interest was purchased during the year recorded in the consolidated income statement? Those of a subsidiary that were disposed of during the year?
10. In what way does the American method of recording pre-acquisition earnings from a subsidiary acquired during the year differ from that applying in Canada?
11. How does the consolidated statement of cash flows differ from that presented by a company that does not have control over or exert significant influence over the affairs of another company?

CASE

CASE 7–1   The Air France — KLM Merger

(A case prepared from Reports in *The Wall Street Journal* as reprinted in *The Globe and Mail* of September 29 and October 1, 2003, and February 12 and May 5, 2004)

On February 12, 2004, the European Union Competition Bureau approved a merger of Air France and KLM subject to certain concessions by the two airlines aimed at promoting competition on certain routes within Europe and across the North Atlantic. The merger, which took effect on May 4, 2004, resulted in the formation of the world's largest airline company based on revenues reported in 2002–2003.

    This followed from the September 27, 2003, announcement that Air France and the Dutch carrier KLM were to merge their operations. The merger was effected by the formation of a new holding company owned as to 44% by the French government, 37% by other French shareholders, and 19% by KLM. Ownership of Air France would be held by a subsidiary of the holding company. To preserve KLM's national character and to safeguard its international landing rights, which had been negotiated in bi-lateral deals with the various countries, ownership of KLM would be by an independent company in which 51% of the voting shares would be held by a special-purpose Dutch Foundation and the balance by the French holding company. The Dutch government would continue to hold its 14.1% interest in KLM, and reserved the right to boost that to 50.1% should it wish to do so over the next three to six years. For the foreseeable future, the two airlines were to maintain their operating hubs at both Amsterdam's Schipol and Paris's Charles de Gaulle airports. Alitalia has announced that it would also like to start negotiations on joining the French holding company.

Advantages of the merger are seen to be that the "SkyTeam" alliance of Air France, Alitalia, Aeromexico, CSA Czech Airlines, Delta Airlines, and Korean Air could add KLM's association with Continental Airlines, Lufthansa, and UAL's United Airlines to the "SkyTeam's" alliance. The alliance allows the participating airlines to sell tickets on each another's flights. For both Air France and KLM, it could also reduce service on presently duplicated and unprofitable air routes. Savings in operating costs of over €1-billion are also expected.

REQUIRED

On the assumption that the same accounting requirements for mergers and consolidations apply in both the European Union and Canada:

1. Determine whether or not this a merger of interests.
2. Explain how the results of operations and assets and liabilities of the two airlines would be treated in the consolidated financial statements of the new holding company to be formed by Air France, should the proposal be effected.

EXERCISES

EXERCISE 7–1

Patch Inc. acquired a 75% interest in Sew Inc. on September 1, 20X4 for $300,000. At December 31, 20X3, Sew had common stock of $240,000 and retained earnings of $120,000. Details of the net income and dividends paid by the two companies for 20X4 through 20X6 were as follows:

		Patch	**Sew**
20X4:	Retained Earnings at January 1	$ 400,000	$120,000
	Net Income from Operations	300,000	60,000
	Dividends Paid (December 10)	(100,000)	(28,000)
20X5:	Net Income from Operations	350,000	80,000
	Dividends Paid (December 12)	(120,000)	(40,000)
20X6:	Net Income from Operations	400,000	60,000
	Dividends Paid (December 8)	(150,000)	(72,000)

REQUIRED

Calculate the consolidated retained earnings of Patch at December 31, 20X6.

EXERCISE 7–2

On October 1, 20X3, Pebble Inc. acquired an 80% interest in Stone Inc. for $1,600,000. Stone prepared financial statements that showed that, on October 1, 20X3, it had common stock of $1,000,000 made up of 200,000 shares of no par value and retained earnings of $800,000. The full equity method was used to account for the investment in Stone.

The following figures were extracted from the ledgers of the two companies for the year ended December 31, 20X4:

	Pebble	Stone
Sales	$4,200,000	$2,000,000
Cost of Goods Sold	1,950,000	800,000
Administration, Selling and Other Expenses	800,000	400,000
Dividends Declared (December 10)	400,000	200,000
Net Income for Three Months Ended December 31, 20X3	—	300,000
Retained Earnings at October 1, 20X3	—	800,000
Retained Earnings at January 1, 20X4	2,240,000	—

REQUIRED

Prepare the consolidated income and retained earnings statement for Pebble for the year ended December 31, 20X4.

EXERCISE 7–3 On September 1, 20X4, Pinch Inc. acquired a 60% interest in Save Inc. for $240,000 when Save had common stock of $200,000. Financial statements were not prepared at the date of acquisition but, at that date, the net assets of Save were considered to be fairly valued except for certain equipment having a five-year remaining life, which was undervalued by $20,000. No impairment of goodwill was recognized in 20X4.

The abbreviated income and retained earnings statements for the two companies for the financial year ended December 31, 20X4 were as follows:

	Pinch	Save
Fees for Services Provided	$900,000	$500,000
Less: Administration and Other Expenses	700,000	440,000
Net Income from Operations	200,000	60,000
Share of Net Income from Save	11,200	—
	211,200	60,000
Dividends Declared and Paid (November 30)	80,000	20,000
	131,200	40,000
Retained Earnings at January 1, 20X4	200,000	100,000
Retained Earnings at December 31, 20X4	$331,200	$140,000

REQUIRED

1. Prepare the combined income and retained earnings statement of Pinch and its subsidiary company for the year ended December 31, 20X4;
2. Give the adjustment to the equipment appearing on the consolidated balance sheet of Pinch at December 31, 20X4.

EXERCISE 7–4 On October 1, 20X6, Price Inc. acquired an 80% interest in Sell Inc. for $160,000 when Sell had common stock of $100,000. On that date, all the assets of Sell were fairly valued except for certain plant and equipment having a five-year life that was considered to be overvalued by $20,000. The goodwill arising on acquisition was considered to be properly valued at December 31, 20X6.

The abbreviated balance sheets and income statements for the two companies for 20X6 were as follows:

BALANCE SHEETS	Price	Sell
Current Assets	$ 500,000	$140,000
Investment in Sell	154,800	—
Plant Equipment (Net)	710,700	110,000
	$1,365,500	$250,000
Accounts Payable	$ 184,700	$ 60,000
Common Stock	1,000,000	100,000
Retained Earnings	180,800	90,000
	$1,365,500	$250,000

	Price	Sell
INCOME STATEMENTS		
Sales	$ 800,000	$400,000
Cost of Goods Sold	$ 350,000	$280,000
Administration and Selling Expenses	330,000	70,000
	$ 680,000	$350,000
Net Operating Income	$ 120,000	$ 50,000
Share of Net Income from Sell	10,800	—
	130,800	50,000
Dividends Paid (November 14)	50,000	20,000
	80,800	30,000
Retained Earnings at January 1, 20X6	100,000	60,000
Retained Earnings at December 31, 20X6	$ 180,800	$ 90,000

REQUIRED

Prepare the consolidated balance sheet and income and retained earnings statement for 20X6.

EXERCISE 7–5

On October 1, 20X4, Polka Inc. acquired a 75% interest in Samba Inc. for $1.2-million. At December 31, 20X3, Samba had common stock of $800,000 made up of 200,000 shares of no par value, and retained earnings of $400,000.

At the date of acquisition, the assets and liabilities amounted to $1.9-million and $540,000 respectively. They were all fairly valued except for an item of equipment that was undervalued by $80,000 and that was expected to have a useful life of an additional five years from the date of acquisition. Goodwill was not written down for impairment in 20X4.

The following figures were extracted from the income and retained earnings statements of the two companies for the year ended December 31, 20X4:

	Polka	Samba
Net Income **from Operations**:		
Nine Months to September 30	$ 600,000	$160,000
Three Months to December 31	450,000	60,000
Dividends Paid (December 10)	300,000	24,000
Retained Earnings at January 1, 20X4	1,800,000	400,000

REQUIRED

1. Give the "Investment in Samba" account in the ledger of Polka using the equity method of accounting;
2. Give the consolidated retained earnings of Polka for the year ended December 31, 20X4;
3. Give the minority interests on the consolidated balance sheet at December 31, 20X4; and
4. Give the adjustment to the equipment on the consolidated balance sheet at December 31, 20X4.

EXERCISE 7–6

On July 1, 20X7, Prey Inc. purchased a 90% interest in Snare Inc. for $810,000. The common stock and retained earnings of Snare on January 1, 20X7 amounted to $600,000 and $200,000 respectively. At the date of acquisition, the assets of Snare were considered to be fairly valued, except for certain equipment having an eight-year life that was undervalued by $40,000.

The reported net income and dividends of the two companies for the two years ended December 31, 20X7 and 20X8 were as follows:

		Prey	Snare
20X7:	Net Income from Operations	$ 800,000	$ 80,000
	Dividends Declared and Paid (October 31)	240,000	60,000

		Prey	Snare
20X8:	Net Income from Operations	1,000,000	120,000
	Dividends Declared and Paid (November 22)	400,000	80,000

At January 1, 20X7, Prey's retained earnings amounted to $1.2-million. The net income of Prey includes the share of net income from Snare. There was no write-down of goodwill for impairment in 20X7 or 20X8.

REQUIRED

Prepare the consolidated retained earnings of Prey and its subsidiary company at December 31, 20X8 using the full equity method.

EXERCISE 7–7   Proceed Inc. purchased an 80% interest in Succeed Inc. for $648,000 on July 1, 20X4. On January 1, 20X4, Succeed had common stock of $620,000 and retained earnings of $50,000. Net income for the year ended December 31, 20X4 amounted to $60,000. On July 1, 20X4, equipment with a five-year remaining life was overvalued by $60,000. Goodwill is accounted for on an impairment basis, and impairment losses of $20,000 in 20X5 and $25,000 in 20X7 were recognized.

The abbreviated income statements and balance sheets for the two companies for the year ended December 31, 20X7 (yes, 20X7) were as follows:

INCOME STATEMENTS	Proceed	Succeed
Sales	$1,000,000	$ 600,000
Cost of Goods Sold	$ 600,000	$ 400,000
Operating Expenses	200,000	100,000
	$ 800,000	$ 500,000
Net Operating Income	$ 200,000	$ 100,000
Share of Net Income from Succeed	64,600	—
Net Income for Year	264,600	100,000
Retained Earnings at January 1, 20X7	800,000	160,000
	1,064,600	260,000
Dividends Paid (November 15)	120,000	10,000
Retained Earnings at December 31, 20X7	$ 944,600	$ 250,000

BALANCE SHEETS		
Cash at Bank	$ 96,200	$ 40,000
Accounts Receivable	800,000	590,000
Inventory	240,000	120,000
Investment in Succeed	770,400	—
Plant and Equipment (Net)	580,000	410,000
	$2,486,600	$1,160,000
Accounts Payable	540,000	290,000
Common Stock	1,000,000	620,000
Retained Earnings	944,600	250,000
	$2,486,600	$1,160,000

REQUIRED

Prepare the consolidated income statement and balance sheet for Proceed for 20X7 on the assumption that at December 31, 20X7 the minority interests appearing on the consolidated balance sheet were $178,200.

EXERCISE 7–8   The comparative consolidated financial statements of Porcupine Inc. for the year ended December 31, 20X5 reflected the following items:

INCOME STATEMENT	20X5	20X4
Share of Net Income from Burrow	$120,000	$ 90,000
Minority Interest Net Income	70,000	65,000

BALANCE SHEET	20X5	20X4
Investment in Burrow	$960,000	$880,000
Minority Interests	760,000	710,000

You are also informed that the minority interests arose from the holding of a 90% interest in Burrow Inc., that had earned net income of $700,000 during 20X5, of which $200,000 had been paid out as a dividend. No goodwill arose from the purchase of the investment in Burrow.

REQUIRED

Explain how the **four items** given above would be reflected on the consolidated statement of cash flows of Porcupine and its subsidiary company at December 31, 20X5 prepared using the indirect method. If, however, you do not feel that any items should not be disclosed, state why you believe this to be the case.

PROBLEMS

PROBLEM 7-1   On October 1, 20X6, Peel Inc. acquired an 80% interest in Strip Inc. for $320,000. At the date of acquisition, the inventory of Strip (which was all sold by December 31, 20X6) was considered to be undervalued by $20,000, while certain of its plant and equipment having a five-year life was considered to be overvalued by $40,000. There was no impairment of goodwill during the period 20X5 through 20X7.

Relevant information relating to the two companies for 20X5 through 20X7 was as follows:

		Peel	Strip
20X5:	Common Stock at December 31	$600,000	$200,000
	Retained Earnings at December 31	200,000	120,000
20X6:	Net Operating Income	240,000	100,000
	Dividends Paid on December 5	100,000	40,000
20X7:	Net Operating Income	300,000	—
	Net Operating Loss	—	60,000
	Dividends Paid on December 7	—	40,000

REQUIRED

1. Give the consolidated net income for the year ended December 31, 20X6;
2. Give the consolidated retained earnings at December 31, 20X7; and
3. Give the minority interests appearing on the consolidated balance sheet at December 31, 20X7.

PROBLEM 7-2   Pie Inc. acquired a 75% interest in Sigh Inc. on September 1, 20X5 for $375,000. Sigh's plant having a five-year remaining life was undervalued by $20,000 at the date of acquisition. At December 31, 20X4, Sigh had common stock of $240,000 and retained earnings of $120,000. Details of the separate net income and dividends paid by Pie and Sigh for the years 20X5 through 20X7 are provided below:

		Pie	Sigh
20X5:	Retained Earnings at January 1, 20X5	$400,000	$120,000
	Net Income	300,000	60,000
	Dividends Declared (Paid December 10)	100,000	28,000
20X6:	Net Income	350,000	80,000
	Dividends Declared (Paid December 12)	120,000	40,000
20X7:	Net Income	400,000	60,000
	Dividends Declared (Paid December 12)	150,000	72,000

Information extracted from the 20X7 income statements of the two companies was as follows:

	Pie	Sigh
Sales	$1,200,000	$400,000
Cost of Goods Sold	$ 650,000	$200,000
Operating Expenses	150,000	140,000
	$ 800,000	$340,000
Net Income from Operations	$ 400,000	$ 60,000

REQUIRED

1. Prepare the consolidated income and retained earnings statement of Pie at December 31, 20X7 on the assumption that there was no impairment of goodwill during the period 20X5 through 20X7; and
2. Give the balance on the "Investment in Sigh" account as it would appear in the ledger of Pie at December 31, 20X7.

PROBLEM 7–3 The abbreviated financial statements of Pussycat Inc. and Mouse Inc. at December 31, 20X4 were as follows:

COMBINED INCOME AND RETAINED EARNINGS STATEMENTS	Pussycat	Mouse
Sales	$10,000,000	$6,000,000
Cost of Goods Sold	$ 6,000,000	$3,600,000
Operating Expenses	2,200,000	1,200,000
	$ 8,200,000	$4,800,000
Net Operating Income	$ 1,800,000	$1,200,000
Share of Net Income from Mouse	900,000	—
	2,700,000	1,200,000
Dividends Declared and Paid	1,000,000	800,000
	1,700,000	400,000
Retained Earnings at January 1, 20X4	3,550,000	1,200,000
Retained Earnings at December 31, 20X4	$ 5,250,000	$1,600,000
BALANCE SHEETS		
Current Assets	$ 5,950,000	$2,400,000
Loan to Mouse	2,000,000	—
Investment in Mouse	3,800,000	—
Plant and Equipment (Net)	6,600,000	4,400,000
	$18,350,000	$6,800,000
Current Liabilities	$ 3,100,000	$1,200,000
Loan from Pussycat	—	2,000,000
Common Stock	$10,000,000	2,000,000
Retained Earnings	5,250,000	1,600,000
	$18,350,000	$6,800,000

You are informed that Pussycat acquired a 75% interest in Mouse on January 1, 20X2 for $3,250,000 when Mouse had retained earnings of $600,000 and land (included in the plant and equipment) having a fair market value of $1.2-million more than its book value. Following a review carried out in 20X3, goodwill was written down by $200,000 for impairment.

You are also informed that during the period January 1, 20X2 to December 31, 20X3, Mouse earned net income of $1-million and paid dividends of $400,000.

REQUIRED

Prepare the consolidated balance sheet and combined income and retained earnings statement at December 31, 20X4.

PROBLEM 7–4

Prowl Inc. acquired an 80% interest in Slink Inc. on April 1, 20X2 for $1,500,000. Financial statements were not prepared at the date of acquisition, but at December 31, 20X1 Slink had common stock of $1,000,000 and retained earnings of $400,000. It was agreed amongst the parties that at the date of acquisition, an item of plant having a 10-year remaining life was undervalued by $125,000.

The abbreviated financial statements of the two companies for 20X2 were as follows:

	Prowl	Slink
BALANCE SHEETS at December 31, 20X2		
Current Assets	$ 860,350	$1,180,000
Investment in Slink	1,584,500	—
Capital Assets (Net)	1,005,400	840,000
	$3,450,250	$2,020,000
Current Liabilities	$ 535,750	$ 420,000
Common Stock	1,800,000	1,000,000
Retained Earnings	1,114,500	600,000
	$3,450,250	$2,020,000

	Prowl	Slink
INCOME AND RETAINED EARNINGS STATEMENTS **for the Year Ended December 31, 20X2**		
Sales	$2,500,000	$1,200,000
Cost of Goods Sold	$ 950,000	$ 660,000
Operating Expenses	850,000	240,000
	$1,800,000	$ 900,000
Net Operating Income	$ 700,000	$ 300,000
Share of Net Income from Slink	164,500	—
Net Income	864,500	300,000
Retained Earnings at January 1, 20X2	750,000	400,000
	1,614,500	700,000
Dividends Paid (November 25)	500,000	100,000
Retained Earnings at December 31, 20X2	$1,114,500	$ 600,000

You are also informed that goodwill was accounted for using the impairment method. On December 31, 20X2, goodwill was written down by $8,000 for impairment.

REQUIRED

Prepare the consolidated balance sheet of Prowl for the year ended December 31, 20X2 and the combined consolidated statement of income and retained earnings for the year ended on that date.

PROBLEM 7–5

On October 1, 20X8, Pierce Inc. acquired a 60% interest in Skewer Inc. for $460,000. Financial statements were not prepared at the date of acquisition, but at January 1, 20X8, Skewer had a capital surplus of $150,000 and retained earnings of $100,000.

At the date of acquisition, all assets and liabilities of Skewer were considered to be fairly valued except for two items that were undervalued: land by $20,000 and inventory by $10,000. All of the inventory on hand at the date of acquisition was sold by December 31, 20X8.

No impairment of goodwill was recognized in 20X8.

The abbreviated balance sheets and combined statements of income and retained earnings statements of Pierce and Skewer at December 31, 20X8 were as follows:

	Pierce	Skewer
BALANCE SHEETS		
Cash	$ 28,750	$ 10,000
Accounts Receivable	331,850	240,000
Inventory	400,000	250,000
Investment in Skewer	459,400	—
Plant and Equipment (Net)	520,000	300,000
	$1,740,000	$800,000
Current Liabilities	$ 158,750	$ 96,000
Common Stock	1,000,000	400,000
Capital Surplus	—	150,000
Retained Earnings	581,250	154,000
	$1,740,000	$800,000

COMBINED INCOME AND RETAINED EARNINGS STATEMENTS		
Sales	$1,200,000	$500,000
Cost of Goods Sold	$ 600,000	$300,000
Operating Expenses	250,000	140,000
	$ 850,000	$440,000
Net Operating Income	$ 350,000	$ 60,000
Share of Net Income from Skewer	3,000	—
Net Income	353,000	60,000
Retained Earnings at January 1, 20X8	328,250	100,000
	681,250	160,000
Dividends Paid (November 15)	100,000	6,000
Retained Earnings at December 31, 20X8	$ 581,250	$154,000

REQUIRED

Prepare the consolidated balance sheet of Pierce at December 31, 20X8 and the combined consolidated statement of income and retained earnings for the year ended on that date.

PROBLEM 7–6

On May 1, 20X5, Part Inc. acquired a 75% interest in Segment Inc. for $642,000. On January 1, 20X5, Segment had common stock of $600,000 and retained earnings of $100,000. At the date of acquisition, all assets and liabilities of Segment were considered to be fairly valued except for an item of plant having a five-year remaining life, which was undervalued by $36,000.

The abbreviated balance sheets and combined statements of income and retained earnings of Part and Segment at December 31, 20X6 were as follows:

COMBINED INCOME AND RETAINED EARNINGS STATEMENTS	Part	Segment
Sales	$1,800,000	$ 320,000
Cost of Goods Sold	$ 880,000	$ 150,000
Operating Expenses	140,000	30,000
	$1,020,000	$ 180,000
Net Operating Income	$ 780,000	$ 140,000
Share of Net Income from Segment	89,600	—
Net Income	869,600	140,000
Retained Earnings at January 1, 20X6	356,400	180,000
	1,226,000	320,000
Dividends Paid (December 2)	240,000	80,000
Retained Earnings at December 31, 20X6	$ 986,000	$ 240,000

	Part	Segment
BALANCE SHEETS		
Cash	$ 60,000	$ 20,000
Accounts Receivable	410,000	490,000
Inventory	235,000	115,000
Investment in Segment	698,000	—
Plant and Equipment (Net)	850,000	570,000
	$2,253,000	$1,195,000
Current Liabilities	$ 267,000	$ 355,000
Common Stock	1,000,000	600,000
Retained Earnings	986,000	240,000
	$2,253,000	$1,195,000

You are further informed that:

(a)　Goodwill was written down for impairment by $10,000 in 20X6.

(b)　During 20X5, Segment earned net income of $120,000. It also paid a dividend of $40,000 on November 30, 20X5.

REQUIRED

Prepare the consolidated balance sheet and combined income and retained earnings statement of Part for 20X6.

PROBLEM 7–7　Preserve Inc. acquired an 80% interest in Save Inc. on April 1, 20X7 for $800,000. Financial statements were not prepared at the date of acquisition, but at December 31, 20X6, Save had common stock of $600,000 made up of 100,000 shares of common stock of no par value and retained earnings of $120,000. It was also agreed amongst the parties that, at the date of acquisition, the plant and equipment of Save was fairly valued except for an item of plant having a remaining seven-year life, which was undervalued by $70,000.

The financial statements of the two companies at December 31, 20X8 were as follows:

COMBINED INCOME AND RETAINED EARNINGS STATEMENT	Preserve	Save
Sales	$1,800,000	$1,000,000
Cost of Goods Sold	1,000,000	600,000
Administration Expenses	300,000	200,000
	$1,300,000	$ 800,000
Net Income from Operations	$ 500,000	$ 200,000
Share of Net Income from Save	132,000	—
Net Income for Year	632,000	200,000
Retained Earnings, January 1, 20X8	606,000	320,000
	1,238,000	520,000
Dividends Paid	200,000	100,000
Retained Earnings, December 31, 20X8	$1,038,000	$ 420,000
BALANCE SHEETS		
Cash	$ 58,000	$ 20,000
Accounts Receivable	480,000	420,000
Inventory	600,000	250,000
Investment in Save	958,000	—
Plant and Equipment (Net)	980,000	540,000
	$3,076,000	$1,230,000
Accounts Payable	538,000	210,000
Common Stock	1,500,000	600,000
Retained Earnings	1,038,000	420,000
	$3,076,000	$1,230,000

You are also informed that:

1. Goodwill was written down for impairment by $20,000 in 20X8.
2. On November 10, 20X7, Save declared and paid dividends of $40,000. Similarly, dividends of $100,000 were declared and paid during November 20X8.
3. The net income of Save accrued evenly throughout 20X7 and 20X8.

REQUIRED

Prepare the consolidated combined income and retained earnings statement and consolidated balance sheet of Preserve for 20X8.

PROBLEM 7–8

Pressure Inc. acquired a 60% interest in Stress Inc. on April 1, 20X7 for $914,000. At that date, the assets and liabilities of Stress were considered to be fairly valued except for an item of plant having a five-year remaining life, which was considered to be undervalued by $100,000. Goodwill was written down by $20,000 for impairment by Pressure in 20X7.

The abbreviated financial statements of the two companies for 20X7 and 20X8 were as follows:

	Pressure		Stress	
BALANCE SHEETS	**20X7**	**20X8**	**20X7**	**20X8**
Cash	$ 140,000	$ 90,000	$ 30,000	$ 150,000
Accounts Receivable	285,000	210,000	500,000	530,000
Inventory	240,000	300,000	390,000	320,000
Investment in Stress	933,000	999,000	—	—
Plant and Equipment (Net)	801,000	1,018,000	360,000	400,000
	$2,399,000	$2,617,000	$1,280,000	$1,400,000
Accounts Payable	250,000	190,000	110,000	100,000
Common Stock	1,200,000	1,200,000	800,000	800,000
Retained Earnings	949,000	1,227,000	370,000	500,000
	$2,399,000	$2,617,000	$1,280,000	$1,400,000
COMBINED INCOME AND RETAINED EARNINGS STATEMENTS				
Sales	$1,700,000	$1,920,000	$1,000,000	$1,100,000
Cost of Goods Sold	$ 680,000	$ 740,000	$ 600,000	$ 580,000
Administration Expenses	250,000	290,000	160,000	270,000
	$ 930,000	$1,030,000	$ 760,000	$ 850,000
Net Income from Operations	$ 770,000	$ 890,000	$ 240,000	$ 250,000
Net Income from Stress	79,000	138,000	—	—
Net Income	849,000	1,028,000	240,000	250,000
Retained Earnings at January 1	600,000	949,000	250,000	370,000
	1,449,000	1,977,000	490,000	620,000
Dividends Paid:				
Interim on March 18	140,000	—	20,000	—
Final on December 15	360,000	750,000	100,000	120,000
Retained Earnings at December 31	$ 949,000	$1,227,000	$ 370,000	$ 500,000

REQUIRED

Prepare the consolidated combined income and retained earnings statements and balance sheets of Pressure for both 20X7 and 20X8.

PROBLEM 7–9

Python Inc. acquired a 75% interest in Snake Inc. on October 1, 20X5 for $570,000. At that date, the assets and liabilities of Snake were considered to be fairly valued except for an item of plant having a 10-year remaining life, which was considered to be undervalued by $96,000. Goodwill was written down by $8,000 for impairment in 20X8.

The abbreviated financial statements of the two companies for 20X5 and 20X6 were as follows:

	Python		Snake	
BALANCE SHEETS	**20X5**	**20X6**	**20X5**	**20X6**
Cash	$ 120,000	$ 110,000	$ 60,000	$ 90,000
Accounts Receivable	200,000	245,000	180,000	230,000
Inventory	180,000	190,000	120,000	130,000
Investment in Snake	568,200	643,000	—	—
Plant and Equipment (Net)	300,000	380,000	370,000	350,000
	$1,368,200	$1,568,000	$730,000	$800,000
Accounts Payable	180,000	190,000	130,000	80,000
Common Stock	800,000	800,000	400,000	400,000
Retained Earnings	388,200	578,000	200,000	320,000
	$1,368,200	$1,568,000	$730,000	$800,000
COMBINED INCOME AND RETAINED EARNINGS STATEMENTS				
Sales	$1,200,000	$1,400,000	$760,000	$920,000
Cost of Goods Sold	$ 600,000	$ 700,000	$400,000	$460,000
Administration Expenses	300,000	360,000	200,000	240,000
	$ 900,000	$1,060,000	$600,000	$700,000
Net Income from Operations	$ 300,000	$ 340,000	$160,000	$220,000
Net Income from Snake	28,200	149,800	—	—
Net Income	328,200	489,800	160,000	220,000
Retained Earnings at January 1	300,000	388,200	120,000	200,000
	628,200	878,000	280,000	420,000
Dividends Paid:				
Interim on June 12	—	—	40,000	—
Final on December 15	240,000	300,000	40,000	100,000
Retained Earnings at December 31	$ 388,200	$ 578,000	$200,000	$320,000

REQUIRED

Prepare the consolidated balance sheets and combined income and retained earnings statements of Python for **20X5 and 20X6.**

PROBLEM 7–10 The abbreviated consolidated financial statements of Print Inc. and its subsidiary, Set Inc., for the two years ended December 31, 20X7 and 20X8 were as follows:

BALANCE SHEETS	**20X8**	**20X7**	**Increase/ (Decrease)**
Cash	$ 150,000	$ 290,000	$(140,000)
Accounts Receivable	1,515,000	1,350,000	165,000
Inventory	380,000	400,000	(20,000)
Investment in Run Inc.	185,000	160,000	25,000
Plant and Equipment (Net)	1,170,000	900,000	270,000
	$3,400,000	$3,100,000	$ 300,000
Accounts Payable	$ 510,000	$ 750,000	$(240,000)
10% Debentures	800,000	600,000	200,000
Minority Interests	190,000	150,000	40,000
Common Stock	1,000,000	900,000	100,000
Retained Earnings	900,000	700,000	200,000
	$3,400,000	$3,100,000	$ 300,000

COMBINED INCOME AND RETAINED EARNINGS STATEMENT
for the Year Ended December 31, 20X8

Sales		$2,500,000
Cost of Goods Sold		$1,140,000
Depreciation Expense		440,000
Administration Expenses		375,000
		$1,955,000
Net Operating Income		$ 545,000
Share of Net Income from Run		35,000
Total Net Income		580,000
Less: Minority Interests		80,000
Consolidated Net Income		500,000
Retained Earnings at January 1, 20X8		700,000
		1,200,000
Dividends Declared and Paid		300,000
Retained Earnings at December 31, 20X8		$ 900,000

Additional Information:

(a)   Set was a 75%-owned subsidiary of Print.

(b)   Print owned a 24% interest in Run, accounted for using the full equity method.

(c)   Dividends received by Print from Set during 20X8 amounted to $120,000, while those from Run amounted to $10,000.

REQUIRED

Prepare the consolidated statement of cash flows for Print for the year ended December 31, 20X8 using:

1.   The direct method; and
2.   The indirect method.

PROBLEM 7–11   The following information relates to Richmond Industries Inc.:

(a)   On November 30, 20X8, Richmond Industries issued 50,000 shares at $2 each for cash. This capital was raised to offset the redemption of 1,000 12% $100 serial bonds.

(b)   During 20X8, Richmond Industries purchased new plant and equipment for $105,000.

(c)   The minority interests on the balance sheet only increased by $20,000 because it was reduced by a dividend from the subsidiary of $10,000.

(d)   Goodwill was written down by $2,000 per impairment in 20X8.

(e)   The following consolidated balance sheets and income statements of Richmond Industries for 20X8:

BALANCE SHEETS	20X8	20X7	Increase/(Decrease)
Cash	$ 130,000	$ 180,000	$ (50,000)
Accounts Receivable	622,000	575,000	47,000
Inventory	540,000	515,000	25,000
Plant and Equipment	980,000	875,000	105,000
Less: Accumulated Depreciation	(390,000)	(310,000)	(80,000)
Goodwill	8,000	10,000	(2,000)
	$1,890,000	$1,845,000	$ 45,000
Accounts Payable	$ 255,000	$ 300,000	$ (45,000)
12% Bonds	300,000	400,000	(100,000)
Minority Shareholders Interests	320,000	300,000	20,000
Common Stock	600,000	500,000	100,000
Retained Earnings	415,000	345,000	70,000
	$1,890,000	$1,845,000	$ 45,000

COMBINED INCOME AND RETAINED EARNINGS STATEMENTS	20X8	20X7
Sales	$1,400,000	$1,300,000
Cost of Goods Sold	$ 750,000	$ 500,000
Depreciation Expense	80,000	75,000
Administrative Expenses	220,000	245,000
	$1,050,000	$ 820,000
Total Net Income	$ 350,000	$ 480,000
Less: Minority Interests	30,000	25,000
Consolidated Net Income	320,000	455,000
Retained Earnings at January 1, 20X8	345,000	255,000
	665,000	710,000
Less: Dividends Declared and Paid	250,000	365,000
Retained Earnings at December 31, 20X8	$ 415,000	$ 345,000

REQUIRED

Prepare the statement of cash flows for Richmond Industries for 20X8 using:

1. The direct method; and
2. The indirect method.

Consolidations: Using the Cost or Equity Method 8

LEARNING OBJECTIVES

After studying this chapter you should be able to:

1. Understand why accountants prefer the cost to the equity method of accounting for longterm investments;
2. Consolidate financial statements using financial statements prepared using the cost method; and
3. Prove the accuracy of the entries where the equity method has been used.

THE EQUITY VERSUS THE COST METHODS OF RECORDING LONGTERM INVESTMENTS

Up to this point, the consolidation process has been explained using illustrations in which the companies used the equity method to account for their longterm investments in companies over which they exerted significant influence. The only reference to the cost method of accounting for longterm investments was in the case of investments over which the investor did not exert significant influence. This may have given the impression that the only acceptable method of **recording** the investment in an investee company is by using the equity method. This is not the case, and the cost method to account for longterm investments is equally suitable.

The requirement to **report** using the equity method is made quite clear by the CICA *Handbook*[1] where, in dealing with the reporting of the effects of exerting significant influence over an investee company, it is stated that shareholders should be informed of the results of operations of the investee, and it is appropriate to include in the results of operations of the investor its share of the income or losses of the investee. This does not, however, mean that the equity method must be used to record investments.

It is only when financial statements are prepared for external reporting purposes that they must be prepared using the equity method. To convert from the cost to the equity method is relatively simple. In fact, most practising accountants believe that the use of the

---

[1] Section 3050.

equity method merely complicates the consolidation process. It appears that the popularity of the equity method in accounting literature (but not necessarily in practice) is because it provides a convenient method of illustrating the similarity between the equity method of accounting and consolidation.

What is important to note is that even though different procedures are used to record the investment and the income from those investments, the consolidated financial statements prepared using the cost method are exactly the same as those prepared using the equity method. This is illustrated later in this chapter.

THE COST METHOD

As outlined earlier, the cost method of recording the interest of an investor company operates by recording the investment at its original cost. This balance remains unchanged until such time that the extent of ownership changes or where there has been a permanent decline in the value of the goodwill arising on acquisition. Income from longterm investments is recognized by the parent company only to the extent that dividends have been declared by the subsidiary company. And, on consolidation, the investor company's share of the income from its subsidiaries is recognized in exactly the same manner as that using the equity method.

THE DIFFERENCES IN RECORDING INVESTMENTS USING THE EQUITY AND COST METHODS

The differences in recording the investment in a subsidiary using the equity and cost methods are presented in Illustration 8–1. This illustration provides the abbreviated financial statements of a parent company on the assumption that it had not made an investment in a subsidiary company and compares this set of financial statements with those of the same parent company if it had made an investment in a subsidiary company using, first, the equity method and, second, the cost method. The abbreviated financial statements of the subsidiary are also provided to illustrate the consolidation process using the equity and cost methods later in this chapter.

Illustration 8–1 shows that the two sets of financial statements of the parent company prepared using the cost and equity methods differ considerably from one another in relation to the retained earnings, the net income for the year, and the actual investment in the subsidiary. These differences are examined further hereunder:

The Retained Earnings of the Investor Company As outlined above and in the previous chapter, where the equity method is used, the income statement of the parent company includes its share of the current net income of the subsidiary as adjusted for the amortization of the fair market value adjustments and any write-down of goodwill for impairment. The share of net income relating to prior years (i.e., from the date of acquisition to the beginning of the current year) is included in the retained earnings of the parent company brought forward at the beginning of the year.

With the cost method, however, the investor company's share of the earnings of the subsidiary company from the date of acquisition to the date of consolidation is limited to its **share of the dividends declared** by the subsidiary company. These differences in retained earnings of the parent company using the cost and equity methods are presented in Illustration 8–2, which uses the information provided in Illustration 8–1.

The Share of Net Income from the Subsidiary Company The differences in income recognized by the parent company are also reflected in Illustration 8–2. Here, the amounts of $240,000 and $320,000 using the equity method represent the share of net income from the subsidiary while the dividends of $80,000 and $120,000 represent the investor company's share of the dividends declared by the subsidiary.

ILLUSTRATION 8–1
DIFFERENCES BETWEEN THE RECORDING OF INVESTMENTS IN A SUBSIDIARY COMPANY
ON THE EQUITY AND COST BASES

On January 1, 20X3, Parent Inc. purchased an 80% interest in Subsidiary Inc. for $820,000 when Subsidiary had common stock of $800,000 and retained earnings of $150,000. During 20X3, the net income earned and dividends paid by Subsidiary amounted to $300,000 and $100,000 respectively. There was no write-down of goodwill for impairment in 20X3 or 20X4.

The abbreviated financial statements at December 31, 20X4 given below are those of Parent on the assumption that no investment in Subsidiary had been made, those of Parent on the assumption that an 80% investment in Subsidiary had been acquired and accounted for on, first, the equity basis and, second, on the cost basis. And, to ensure that the difference between the two methods is fully understood, the financial statements of Subsidiary are also provided. Details of the share of net income from Subsidiary are provided in Illustration 8–2.

	Parent with No Investment in Subsidiary	Parent with Investment in Subsidiary on		Subsidiary
		Equity Basis	**Cost Basis**	
COMBINED INCOME AND RETAINED EARNINGS STATEMENTS				
Net Operating Income	$1,000,000	$1,000,000	$1,000,000	$ 400,000
Share of Net Income from Subsidiary	—	320,000	—	—
Dividends from Subsidiary	—	—	120,000	—
	1,000,000	1,320,000	1,120,000	400,000
Less: Dividends Declared and Paid	450,000	450,000	450,000	150,000
	550,000	870,000	670,000	250,000
Retained Earnings at January 1, 20X4	1,200,000	1,440,000	1,280,000	350,000
Retained Earnings at December 31, 20X4	$1,750,000	$2,310,000	$1,950,000	$ 600,000
BALANCE SHEETS				
Current Assets — see note below	$1,300,000	$ 680,000	$ 680,000	$ 500,000
Investment in Subsidiary	—	1,180,000	820,000	—
Plant Assets	3,750,000	3,750,000	3,750,000	1,020,000
	$5,050,000	$5,610,000	$5,250,000	$1,520,000
Current Liabilities	$ 300,000	$ 300,000	$ 300,000	$ 120,000
Common Stock	3,000,000	3,000,000	3,000,000	800,000
Retained Earnings	1,750,000	2,310,000	1,950,000	600,000
	$5,050,000	$5,610,000	$5,250,000	$1,520,000

Note: The current assets of $680,000 are made up of the original amount of $1,300,000 minus the purchase consideration of $820,000 and the addition of the dividends of $80,000 and $120,000 (i.e., $1,300,000 − $820,000 + $80,000 + $200,00 = $680,000).

The Investment Account With the cost method, the "Investment in Subsidiary Account" in Illustration 8–1 is merely shown as the amount of the interest in the investee company at the date of acquisition. As explained earlier, this amount remains unchanged until there is a change in ownership or the goodwill is adjusted downwards to reflect its current value. Where the equity method is used, the investment account is adjusted for its annual share of net income and dividends as follows:

Investment in Subsidiary Inc.

20X3				
Jan. 1	Purchase Consideration	820,000		820,000
Dec. 31	Dividends		80,000	
	Net Income	240,000		980,000
20X4				
Dec. 31	Dividends		120,000	
	Net Income	320,000		1,180,000

ILLUSTRATION 8–2
THE DIFFERENCES IN RETAINED EARNINGS USING THE EQUITY AND
COST METHODS OF RECORDING LONGTERM INVESTMENTS

As outlined in Illustration 8–1, it was on January 1, 20X3 that Parent Inc. purchased an 80% interest in Subsidiary Inc. for $820,000 when Subsidiary had common stock of $800,000 and retained earnings of $150,000. During 20X3, the net income earned and dividends paid by Subsidiary amounted to $300,000 and $100,000 respectively. There was no write-down of goodwill for impairment in 20X3 or 20X4.

The differences in retained earnings at December 31, 20X4 using the cost and equity methods are as follows:

	Equity Method	Cost Method
Balance retained earnings with no investment in Subsidiary at December 31, 20X3	$1,200,000	$1,200,000
Add: Share of Net Income from Subsidiary — 20X3	240,000	—
Dividends from Subsidiary — 20X3	—	80,000
Balance at December 31, 20X3	1,440,000	1,280,000
Add: Net Income from Parent — 20X4	1,000,000	1,000,000
Less: Dividends Paid by Parent	(450,000)	(450,000)
Add: Share of Net Income from Subsidiary — 20X4	320,000	—
Dividends from Subsidiary — 20X4	—	120,000
Balance at December 31, 20X4	$2,310,000	$1,950,000

THE ACTUAL CONSOLIDATION PROCESS USING THE COST METHOD

The consolidation process using the cost method differs very little from that using the equity method. It is outlined in Illustration 8–3 using the information provided in Illustrations 8–1 and 8–2.

This method is essentially the same. However, to carry out the consolidation, the retained earnings at the beginning of the year in which the financial statements are being consolidated must be restated to reflect the correct amount at that date **as if** the equity method had been used. This means that any amounts included as dividend income from the subsidiary company must be excluded and replaced by the parent company's share of the net income from the subsidiary, less any adjustments for any impairment of goodwill, amortization of the fair market values assigned to assets, etc. These adjustments are required to give the same retained earnings as that provided by the equity method. This is reflected by the reconciliation of the retained earnings of the parent company at January 1, 20X4 given in Illustration 8–3.

It should be noted that the amounts required to reconcile the retained earnings using the cost method with that using the equity method all appear in the investment account prepared using the equity method. The only difference between the cost and equity methods lies with the subsidiary's undistributed earnings since acquisition. All that is, therefore, required is to prepare the investment account and extract the necessary figures. For example, using the information provided in the investment account for the subsidiary in Illustration 8–1, the retained earnings account may be reconciled with that using the equity method by deducting the dividends of $80,000 already included in the retained earnings and adding the net income of $240,000. The reconciliation is then $1,280,000 + $240,000 – $80,000 = $1,440,000. The difference of $160,000 ($1,440,000 – $1,280,000) represents the undistributed income for 20X3 of net come of $240,000 less the dividends received of $80,000.

It is important to note that to be able to reconcile the retained earnings at the beginning of the year, full information on the net income and dividends declared and paid by the subsidiary company since acquisition must be known. In practice, this poses no problem because the consolidation of financial statements is an annual process and the information required is available in the working papers from year to year.

ILLUSTRATION 8–3
ILLUSTRATION OF THE CONSOLIDATION PROCESS USING THE COST METHOD

On January 1, 20X3, Parent Inc. purchased an 80% interest in Subsidiary Inc. for $820,000 when Subsidiary had common stock of $800,000 and retained earnings of $150,000. During 20X3, the net income earned and dividends paid by Subsidiary on November 30 amounted to $300,000 and $100,000 respectively. Goodwill was written down by $5,000 for impairment in 20X3.

The abbreviated financial statements of Parent and Subsidiary at December 31, 20X4 were as follows:

	Parent	Subsidiary
BALANCE SHEETS		
Current Assets	$ 680,000	$ 500,000
Investment in Subsidiary	820,000	—
Plant Assets (Net)	3,750,000	1,020,000
	$5,250,000	$1,520,000
Current Liabilities	$ 300,000	$ 120,000
Common Stock	3,000,000	800,000
Retained Earnings	1,950,000	600,000
	$5,250,000	$1,520,000
COMBINED INCOME AND RETAINED EARNINGS STATEMENTS		
Net Operating Income	$1,000,000	$ 400,000
Dividends from Subsidiary	120,000	—
	1,120,000	400,000
Less: Dividends Declared and Paid	450,000	150,000
	670,000	250,000
Retained Earnings at January 1, 20X4	1,280,000	350,000
Retained Earnings at December 31, 20X4	$1,950,000	$ 600,000

The consolidation of the financial statements using the cost method is carried out in the following manner:

The Establishment of the Retained Earnings at January 1, 20X4:

Balance of Retained Earnings at January 1, 20X4		$1,280,000
Less: Dividends Received during 20X3 (i.e., 80% of $100,000)		80,000
		1,200,000
Add: Share of Net Income from Subsidiary — 20X3 (i.e., 80% of $300,000)	$ 240,000	
Less: Impairment of Goodwill — 20X3	5,000	235,000
Adjusted Retained Earnings at January 1, 20X4		$1,435,000

Analysis of Equity:

	Total	Parent 80%	Minority Interests
At Acquisition:			
Common Stock	$ 800,000	$ 640,000	$ 160,000
Retained Earnings	150,000	120,000	30,000
		760,000	
Purchase Consideration		820,000	
Goodwill		$ 60,000	

Goodwill Impairment of $5,000 in 20X3

	Total	Parent 80%	Minority Interests
Since Acquisition:			
Net Income — 20X3	$ 300,000	$ 240,000	$ 60,000
Less Dividends	(100,000)	(80,000)	(20,000)
Net Income — 20X4	400,000	320,000	80,000
Less Dividends	(150,000)	(120,000)	(30,000)
Total Minority Interests			$ 280,000

ILLUSTRATION 8–3 (Continued)

The Preparation of the Consolidated Financial Statements:

BALANCE SHEET

Current Assets (680,000 + 500,000)	$1,180,000
Plant Assets (3,750,000 + 1,020,000)	4,770,000
Goodwill (60,000 − 5,000)	55,000
	$6,005,000
Current Liabilities (300,000 + 120,000)	$ 420,000
Minority Interests	280,000
Common Stock	3,000,000
Retained Earnings	2,305,000
	$6,005,000

COMBINED INCOME AND RETAINED EARNINGS STATEMENT

	Consolidated	Parent	Subsidiary
Net Operating Income	$1,400,000	$1,000,000	$ 400,000
Less: Minority Interests	80,000	—	80,000
Consolidated Net Income	1,320,000	$1,000,000	$ 320,000
Retained Earnings at January 1, 20X4	1,435,000		
	2,755,000		
Less: Dividends Paid	450,000		
Retained Earnings at December 31, 20X4	$2,305,000		

It should be stressed, once again, that there is no difference between the consolidated financial statements prepared using the cost and equity methods of consolidation. The equity method of accounting for an investment in a subsidiary company provides the correct amount of retained earnings for the investor company and, therefore, the correct consolidated net income. This is why the equity method of accounting for an investment is referred to as a "one-line consolidation".

COMPLICATIONS ARISING FROM THE CHANGE IN ACCOUNTING FOR GOODWILL

The change from the amortization to the impairment method of accounting for goodwill may give rise to minor complications in establishing the retained earnings of the parent company at the beginning of the 2002 reporting period. This is because the impairment method is **not applied retroactively**, and the determination of retained earnings brought forward would require the recognition of any amortization of goodwill up to the date on which the impairment method became effective (i.e., for companies having financial years beginning after January 1, 2002).

The amortization of goodwill must cease from the commencement of the period in which the impairment method came into effect. The goodwill remaining must be carried forward and, within six months, the value of the goodwill must be assessed for impairment by carrying out a review of the value of the net assets. Any impairment losses arising from the assessment must be written off in the normal manner as goodwill charges. Such a situation is presented in Illustration 8–4 which reflects the determination of retained earnings brought forward in a case where goodwill was accounted for using both the amortization and impairment methods.

ILLUSTRATION 8–4
DETERMINATION OF THE RETAINED EARNINGS BROUGHT FORWARD IN SITUATIONS WHERE THERE HAS BEEN A CHANGE IN THE ACCOUNTING FOR GOODWILL

Goodwill of $75,000 arose from the purchase by Parent Inc. of a 75% interest in Subsidiary Inc. on May 1, 20X0. At the date of acquisition, an item of plant having a remaining life of eight years was considered to be undervalued by $120,000.

Up to December 31, 20X1, Parent had amortized any goodwill arising on acquisition over a 10-year period. On January 1, 20X2 (20 months later), the impairment method of accounting for goodwill became mandatory. In accordance with the requirements of CICA *Handbook*, a review of the value of goodwill was carried out in June 20X2 that indicated that the goodwill was overvalued by $10,000. The goodwill was, consequently, written down by that amount.

Relevant information relating to Parent and Subsidiary for the three years ended December 31, 20X2 was as follows:

		Parent	Subsidiary
20X0:	Net Income (including Dividends Received)	$ 960,000	$ 300,000
	Dividends Paid (December 10)	240,000	80,000
20X1:	Net Income (including Dividends Received)	1,080,000	400,000
	Dividends Paid (December 12)	300,000	100,000
20X2:	Net Income (including Dividends Received)	1,100,000	420,000
	Dividends Paid (December 9)	320,000	140,000
	Retained Earnings at December 31	1,600,000	900,000

The determination of the Consolidated Retained Earnings of Parent at January 1, 20X3 (i.e., December 31, 20X2) to appear on the Consolidated Income Statement of Parent for the year ended December 31, 20X3 would have been as follows:

Retained Earnings of Parent at December 31, 20X2:			$1,600,000
Add:	Net Income less Dividends from Subsidiary — 20X0[1]	90,000	
	($[75\% \times \$300,000 \times 8/12] - [75\% \times \$80,000]$)		
	Net Income less Dividends from Subsidiary — 20X1	225,000	
	($[75\% \times \$400,000] - [75\% \times \$100,000]$)		
	Net Income less Dividends from Subsidiary — 20X2		
	($[75\% \times \$420,000] - [75\% \times \$140,000]$)	210,000	525,000
			2,125,000
Less:	Goodwill Amortization — 20X0 ($\$75,000/10$ years $\times 8/12$)[2]	5,000	
	Goodwill Amortization — 20X1 ($\$75,000/10$ years)	7,500	
	Goodwill Impairment — 20X2	10,000	22,500
			2,102,500
Less:	Fair Market Value Adjustments — Plant		
	20X0 — $75\% \times \$120,000/8$ years $\times 8/12$[3]	7,500	
	20X1 — $75\% \times \$120,000/8$ years	11,250	
	20X2 — $75\% \times \$120,000/8$ years	11,250	30,000
Consolidated Retained Earnings of Parent at December 31, 20X2			$1,072,500

Notes:
[1] The net income from Subsidiary recognized by Parent would be for the 8 months from the date of acquisition.
[2] Goodwill amortization using the straight-line method was for the period since acquisition.
[3] The fair market value adjustments for the plant were from May 1, 20X0.

THE INCOMPLETE USE OF THE EQUITY METHOD

Up to this point, it has been safe to assume that the share of net income from an investee or subsidiary company and the amounts reflected on the balance as the cost of the investment was correct. However, from this point on you may not do so because the figures reflected for these two items may not have been correctly determined because of the omission of some or other adjustment. Where this has occurred, this is referred to as the incomplete use of the equity method and it is, therefore, necessary to establish the correctness of these amounts and, if necessary, make adjustments to the share of net income and investment accounts.

The incomplete use of the equity method poses the problem of analyzing and reconciling the investment account to establish exactly what entries have been entered in that account. For example, all entries may have been entered except those relating to the impairment of goodwill. However, until such time as the investment account has been analyzed and reconciled, there is no way of knowing exactly what entries have been and which have not been put through the books of the company. It is, therefore, necessary to reconstruct the investment account using the three-step procedure explained in the following section.

THREE-STEP PROOF OF THE FULL USE OF THE EQUITY METHOD

The way in which the full use of the equity method is proved is to work through the following three steps:

(a) The equity of the subsidiary company must first be analyzed to establish the amortization of the fair market value adjustments, and the parent company's share of the post-acquisition net income and dividends paid. At this stage, it must be established whether any write-downs of goodwill for impairment have occurred.

(b) The next step is to analyze the share of the net income from the subsidiary company reflected on the income statement of the parent company. The reason for this is that it indicates which adjustments are necessary.

(c) Finally, the third step consists of the reconstruction of the investment account to confirm that these amounts have, in fact, been omitted.

The reconciliation of the share of net income and investment account only takes a few moments because all the figures required are presented in the analysis of equity.

WHERE THE INVESTOR AND INVESTEE COMPANIES HAVE DIFFERENT FINANCIAL YEAR ENDS

The financial year ends of the investor and the investee companies do not always coincide. Ideally, this should be rectified as soon as possible after acquisition by changing the year end of the investee company. However, this may not always be possible for one reason or another, because the jurisdiction in which the investee company is registered may not allow a change in the financial year in question.

Obviously, where it is possible to do so, the investee company should prepare financial statements corresponding with the financial year of its parent company. In those cases where this is not possible as, for example, in the year of acquisition, the consolidation process should be carried out using the financial statements having different year ends. However, attention to this fact must be disclosed in the consolidated financial statements.[2] Furthermore, any material post-balance sheet events relating to subsidiary companies having year ends different from that of the parent company should be disclosed.

---

2 CICA *Handbook*, section 1600.

STATEMENTS PREPARED ON A COST BASIS

Notwithstanding the requirement that consolidated financial statements should always be prepared, there are cases where the presentation of **financial statements prepared on a cost basis are recognized as being appropriate** for reporting purposes.[3] In this respect, the financial statements comply with generally accepted accounting principles except that the parent company's interest in the results of operations of investee companies or subsidiaries would not have been prepared using the equity method or consolidated with those of the parent company.[4]

The most common example is where a company that prepares consolidated financial statements for reporting to shareholders prepares financial statements on a cost basis **for income tax purposes**. A similar set of financial statements may also be required by the company's bankers to **assess its credit rating or to extend a bank loan**. This latter situation often exists where money has been advanced to the company against the security of certain assets and the lender needs to assess the extent of its security without the position being clouded by the consolidated position.

This also applies to private or closely held companies where the owners have access to all information on the results of operations and resources of the group and all owners, including those holding non-voting securities, have unanimously agreed to the presentation of non-consolidated financial statements. In these cases, the information is normally provided by preparing financial statements of the individual companies making up the group.

Irrespective of the reasons for doing so, these financial statements must include additional information giving the reason consolidated financial statements have not been presented, that they have not been prepared for general use, and that, other than the lack of consolidated financial statements or the use of the equity method, they have been prepared using GAAP. It also specifically requires that where the cost method has been used, any gains or losses arising from intercompany transactions should be disclosed.

SUMMARY

In this chapter, the differences between the cost and equity methods of recording longterm investments are outlined. Even though it is often suggested that the equity method should be used to record longterm investments over which control is exercised, the cost method provides an equally acceptable method of accounting for these investments. The choice of the method is entirely a matter of personal preference because the consolidated financial statements prepared using the two different methods are exactly the same. The major difference between the methods is that the use of the equity method provides the figure for the consolidated retained earnings at the beginning of the year, while with the cost method, this figure has to be established as part of the consolidation process.

The incomplete use of the equity method of accounting for longterm investments may also be encountered in practice. It is, therefore, always necessary to establish whether or not the figures provided for retained earnings at the beginning of the year, the investment account, and the share of net income from the investee company appearing in the financial statements of the investor company include all the necessary adjustments. This is achieved through a three-step reconstruction of the investment account.

---

[3] For example, those situations recognized in section 3050 of the CICA *Handbook*.
[4] The CICA is in the process of formalizing this situation and is to issue a new CICA *Handbook* section, entitled "Differential Reporting", covering the issue of financial statements prepared on a cost basis.

SELF-STUDY PROBLEM

(covering current chapter and certain aspects of Chapter Seven)

PROBLEM 8A†   Piper Inc. purchased a 75% interest in Scot Inc. on April 1, 20X4 for $1,380,000. Financial statements were not prepared at the date of acquisition, but at January 1, 20X4, the retained earnings of Scot had amounted to $500,000. At December 31, 20X5, the abbreviated financial statements of Piper and Scot were as follows:

COMBINED INCOME AND RETAINED EARNINGS STATEMENTS	Piper	Scot
Sales	$5,560,000	$2,870,000
Interest Revenue	10,000	—
Total Revenues	$5,570,000	$2,870,000
Cost of Goods Sold	$1,830,000	$1,390,000
Operating Expenses	1,920,000	1,160,000
Interest Expense	—	10,000
	$3,750,000	$2,560,000
Net Operating Income	$1,820,000	$ 310,000
Dividends from Scot	60,000	—
Net Income for Year before Extraordinary Item	1,880,000	310,000
Extraordinary Item	—	100,000
Net Income for Year	1,880,000	410,000
Retained Earnings at January 1, 20X5	1,630,000	820,000
	3,510,000	1,230,000
Less: Dividends Paid	500,000	80,000
Retained Earnings at December 31, 20X5	$3,010,000	$1,150,000

BALANCE SHEETS		
Cash	$ 218,000	$ 85,000
Accounts Receivable	1,885,000	670,000
Inventory	955,000	490,000
Investment in Scot	1,380,000	—
10% Loan to Scot	100,000	—
Capital Assets (Net)	2,592,000	1,350,000
	$7,130,000	$2,595,000
Accounts Payable	$ 920,000	$ 345,000
10% Loan from Piper	—	100,000
Common Stock	3,200,000	1,000,000
Retained Earnings	3,010,000	1,150,000
	$7,130,000	$2,595,000

Additional Information:

1. At the date of acquisition, all the assets of Scot were considered to be fairly valued except for plant having a six-year remaining life that was undervalued by $80,000.
2. The assets acquired also included a non-renewable capital lease that was to expire on March 31, 20X6. The lease was considered to be undervalued by $48,000 at the date of acquisition and was to be recorded as an asset on the balance sheet of Scot.
3. The after tax extraordinary item of $100,000 for Scot arose in 20X5 from the expropriation of land.

---

† The solution is provided in Appendix B to this text.

4. In 20X4, Scot had earned $400,000 and declared a dividend of $80,000 on November 25.
5. Goodwill was written down for impairment by $8,000 in 20X4 and a further $2,000 in 20X5.
6. On January 1, 20X5, Piper had lent $100,000 to Scot at an annual interest rate of 10%.

REQUIRED

Prepare the consolidated balance sheet and combined income and retained earnings statement of Piper and its subsidiary for the year ended December 31, 20X5.

REVIEW QUESTIONS

1. Why is the cost method of accounting for an investment in a subsidiary company preferred by some accountants? Is it a valid reason?
2. Why do the consolidated financial statements prepared using the cost and equity methods of accounting for the investment in a subsidiary company give the same consolidated results of operations and financial position?
3. Explain how the consolidated retained earnings at the beginning of the year in which the consolidation takes place is established.
4. Describe what occurs when the incomplete use of the equity method of recording a longterm investment is used.
5. Describe the three-step process of proving the correct retained earnings and net income for the current year from the subsidiary company where the incomplete equity method has been used.
6. In what circumstances are financial statements prepared on a cost basis considered appropriate?

EXERCISES

EXERCISE 8–1 No goodwill arose on the acquisition by Page Inc. of a 60% interest in Sheet Inc. for $120,000 on July 1, 20X5 when Sheet had retained earnings of $30,000. At the date of acquisition, all assets and liabilities were fairly valued except for a single item of plant having a five-year remaining life that was undervalued by $10,000 and amortized using the straight-line method. Page accounts for its investment in Sheet using the cost method.

Additional relevant information relating to the two companies for the year ended December 31, 20X6 was as follows:

	Page	Sheet
Net Operating Income	$200,000	$100,000
Retained Earnings at January 1	240,000	70,000
Dividends Paid on November 1	80,000	20,000

REQUIRED

Indicate which of the following possible answers are correct.

1. The consolidated net income of Page for 20X6 was:

(a) $258,800
(b) $257,800
(c) $248,400
(d) $245,100
(e) None of the above

2. The consolidated retained earnings of Page at January 1, 20X6 was:

   (a) $279,000   (b) $268,500
   (c) $261,000   (d) $262,500
   (e) None of the above

3. The minority interest net income for 20X6 was:

   (a) $40,000   (b) $38,500
   (c) $37,000   (d) $25,000
   (e) None of the above

4. The consolidated retained earnings at December 31, 20X6 was:

   (a) $449,200   (b) $440,700
   (c) $429,500   (d) $417,000
   (e) None of the above

EXERCISE 8–2 Goodwill of $90,000 arose from the purchase by Picture Inc. of a 75% interest in Scene Inc. on April 1, 20X1. At the date of acquisition an item of plant having a 10-year remaining life was considered to be undervalued by $80,000.

The abbreviated income and retained earnings statements of the two companies at December 31, 20X2 were as follows:

INCOME AND RETAINED EARNINGS STATEMENTS	Picture	Scene
Sales	$2,500,000	$1,200,000
Cost of Goods Sold	$ 900,000	$ 600,000
Operating Expenses	850,000	240,000
	$1,750,000	$ 840,000
Net Operating Income	$ 750,000	$ 360,000
Dividends Received from Scene	150,000	—
Net Income	900,000	360,000
Retained Earnings at January 1, 20X2	670,000	320,000
	1,570,000	680,000
Dividends Paid (November 25)	500,000	200,000
Retained Earnings at December 31, 20X2	$1,070,000	$ 480,000

You are also informed that:

(a) Goodwill was written down for impairment by $4,000 in June 20X1 and $6,000 in November 20X2.
(b) During 20X1, Scene had earned net income of $160,000 and paid a dividend of $100,000 on November 20.

REQUIRED

Prepare the combined consolidated statement of income and retained earnings for the year ended December 31, 20X2.

EXERCISE 8–3 Pike Inc. purchased an 80% interest in Staff Inc. on July 1, 20X2 for $1,500,000. Financial statements had not been prepared at the date of acquisition but at December 31, 20X1, Staff had retained earnings of $400,000 and during 20X2, Staff had earned net income of $300,000 and paid a dividend of $100,000 on November 15. At the date of acquisition, the assets of Staff were considered to be fairly valued. Pike amortizes goodwill using the impairment method and in July 20X2 and December 20X3, goodwill was written down by $10,000 and $20,000 respectively.

At December 31, 20X3, the abbreviated balance sheets and income and retained earnings statements of the two companies were as follows:

COMBINED INCOME AND RETAINED EARNINGS STATEMENTS	Pike	Staff
Sales	$4,000,000	$2,000,000
Cost of Goods Sold	$2,000,000	$ 920,000
Administration Expenses	1,400,000	760,000
Total Expenses	$3,400,000	$1,680,000
Operating Income	$ 600,000	$ 320,000
Dividends Received from Staff	32,000	—
Net Income for Year	632,000	320,000
Retained Earnings at January 1, 20X3	712,000	600,000
	1,344,000	920,000
Dividends Paid (December 15)	400,000	40,000
Retained Earnings at December 31, 20X3	$ 944,000	$ 880,000

BALANCE SHEETS		
Current Assets	$1,000,000	$ 720,000
Investment in Staff	1,500,000	—
Plant and Equipment (net)	900,000	1,240,000
	$3,400,000	$1,960,000
Accounts Payable	456,000	180,000
Common Stock	2,000,000	900,000
Retained Earnings	944,000	880,000
	$3,400,000	$1,960,000

REQUIRED

Prepare the consolidated balance sheet at December 31, 20X3, and the consolidated income and retained earnings statement for the year ended on that date.

EXERCISE 8–4   Plain Inc. acquired an 80% interest in Sailing Inc. on January 1, 20X5 for $1-million when Sailing had retained earnings of $200,000.

The abbreviated financial statements of Plain and Sailing at December 31, 20X6 were as follows:

BALANCE SHEETS	Plain	Sailing
Current Assets	$1,450,000	$ 970,000
Investment in Sailing	1,000,000	—
Plant and Equipment (Net)	3,290,000	1,350,000
	$5,740,000	$2,320,000
Current Liabilities	$ 280,000	$ 490,000
Common Stock	2,000,000	800,000
Retained Earnings	3,460,000	1,030,000
	$5,740,000	$2,320,000

COMBINED INCOME AND RETAINED EARNINGS STATEMENTS		
Sales	$7,300,000	$5,120,000
Cost of Goods Sold	(4,050,000)	(2,890,000)
Administration and Other Expenses	(2,090,000)	(1,650,000)
Net Operating Income	$1,160,000	580,000
Retained Earnings at January 1, 20X6	2,300,000	450,000
Retained Earnings at December 31, 20X6	$3,460,000	$1,030,000

You are provided with the following additional information:

(a)   No dividends had been paid by Sailing since the controlling interest had been acquired by Plain;

(b) Goodwill was written down for impairment by $10,000 in 20X5 and a further $20,000 in 20X6.

(c) The assets and liabilities of Sailing were fairly valued at the date of acquisition.

REQUIRED

Prepare the consolidated balance sheet and combined income and retained earnings statement of Plain at December 31, 20X6.

EXERCISE 8–5   The following figures were extracted from the income and retained earnings statements of Peer Inc. and See Inc. for the year ended December 31, 20X4:

	Peer	See
Net Income from Operations	$ 955,000	$240,000
Dividends Paid (December 31)	300,000	80,000
Retained Earnings at January 1, 20X4	2,300,000	600,000

On October 1, 20X4, Peer had acquired a 75% interest in See for $1.5-million. At December 31, 20X3, See had common stock of $1-million and retained earnings of $600,000.

At the date of acquisition, all assets and liabilities were fairly valued except for the undervaluation of plant by $80,000. The undervalued plant was expected to have a useful life of five years from the date of acquisition.

You are also informed that Peer accounts for its investment in See using the cost method and goodwill on an impairment basis.

REQUIRED

1. Prepare the consolidated net income of Peer for the year ended December 31, 20X4 on the assumption that goodwill was written down by $15,000 for impairment during the year;

2. Give the consolidated retained earnings of Peer for the year ended December 31, 20X4; and

3. Give the "Investment in See" account as it would appear in the ledger of Peer at December 31, 20X4.

EXERCISE 8–6   Pop Inc. acquired an 80% interest in Soda Inc. on July 1, 20X1 for $700,000. At January 1, 20X1, Soda had common stock of $600,000 and retained earnings of $125,000. The net income of Soda for 20X1, which was not included in the retained earnings given below, amounted to $30,000. At the date of acquisition, it was determined that the plant assets having a 10-year remaining useful life were undervalued by $50,000. Land owned by Soda was also undervalued by $10,000. No write-down of goodwill for impairment occurred in 20X1 and 20X2.

The following information appeared on the balance sheets and income statements of Pop and Soda at December 31, 20X2.

	Pop	Soda
Common Stock	$1,200,000	$600,000
Retained Earnings at January 1, 20X2	720,000	155,000
Net Income from Operations	300,000	100,000
Share of Net Income from Soda	76,000	—
Dividends Declared	120,000	40,000
Investment in Soda	754,000	—

REQUIRED

Determine whether or not Pop has used the "full" equity method of recording its investment in Soda.

EXERCISE 8–7 Goodwill of $20,000 arose on the acquisition by Picket Inc. of a 60% interest in Strike Inc. on October 1, 20X4. At that date, all assets and liabilities were considered fairly valued except for current liabilities that were undervalued by $20,000.

The following information relates to Picket and Strike for the years ended December 31, 20X4 and 20X5:

		Picket	Strike
20X4:	Retained Earnings at January 1	$400,000	$200,000
	Total Net Income for Year	300,000	100,000
	Dividends Paid (November 30)	100,000	40,000
20X5:	Total Net Income for Year	420,000	150,000
	Dividends Paid (December 4)	120,000	60,000

You are **further informed** that Picket accounts for its longterm investments using the cost method and that goodwill was written down by $5,000 for impairment in 20X5.

REQUIRED

Prepare the consolidated retained earnings of Picket at December 31, 20X5.

EXERCISE 8–8 Goodwill of $72,000 arose as a result of the purchase by Port Inc. of a 90% interest in Sherry Inc. on July 1, 20X7. At the date of acquisition, the assets of Sherry were considered to be fairly valued.

At January 1, 20X7, Port had retained earnings of $900,000 while Sherry had an accumulated loss of $200,000.

The reported net income and dividends paid by the two companies for the two years ended December 31, 20X7 and 20X8 were as follows:

		Port	Sherry
20X7:	Net Income (including dividend revenue)	$600,000	$ 80,000
	Dividends Paid (October 25)	180,000	40,000
20X8:	Net Income (including dividend revenue)	750,000	120,000
	Dividends Paid (November 1)	300,000	80,000

You are informed that Port accounts for its investment in Sherry using the cost method and that goodwill was written down by $6,000 for impairment in 20X7.

REQUIRED

Prepare the consolidated retained earnings of Port and its subsidiary company at December 31, 20X8.

PROBLEMS

PROBLEM 8–1 The abbreviated financial statements of Parent Inc. and Son Inc. at December 31, 20X4 were as follows:

BALANCE SHEETS	Parent (000s)	Son (000s)
Current Assets	$ 73,500	$24,000
Investment in Son	35,500	—
Land	20,000	10,000
Plant and Equipment (Net)	44,000	34,000
	$173,000	$68,000
Current Liabilities	$ 29,000	$28,000
Common Stock	100,000	20,000
Retained Earnings	44,000	20,000
	$173,000	$68,000

COMBINED INCOME AND RETAINED EARNINGS STATEMENT	Parent (000s)	Son (000s)
Sales	$100,000	$60,000
Cost of Goods Sold	$ 60,000	$32,000
Operating Expenses	22,000	12,000
	$ 82,000	$44,000
Net Operating Income	$ 18,000	$16,000
Dividends from Son	6,000	—
Net Income	24,000	16,000
Dividends Paid	10,000	8,000
	14,000	8,000
Retained Earnings at January 1, 20X4	30,000	12,000
Retained Earnings at December 31, 20X4	$ 44,000	$20,000

Parent had acquired a 75% interest in Son on January 1, 20X2 when Son had retained earnings of $6-million. At the date of acquisition, land (included in plant and equipment) was undervalued by $8-million. You are informed that no dividends had been paid by Son during 20X2 and 20X3 and that goodwill had been written down for impairment by $5-million in 20X2 and a further $2-million in 20X4. The net income of Son for 20X2 and 20X3 was $3-million in each year.

REQUIRED

Prepare consolidated balance sheet and combined income and retained earnings statement for Parent at December 31, 20X4, from the above information.

PROBLEM 8–2 Pat Inc. acquired a 75% interest in Sat Inc. on April 1, 20X5 for $4.5-million. At that date, certain plant belonging to Sat having a five-year remaining useful life was overvalued by $2.4-million.

The abbreviated financial statements of Pat and Sat at December 31, 20X7 were as follows:

COMBINED INCOME AND RETAINED EARNINGS STATEMENTS	Pat	Sat
Sales	$ 20,850,000	$ 12,600,000
Cost of Goods Sold	(12,710,000)	(7,300,000)
Expenses	(4,540,000)	(2,900,000)
Net Operating Income	3,600,000	2,400,000
Share of Net Income from Sat	1,800,000	—
Net Income	5,400,000	2,400,000
Dividends Declared and Paid	2,000,000	1,600,000
	3,400,000	800,000
Retained Earnings at January 1, 20X7	6,600,000	2,400,000
Retained Earnings at December 31, 20X7	$ 10,000,000	$ 3,200,000

BALANCE SHEETS		
Current Assets	$ 12,380,000	$ 5,080,000
Loan to Sat	4,200,000	—
Investment in Sat	5,300,000	—
Plant and Equipment	17,120,000	11,920,000
Less: Accumulated Amortization	(4,000,000)	(3,200,000)
	$ 35,000,000	$ 13,800,000
Current Liabilities	$ 5,000,000	$ 1,200,000
Loan from Pat	—	4,200,000
Common Stock	20,000,000	5,200,000
Retained Earnings	10,000,000	3,200,000
	$ 35,000,000	$ 13,800,000

You are also informed that:

(a) On January 1, 20X5, Sat had retained earnings of $1.2-million.
(b) Goodwill was written down by $400,000 for impairment in 20X5.
(c) The trading results and dividends paid by Sat for 20X5 and 20X6 were as follows:

	20X5	20X6
Net Income	$1,600,000	$2,400,000
Dividends Paid (October)	1,200,000	1,600,000

REQUIRED

Prepare the consolidated financial statements of Pat at December 31, 20X7.

PROBLEM 8–3

Phase Inc. acquired a 75% interest in Stage Inc. on January 1, 20X7 for $525,000 when the common stock of Stage amounted to $500,000 made up of 100,000 shares of common stock of no par value and retained earnings of $40,000. At the date of acquisition, the plant and equipment of Stage was considered to be fairly valued except for an item of plant having a remaining five-year life which was undervalued by $80,000.

The financial statements of the two companies at December 31, 20X8 were as follows:

BALANCE SHEETS	Phase	Stage
Cash	$ 45,000	$ 20,000
Accounts Receivable	550,000	290,000
Inventory	280,000	210,000
Investment in Stage	525,000	—
Land	—	80,000
Plant and Equipment (Net)	1,060,000	370,000
	$2,460,000	$970,000
Accounts Payable	$ 400,000	$150,000
Common Stock	1,500,000	500,000
Retained Earnings	560,000	320,000
	$2,460,000	$970,000

COMBINED INCOME AND RETAINED EARNINGS STATEMENTS	Phase	Stage
Sales	$1,720,000	$900,000
Cost of Goods Sold	$1,100,000	$400,000
Administration Expenses	200,000	120,000
Depreciation Expense	120,000	80,000
	$1,420,000	$600,000
Net Income from Operations	$ 300,000	$300,000
Dividends from Stage	60,000	—
Net Income for Year	360,000	300,000
Retained Earnings at January 1, 20X8	400,000	100,000
	760,000	400,000
Dividends Paid	200,000	80,000
Retained Earnings at December 31, 20X8	$ 560,000	$320,000

You are also informed that:

(a) Goodwill was written down by $5,000 for impairment in 20X7.
(b) At December 31, 20X8 Stage owed Phase $20,000 on open account.

REQUIRED

Prepare the consolidated income and retained earnings statement (individual or combined) and consolidated balance sheet of Phase for 20X8.

PROBLEM 8–4   Platinum Inc. acquired an 80% interest in Silver Inc. on April 1, 20X2 for $660,000 when Silver had common stock of $600,000. Financial statements had not been pre-pared at the date of acquisition, but the equity section of the balance sheet of Silver at December 31, 20X1 reflected retained earnings of $60,000. It was also agreed that at the date of acquisition, an item of plant having an eight-year remaining life was undervalued by $80,000.

The abbreviated financial statements of the two companies for 20X4 were as follows:

	Platinum	Silver
BALANCE SHEETS		
Cash	$ 70,000	$ 140,000
Accounts Receivable	400,000	300,000
Inventory	300,000	280,000
Investment in Silver	660,000	—
Plant and Equipment (Net)	520,000	460,000
	$1,950,000	$1,180,000
Current Liabilities	$ 280,000	$ 100,000
Common Stock	1,000,000	600,000
Retained Earnings	670,000	480,000
	$1,950,000	$1,180,000
INCOME AND RETAINED EARNINGS STATEMENTS		
Sales	$1,400,000	$ 900,000
Cost of Goods Sold	$ 700,000	$ 400,000
Operating Expenses	250,000	240,000
	$ 950,000	$ 640,000
Net Operating Income	$ 450,000	$ 260,000
Dividends Received	80,000	—
Net Income	530,000	260,000
Retained Earnings at January 1, 20X4	390,000	320,000
	920,000	580,000
Dividends Paid (November 15)	250,000	100,000
Retained Earnings at December 31, 20X4	$ 670,000	$ 480,000

You are also informed that:

(a)   The trading results and dividends paid by the two companies for 20X2 and 20X3 were as follows:

		Platinum	Silver
20X2:	Net Income from Operations	$200,000	$160,000
	Dividends Paid (December 5)	120,000	40,000
20X3:	Net Income from Operations	360,000	$220,000
	Dividends Paid (November 30)	200,000	80,000

(b)   Goodwill was amortized in 20X2 on a straight-line basis over a six-year period.
(c)   With effect from January 1, 20X3, the impairment method was used and an impairment loss of $8,000 was recognized in 20X3.

REQUIRED

Prepare the consolidated balance sheet of Platinum for the year ended December 31, 20X4 and the combined consolidated statement of income and retained earnings for the year ended on that date.

PROBLEM 8–5   On October 1, 20X4, Putt Inc. acquired an 80% interest in Sink Inc. for the sum of $800,000 after agreement that certain plant having a 10-year remaining life was undervalued by $50,000 and that the debentures issued by Sink were overvalued by $40,000. Financial statements of Sink were not prepared at the date of acquisition but on January 1, 20X4, Sink had common stock of $550,000 (100,000 shares of no par value) and retained earnings of $50,000. You are also informed that goodwill was written down by $10,000 for impairment in 20X5.

The trading operations of Sink were cyclical in pattern, and over the years it had been established that 40% of the sales were made in the first six months of the year and 60% in the second six months. Sales and profits, however, accrued evenly within each six-monthly period.

Trading activities and dividends paid for the two years ended December 31, 20X5 were as follows:

	Putt	Sink
20X4:		
Net Income from Operations	$ 600,000	$ 300,000
Dividends Declared and Paid (November 30)	200,000	—
20X5:		
Net Income from Operations	750,000	250,000
Dividends Declared and Paid (December 4)	300,000	100,000

The abbreviated financial statements of Putt and Sink at December 31, 20X6 were as follows:

BALANCE SHEETS	Putt	Sink
Current Assets	$ 950,000	$ 800,000
Investment in Sink	800,000	—
Plant and Equipment (Net)	1,250,000	1,555,000
	$3,000,000	$2,355,000
Current Liabilities	$ 500,000	$ 280,000
10% Debentures (Maturity date: September 30, 20X8)	—	800,000
Common Stock	1,000,000	550,000
Retained Earnings	1,500,000	725,000
	$3,000,000	$2,355,000

COMBINED INCOME AND RETAINED EARNINGS STATEMENTS	Putt	Sink
Sales	$2,500,000	$ 900,000
Cost of Goods Sold	$1,200,000	$ 330,000
Expenses	400,000	220,000
	$1,600,000	$ 550,000
Net Operating Income	$ 900,000	$ 350,000
Dividends Received from Sink	100,000	—
Net Income	1,000,000	350,000
Retained Earnings at January 1, 20X6	800,000	500,000
	1,800,000	850,000
Dividends Declared and Paid	300,000	125,000
Retained Earnings at December 31, 20X6	$1,500,000	$ 725,000

REQUIRED

Prepare the consolidated balance sheet and combined income and retained earnings statement of Putt at December 31, 20X6.

PROBLEM 8–6 Par Inc. acquired a 75% interest in Standard Inc. on October 1, 20X5 for $960,000. At that date, the assets and liabilities of Standard were considered to be fairly valued except for an item of plant having a 10-year remaining life that was considered to be undervalued by $80,000.

Financial statements were not prepared at the date of acquisition. However, at January 1, 20X5, Standard had retained earnings of $200,000, common stock of $800,000, and its income statement for the year ended December 31, 20X5 disclosed net income of $160,000, and the payment of a dividend of $80,000 on December 10.

You are also informed that goodwill was written down by $12,000 for impairment in 20X6.

The abbreviated financial statements of the two companies for the year ended December 31, 20X6 were as follows:

	Par	Standard
BALANCE SHEETS		
Cash	$ 110,000	$ 60,000
Accounts Receivable	230,000	480,000
Inventory	260,000	330,000
Investment in Standard	1,045,500	—
Plant and Equipment (Net)	310,000	550,000
	$1,955,500	$1,420,000
Accounts Payable	210,000	60,000
10% Bonds (Repayable 20X9)	—	100,000
Common Stock	1,000,000	800,000
Retained Earnings	745,500	460,000
	$1,955,500	$1,420,000
COMBINED INCOME AND		
RETAINED EARNINGS STATEMENTS		
Sales	$1,500,000	$1,280,000
Cost of Goods Sold	$ 800,000	$ 740,000
Administration Expenses	350,000	300,000
Total Expenses	$1,150,000	$1,040,000
Net Income from Operations	$ 350,000	$ 240,000
Extraordinary Item	—	20,000
Net Income	350,000	260,00
Share of Net Income from Standard:		
From Operations	162,000	—
Extraordinary Item	15,000	—
Net Income after Extraordinary Item (arising on November 30)	527,000	260,000
Retained Earnings at January 1	618,500	280,000
	1,145,500	540,000
Dividends Paid (December 15)	400,000	80,000
Retained Earnings at December 31	$ 745,500	$ 460,000

REQUIRED

1. Analyze the share of net income from Standard for 20X6;
2. Reconcile the "Investment in Standard" at December 31, 20X6;
3. Prepare the consolidated combined income and retained earnings statement and balance sheet of Par for the year ended December 31, 20X6.

PROBLEM 8–7   The following information appeared on the balance sheets and income statements of Plunge Inc. and Sink Inc. at December 31, 20X1.

	Plunge	Sink
Common Stock (1,200,000 shares)	$1,200,000	
Common Stock (480,000 shares)		$480,000
Retained Earnings at January 1, 20X1	720,000	120,000
Net Income from Operations	320,000	100,000
Share of Net Income from Sink	32,000	—
Dividends Declared	120,000	40,000
Investment in Sink	316,000	—

Plunge acquired a 40% interest in Sink on January 1, 20X1 for $300,000. At the date of acquisition, it was determined that plant assets having a 10-year remaining useful life were undervalued by $50,000. In 20X1, the policy of Plunge was to amortize any goodwill arising on acquisition over five years, as the amortization method of accounting for goodwill still applied.

REQUIRED

1. Using the three-step procedure, determine whether Plunge has used the "full" equity method of recording its investment in Sink; and
2. Determine the retained earnings of Plunge at December 31, 20X1.

9 Consolidations: Intercompany Transactions in Inventories

LEARNING OBJECTIVES

After studying this chapter you should be able to:

1. Understand the nature of transfer pricing as it applies to inventories;
2. Recognize the need to eliminate intercompany transactions and unrealized profits in inventories;
3. Apply the techniques required to eliminate unrealized profits in inventories in both upstream and downstream situations;
4. Adjust the income tax expense/future taxes arising from the elimination of unrealized profits; and
5. Appreciate the theoretical inconsistencies in eliminating unrealized profits in inventories.

THE NEED TO ELIMINATE INTERCOMPANY TRANSACTIONS

Where transactions involving the purchase and sale of inventory between companies affiliated in a parent-subsidiary company relationship have taken place, these transactions and their effects on the individual companies must be recognized and eliminated in the consolidation process. This is necessary to ensure that the financial position and results of operations of the group of companies are not distorted by including these intercompany transfers in sales and recognizing unrealized profits on such transfers. This chapter outlines the procedures necessary to eliminate intercompany inventory purchases and sales and the effects of these transactions on the consolidated financial statements.

ELIMINATING INTERCOMPANY SALES

The objective of the elimination process is to exclude the intercompany sales from the income statements of the companies concerned. This is carried out by deducting them from the sales appearing on the income statement of the selling company and by deducting the same amount from the cost of goods sold in the purchasing company. However, no matter how correct this treatment may appear to be, this results in the restatement of the trading results of the

ILLUSTRATION 9–1

THE ELIMINATION OF INTERCOMPANY PURCHASES AND SALES

The following figures appeared in the income statement of two companies associated in a parent-subsidiary company relationship.

	Parent	Subsidiary
Sales	$500,000	$300,000
Cost of Goods Sold	300,000	200,000
Gross Profit	$200,000	$100,000

If sales by the parent company to the subsidiary amounted to $50,000 during the year, the elimination of these intercompany transactions in the consolidated working papers would be as follows:

	Consolidated	Parent	Subsidiary
Sales		$500,000	$300,000
Less: Intercompany Sales		50,000	—
Sales	$750,000	$450,000	$300,000
Cost of Goods Sold		$300,000	$200,000
Less: Intercompany Purchases		50,000	—
Cost of Goods Sold	450,000	$250,000	$200,000
Gross Profit	$300,000	$200,000	$100,000

However, if the elimination of the intercompany purchases and sales had been carried out by deducting the intercompany sales from the company effecting the sale and by deducting the intercompany purchases from the company purchasing the goods, the resulting figures would have been as follows:

	Consolidated	Parent	Subsidiary
Sales		$500,000	$300,000
Less: Intercompany Sales		50,000	—
Sales	$750,000	$450,000	$300,000
Cost of Goods Sold		$300,000	$200,000
Less: Intercompany Purchases		—	50,000
Cost of Goods Sold	450,000	$300,000	$150,000
Gross Profit	$300,000	$150,000	$150,000

individual companies in a manner that bears little resemblance to those prior to the making of the adjustments. It is, therefore, necessary to make the adjustment for intercompany sales and purchases against the same company. This ensures that financial statements continue to reflect the trading results of the companies concerned before the adjustments were made.

The deduction of the intercompany purchases and sales against the same company is reflected in Illustration 9–1, where it is shown that the gross profit of $200,000 for the parent company and the $100,000 of the subsidiary company remain unchanged after the elimination of these intercompany transactions. Where the deductions for intercompany transactions are against the sales of the selling company and the cost of goods sold of the company receiving the goods, the gross profit reflected by the parent and subsidiary companies becomes $150,000 in both companies. Even though the consolidated figures remain unchanged at $300,000 (i.e., 2 × $150,000 and not the $200,00 + $100,000 before adjustment), the entire trading results are so distorted that they no longer represent those of the separate companies before the exclusion of these transactions.

It should also be noted that the adjustment for intercompany sales and purchases can be made in either company. All that is necessary is that **both adjustments are made in the same company**.

THE ELIMINATION OF UNREALIZED GAINS OR LOSSES IN INTERCOMPANY TRANSACTIONS

Where intercompany sales of inventory have taken place, it is also necessary to eliminate any unrealized gains or losses arising from these transactions because they affect the value of the closing inventory and the net income of the consolidated entity. The inflation or deflation of the prices at which goods are sold between companies in a group is referred to as "transfer pricing".

The use of transfer pricing is considerably more common than is generally believed. It is often used to conceal the level of profits where there is a divisionalization of operations within a group. It is also frequently used in the case of foreign subsidiaries, particularly where monetary exchange control regulations are in force, as a means of transferring funds that would otherwise remain in the foreign country.[1] It also provides the means of utilizing income tax losses in the companies in the group and, with international operations, to avoid the payment of income taxes through the reduction of taxable profits in those countries where they are subject to taxes at higher rates.

The adjustment for transfer pricing only applies to the unrealized profits or losses arising from the "internal markup or markdown" of the goods that are unsold at the end of the accounting period. This is an inventory valuation problem because, irrespective of how the intercompany trading activities have been conducted during the year, the ending inventory of the affiliated group must be correctly valued for both balance sheet and income statement purposes. Goods purchased by one company from another in an affiliated group that have been sold to outside parties do not concern the consolidation process because they represent goods on which gains or losses have been realized.

The reason it is necessary to eliminate intercompany sales and the unrealized gains (or losses) remaining in inventory at the end of the accounting period, is to ensure that the consolidated trading results of the group are not inflated (or deflated) through fictitious sales. For example, if A Inc. and B Inc. sold goods to one another back and forth throughout the year at a profit, the companies would both show healthy but fictitious profits on the sales between themselves.

The elimination of intercompany sales and unrealized profits **do not** apply to any transactions effected between companies **before they became affiliated** in a parent company-subsidiary company relationship because these transactions are considered to have been carried out at arm's length between the parties concerned. It is, therefore, only those intercompany sales entered into subsequent to the acquisition that are transactions between related parties, and are those to which the elimination process applies.

Transfer pricing should not be confused with **dumping**, which is the selling of goods by companies in foreign countries at prices below their manufactured cost. It is usually carried out to establish a market in a foreign country or to earn foreign exchange. It is a practice that is outlawed by international trade agreements, as well as by individual countries (e.g., Canada) because it can cause considerable damage to the industrial bases of countries.

---

[1] Transfer pricing applies worldwide. *The Globe and Mail* of November 25, 1996, in reprinting an article from *The Wall Street Journal*, reported that the Japanese revenue authorities are stepping up their claims for back taxes from foreign companies suspected of using transfer pricing to avoid the high Japanese rate of corporate taxes. Corporations pay roughly 50% of their annual earnings in corporate taxes in Japan, compared with 41% in the USA and 33% in Britain, and current litigation involves Coca-Cola, the Goodyear Tire & Rubber Company, Procter & Gamble, and the Swiss pharmaceutical company, Roche Holding AG.

THE ELIMINATION OF GAINS OR LOSSES IN INVENTORY IN THE YEAR OF SALE

The elimination of unrealized gains and losses in inventory in the year of sale depends upon three factors: first, the markup at which the intercompany sales were made; second, the amount of inventory on hand at the end of the year resulting from intercompany sales; and, third, which company in the group sold the goods. These three factors are dealt with hereunder.

The Markup and Extent of the Unsold Inventory

As the objective is to eliminate any unrealized gains or losses in inventory resulting from intercompany transactions, it is necessary to know the markup at which the goods were sold and the amount of these goods held as inventory at the end of the accounting cycle.

These markups may be expressed as applying to either the cost of the goods or their selling price. For example, if a company in a parent company-subsidiary company relationship sells goods to an associated company at a markup of 25% on cost and, at balance sheet date, $10,000 worth of that inventory is still on hand, the unrealized gain included in the inventory to be eliminated from the consolidated financial statements at the end of the year would be $2,000 (i.e., 25/125 × $10,000). If, on the other hand, the markup was 25% of the selling price, the unrealized profit to be eliminated would be $2,500 (i.e., 25/100 × $10,000).

The Accounting Treatment

The full amount of the unrealized gain (or loss) is eliminated on consolidation by reducing (or increasing) the ending inventory of the company concerned by that amount. The reason for this treatment is explained in the following section.

The accounting treatment is, however, affected by which company sold the goods. Sales by the parent company to a subsidiary are known as "**downstream sales**" because of their direction in a parent company-subsidiary company relationship. In these cases, unrealized gains or losses on downstream sales of inventory apply **only to the parent company**. This is because the full amount of the unrealized gain or loss is included in the net income of the parent company and is eliminated in full from the net income of the parent company. On the other hand, sales from a subsidiary company to its parent company are referred to as "**upstream sales**" to reflect the movement of the goods in relation to the structure of the affiliated group of companies. As explained below, the adjustment for these unrealized profits is against the net income of the subsidiary company. If the sales are made by a subsidiary to another subsidiary within the group that are neither upstream nor downstream sales, they are known as "**lateral sales**", and affect both the selling and receiving companies. However, as these adjustments only apply to complicated groups of companies, consideration of this aspect is deferred to a later chapter.

The accounting for upstream sales affects **both** the parent and the subsidiary companies, because **the adjustment for unrealized gains is apportioned between the parent company and the minority interests**. The elimination is also against the cost of goods sold but, in this case, it affects the share of net income attributable to **both** the parent company and the subsidiary. This is reflected in Illustration 9–3 using the same figures as those used in Illustration 9–2 dealing with downstream sales.

The adjustment to eliminate unrealized gains or losses in inventories is effected by deducting the unrealized gains or losses from the inventories of **the companies making the sales and not from the companies holding the goods as inventory**. This adjustment is designed to either increase or decrease the net income of the company that made the sale by the unrealized gain or loss on the unsold inventory. In this respect, a reduction in the net income of

ILLUSTRATION 9–2

ELIMINATION OF INTERCOMPANY SALES AND UNREALIZED PROFITS IN INVENTORIES ARISING FROM DOWNSTREAM SALES

Parent Inc. had acquired a 75% interest in Subsidiary Inc. for $225,000 on its formation some years before. Parent accounts for its investment using the cost method. During 20X2, Parent sold goods to Subsidiary for $20,000, which included a markup of 25% on cost. At balance sheet date, the inventory of Subsidiary included $10,000 of these goods.

The abbreviated financial statements of the two companies for 20X2 were as follows:

Income and Retained Earnings Statement	Parent	Subsidiary
Sales	$860,000	$610,000
Cost of Goods Sold	$790,000	$560,000
Expenses	26,000	18,000
	$816,000	$578,000
Net Operating Income	$ 44,000	$ 32,000
Retained Earnings at January 1, 20X2	96,000	48,000
Retained Earnings at December 31, 20X2	$140,000	$ 80,000

Balance Sheet

	Parent	Subsidiary
Cash and Accounts Receivable	$175,000	$190,000
Inventory	75,000	85,000
Investment in Subsidiary (75% × $300,000)	225,000	—
Capital Assets (Net)	240,000	180,000
	$715,000	$455,000
Accounts Payable	$125,000	$ 75,000
Common Stock (no par value shares)	450,000	300,000
Retained Earnings	140,000	80,000
	$715,000	$455,000

The elimination of the intercompany sales and unrealized profit (i.e., $2,000 = $10,000 × 25/125) in inventories on consolidation was as follows:

Consolidated Income and Retained Earnings Statement

	Consolidated	Parent	Subsidiary
Sales		$860,000	$610,000
Less Intercompany Sales		20,000	—
	$1,450,000	$840,000	$610,000
Cost of Goods Sold		$790,000	$560,000
Less Intercompany Purchases		20,000	—
		770,000	560,000
Add: Unrealized Profit in Inventory		2,000	—
Cost of Goods Sold	1,332,000	$772,000	$560,000
Gross Profit	118,000	$ 68,000	$ 50,000
Expenses	44,000	26,000	18,000
Net Operating Income	$ 74,000	$ 42,000	$ 32,000
Less: Minority Interests (25%)	8,000	—	8,000
Consolidated Net Income	66,000	$ 42,000	$ 24,000
Retained Earnings at January 1, 20X2	132,000		
Retained Earnings at December 31, 20X2	$ 198,000		

Consolidated Balance Sheet

Cash and Accounts Receivable	$ 365,000	($175,000 + $190,000)
Inventory	158,000	($75,000 + $85,000 − $2,000)
Capital Assets	420,000	($240,000 + $180,000)
	$ 943,000	
Accounts Payable	200,000	($125,000 + $75,000)
Minority Interests	95,000	(25% × [$300,000 + $80,000])
Common Stock	450,000	
Retained Earnings	198,000	
	$ 943,000	

ILLUSTRATION 9–3
ELIMINATION OF INTERCOMPANY SALES AND UNREALIZED PROFITS IN INVENTORIES ARISING FROM UPSTREAM SALES

This illustration uses exactly the same information as that applying to Illustration 9–2, except that during 20X2, the intercompany sale of goods for $20,000 was from Subsidiary to Parent and that at balance sheet date, the inventory of Parent included $10,000 worth of these goods.

The elimination of the intercompany sales and the unrealized profits (i.e., $2,000 = $10,000 × 25/125) in inventories on consolidation in 20X2 would have been as follows:

Consolidated Income and Retained Earnings Statement

	Consolidated	Parent	Subsidiary
Sales		$860,000	$610,000
Less: Intercompany Sales		20,000	—
	$1,450,000	$840,000	$610,000
Cost of Goods Sold		$790,000	$560,000
Less: Intercompany Purchases		20,000	—
		770,000	560,000
Add: Unrealized Profit in Inventory		—	2,000
Cost of Goods Sold	1,332,000	$770,000	$562,000
Gross Profit	118,000	$ 70,000	$ 48,000
Expenses	44,000	26,000	18,000
Net Operating Income	$ 74,000	$ 44,000	$ 30,000
Less: Minority Interests (25%)	7,500	—	7,500
Consolidated Net Income	66,500	$ 44,000	$ 22,500
Retained Earnings at January 1, 20X2	132,000		
Retained Earnings at December 31, 20X2	$ 198,500		

Consolidated Balance Sheet

The consolidated balance sheet would have been the same as that given in Illustration 9–2 except that the minority interests and retained earnings would be different. These would have changed because the unrealized profit of $2,000 was apportioned as to $1,500 to Parent (to give retained earnings of $198,500) and $500 to the minority interests. The minority interests appearing on the consolidated balance sheet would, consequently, now be $94,500 (i.e., 25% × [$300,000 + $80,000] − [25% × $2,000]).

The Position in 20X3

In 20X3, the unrealized profit of $2,000 would be reversed, giving a cost of goods sold figure of $2,000 less. The reason for this is that any adjustment that reduces or increases the cost of goods sold in one year must be reversed in the following year. If, for example, the cost of goods sold in 20X3 was $$600,000, the adjustment in the consolidated workings for Subsidiary would be as follows:

Cost of Goods Sold	$ 600,000
Less: Unrealized Profit in Inventory	(2,000)
Cost of Goods Sold	$ 598,000

the selling company is effected by reducing the ending inventory of the selling company so that **a larger cost of goods sold is matched against sales in the period involved**.

The actual elimination of the unrealized profit is shown as an increase in the cost of goods sold and as a reduction of the consolidated inventory on the balance sheet by the same amount. This treatment is based on the assumption that the **perpetual system of recording inventories** is used by both the parent and subsidiary companies. With such a system, purchases and issues of inventory are recorded directly in the inventory account as they occur so that at any time, the balance on the inventory account represents the actual inventory on hand, and the inventory issued represents the actual cost of goods sold.

ILLUSTRATION 9–4
A COMPARISON OF ADJUSTING THE COST OF GOODS SOLD FOR UNREALIZED PROFITS WITH
PERIODIC AND PERPETUAL SYSTEMS OF RECORDING INVENTORIES

The adjustments to inventory using the periodic and perpetual inventory system are illustrated hereunder using a typical business situation:

If the inventory records had been maintained using **a periodic inventory system**, the trading section of the income statement would have been as follows:

		Subsidiary
Sales		$1,800,000
Beginning Inventory		$ 134,000
Purchases		1,460,000
		1,594,000
Ending Inventory	114,000	
Less: Unrealized Profit (i.e., $40,000 × 25/125)	8,000	106,000
Cost of Goods Sold		$1,488,000
Gross Profit		$ 312,000

With **a perpetual inventory system**, however, the trading section of the income statement is:

	Subsidiary
Sales	$1,800,000
Cost of Goods Sold before Adjustment (i.e., $134,000 + $1,460,000 − $114,000)	$1,480,000
Add: Unrealized Profit in Inventory	+ 8,000
Cost of Goods Sold after Adjustment	$1,488,000
Gross Profit	$ 312,000

A comparison of the adjustment for unrealized profits in inventory using the periodic and perpetual methods is presented as Illustration 9–4. This shows that, even though both methods give the same cost of goods sold, the addition of the unrealized profit to the cost of goods sold provides a simpler method of achieving the same result.

It should also be noted that in Illustration 9–3, the intercompany sales and purchases have been deducted from the sales and cost of goods sold of Parent and not Subsidiary. This is because, provided the deductions are both made in the same company, the final result is exactly the same and the deductions are made wherever it is convenient to do so.

YEAR TO YEAR ADJUSTMENTS OF UNREALIZED GAINS OR LOSSES

In accounting, it is generally understood that **the over- or under-valuation of inventory adjusts itself over a period of time** provided the inventory is all sold during the period concerned. An under-valuation of closing inventory in one year of, say, $500, results in the understatement of net income in that year by the same amount. However, this understatement is adjusted by a corresponding overstatement of net income in the following period by an equivalent amount. As a result, the total net income of the company over the two years involved remains the same (i.e., + $500 − $500 = 0).

In accounting for unrealized gains and losses in inventory, however, it is necessary to eliminate these gains or losses in the periods to which they relate. This requires a **corresponding adjustment in the following year** to ensure that the elimination of the unrealized gain or loss arising in the previous period is cancelled out.

For example, the adjustment made in year one to eliminate an unrealized gain of $500 arising from intercompany inventory sales would be to reduce the ending inventory and increase the cost of goods sold by this amount (i.e., through the reduction of the value of closing inventory of $500). In year two, this adjustment reverses itself because what has happened is that the elimination of the unrealized profit of $500 was achieved by reducing the closing inventory by $500 to give a higher cost of goods sold in that year. The opening inventory in the following year is, therefore, $500 dollars less than the original unadjusted figure, which results in a smaller cost of goods sold. The consolidation adjustment in the year in which the elimination takes place is, therefore, to reduce the closing inventory on the balance sheet and in the income statement by $500. In the following year, the adjustment is to reduce both the opening inventory and the opening retained earnings by $500.

The adjustment in the following year is **against the retained earnings** because the reduction in closing inventory would have reduced the net income by $500 (through the increased cost of goods sold) which, in turn, would have reduced the retained earnings at the end of that year by the same amount. What occurs is that the elimination of the unrealized profit in inventory at the year end results in a smaller amount of consolidated net income and, in turn, a reduced consolidated retained earnings figure.

The **rule** to be followed in eliminating these unrealized gains or losses is to **assume that all the inventory present at the end of one period is sold in the period following that in which the adjustment was made**. That means that the entire adjustment is reversed at the beginning of the following period, and the position relating to unrealized gains in inventory is reassessed when the consolidated financial statements are prepared at the end of the following period. This assumption is reasonable because inventory turnover is normally at least once per year even in those businesses, like stone masonry, where inventory turnover is extremely slow.

The entries relating to the elimination of unrealized profit in inventory resulting from upstream sales **also affect the value of the investment in the ledger of the parent company**. The reduction in **the net income from the subsidiary** in the year in which the unrealized profit is eliminated must be reversed in the following year. An illustration of the way in which this is carried out is provided in Illustration 9–5. In this case, if the cost of goods sold of Subsidiary Inc. for 20X5 was $300,000 and that for 20X6 was $400,000, the adjustments made on the spreadsheets for 20X5 and 20X6 would be as follows:

	20X5	20X6
Cost of Goods Sold	$300,000	$400,000
Add/Less Adjustment for Unrealized Profit/Loss in Inventory in 20X5 (i.e., 80% of [$6,000 × 20/120])	800	(800)
Add Adjustment for Unrealized Profit/Loss in Inventory in 20X6 (i.e., 80% of [$9,000 × 20/120])		1,200
	$300,800	$400,400

The adjustment is carried out by adding the amount of the unrealized profit to the cost of goods sold and deducting the same amount from the inventory on the consolidated balance sheet. The adjustments are necessary to show the larger cost of goods sold in 20X5 occasioned by the **smaller closing inventory figure** and, for 20X6, **the smaller cost of goods sold figure** resulting from the **smaller opening inventory figure**. And, as the intercompany sales of inventory in this illustration are upstream sales, adjustments to both the net income, retained earnings and minority interests are necessary. **The current year's adjustment is made automatically in establishing the minority interest in the net income for the year.** However, that applying to the previous year requires an adjustment to the retained earnings brought forward. For example, in Illustration 9–5, the adjustment to the consolidated retained earnings brought forward in 20X6 would be $800 being 80% of the unrealized profits of $1,000 at the end of 20X5.

Also, as the adjustment for unrealized profits in inventory of $800 in 20X5 is reversed in the following year, recording of the unrealized profit adjustments is often ignored, giving rise to the incomplete use of the equity method.

ILLUSTRATION 9–5
ACCOUNTING FOR UNREALIZED GAINS ON INVENTORY SALES USING
THE FULL EQUITY METHOD

Parent Inc. acquired an 80% interest in Subsidiary Inc. on January 1, 20X5 for $200,000, which did not include any amount paid for goodwill. The net income of Subsidiary and dividends paid (on November 30) during the financial years ended December 31, 20X5 and 20X6 were as follows:

	Net Income	Dividends Declared and Paid
20X5	$ 80,000	$ 30,000
20X6	100,000	40,000

During 20X5 and 20X6, Subsidiary sold goods to Parent at cost plus 20%. At December 31, 20X5 and 20X6, the value of the goods held as inventory by Parent amounted to $6,000 and $9,000 respectively.

The investment account using the full equity method would be as follows:

Investment in Subsidiary

20X5				
Jan. 1	Purchase Consideration	200,000		200,000
Nov. 30	Dividends Received		24,000	176,000
Dec. 31	Net Income	64,000		
	Adjustment for Unrealized Profit in Inventory		800	229,200
20X6				
Jan. 1	Reversal of Unrealized Profit	800		230,000
Nov. 30	Dividends Received		32,000	198,000
Dec. 31	Net Income	80,000		
	Adjustment for Unrealized Profit		1,200	276,800

The journal entries recording the unrealized profits and the reversal of this adjustment in 20X6 in the "Investment in Subsidiary" account in the ledger of Parent would have been as follows:

20X5			
Dec. 31	Net Income from Subsidiary	800	
	Investment in Subsidiary		800
	Elimination of Unrealized Profit in Inventory — 80% × (20/120 × 6,000)		
20X6			
Jan. 1	Investment in Subsidiary	800	
	Net Income from Subsidiary		800
	Reversal of Unrealized Profit in Inventory at December 31, 20X5		
Dec. 31	Net Income from Subsidiary	1,200	
	Investment in Subsidiary		1,200
	Elimination of Unrealized Profit in Inventory — (80% × 20/120 × 9,000)		

YEAR END ADJUSTMENT TO MINORITY INTERESTS

The minority interests at the year end must also be adjusted for any unrealized profits or losses in inventory arising from **upstream intercompany sales** of inventory. The reason is that in these cases, **the adjustment for unrealized gains or losses is against the parent company and the minority interests** in accordance with their shareholdings. These transactions are also related party transactions that must be eliminated in the consolidation process by section 3840 of the CICA *Handbook*.

For example, using the information provided in Illustration 9–3, the adjustment of the gain of $2,000 arising from the upstream sale of inventory in the 75%-owned subsidiary, the apportionment is $1,500 to the parent company (i.e., 75% × $2,000) and $500 to the minority interests. In this case, the total reduction in the value of the inventory on the consolidated balance sheet would be $2,000. The parent company's share of the adjustment (i.e., the $1,500) is included as part of the adjustments to the income statement (i.e., the $2,000 less the minority's share of $500) and is, subsequently, reflected as a reduction of the same amount in the retained earnings. However, no such adjustment occurs with the minority's share of $500, and this amount must be deducted from the minority interest appearing on the consolidated balance sheet. On making this adjustment, the reduction in inventory of $2,000 is balanced by a reduction of $1,500 in the consolidated retained earnings and $500 from the minority interests.

It should be noted that there are no adjustments to the minority interests with downstream sales. This is because the adjustment is against the net income of the parent company and there is an equal reduction in the value of the inventory and the consolidated retained earnings.

INCOME TAX IMPLICATIONS ARISING FROM THE ELIMINATION

The adjustments to eliminate intercompany transactions affect the reported net income of the companies concerned and, consequently, the calculation of the taxes reflected as being payable on the consolidated net income. If the results of operations of the consolidated entity are not to be distorted, the income tax expense must be adjusted accordingly. This adjustment is carried out by treating the difference in the income tax expense as an adjustment to the future taxes account. This adjustment does not affect the actual income taxes payable by the individual companies, but merely adjusts the income tax expense applying to the consolidated net income.

Every attempt has been made in this text to eliminate unnecessary complications in presenting the issues under consideration. The amounts reflected as the amortization of capital assets are, therefore, **assumed to correspond** with the capital cost allowances allowed for income tax purposes.

To appreciate the income tax effects of transfer pricing, an understanding of the calculation of income taxes by companies is necessary. For those who lack a full understanding of the way this is carried out, a brief explanation of the calculation and presentation of income tax balances of companies is provided as Appendix 9A to this chapter.

The Accounting Problems

Transfer pricing can apply equally to either the parent or subsidiary companies. However, it normally applies to transfers of inventories from the parent to the subsidiary company. In many cases, the company receiving the goods may be totally unaware that they are subject to transfer pricing. This occurs if it has been carried to limit managerial bonuses based on profit levels or where transfer pricing is used to circumvent monetary control regulations or the manipulation of income taxes payable on foreign operations. In all cases, however, the parent company would be fully aware of the existence of unrealized profits in inventories, and it is its responsibility to make the necessary adjustments.

The income tax adjustments are relatively straightforward. All that is necessary is to re-calculate the income tax expense for the companies concerned after the elimination of the unrealized profits to give the consolidated income tax expense for the year. The difference between the original income tax expense and the re-calculated consolidated income tax expense for the year under review is the amount by which the future income taxes must be adjusted.

Two matters should be borne in mind in making the adjustments to the consolidated financial statements. First, the re-calculation of the income tax expense is **only affected by the**

ILLUSTRATION 9–6
INCOME TAX ADJUSTMENTS RELATING TO THE ELIMINATION OF UNREALIZED PROFITS IN INVENTORY IN AN UPSTREAM SITUATION

The following information relates to the trading operations and income tax calculations of Parent Inc. and its 80%-owned subsidiary company for the two years ended December 31, 20X6:

	Parent		Subsidiary	
	20X5	**20X6**	**20X5**	**20X6**
Net Income from Operations for Year	$1,000,000	$1,200,000	$460,000	$500,000
Income Tax Expense (50%)	500,000	600,000	230,000	250,000
	500,000	600,000	230,000	250,000
Share of Net Income from Subsidiary (80%)	184,000	200,000	—	—
Reported Net Income for Year	$ 684,000	$ 800,000	$230,000	$250,000

In 20X5, Subsidiary commenced selling goods to Parent at cost plus 50%. At December 31, 20X5, goods costing $30,000 were still in the inventory of Parent. The corresponding figure for 20X6 was $75,000.

Net Income and Income Tax Adjustments:

Step 1: The income tax adjustments applying to the consolidated financial statements arising from the changes to the net income of Subsidiary in 20X5 and 20X6 are as follows:

	20X5	**20X6**
Net Income before Recognition of Unrealized Profits and Any Impairment of Goodwill	$460,000	$500,000
Adjustment for Unrealized Profit in Inventory in 20X5	(10,000)	—
Reversal of 20X5 Unrealized Profit in Inventory	—	+10,000
Adjustment for Unrealized Profit in Inventory in 20X6	—	(25,000)
Adjusted Accounting Income at December 31	$450,000	$485,000
Income Tax Expense at a Tax Rate of 50%	$225,000	$242,500

Step 2: The adjustments would be disclosed on the balance sheet as an adjustment to short-term future income taxes. In this case, assume that **the unadjusted future income tax balances** on the balance sheets of the two companies **were credit balances of** $40,000 for 20X5 and $50,000 for 20X6:

The adjustments on the consolidated balance sheet would, therefore, be as follows:

20X5:   Future Income Taxes of $40,000 − $5,000 = $35,000
20X6:   Future Income Taxes of $50,000 − $12,500 = $37,500

Note: Adjustments to the future taxes on the consolidated balance are only those that apply to the current year's adjustment to the consolidated net income.

---

unrealized profits adjustments because the write-down of goodwill for impairment and the fair market value adjustments arising from revalued assets at the date of acquisition are **merely book entries** and, consequently, they do not affect the income taxes payable. Second, the adjustments to the income tax expense and future taxes **only affect the consolidated financial statements for the current year**, and there is **no carry-forward** from one year to the next. It should also be borne in mind that the income tax adjustments are only made in the consolidated workings and nowhere else.

An example of the income tax adjustments arising from the elimination of unrealized profits in inventory is provided by Illustration 9–6, which shows the adjustment for each of the two years relating to upstream sales of inventory in 20X5 and 20X6. In this case, the income tax adjustments relating to 20X5 arise from the elimination of unrealized profits of $10,000 to give a reduction in income tax expense of $5,000 (i.e., 50% of $10,000) to reduce the income tax expense for the subsidiary for consolidation purposes from $230,000 to $225,000 in that year. The corresponding adjustment to the future income taxes is also $5,000. Illustration 9–6 continues to show that in the consolidated workings for 20X6, the $10,000 inventory adjustment for 20X5 is reversed and the elimination of unrealized profits in 20X6 of $25,000 is deducted, reducing the current net income by $15,000. The adjustment to the consolidated income tax expense for 20X6 is, therefore, $7,500 (i.e., 50% × [$25,000 – $10,000]), while the adjustment to the future taxes is $12,500 being 50% of the current year's adjustment to inventory of $25,000. To recap, **the adjustments are merely the recognition of the difference between the unadjusted and adjusted income tax expense on the consolidated income statement for the year under review** and adding or deducting it, as the case may be, from the consolidated future income taxes reflected on the consolidated balance sheet.

THEORETICAL INCONSISTENCIES IN ELIMINATING UNREALIZED PROFITS

As outlined earlier in the text, **the proprietary ownership theory** is used for the presentation of consolidated and other financial statements. With this ownership theory the emphasis of the reporting is to present the performance of the entity and its financial position as it affects the interests of the owners (i.e., the shareholders).

Consolidated net income is, therefore, determined after deducting, from the total net income, the portion attributable to the minority interests. The equity of the consolidated entity is presented by reflecting the shareholders' equity and that attributable to the minority interests as two separate amounts. Furthermore, if inventory or some other asset is over- or undervalued at the date of acquisition, only the parent company's share of the adjustment is recognized in the analysis of equity. One would, therefore, have assumed that the proprietary ownership theory would also apply to the elimination of unrealized profits in inventory. In such circumstances, the need to distinguish between upstream and downstream sales falls away, and the adjustment for the unrealized gain is against the net income of the parent company only. This is, however, not the case because **the entity ownership theory** is applied to the elimination of unrealized profits in inventory.

To illustrate this position, assume that a 75%-owned subsidiary company transfers inventory to its parent company at cost plus 25% and, at balance sheet date, inventory held by the parent company included unrealized profits of $60,000. Using the proprietary ownership theory, all that would be necessary would be to eliminate $45,000 from the net income of the parent company in the consolidated workings and to leave the share of net income of the subsidiary company unchanged. If, as is the case, the entity ownership theory applies, the full $60,000 would be deducted from the subsidiary company's net income so that on consolidation, the parent company's share of the net income would be reduced by $45,000 and that of the minority interests by $15,000. In both cases the share of net income attributable to the parent company is the same but, with the entity ownership theory, the minority interests share of net income and the amount appearing as minority interests on the balance sheet is $15,000 less than that using the proprietary ownership theory.

No reason for this inconsistency is given. One can, therefore, only assume that the objective of the current position is conservatism because it results in a lower figure for both inventory and minority interests on the consolidated balance sheet.

SUMMARY

This chapter covers the accounting for intercompany purchases and sales of inventories between affiliated companies and the adjustments relating to any unrealized profits included in inventories. Intercompany transactions of this nature must be eliminated in the consolidation process to ensure that the consolidated results of operations are not distorted by the inclusion of fictitious sales and purchases and profits on intercompany sales.

Intercompany sales and purchases are eliminated in the consolidation process by deducting the amounts involved from the sales and cost of goods sold in the same company. However, adjustments necessitated by the existence of unrealized profits in inventories at the year end depend upon whether the sales of inventories are "upstream sales", "downstream sales" or "lateral sales". "Upstream sales" are from the subsidiary company to its parent whereas "downstream sales" are from the parent company to its subsidiary; "lateral sales" are between subsidiaries in the same group. The actual adjustment is to reduce the closing inventory on both the balance sheet and in the income statement of the company initiating the transaction. This means that with "upstream sales", the adjustment is against the subsidiary's cost of goods sold while with "downstream sales", the adjustment is against the cost of goods sold of the parent company. With "lateral sales", the adjustment is against the initiating company's cost of goods sold. In the following year, the adjustment for unrealized profits must be reversed because it is always assumed that the inventory on hand at the end of one year is all sold in the following year. Finally, the chapter covers the adjustments to income tax expense resulting from the elimination of unrealized profits in inventories in the consolidation process.

APPENDIX 9A: CORPORATE INCOME TAXES

Taxes are payable by companies on their **taxable income**, which is the amount of income that is subject to taxation in terms of the *Income Tax Act*. The taxable income of a company is established by including in income all amounts that are subject to income tax and by deducting from that amount those revenues and expenses that are allowable as income tax deductions.

Income from an income tax point of view is much the same as revenue in an accounting sense. Similarly, the deductions from income for income tax purposes correspond largely with the expenses deducted from revenues to arrive at accounting net income. Generally speaking, the major difference is that accrual accounting does not normally apply. In this respect, it is usually the full amount of income receivable and the full amount of expenses actually incurred that are, respectively, included in or allowable as deductions from taxable income. As a result, certain expenses allowed for income taxes are only included in accounting net income at a later date. Additional adjustments arise when the period over which certain expenses, like the amortization of capital assets, differ from the period over which capital cost allowances (i.e., the income tax equivalent of the amortization of capital assets) allowed by the *Income Tax Act* may be deducted. These adjustments are referred to as **temporary differences**. In addition, **permanent differences** arise where certain revenues or expenses that have been included in the determination of the accounting net income are not subject to income tax: for example, the impairment of goodwill or the receipt of dividends from Canadian companies that are paid out as dividends by the recipient company.

In calculating the income taxes payable, permanent differences are merely deducted from the amounts subject to income tax. Temporary differences, on the other hand, are recognized for accounting purposes in one period but are subject to income taxes in another period. Over a period of time, temporary differences cancel one another out; amounts excluded in one period are included in the next and subsequent periods so that over a period of years, the same total amounts appear as adjustments to the accounting net income and taxable income.

The determination of the taxable income of a company normally begins with the reported accounting net income that is adjusted by the various inclusions and exclusions to arrive at the taxable income. An illustration of the way this is carried out is given as Illustration 9A–1.

The rates of corporate tax are normally fixed and are applied to the taxable income. For example, where the taxable income of a company is $200,000 and the rate of company tax is 45% (or 45 cents in the dollar), the income taxes payable by that company would be $90,000. The amount of income tax expense is, however, only established when the income taxes payable have been **assessed** by the Canada Revenue Agency. Up until that time, the amount reflected as income tax expense on the income statement is nothing more than a good estimate of the amount of income tax that will be payable in the future.

Capital gains arising from the sale of capital assets, the redemption of preferred shares, bonds and the like, are also subject to income tax. At present, 50% of a capital gain is subject to income tax.

ILLUSTRATION 9A–1
DETERMINATION OF TAXABLE INCOME OF A COMPANY

Reported Net Income from Income Statement	$xxx,xxx
Less: Permanent Differences	xxx,xxx
Amount on which Income Taxes are Payable Sometime in the Future	xxx,xxx
Less: Temporary Differences (e.g., the differences between the Amortization of Capital Assets and Capital, Cost Allowances and/or between Allowances for Warranty Expenses and Actual Warranty Expenses)	xxx,xxx
Taxable Income	$xxx,xxx

Income Statement Presentation

It is generally accepted that income taxes are an expense of carrying on business. Income tax expense must, therefore, be included in the income statement as a deduction from net income. The income statement must also be presented in a way that reflects the net income (or loss) from its normal operations as well as the income tax effects arising from discontinued operations and extraordinary items. This procedure is referred to as intraperiod and interperiod income tax allocation.

Intraperiod income tax allocation refers to the allocation of income taxes to the various items or sections of the income statement of a company for the reporting period. The information is required to be presented in this manner by section 1520 of the CICA *Handbook*, so that it is possible to compare its trading operations from one year to another. The way this is carried out is to reflect the income taxes applicable to trading operations as an expense (or deduction from net income) to give the net income from trading operations and, to add to this figure, the net gains or losses (i.e., after deduction of the income tax expense or benefits) from discontinued operations or extraordinary items.

Interperiod income tax allocation refers to the complex area of allocating income tax expense to the accounting income over the various periods to which temporary differences apply. It involves the following three steps:

(a) Calculation of the **income tax expense** for the period recognizing permanent differences but **excluding** temporary differences.
(b) Calculation of the **income taxes payable** for the same period by recognizing **both** permanent and temporary differences.
(c) Deferring the difference (as **future income taxes**) between the two amounts calculated above as an adjustment to the income taxes payable in future periods.

For example, assume that a company has net income of $200,000 and a taxable income of only $180,000 due to temporary differences. If the rate of income tax is 40%, the journal entry recording the income tax expense, income taxes payable, and the effect of the deferral of temporary differences would be as follows:

Income Tax Expense ($200,000 × 40%)	80,000	
Income Taxes Payable ($180,000 × 40%)		72,000
Future Income Taxes Payable		8,000

The way interperiod income tax allocation is carried out is a highly contentious issue amongst accountants. In Canada, like the USA, a liability method of allocating income taxes is used. This method treats future taxes as liabilities of the reporting company, and operates as outlined hereunder.

Income Tax Allocation Using the Liability Approach

Canada has adopted a comprehensive income tax allocation approach using the liability method. The principle on which this approach is based is that it assumes that in the preparation of financial statements, all assets will be realized for at least their carrying value giving rise to future economic benefits. As a result, the realization of such assets will give rise to either an increase or decrease in the amount of income taxes payable in the period of realization, depending upon **the differences between** the assets carrying values and their income tax values resulting from permanent and temporary differences. This approach, based on the inflows or outflows of resources from the realization of assets or liabilities, meets the definition of assets and liabilities and the approach is, therefore, referred to as the liability method.

From a conceptual viewpoint, the realization of the assets and liabilities subject to temporary differences that are expected to reverse will give rise to an increase or decrease in the amount of taxes payable, depending upon their carrying and income tax values. The practical application of this approach is that, generally speaking, the temporary differences multiplied by the current rate of income tax would at any one time give the future income tax on the balance sheet. For example, take the case of a company having assets with **a carrying value of $1-million** and a **tax value of $600,000**. If the tax rate is 40%, the liability for future taxes reflected on the balance sheet would be $160,000 (i.e., [$1,000,000 – $600,000] × 40%).

In practice, the income tax expense, income taxes payable and the adjustment to future taxes are calculated each year in the normal manner. The balance on the future taxes account should then reflect the total temporary differences multiplied by the income tax rate. If not, it is adjusted accordingly by writing off any shortfalls or excesses through the income statement. The successful operation of this approach, therefore, requires the maintaining of detailed records of the differences between the carrying and tax values of assets and liabilities, and the temporary differences relating to current assets and liabilities.

SELF-STUDY PROBLEMS
(covering transfer pricing in inventories with and without income tax effects)

PROBLEM 9A†   On July 1, 20X4, Pension Inc. acquired a 75% interest in Stipend Inc. for $620,000. Financial statements were not prepared at the date of acquisition but at January 1, 20X4, Stipend had retained earnings of $60,000. No dividends were declared by Stipend during 20X4.

The abbreviated balance sheets and combined income and retained earnings statements of Pension and Stipend at December 31, 20X5 were as follows:

	Pension	Stipend
BALANCE SHEETS		
Cash	$ 150,000	$ 10,000
Accounts Receivable	210,000	590,000
Inventory	133,000	272,000
Investment in Stipend	620,000	—
Plant and Equipment (Net)	590,000	110,000
	$1,703,000	$982,000
Current Liabilities	$ 410,000	$250,000
Common Stock	1,000,000	600,000
Retained Earnings	293,000	132,000
	$1,703,000	$982,000
COMBINED INCOME AND RETAINED EARNINGS STATEMENTS		
Sales	$ 900,000	$180,000
Cost of Goods Sold	$ 580,000	$110,000
Operating Expenses	40,000	30,000
	$ 620,000	$140,000
Net Operating Income	$ 280,000	$ 40,000
Dividends from Stipend	6,000	—
Net Income	286,000	40,000
Retained Earnings at January 1, 20X5	47,000	100,000
	333,000	140,000
Dividends Paid (December 2)	40,000	8,000
Retained Earnings at December 31, 20X5	$ 293,000	$132,000

---

† The solution is provided in Appendix B to this text.

Additional Information:

1. At the date of acquisition it was agreed amongst the parties that all assets and liabilities were fairly valued, except for a certain item of plant of Stipend having a three-year remaining life that was undervalued by $40,000.
2. Goodwill is accounted for on an impairment basis. Impairment losses of $5,000 and $10,000 were recognized in 20X4 and 20X5 respectively.
3. From the date of acquisition, the two companies had traded actively with one another. All sales were made at a markup of 25% on cost, and an examination of the records of the two companies disclosed the following position:

Sales	Amount	Amount in Inventory at December 31
Pension to Stipend — 20X4	$60,000	$10,000
Stipend to Pension — 20X4	$40,000	$20,000
20X5	$50,000	$30,000

REQUIRED

Ignoring income tax effects, prepare the consolidated balance sheet and combined income and retained earnings statement for 20X5.

PROBLEM 9B† Penn Inc. acquired an 80% interest in Sylvania Inc. for $1,080,000 on January 1, 20X4 when Sylvania had retained earnings of $250,000. At the date of acquisition, all the assets of Sylvania were considered to be fairly valued except for land that was overvalued by $20,000.

At December 31, 20X5, the abbreviated financial statements of Penn and Sylvania were as follows:

COMBINED INCOME AND RETAINED EARNINGS STATEMENT	Penn	Sylvania
Sales	$6,000,000	$2,200,000
Cost of Goods Sold	$3,600,000	$1,040,000
Operating Expenses	1,312,000	720,000
	$4,912,000	$1,760,000
Net Income from Operations	$1,088,000	$ 440,000
Dividends from Sylvania	64,000	—
Net Income Before Income Tax	1,152,000	440,000
Income Tax Expense (50%)	544,000	220,000
Net Income After Income Tax	608,000	220,000
Retained Earnings at January 1, 20X5	600,000	330,000
	1,208,000	550,000
Less: Dividends Paid	240,000	80,000
Retained Earnings at December 31, 20X5	$ 968,000	$ 470,000

BALANCE SHEETS	Penn	Sylvania
Current Assets	$1,354,000	$ 700,000
Investment in Sylvania	1,080,000	—
Land	200,000	120,000
Plant (Net)	876,000	980,000
	$3,510,000	$1,800,000
Current Liabilities	$ 922,000	$ 290,000
Future Income Taxes	120,000	40,000
Common Stock (shares of no par value)	1,500,000	1,000,000
Retained Profits	968,000	470,000
	$3,510,000	$1,800,000

† The solution is provided in Appendix B to this text.

Additional Information:

(a) During 20X4, Penn sold goods for resale to Sylvania for $300,000 that included a markup of 25% on cost. Fifty percent of these goods were still on hand on December 31, 20X4. By December 31, 20X5, all of these goods had been sold.

(b) Sylvania sold goods costing $200,000 to Penn in 20X4 at a markup of 25% on cost. At December 31, 20X4, $50,000 of these goods held by Penn had not been sold. Comparative figures for 20X5 were $300,000 and $60,000.

(c) The net income of Sylvania in 20X4 was $130,000, out of which it had paid a dividend of $50,000 on December 1, 20X4.

(d) The rate of income tax is 50%.

(e) Goodwill was written down for impairment by $12,000 in 20X4.

REQUIRED

Prepare the consolidated balance sheet and combined consolidated income and retained earnings statement of Penn for 20X5.

REVIEW QUESTIONS

1. Why do we eliminate intercompany sales from the consolidated income statement?

2. What is meant by the term "transfer pricing"?

3. Explain what advantages flow to a firm from using transfer pricing?

4. A 60% interest in Subsidiary Inc. was acquired by Parent Inc. on July 1, 20X3. If $80,000 worth of goods had been sold each month by Parent to Subsidiary at cost plus 20% during the period January 1, 20X3 to October 31, 20X3, what adjustments (if any) for intercompany sales and unrealized profits are necessary for the financial year ended December 31, 20X3?

5. What are "upstream sales"? "Downstream sales"?

6. Parent Inc. sold inventory for $120,000 to Subsidiary Inc., an 80%-owned subsidiary, which included a markup of 25% on cost. What would be the effect on the minority interest net income if $20,000 worth of these goods were still on hand at the end of the financial year? Would the position have been any different if the sale of inventory had been by Subsidiary to Parent?

7. If $40,000 worth of inventory purchased by a company affiliated in a "parent company-subsidiary company" relationship that was held as inventory at the beginning of the year was still unsold at the year end, would any adjustment be necessary if it included a markup of 20% on cost?

8. Explain what adjustment is necessary in the consolidated financial statements in 20X5 if an adjustment for unrealized profits of $12,000 in inventory held at the end of the financial year was made on December 31, 20X4.

9. Why is the adjustment to eliminate unrealized profits in inventory added to the cost of goods sold of the company selling the goods in the year of occurrence?

10. If $50,000 in unrealized profits in inventory is excluded from the consolidated net income, what adjustment is necessary to the income tax expense if income tax is chargeable at the rate of 40 cents in the dollar?

11. If, on the acquisition of a 75% interest in a subsidiary, inventory held by the subsidiary is overvalued by $100,000, how much of this overvaluation of inventory would enter into the establishment of the figure for goodwill and be amortized against revenues in the year of acquisition? Does accepted accounting treatment of such a write-off represent the application of the proprietary or entity ownership theory?

CASE

CASE 9–1

Norman-Ellis Components Ltd.

The happy mood in which David Lee, assistant accountant at Norman-Ellis Components Ltd., had arrived at work was broken by a telephone call from the group controller, Mike Ivanov, asking him to drop everything he was doing and to come down to his office. It was the second Wednesday of the month and David knew that Mike was to report to the board of directors at 10.00 am on the company's cash, financial, and other related matters.

On entering the office, Mike asked him to be seated and, after an exchange of greetings, handed him a letter from the Canada Revenue Agency. The relevant parts of the letter were as follows:

(a) As you are no doubt aware, this office has been concerned for some time that certain companies have been avoiding the payment of income taxes on their transactions with their American subsidiaries through the use of transfer pricing. We note that, during the past two years, your company has sold goods with invoice prices in excess of $1.2-million to your American subsidiary company, Norman-Ellis USA Inc. We are also concerned about the amounts charged by your company to Norman-Ellis USA Inc. for managerial services.

(b) In accordance with the authority conferred upon us in terms of the *Income Tax Act*, your company has been selected for audit.

(c) The project manager will be Ms. Celine Thomas, who shall be contacting you within the next two weeks.

REQUIRED

From the viewpoint of Norman-Ellis, outline the evidence that would be required to justify:

1. The company's policies related to the pricing of goods for resale sold to Norman-Ellis USA Inc.; and
2. The company's policy of charging its subsidiary companies a fee for managerial services.

EXERCISES

EXERCISE 9–1

Pun Inc. paid $400,000 for its 80% interest in Satire Inc. on January 1, 20X6, which included an amount of $80,000 for goodwill that was being accounted for on an impairment basis. At the date of acquisition, Satire had retained earnings of $40,000. During 20X6, Satire's net income amounted to $200,000, out of which it paid a dividend of $120,000. Pun uses the full equity method of accounting for its investment in Satire.

During 20X6 and 20X7, Satire sold goods for resale to Pun that included a markup of 20% on cost. At December 31, 20X6, Pun held $72,000 worth of these goods in inventory while, at the end of 20X7, it had sold all of the goods purchased from Satire except for items that cost Pun $90,000.

The abbreviated combined income and retained earnings statements of Pun and Satire for the year ended December 31, 20X7 were:

	Pun	Satire
Net Operating Income	$ 600,000	$400,000
Share of Net Income from Satire	309,600	—
Net Income	909,600	400,000
Retained Earnings at January 1, 20X7	300,000	120,000
	1,209,600	520,000
Dividends Declared and Paid	500,000	200,000
Retained Earnings at December 31, 20X7	$ 709,600	$320,000

REQUIRED

Ignoring income tax effects, give:

1. The reconciliation of the net income from Satire for 20X7 if goodwill had been written down by $8,000 for impairment in 20X7;
2. The consolidated retained earnings of Pun at December 31, 20X7; and
3. The "Investment in Satire" account as it would appear in the ledger of Pun at December 31, 20X6 and 20X7 using the full equity method.

EXERCISE 9–2   You are furnished with the following abbreviated combined income and retained earnings statements at December 31, 20X7 of Pry Inc. and Spy Inc.:

	Pry	Spy
Net Operating Income	$150,000	$125,000
Dividends from Spy	40,000	—
Net Income	190,000	125,000
Retained Earnings at January 1, 20X7	110,000	45,000
	300,000	170,000
Dividends Paid	100,000	50,000
Retained Earnings at December 31, 20X7	$200,000	$120,000

Goodwill of $10,000 arose on the acquisition by Pry of its interest in Spy on July 1, 20X5, which was being accounted for on an impairment basis. At the date of acquisition, Spy had retained earnings of $20,000. No dividends had been paid by Spy during the period July 1, 20X5 to December 31, 20X6.

During 20X6 and 20X7, Spy sold goods for resale to Pry that included a markup of 20% on cost. At December 31, 20X6, Pry held $30,000 worth of these goods in inventory while, at the end of 20X7, it had sold all of the goods purchased from Spy except for items that cost Pry $15,000.

REQUIRED

Ignoring income tax effects, give:

1. The consolidated net income for 20X7 if goodwill had been written down for impairment in 20X7 by 10%;
2. The consolidated retained earnings brought forward from 20X6 at January 1, 20X7;
3. The consolidated retained earnings at December 31, 20X7.

EXERCISE 9–3   Pine Inc. acquired its 80% interest in Spruce Inc. on January 1, 20X7 when Spruce had retained earnings of $60,000. No goodwill arose on acquisition, and no dividends were paid by Spruce during 20X7.

You are furnished with the following abbreviated combined income and retained earnings statements of Pine and Spruce for the year ended December 31, 20X8:

	Pine	Spruce
Sales	$2,400,000	$1,000,000
Cost of Goods Sold	$1,700,000	$ 750,000
Operating and Other Expenses	500,000	100,000
	$2,200,000	$ 850,000
Net Operating Income	$ 200,000	$ 150,000
Dividend Income from Spruce	80,000	—
Net Income	280,000	150,000
Retained Earnings at January 1, 20X8	200,000	80,000
	480,000	230,000
Dividends Declared and Paid	200,000	100,000
Retained Earnings at December 31, 20X8	$ 280,000	$ 130,000

During 20X7, Pine had sold goods that cost $40,000 to Spruce at a markup of 25%. At December 31, 20X7, some of these goods having a selling price of $10,000 were still in inventory. Spruce also sold goods to Pine at a set markup of 25% on cost. The transfers during 20X7 and 20X8 were $125,000 and $200,000 respectively. At the end of 20X7, $75,000 of these goods were still on hand, while the corresponding figure for 20X8 was $50,000.

REQUIRED

Ignoring income tax effects, prepare the consolidated net income and consolidated retained earnings statement of Pine for the year ended December 31, 20X8.

EXERCISE 9–4   Say Inc. had become a subsidiary of Pay Inc. when Say had retained earnings of $40,000. No goodwill arose on acquisition. The operations of Say were such that its first dividend was only paid in 20X7.

The two companies traded actively with one another and, in 20X6 and 20X7, Say sold goods for resale to Pay, for $60,000 and $80,000 respectively, that included a markup of 20% on cost. At December 31, 20X6, Pay held $42,000 worth of these goods in inventory while, at the end of 20X7, it had sold all of the goods purchased from Say except for items costing Pay $12,000.

The abbreviated combined income and retained earnings statements of Pay and Say for the financial year ended at December 31, 20X7 were as follows:

	Pay	Say
Sales	$1,000,000	$800,000
Cost of Goods Sold	$ 600,000	$550,000
Operating and Other Expenses	250,000	150,000
	$ 850,000	$700,000
Net Operating Income	$ 150,000	$100,000
Dividend Income from Say	64,000	—
Net Income	214,000	100,000
Retained Earnings at January 1, 20X7	180,000	120,000
	394,000	220,000
Dividends Declared and Paid	200,000	80,000
Retained Earnings at December 31, 20X7	$ 194,000	$140,000

REQUIRED

Ignoring income tax effects, prepare the combined consolidated income and retained earnings statement of Pay for 20X7.

EXERCISE 9–5   You are furnished with the following abbreviated combined income and retained earnings statements of Prize Inc. and Select Inc. for the year ended December 31, 20X8:

	Prize	Select
Sales	$5,200,000	$2,000,000
Cost of Goods Sold	$3,400,000	$1,500,000
Operating and Other Expenses	1,000,000	200,000
	$4,400,000	$1,700,000
Net Operating Income	$ 800,000	$ 300,000
Less: Income Tax Expense (50%)	400,000	150,000
	400,000	150,000
Dividend Income from Select	80,000	—
Net Income for Year	480,000	150,000
Retained Earnings at January 1, 20X8	400,000	160,000
	880,000	310,000
Dividends Declared and Paid	300,000	100,000
Retained Earnings at December 31, 20X8	$ 580,000	$ 210,000

You are informed that:

(a)   Prize acquired its 80% interest in Select on January 1, 20X7 when Select had retained earnings of $120,000. No goodwill arose on acquisition, and no dividends were paid by Select during 20X7.

(b)   The companies traded actively with one another and goods were transferred between the two companies at cost plus 25%. Details of these activities are:

	Activity	Amount	Balance in Inventory at December 31
20X7:	Sales from Prize to Select	$ 80,000	$ 40,000
	Sales from Select to Prize	250,000	150,000
20X8:	Sales from Select to Prize	400,000	100,000

(c)   The dividend income from Select was not subject to income taxes.

REQUIRED

1.   Prepare the consolidated net income and consolidated retained earnings of Prize for the year ended December 31, 20X8.

2.   Give the adjustments to minority interests, inventory and future income taxes on the balance sheet at December 31, 20X8.

EXERCISE 9–6   At December 31, 20X7, the abbreviated combined income and retained earnings statements of Pseudo Inc. and Sham Inc. were as follows:

	Pseudo	Sham
Sales	$3,900,000	$2,000,000
Cost of Goods Sold	$2,550,000	$1,500,000
Operating and Other Expenses	750,000	200,000
	$3,300,000	$1,700,000
Net Operating Income	$ 600,000	$ 300,000
Less: Income Tax Expense (50%)	300,000	150,000
	300,000	150,000
Dividends from Sham	80,000	—
Net Income after Income Taxes	380,000	150,000
Retained Earnings at January 1, 20X7	680,000	200,000
	1,060,000	350,000
Dividends Declared and Paid	400,000	100,000
Retained Earnings at December 31, 20X7	$ 660,000	$ 250,000

You are informed that:

(a)   Pseudo acquired an 80% interest in Sham at cost (i.e., no goodwill arose on acquisition) when Sham had retained earnings of $120,000.

(b)   Since the date of acquisition to December 31, 20X6, Sham had earned net income of $280,000 and paid dividends of $200,000.

(c)   During 20X6, Pseudo had sold goods costing $96,000 to Sham at a markup of 50% on cost. At December 31, 20X6, some of these goods having a selling price of $24,000 were still in inventory.

(d)   Sham transferred part of its production to Pseudo at a set markup of 25% on manufactured cost. The transfers during 20X6 and 20X7 were $250,000 and $320,000 respectively. At the end of 20X6 the transferred goods on hand amounted to $120,000 while the corresponding figure for 20X7 was $170,000.

REQUIRED

1.   Prepare the combined consolidated income and retained earnings statement of Pseudo for 20X7.

2. Give the adjustments to future income taxes, inventory and minority interests at December 31, 20X7.

PROBLEMS

PROBLEM 9–1

Press Inc. acquired a 75% interest in Seal Inc. on January 1, 20X3 for $180,000 when Seal had common stock of $200,000 and retained earnings of $40,000. Up to January 1, 20X5, Seal had earned net income of $80,000 and paid dividends of $60,000.

The two companies traded actively with one another. All intercompany sales were at cost plus 25% and details of these transactions were as follows:

20X4	Sales amounted to $100,000 of which $40,000 were still in inventory at December 31, 20X4.
20X5	Sales amounted to $120,000 of which $30,000 were still in inventory at December 31, 20X5.

The combined income and retained earnings statements of the two companies at December 31, 20X5 were as follows:

	Press	Seal
Sales	$800,000	$600,000
Cost of Goods Sold	$500,000	$400,000
Operating and Other Expenses	100,000	80,000
	$600,000	$480,000
Net Operating Income	$200,000	$120,000
Dividends from Seal	30,000	—
Net Income	230,000	120,000
Retained Earnings at January 1, 20X5	100,000	60,000
	330,000	180,000
Dividends Declared and Paid	45,000	40,000
Retained Earnings at December 31, 20X5	$285,000	$140,000

REQUIRED

Ignoring income tax effects, prepare the combined consolidated income and retained earnings statement for Press at December 31, 20X5 on the assumption that:

1. All intercompany sales were from Press to Seal.
2. All intercompany sales were from Seal to Press.

PROBLEM 9–2

The financial statements of Peel Inc. and Skin Inc. at December 31, 20X8 were as follows:

COMBINED INCOME AND RETAINED EARNINGS STATEMENT	Peel	Skin
Sales	$1,720,000	$900,000
Cost of Goods Sold	$1,100,000	$400,000
Administration Expenses	200,000	120,000
Amortization of Capital Assets	120,000	80,000
	$1,420,000	$600,000
Net Income from Operations	$ 300,000	$300,000
Dividends from Skin	60,000	—
Net Income for Year	360,000	300,000
Retained Earnings, January 1, 20X8	400,000	100,000
	760,000	400,000
Dividends Paid	200,000	80,000
Retained Earnings, December 31, 20X8	$ 560,000	$320,000

BALANCE SHEETS

Cash	$ 45,000	$ 20,000
Accounts Receivable	550,000	290,000
Inventory	280,000	210,000
Investment in Skin	525,000	—
Plant and Equipment (net)	1,060,000	450,000
	$2,460,000	$970,000
Accounts Payable	$ 400,000	$150,000
Common Stock	1,500,000	500,000
Retained Earnings	560,000	320,000
	$2,460,000	$970,000

Peel had acquired a 75% interest in Skin Inc. on January 1, 20X7 for $525,000 when the common stock of Skin amounted to $500,000 made up of 100,000 shares of common stock of no par value and retained earnings of $40,000 (i.e., when the net assets of Skin amounted to $540,000). At the date of acquisition, the plant and equipment of Skin was considered to be fairly valued except for an item of plant having a remaining five-year life that was undervalued by $80,000.

You are also informed that:

(a) During 20X7, Peel sold goods costing $40,000 to Skin at cost plus 25% and at December 31, 20X7, Skin held 50% of these goods in inventory. In 20X8, Skin also sold goods to Peel for $300,000 at a markup of 20% on cost. At December 31, 20X8, $60,000 of these goods were still held by Peel.

(b) Goodwill was written down for impairment by $6,000 in 20X7.

(c) At December 31, 20X8, Skin owed Peel $20,000 on open account.

(d) No dividends had been paid by Skin during 20X7.

REQUIRED

Ignoring income tax effects, prepare the consolidated income and retained earnings statement and consolidated balance sheet of Peel for 20X8.

PROBLEM 9–3 Goodwill of $20,000 arose on the acquisition by Pizza Inc. of its interest in Salami Inc. on July 1, 20X5. At the date of acquisition, Salami had retained earnings of $40,000. Plant of Salami, which was being amortized on a straight-line basis over 10 years, having a 10-year life that was undervalued by $25,000. No dividends had been paid by Salami during the period July 1, 20X5 and December 31, 20X6.

The abbreviated combined income and retained earnings statements of Pizza and Salami at December 31, 20X7 were as follows:

	Pizza	Salami
Sales	$2,000,000	$1,000,000
Cost of Goods Sold	$1,200,000	$ 600,000
Operating and Other Expenses	500,000	150,000
	$1,700,000	$ 750,000
Net Operating Income	$ 300,000	$ 250,000
Dividends from Salami	80,000	—
Net Income	380,000	250,000
Retained Earnings at January 1, 20X7	220,000	90,000
	600,000	340,000
Dividends Declared and Paid	200,000	100,000
Retained Earnings at December 31, 20X7	$ 400,000	$ 240,000

During 20X6 and 20X7, Salami sold goods for resale to Pizza for $120,000 and $200,000 respectively that included a markup of 20% on cost. At December 31, 20X6, Pizza held $60,000 worth of these goods in inventory while, at the end of 20X7, it had sold all of the goods purchased from Salami except for items costing Pizza $30,000.

REQUIRED

Ignoring income tax effects, prepare the combined consolidated income and retained earnings statement of Pizza for 20X7 if goodwill was written down for impairment by $2,000 in 20X7.

PROBLEM 9–4   On January 1, 20X6, Plate Inc. acquired an 80% interest in Slate for $240,000 when Slate had common stock of $200,000 and retained earnings of $10,000.

The abbreviated income and retained earnings statements and balance sheets for the two companies for 20X7 were as follows:

INCOME AND RETAINED EARNINGS STATEMENTS	Plate	Slate
Sales	$1,200,000	$600,000
Cost of Goods Sold	$ 525,000	$375,000
Operating and Administrative Expenses	495,000	105,000
	$1,020,000	$480,000
Net Operating Income	$ 180,000	$120,000
Share of Net Income from Slate	96,000	—
	276,000	120,000
Retained Earnings at January 1, 20X7	222,000	50,000
	498,000	170,000
Dividends Declared and Paid	80,000	60,000
Retained Earnings at December 31, 20X7	$ 418,000	$110,000

BALANCE SHEETS		
Cash	$ 148,000	$ 95,000
Accounts Receivable	300,000	130,000
Inventory	210,000	85,000
Investment in Slate	320,000	—
Plant and Equipment (Net)	150,000	75,000
	$1,128,000	$385,000
Accounts Payable	$ 110,000	$ 75,000
Common Stock	600,000	200,000
Retained Earnings	418,000	110,000
	$1,128,000	$385,000

You are also informed that:

(a)   During 20X6, Slate's net operating income was $100,000 and dividends of $60,000 were declared and paid.

(b)   During 20X6, sales by Plate to Slate amounted to $60,000, which included a markup of 20% on cost. At December 31, 20X6, 40% of these goods were still on hand.

(c)   Goods that cost $30,000 were sold by Slate to Plate during 20X7 at a markup of 50% on cost. At December 31, 20X7, the inventory of Plate included half of these goods.

(d)   On December 31, 20X7, Plate owed Slate $10,000.

(e)   Goodwill was written down for impairment by $5,000 in 20X6.

REQUIRED

Ignoring income tax effects, prepare the consolidated income and retained earnings statement and balance sheet for 20X7.

PROBLEM 9–5   Power Inc. acquired an 80% interest in Speed Inc. on January 1, 20X4 when Speed had retained earnings of $60,000. At the date of acquisition, the net assets of Speed were considered to be fairly valued except for land that was undervalued by $30,000.

During 20X4, Speed earned net income of $150,000 and paid a dividend of $100,000. Goodwill was written down for impairment by $6,000 in 20X4 and by a further $2,000 in 20X5.

The abbreviated financial statements of the two companies at December 31, 20X5 were as follows:

INCOME AND RETAINED EARNINGS STATEMENTS	Power	Speed
Sales	$1,200,000	$600,000
Cost of Goods Sold	$ 700,000	$350,000
Operating and Other Expenses	305,000	180,000
	$1,005,000	$530,000
Net Operating Income	$ 195,000	$ 70,000
Dividends from Speed	24,000	—
	219,000	70,000
Extraordinary Gain	—	20,000
Net Income for Year	219,000	90,000
Retained Earnings at January 1, 20X5	160,000	110,000
	379,000	200,000
Dividends Declared and Paid	104,000	30,000
Retained Earnings at December 31, 20X5	$ 275,000	$170,000

BALANCE SHEETS	Power	Speed
Cash	$ 26,000	$ 35,000
Accounts Receivable	195,000	55,000
Inventory	116,000	40,000
Investment in Speed	268,000	—
Land	100,000	50,000
Plant Assets (Net)	600,000	250,000
	$1,305,000	$430,000
Accounts Payable	$ 230,000	$ 60,000
Common Stock	800,000	200,000
Retained Earnings	275,000	170,000
	$1,305,000	$430,000

You are also provided with the following information:

(a)   All intercompany sales were at cost plus 25%.
(b)   The extraordinary item was received on July 1, 20X5.
(c)   The companies traded actively with one another, and transactions between the two companies since they became affiliated were as follows:

	Sales by Power to Speed		Sales by Speed to Power	
Year	Total Sales	Amount in Inventory at December 31	Total Sales	Amount in Inventory at December 31
20X4	$10,000	—	$20,000	$10,000
20X5	20,000	$ 8,000	30,000	6,000

REQUIRED

Ignoring income tax effects, prepare the consolidated balance sheet and combined income and retained earnings statement of Power at December 31, 20X5.

PROBLEM 9–6   Plush Inc. acquired an 80% interest in Sumptuous Inc. on January 1, 20X7 for $820,000 when the common stock of Sumptuous amounted to $600,000 made up of 100,000 shares of common stock of no par value and retained earnings of $200,000. At the date of acquisition, the plant and equipment of Sumptuous was considered to be fairly valued except for an item of plant having a remaining five-year life that was undervalued by $125,000.

The financial statements of the two companies at December 31, 20X8 were as follows:

COMBINED INCOME AND RETAINED EARNINGS STATEMENT	Plush	Sumptuous
Sales	$2,400,000	$1,000,000
Cost of Goods Sold	$1,500,000	$ 600,000
Administration Expenses	300,000	200,000
	$1,800,000	$ 800,000
Net Income from Operations	$ 600,000	$ 200,000
Dividends from Sumptuous	80,000	—
Net Income for Year	680,000	200,000
Retained Earnings, January 1, 20X8	600,000	300,000
	1,280,000	500,000
Dividends Paid	200,000	100,000
Retained Earnings, December 31, 20X8	$1,080,000	$ 400,000

BALANCE SHEETS		
Cash	$ 30,000	$ 20,000
Accounts Receivable	500,000	320,000
Inventory	700,000	280,000
Investment in Sumptuous	820,000	—
Plant and Equipment (net)	1,200,000	600,000
	$3,250,000	$1,220,000
Accounts Payable	$ 170,000	$ 220,000
Common Stock	2,000,000	600,000
Retained Earnings	1,080,000	400,000
	$3,250,000	$1,220,000

You are also informed that:

1. During 20X7, Sumptuous had sold goods to Plush for $240,000 and at December 31, 20X7, Plush had held $42,000 of these goods in inventory. These goods were sold by Sumptuous at a markup of 20% on cost.
2. In 20X8, Sumptuous once again sold goods to Plush for $300,000 on the same basis. At December 31, 20X8, $12,000 of these goods were still held by Plush.
3. Goodwill was written down for impairment by $8,000 in 20X8.
4. During 20X7, Sumptuous paid dividends of $60,000.

REQUIRED

Ignoring income tax effects, give the consolidated income and retained earnings statement and consolidated balance sheet of Plush for 20X8.

PROBLEM 9–7   Prop Inc. acquired an 80% interest in Support Inc. on October 1, 20X5 for $1,040,000. At that date, the assets and liabilities of Support were considered to be fairly valued except for an item of plant having a 10-year remaining life, which was considered to be undervalued by $100,000.

Additional Information:

(a) Goodwill was written down for impairment by $5,000 in 20X6.
(b) From the date of acquisition, Prop purchased goods from Support at cost plus 25%, and goods having selling prices of $100,000 and $160,000 were sold by Support to Prop during 20X5 and 20X6 respectively. At December 31, 20X5, Prop

held goods purchased for $50,000 in inventory whereas at December 31, 20X6, only $40,000 of the goods purchased by Prop during 20X6 remained unsold.

The abbreviated financial statements of the two companies for 20X5 and 20X6 were as follows:

	Prop		Support	
BALANCE SHEETS	**20X5**	**20X6**	**20X5**	**20X6**
Cash	$ 80,000	$ 200,000	$ 180,000	$ 220,000
Accounts Receivable	320,000	360,000	400,000	430,000
Inventory	270,000	300,000	290,000	280,000
Investment in Support	1,040,000	1,040,000	—	—
Plant and Equipment (Net)	310,000	348,000	400,000	550,000
	$2,020,000	$2,248,000	$1,270,000	$1,480,000
Accounts Payable	$ 250,000	$ 400,000	$ 70,000	$ 60,000
Common Stock	1,000,000	1,000,000	800,000	800,000
Retained Earnings	770,000	848,000	400,000	620,000
	$2,020,000	$2,248,000	$1,270,000	$1,480,000

COMBINED INCOME AND RETAINED EARNINGS STATEMENTS

	Prop		Support	
Sales	$1,500,000	$1,600,000	$ 900,000	$1,000,000
Cost of Goods Sold	$ 680,000	$ 900,000	$ 460,000	$ 470,000
Administration Expenses	240,000	350,000	240,000	250,000
	$ 920,000	$1,250,000	$ 700,000	$ 720,000
Net Income from Operations	$ 580,000	$ 350,000	$ 200,000	$ 280,000
Dividends from Support	20,000	48,000	—	—
Net Income	600,000	398,000	200,000	280,000
Retained Earnings at January 1	430,000	770,000	250,000	400,000
	1,030,000	1,168,000	450,000	680,000
Dividends Paid:				
Interim on June 12	(100,000)	(100,000)	(25,000)	(25,000)
Final on December 15	(160,000)	(220,000)	(25,000)	(35,000)
Retained Earnings at Dec. 31	$ 770,000	$ 848,000	$ 400,000	$ 620,000

REQUIRED

Ignoring income tax effects, prepare the consolidated combined income and retained earnings statements and balance sheets of Prop for the two years ended December 31, 20X5 and 20X6.

PROBLEM 9–8 On July 1, 20X4, Possess Inc. acquired a 75% interest in Seize Inc. for $675,000. Financial statements were not prepared at the date of acquisition, but at January 1, 20X4, Seize had retained earnings of $120,000. No dividends were declared by Seize during 20X4.

You are informed that:

1. At the date of acquisition it was agreed amongst the parties that all assets and liabilities were fairly valued.
2. The rate of income tax is 50%.
3. Goodwill was written down for impairment by $20,000 in 20X5.
4. From the date of acquisition, the two companies had traded actively with one another. All sales were made at a markup of 25% on cost and an examination of the records of the two companies disclosed the following position:

Sales			Amount	Balance in Inventory at December 31
Possess to Seize	—	20X4	$640,000	$100,000
Seize to Possess	—	20X4	$860,000	$250,000
		20X5	$920,000	$300,000

The abbreviated balance sheets and combined statements of income and retained earnings of Possess and Seize at December 31, 20X5 were as follows:

COMBINED INCOME AND RETAINED EARNINGS STATEMENTS	Possess	Seize
Sales	$2,800,000	$1,600,000
Cost of Goods Sold	$1,160,000	$ 720,000
Operating Expenses	1,080,000	600,000
	$2,240,000	$1,320,000
Net Operating Income	$ 560,000	$ 280,000
Dividends from Seize	60,000	—
Net Income Before Income Taxes	620,000	280,000
Income Tax Expense (50%)	280,000	140,000
Net Income After Income Taxes	340,000	140,000
Retained Earnings at January 1, 20X5	580,000	160,000
	920,000	300,000
Dividends Paid (December 2)	180,000	80,000
Retained Earnings at December 31, 20X5	$ 740,000	$ 220,000

BALANCE SHEETS		
Cash	$ 45,000	$ 20,000
Accounts Receivable	510,000	590,000
Inventory	135,000	275,000
Investment in Seize	675,000	—
Plant and Equipment (Net)	790,000	170,000
	$2,155,000	$1,055,000
Current Liabilities	$ 315,000	$ 190,000
Future Income Taxes	100,000	45,000
Common Stock	1,000,000	600,000
Retained Earnings	740,000	220,000
	$2,155,000	$1,055,000

REQUIRED

Prepare the consolidated balance sheet and combined income and retained earnings statement for Possess for 20X5.

PROBLEM 9–9

Penal Inc. acquired an 80% interest in Severe Inc. on January 1, 20X7 for $820,000 when the common stock of Severe amounted to $600,000 made up of 100,000 shares of common stock of no par value and retained earnings of $200,000. At the date of acquisition, the plant and equipment of Severe was considered to be fairly valued.

The financial statements of the two companies at December 31, 20X8 were as follows:

COMBINED INCOME AND RETAINED EARNINGS STATEMENT	Penal	Severe
Sales	$4,800,000	$2,000,000
Cost of Goods Sold	$3,000,000	$1,200,000
Administration Expenses	600,000	400,000
	$3,600,000	$1,600,000
Net Income from Operations	$1,200,000	$ 400,000
Dividends from Severe	80,000	—
Net Income Before Income Tax	1,280,000	400,000
Income Tax Expense (50%)	600,000	200,000
Net Income for Year	680,000	200,000
Retained Earnings, January 1, 20X8	600,000	300,000
	1,280,000	500,000
Dividends Paid	200,000	100,000
Retained Earnings, December 31, 20X8	$1,080,000	$ 400,000

BALANCE SHEETS	Penal	Severe
Cash	$ 30,000	$ 20,000
Accounts Receivable	500,000	320,000
Inventory	700,000	280,000
Investment in Severe	820,000	—
Plant and Equipment (Net)	1,200,000	600,000
	$3,250,000	$1,220,000
Accounts Payable	$ 140,000	$ 195,000
Future Income Taxes	30,000	25,000
Common Stock	2,000,000	600,000
Retained Earnings	1,080,000	400,000
	$3,250,000	$1,220,000

You are also informed that:

1. During 20X7, Severe had sold goods to Penal for $480,000 and at December 31, 20X7, Penal had held $84,000 of these goods in inventory. These goods were sold by Severe at a markup of 20% on cost.
2. In 20X8, Severe once again sold goods to Penal for $600,000 on the same basis. At December 31, 20X8, $24,000 of these goods were still held by Penal.
3. Goodwill was written down for impairment by $20,000 in 20X7 and $5,000 in 20X8.
4. During 20X7, Severe paid dividends of $60,000.
5. The rate of income tax is 50%.

REQUIRED

Prepare the consolidated income and retained earnings statement and consolidated balance sheet of Penal for 20X8.

PROBLEM 9–10 Prune Inc. acquired an 80% interest in Shear Inc. on October 1, 20X5 for $1,020,000. At that date, the assets and liabilities of Shear were considered to be fairly valued.
Additional Information:

(a) Goodwill was written down for impairment by $10,000 in 20X6.
(b) From the date of acquisition, Prune purchased goods from Shear at cost plus 25%. Goods having selling prices of $200,000 and $320,000 were sold by Shear to Prune during 20X5 and 20X6 respectively. At December 31, 20X5, Prune held goods purchased for $100,000 in inventory, whereas at December 31, 20X6, only $80,000 of the goods purchased by Prune during 20X6 remained unsold.
(c) The rate of income tax is 50%.

The abbreviated financial statements of the two companies for 20X5 and 20X6 were as follows:

	Prune		Shear	
BALANCE SHEETS	20X5	20X6	20X5	20X6
Cash	$ 80,000	$ 188,000	$ 180,000	$ 220,000
Accounts Receivable	380,000	360,000	400,000	430,000
Inventory	290,000	320,000	290,000	280,000
Investment in Shear	1,020,000	1,020,000	—	—
Plant and Equipment (Net)	770,000	900,000	410,000	550,000
	$2,540,000	$2,788,000	$1,280,000	$1,480,000
Accounts Payable	$ 250,000	$ 400,000	$ 75,000	$ 40,000
Future Income Taxes	120,000	140,000	5,000	20,000
Common Stock	1,000,000	1,000,000	800,000	800,000
Retained Earnings	1,170,000	1,248,000	400,000	620,000
	$2,540,000	$2,788,000	$1,280,000	$1,480,000

COMBINED INCOME AND RETAINED EARNINGS STATEMENTS	Prune		Shear	
	20X5	20X6	20X5	20X6
Sales	$3,000,000	$3,200,000	$1,800,000	$2,000,000
Cost of Goods Sold	$1,360,000	$1,800,000	$ 920,000	$ 940,000
Administration Expenses	480,000	700,000	480,000	500,000
	$1,840,000	$2,500,000	$1,400,000	$1,440,000
Net Income from Operations	$1,160,000	$ 700,000	$ 400,000	$ 560,000
Dividends from Shear	20,000	48,000	—	—
Net Income Before Income Taxes	1,180,000	748,000	400,000	560,000
Income Tax Expense (50%)	580,000	350,000	200,000	280,000
Net Income After Income Taxes	600,000	398,000	200,000	280,000
Retained Earnings at January 1	830,000	1,170,000	250,000	400,000
	1,430,000	$1,568,000	$ 450,000	$ 680,000
Dividends Paid:				
Interim on June 12	(100,000)	(100,000)	(25,000)	(30,000)
Final on December 15	(160,000)	(220,000)	(25,000)	(30,000)
Retained Earnings at December 31	$1,170,000	$1,248,000	$ 400,000	$ 620,000

REQUIRED

Prepare the consolidated combined income and retained earnings statements and balance sheets of Prune for the two years ended December 31, 20X5 and 20X6.

10

Consolidations: Intercompany Transactions in Capital Assets

LEARNING OBJECTIVES

After studying this chapter you should be able to:

1. Understand the nature of transfer pricing as it applies to capital assets;
2. Apply the techniques required to eliminate unrealized profits in capital assets in both upstream and downstream situations;
3. Adjust the income taxes payable arising from the elimination of unrealized profits arising from intercompany transfers of capital assets; and
4. Recognize the theoretical inconsistencies applying to the elimination of unrealized profits from intercompany sales of capital assets at a profit.

THE NEED TO ACCOUNT FOR INTERCOMPANY SALES OF CAPITAL ASSETS

From time to time, it is necessary to create conditions where divisions of companies compete with one another on equal grounds. For example, a company having two divisions may find that one operates through a factory built some years ago, and the other through a new factory. In such a case, the fixed overhead of the older factory may be considerably less than that of the division operating through the newer factory. To place the two divisions on an equal footing would, therefore, require an adjustment to the fixed overhead. One of the ways in which this could be achieved is through the transfer of capital assets to the older factory at inflated prices.

As with intercompany sales of inventory, it is necessary to eliminate the effects of any intercompany transactions involving capital assets from the consolidated financial statements. It is, however, **only those capital assets sold by one company to another at a profit or loss that require adjustment**. This is because any unrealized profits (or losses) on the sale of assets affects the net income (and/or retained earnings) of the consolidated entity and the amount at which the assets are reflected on the consolidated balance sheet. Any sales of capital assets at cost do not require adjustment because these sales represent nothing more than normal transfers of assets between companies in affiliated groups.

This chapter outlines the procedures necessary to eliminate the effects of intercompany transactions involving fixed assets sold at a profit or loss.

240

ILLUSTRATION 10–1
THE ELIMINATION OF UNREALIZED PROFITS ON INTERCOMPANY SALES OF LAND

Parent Inc. acquired a 75% interest in Subsidiary Inc. on its formation. At December 31, 20X6, the income statements of Parent and Subsidiary reflected net income of $400,000 and $200,000 respectively.

During 20X6, land having a book value of $60,000 was sold for $80,000. If the sale was "downstream" from Parent to Subsidiary, the consolidated income statement for 20X6 would be as follows:

	Consolidated	Parent	Subsidiary
Net Income before Adjustment		$400,000	$200,000
Less: Unrealized Profit on Sale of Land		20,000	—
Net Income	$580,000	380,000	200,000
Less: Minority Interests	50,000	—	50,000
Consolidated Net Income	530,000	$380,000	$150,000
Retained Earnings at January 1, 20X6	340,000		
Retained Earnings at December 31, 20X6	$870,000		

If, however, the sale of land had been "upstream" from Subsidiary to Parent, the position would have been as follows:

	Consolidated	Parent	Subsidiary
Net Income before Adjustment		$400,000	$200,000
Less: Unrealized Profit on Sale of Land		—	20,000
Net Income	$580,000	400,000	180,000
Less: Minority Interests	45,000	—	45,000
Consolidated Net Income	535,000	$400,000	$135,000
Retained Earnings at January 1, 20X6	340,000		
Retained Earnings at December 31, 20X6	$875,000		

Note: In both cases, the value of the land on the consolidated balance sheet must be reduced by the full amount of $20,000. However, with the upstream sale, the minority interests on the balance sheet would also have to be adjusted downwards by their $5,000 share of the unrealized profit.

INTERCOMPANY SALES OF NONDEPRECIABLE ASSETS

As outlined above, any profit or loss arising from intercompany sales of land or other **nondepreciable assets** must be eliminated in the consolidation process. The adjustment is relatively straightforward and depends upon the date on which the sale took place.

If the sale occurred during the current year, the adjustment is merely to eliminate the profit (or loss) arising from the sale of land in the income statement of the company concerned and to adjust the cost of the land by the same amount on the balance sheet. **The adjustment is made, as with the elimination of unrealized gains or losses in inventory, against the net income of the selling company** because it is this company that initiated the transaction and made the gain or loss. With downstream sales, the adjustment is against the parent company's net income. With upstream sales, the adjustment is against the subsidiary company's net income so that on consolidation, the unrealized gain is automatically allocated between the majority and minority interests in the subsidiary.

An illustration of an adjustment for unrealized profits on the sale of land in the current year is provided in Illustration 10–1. This illustration shows that the full unrealized gain of $20,000 is eliminated from the net income of the parent company in the case of downstream sales and against the net income of the subsidiary company with upstream sales.

Where the sale of the land took place some years prior to the year for which consolidated financial statements are being prepared, **the adjustment is against the post-acquisition retained earnings of the company concerned.** This is because the profit or loss would already

ILLUSTRATION 10–2
ADJUSTMENTS FOR UNREALIZED PROFITS ON INTERCOMPANY SALES OF
NONDEPRECIABLE ASSETS IN PRIOR YEARS

Parent Inc. acquired a 75% interest in Subsidiary Inc. on its formation on January 1, 20X5. The following information was extracted from the financial statements of the two companies for the year ended December 31, 20X6:

	Parent	Subsidiary
Net Income for Year	$400,000	$200,000
Retained Earnings at January 1, 20X6	340,000	120,000

If land having a book value of $60,000 was sold for $80,000 during 20X5, the adjustments to consolidated net income would, therefore, be as follows:

	Downstream Sales	Upstream Sales
Consolidated Net Income		
($400,000 + $200,000 − Minority Interest Net Income of $50,000)	$550,000	$550,000
Retained Earnings at January 1, 20X6		
(i.e., less the Share of Unrealized Profit on Land from 20X5)		
($340,000 − Unrealized Profit of $20,000)	320,000	—
($340,000 − 75% of Unrealized Profit of $20,000)	—	325,000
Retained Earnings at December 31, 20X6	$870,000	$875,000

have been included in the net income of the selling company for the year in which the sale took place, and would be reflected as part of the retained earnings at the beginning of the year in which the consolidation takes place.

This position is outlined in Illustration 10–2, which shows that the unrealized profit on the sale of land is eliminated in full with downstream sales from the retained earnings of the parent company. With upstream sales, however, the elimination of the unrealized gain depends upon the extent of the interest in the subsidiary. In this latter case, the elimination was 75% against the retained earnings of the subsidiary attributable to the parent company and 25% against the minority interests. In either case, the cost of the land on the consolidated balance sheet must be reduced by the full amount of the unrealized gain.

INTERCOMPANY SALES OF DEPRECIABLE ASSETS

Where intercompany sales of **depreciable capital assets** at a profit (or loss) have taken place, two adjustments are necessary. The elimination of the excess (or under) amortization on these assets is required as well as any profit or loss arising from the sale of these assets.

The problem is that where the intercompany sales have been made at a profit, the purchasing company will hold an asset that is recorded at an **inflated value**. The amortization charged against the net income of the purchasing company would, as a result, have been calculated on this inflated value. This must, therefore, be reduced to the correct figure on the consolidated balance sheet. In many cases, the company purchasing the depreciable asset may be unaware that it was sold to it at a profit.

In the case of a downstream sale of a depreciable asset sold at a profit during the current year, the adjustments are threefold in nature: two affecting the income statement and one affecting the balance sheet. The two adjustments to the income statement are that, first, **the unrealized gain must be eliminated from the net income of the selling company** in the year of sale. Second, **the amortization charged on the value at which the asset was recorded in the records of the purchasing company must be reduced by the amount of amortization on the unrealized profit**. This latter adjustment is made by the **selling company** so that the

ILLUSTRATION 10–3
ELIMINATION OF INTERCOMPANY PROFITS ON THE SALE OF
DEPRECIABLE ASSETS DURING THE YEAR

Parent Inc. acquired an 80% interest in Subsidiary Inc. on its formation. The abbreviated combined income and retained earnings statements of the two companies for the year ended December 31, 20X1 **using the equity method**, are given below. On April 1, Subsidiary had sold equipment costing $80,000 to Parent for $120,000; the equipment is expected to last 10 years and have no residual value at the end of its useful life.

	Parent	Subsidiary
Net Operating Income	$400,000	$140,000
Profit on Sale of Equipment	—	40,000
Share of Net Income from Subsidiary	114,400	—
Net Income	514,400	180,000
Retained Earnings at January 1, 20X1	420,000	300,000
Retained Earnings at December 31, 20X1	$934,400	$480,000

The unrealized profit on the sale of the equipment and the excess amortization would be eliminated in the consolidated income statement for 20X1 as follows:

	Consolidated	Parent	Subsidiary
Net Income		$400,000	$180,000
Less Profit on Sale of Equipment		—	(40,000)
		400,000	140,000
Addback Excess Amortization of Capital Gain [10% of ($120,000 − 80,000) × 9/12]		—	3,000
Net Operating Income	$543,000	400,000	143,000
Less Minority Interests	28,600	—	28,600
Consolidated Net Income	514,400	$400,000	$114,400
Retained Earnings at January 1, 20X1	420,000		
Retained Earnings at December 31, 20X1	$934,400		

Notes:

[1] Two additional adjustments are necessary. First, as the sale was upstream, the minority interests on the balance sheet must be reduced by the proportionate share of the adjustments relating to the unrealized profit of $7,400 (i.e., 20% of $37,000). Second, it is also necessary to reduce the consolidated plant and equipment and accumulated amortization on the balance sheet by $40,000 and $3,000 respectively.

[2] The statement given above that the equipment will "have no residual value at the end of its useful life" has no effect on the unrealized profit adjustment because it only affects the calculation of the normal amortization expense.

unrealized gain is written off over the life of the asset to which it applies. And, third, **the asset value and balance of accumulated amortization appearing on the consolidated balance sheet must be adjusted accordingly.** With upstream sales, there also is **an additional adjustment to the minority interests** appearing on the balance sheet for its share of the unrealized gain (or loss).

These adjustments are outlined in Illustration 10–3, which shows the two adjustments to the net income of the selling company. In this case, the sale is an upstream sale and the adjustment is to the net income of Subsidiary Inc. This involves the elimination of the unrealized profit of $40,000 on the sale of the equipment less the addback of the excess amortization of $3,000 on the asset sold. The net adjustment to the consolidated net income is $29,600, representing 80% of the net adjustment of $37,000 (i.e., $40,000 − $3,000). An adjustment of $7,400 (i.e., 20% of the $37,000) to the minority interests is also required because the sale is upstream. And, finally, Illustration 10–3 draws attention to the fact that the plant and equipment on the consolidated balance sheet must be reduced by $40,000 and the accumulated amortization on the plant and equipment reduced by $3,000.

Where the sale of a depreciable capital asset is downstream, the adjustments are against the net income of the parent company. The gain (or loss) and the amortization adjustments are, once again, adjusted against the plant and equipment and accumulated amortization on the balance sheet.

ADJUSTMENTS ARISING SOME TIME AFTER THE DATE OF SALE

Where the consolidation is carried out some time after the sale of the asset, the three adjustments are still necessary, but **the elimination of the unrealized gain is against the retained earnings** of the selling company. In these cases, the selling company's post-acquisition retained earnings must first be reduced by the amount of the unrealized profit on the sale of the asset concerned **less** the amount by which the excess asset value has been amortized since the date of sale. The amortization charged by the selling company in the current year must then be reduced by the amortization applying to the increased asset value (i.e., on the unrealized gain). And, finally, the value and accumulated amortization of the asset to which the unrealized profit applies must be adjusted on the consolidated balance sheet.

These adjustments are outlined in Illustration 10–4, which shows that midway through 20X2, the subsidiary company sold equipment having a 10-year life to its parent company at a price that included an unrealized profit of $40,000. When the financial statements of the two companies were consolidated 30 months later (i.e., on December 31, 20X4), the unrealized profit on this asset would have been reduced by $6,000 to $34,000 as follows:

Amount by which Asset Value was inflated			$40,000
Less: Accumulated Amortization of Unrealized Profit:			
20X2 — 10% × ($40,000 × 6/12)		$ 2,000	
20X3 — 10% × $40,000		4,000	6,000
"Unamortized" Unrealized Profit at December 31, 20X3			$34,000

The adjustments required to account for these amounts in consolidating the financial statements at December 31, 20X4 were:

(a) The consolidated retained earnings at January 1, 20X4 was reduced by the parent company's share of the "unamortized" unrealized profit. Here, as the sale was upstream, the adjustment was $27,200 being 80% of $34,000.

(b) The excess amortization of $4,000 for 20X4 was adjusted in Illustration 10–4 in the normal manner for upstream sales in the income statement against the subsidiary company. As outlined earlier, what occurred was that on calculation of the minority interests in the net income, the $4,000 excess amortization was apportioned as to $3,200 to the parent (i.e., 80% of $4,000), and $800 to the subsidiary (i.e., 20% of $4,000).

(c) At December 31, 20X4, two further adjustments were necessary. First, both the assets and the accumulated amortization on the consolidated balance sheet had to be reduced. Here, the assets were reduced by the $40,000 unrealized profit, and the accumulated amortization by $10,000 (i.e., the $2,000 excess amortization from 20X2 and the $4,000 from both 20X3 and 20X4).

In addition, the **minority interests** would have been reduced by their share of the "unamortized" unrealized profit. In this case, the balance remaining at December 31, 20X4 was $30,000 (i.e., the $40,000 less accumulated amortization of $10,000), of which 20% was attributable to them. The minority interests appearing on the consolidated balance sheet was, therefore, reduced by $6,000.

It should, however, be noted that the $6,000 adjustment to the minority interests, like that applying to the retained earnings at the beginning of the year, is reduced each year over the life of the asset to which the unrealized profit applies. In this case, the adjustment to the

ILLUSTRATION 10–4
THE INTERCOMPANY SALE OF DEPRECIABLE ASSETS AT A PROFIT SOME YEARS
PRIOR TO CONSOLIDATION

Parent Inc. acquired an 80% interest in Subsidiary Inc. at cost. The income statements of the two companies for the year ended December 31, 20X4 prepared using the full equity method are given below. On July 1, 20X2, Subsidiary had sold equipment costing $80,000 to Parent for $120,000; the equipment was expected to last 10 years and have no residual value at the end of its useful life.

	Parent	Subsidiary
Net Operating Income	$480,000	$240,000
Share of Net Income from Subsidiary	195,200	—
Net Income	675,200	240,000
Retained Earnings at January 1, 20X4 (full equity basis)	292,800	200,000
Retained Earnings at December 31, 20X4	$968,000	$440,000

The consolidated income statement for the year ended December 31, 20X4 would be as follows:

	Consolidated	Parent	Subsidiary
Net Operating Income		$480,000	$240,000
Addback: Excess Amortization of Capital Gain of 10% of ($120,000 − $80,000)		—	4,000
Total Net Income	$724,000	480,000	244,000
Less: Minority Interests	48,800	—	48,800
Consolidated Net Income	675,200	$480,000	$195,200
Retained Earnings at January 1, 20X4	292,800		
Retained Earnings at December 31, 20X4	$968,000		

It is important to note that the retained earnings at January 1, 20X4 would have been calculated as follows:

Balance before Adjustments would, therefore, have been		$320,000
Less: Unrealized Gain on Sale of Plant and Equipment of 80% of $40,000	$ 32,000	
Less: Excess Amortization Addback of 80% of ($2,000 [20X2] + $4,000 [20X3])	4,800	27,200
Retained Earnings at December 31, 20X3		$292,800

Note: For convenience, the adjustment to the unrealized gain on the plant and equipment may be calculated by merely taking the parent company's share of the net amount remaining. In this case, the adjustment would be 80% of ($40,000 − [10% of 40,000 × 1.5 years]) = $27,200.

The following additional adjustments would also be necessary:

(a) Minority interests would also be adjusted downwards at the end of the year by their share of the net remaining gain on the unrealized profit on the sale of the plant and equipment of $6,000 (i.e., 20% of $40,000 − 20% of the excess amortization of $10,000, which is $6,000 [20X2 and 20X3] + $4,000 [20X4]).

(b) The cost of the consolidated plant and equipment would be reduced by $40,000.

(c) The accumulated amortization for the consolidated capital assets would be reduced by $10,000 (2,000 + 4,000 + 4,000).

minority interests through the period July 1, 20X2 to December 31, 20X4 would be reduced in the following manner:

July 1, 20X2:	20% of Unrealized Profit of $40,000	$8,000
December 31, 20X2:	Less: Amortization of 10% × ($40,000 × 6/12 × 20%)	400
	Balance "Unamortized" Unrealized Profit	7,600
December 31, 20X3:	Less: Amortization of 10% × ($40,000 × 20%)	800
	Balance "Unamortized" Unrealized Profit	6,800
December 31, 20X4:	Less: Amortization of 10% × ($40,000 × 20%)	800
	Balance "Unamortized" Unrealized Profit	$6,000

FLOW THROUGH OF ADJUSTMENTS

All the effects on consolidation arising from the intercompany sale of an asset at a profit are eliminated over the life of the asset concerned. For example, if Parent Inc. sold equipment having a book value of $80,000 and a five-year remaining life and no residual value to Subsidiary Inc. for $100,000 on July 1, 20X1, all effects of the transaction would be eliminated from the consolidated financial statements by the end of the five-year period. The elimination in the consolidated workings would be as follows:

1. The unrealized profit would first be excluded by reducing the net income by $20,000 and equipment by the same amount in the year of sale, which is 20X1.
2. The annual amortization expense would be reduced by the difference between the amount calculated using the selling price of the equipment of $100,000 (i.e., $20,000) and that calculated on the original cost of the equipment of $80,000 (i.e., $16,000). The adjustments to the amortization expense in the income statement over the life of the equipment would, consequently, be reduced by $4,000 × 6/12 = $2,000 in 20X1 and 20X6, and by $4,000 in 20X2 through 20X5 until such time as the unrealized profit of $20,000 has been reduced to zero.
3. During the period January 1, 20X2 through December 31, 20X6, the consolidated retained earnings brought forward each year would be reduced by the net adjustment of the unrealized profit less the amortization adjustment at that date. For example, the adjustment at January 1, 20X4 would be $10,000 (i.e., $20,000 – [$2,000 + $4,000 + $4,000]).
4. At the end of each of the years 20X1 through 20X6, the equipment appearing on the consolidated balance sheet would be reduced until amortized (i.e., depreciated) down to zero. In each case the deduction would be the $20,000 from the equipment and the accumulated amortization to date.

ADJUSTMENTS ARISING FROM USING THE EQUITY METHOD

Where unrealized profits have arisen from intercompany sales of capital assets and the equity method is used by the parent company to record its investment in the subsidiary, adjustments to the investment account are also necessary.

These adjustments must be made to, first, reflect the correct figure for the "net income from subsidiary" so that the income statement of the parent company reflects the total net income of the group in accordance with the "one-line consolidation" concept. Second, the "investment in subsidiary" account appearing on the balance sheet of the parent company (i.e., its own and not the consolidated balance sheet) should reflect the correct value of the investment.

The adjustments in the case of upstream sales are quite straightforward. The unrealized profit is eliminated in the year in which it occurs and, thereafter, the excess amortization adjustments are made every year until the figure for unrealized profit is reduced to zero. For example, assume that an unrealized profit of $20,000 arose on January 1, 20X2 from the sale of capital assets being amortized over five years on the straight-line basis by a 75%-owned subsidiary. The unrealized profit of $15,000 (i.e., 75% of $20,000) would be eliminated from both the "net income from subsidiary" and "investment in subsidiary" account on January 1, 20X2, and excess amortization of $3,000 would be deducted therefrom on December 31 in each of the five years from 20X2 to 20X6.

With downstream sales, the adjustments are also against the "investment in subsidiary" and "net income from subsidiary" accounts even though the adjustments are, in reality, adjustments to the parent company's net income. This is because, with the equity method of accounting for longterm investments, there is no other place to make these adjustments.

To illustrate the recording of these adjustments in the ledger of the parent company, assume that the cost of a 60% interest in a subsidiary on January 1, 20X5 was $300,000. No goodwill arose on acquisition and during 20X5, the subsidiary earned net income of $160,000 but paid no dividends. On January 1, 20X5, the parent company sold capital assets that were to be amortized on the straight-line basis over 10 years at a profit of $40,000. The "investment in subsidiary" and "net income from subsidiary" accounts would be as follows:

Investment in Subsidiary

20X5					
Jan. 1	Purchase Consideration	300,000			300,000
Dec. 31	Net Income (60% of $160,000)	96,000			
	Unrealized Profit on Capital Assets		40,000		
	Excess Amortization Adjustment	4,000			360,000

Net Income from Subsidiary

20X5					
Dec. 31	Net Income		96,000		
	Unrealized Profit on Capital Assets	40,000			
	Excess Amortization Adjustment		4,000		60,000
	Income Summary	60,000			Nil

Note: One hundred percent of the unrealized profit on the capital assets is recorded less excess amortization of $4,000, thereon is because the sale was downstream in nature and there is no apportionment between the parent company and the minority.

WHERE INTERCOMPANY SALES ARE NORMAL TRADING ACTIVITIES

Normally, intercompany transfers or sales of capital assets result in the recognition and subsequent elimination of any gains or losses on the sale of the asset. However, where the selling company **actually trades in the assets sold**, the sale represents an intercompany sale that must be eliminated from both the sales and the purchases in the income statement of the selling company in the year of sale as part of the consolidation process.

For example, assume that the subsidiary company is a motor dealer and it sells a delivery truck that cost $15,000 to its parent company for $18,000. The elimination process would, therefore, require that $18,000 be deducted from sales and $15,000 from purchases in the income statement of the selling company in the year of sale. This adjustment also eliminates the gain of $3,000 because the revenues of the selling companies are automatically decreased by the equivalent amount of $3,000 (i.e., $18,000 – $15,000). In subsequent years, the adjustment to the retained earnings would be effected by the elimination of the gain of $3,000 less the deductions for the addback of the excess amortization.

INTERCOMPANY LEASING OF CAPITAL ASSETS

From time to time, companies within a group may lease capital assets from each other. These leases normally take the form of operational leases (i.e., the lease of office space, factory buildings, etc.) for a monthly rental. However, they can also be financial leases covering motor vehicles or equipment or the sale and leaseback of buildings and other capital assets.

With **operating leases**, all that is required is the elimination of the rental charges in the consolidated workings. For example, the receipt of rental revenues by one company of, say $24,000, is merely offset against the rental expense of $24,000 of another company.

Financial leases must also be eliminated in the consolidation process. Here, as the financing and leasing charges are made up of both interest and capital, both the intercompany charges should be eliminated by offsetting receipts against the payments in the consolidated workings.

INCOME TAX EFFECTS RELATING TO CAPITAL ASSETS

Those Relating to Unrealized Profits on Sales of Capital Assets

As with inventories, adjustments to the income tax expense and future income taxes are necessary when unrealized profits on intercompany sales of capital assets are eliminated in the consolidation process. The adjustments are straightforward because **they are treated as timing differences** extending over the life of the capital asset to which they relate. These adjustments also **only affect the consolidated income tax expense and future income taxes** because the liability for the payment of income taxes remains unchanged.

The elimination process consists of an initial adjustment to the income tax expense on the exclusion of the unrealized profit (or loss) on the sale of the capital asset in the year of sale and, thereafter, the annual amortization of the adjustment until the effects of the unrealized gain are reduced to zero. As outlined in the previous chapter, the company receiving the asset at an inflated price may be totally unaware of the existence of the unrealized profit.

The income tax effects of an upstream sale of equipment by a 75%-owned subsidiary to its parent company are outlined in Illustration 10–5. In this case, the equipment having an expected five-year remaining life with no residual value was sold halfway through 20X3. In 20X3, the elimination of the effects of the sale of $18,000 (i.e., unrealized profit of $20,000 less the half-year amortization of the unrealized profit of $2,000) gives rise to a reduction of both the consolidated income tax expense and the consolidated future income taxes of $9,000 (i.e., 50% × $18,000). In 20X4, there is a further drawdown of the consolidated future income taxes adjustment with a corresponding increase in the consolidated income tax expense of $2,000 (i.e., 50% of $4,000). This position would be repeated in 20X5, 20X6 and 20X7 until the final drawdown of $1,000 in 20X8 occurs that reduces the income tax effect of the sale to zero.

It is important to note that **adjustments arising from the revaluation of capital assets on acquisition of an interest in a subsidiary in the analysis of equity are not subject to income taxes** because these adjustments are, in effect, nothing more than an adjustment to the amount appearing as goodwill. And, as pointed out earlier, the amortization of goodwill arising on consolidation is not allowable as a deduction for income tax purposes.

Adjustments to Future Taxes on Assigned Values at Date of Acquisition

A further complication in the accounting for income taxes in relation to capital assets arises from the accounting for the fair market values allocated to the assets and liabilities of a subsidiary company at the date of acquisition. The complication arises because paragraph 1581.47 of the CICA Handbook states, *inter alia*, that:

> ... the tax effects of differences between the assigned values of the identifiable assets and liabilities acquired and their tax bases [must] be recognized as future income tax assets and liabilities and included in the allocation of the cost of the purchase.[1]

This means that future taxes must be calculated on **the differences between the fair market values assigned to the assets and liabilities at the date of acquisition and their values for income tax purposes.** Where recognized, these future taxes must be treated as additional assets

---

[1] The issue is further examined in section 3465 of the CICA *Handbook*.

ILLUSTRATION 10–5
INCOME TAX EFFECTS OF THE ELIMINATION OF UNREALIZED PROFITS ARISING FROM THE INTERCOMPANY SALE OF CAPITAL ASSETS

A 75%-owned subsidiary sold an item of plant having a five-year remaining life (and no residual value) and a book value of $80,000 to its parent company on July 1, 20X3 at $100,000. The equipment sold had originally cost $120,000. Both companies have financial years ending on December 31 and the differences between net income and taxable income are all due to timing differences.

The reported net income and income tax expense for the two companies for the financial years ended December 31, 20X3 and 20X4 were as follows:

	Parent		Subsidiary	
Trading Operations:	**20X3**	**20X4**	**20X3**	**20X4**
Net Income from Operations for Year	$ 840,000	$ 920,000	$240,000	$300,000
Share of Net Income from Subsidiary — Note 1	180,000	225,000	—	—
Gain on Sale of Equipment — Note 2	—	—	20,000	—
	1,020,000	1,145,000	260,000	300,000
Less Income Tax Expense (50%)	420,000	460,000	130,000	150,000
Net Income for Year	$ 600,000	$ 685,000	$130,000	$150,000

Notes:

[1] The share of net income from the subsidiary, like dividends from a subsidiary, is not subject to income tax.

[2] The gain on the sale of equipment is considered to be taxable because it represents a recovery of the amortization of capital assets/capital cost allowances allowable for income tax purposes in previous years.

Net Income and Income Tax Adjustments:

The income tax adjustments applying to the consolidated financial statements arising from the elimination of the unrealized profit on the sale of capital assets against the net income of Subsidiary are as follows:

	20X3	20X4
Unadjusted Net Income from Operations for Year **excluding** the Unrealized Gain of $20,000 given above	$240,000	$300,000
Amortization of Unrealized Gain (i.e., Excess Amortization of Capital Assets)		
20X3 — $20,000/5 × 6/12	(2,000)	
20X4 — $20,000/5		(4,000)
Adjusted Net Income before Taxes	$242,000	$304,000
Income Tax Expense at Rate of 50%	$121,000	$152,000

Adjustment to Future Income Taxes on Balance Sheet:

If the total unadjusted future income taxes of the two companies had a credit balance of $120,000 in 20X3, and this amount remained unchanged in 20X4 and 20X5, the adjustments to these figures would be as follows:

20X3:	$120,000 − (50% of [$20,000 − $2,000])	=	$111,000
20X4:	$120,000 − (50% of [$20,000 − $2,000 − $4,000])	=	$113,000
20X5:	$120,000 − (50% of [$20,000 − $2,000 − {2 × $4,000}])	=	$115,000

Note: The adjustment on the income statement is an increase in income tax expense for the elimination of the excess amortization (i.e., the tax rate × excess amortization eliminated). The adjustment to the future income taxes is for the amount of the net unrealized profit at the year end (i.e., the tax rate × the net unrealized profit).

(or liabilities) of the subsidiary company in the analysis of equity and written off (i.e., referred to as drawdowns) over the periods corresponding to the lives of the assets to which they apply along the same lines as that applying to the undervalued assets. For example, if the tax effects of an undervalued asset in a 75%-owned subsidiary were $20,000, the adjustment would have been an increase in the equity acquired of $15,000 and an increase in future tax assets of

$15,000. And, if the life of the asset to which the tax effects applied was three years, the income tax expense on the income statement would be increased by $5,000 and the future tax assets reduced (i.e., drawn down) by the same amount in each of the three years. The drawdown of future taxes is added to the income tax expense in the consolidated workings.

The inclusion and subsequent recognition of the drawdown of these assets and liabilities are explained in Illustration 10–6. Here, the analysis of equity shows that the equity acquired by Parent is increased by its $40,000 share of the income tax effects of $50,000 and an increase of $40,000 in the future tax assets. These adjustments are treated as temporary differences arising from the differences between the carrying amounts of assets and liabilities of each enterprise and the appropriate tax value. What occurs is that when the carrying amount of an asset is increased to fair value but the tax value of the asset is not adjusted, a taxable temporary difference arises, resulting in a future income tax liability. As the life of the asset to which the tax effects apply is four years, the amortization expense would be increased by $10,000 per year with a corresponding reduction in the future tax asset until it is completely written off.

A FINAL NOTE ON THESE ADJUSTMENTS

The adjustments described in this chapter, up to this point, automatically eliminate the unrealized profit on the sale of capital assets over the life of the asset concerned. They also automatically adjust the amounts accruing to the parent company and the minority interests because the adjustments are made to the income statement of the company benefiting from the sale. In this respect, the adjustments to the amortization expense over the life of the asset must always equal the amount of unrealized profit on the sale of the asset and reduce the unrealized profit to zero. The income tax adjustments, likewise, cancel one another out over the life of the capital asset to which they apply.

THEORETICAL INCONSISTENCIES IN THE TREATMENT OF CAPITAL ASSETS

As with inventories, there are certain theoretical inconsistencies in the treatment of capital assets in the consolidation process. In certain cases the proprietary ownership theory is applied, whereas in others the entity ownership theory applies.

On acquisition of an interest in a subsidiary, any under or overvalued capital assets at the date of acquisition are brought into account using **the proprietary ownership theory.** For example, if plant is undervalued by $100,000 on the acquisition of a 60%-owned subsidiary, only 60% of the undervaluation is recognized in determining the parent company's share of the equity acquired in the analysis of equity. The plant on the consolidated balance sheet is, therefore, increased in value by $60,000 and amortized over the remaining life of the asset. As outlined earlier, the justification of this partial recognition of the value of the plant is based on the contention that the value of the individual shares held by the minority are worth less than those of the majority and, consequently, this treatment reflects their lower value. The standard setting bodies take the position that only 60% of this change in value is recognized because the parent company owns only 60% of the shares in the subsidiary. The only exception is with push-down accounting, where 100% of the change in value is recognized.

Adjustments arising from intercompany transfers of assets at a gain or loss are, however, eliminated using **the entity ownership theory.** In this respect, it is the full unrealized profit or loss that is eliminated and not merely the amount applicable to the parent company. For example, if an unrealized profit of $40,000 arose from an upstream sale of plant by a 75%-owned subsidiary, the elimination would be against both companies (i.e., $30,000 against the

ILLUSTRATION 10–6

INCOME TAX EFFECTS OF THE APPLICATION OF FAIR MARKET VALUES TO ASSETS AND LIABILITIES OF SUBSIDIARIES AT THE DATE OF ACQUISITION

Parent Inc. acquired an 80% interest in Subsidiary Inc. on April 1, 20X4 for $3,000,000. Financial statements were not prepared at that date, but at December 31, 20X3, Subsidiary had common stock of $2,000,000 and retained earnings of $800,000. In 20X4, Subsidiary earned net income of $600,000 and paid a dividend of $200,000 on November 30.

Following a review of the value of the assets and liabilities carried out on April 1, 20X4, it was established that a single item of equipment with a four-year remaining life having a book value of $120,000 and a tax value of $95,000 was undervalued by $100,000. All other assets and liabilities were properly valued. At the date of acquisition, the rate of income tax was 40%.

The analysis of equity of Subsidiary at December 31, 20X4 was as follows:

	Total	Parent 80%	Subsidiary
At Acquisition:			
Common Stock	$2,000,000	$1,600,000	$400,000
Retained Earnings	800,000	640,000	160,000
Net Income for 20X4 (3/12)	150,000	120,000	30,000
Fair Market Value Adjustment — Equipment	100,000	80,000	—
Future Income Taxes on Undervalued Equipment	50,000	40,000	—
(40% × [$120,000 + $100,000 − $95,000])			
		2,480,000	
Purchase Consideration		3,000,000	
Goodwill		$ 520,000	

> Fair Market Value Adjustment = $80,000/4 = $20,000/year
> Future Taxes (40%) = $40,000/4 = $10,000/year

Since Acquisition:			
Net Income for 20X4 (9/12)	450,000	$ 360,000	90,000
Dividends Paid (November 30)	(200,000)	(160,000)	(40,000)
Minority Interests			$640,000

The adjustments to the consolidated workings and financial statements necessitated by the inclusion of the future taxes would be:

1. An increase in the Future Tax Assets of $40,000, which is the asset side of the adjustment to the equity acquired.
2. A draw down of the future taxes of $7,500 in 20X4 (9/12 × $10,000) and $10,000 in 20X5, 20X6, and a final draw down of $2,500 in 20X8 to reduce the increase in future income tax assets of the $40,000 to zero. These amounts would be adjusted as an increase (or decrease) in the income tax expense. There would also be a corresponding increase in the amortization of capital assets on the income statement in each of the five years 2004 through 2008.

The normal write down of the fair market value adjustment to the equipment of $80,000 over its four-year life would, of course, still apply.

parent company and $10,000 against the subsidiary). However, if the proprietary ownership theory applied, all that would be necessary would be to eliminate $30,000 from the parent company's share of the subsidiary's net income.

Once again, no reason is given for this inconsistent treatment. Perhaps, as with the elimination of unrealized profits in inventories, the reason is that it is conservative because it results in a lower amount for minority interests.

The use of these inconsistent practices in the consolidation process is considered by some to represent the application of a "parent theory of consolidation". The term is, however, neither explanatory nor properly descriptive of the situation and it is, consequently, not used in this text.

SUMMARY

This chapter outlines the elimination of unrealized profits or losses on the sale of capital assets between companies affiliated in parent company-subsidiary company relationships. With nondepreciable assets, like land, the adjustment in the year of occurrence is carried out by reducing the selling company's net income and the value of the land on the consolidated balance sheet by the same amount. In subsequent years, however, the adjustment is more complicated and depends upon whether the sales were upstream or downstream. With downstream sales, the adjustment is against the value of the land and the retained earnings of the selling company. With upstream sales, the adjustment is against the minority interests as well as the consolidated retained earnings in proportion to the ownership of the subsidiary.

In the case of depreciable assets, any unrealized profits or losses are eliminated over their useful lives through the addback of excess amortization. The adjustments in later years are, likewise, against the retained earnings of the parent company and, where the sale was upstream, also against the minority interests.

Finally, it is explained that where the equity method of accounting is used by the parent company to account for its investment in a subsidiary, the adjustments arising from the unrealized profit and the excess amortization are recorded by the parent company in the investment account and against the net income from the subsidiary irrespective of whether they are upstream or downstream in nature.

SELF-STUDY PROBLEMS
(covering transfer pricing on capital assets with and without income tax effects)

PROBLEM 10A†   Pal Inc. acquired an 80% interest in Sal Inc. for $360,000 on July 1, 20X4. At January 1, 20X4, Sal had retained earnings of $50,000. At the date of acquisition, certain plant and equipment having a useful life of six years was undervalued by $45,000.

You are also informed that:

(a)   During 20X4, Sal did not pay any dividends.

(b)   On October 1, 20X4, Pal sold plant and equipment that it had purchased for $32,000 to Sal for $48,000. This plant and equipment was expected to have a useful life of eight years and no salvage value.

(c)   On July 1, 20X5, Sal sold plant with a 10-year life costing $40,000 to Pal for $60,000 as part of its normal trading activities, which was treated as the purchase of plant by Pal.

(d)   Goodwill was written down by $4,000 for impairment in 20X4.

You are furnished with the following abbreviated financial statements of Pal and Sal for the year ended December 31, 20X5:

	Pal	Sal
BALANCE SHEETS		
Current Assets	$ 640,000	$280,000
Investment in Sal	360,000	—
Plant and Equipment	800,000	400,000
Accumulated Amortization	(250,000)	(80,000)
	$1,550,000	$600,000
Accounts Payable	$ 120,000	$110,000
Common Stock	800,000	300,000
Retained Earnings	630,000	190,000
	$1,550,000	$600,000

† The solution is provided in Appendix B to this text.

COMBINED INCOME AND RETAINED EARNINGS STATEMENTS	Pal	Sal
Sales	$1,200,000	$800,000
Cost of Goods Sold	$ 600,000	$500,000
Operating Expenses	250,000	100,000
	$ 850,000	$600,000
Net Operating Income	$ 350,000	$200,000
Dividends from Sal	80,000	—
Net Income	430,000	200,000
Retained Earnings at January 1, 20X5	520,000	90,000
	950,000	290,000
Dividends Declared and Paid	320,000	100,000
Retained Earnings at December 31, 20X5	$ 630,000	$190,000

REQUIRED

Ignoring income tax effects, prepare the consolidated income and retained earnings statement and balance sheet of Pal and its subsidiary company for the year ended December 31, 20X5.

PROBLEM 10B†   You are informed that:

1. Psychic Inc. acquired a 75% interest in See Inc. on July 1, 20X4 for $2,545,000. Financial statements were not prepared at the date of acquisition but at January 1, 20X4, See had retained earnings of $600,000. At the date of acquisition, a plant having a book value of $200,000 and a remaining useful life of five years held by See was considered to be undervalued by $60,000. The income tax value of this undervalued asset was $100,000.
2. During 20X4, See earned net income of $400,000 of which $80,000 was paid out as a dividend on December 10, 20X4.
3. Goodwill was written down for impairment by $20,000 in 20X4.
4. On July 1, 20X5, See sold plant to Psychic at a profit of $60,000. This plant had an expected remaining five-year life with no residual value.
5. The rate of income tax was 50%.
6. The abbreviated financial statements of Psychic and its 75%-owned subsidiary, See, at December 31, 20X5, were as follows.

COMBINED INCOME AND RETAINED EARNINGS STATEMENT	Psychic	See
Sales	$5,110,000	$3,290,000
Cost of Goods Sold	$1,700,000	$1,420,000
Operating and Other Expenses	1,810,000	1,330,000
	$3,510,000	$2,750,000
Net Operating Income	$1,600,000	$ 540,000
Gain on Sale of Capital Asset	—	60,000
Dividends from See	75,000	—
Net Income before Income Taxes	1,675,000	600,000
Income Tax Expense (50%)	800,000	300,000
Net Income after Income Taxes	875,000	300,000
Less: Dividends Paid	200,000	100,000
	675,000	200,000
Retained Earnings, January 1, 20X5	1,495,000	920,000
Retained Earnings, December 31, 20X5	$2,170,000	$1,120,000

---

† The solution is provided in Appendix B to this text.

BALANCE SHEETS	Psychic	See
Cash	$ 130,000	$ 220,000
Accounts Receivable	365,000	940,000
Inventory	800,000	880,000
Investment in See	2,545,000	—
Plant and Equipment (Net)	3,970,000	1,940,000
	$7,810,000	$3,980,000
Accounts Payable	$ 580,000	$ 740,000
Future Income Taxes	60,000	120,000
Common Stock (shares of no par value)	5,000,000	2,000,000
Retained Earnings	2,170,000	1,120,000
	$7,810,000	$3,980,000

REQUIRED

Prepare the consolidated balance sheet and combined income and retained earnings statement for 20X5.

REVIEW QUESTIONS

1. Why are assets transferred between companies affiliated in a parent company-subsidiary company relationship at a profit or loss?
2. Explain what adjustments, if any, are required as a result of the transfer of assets between affiliated companies at amounts in excess of their book values?
3. Why do we only concern ourselves with intercompany sales of plant and equipment that are sold at either a profit or a loss?
4. Explain the three steps that are necessary to eliminate the effects of an intercompany sale of depreciable plant in the current year at a loss.
5. Why are the adjustments for unrealized profits or losses and amortization of capital assets made in the same company?
6. Explain what adjustments are necessary in the current year to eliminate the effects of an upstream intercompany sale of plant that occurred two years before accounted for using the cost method.
7. What adjustments are necessary for intercompany sales of plant and equipment at either a profit or a loss using the full equity method?
8. In what way does the adjustment for intercompany sales of equipment differ where the intercompany sale is part of the normal trading activities of the selling company?
9. Explain what adjustments to the income tax expense and future income taxes are necessary in the year following the upstream sale of a capital asset at a profit.
10. What theoretical inconsistencies apply to adjustments affecting the capital assets of companies?

EXERCISES

EXERCISE 10–1   Pull Inc. acquired an 80% interest in Shove Inc. on the formation of Shove on January 1, 20X8. On April 1, 20X9, Shove sold equipment it had just purchased for $80,000 to Pull for $100,000. Pull amortized this equipment at the rate of 10% per year on the straight-line basis. During the period since acquisition to December 31, 20X8, Shove earned net income from operations of $180,000 and paid dividends of $60,000. No dividends were paid by either company during 20X9.

At December 31, 20X9, the abbreviated income statements of the two companies prepared on the cost basis were as follows:

	Pull	Shove
Sales	$1,000,000	$780,000
Gain on Sale of Equipment	—	20,000
	$1,000,000	$800,000
Cost of Goods Sold	$ 500,000	$400,000
Amortization of Equipment	50,000	40,000
Other Expenses	250,000	180,000
	$ 800,000	$620,000
Net Income	$ 200,000	$180,000
Retained Earnings at January 1, 20X9	300,000	120,000
Retained Earnings at December 31, 20X9	$ 500,000	$300,000

REQUIRED

Ignoring income tax effects:

1. Prepare the consolidated income and retained earnings statement for the year ended December 31, 20X9; and
2. Explain what other adjustments to the consolidated financial statements are necessary.

EXERCISE 10–2 Page Inc. purchased a 60% interest in Sage Inc. on January 1, 20X2 at cost. Sage's net income for 20X2, 20X3 and 20X4 were $80,000, $100,000 and $120,000 respectively — no dividends were paid by Sage during this time.

Page had retained earnings of $120,000 at January 1, 20X2, and details of its net income and dividends paid for 20X2 through 20X4 were as follows:

	Net Income	Dividends
20X2	$200,000	$ 80,000
20X3	250,000	100,000
20X4	300,000	120,000

On July 1, 20X2, Page had sold land with a book value of $40,000 to Sage for $50,000 and, on October 1 of the same year, Sage had sold equipment having a five-year life to Page at a profit of $40,000.

REQUIRED

Ignoring income tax effects, prepare:

1. A detailed analysis of the consolidated retained earnings of Page at December 31, 20X4; and
2. The adjustments to the minority interests at December 31, 20X4.

EXERCISE 10–3 You are furnished with the following abbreviated combined income and retained earnings statements of Pewter Inc. and Silver Inc. at December 31, 20X7:

	Pewter	Silver
Net Operating Income	$1,000,000	$600,000
Dividends from Silver	160,000	—
Net Income	1,160,000	600,000
Retained Earnings at January 1, 20X7	640,000	280,000
Retained Earnings at December 31, 20X7	1,800,000	880,000
Less: Dividends Declared and Paid	600,000	200,000
Retained Earnings at December 31, 20X7	$1,200,000	$680,000

You are provided with the following additional information:

(a) Goodwill of $80,000 arose on the acquisition by Pewter of an 80% interest in Silver on January 1, 20X5. At the date of acquisition, Silver had retained earnings of $120,000 and plant having a 10-year remaining life that was under-valued by $160,000.

(b) On July 1, 20X6, Silver sold plant with a book value of $450,000 to Pewter for $500,000. This plant was expected to have a five-year remaining life from the date of sale and no residual value. The gain on the sale was included in net operating income in 20X6.

(c) Both Pewter and Silver amortize assets using the straight-line method.

(d) During the two years ended December 31, 20X6, Silver earned net income of $240,000 and paid dividends of $80,000.

(e) Goodwill was written down for impairment by $8,000 in 20X5 and $10,000 in 20X7.

REQUIRED

Ignoring income tax effects, calculate:

1. The consolidated net income for 20X7;
2. The consolidated retained earnings brought forward at January 1, 20X7; and
3. The consolidated retained earnings at December 31, 20X7.

EXERCISE 10–4 You are provided with:

1. The following abbreviated analysis of equity of Submerge Inc., an 80%-owned subsidiary of Plunge Inc. acquired on January 1, 20X2:

	Total	80%	Minority Interests
Common Stock	$400,000	$320,000	$ 80,000
Retained Earnings	50,000	40,000	10,000
		360,000	
Purchase Consideration		400,000	
Goodwill		$ 40,000	

Goodwill Impairment of $4,000 in 20X2 and $4,000 in 20X3

Retained Earnings	30,000	24,000	6,000
Net Income — 20X3	120,000	96,000	24,000
Dividends Paid	(40,000)	(32,000)	(8,000)
Minority Interests			$112,000

2. The abbreviated combined income and retained earnings statements of the two companies for the year ended December 31, 20X3:

	Plunge	Submerge
Sales	$1,000,000	$660,000
Cost of Goods Sold	$ 500,000	$300,000
Operating Expenses	250,000	240,000
	$ 750,000	$540,000
Net Operating Income	$ 250,000	$120,000
Dividends Received	32,000	—
Net Income	282,000	120,000
Retained Earnings at January 1, 20X3	48,000	80,000
	330,000	200,000
Dividends Paid (November 15)	50,000	40,000
Retained Earnings at December 31, 20X3	$ 280,000	$160,000

You are also informed that on July 1, 20X2, Submerge had sold equipment with a book value of $50,000 to Plunge for $70,000. On the date of sale, this equipment had an expected useful life of five years with no residual value.

REQUIRED

Ignoring income tax effects:

1. Prepare the consolidated combined income and retained earnings statement for 20X3;
2. Determine the minority interests appearing on the consolidated balance sheet at December 31, 20X3: and
3. Give the adjustment to the equipment appearing on the consolidated balance sheet at December 31, 20X3.

EXERCISE 10–5 **REQUIRED**

Answers to the following two situations:

1. On July 1, 20X2, Silvia Inc., a 75%-owned subsidiary of Peter Inc. transferred an item of plant having a five-year life it had purchased for $50,000 to Sheila Inc., a 60%-owned subsidiary of Peter Inc. The transfer was at $45,000. What adjustments, if any, must be made to the consolidated financial statements of Peter at December 31, 20X2?
2. Sally's Truck Sales Inc., a dealer in motor trucks, was a 75%-owned subsidiary of Pal Enterprises Ltd., an investment company having widespread and diverse interests. On October 1, 20X2, Sally's Auto Sales sold two trucks to Sam's Farms Inc., an 80%-owned subsidiary of Pal Enterprises Ltd. The cost of the trucks had been $40,000 each and they had been sold for $48,000 each and were expected to have a useful life of 10 years. What adjustments, if any, would have to be made to eliminate the effects of these transactions in the consolidated workings at December 31, 20X2?

EXERCISE 10–6 Goodwill of $20,000 arose as a result of the purchase by Patch Inc. of a 75% interest in Sew Inc. on January 1, 20X1. On January 1, 20X1, Sew had retained earnings of $30,000. During the period from acquisition to December 31, 20X4, Sew had incurred losses of $20,000 and had not paid any dividends. During the same period, Patch had written down the goodwill arising on acquisition by $5,000 for impairment.

On July 1, 20X3, Sew had sold equipment costing $100,000 to Patch for $120,000. This equipment was amortized by Patch at the rate of 20% per year on a straight-line basis.

At December 31, 20X5, the income statements of the two companies were as follows:

	Patch	Sew
Sales	$2,400,000	$600,000
Cost of Goods Sold	$1,000,000	$300,000
Operating Expenses	800,000	120,000
	$1,800,000	$420,000
Net Income	$ 600,000	$180,000
Dividends from Sew	45,000	—
	645,000	180,000
Retained Earnings at January 1, 20X5	120,000	10,000
	765,000	190,000
Dividends Declared and Paid	200,000	60,000
Retained Earnings at December 31, 20X5	$ 565,000	$130,000

REQUIRED

Ignoring income tax effects, prepare:

1. The combined consolidated income statement and statement of retained earnings at December 31, 20X5.
2. The adjustment to the minority interests at December 31, 20X5

3. The adjustment to the equipment on December 31, 20X5 arising from the intercompany sale.

EXERCISE 10–7 The following information relates to the financial records of Pain Inc. and its 80%-owned subsidiary, Suffer Inc., at December 31, 20X3 and 20X4:

	Pain	Suffer
Amount of goods in inventory sold by Suffer to Pain at cost plus		—
25% at December 31, 20X4	$ 60,000	
Unrealized profit on sale of equipment having a six-year life by		
Suffer to Pain on September 1, 20X4	—	$ 36,000
Future tax liability at December 31, 20X4	380,000	295,000

REQUIRED

Give the liability for future taxes on the consolidated balance sheet of Pain at December 31, 20X4, if income tax was at the rate of 50%.

EXERCISE 10–8 Polish Inc. acquired an 80% interest in Spit Inc. on April 1, 20X4. Financial statements were not prepared at the date of acquisition, but at January 1, 20X4 Spit had retained earnings of $60,000. At the date of acquisition, the net assets of Spit were considered to be fairly valued.

The abbreviated financial statements of the two companies at December 31, 20X5 were as follows:

	Polish	Spit
BALANCE SHEETS		
Current Assets	$ 330,000	$ 140,000
Investment in Spit	256,000	—
Plant Assets (net)	718,000	260,000
	$1,304,000	$ 400,000
Accounts Payable	$ 121,000	$ 40,000
Future Income Taxes	85,000	20,000
Common Stock	800,000	200,000
Retained Earnings	298,000	140,000
	$1,304,000	$ 400,000
COMBINED INCOME AND		
RETAINED EARNINGS STATEMENTS		
Sales	$2,400,000	$1,160,000
Gain on Sale of Equipment	—	20,000
Total Revenues	$2,400,000	$1,180,000
Cost of Goods Sold	$1,400,000	$ 640,000
Operating and Other Expenses	568,000	360,000
	$1,968,000	$1,000,000
Total Income	$ 432,000	$ 180,000
Dividends from Spit	24,000	—
Net Income for Year before Income Taxes	456,000	180,000
Income Tax Expense (50%)	216,000	90,000
Net Income for Year	240,000	90,000
Retained Earnings at January 1, 20X5	178,000	80,000
	418,000	170,000
Dividends Declared and Paid	120,000	30,000
Retained Earnings at December 31, 20X5	$ 298,000	$ 140,000

You are also provided with the following information:

1 (a) On July 1, 20X4, Polish had sold plant having a five-year remaining life and a book value of $30,000 to Spit for $50,000. At the end of the five-year life, this plant was not expected to have any residual value.

(b) On January 1, 20X5, Spit sold an item of plant with a book value of $60,000 to Polish for $80,000. This plant was expected to have a four-year life and no residual value.

2. Amortization of plant assets is calculated using the straight-line method.

3. During 20X4, Spit had net income of $40,000 and paid a dividend of $20,000 on December 10, 20X4.

4. In 20X5, goodwill was written down by $8,000 for impairment.

REQUIRED

Prepare the consolidated balance sheet and combined income and retained earnings statement of Polish at December 31, 20X5.

EXERCISE 10–9 Goodwill of $120,000 arose from the acquisition by Pan Inc. of a 75% interest in Skillet Inc. on January 1, 20X5. At that date, the assets and liabilities of Skillet were considered to be fairly valued, and it had retained earnings of $200,000.

The following information was extracted from the financial statements of the two companies at December 31, 20X6:

	Pan	Skillet
Sales	$5,800,000	$1,960,000
Cost of Goods Sold	2,160,000	800,000
Operating Expenses	2,600,000	560,000
Gain on Sale of Equipment	96,000	—
Income Tax Expense (50%)	568,000	300,000
Retained Earnings at January 1, 20X6	960,000	400,000

You are also informed that:

(a) During 20X5, Skillet had earned after-tax income of $200,000 and paid no dividends.

(b) On July 1, 20X5, Skillet had sold an item of equipment to Pan at a profit of $40,000. At the date of sale, this equipment had an estimated 10-year useful life with no residual value.

(c) The "gain on the sale of equipment of $96,000" appearing on the income statement of Pan relates to the sale of an item of equipment to Skillet on April 1, 20X6. At the date of sale, this equipment was expected to have a useful life of eight years and no residual value.

(d) Goodwill was written down for impairment by $10,000 in 20X5 and $5,000 in 20X6.

REQUIRED

1. Prepare the consolidated combined Income and retained earnings statement of Pan for the year ended December 31, 20X6.

2. Determine the net equipment appearing on the consolidated balance sheet of Pan at December 31, 20X6 if the balance sheets of Pan and Skillet at that date reflected net equipment of $1,560,000 and $1,064,000 respectively.

3. Give the minority interests appearing on the consolidated balance sheet of Pan at December 31, 20X6 if the total equity appearing on the balance sheet of Skillet at that date amounted to $1.2-million.

4. Calculate the future income tax balance if the future taxes appearing on the individual balance sheets of Pan and Skillet at December 31, 20X6 were $210,000 and $186,000 respectively.

PROBLEMS

PROBLEM 10–1 Goodwill of $80,000 arose on the acquisition by Pin Inc. of an 80% interest in Sin Inc. on January 1, 20X5 for $2,100,000.

You are also informed that:

(a) During 20X5, Sin had earned net income of $600,000 and had paid a dividend of $300,000 on November 4.

(b) Sin sold equipment with a five-year life with a book value of $500,000 to Pin for $600,000 on October 1, 20X5.

(c) On July 1, 20X6, Pin had sold equipment with a 10-year life to Sin for $800,000 that included a markup of one-third on cost.

(d) Goodwill was written down for impairment by $15,000 in both 20X5 and 20X6.

(e) At December 31, 20X6, the abbreviated income and retained earnings statements of the two companies were as follows:

	Pin	Sin
Net Operating Income	$1,240,000	$ 800,000
Share of Net Income from Sin	451,000	—
Net Income	1,291,000	800,000
Retained Earnings at January 1, 20X6	920,000	700,000
	2,211,000	1,500,000
Dividends Declared and Paid (November 5)	800,000	400,000
Retained Earnings at December 31, 20X6	$1,411,000	$1,100,000

REQUIRED

Ignoring income tax effects:

1. Reconcile the "Income from Sin" of $451,000 appearing on the income statement of Pin at December 31, 20X6.

2. Give the "Investment in Sin" account as it would appear in the ledger of Pin at December 31, 20X6.

PROBLEM 10–2 REQUIRED

Ignoring income tax effects, prepare the consolidated balance sheet and combined consolidated income and retained earnings statement of Post Inc. and its subsidiary company, Send Inc., at December 31, 20X5, from the following information:

(a) Post acquired an 80% interest in Send on January 1, 20X3 for $268,000 when Send had common stock of $200,000 and retained earnings of $90,000. At the date of acquisition, the net assets of Send were considered to be fairly valued.

(b) Goodwill arising on acquisition was written down for impairment by $7,200 in 20X3 and $3,600 in 20X5.

(c) The retained earnings of Send at December 31, 20X4 reflected the addition of net income of $120,000 earned since acquisition less dividends paid of $100,000.

(d) On January 1, 20X4, Send sold plant assets with an expected life of four years to Post at a profit of $20,000.

(e) Post accounts for its investment in Send using the incomplete equity method.

The abbreviated financial statements of Post and Send for the financial year ended December 31, 20X5, are given below:

BALANCE SHEETS	Post	Send
Cash	$ 24,000	$ 25,000
Accounts Receivable	195,000	45,000
Inventory	100,000	40,000
Investment in Send	316,000	—
Plant Assets (Net)	700,000	300,000
	$1,335,000	$410,000
Accounts Payable	$ 180,000	$ 60,000
Common Stock	800,000	200,000
Retained Earnings	355,000	150,000
	$1,335,000	$410,000

COMBINED INCOME AND RETAINED EARNINGS STATEMENTS	Post	Send
Sales	$1,200,000	$600,000
Cost of Goods Sold	$ 700,000	$350,000
Operating Expenses	240,000	160,000
Amortization of Plant Assets	65,000	20,000
	$1,005,000	$530,000
Net Operating Income	$ 195,000	$ 70,000
Share of Net Income from Send	56,000	—
Net Income	251,000	70,000
Retained Earnings at January 1, 20X5	224,000	110,000
	475,000	180,000
Dividends Declared and Paid	120,000	30,000
Retained Earnings at December 31, 20X5	$ 355,000	$150,000

PROBLEM 10–3 You are provided with the following information:

(a) Goodwill of $40,000 arose on the acquisition by Pisa Inc. of an 80% interest in Sienna Inc. on January 1, 20X5. At the date of acquisition, Sienna had retained earnings of $60,000 and plant having a 10-year remaining life that was undervalued by $80,000.

(b) The net income earned by Sienna (including any profits arising from the intercompany sales of capital assets) and dividends declared and paid during 20X5 and 20X6 were as follows:

	20X5	20X6
Net Income	$100,000	$120,000
Dividends	60,000	80,000

(c) On July 1, 20X6, Sienna sold plant with a book value of $240,000 to Pisa for $270,000. This plant was expected to have a five-year remaining life from the date of sale and no residual value.

(d) The policy of both Pisa and Sienna is to amortize assets using the straight-line method.

(e) During 20X6, Pisa sold goods to Sienna at a markup of 50% on cost. During 20X6 sales of these goods amounted to $150,000 and at December 31, 20X6, some of these goods having a selling price of $30,000 were still in inventory.

(f) Sienna also transferred part of its production to Pisa at a set markup of 25% on manufactured cost. These transfers for 20X6 and 20X7 were $200,000 and $300,000 respectively. At the end of 20X6 Pisa held $35,000 of these goods in inventory, while the corresponding figure for 20X7 was $130,000.

(g) The abbreviated combined income and retained earnings statements of Pisa and Sienna at December 31, 20X7 were as follows:

	Pisa	Sienna
Sales	$2,000,000	$1,200,000
Cost of Goods Sold	$1,250,000	$ 800,000
Operating Expenses	250,000	100,000
	$1,500,000	$ 900,000
Net Operating Income	$ 500,000	$ 300,000
Dividends from Sienna	80,000	—
Net Income	580,000	300,000
Retained Earnings at January 1, 20X7	320,000	140,000
	900,000	440,000
Dividends Declared and Paid	300,000	100,000
Retained Earnings at December 31, 20X7	$ 600,000	$ 340,000

REQUIRED

Ignoring income tax effects, prepare the combined consolidated income and retained earnings statement of Pisa for 20X7 if the goodwill arising on acquisition was written down for impairment in 20X5 by $5,000.

PROBLEM 10–4

Plant Inc. purchased an 80% interest in Shop Inc. on January 1, 20X4 for $1,080,000 when Shop had 100,000 shares of common stock of no par value (issued at $10 per share) and retained earnings of $250,000. At the date of acquisition, all the assets of Shop were considered to be fairly valued except for land that was overvalued by $20,000 and a non-renewable operating lease, which was undervalued by $30,000. The lease was not recorded on the balance sheet of Shop, but it still had two years to run to December 31, 20X5.

Additional Information:

1. On October 1, 20X4, Shop had sold equipment with a book value of $60,000 to Plant for $80,000. At the date of sale, this equipment had an estimated useful life of five years with no residual value.
2. On April 1, 20X5, Shop had sold a further item of plant to Plant for $60,000. This item of plant had a book value of $40,000 and was expected to have an eight-year remaining useful life and no residual value.
3. During 20X4, Shop had earned $140,000 and paid dividends of $60,000.
4. Goodwill was written down for impairment in 20X4 by $7,000.

At December 31, 20X5, the abbreviated financial statements of Plant and Shop were as follows:

	Plant	Shop
BALANCE SHEETS		
Current Assets	$1,356,000	$ 800,000
Investment in Shop	1,080,000	—
Land and Other Plant Assets (Net)	652,000	1,000,000
	$3,088,000	$1,800,000
Current Liabilities	$ 920,000	$ 410,000
Common Stock	1,500,000	1,000,000
Retained Earnings	668,000	390,000
	$3,088,000	$1,800,000
COMBINED INCOME AND RETAINED EARNINGS STATEMENTS		
Sales	$3,000,000	$1,000,000
Cost of Goods Sold	$1,800,000	$ 520,000
Operating Expenses	656,000	360,000
	$2,456,000	$ 880,000
Net Operating Income	$ 544,000	$ 120,000
Gain on Sale of Capital Asset	—	20,000
Dividends from Shop	64,000	—
Net Income for Year	608,000	140,000
Retained Earnings at January 1, 20X5	300,000	330,000
	908,000	470,000
Less: Dividends Paid	240,000	80,000
Retained Earnings at December 31, 20X5	$ 668,000	$ 390,000

REQUIRED

Ignoring income tax effects, prepare the consolidated balance sheet and combined income and retained earnings statement of Plant and its subsidiary for the year ended December 31, 20X5.

PROBLEM 10–5

The abbreviated financial statements of Play Inc. and its 60%-owned subsidiary, Shuffle Inc., at December 31, 20X5 were as follows.

	Play	Shuffle
BALANCE SHEETS		
Cash	$ 150,000	$ 200,000
Accounts Receivable	350,000	100,000
Inventory	200,000	80,000
Investment in Shuffle	404,000	—
Land	220,000	100,000
Buildings	530,000	300,000
Plant and Equipment (Net)	564,000	500,000
	$2,418,000	$1,280,000
Accounts Payable	$ 248,000	$ 380,000
Common Stock (100,000 shares of no par value)	1,200,000	600,000
Retained Earnings	970,000	300,000
	$2,418,000	$1,280,000
COMBINED INCOME AND		
RETAINED EARNINGS STATEMENT		
Sales	$2,000,000	$1,200,000
Cost of Goods Sold	$ 700,000	$ 750,000
Operating and Other Expenses	500,000	350,000
	$1,200,000	$1,100,000
Net Operating Income	$ 800,000	$ 100,000
Dividends from Shuffle	30,000	—
Net Income	830,000	100,000
Less: Dividends Paid	200,000	50,000
	630,000	50,000
Retained Earnings, January 1, 20X5	340,000	250,000
Retained Earnings, December 31, 20X5	$ 970,000	$ 300,000

You are also informed that:

1. Play acquired its interest in Shuffle on July 1, 20X3 for $404,000 when Shuffle had **an accumulated loss of $200,000**. On that date, certain plant and equipment of Shuffle having a remaining useful life of six years was overvalued by $60,000.
2. Goodwill was written down for impairment by $20,000 in 20X3 and $10,000 in $20X5.
3. On October 1, 20X4, Shuffle which was a motor dealer, had sold a motor truck with a book value of $48,000 and having a six-year remaining life (with no residual value) to Play for $72,000.
4. On July 1, 20X5, Shuffle had sold an additional motor truck to Play at a profit of $20,000. This motor truck had cost $60,000 and an expected five-year life with no residual value.
5. No dividends were paid by Shuffle during the period between July 1, 20X3 and December 31, 20X4.

REQUIRED

Ignoring income tax effects, prepare the consolidated balance sheet and combined income and retained earnings statement for 20X5.

PROBLEM 10–6 Partition Inc. acquired a 75% interest in Screen Inc. on July 1, 20X5 for $685,000. At that date, the assets and liabilities of Screen were considered to be fairly valued except for an item of plant having a 10-year remaining life that was considered to be undervalued by $100,000. Goodwill arising on acquisition was written down for impairment by $5,000 in 20X5.

The abbreviated financial statements of the two companies for 20X5 and 20X6 were as follows:

	Partition		Screen	
BALANCE SHEETS	**20X5**	**20X6**	**20X5**	**20X6**
Cash	$ 128,000	$ 18,000	$104,000	$ 94,000
Accounts Receivable	300,000	345,000	160,000	250,000
Inventory	180,000	190,000	220,000	230,000
Investment in Screen	685,000	685,000	—	—
Plant and Equipment (Net)	325,000	505,000	370,000	350,000
	$1,618,000	$1,743,000	$854,000	$924,000
Accounts Payable	$ 310,000	$ 215,000	$110,000	$ 60,000
Common Stock	1,000,000	1,000,000	500,000	500,000
Retained Earnings	308,000	528,000	244,000	364,000
	$1,618,000	$1,743,000	$854,000	$924,000

COMBINED INCOME AND RETAINED EARNINGS STATEMENTS

	Partition		Screen	
Sales	$1,150,000	$1,460,000	$760,000	$920,000
Cost of Goods Sold	$ 600,000	$ 700,000	$400,000	$460,000
Administration Expenses	300,000	345,000	200,000	240,000
	$ 900,000	$1,045,000	$600,000	$700,000
Net Income from Operations	$ 250,000	$ 415,000	$160,000	$220,000
Gain on Sale of Plant	8,000	—	24,000	—
Dividends from Screen	45,000	75,000	—	—
Net Income	303,000	490,000	184,000	220,000
Retained Earnings at January 1	245,000	308,000	120,000	244,000
	548,000	798,000	304,000	464,000
Dividends Paid (December 15)	240,000	270,000	60,000	100,000
Retained Earnings at December 31	$ 308,000	$ 528,000	$244,000	$364,000

You are also informed that:

(a) On October 1, 20X5, Partition sold new equipment with a book value of $40,000 and having a 10-year expected life (and no residual value) to Screen for $48,000.

(b) On September 1, 20X5, Screen sold equipment having a book value of $72,000 (and having a five-year expected life and no residual value) to Partition for $96,000.

REQUIRED

Ignoring income tax effects, prepare the consolidated balance sheets and combined income and retained earnings statements of Partition for **20X5 and 20X6**.

PROBLEM 10–7   Phonetic Inc. acquired a 75% interest in Speech Inc. on July 1, 20X5 for $850,000. At that date, the assets and liabilities of Speech were considered to be fairly valued except for an item of plant having a 10-year remaining life that was considered to be undervalued by $100,000.

Financial statements were not prepared at the date of acquisition but at January 1, 20X5, Speech had retained earnings of $244,000. During 20X5, Speech had earned **after tax** net income of $280,000 and paid dividends of $80,000 on December 5.

You are further informed that:

(a) On July 1, 20X5, Speech sold new equipment costing $40,000 and having a five-year remaining life (and no residual value) to Phonetic for $80,000. The after tax gain of $20,000 from this sale was included in the retained earnings of Speech for 20X5 of $464,000.

(b) The rate of income tax was 50%.

(c) Goodwill arising on acquisition was written down for impairment in 20X6 by $12,000.

The abbreviated financial statements of the two companies for 20X6 were as follows:

COMBINED INCOME AND RETAINED EARNINGS STATEMENTS	Phonetic	Speech
Sales	$4,240,000	$1,960,000
Cost of Goods Sold	$1,665,000	$ 770,000
Administration Expenses	1,715,000	870,000
	$3,380,000	$1,640,000
Net Income from Operations	$ 860,000	$ 320,000
Dividends from Speech	75,000	—
Net Income before Income Taxes	935,000	320,000
Income Tax Expense	430,000	160,000
Net Income after Income Taxes	505,000	160,000
Retained Earnings at January 1	1,100,000	464,000
	1,605,000	624,000
Dividends Paid (December 15)	300,000	100,000
Retained Earnings at December 31	$1,305,000	$ 524,000

BALANCE SHEETS		
Current Assets	$1,045,000	$ 870,000
Investment in Speech	850,000	—
Plant and Equipment (Net)	2,025,000	425,000
	$3,920,000	$1,295,000
Current Liabilities	$ 325,000	$ 205,000
Future Income Taxes	290,000	66,000
Common Stock	2,000,000	500,000
Retained Earnings	1,305,000	524,000
	$3,920,000	$1,295,000

REQUIRED

Prepare the consolidated balance sheet and combined income and retained earnings statement of Phonetic for 20X6.

PROBLEM 10–8 Priest Inc. purchased an 80% interest in Sermon Inc. on January 1, 20X4 for $2,620,000 when Sermon had 1,000,000 shares of common stock of no par value and retained earnings of $750,000. At the date of acquisition, all the assets of Sermon were considered to be fairly valued except for land that was overvalued by $100,000.

At December 31, 20X5, the abbreviated financial statements of Priest and Sermon were as follows:

COMBINED INCOME AND RETAINED EARNINGS STATEMENTS	Priest	Sermon
Sales	$9,000,000	$4,000,000
Cost of Goods Sold	$5,400,000	$2,000,000
Operating Expenses	2,000,000	1,000,000
	$7,400,000	$3,000,000
Net Operating Income	$1,600,000	$1,000,000
Gain on Sale of Capital Asset	—	80,000
Dividends from Sermon	160,000	—
Net Income for Year before Income Taxes	1,760,000	1,080,000
Income Tax Expense (50%)	800,000	540,000
Net Income after Income Taxes	960,000	540,000
Retained Earnings at January 1, 20X5	920,000	1,230,000
	1,880,000	1,770,000
Less: Dividends Paid	400,000	200,000
Retained Earnings at December 31, 20X5	$1,480,000	$1,570,000

BALANCE SHEETS	Priest	Sermon
Current Assets	$1,390,000	$1,800,000
Investment in Sermon	2,620,000	—
Land and Other Plant Assets (Net)	2,150,000	2,295,000
	$6,160,000	$4,095,000
Current Liabilities	$ 920,000	$ 415,000
Future Income Taxes	260,000	110,000
Common Stock	3,500,000	2,000,000
Retained Earnings	1,480,000	1,570,000
	$6,160,000	$4,095,000

Additional Information:

1. On October 1, 20X4, Sermon had sold equipment with a book value of $360,000 to Priest for $400,000. At the date of sale, this equipment had an estimated useful life of five years with no residual value.
2. On April 1, 20X5, Sermon had sold a further item of plant to Priest for $290,000. At the date of sale, it had a book value of $210,000. This item was expected to have an eight-year remaining useful life and no residual value.
3. During 20X4, Sermon had earned after tax net income of $600,000 and paid dividends of $120,000.
4. Goodwill arising on acquisition was written down for impairment by $20,000 in 20X4 and $5,000 in 20X5.
5. The rate of income tax is 50%.

REQUIRED

Prepare the consolidated balance sheet and combined income and retained earnings statement of Priest and its subsidiary for the year ended December 31, 20X5.

PROBLEM 10–9   Pitcher Inc. acquired a 75% interest in Stein Inc. on July 1, 20X5 for $1,820,000. At that date, the assets and liabilities of Stein were considered to be fairly valued except for an item of plant having a 10-year remaining life that was considered to be undervalued by $100,000. Goodwill arising on acquisition was written down for impairment by $20,000 in 20X6.

You are also informed that:

(a) On October 1, 20X5, Pitcher sold new equipment costing $40,000 and having a 10-year expected life (and no residual value) to Stein for $80,000.
(b) On December 1, 20X5, Stein sold equipment with a book value of $80,000 (and having a five-year expected life and no residual value) to Pitcher for $128,000.
(c) The rate of income tax was 50%.

The abbreviated financial statements of the two companies for 20X5 and 20X6 were as follows:

	Pitcher		Stein	
BALANCE SHEETS	20X5	20X6	20X5	20X6
Cash	$ 108,000	$ 270,000	$ 175,000	$ 80,000
Accounts Receivable	642,000	745,000	560,000	850,000
Inventory	760,000	860,000	745,000	730,000
Investment in Stein	1,820,000	1,820,000	—	—
Plant and Equipment (Net)	2,220,000	1,925,000	950,000	1,050,000
	$5,550,000	$5,620,000	$2,430,000	$2,710,000
Accounts Payable	$ 630,000	$ 635,000	$ 406,000	$ 460,000
Future Income Taxes	590,000	540,000	140,000	156,000
Common Stock	3,000,000	3,000,000	1,000,000	1,000,000
Retained Earnings	1,330,000	1,445,000	884,000	1,094,000
	$5,550,000	$5,620,000	$2,430,000	$2,710,000

COMBINED INCOME AND RETAINED EARNINGS STATEMENTS	Pitcher		Stein	
	20X5	**20X6**	**20X5**	**20X6**
Sales	$4,150,000	$4,310,000	$3,420,000	$3,920,000
Cost of Goods Sold	$1,650,000	$1,685,000	$1,340,000	$1,560,000
Administration Expenses	1,850,000	1,945,000	1,520,000	1,740,000
	$3,500,000	$3,630,000	$2,860,000	$3,300,000
Net Income from Operations	$ 650,000	$ 680,000	$ 560,000	$ 620,000
Dividends from Stein	75,000	75,000	—	—
Gain on Sale of Plant	40,000	—	48,000	—
Net Income before Income Taxes	765,000	755,000	608,000	620,000
Income Tax Expense	345,000	340,000	304,000	310,000
Net Income after Income Taxes	420,000	415,000	304,000	310,000
Retained Earnings at January 1	1,150,000	1,330,000	680,000	884,000
	1,570,000	1,745,000	984,000	1,194,000
Dividends Paid (December 15)	240,000	300,000	100,000	100,000
Retained Earnings at December 31	$1,330,000	$1,445,000	$ 884,000	$1,094,000

REQUIRED

Prepare the consolidated balance sheets and combined income and retained earnings statements of Pitcher for **20X5 and 20X6**.

PROBLEM 10–10 Plate Inc. acquired an 80% interest in Saucer Inc. on July 1, 20X2 for $3-million. Financial statements were not prepared at the date of acquisition, but at December 31, 20X1 Saucer had common stock of $2-million made up of 1,000,000 shares of common stock of no par value and retained earnings of $800,000. At the date of acquisition, the assets and liabilities of Saucer were considered to be fairly valued.

The financial statements of the two companies at December 31, 20X3 were as follows:

COMBINED INCOME AND RETAINED EARNINGS STATEMENT	Plate	Saucer
Sales	$12,400,000	$8,000,000
Cost of Goods Sold	$ 5,500,000	$3,600,000
Administration Expenses	3,300,000	2,000,000
	$ 8,800,000	$5,600,000
Net Income from Operations	$ 3,600,000	$2,400,000
Dividends from Saucer	400,000	—
Net Income for Year Before Income Taxes	4,000,000	2,400,000
Income Tax Expense (50%)	1,800,000	1,200,000
Net Income After Income Taxes	2,200,000	1,200,000
Retained Earnings, January 1, 20X3	2,600,000	1,400,000
	4,800,000	2,600,000
Dividends Paid (September 15)	800,000	500,000
Retained Earnings, December 31, 20X3	$ 4,000,000	$2,100,000

Balance Sheets:

	Plate	Saucer
Current Assets	$ 3,780,000	$2,820,000
Investment in Saucer	3,000,000	—
Plant and Equipment (Net)	3,400,000	3,190,000
	$10,180,000	$6,010,000
Accounts Payable	$ 1,790,000	$1,810,000
Future Taxes	190,000	100,000
Common Stock	4,200,000	2,000,000
Retained Earnings	4,000,000	2,100,000
	$10,180,000	$6,010,000

You are also informed that:

(a)   No dividends were paid by Saucer in 20X2.
(b)   Following a review of the value of assets and liabilities carried out in July 20X2, it was established that equipment having a five-year remaining life and a book value of $340,000 and an income tax value of $290,000 was undervalued by $150,000.
(c)   Goodwill was written down for impairment by $30,000 in 20X3.

REQUIRED

Prepare the consolidated income and retained earnings statement and consolidated balance sheet of Plate for 20X3.

Consolidations: Accounting for Intercompany Financial Holdings

11

LEARNING OBJECTIVES

After studying this chapter you should be able to:

1. Understand the need to effectively retire intercompany bond holdings between companies in the same group of companies and make such adjustments as part of the consolidation procedure;
2. Recognize the effects of intercompany holdings of preferred shares and their elimination from the consolidated financial statements; and
3. Identify the cases where the holding of treasury shares affects the extent of ownership and the treatment of those changes.

ADJUSTMENTS RELATING TO BONDS, PREFERRED SHARES AND TREASURY STOCK

Even though the issuing of bonds as a means of raising capital is not as popular in Canada as it is in the USA, bonds are commonplace in the operation of Canada's capital markets. In fact, there is an active "over the counter" bond market in Toronto.[1] Preferred shares have also been issued by companies for many years as a means of financing part of their capital requirements.

Bonds and preferred shares are normally issued to yield a set amount of interest or dividends respectively. For example, bonds may be issued to yield, say, 10% on their stated (par or face) value, whereas fixed-rate preferred stock is issued to pay, say, a dividend of $10 on

---

[1] *The Globe and Mail* of January 16, 1996, reported that the trading in bonds in Canada amounts to about $14-billion per day compared with that of shares which, only amounts to about $1-billion. Up until now, the trading in bonds has been relatively unregulated but, during May 1996, the Ontario Securities Commission announced that henceforth, a new bond pricing service would apply to the trading in bonds. CanPx, a partnership between the Investment Dealers Association of Canada and the Interdealer Brokers of Canada, will supply previously unavailable pricing data on Canada's market for bonds and "money market paper" (e.g., treasury bills) that adds about another $26-billion dollars per day. From now on, the IDA will also compel bond brokers in Canada to provide data to CanPx on the lowest and highest bid prices and the prices at which they last changed hands for the most frequently traded bonds and treasury bills. This information will then be made available to all subscribers in much the same way as that applying to share prices.

their stated value. Both bonds and preferred shares are, therefore, referred to as fixed income securities. And, as the price paid for such securities is based on their yield in relation to other securities, the prices at which they are traded may differ considerably from their stated values. As a result, when the price at which these securities are traded drops below their redemption value, they may represent a good investment and be purchased by the issuing company. Intercompany holdings of bonds and preferred stock may, therefore, arise between members of an affiliated group of companies.

As with other intercompany transactions, these intercompany holdings must be eliminated in the consolidation process to ensure that the consolidated trading results and the assets and liabilities appearing on the consolidated balance sheet are correctly stated. This chapter outlines how intercompany holdings of bonds and preferred shares are eliminated in the consolidation process.

This chapter also examines the effects of holding treasury stock on the consolidation of financial statements. And, for those whose skills in accounting for bonds require updating, a brief illustration of the accounting for bonds is provided as an appendix to this chapter.

A. ACCOUNTING FOR INTERCOMPANY BOND HOLDINGS

The Need to Eliminate Reciprocal Bond Holdings

Intercompany holdings of bonds within a group of affiliated companies give rise to **reciprocal assets and liabilities**. The accounting treatment is to offset the bonds issued by one company but held by another company in the same affiliated group of companies against each other on consolidation along the lines applicable to the elimination of intercompany loans. Failure to do so would result in the overstatement of assets and liabilities on the consolidated balance sheet and lead to the inclusion of both interest revenue and interest expense from the same bond issue on the consolidated income statement.

The Effective Retirement of Bonds

Unlike shares of common or preferred stock that may normally be cancelled by the issuing company, **bonds can usually only be retired on their maturity dates**. This depends, of course, on the conditions of the bond issue, but it usually means that where the bonds issued by one company are held as an investment by another company in the same group, the bonds are held by the purchasing company until they are retired or sold.

The consolidation process requires that these investments in bonds are offset against the bond liability as if the bonds had been retired. Reciprocal bond holdings are, therefore, **effectively but not actually retired insofar as the consolidated financial statements are concerned**. However, they remain on the books of the purchasing and issuing companies and appear on their respective balance sheets until retirement. Effective gains or losses are also referred to as **"constructive" gains or losses**.

To illustrate the effective retirement of bonds, assume that a subsidiary company purchased, on the date of issue, 20% of the 10,000 12% $100 bonds issued by its parent company for $200,000. On consolidation, the investment in bonds of $200,000 would merely be offset against the bond liability of $1-million to give a bond liability of $800,000 on the consolidated balance sheet. However, the balance sheets of the parent and subsidiary companies would continue to reflect a bond liability of $1-million and investment in bonds of $200,000 respectively. The bond interest revenue of the subsidiary would, likewise, be offset against the bond interest expense in the consolidated income statement to reflect only the interest on the bond liability of $800,000 for the year (or period of time) concerned.

Establishing the Cost of the Bonds

The problem of accounting for reciprocal bond holdings is that bonds are seldom purchased by one company at a price that equals the amount at which they are carried in the books of the issuing company. As a result, **a gain or loss, which is referred to as an effective gain or loss, arises on the elimination of the intercompany bond holding**s. From a consolidation point of view, there is no difference between effective and actual gains or losses, and the amount reflected on the consolidated income statement is referred to as a **"Gain (or Loss) on the Extinguishment of Debt"**.

At this stage, it should be noted that **an effective gain or loss arises because the amount paid for the bonds purchased is offset against the amount at which the bonds payable are carried in the books of the issuing company**. The effective gain (or loss) is, therefore, the difference between the cost of the bonds purchased and the proportionate share of the value at which those bonds appear on the balance sheet of the company that issued the bonds. It is, therefore, necessary to calculate the value at which the bonds are held by the issuing company at the date of purchase.

The calculation of the value at which the bonds are held by the issuing company depends upon whether the bonds were originally issued at a premium or a discount. In these circumstances, the premium or discount is amortized over the life of the bonds against the interest expense so that at retirement date, the bond liability equals the face (or par) value of the bonds.

There are two ways in which the discount or premium on bonds may be amortized: the straight-line or effective-interest methods.

With the **straight-line method**, the discount or premium is amortized over the life of the bonds by writing off an equal amount at each interest payment date. For example, assume that 1,000 $100 12% 10-year bonds were issued on January 1, 20X1 at 98% with interest being paid semi-annually on June 30 and December 31 in each year. In this case, the discount of $2,000 (i.e., $100,000 – [$100,000 × 98%]) would be amortized over the 10-year period by writing off $100 at each of the 20 interest payment dates. At June 30, 20X1, the outstanding bond liability would be $98,100 (i.e., $100,000 – [$2,000 – $100]) and $98,200 (i.e., $100,000 – [$2,000 – $100 – $100]) at December 31, 20X1, so that on redemption date, the bond liability would be exactly $100,000.

The theoretically correct method of establishing the amount of bond premium or discount to be amortized is by using the **effective-interest method**. With this method, the issue price of the bonds represents the present value of the face value of the bonds plus the present value of an ordinary annuity of the interest payments over the tenure of the bonds calculated at the effective (or market rate) of interest.

If, for example, 100 $1,000 11% five-year bonds having June 30 and December 31 interest payment dates had been issued to yield an effective interest rate of 12%, the bonds would have been issued at a discount of $3,681 calculated as follows:[2]

Stated Value of Bonds (100 × $1,000)		$100,000
Issue Price:		
Present Value of $100,000 for 10 periods at 6% interest = $100,000 × 0.55839 =	$55,839	
Present Value of an Ordinary Annuity of $5,500 for 10 periods at 6% interest = $5,500 × 7.36009[2] =	40,480	96,319
Discount at Date of Issue		$ 3,681

2

$$\text{PV of an annuity} = \frac{1 - \dfrac{1}{(1+n)^n}}{i}$$

In this case, the amortization of the discount for the six months ended June 30, 20X1 would be $280 arrived at by deducting the value of bond liability at January 1, 20X1 of $96,319 from that at June 30, 20X1 of $96,599.[3]

Irrespective of the theoretical correctness of the effective interest method, this chapter is concerned with the accounting treatment of intercompany bond transactions as they affect the consolidation process, and not a detailed explanation of accounting for longterm liabilities. For simplicity's sake, the premium or discount arising on the issue of the bonds is, therefore, amortized using the straight-line method in all illustrations and examples provided in this text.

Approaches to Accounting for Intercompany Bonds

Four different approaches to accounting for effective gains or losses on bond transactions arising from intercompany bond transaction have been suggested. These are:

1. The entire gain or loss should be **allocated to the issuing company**. This position is referred to as the **agency approach** because it is based on the viewpoint that as the companies are under common control, the company purchasing the bonds is acting as the agent of the issuing company. This is the approach used in this text because it recognizes the offsetting of the carrying values of an asset and a liability within the group of companies to establish the effective gain or loss.
2. The entire gain should be **allocated to the purchasing company** because the gain or loss arose as a result of the purchase of the bonds. This approach treats the purchase and sale of the bonds as if they had actually been retired which is, of course, not the case.
3. The entire gain or loss should be **allocated to the controlling interest**. The argument for this treatment is that as the parent company controls the companies to which the bond transactions applied, the gain or loss on these transactions accrues to the parent company. This approach also treats the bonds as if they had been retired.
4. The gain or loss should be **allocated to both the issuing and purchasing companies**. This treatment recognizes that the gain or loss arises from two components — the unamortized discount or premium arising from the original bond issue and the discount or premium resulting from the purchase of the bonds. In these cases, the gain or loss is allocated to the issuing and purchasing companies based on the difference between the par value of the bonds and the amounts at which the bonds are held by the two companies. It is referred to as the **par value approach**, and enjoys some support amongst accountants.

Calculation of the Effective Gain or Loss

As outlined earlier, the amount of the effective gain or loss will vary depending upon the purchase price of the bonds and the amount at which the bonds are held by the issuing company. This is outlined in Illustration 11–1 which shows how an effective loss on the purchase of the bonds is calculated using the straight-line method. The information used in this Illustration is the same as that provided in the Appendix to this chapter so that the transaction may be carried through from start to finish.

In Illustration 11–1, 20% of the bond liability appearing on the balance sheet of the issuing company has been offset against the purchase price of the bonds held as an investment. The difference represents a "Loss on Retirement of Debt of $5,850" on the consolidated income statement.

---

[3] Present value of $100,000 for 9 periods at 6% = $100,000 × 0.59190   = $59,190
Present value of an annuity of $5,500 for 9 periods at 6% = $5,500 × 6.80169   =   37,409
             $96,599

ILLUSTRATION 11–1
CALCULATION OF AN EFFECTIVE LOSS

Jay Inc. issued $500,000 20-year 12% bonds on July 1, 20X4 at 98. Interest on these bonds was payable semi-annually on June 30 and December 31 in each year. On January 1, 20X5, Kay Inc., the 80%-owned subsidiary of Jay, purchased $100,000 of these bonds on the open market for $103,900. The effective loss arising on the purchase of bonds with a face value of $100,000 by Kay is calculated as follows:

Proportionate value of the bonds purchased by Kay appearing on the balance sheet of Jay on January 1, 20X5 of 20% of (500,000 − $9,750 [i.e., the total discount of $10,000 less the amortization to date of $250])	$ 98,050
Purchase Consideration	103,900
Effective Loss	$ 5,850

Using the **par value approach** of recognizing the effective loss of $5,850, the position would be that the total effective gain of $5,850 (i.e., $103,900 − $98,050) would be apportioned as to $3,900 to Jay (i.e., $103,900 − $100,000) and $1,950 (i.e., $100,000 − $98,050) to Kay. The loss is, in both cases, related to the par value of the bonds.

As this text uses the straight-line method and **the agency approach**, the effective loss of $5,850 would be written off over the remaining life of the bonds (i.e., the 19½ years to their maturity date). This is spread over the 39 interest payments remaining (i.e., $5,850 − [39 × $150] = 0).

A review of the position is that **the effective gain or loss** arising on the elimination of intercompany bond holdings is, in effect, **merely a transitional balance because it is the difference between an asset and a liability at a point in time**. This amount must be amortized over the remaining life of the bonds so that **at their retirement date**, the difference between them will **be zero**. The effective gain or loss is, therefore, amortized proportionately over the remaining life of the bonds against the bond interest expense. This amortization is referred to as a "step amortization", and is carried out in a similar manner as that applying to the amortization of bond discounts or premiums.

An effective gain is, therefore, eliminated by debiting (i.e., increasing) the interest expense with the annual amortization of the effective gain; whereas with an effective loss, the elimination is by crediting the interest expense accordingly. Using the information provided in Illustration 11–1, the loss on the effective retirement of the bonds of $5,850 is amortized at the rate of $300 per year (or by $150 per each semi-annual interest payment) over the remaining nineteen and a half year life of the bonds.

The effects of accounting for effective gains or losses on the income statement are outlined in Illustration 11–3, which also uses the information provided in Illustrations 11–1 and 11–2 and Appendix 11A. In this illustration, the "Loss on the Extinguishment of Debt" is brought into account on the consolidated income statement as a separately disclosable item, and the proportionate amount of this loss is deducted from the bond interest expense for the year.

The Balance Sheet Treatment

As far as the balance sheet is concerned, the correct net liability to bondholders must be reflected on the consolidated balance sheet. This figure is the balance of the bonds remaining after effectively retiring those held as an investment by other companies within the group. Using the information provided by Illustration 11–1 (and Appendix 11A), the bonds would be reflected on the consolidated balance sheet at December 31, 20X5 at $392,600 which is 80%

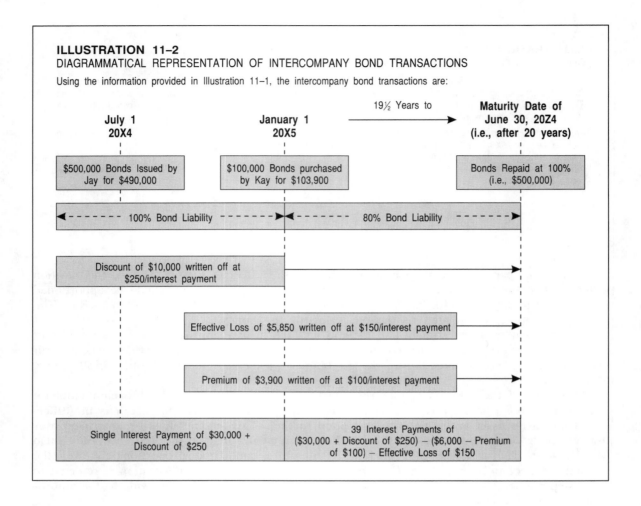

ILLUSTRATION 11–2
DIAGRAMMATICAL REPRESENTATION OF INTERCOMPANY BOND TRANSACTIONS

Using the information provided in Illustration 11–1, the intercompany bond transactions are:

of the value of the bond liability appearing on the balance sheet of Jay at that date (i.e., 80% of [$500,000 – $9,250] = $392,600).

Furthermore, at any balance sheet date until the redemption of the bonds, the difference between the amount reflected for the investment in bonds on the balance sheet of the purchasing company and the proportionate reduction of the liability for the outstanding bonds on the balance sheet of the issuing company will equal the unamortized effective gain or loss on retirement of the bonds. For example, the difference between 20% of the bonds of $490,750 outstanding at December 31, 20X5 (i.e., $98,150) less the amount at which the investment in bonds is reflected on the balance sheet of the purchasing company of $103,700 on that date (i.e., $103,900 – [$200 for two interest payments]) equals the unamortized effective loss of $5,550 (i.e., $5,850 – $300) on that date.

Diagrammatical Representation of Intercompany Bond Transactions

The understanding of accounting for intercompany bond transactions is considerably easier when viewed as a sequence of events over the period over which the bonds are held. Using the information provided in Illustration 11–1, the transactions in the bonds as they affect the consolidated financial statements of Jay Inc., the parent company, are diagrammatically presented and annotated in Illustration 11–2.

Illustration 11–2 shows that the liability for the bonds issued by Jay (the parent company) is reduced to 80% on the effective retirement of the 20% purchased by Kay (the subsidiary) on January 1, 20X5. This is required because it is only those transactions with parties outside the affiliated group that are reflected in the consolidated financial statements, and only 80% of the bonds are reflected as a liability on the consolidated balance sheet from that point onwards.

The effective loss of $5,850 arising from the effective retirement is written off on a straight-line basis over the 19½ years of life remaining life of the bonds as part of the interest expense. In this case, the semi-annual interest payment appearing on the consolidated income statement is $24,200 after adjustment for the write-off of the bond discount by Jay and the bond premium by Kay.

The Income Tax Effects

The issue of whether income tax adjustments arising from the elimination of effective gains or losses from intercompany bond transactions should be recognized is debatable. Those who believe that these adjustments are necessary assume that because the reported consolidated net income has been changed, recognition of the income tax effects of those changes is also necessary. On the other hand, those who disagree point out that effective gains and losses are not taxable because they are merely adjusting entries arising from the offsetting of two balances. The application of income taxes to such balances is, therefore, unnecessary and only complicates the consolidation process.

The recognition of income tax effects as they apply to inventories and capital assets must be eliminated on consolidation. However, no reference to effective gains or losses on intercompany bond transactions is made. As a result, the question of whether they should be adjusted for financial reporting purposes remains unanswered.

If the income tax effects of effective gains and losses are recognized, the adjustments are exactly the same as those applying to the elimination of capital assets. They are treated as timing differences spread over the tenure of the bonds. The gain or loss is included or deducted from taxable income, as the case may be, in the year of occurrence and, thereafter, the annual write-off of the gain or loss is added back or deducted from taxable income until it is reduced to zero. At this stage it should also be noted that **neither the annual write-off of bond discount nor the premium on the issue of bonds is subject to income tax**.

Supporters of adjusting income taxes suggest that, as the income tax effects of unrealized profits in inventories and capital assets are recognized, the same should apply to effective gains and losses. The most compelling argument is that if the company issuing the bonds had repurchased the bonds itself, it would have recognized a gain (or loss) on the retirement of its debt. Obviously, the materiality of the amounts involved is also important. However, notwithstanding the fact that the issue is unresolved, the position relating to the recognition of income tax effects from effective gains or losses has been provided in Illustration 11–3 and is continued in Illustration 11–4.

Illustration 11–3 shows that a "loss on retirement of debt" of $5,850 would be treated as a timing difference spread over 19½ years. In 20X4, the income tax effect would be to decrease the income tax expense by $2,775 (i.e., 50% × [$5,850 – $300]) with a corresponding debit to future income taxes. This decrease in income tax expense of $2,775 is reflected by the difference between the total income tax expense of the two companies of $433,150 (i.e., $244,750 from Jay + $188,400 from Kay) less the consolidated income tax expense of $430,375. In the following 18½ years, the income tax expense would be increased by $75 with a corresponding credit to future income taxes on each of the 37 remaining interest payment dates.

ILLUSTRATION 11–3
THE INCOME STATEMENT TREATMENT OF EFFECTIVE GAINS OR LOSSES WHERE INCOME TAX EFFECTS ARE RECOGNIZED

Kay Inc. was an 80%-owned subsidiary of Jay Inc. The abbreviated income statements of the two companies at December 31, 20X5 were as follows:

	Jay	Kay
Sales	$1,900,000	$1,100,000
Bond Interest Revenue	—	11,800
Total Revenues	$1,900,000	$1,111,800
Cost of Goods Sold	$ 900,000	$ 400,000
Bond Interest Expense	60,500	—
Other Financing and Administration Expenses	450,000	335,000
Total Expenses	$1,410,500	$ 775,000
Net Income before Income Taxes	$ 489,500	$ 376,800
Income Tax Expense (50%)	244,750	188,400
Net Income for Year	$ 244,750	$ 188,400

The preparation of the consolidated income statement incorporating the information provided in Illustration 11–1 that an effective loss of $5,850 arose from the purchase by **Kay** of 20% of a 12% bond issue of $500,000 by **Jay** on January 1, 20X5 (i.e., 19½ years before redemption date) is provided hereunder:

	Consolidated	Jay	Kay
Sales	$3,000,000	$1,900,000	$1,100,000
Less Loss on Retirement of Debt (from Illustration 11–1)	5,850	5,850	—
Total Revenues	$2,994,150	$1,894,150	$1,100,000
Cost of Goods Sold	$1,300,000	$ 900,000	$ 400,000
Bond Interest Expense (from ledger accounts in Illustration 11A–1)	48,400	60,500	(11,800)
Amortization of Effective Loss		(300)	—
Other Financing and Administration Expenses	785,000	450,000	335,000
Total Expenses	$2,133,400	$1,410,200	$ 723,200
Net Income before Income Taxes	$ 860,750	$ 483,950	$ 376,800
Income Tax Expense (50%)	430,375	241,975	188,400
Total Net Income	430,375	241,975	188,400
Less Minority Interests (20%)	37,680		37,680
Consolidated Net Income	$ 392,695	$ 241,975	$ 150,720

Note: The interest expense and interest revenue of the two companies has been restated so that they can be offset against each other in the consolidated working papers and adjusted by the amortization of the effective loss.

Review of the Accounting for Intercompany Bond Holdings

The issues relating to the accounting for these effective gains or losses are summarized in the following seven points:

(a) Effective gains or losses apply to **the company that issued the bonds** because the consolidation process assumes that the bonds have been (effectively but not actually) retired at the price paid for them by the company purchasing the bonds.

(b) The effective gain or loss must be amortized over the period from the date of purchase of the bonds to the retirement date. In Illustration 11–1, the tenure of the bonds from the date of purchase by Kay Inc. is 19 ½ years, and the effective loss must, therefore, be amortized by $300 per year (i.e., $5,850/19 ½ years).

(c) It is not necessary to concern oneself with the accounting for the individual bond issues or holdings of investments in the consolidation process because the amortization of discounts or premiums will be carried out by the companies concerned without consideration of the problems caused by intercompany bond transactions.

(d) The amortization of the effective gain or loss is against the bond interest expense on the consolidated income statement.

(e) The interest expense and interest revenue figures are adjusted by the individual companies for the amortization of the bond discount or premium, and require no further adjustment other than the amortization of the effective gain (or loss) in the consolidation process.

(f) Where income tax adjustments are recognized, these adjustments are treated as timing differences extending over the remaining tenure of the bonds.

(g) The bond liability appearing on the consolidated balance sheet is the net amount remaining after effectively retiring the intercompany purchase.

ACCOUNTING FOR EFFECTIVE GAINS OR LOSSES ON BONDS IN SUBSEQUENT PERIODS

The accounting for effective gains or losses on intercompany bond transactions in years subsequent to that in which they took place involves adjustments to the retained earnings of the consolidated entity and, depending upon which company issued the bonds, to the minority interests. These adjustments are as follows:

(a) The retained earnings of the company that originally issued the bonds is adjusted by the amount of the unamortized effective gain or loss at the beginning of the year in question. This adjustment decreases every year as the effective gain or loss is amortized over the life of the bonds.

(b) The annual amount required to amortize the effective gain or loss is brought into account on the income statement of the company that originally issued the bonds as an adjustment to the interest expense.

A comprehensive illustration covering those aspects of intercompany bond transactions affecting the income statement over a period of six years is provided by Illustration 11–4.

SUBSEQUENT SALE OF BONDS ON WHICH EFFECTIVE GAINS OR LOSSES HAVE BEEN RECOGNIZED

From time to time bonds on which an effective gain or loss has been recognized are sold. In these cases, the gain or loss on the sale is recognized by the company selling the bonds (i.e., the issuing company) in the normal manner. This has the net effect of eliminating the balance of the effective gain or loss in the consolidated retained earnings. In effect, all that occurs is that there is a change from an effective to an actual gain or loss.

RECORDING ADJUSTMENTS TO BONDS USING THE EQUITY METHOD

As with adjustments relating to intercompany sales of inventory and plant and equipment, the adjustments for intercompany bond transactions must be included in the "Investment in Subsidiary" account in the ledger of the parent company where the equity method is used. This is necessary irrespective of which company issued or purchased the bonds because there is no

ILLUSTRATION 11–4

COMPREHENSIVE ILLUSTRATION OF THE EFFECTS OF INTERCOMPANY BOND TRANSACTIONS AND INCOME TAXES ON THE INCOME STATEMENT OVER A SIX-YEAR PERIOD

Parent Inc. holds an 80% interest in Subsidiary Inc. On April 1, 20X2, Subsidiary issued 1,000 five-year 12% bonds of $1,000 each at 102. Interest was payable on these bonds semi-annually on April 1 and October 1 in each year. On April 1, 20X4, Parent purchased 100 of these bonds at 97. The net income for each of these years before making any adjustments for the bond issue (i.e., interest expense, interest revenue and effective gains or losses, or amortization) was $600,000 for Parent and $300,000 for Subsidiary.

The consolidated income statements of Parent for the financial years ended December 31, 20X2 through 20X7 are given hereunder:

	Consolidated	**Parent**	**Subsidiary**
20X2:			
Net Income before Adjustments	$900,000	$600,000	$300,000
Bond Interest Expense (9/12)	(87,000)	—	(90,000)
Bond Premium Amortization — Note 1	—	—	3,000
Total Net Income before Income Taxes	813,000	600,000	213,000
Income Tax Expense (50%)	405,000	300,000	105,000
Total Net Income after Income Taxes	408,000	300,000	108,000
Minority Interests (20%)	21,600	—	21,600
Consolidated Net Income	$386,400	$300,000	$ 86,400
20X3:			
Net Income before Adjustments	$900,000	$600,000	$300,000
Bond Interest Expense	(116,000)	—	(120,000)
Bond Premium Amortization — Note 2	—	—	4,000
Total Net Income	784,000	600,000	184,000
Income Tax Expense (50%)	390,000	300,000	90,000
Total Net Income after Income Taxes	394,000	300,000	94,000
Minority Interests (20%)	18,800	—	18,800
Consolidated Net Income	$375,200	$300,000	$ 75,200
20X4:			
Net Income before Adjustments	$900,000	$600,000	$300,000
Gain on Extinguishment of Debt — Note 3	4,200	—	4,200
	904,200	600,000	304,200
Bond Interest Expense	(107,300)		(120,000)
Bond Interest Revenue — Note 4		9,000	—
Bond Discount Amortization — Note 5		750	—
Bond Premium Amortization		—	4,000
Amortization of Effective Gain — Note 6	—	—	(1,050)
Total Net Income	796,900	609,750	187,150
Income Tax Expense (50%)	396,075	304,500	91,575
Total Net Income after Income Taxes	400,825	305,250	95,575
Minority Interests (20%)	19,115	—	19,115
Consolidated Net Income	$381,710	$305,250	$ 76,460
20X5 and 20X6:			
Net Income before Adjustments	$900,000	$600,000	$300,000
Bond Interest Expense	(104,400)		(120,000)
Bond Interest Revenue		12,000	—
Bond Discount Amortization		1,000	—
Bond Premium Amortization — Note 7		—	4,000
Amortization of Effective Gain	—	—	(1,400)
Total Net Income	795,600	613,000	182,600
Income Tax Expense (50%)	395,300	306,000	89,300
Total Net Income after Income Taxes	400,300	307,000	93,300
Minority Interests (20%)	18,660	—	18,660
Consolidated Net Income	$381,640	$307,000	$174,640

ILLUSTRATION 11–4 (Continued)

	Consolidated	Parent	Subsidiary
20X7:			
Net Income before Adjustments	$900,000	$600,000	$300,000
Bond Interest Expense (3/12)	(26,100)	—	(30,000)
Bond Interest Revenue		3,000	
Bond Discount Amortization — Note 8		250	
Bond Premium Amortization — Note 9		—	1,000
Amortization of Effective Gain — Note 10	—	—	(350)
Total Net Income	873,900	603,250	270,650
Income Tax Expense (50%)	436,325	301,500	134,825
Total Net Income after Income Taxes	437,575	301,750	135,825
Minority Interests (20%)	27,165	—	27,165
Consolidated Net Income	$410,410	$301,750	$108,660

Notes:

[1] The premium on the issue of the bonds of $20,000 is amortized on the straight-line basis over the tenure of the bonds. In this illustration the amounts amortized are $2,000 per each of the 10 interest payments (i.e., over the five years involved). This means that in 20X2 the amortization is $3,000 (i.e., the amortization of $2,000 on October 1 plus $1,000 for the three months ending December 31, 20X2).

[2] The $4,000 represents the amortization of the premium for the entire year.

[3] The "Gain on the Extinguishment of Debt" is the effective gain arising from the purchase of bonds by Parent calculated as follows:

Book Value of Bonds Sold:		
10% of $1,000,000	=	$100,000
10% of Premium of ($20,000 − [4 × $2,000])	=	1,200
		101,200
Purchase Price of Bonds		97,000
Gain on Extinguishment of Debt		$ 4,200

[4] The $9,000 for bond interest revenue is the interest on $100,000 at 12% for 9 months.

[5] The bond discount amortization of $750 represents the amortization of the $3,000 discount (i.e., $100,000 × $97,000) on the purchase of the bonds over the nine months to December 31. It is made up of the amortization at the interest payment date of the discount of $500 plus the accrual for the three months to the end of the financial year.

[6] The "gain on extinguishment of debt" of $4,200 is amortized over the remaining three-year life of the bonds. As only 9 months apply in 20X4, the amount is $1,050 (i.e., $4,200/3 × 9/12 months).

[7] For 20X5 and 20X6, the amortization of the discount on the purchase of the bonds by Parent, the amortization of the premium on sale of the bonds by Subsidiary, and the amortization of the "gain on the extinguishment of debt" by Subsidiary cover the full 12 months.

[8] The bond discount of $250 represents the discount on the bonds payable for the three months to March 31, 20X7.

[9] The amortization of the bond premium is the amount covering the three months ending March 31, 20X7.

[10] As with the bond discount and bond premium, the amortization of effective gain is for the three-month period.

other way the adjustments for intercompany bond transactions can be reflected in the records of the parent company.

These adjustments are quite straightforward. The only thing to remember is that where the effective gain and its subsequent amortization are upstream adjustments, it is only the proportionate share of the gain and amortization that are recorded in the investment account and against the share of net income from the subsidiary company.

B. PREFERRED SHARES

Preferred shares consist of that class of shares issued by a company that have **preferential rights to either the repayment of capital in the event of the liquidation of a company or the payment of a dividend or both**. These preferential rights depend upon the conditions of the share issue that, in turn, is dependent upon the types of preferred shares the company is authorized to issue by its charter or memorandum of association.

Preferred shares may be issued either for an indefinite period or a specific period after which they are retired. They carry set dividends and, where the shares are redeemable, they are retired at their redemption values. They may be issued on the condition that the preferential rights to dividends may be cumulative which means that all preferred dividends in arrears must be paid before any dividends are paid to the common shareholders. They may also be issued as participating preferred shares which means that in addition to the regular dividend paid, these shares may participate in the distribution of profits as dividends over and above the stated dividend once the distribution to common shareholders reaches a certain level.

As preferred shares do not form part of the residual equity of a company, they do not, other than in certain exceptional circumstances, enjoy voting rights. For example, limited voting rights may be conferred upon preferred shareholders when the preferred shares are cumulative in relation to dividends and the dividends are in arrears. These rights may even be extended to the election of directors in cases where the company is in receivership. However, these voting rights are usually severely restricted and only apply to voting on matters affecting their rights.[4] The holding of preferred shares does **not**, therefore, normally affect ownership interests, and they are not taken into account in determining the extent of ownership in an investee company.

The use of preferred shares as a source of capital is declining in popularity because it has an income tax disadvantage when compared with the use of bonds for this purpose. This is because the interest on bonds is an allowable expense for income tax purposes, while preferred dividends are paid out of "after tax" net income. However, there is a market for these shares because certain investors find these investments attractive because of the lower risk involved and the dividend tax credit that applies to preferred dividends.

From a financial instrument perspective, preferred shares may be classified as either equity instruments or liabilities by the issuing company.[5] Basically, the distinction is based on whether there is a contractual obligation to **retract or redeem** the preferred shares. The term **retract** refers to the right of the holder of the preferred shares to demand repayment from the issuing company, whereas the term **redeem** refers to the right of the issuing company to call in the preferred shares.

Where preferred shares are retractable (on either a specific date or at the discretion of the holder), they meet the definition of a liability because the issuer has an obligation to transfer financial assets to the holder of the share. On the other hand, **preferred shares that give the issuer the option to redeem them** sometime in the future do not fit the definition of a liability because, until such time as the option is exercised, the issuer does not have an obligation to transfer financial assets to the holders of those shares.

Additional requirements apply to non-redeemable preference shares. Here, the position is that they are equity instruments if they are (1) non-redeemable, and (2) the payment of dividends on those shares is at the discretion of the issuing company. However, where the

---

4   In an interesting development, *The Globe and Mail* of November 30, 1995, reported that Canada Trustco Mortgage Company was to issue "rare preferred shares" that will pay a fixed dividend but also carry voting rights. In commenting on the issue, Paul Derksen, senior vice-president with Canada Trustco, stated that the complex preferred shares were designed to balance the reluctance of its controlling shareholder at that time, Imasco Ltd., to reduce its equity stake in the company to 65% to comply with federal restrictions on the ownership of financial institutions.

5   CICA *Handbook*, section 3860 and *Emerging Issue Committee Abstract of Issues Discussed No. 69*.

payment of dividends on those shares is specified, the preferred shares are liabilities because the purchase is of a future income stream in perpetuity and the purchase price represents the discounted value of the future income stream.

The issue of reclassification of preferred shares is a contentious one amongst accountants. However, these provisions apply to all public companies (i.e., those listed on a recognized stock exchange), deposit taking institutions (i.e., banks and similar financial institutions), co-operatives, and life insurance companies.

ACCOUNTING FOR PREFERRED SHARES

The Accounting Treatment

The accounting for preferred shares on consolidation is dependent upon four factors. First, it depends upon which company in an affiliated group issued the preferred shares. Second, it depends on the ownership of these shares. In this respect, the accounting treatment varies according to whether the preferred shares are held by the minority shareholders or, in whole or in part, by the parent company. Third, it depends upon whether the shares were issued for an indefinite or set period. This dictates whether or not it is possible for the issuing company to redeem or retire its preferred shares. And, fourth, it depends upon whether the preferred shares are cumulative in relation to the payment of dividends and whether those dividends are in arrears. If the preferred shares are not cumulative in relation to dividends, the claims of the preferred shareholders against the company in the event of liquidation are limited to their capital contributions.

Intercompany holdings of preferred shares are **either retired or treated as having been effectively retired by the companies concerned on consolidation**. If the conditions of the share issue allow the companies concerned to do so, intercompany holdings of preferred shares are normally retired before their redemption dates. If not, these shares are held by the companies concerned until they are sold.

Where the dividends on preferred shares are cumulative, **provision should always be made for the payment of these dividends in the allocation of net income in the analysis of equity**. This is carried out by merely deducting any dividends in arrears from the net income before allocating it between the parent company and the minority interests.

Where the Preferred Shares Have Been Issued by a Subsidiary to Outside Shareholders

Where the preferred shares have all been issued by a subsidiary company to investors outside the affiliated group, the preferred shares are merely treated as part of the minority interests in the analysis of equity. This occurs irrespective of when the preferred shares were issued, as outlined in Illustration 11–5.

Illustration 11–5 shows that the preferred shares are merely allocated to the minority interests and, where the preferred shares are cumulative in relation to dividends, provision for the preferred dividends must be made before the net income is apportioned between the parent company and minority interests. Where amounts have been set aside to cover preferred dividends, these amounts may be either credited to the minority interests or treated as a deferred credit on the balance sheet of the company to which they relate.

Where Preferred Shares Have Been Issued by the Parent Company

Where preferred shares have been issued by the parent company, they appear as part of the equity of the parent company on the consolidated balance sheet. As outlined earlier, where some of the preferred shares issued by the parent company are held by its subsidiaries,

ILLUSTRATION 11–5
THE ELIMINATION OF PREFERRED SHARES ISSUED BY A SUBSIDIARY TO
ITS MINORITY SHAREHOLDERS

Parent Inc. acquired 80% of the common shares of Subsidiary Inc. for $380,000 on January 1, 20X4. At that date Subsidiary had common shares of $400,000, 12% cumulative preferred shares of $300,000 and retained earnings of $48,000 before provision of the semi-annual preferred dividend, which had not yet been paid.

The cumulative preferred shares are eliminated on consolidation through the analysis of equity in the following manner:

Analysis of Equity at Acquisition:

		Total	Parent	Minority Interests
Common Shares		$400,000	$320,000	$ 80,000
12% Cumulative Preferred Shares		300,000	—	300,000
Retained Earnings	$48,000			
Less: Preferred Dividend (6/12 × 12% × $300,000)	18,000	30,000	24,000	6,000
Preferred Dividend Payable		+18,000	—	18,000
			344,000	
Purchase Consideration			380,000	
Goodwill			$ 36,000	—
Minority Interests				$404,000

they are either retired or, if the issue is for an indefinite period, treated as if they had been effectively retired. In either case, it is only the net amount of the preferred shares issued by the parent company that appears on the consolidated balance sheet.

In practice, and in view of the problems posed by intercompany holdings of preferred shares, companies usually divest themselves of these intercompany holdings of shares as soon as possible.

Where the Entire Issue of Preferred Shares Are Held by Another Company in the Affiliated Group

This situation applies equally to the parent and subsidiary companies and occurs where, for some reason or other, the entire issue of preferred shares is taken up or purchased at a later date by another company in the group. If possible, the preferred shares are retired in these cases. If not, then the preferred shares are treated as if they had been effectively retired on consolidation.

Where Some of the Preferred Shares Issued by a Member of an Affiliated Group Are Held by Another Company in That Group

In these cases, the accounting treatment is essentially the same as where the entire issue of preferred shares are held by another member of the group. The only difference is that after retiring or effectively retiring the intercompany holdings of preferred shares, the remaining preferred shares must be accounted for by the issuing company. If the preferred shares were issued by the parent company, then the remaining preferred shares would be reflected on the consolidated balance sheet as part of the equity of the parent company. On the other hand, if a subsidiary company had issued the preferred shares, the remaining preferred shares would be included with the minority interests.

The following table provides a summary of the position:

Preferred Stock Issued by:	Treatment
P ⟶ S	Effective retirement of the preferred stock held by the subsidiary and any balance remaining is reflected as part of the consolidated equity.
P ⟶ Minority Interests	All reflected as part of the consolidated equity.
S — (100%) ⟶ P	All effectively retired.
S — (50%) ⟶ P	50% issued to parent effectively retired; balance shown as part of minority interests.
S — (100%) ⟶ Minority Interests	All allocated as part of the minority interests in the analysis of equity at date of acquisition.

RETIREMENT OR EFFECTIVE RETIREMENT OF PREFERRED SHARES

The simplest case of retiring or effectively retiring preferred shares is where the preferred shares are all taken up by one company in the affiliated group on the date of issue. In these cases, the issue and purchase price are the same, and the elimination of the preferred shares is to offset them against one another in exactly the same manner as the elimination of intercompany loans.

If, however, the preferred shares were purchased some time after their issue, the treatment is somewhat more complicated. This is because there is normally a difference between the price at which the preferred shares were issued and the price at which they were purchased. This difference gives rise to **a gain or loss on retirement or effective retirement** of part of the **capital** of the issuing company, and must be accounted for in accordance with the requirements of the CICA *Handbook*[6] covering the redemption of shares at a gain or loss.

Irrespective of whether the preferred shares are retired or effectively retired, this normally results in **a capital gain or loss**. If it is a gain it must be treated as "additional contributed capital" by the issuing company, and is taxable as a capital gain.[7] If it results in a loss, the treatment is to write it off against any "additional contributed capital" or other contributed surplus, and where no such account balance exists, to write it off against retained earnings.[8] For income tax purposes, capital losses are offset against existing capital gains or carried forward to be offset against capital gains arising in the future.

The gain or loss is the difference between the price at which the preferred shares are purchased and their book value at the date of sale because dividends only accrue to preferred shareholders when declared. There is, consequently, no proportionate adjustment for the unpaid dividends. An illustration of the calculation of a gain on the retirement of preferred shares is provided in Illustration 11–6.

The rule to be followed is that, as with the treatment of unrealized profits arising from intercompany sales or the effective retirement of bonds, **it is the issuing company that**

---

[6] Section 3240.
[7] CICA *Handbook*, section 3240.
[8] *Ibid.*

ILLUSTRATION 11–6
ACCOUNTING FOR A CAPITAL GAIN ARISING FROM THE RETIREMENT OR
EFFECTIVE RETIREMENT OF PREFERRED SHARES IN AN UPSTREAM SITUATION

Subsidiary Inc. is an 80%-owned subsidiary of Parent Inc. On January 1, 20X5, Subsidiary issued 100,000 preferred shares of no par value for $50 per share that were redeemable at $50, 10 years from their date of issue. On June 30, 20X8, Parent purchased 20% of these shares (i.e., 20,000 shares) on the open market for $45 per share.

   The transactions relating to the preferred shares would be accounted for on the consolidated balance sheet at December 31, 20X8 were in the following manner:

Calculation of the Gain on Retirement or Effective Retirement of the Preferred Shares:

Book Value of Preferred Shares (100,000 × $50)	$5,000,000
20% thereof	$1,000,000
Purchase Consideration (20,000 × $45)	900,000
Gain on Retirement or Effective Retirement	$ 100,000

Apportionment of the Gain:
As the gain arose from an upstream situation, it is apportioned as:

Additional Contributed Capital (80% × $100,000)	$ 80,000
Minority Interests (20% × $100,000)	20,000
Gain or Effective Gain	$ 100,000

Treatment of the Balance of the Preferred Shares:

The remaining preferred shares of $4,000,000 (i.e., 80% of issue) are added to the Minority Interests.

---

recognizes the gain or loss on retirement. Therefore, where the parent company is the issuing company, a downstream situation exists and the whole amount is credited (or debited) to its "additional contributed capital" account. On the other hand, if a subsidiary company issued the preferred shares, any gain (or loss) must be appropriated proportionately to the parent company's additional contributed capital account and the minority interests. This is because in this latter case, it is the subsidiary company that has effectively retired the preferred shares, and the minority must be allocated its share of the effective gain. For example, if the entire issue of preferred shares of $400,000 issued by a 60%-owned subsidiary is acquired by its parent company at 95% of the issue price, the subsidiary would recognize a gain on the effective retirement of those preferred shares of $20,000. This gain would then be apportioned as to $12,000 (60%) to the parent company as additional contributed capital and $8,000 (40%) to the minority interests.

THE TREATMENT OF PREFERRED DIVIDENDS

It should be noted that preferred dividends received are offset in the consolidation process against the dividends paid in exactly the same manner as bond interest where there are intercompany bond holdings.

   Where the preferred shares are cumulative as to the payment of dividends, an amount equal to any preferred dividends that are unpaid or in arrears must be deducted from the net income of the issuing company before there is any recognition of the net income applicable to the consolidated entity. This is necessary to ensure that it is only the net income to which the common shareholders of the parent company have a right that is reflected in the consolidated financial statements.

C. TREASURY STOCK TRANSACTIONS

A company may purchase its own shares for a number of reasons. For example, it may want to effect a permanent decrease in its issued share capital[9,10] or to acquire shares to carry out the terms of a stock option plan or other shareholder agreement.

Where the treasury stock has been purchased from the minority shareholders by a subsidiary company to reduce its issued share capital, this decreases the interests of the minority and results in a corresponding increase in the interest of the parent company because this gives the parent company a greater proportionate interest in the subsidiary. For example, if a 60%-owned subsidiary having 600,000 no par value shares outstanding purchases 40,000 shares from the minority shareholders and cancels them, the interest of the parent company would increase to 64.29% (i.e., 360,000/[600,000 − 40,000] × 100).

Where treasury stock is cancelled, two adjustments are necessary. First, the purchase of the treasury stock should be treated as an additional acquisition (see later chapter). Second, the treasury stock should be cancelled. Any gains on the cancellation of the treasury stock must be credited to the "capital surplus" or contributed surplus account and not taken into revenue. Losses must similarly be written off against the "capital surplus", if such a surplus exists or treated as a capital loss against retained earnings if no capital surplus exists.[11] Gains arising from treasury stock transactions are also subject to income tax as "deemed dividends" but because this area involves an in-depth knowledge of Canadian income tax, any consideration of the topic is beyond the scope of this chapter.

Treasury stock held by a subsidiary may also be sold by it to its parent company. In these cases, the purchase of treasury stock is accounted for as a step acquisition and the cost of these shares is debited to the investment account.

In those cases where the subsidiary has purchased treasury stock to meet its commitments in terms of stock option plans or other shareholder agreements, the purchase and sale of treasury stock is normally ignored in the consolidation process because it is only held on a temporary basis. In these cases, the only problem relates to the reflection of any treasury stock held by the subsidiary at balance sheet date. If the amount is material, it must be reflected on the consolidated balance sheet as a deduction from the total consolidated equity as "Treasury Stock of Subsidiary" in proportion to the parent company's interest in the subsidiary; that applicable to the minority is deducted from the minority interests. Where the amount is immaterial, it can be included with other amounts with suitable note disclosure.

SUMMARY

Where there are intercompany holdings of bonds or preferred shares, these must be eliminated in the consolidation process to reflect the net indebtedness of investments in these securities by the consolidated entity.

---

[9] For example, Manulife Financial Corporation announced that it was prepared to purchase up to five percent of its issued share capital from existing shareholders (i.e., 25-million shares) in order to improve the return on the remaining issued shares (*The Globe and Mail*, October 25, 1999).

[10] Purchases by a company of its own shares are, however, strictly controlled by securities legislation. They take place under what is referred to as "a normal course issuer bid" for its own shares. Notice of the company's intention to purchase its own shares must be filed with the applicable stock exchange and must state how many shares the company wishes to buy, the price at which it is prepared to purchase shares, and the period of time over which the purchases are to take place. Similar provisions also relate to the sale of its shares. The Toronto Stock Exchange limits the buyback of shares to five percent of a company's outstanding shares in any one year.

[11] CICA *Handbook*, section 3240.

As bonds can normally only be cancelled on their maturity dates, bonds issued by one company and held by another in the affiliated group are only effectively retired. This means that reciprocal holdings of bonds are offset against one another in the consolidation process to give a "Gain (or Loss) on the Retirement of Debt" in exactly the same manner as that which would have occurred if the intercompany holdings of bonds had actually been retired. As the effective retirement of bonds may affect the consolidated income tax expense, adjustments to this amount may be necessary to reflect the correct consolidated net income.

With preferred shares, however, the redemption or retirement depends upon the conditions of the issue and by whom they are held. Preferred shares held by outside shareholders are merely added to the interests of the minority. However, where they are jointly held by the outside shareholders and the companies within the group and cannot be retired, they are effectively retired and treated as capital transactions. In view of the accounting difficulties posed by intercompany holdings of preferred shares, the companies should preferably divest themselves of these holdings as soon as they can.

Treasury stock may be purchased by the subsidiary company to reduce its issued share capital. Irrespective of whether these shares are cancelled by the subsidiary company or sold to the parent company, they result in an increase in the parent company's interest in the subsidiary and are accounted for as effective or step acquisitions. On the other hand, treasury stock transactions relating to the purchase and re-issue of shares in accordance with stock option plans or other shareholder agreements are normally ignored in the consolidation process.

APPENDIX 11A: ACCOUNTING FOR BONDS

Bonds may be issued at par, at a discount, or at a premium. Issues at par are, however, somewhat rare because the price at which bonds are issued is largely dependent upon the market rate of interest in relation to the interest payable on the bonds at the date of issue. If the market rate is higher than the bond interest rate, the bonds are issued at a discount to increase the effective rate of interest to the purchaser. On the other hand, when the bond interest rate is higher than the market rate, the bonds are issued at a premium.

The bond discount or premium is amortized by the issuing company against the interest expense relating to the bonds over the life of the bonds by either increasing or decreasing the bond interest expense as the case may be. The total interest charge then reflects the effective rate of interest on the bonds.

Insofar as the purchaser of the bonds is concerned, it is assumed that the bonds will be held until their retirement date and the discount or premium at which the bonds were acquired is likewise amortized against the interest over the life of the bonds. This treatment is reflected in Illustration 11A–1, which provides a simple illustration of the accounting treatment of bonds using the straight-line method.

The important aspect to bear in mind is that the discount or premium arising on the issue or purchase of bonds is written-off over the life of the bonds. This is necessary to ensure that at the maturity date of the bonds, the redemption of the bonds is at their face value.

Where bonds are sold or retired before maturity date, any premium or discount applicable to the bonds must be accrued up to the date of sale to give the correct cost of the bonds sold or retired. It is also necessary to adjust for the portion of the interest sold by recognizing interest up to and including the date of sale by reducing the selling price by the amount of interest accrued up to that date and included as part of the purchase price. The difference between the cost of the bond sold and the selling price (as adjusted for any interest) represents a gain or loss on the sale of the bonds.

ILLUSTRATION 11A–1
ACCOUNTING FOR BOND TRANSACTIONS USING THE STRAIGHT-LINE METHOD

Jay Inc. issued $500,000 20-year 12% bonds on July 1, 20X4 at 98. Interest on these bonds was payable semi-annually on June 30 and December 31 in each year. On January 1, 20X5, Kay Inc. purchased $100,000 of these bonds on the open market for $103,900. The transactions for 20X4 and 20X5 relating to the issue and purchase of these bonds by the respective companies using the straight-line method of accounting for the amortization of discounts and premiums are given hereunder in journal entry and ledger account form.

Journal of Jay:

20X4

July 1	Cash		490,000	
	Discount		10,000	
	Bonds Payable			500,000
	Issue of Bonds at 98%			
Dec. 31	Interest Expense		30,000	
	Cash			30,000
	Half-yearly interest at 12%			
	Interest Expense		250	
	Bond Discount			250
	Write-off of proportionate amount of discount over tenure of bonds (i.e., 1/40th of $10,000)			
	Income Summary		30,250	
	Interest Expense			30,250
	Transfer to close			
20X5				
June 30	Interest Expense		30,000	
	Cash			30,000
	Half-yearly interest at 12%.			
	Interest Expense		250	
	Bond Discount			250
	Write-off of proportionate amount of discount over tenure of bonds.			
Dec. 31	Interest Expense		30,000	
	Cash			30,000
	Half-yearly interest at 12%.			
	Interest Expense		250	
	Bond Discount			250
	Write-off of proportionate amount of discount over tenure of bonds.			
	Income Summary		60,500	
	Interest Expense			60,500
	Transfer to close			

The above transactions are illustrated in three column ledger accounts as follows:

12% Bonds Payable

20X4				
July 1	Cash from Bond Issue		500,000	500,000

Discount on 12% Bond Issue

20X4				
July 1	Bond Discount	10,000		10,000
Dec. 31	Interest Expense ($10,000/40)		250	9,750

ILLUSTRATION 11A–1 (Continued)

Discount on 12% Bond Issue

20X5				
June 30	Interest Expense		250	9,500
Dec. 31	Interest Expense		250	9,250

Bond Interest Expense

Dec. 31	Cash	30,000		
	Discount Amortization	250		30,250
	Income Summary		30,250	Nil
20X5				
June 30	Cash	30,000		
	Discount Amortization	250		30,250
Dec. 31	Cash	30,000		
	Discount Amortization	250		60,500
	Income Summary		60,500	Nil

Journal of Kay:

20X5			
Jan. 1	Investment in 12% Bonds	100,000	
	Premium on Bonds Purchased	3,900	
	Cash		103,900
	Purchase of Bonds		
June 30	Cash	6,000	
	Interest Revenue		6,000
	Half-yearly interest on Bonds		
	Interest Revenue	100	
	Premium on Bonds		100
	Write-off of proportionate amount of premium over tenure of bonds (i.e., 1/39 of $3,900)		
Dec. 31	Cash	6,000	
	Interest Revenue		6,000
	Half-yearly interest on Bonds		
	Interest Revenue	100	
	Premium on Bonds		100
	Write-off of proportionate amount of premium over tenure of bonds (i.e., 1/38th of $3,800)		
	Interest Revenue	11,800	
	Income Summary		11,800
	Transfer to close.		

These entries would be recorded in the ledger of Kay as follows:

Investment in Jay 12% Bonds

20X5				
Jan. 1	Cash	100,000		100,000

ILLUSTRATION 11A–1 (Continued)

Premium on Jay Bonds

20X5				
Jan. 1	Cash	3,900		3,900
June 30	Interest Revenue (1/39 × $3,900)		100	3,800
Dec. 31	Interest Revenue (1/38 × $3,800)		100	3,700

Interest Revenue

20X5				
June 30	Cash		6,000	
	Bond Premium Amortization	100		5,900
Dec. 31	Cash		6,000	
	Bond Premium Amortization	100		11,800
	Income Summary	11,800		Nil

Balance Sheet Presentation of Bonds on the Balance Sheets of the Companies Concerned at December 31

Balance Sheet of Jay:
Longterm Liability of 12% Bonds Payable ($500,000 − $9,250 [i.e., $10,000 − {3 × $250}]) $490,750

Balance Sheet of Kay:
Investment in 12% Bonds of Jay ($100,000 + $3,700 [i.e., $3,900 − {2 × $100}]) $103,700

SELF-STUDY PROBLEMS
(covering effective gains or losses on bond transactions without [11A] and with income tax effects [11B])

PROBLEM 11A† On July 1, 20X4, Punish Inc. purchased 100 $1,000 8% 10-year bonds issued by Scold Inc., its 80%-owned subsidiary, for $95,500. One thousand of these bonds had been issued by Scold Inc. on January 1, 20X2 at 98 and pay interest on July 1 and December 31 in each year.

REQUIRED

1. Calculate the effective gain or loss on the bonds on the assumption that the discount on bonds was amortized by Scold using the straight-line method;
2. Give the amounts appearing on the consolidated income statement for interest and any other amounts relating to the bonds for the year ended December 31, 20X4;
3. Explain how, if at all, the effective gain would be reflected on the consolidated income statement in 20X4 and thereafter until the bonds are redeemed; and
4. Show how the bonds would be disclosed on the consolidated balance sheet at December 31, 20X4

PROBLEM 11B† Primary Inc. purchased an 80% interest in Secondary Inc. on January 1, 20X1 for $1.2-million. At the date of acquisition, Secondary had retained earnings of $250,000 and assets that were considered to be fairly valued.

---

† The solution is provided in Appendix B to this text.

The abbreviated income statements of the two companies for 20X3 were as follows:

BALANCE SHEETS	Primary	Secondary
Current Assets	$1,143,000	$ 637,200
Investment in Secondary	1,200,000	—
8% Bonds	—	388,000
Capital Assets (Net)	4,672,000	910,000
	$7,015,000	$1,935,200
Current Liabilities	$ 400,000	$ 236,400
Deferred Income Taxes	280,000	165,000
8% Bonds	2,030,000	—
Common Stock	3,000,000	1,000,000
Retained Earnings	1,305,000	533,800
	$7,015,000	$1,935,200

INCOME STATEMENTS

	Primary	Secondary
Sales	$3,600,000	$2,400,000
Dividend Revenue	200,000	—
Interest Revenue ($16,000 + $800)	—	16,800
Total Revenues	$3,800,000	$2,416,800
Cost of Goods Sold	$1,020,000	$ 800,000
Administration and Operating Expenses	1,250,000	900,000
Interest Expense ($160,000 − $4,000)	156,000	—
Total Expenses	$2,426,000	$1,700,000
Net Income Before Income Taxes	$1,374,000	$ 716,800
Income Tax Expense (50%) — see note	589,000	358,000
Net Income After Income Taxes	785,000	358,800
Retained Earnings at January 1, 20X3	920,000	425,000
	1,705,000	783,800
Dividends Paid	400,000	250,000
Retained Earnings at December 31, 20X3	$1,305,000	$ 533,800

You are informed that:

(a)   On July 1, 20X1, Primary had issued 20,000 $100 8% 10-year bonds having interest dates of December 31 and June 30 at 102%. Four-thousand of these bonds had been purchased by Secondary on July 1, 20X3 for $387,200. All entries relating to the bonds had been put through the books of the individual companies, but no consolidated financial statements had been prepared.

(b)   Income tax expense was $589,000 (i.e., 50% × [$1,374,000 − $200,000 + $4,000]) and $358,000 (i.e., 50% × [$716,800 − $800]) for Primary and Secondary respectively.

(c)   Goodwill was written down for impairment by $20,000 in 20X1.

REQUIRED

Prepare the consolidated income and retained earnings statement and consolidated balance sheet for 20X3 from the above information.

REVIEW QUESTIONS

1.   Why do we use the term "effective gain or loss" when referring to the elimination of intercompany bond holdings between affiliated companies?

2.   Do all intercompany bond transactions give rise to effective gains or losses?

3. Explain what adjustments, if any, have to be made to the values of the bonds and the bond interest expense (or revenue) reflected in the financial statements of the individual affiliated companies before an effective gain or loss can be established?

4. An effective gain of $10,000 arose on the purchase of bonds having a remaining life of five years in an upstream situation between two affiliated companies. What adjustments would have to be made to the consolidated financial statements two years later if the subsidiary company was 80%-owned?

5. If the entire issue of bonds of a parent company is purchased at a gain of $5,000 by a 60%-owned subsidiary, how much of the gain is attributable to:
   (a) The parent company? and
   (b) The subsidiary company?

6. Bonds with a face value of $100,000 were purchased for $110,000 exactly three years before their redemption date. They were sold for $108,000 one year later. Were the bonds sold at a profit or loss?

7. Why does the treatment of preferred shares in the consolidation process differ depending upon which company holds the preferred stock?

8. A 75%-owned subsidiary company purchased 100 shares of 12% preferred shares with a face value of $100 per share issued by its parent company for $95 each on the last day of the financial year of the companies concerned. How would the purchase be treated by the subsidiary company if the purchase amounted to 10% of the preferred shares issued?

9. If a company has to choose between issuing preferred shares and bonds, which one would the issuing company choose? Why?

10. In what conditions, if any, do preferred shares enjoy voting rights?

11. Why are intercompany preferred shares cancelled in certain cases and held until their redemption date in others?

12. How are gains or losses on the retirement or effective retirement of preferred shares calculated?

13. If a parent company holds a 75% interest in a subsidiary that, in turn, holds a substantial number of shares as treasury stock, what adjustments may the parent company have to make to its interests in the subsidiary for consolidation purposes?

EXERCISES

EXERCISE 11–1   On July 1, 20X1, Sacramento Inc. issued 1,000 10-year $1,000 12% bonds at 98%. Interest was paid each year on July 1 and December 31.

Exactly two and a half years later, on January 1, 20X4, Pasadena Inc. acquired an 80% interest in Sacramento. In view of the attractive price at which Sacramento's bonds were being traded, Pasadena purchased 300 of Sacramento's bonds on July 1, 20X5 at 96% on the open market.

REQUIRED

Ignoring income considerations, calculate

1. The effective gain or loss on the purchase by Pasadena of Sacramento's bonds on July 1, 20X5;

2. The bond interest revenue or expense for 20X5 appearing on:
   i.   The income statement of Pasadena;
   ii. The income statement of Sacramento; and
   iii. The consolidated income statement of Pasadena.

3. The adjustment to the consolidated retained earnings of Pasadena at January 1, 20X6 relating to the effective gain or loss on the bonds.

EXERCISE 11–2   You are provided with the following information:

(a)   Pew Inc. owned an 80% interest in Seat Inc.

(b)   At December 31, 20X5, the following items appeared on the balance sheets of Pew and Seat:

	Pew	Seat
12% Bonds Payable (repayable at par on December 31, 20X7)	—	$500,000
Less: Discount		600
		499,400
Investment in Seat's 12% Bonds	$192,000	—

(c)   The bonds pay interest on June 30 and December 31 in each year. They were issued by Seat eight years ago.

(d)   On July 1, 20X5, Pew had purchased 40% of the issue at 95%. Pew amortizes any discount or premium arising on the purchase of bonds and any effective gains or losses from the "extinguishment of debt" using the straight-line method.

REQUIRED

1.   Calculate the effective "Gain on Retirement of Bonds" gain on the purchase of the bonds.

2.   Give the total (or net) interest expense appearing on the consolidated income statement for the year ended December 31, 20X5.

3.   Explain how (if at all) the "Gain (or Loss) on Retirement of Bonds" would be reflected on the consolidated income statement of Pew in 20X5 and thereafter until fully amortized.

4.   At what amount (if any) would the Bonds Payable be reflected on the consolidated balance sheet at December 31, 20X5?

EXERCISE 11–3   Pet Inc. owns 80% of the common shares of Set Inc., which it records using the cost method. On January 1, 20X4, Pet issued $100,000 10-year 12% bonds at 104. On December 31, 20X7, Set purchased $30,000 par value of these bonds for $30,420.

Additional information relating to the years ended December 31, 20X7 and 20X8 was as follows:

	Pet		Set	
	20X7	**20X8**	**20X7**	**20X8**
Net Income after bond Interest adjustments and bond revenue	$120,000	$150,000	$40,000	$50,000
Dividends paid	40,000	50,000	20,000	25,000

REQUIRED

1.   Calculate the consolidated net income **before income taxes** of Pet for 20X7 and 20X8.

2.   Give the amounts reflected in the individual income statements of Pet and Set for the interest paid or received on the bonds for 20X7 and 20X8.

3.   Determine the interest expense relating to the bonds appearing on the consolidated income statement for 20X9.

EXERCISE 11–4   On January 1, 20X5, Pan Inc. purchased an 80% interest in San Inc. for $400,000 when San had common shares of $400,000 and retained earnings of $100,000. Included amongst the investments of San on that date were 100 $1,000 12% 10-year bonds issued by Pan on July 1, 20X2 at 97%. These bonds had been purchased by San on January 1, 20X4 for $91,500. The bond issue by Pan had consisted of 1,000 bonds on which interest was payable on December 31 and June 30 in each year.

At January 1, 20X5, the retained earnings of Pan were $300,000 and the trading results and dividends paid by the two companies during 20X5 were as follows:

	Pan	San
Net Income after bond interest but before adjustments for the effective gain or loss	$300,000	$200,000
Dividends paid	120,000	40,000

REQUIRED

Ignoring income taxes:

1. Calculate the effective gain or loss on the bonds at January 1, 20X5;
2. Give the amounts to be reflected on the consolidated income statement for 20X5 to record the effective retirement of the bonds and the interest payable on the bonds;
3. Give the "Investment in San" account in the ledger of Pan at December 31, 20X5 on the assumption that the full equity method of accounting is used for its investment in San; and
4. Show what amount would be reflected on the income statement of Pan as "Income from Subsidiary Company" for 20X5.

EXERCISE 11–5   The following information appeared on the adjusted trial balances of Push Inc. and its 80%-owned subsidiary, Shove Inc., at December 31, 20X4:

	Push	Shove
Net **Operating** Income for Year (on Cost Basis)	$300,000	$100,000
Dividends Paid	100,000	Nil
Investment in Shove 12% Bonds	50,000	—
Discount on Bonds Purchased	5,040 Cr.	—
12% Bonds Payable (Due July 1, 20X8)	—	200,000
Premium on Bonds	—	12,600

REQUIRED

1. Calculate the "Effective Gain or Loss" on the bonds if Push had purchased the bonds on July 1, 20X3;
2. Give the amount that would appear as "Interest Expense" on the consolidated income statement of Push for the year ended December 31, 20X4 on the assumption that interest on the bonds is payable on July 1 and December 31 in each year; and
3. Give the consolidated net income of Push for the year ended December 31, 20X4 on the assumption that the net operating income given above does not include interest on the bonds and the income tax rate is 50%.

EXERCISE 11–6   Pot Inc. acquired a 75% interest in Shot Inc. on July 1, 20X4 for $265,000. The equity sections of Pot and Shot at December 31, 20X3 were as follows:

	Pot	Shot
Common Shares	$400,000	$200,000
Preferred Shares (10,000 8% shares redeemable on December 31, 20X8 at $10 each)		100,000
Retained Earnings	80,000	60,000
	$480,000	$360,000

Additional Information:

(a) The after tax net income of Shot for 20X4 amounted to $80,000.
(b) The preferred shares are preferred in relation to dividends, and that right is cumulative.
(c) Dividends on the preferred shares are payable on June 30 and December 31 in each year. All dividends had been paid when due.

REQUIRED

1. **Assuming** that all the preferred shares were held by the minority, calculate:
   i. The goodwill arising on the purchase of the 75% interest in Shot; and
   ii. The minority interests in Shot at December 31, 20X4.

2. Explain how the preferred shares of Shot would be reflected in the consolidated financial statements for 20X4 if the preferred shares had all been purchased by Pot on October 1, 20X4 for $100,000.

3. Explain how the preferred shares of Shot would be reflected in the consolidated financial statements for 20X4 if the preferred shares had all been purchased by Pot on July 1, 20X4 for $98,200.

4. What would be the position if, in part (3) above, Pot had acquired only 60% of the preferred shares on October 1, 20X4 for $58,920?

PROBLEMS

PROBLEM 11–1   Solve Inc., which was an 80%-owned subsidiary of Prove Inc., issued 100 $1,000 10-year 12% bonds at 96% on January 1, 20X1. Interest was payable on June 30 and December 31 in each year.

Exactly two years later (i.e., on January 1, 20X3), Prove purchased 30% of the outstanding bonds of Solve for $28,240.

REQUIRED

1. Record the transactions relating to both the issue and purchase of bonds in the ledgers of the companies concerned up to and including the year ended December 31, 20X3 on the assumption that any discount or premium arising on the issue or purchase of the bonds is amortized using the straight-line method.
2. Calculate the effective gain or loss on the purchase of the bonds on January 1, 20X3.
3. Determine the amount of the bond interest expense appearing on the consolidated income statement for the year ended 20X3.

PROBLEM 11–2   Pepper Inc. purchased an 80% interest in Salt Inc. on January 1, 20X3 for $600,000. No goodwill arose on the acquisition, and the assets of Salt were fairly valued at the date of acquisition. At January 1, 20X3, the retained earnings of Pepper amounted to $420,000.

The trading results and dividends paid by Pepper and Salt for 20X3 and 20X4 were as follows:

		Pepper	**Salt**
20X3:	Net Operating Income	$300,000	$200,000
	Dividends Paid	120,000	100,000
20X4:	Net Operating Income	250,000	240,000
	Dividends Paid	120,000	120,000

You are informed that on July 1, 20X1, Pepper had issued 5,000 $100 12% 10-year bonds having interest dates of December 31 and June 30 at 102%. One-thousand of these bonds had been purchased by Salt on July 1, 20X3 for $96,800. All entries relating to the bonds had been put through the books of the individual companies, but no consolidated financial statements had been prepared.

REQUIRED

Ignoring income taxes:

1. Calculate the consolidated retained earnings at December 31, 20X4 of Pepper and its subsidiary company.

2. Give the "Investment in Salt" account in the ledger of Pepper at December 31, 20X4 using the full equity method of accounting for the investment in Salt.

PROBLEM 11–3   The following three items appeared on the balance sheets of Part Inc. and Start Inc. at December 31, 20X6.

	Part	Start
Investment in Start's Bonds	$155,250	—
9% Bonds Payable (5,000 units of $100 each)	—	$500,000
Discount on Bonds	—	12,500

Additional Information:

(a) Start is a 90%-owned subsidiary of Part.
(b) On January 1, 20X2, Part had purchased 30% of the bonds issued by Start.
(c) The bonds issued by Start pay interest semi-annually on June 30 and December 31 in each year. The bonds are repayable on June 30, 20X9 and were issued for $45,000.

REQUIRED

WIth the infomration provided, give

1. The price paid by Part for its 30% investment in the bonds of Start;
2. The effective loss on the purchase of the bonds;
3. The annual bond interest expense appearing on the income statement of Start since the issue of the bonds;
4. The annual interest revenue accruing to Part from the bonds purchased since 20X2; and
5. The annual bond interest expense appearing on the consolidated income statement since 20X2.

PROBLEM 11–4   The following balances relating to bond transactions were extracted from the adjusted trial balance of Pain Inc. and its 80%-owned subsidiary, Sore Inc., at December 31, 20X6:

	Pain	Sore
Bonds Payable (12%)	—	$200,000
Bond Premium	—	2,000
Interest Expense	—	23,000
Interest Receivable	$ 4,800	—
Interest Revenue	10,100	—
Investment in Sore's Bonds (40%)	79,000	—

The bonds were purchased by Pain on July 1, 20X5. Interest on the bonds is payable on June 30 and December 31 in each year.

You are provided with the following additional information:

(a) The bonds are redeemable at par on December 31, 20X8.
(b) The rate of income tax is 50%.
(c) The trading results and dividends paid were as follows:

	Pain 20X5	Pain 20X6	Sore 20X5	Sore 20X6
Net income from operations	$200,000	$240,000	$48,000	$60,000
Dividend income from Sore	16,000	20,000	—	—
Dividends paid	120,000	150,000	20,000	25,000

REQUIRED

Using the above information, prepare the consolidated income statement of Pain for 20X5.

12 Consolidations: Acquisitions and Disposals of Part Interests in Subsidiaries

LEARNING OBJECTIVES

After studying this chapter you should be able to:

1. Understand the restrictions placed on step acquisitions of interests in subsidiaries by securities legislation in Canada;
2. Apply the techniques necessary to account for step acquisitions where the first acquisition allows the investor company to exert significant influence over the affairs of the investee company;
3. Apply the techniques necessary to account for step acquisitions where the first acquisition represents the acquisition of a portfolio investment only; and
4. Understand and apply the techniques necessary to account for the sale of part interests in a subsidiary company or a company over which the investor exerts significant influence.

INTRODUCTION

Up to this point, the acquisition of an interest in a subsidiary or investee company has been assumed to have occurred as the result of a single purchase of shares. Although this may occur in certain circumstances, acquisitions of controlling interests in companies often take place over a period of time through a number of purchases of shares in the company. Where this occurs it is referred to as a step (or step-by-step) acquisition. Similarly, the sale of an interest in a subsidiary may also be through a number of different transactions.

This chapter outlines the procedures to be followed when an acquisition of an interest in a company takes place in more than one transaction and the disposals of part interests in subsidiaries during the year.

INSIDER TRADING AND THE ACQUISITION OF ADDITIONAL INTERESTS IN SUBSIDIARIES

At one time investors could increase their holdings in corporations by merely purchasing shares on securities markets. However, to ensure that investors receive a fair price for their shares, the entire area of increasing individual holdings of shares in companies is now strictly controlled by securities legislation.

For example, the Ontario *Securities Act*[1] requires that any company or individual holding a 10% interest in the voting shares of a company is classified as an "insider" together with the directors and senior officers of that company. **This means that these persons (or companies) are considered to be privy to information regarding the investment that is not readily available to the investing public and they must, therefore, report any changes in their shareholdings to the Ontario Securities Commission (OSC).** This information is included in a weekly "insider trading report", which is available for public scrutiny. Persons privy to insider information who use that information for their own benefit can be held criminally liable for their actions in terms of securities legislation.[2]

With **acquisitions of additional interests in companies,** there is also an "early warning requirement". This requires that any person who acquires a 10% or greater interest in the voting shares or votes attached to a class of shares in a company must immediately issue a press release and file a report with the OSC.[3] Any additional acquisitions of two percent or more of the voting shares or votes attached to a class of shares in the company also requires the issuing of a press release.[4,5] The conditions relating to banks are even more strictly applied. Banks can only hold a maximum of 10% of the voting shares in a company or 25% of its total equity except where the shareholdings relate to temporary holdings of shares arising from actions relating to troubled loans made by them to the companies concerned.

Where a parent company holds over 90% of the shares in a subsidiary, it can force the remaining shareholders to sell their shares to it.[6] All the company has to do is make application to the Supreme Court in the jurisdiction where the company is registered and, once the necessary approval has been obtained, notify the shareholders of the price at which it intends to pay for the shares. If the shareholders accept the offer then the acquisition goes ahead. If, however, the shareholders do not accept the offer, they may launch "dissenting proceedings" through the courts, which eventually ensures, through arbitration or direct ruling, a fair price for the shares.

ACQUISITIONS AND TAKEOVERS

The acquisition of an interest in a company may be for investment or marketing purposes, to guarantee a supply of raw materials, or for some other reason, like the belief that the combined entity would be able to operate more efficiently and effectively than the individual businesses themselves. If the combination is through a share exchange or outright purchase of shares, it is referred to as a merger. It is called a take-over if one of the parties to the combination is the dominant party.

---

[1] Section 1.
[2] The lack of action by both the Ontario Securities Commission and the Toronto Stock Exchange on the issue of insider trading is, however, a matter of great concern. In this respect, an investigation into insider trading revealed that of the 28 friendly mergers or acquisitions announced in the year ended July 31, 1999, the share price of almost half of the target companies rose more than 25% between the times the companies first started talking and the night before the deal was announced publicly (*The Globe and Mail*, October 26, 1999). Since these findings were released, both the OSC and the TSE have, however, announced that action on the issue is to be taken. Perhaps this is why *The Globe and Mail* of October 8, 2002, reported that the securities commissions of Ontario, Alberta, and British Columbia have formed a task force to examine recent major corporate announcements to assess the extent to which insider trading has taken place.
[3] *Ontario Securities Act*, section 100(1).
[4] *Ibid.*, section 100a(1)
[5] The insider provisions and early warning requirements required by the *Securities Act* in the USA are even stricter and apply to a 5% holding and all additional increases of one percent or more.
[6] For example, in terms of section 206(2) of the *Canada Business Corporations Act*.

Friendly and Hostile Takeovers

Takeovers are either friendly or hostile. What this means is that if the management and shareholders of the company being "taken over" are in favour of the move, it is referred to as a friendly takeover. On the other hand, hostile takeovers occur where the management of a company and its shareholders oppose the takeover. Hostile takeovers are, therefore, usually bitterly opposed by management and, if the takeover succeeds, the entire management team is usually replaced by the acquiring company. From time to time, a **"white knight"** appears, which is the name given to a friendly bidder for the target company's shares to save the target company from being taken over by an unwelcome suitor. These "white knights" may either be in the form of another company in the same line of business or a corporate raider, which is a company looking for a quick profit on the sale of the shares or assets of the acquired company.

To **obstruct a hostile takeover bid**, the directors of a company may use what they refer to as a **shareholder protection rights plan** (also known as a "the poison pill").[7] The plan is designed to require anyone who seeks to acquire 15% or more of a company to negotiate with the target company's board of directors to terminate the plan. If no agreement is reached, the board may issue shares to any or all the shareholders other than the shareholder making the offer at a substantial discount (say of 50% of the present market price). Plans vary, but they normally provide for the shares to be offered to the existing shareholders in proportion to their current share holdings.

The objective of the rights plan is to increase the number of shares in order to dilute the potential acquiror's interest in the target company and make a takeover bid prohibitively expensive. It is supposed to be used where the directors believe that the takeover bid is unfair to shareholders or, in particular, to any one group of shareholders: for example, an offer to buy shares from, say, the American but not the Canadian shareholders.

The adoption of a shareholder rights plan requires shareholder approval and that the articles of association of the company empower the directors to use a shareholder rights plan. The use of such a plan is subject to approval by the relevant securities commission, which can either approve or "dissolve" the poison pill depending upon its assessment of the takeover bid.

Companies have used different strategies to lessen the chances of a "poison pill" being disallowed by a securities commission. For example, on being faced with a hostile takeover, a company may threaten to sell off a key division of the company or investment. These "spin-offs", as they are known, can drastically change the nature of the company. If the hostile take-over is not thwarted by this action, the division or investment can be sold with the proceeds being distributed to the shareholders by way of a cash or stock dividend.[8] A cash dividend could be used to deplete liquid reserves, whereas a stock dividend could be declared to reduce the value of the shares in cases where the company initiating the takeover has specified a price at which the shares of the target company would be acquired.

Leveraged Buyouts

A "leveraged buyout" is the term given to the purchase of a controlling interest in a company where the money raised to finance the acquisition is secured over the assets of the acquired company and not over the assets of the acquiring party. **Leveraged buyouts**

---

[7] *The Globe and Mail* of November 13, 1995 reported that the board of Slocan Forest Products Ltd. of Richmond, B.C. had adopted a "poison pill" to thwart any unwanted takeover bid. The "poison pill" would be activated if any investor tries to acquire 20% or more of the company without its approval and would operate by allowing existing shareholders to purchase new stock at a 50% discount to the market price. This would then flood the market with new shares, making the takeover prohibitively expensive. A different plan applies for the Hudson's Bay Company, where the poison pill requires that any single shareholder must make an offer to purchase the entire share issue as soon as they acquire 20% of the shares in issue (*The Globe and Mail*, May 3, 2004).

[8] The advantage of declaring a dividend is that once has been declared, it cannot be recalled.

occur where the existing shareholders have indicated their willingness to divest themselves of their interests in the company. They can, therefore, represent mergers of interests between companies or merely changes in ownership. This form of takeover was extremely popular in the 1980s because it allowed either the purchasing company or the managers or directors of companies to acquire control of a company with very little risk to themselves.

With leveraged buyouts, the persons acquiring the shares rely on the success of the company to cover the interest and capital repayments through the payment of dividends and, in the case of the purchase of the shares by managers, any directors' fees and managerial bonuses. The problem is that where the company is not successful, the cash flows to the purchasers of the shares may be insufficient to service the debt, and the creditors look to the company's assets to recover the amounts owing. Experience has shown that to stave off the possibility of claims against the purchasing company, the non-essential assets of the acquired company are often sold. As a result, a significant downsizing of the company's operations often occurs. Since the onset of the economic downturn of the 1990s, however, leveraged buyouts have virtually disappeared.

ACCOUNTING FOR PART INTERESTS IN SUBSIDIARIES ACQUIRED DURING THE YEAR

With step (or step-by-step) acquisitions of interests in companies, **the cost method is used to account for the investment until such time as the use of the equity method becomes necessary.** At that point, the investment is accounted for using the equity method in exactly the same way as that outlined in Chapter Five. **A further adjustment is necessary when the purchase of an additional interest in an investee company results in a change from the use of the equity method to consolidation.** In these cases, the equity method is used to account for the investment up to the date on which control is exercised and, thereafter, the results of operations are consolidated with those of the parent company.

The various steps in accounting for step acquisitions and the way this differs from that relating to acquisitions resulting from a single purchase are explained and illustrated in the following subsections.

THE SIMPLEST CASE OF STEP ACQUISITIONS — WHERE SIGNIFICANT INFLUENCE MAY BE EXERTED AFTER THE FIRST ACQUISITION

Where the initial purchase of an interest in an investee company in a step acquisition allows the investor company to exert significant influence over the affairs of the investee company, the consolidation process is relatively straightforward because each acquisition is treated as **a separate purchase of shares**. All that is required is to analyze the equity at the date of each acquisition through a multiple analysis of equity.

This is outlined in Illustration 12–1 that shows how the analysis of equity covering the acquisition of a controlling interest in two separate purchases is carried out. In this particular case, 75% of the equity of Subsidiary Inc. is purchased by Parent Inc. in two separate transactions. With the first acquisition, the analysis is exactly the same as with a single acquisition. However, with the second and any subsequent acquisitions, equity is analyzed in proportion to the additional interests acquired.

It is important to note that with step acquisitions, the income attributable to the parent company is limited to the proportionate amount of net income earned from the date of each acquisition. This is because any net income earned prior to the date of acquisition must be capitalized as part of the equity acquired. In Illustration 12–1, the net income attributable to Parent for the year in which the acquisition took place is, therefore, limited to $12,500.

ILLUSTRATION 12–1
STEP ACQUISITION OF A SUBSIDIARY IN THOSE CASES WHERE
SIGNIFICANT INFLUENCE IS EXERCISED FROM THE FIRST PURCHASE

Parent Inc. acquired a 75% interest in Subsidiary Inc. in two purchases. The first was the purchase of a 25% interest for $25,000 on formation of Subsidiary on January 1, 20X8 when its equity only consisted of common stock of $100,000. The second was an additional 50% interest acquired for $80,000 on December 31, 20X8. The net income for 20X8 amounted to $50,000. Significant influence could be exercised after the first acquisition.

The two acquisitions are treated as being allocations of the equity applying to the dates on which the shares were purchased:

	Total	First Acquisition (25%)	Second Acquisition (50%)	Minority Interests
Common Stock	$100,000	$25,000	$50,000	$25,000
Purchase Consideration		25,000		
Goodwill		$ Nil		
Net Income	50,000	12,500	25,000	12,500
			75,000	
Purchase Consideration			80,000	
Goodwill			$ 5,000	
Minority Interests				$37,500

With the second and subsequent acquisitions, net income is also recognized from the actual dates of acquisition. For example, if the net income of Subsidiary for 20X9 amounted to $80,000 and Parent purchased an additional five percent interest in Subsidiary on October 1, 20X9, Parent's share of the reported net income of Subsidiary for 20X9 would be $61,000 made up as follows:

75% of $80,000 for 9 months	=	75% of 9/12 × $80,000	=	$45,000
80% of $80,000 for 3 months	=	80% of 3/12 × $80,000	=	16,000
				$61,000

As the individual acquisitions of interests in a subsidiary are treated independently of one another, **any fair market value adjustments to the net assets arising on the various acquisitions are treated as separate amounts** and amortized on an individual basis from the dates on which the acquisitions took place. For example, if an acquisition of an interest in a subsidiary occurred in two transactions on March 1 and September 1 of the same year, any fair market value adjustments would be amortized independently from one another from those dates.

The position with **goodwill** is, however, somewhat different. Notwithstanding the fact that each purchase of shares is treated as a separate acquisition, the amounts determined for goodwill are **not kept separate** but aggregated and reflected on the balance sheet as a single figure and assessed for impairment in the normal manner.

A comprehensive example of consolidation where an interest in a subsidiary is acquired on a step basis and where significant influence may be exerted over the investee company after the first purchase of an interest is given in Illustration 12–2. Here, the multiple analysis of equity is relatively simple and has been illustrated by allocating the equity acquired over the two acquisitions. The only complications are those arising from the change from accounting for the investment from the equity basis to consolidation.

In this illustration, the fair market value adjustment at the second acquisition is based on the plant that was undervalued by $20,000. This is because the parent company's share of the fair market values assigned to the net assets must be in proportion to its interest in the

ILLUSTRATION 12–2

CONSOLIDATION IN A STEP ACQUISITION WHERE SIGNIFICANT INFLUENCE
IS EXERCISABLE AFTER THE FIRST ACQUISITION AND CONTROL IS EXERCISABLE
AFTER THE SECOND ACQUISITION

On January 1, 20X4, Parent Inc. purchased a 40% interest in Subsidiary Inc. for $60,000 when Subsidiary had common stock of $100,000 and retained earnings of $20,000. This purchase permitted Parent to exert significant influence over the affairs of Subsidiary.

At the date of acquisition, the assets and liabilities of Subsidiary were properly valued except for plant having a five-year life, which was undervalued by $15,000. All revenues and expenses accrued evenly throughout the year.

On April 1, 20X4, Parent purchased a further 20% interest in Subsidiary for $41,000. At that date, it was established that all assets and liabilities of Subsidiary were fairly valued except for the undervalued plant at January 1, 20X4, and an additional item of plant that was considered to be undervalued by $20,000 and to be written off over five years. The total value of the goodwill is assessed whenever an event occurs that indicates that its value may have been impaired. Following such an assessment carried out in October 20X4, the goodwill was written down for impairment by $4,000.

The abbreviated financial statements of the two companies at December 31, 20X4 were as follows:

	Parent	Subsidiary
BALANCE SHEETS		
Current Assets	$203,000	$100,000
Investment in Subsidiary	116,200	—
Plant and Equipment (Net)	350,000	150,000
	$669,200	$250,000
Current Liabilities	$102,000	$ 90,000
Common Stock	300,000	100,000
Retained Earnings	267,200	60,000
	$669,200	$250,000
COMBINED INCOME AND RETAINED EARNINGS STATEMENTS		
Gross Profit	$400,000	$130,000
Operating Expenses	220,000	70,000
Net Operating Income	180,000	60,000
Net Income from Subsidiary	27,200	—
Net Income for Year	207,200	60,000
Dividends Paid (December 15)	60,000	20,000
	147,200	40,000
Retained Earnings at January 1, 20X4	120,000	20,000
Retained Earnings at December 31, 20X4	$267,200	$ 60,000

As it is first necessary to analyze the equity at each acquisition date, this is illustrated hereunder:

Analysis of Equity:

	Total	First Acquisition (40%)	Second Acquisition (20%)	Minority Interests
At Acquisition:				
Common Stock	$100,000	$40,000	$20,000	$40,000
Retained Earnings	20,000	8,000	4,000	8,000
Fair Market Value Adjustment	15,000	6,000	—	—
		54,000		
Purchase Consideration		60,000		
Goodwill		$ 6,000		
Since First Acquisition:				
Net Income — 3 months	$15,000	$ 6,000	$ 3,000	$ 6,000
At Second Acquisition (+20%):				
Fair Market Value Adjustment	20,000	—	4,000	—
			31,000	
Purchase Consideration			41,000	
Goodwill			$10,000	
Since Second Acquisition:				
Net Income — 9 months	45,000	18,000	9,000	18,000
Dividends Paid	(20,000)	(8,000)	(4,000)	(8,000)
Minority Interests				$64,000

ILLUSTRATION 12–2 (Continued)

Adjustments for 20X4 Arising from First and Second Acquisitions:

Fair Market Value Adjustments — First Acquisition	$6,000/5	=	$1,200
Fair Market Value Adjustments — Second Acquisition	$4,000/5 × 9/12	=	$ 600
Goodwill Impairment of $4,000 in 20X4			

Reconciliation of the Investment Account:

Investment in Subsidiary

20X4				
Jan. 1	Purchase Consideration	60,000		60,000
Apr. 1	Purchase Consideration	41,000		101,000
Oct. 1	Goodwill Impairment		4,000	97,000
Dec. 15	Dividends Received (8,000 + 4,000)		12,000	85,000
31	Net Income (6,000 + 18,000 + 9,000)	33,000		
	Fair Market Value Adjustments ([300 + 900] + 600)		1,800	116,200

Consolidated Financial Statements:

Balance Sheets:

Current Assets (203,000 + 100,000)	$303,000
Plant and Equipment (350,000 + 150,000 + 6,000 + 4,000 − [300 + 900] − 600)	508,200
Goodwill ([6,000 + 10,000 − 4,000)	12,000
	$823,200
Current Liabilities (102,000 + 90,000)	$192,000
Minority Interests	64,000
Common Stock	300,000
Retained Earnings	267,200
	$823,200

Combined Income and Retained Earnings Statement:

	Consolidated	Parent	Subsidiary (9/12)
Gross Profit	$497,500	$400,000	$97,500
Less: Operating Expenses	$272,500	$220,000	$52,500
Fair Market Value Adjustment ([9/12 × 1,200] + 600)	1,500	1,500	—
Total Expenses	$274,000	$221,500	$52,500
Total Operating Net Income	$223,500	$178,500	$45,000
Less: Minority Interests	18,000	—	18,000
Net Operating Income before Goodwill Amortization	205,500	$178,500	$27,500
Goodwill Charges	4,000		
Net Operating Income	201,500		
Share of Net Income from Investee Company — see note	5,700		
Consolidated Net Income	207,200		
Retained Earnings at January 1, 20X4	120,000		
	327,250		
Dividends Paid	60,000		
Retained Earnings at December 31, 20X4	$267,200		

Note on Share of Net Income from Investee Company:

In terms of section 1600 of the CICA *Handbook*, net income from the investee company must be disclosed on the income statement using the equity method up to the date on which consolidation is required. In this case, this applies to the period January 1 to March 31, 20X4, in which period there was no impairment of goodwill, and is calculated as follows:

Share of Net Income (3/12 × $60,000)	$15,000
Less: Minority Interests therein (i.e., 60%)	9,000
Share of Net Income from Investee Company	6,000
Less: Fair Market Value Adjustment (3/12 × $1,200)	300
Net Income from Investee Company	$ 5,700

subsidiary acquired which, in this case, is an additional 20% interest. And, because the fair market value adjustments are recognized from different dates, the excess amortization adjustments must be calculated from the dates on which these changes in asset or liability values are recognized.

As the investment changed from one over which significant influence was exercised to where the parent company exercised control, the trading results of Subsidiary must be presented using the equity method up to the date on which control may be exercised and then consolidated. This complication, obviously, only arises in the year in which control is exercised. This is reflected in Illustration 12–2 where the consolidated figures only include the trading operations of Subsidiary for the last nine months of the year and the amount of $5,700 for the first three months appears as the "net income from investee company".

STEP ACQUISITIONS WHERE SIGNIFICANT INFLUENCE OR CONTROL IS ONLY EXERCISABLE AFTER THE SECOND OR SUBSEQUENT PURCHASE

The Change from the Cost to the Equity Method

Where significant influence (or control) over the affairs of an investee company is only exercised by the investor company after the second or subsequent purchase of an interest, the consolidation process is somewhat more complicated. This is because longterm investments are accounted for using the cost method up to the point in time when significant influence may be exercised by the investor company. From that point onwards, the investment must be reported using the equity method.

The procedure followed is the cost method where the investor company only recognizes dividends from the investee company up to the time significant influence or control is exercisable. From that point onwards, the investor (or parent) company recognizes its share of net income from the investee (or subsidiary) company **without any retroactive adjustment of earnings**. This treatment is based on the contention in the CICA *Handbook*[9] that a change in the initial adoption or alteration of an accounting policy necessitated by events or transactions that are clearly different in substance from those previously occurring **is not a change in accounting policy**. And, since a change from the cost to the equity method is only considered **a change in substance**, there is **no retroactive adjustment** of earnings irrespective of how material the effects of such a change may be.

The position taken by the CICA is outlined in Illustration 12–3 where a 55% interest in an investee company having a December 31 year end was acquired in two purchases: a 10% on January 1, 20X8, and a further 45% on July 1, 20X9. During 20X8, the investee company earned net income of $100,000 and declared and paid a dividend of $20,000 in August of that year. In 20X9, the investee company earned net income of $60,000 in the first six months of the year and $80,000 in the last six months; a dividend of $20,000 was declared and paid on June 15. Significant influence and control was only exercisable after the second acquisition.

The breakdown of the position is once again through a multiple analysis of equity. However, it differs from the position outlined in Illustration 12–2 in that the first acquisition does not allow the investor company to exert significant influence over the investee, and the cost method must be used. As a result, only dividend revenue may be recognized. The way this is carried out is to allocate 10% of the net income (i.e., $10,000) to the first acquisition to cover the dividend attributable to the investor of $2,000. The excess of $8,000 **is considered part of**

---

[9] Section 1506.

ILLUSTRATION 12–3

CALCULATION OF FAIR MARKET VALUE ADJUSTMENTS AND GOODWILL IN AN ACQUISITION WHERE SIGNIFICANT INFLUENCE (OR CONTROL) IS ONLY EXERCISABLE AFTER THE SECOND ACQUISITION

A 55% interest in an investee company having a December 31 financial year end was acquired in two purchases; a 10% interest was acquired on January 1, 20X8 for $25,000 and an additional 45% was acquired on July 1, 20X9 for $155,000. After the second acquisition, the investor company was able to exercise significant influence over the affairs of the investee company. At the date of the first acquisition, the equity of the investee company was $200,000, which had increased by $120,000 by the second acquisition on July 1, 20X9.

The increase in equity was due to net income of $100,000 earned during 20X8 less dividends of $20,000 paid in August 20X8, plus net income of $60,000 earned during the first six months of 20X9 less the payment of a dividend of $20,000 paid on June 15, 20X9. Earnings for the last six months of 20X9 were $80,000.

The fair market values of the net assets of the investee company could not be determined at December 31, 20X7, but on June 30, 20X9, the fair market values of the net assets were $20,000 greater than their book value.

The analysis of equity of the investee company would be as follows:

	Total	First Acquisition 10%	Second Acquisition 45%	Minority Interests
			(Treat as 55%)	
Equity at First Acquisition	$200,000		$110,000	$ 90,000
Net Income — 20X8	100,000	10,000	45,000	45,000
Dividends — 20X8	(20,000)	(2,000)	(9,000)	(9,000)
Transfer to Minority Interests — Note 1		–$ 8,000		+8,000
Current Period Adjustments:				
Net Income — 20X9 (6 months)	60,000	6,000	27,000	27,000
Dividends — 20X9	(20,000)	(2,000)	(9,000)	(9,000)
Transfer to Minority Interests — Note 1		–$ 4,000		+4,000
			164,000	
Fair Market Value Adjustment (55% of $20,000)	20,000		11,000	
Total Equity Purchased			175,000	
Purchase Consideration ($25,000 + $155,000)			180,000	
Goodwill			$ 5,000	
		(revert to 10% and 45%)		
Net Income — 20X9 (6 months)	80,000	8,000	36,000	$ 36,000
Total Minority Interests				$192,000

The workings for the consolidated income statement of for 20X9 are given belowoin the assumption that there were fair market value adjustments and the impairment of goodwill of $550 and $1,000 respectively. What should also be noted is that the consolidated income statement includes the $2,000 dividend received from the 10% interest in the investee company before the additional 45% interest was acquired.

	Consolidated	Investor	Investee (6/12)
Total Net Income — see Note below	$880,000	$800,000	$ 80,000
Less: FMV Adjustments	550	550	—
	879,450	799,450	80,000
Less: Minority Interest	36,000	—	36,000
Net Income before Goodwill Charges — Note 2	843,450	$799,450	$ 44,000
Goodwill Charges	1,000		
	842,450		
Add: Dividends from Investee Company	2,000		
Consolidated Net Income for Year	$844,450		

Notes:

[1] The net income less dividends applicable to the first acquisition of $8,000 and $4,000 are transferred to the minority interests.

[2] The net income before goodwill charges of $44,000 from Investee for the last six months of the year is the allocation of the $8,000 from the first acquisition plus the $36,000 from the second acquisition.

the minority interests in the investee company and is transferred to that column.[10] The position is the same for the first six months of 20X9, where an allocation of net income of $6,000 is to the first acquisition to cover the dividend of $2,000 and a subsequent transfer of the difference of $4,000 to the minority interests.

As control is only exercised after the second acquisition, the net income and dividends for the second six months of 20X9 are allocated as to 10% to the first acquisition (i.e., $8,000), 45% to the second acquisition (i.e., $36,000), and the balance of 45% to the minority interests. The total revenues from the investor's 10% interest recognized in 20X8 is, therefore, restricted to the dividend of $2,000 and that from its 55% interest for 20X9 was $44,000 (i.e., $8,000 + $36,000).

The Assignment of Fair Market Values to the Net Assets and the Treatment of Goodwill

It is also necessary to assign fair market values to the assets and liabilities of the investee company at the date of each acquisition. Ideally, these values should be assigned to the assets at the date of the original investment, even though significant influence could not be exercised by the investor company at that stage. However, the practical problem arises that access to the books and records of the investee company is only possible once significant influence can be exercised. Therefore, fair market values can only be assigned to the assets from the date on which it is possible to exert significant influence over the investee company and on the date of each additional major purchase thereafter. Where numerous purchases of small numbers of shares take place, these may be grouped together and treated as a single purchase.[11]

As outlined in the previous section, the fair market values assigned to the assets and liabilities at each major purchase date remain unchanged. The values at which the assets are carried for consolidation purposes are, therefore, not adjusted by subsequent acquisitions and the values assigned to the assets and liabilities differ depending upon the date on which the interests are acquired. As a result, the fair market value adjustments and amortization thereon must be calculated separately for each acquisition.

Furthermore, because the amount of goodwill arising on acquisition is dependent upon the assignment of fair market values to assets, goodwill is also only calculated from the date on which significant influence may be exercised. The amounts paid to acquire the interests in the subsidiary or investee company up to that date are added together and offset against the total equity purchased. From then onwards, goodwill is calculated for each additional purchase. This treatment is outlined in Illustration 12–3 where significant influence is only exercisable after the second purchase.

---

[10] The difference between the net income allocated to the 10% interest acquired and the dividends paid in Illustration 12–2 can only be transferred to the minority interests column. This is because this difference does not accrue to the 10% interest acquired by the parent company because the only amount that can be recognized by the parent company is limited to the dividends paid. As outlined later in the chapter, this situation is recognized in the USA where these differences are treated as prior period adjustments as soon as sufficient voting shares are acquired to allow the exercise of significant influence or control. And, because of the position taken by the CICA, this difference can only be considered part of the minority interests.

Any suggestion that the difference should be added or allocated to the equity acquired in subsequent share purchases is incorrect because such action would cause the additional equity acquired to be overstated. This problem does not arise using the old worksheet approach to consolidating financial statements because with that approach there is no complete analysis of the allocation of the net income over the various acquisitions. All that occurs with this approach is that amounts corresponding to the parent company's interests are calculated and deducted from the total net income on the worksheet.

[11] CICA *Handbook*, section 1600.

The multiple analysis of equity presented in Illustration 12–3 differs from the normal analysis insofar as the apportionment of the equity over the various purchases is concerned. As outlined above, the first acquisition of a 10% interest did not allow the parent company to exert significant influence and, as a result, it was only with the second acquisition that the goodwill and fair market value adjustments were recognized.

The Difference between the Canadian and American Positions

The Canadian position relating to the application of the cost and equity method differs from that applying in the USA, which is outlined in APB *Opinion No. 18: The Equity Method of Accounting for Investments in Common Stock* (1971) and *Accounting Research Bulletin No. 51: Consolidated Financial Statements* (1959).[12] APB *Opinion No. 18*[13] states that where an investment qualifies for the use of the equity method, "The investment, results of operations (current and prior periods presented), and retained earnings of the investor should be adjusted **retroactively** in a manner consistent with the accounting for step-by-step acquisitions of a subsidiary" (emphasis added). The position relating to step acquisitions is clarified by *ARB No. 51*[14] (1959), where it states:

> ... if a 45% interest was acquired on October 1, 1957, and a further 30% interest was acquired on April 1, 1958, it would be appropriate to include in consolidated net income for the year ended December 31, 1958, 45% of the **earnings** of the subsidiary for the three months ended March 31, and 75% of the **earnings** for the nine months ended December 31, and to credit consolidated earned surplus in 1958 with 45% of the undistributed earned surplus in 1958 with 45% of the **undistributed earnings** of the subsidiary for the three months ended December 31, 1957 (emphasis added).

The specific use of the term "earnings" shows that the retroactive adjustment applies to the "share of net income" from the subsidiary. Here, the position in the USA is that the moment significant influence is exercisable by the investor company in a step acquisition, the recognition of revenue from the investee company must be applied retroactively to its share of the investee company's earnings earned prior to that date and, unlike the position in Canada, it is **not** merely restricted to the dividends received. This means that the change from the cost to an equity basis in the USA is considered to be **a change in accounting policy, and is accounted for retroactively from the date of the original acquisition** and not merely from the date on which significant influence or control is exercised.

Using the information provided above and in Illustration 12–3, the position in the USA would have been the same as that outlined in Illustration 12–3 for 20X8 but, in 20X9, it would have differed in two respects. First, the difference of $8,000, between the allocation of net income of $10,000 and the dividend paid $2,000, would have been treated as a prior period adjustment. Second, the full amount of net income of $6,000 would have been recognized in the first six-month period. Allocations for the second six-month period would be unchanged.

The effect of the American adjustments is that the recognition of its revenues from its investment in the investee company would have been:

10% of net income of $100,000 from the first acquisition in 20X8	$10,000
10% of net income of $ 60,000 from the first acquisition in the first six months of 20X9	6,000
55% of net income of $ 80,000 from the second acquisition in second six months of 20X9	44,000
Total revenues since acquisition	$60,000

---

12 Both issued by the American Institute of Certified Public Accountants.
13 Para. 19 (m).
14 Section 10.

The Canadian position, however, is that only $48,000 is recognized made up of dividends of $2,000 in 20X8, dividends of $2,000 in the first six months of 20X9, and net income of $44,000 in the second six months of 20X9 (i.e., $8,000 + $36,000). It also fails to allow the minority interests to be the amount representing their ownership percentage multiplied by the shareholders' equity in the subsidiary.

The position taken by the CICA is difficult to understand because it is ultra-conservative and fails to reflect economic reality. In this case, a 10% investment does not mean that the investor is entitled to 10% of the net income of the investee company. It also leaves the question of whether the additional $12,000 allocated to the minority interests in the analysis of equity in 20X8 and 20X9 represents part of the equity to be allocated to any additional purchases of interests in the investee company or whether it remains part of the minority interests indefinitely.

THE SALE OF A PART INTEREST IN A SUBSIDIARY

Where a part interest in a subsidiary is sold, it is necessary to analyze the equity at the date of sale to establish exactly what has been realized. This is required to, first, determine whether the shares were sold at a gain or loss and, second, to establish exactly what made up the equity sold so that the consolidated financial statements can be properly adjusted in the year of sale. This latter step is necessary because the disposal of a part interest in a subsidiary affects the right of the parent company to receive any net income from a subsidiary earned prior to the date of sale. Adjustments to the consolidated retained earnings at the beginning of the year in which the disposal took place are, therefore, necessary. To explain what occurs, an illustration of such a disposal of interests is provided as Illustration 12–4.

In Illustration 12–4, the parent company sold one-quarter of its interest in a subsidiary for the sum of $40,000. The analysis of equity shows that the equity sold amounts to $34,000, but this amount does not take into account the sale of a portion of goodwill arising on consolidation or any fair market value adjustments, nor does it take the sale of its right to retained earnings into account.

The establishment of exactly what equity is sold in the disposal of a part interest in a subsidiary is examined and explained in the following section.

ACCOUNTING FOR THE DISPOSAL OF AN INTEREST IN A SUBSIDIARY

The Analysis of the Investment Account

Where the full equity method of accounting is used, the investment account would automatically reflect the information required to establish the actual equity sold. However, where the cost method has been used, the investment account must be reconstructed to reflect the position as if the full equity method had been used.

In Illustration 12–4, the investment account shows that the equity actually sold amounted to $35,750. This amount represents the proportionate amount of the value of the investment in the subsidiary at the date of sale (i.e., 25% of $143,000). As explained in the following subsection, it also includes the sale of part of the goodwill that arose on the acquisition of the investment.

As far as the gain or loss on the sale of the investment is concerned, this depends upon the selling price of the investment. In this case, the selling price of part of the investment in Subsidiary was $40,000, giving a "Gain on the Sale of Investment" of $4,250 (i.e., $40,000 – $35,750).

The gain or loss on the sale of the investment is also affected by any payment of a pre-acquisition dividend in prior years. As outlined in an earlier chapter, pre-acquisition dividends represent a repayment of part of the purchase consideration and, consequently, this reduction in the cost of the investment must be recognized when the equity is sold.

ILLUSTRATION 12–4

THE ANALYSIS OF EQUITY AND RECONSTRUCTION OF THE INVESTMENT ACCOUNT
WHERE THERE IS A DISPOSAL OF A PART INTEREST IN A SUBSIDIARY

Parent Inc. acquired an 80% interest in Subsidiary Inc. on January 1, 20X3 for $120,000 when Subsidiary had common stock of $100,000 and retained earnings of $40,000. Following a review for impairment, goodwill was written down by $1,000 in October 20X3.

On April 1, 20X5, Parent sold one-quarter of its interest in Subsidiary for $40,000. The retained earnings of Subsidiary at January 1, 20X5 amounted to $60,000; the increase of $20,000 since the date of acquisition was made up of net income $60,000 less the payment of dividends of $40,000. The net income of Subsidiary for the year ended December 31, 20X5 was $40,000.

Analysis of Equity:

The analysis of equity would be as follows:

	Total	Acquisition of 80%	Sale of One-quarter†	Minority Interests
At Acquisition:				
Common Stock	$100,000	$ 80,000	$20,000	$20,000
Retained Earnings	40,000	32,000	8,000	8,000
		112,000	28,000	28,000
Purchase Consideration		120,000		
Goodwill		$ 8,000		
Goodwill Impairment of $1,000 in 20X3				
Since Acquisition:				
Net Income 20X3–20X4	60,000	48,000	12,000	12,000
Dividends Paid 20X3–20X4	(40,000)	(32,000)	(8,000)	(8,000)
Net Income 20X5 (3 months)	10,000	8,000	2,000	2,000
				34,000
Sale of 20,000 shares		(−34,000)	$34,000	+34,000

Now 60%

	Total	Acquisition of 80%	Sale of One-quarter†	Minority Interests
Since Sale of Shares:				
Net Income 20X5 (9 months)	30,000	18,000		12,000
Minority Interests				$80,000

In this case, the Investment Account would reflect the following position:

Investment in Subsidiary

20X3					
Jan. 1	Purchase Consideration	120,000			120,000
Oct. 31	Goodwill Impairment		1,000		119,000
20X3–20X4	Net Income	48,000			
	Dividends Received		32,000		135,000
20X5					
Mar. 31	Net Income	8,000			143,000
	Sale of 1/4 of $143,000		35,750		107,250
Dec. 31	Net Income (60% of $30,000)	18,000			126,250

Reconciliation of Equity Sold on Analysis of Equity with that on Investment Account:

The adjustment to the equity sold on the Analysis of Equity does not include the share of goodwill sold. The reconciliation is, therefore, as follows:

Equity Sold, per Analysis of Equity	$34,000
Add: Goodwill Sold − 25% of $7,000 (i.e., $8,000 − $1,000)	1,750
Equity Sold, per Investment Account	$35,750

† The figures reflected in the box given below are purely for illustrative purposes.

The Sale of Part of the Goodwill

Where the purchase of an interest in a subsidiary company is at a price in excess of the value of the equity acquired, the purchase consideration includes an amount paid for goodwill. Therefore, for so long as the goodwill has not been completely written down for impairment, any sale of part of the investment includes the sale of part of the remaining goodwill at the date of sale. In this respect, the amount of goodwill sold is equal to the proportion of the number of shares sold bears to the total number of shares held prior to the sale.

Fair Market Value Adjustments with Disposals

If the values of the assets had been adjusted for fair market values at the date of acquisition, these would also have been treated as part of the equity sold. This requires a proportionate adjustment to the annual amortization of the fair market value adjustment.

For example, assume the parent company's allocation of the fair market value adjustment to undervalued plant and equipment was $40,000 (with a five-year remaining life) in the analysis of equity at the date of acquisition. If the parent company sold 20% of its interest in the subsidiary two years after acquisition, the net adjustment to the consolidated plant and equipment of $24,000 would be reduced by 20% to $19,200 (i.e., 80% of [$40,000 – $16,000]).

The Amount of Net Income from the Subsidiary
Attributable to the Parent Company

Unlike the position with step acquisitions, where the net income earned up to the date of each acquisition is capitalized, the post-acquisition retained earnings and net income of a subsidiary company accruing to the parent company after the disposal of a part interest is limited to the **interest held at the end of the year**. This is in accordance with the principle that **a company cannot recognize income to which it has no right**.

For example, in Illustration 12–4, the post-acquisition retained earnings of Subsidiary Inc. at January 1, 20X5 amounted to $60,000 and the net income for 20X5 was $40,000. As the extent of Parent's interest in Subsidiary was reduced from 80% to 60% by the sale of one-quarter of its interest, Parent only has a right to 60% of the post-acquisition retained earnings (i.e., $36,000) and 60% of the current net income (i.e., $24,000). The differences in post-acquisition retained earnings of $12,000 (i.e., 25% of 80% of $60,000) and the share of the first three months' current net income of $2,000 (i.e., 25% of 80% of $10,000) are treated as retained earnings and net income that have been sold.

This adjustment for the sale of part of the post-acquisition retained earnings and net income earned by Subsidiary is established by analyzing the equity sold into its three components, namely, investment cost, retained earnings and current net income. The breakdown of the part of the investment sold in Illustration 12–4 of $35,750 was as follows:

Cost of the Investment Sold (i.e., 25% of):		$29,750
Purchase Consideration	$120,000	
Less: Impairment of Goodwill	1,000	
	$119,000	
Post-Acquisition Retained Earnings to January 1, 20X5 Sold (i.e., 25% of $48,000)	$ 12,000	
Less: Adjustment for Dividends Received		
(i.e., $32,000 [i.e., 80% of $40,000] – $24,000 [i.e., 60% of $40,000])	8,000	4,000
Net Income for Period January 1–March 31, 20X5 Sold (i.e., 25% of $8,000)		2,000
Total Equity Sold		$35,750

This analysis is necessary for three reasons.

(a) It is necessary to **keep track of the balance of the purchase consideration** less the necessary amortization of goodwill and adjustments to the fair market value of the net assets.

It is also necessary **to ensure that any pre-acquisition dividends paid by the subsidiary have been applied in reducing the cost of the investment**.

(b) **The consolidated retained earnings at the beginning of the year in which the disposal takes place must be adjusted to reflect the effect of the sale of the parent company's share of the post-acquisition retained earnings at the end of the previous year.**

(c) The share of the net income earned during the current year up to the date of sale must be calculated to adjust the investment account and to establish the actual net income of the subsidiary attributable to the parent company. This latter adjustment is automatically carried out by calculating the minority's share of net income in the consolidated income statement using the minority's percentage interest in the subsidiary **at the end of the year** (i.e., 60% of $40,000).

As outlined above, the share of the post-acquisition retained earnings sold in this example was only $4,000 because, of the $36,000 (i.e., 75% × $48,000) to which it is entitled, it had already received $32,000 by way of dividends from Subsidiary. Therefore, if the consolidated retained earnings of Parent at December 31, 20X4 amounted to $260,000 (i.e., $212,000 from Parent and $48,000 from Subsidiary), the opening balance at January 1, 20X5 must also be $260,000 but subject to adjustment for the share of retained earnings due from Subsidiary that has been sold. In this case, the consolidated retained earnings at January 1, 20X5 would have to be disclosed as follows:

Consolidated Retained Earnings at January 1, 20X5	$260,000
Less: Proportion of Post-Acquisition Retained Earnings of	
Subsidiary Sold on April 1 (i.e., 25% of $48,000)	12,000
Adjusted Consolidated Retained Earnings	$248,000

The adjustment is $12,000 and is, as outlined above, 25% of the parent company's share of the post-acquisition net income of $48,000.

WHERE A DISPOSAL RESULTS IN A REVERSION TO THE COST METHOD

In the section dealing with the necessity to change from a cost to an equity method of recording longterm investments, it was pointed out that in Canada the earnings of affected companies are not adjusted retroactively. The same applies when the opposite occurs (i.e., conversion from an equity to a cost method). There is, consequently, no change and earnings which were previously treated as the parent company's share of net income from the subsidiary remain as part of the carrying value of the investment. In this respect, the CICA *Handbook*[15] states quite explicitly that:

> When an investment no longer qualifies for the equity method an investor will discontinue accruing its share of the income and losses of the investee. The income and losses that relate to the shares retained by the investor and that were previously accrued would remain as a part of the carrying value of the investment. The investment account would **not be adjusted retroactively** under these conditions. However, accumulated dividends received by the investor in subsequent periods that exceed its share of accumulated earnings for such periods would be applied [as pre-acquisition dividends] in reduction of the carrying value of the investment.

---

[15] The explanatory material in para. 3050.24 as recommended in para. 3050.25.

SUMMARY

This chapter deals with step acquisitions and disposals of part interests in subsidiaries. With step acquisitions, the cost method is used to account for the acquisition until such time as significant influence is exercisable over the investee company, at which time the equity method must be used. The preparation of the consolidated income statement differs in the year of acquisition depending upon whether the change to control is from a cost to an equity basis.

With disposals of part interests in a subsidiary, it is necessary to analyze the investment in the subsidiary to establish exactly what equity has been sold. This is because sales of part interests in subsidiaries include not only the cost of the investment (and part of the goodwill) but also the parent company's right to receive a portion of the subsidiary's post-acquisition retained earnings.

Finally, the chapter examines the position relating to the reversion from an equity to a cost method of recording longterm investments. In these cases, there are no retroactive adjustments to retained earnings. Any earnings recognized as the parent company's share of net income from the subsidiary remain as part of the carrying value of the investment.

SELF-STUDY PROBLEMS

(Problem 12A covers step acquisitions where significant influence is exercisable after the first acquisition and control after the second, and Problem 12B covers step acquisitions where control is only exercisable after the second acquisition.)

PROBLEM 12A†   Pivot Inc. acquired a 40% interest in Shaft Inc. on July 1, 20X7 for $1,460,000. Financial statements were not prepared at the date of acquisition but at January 1, 20X7, Shaft had retained earnings of $650,000. At the date of acquisition, the plant and equipment of Shaft was considered to be fairly valued except for an item of plant having a five-year remaining life and no residual value that was undervalued by $200,000.

On October 1, 20X8, Pivot acquired a further 20% interest in Shaft for $978,000. At that date, all assets were considered to be fairly valued except for an item of plant that had a three-year remaining life and was undervalued by $120,000.

The financial statements of the two companies at December 31, 20X8 were as follows:

COMBINED INCOME AND RETAINED EARNINGS STATEMENT	Pivot	Shaft
Sales	$5,800,000	$3,600,000
Cost of Goods Sold	$2,500,000	$1,240,000
Administration Expenses	1,600,000	1,400,000
	$4,100,000	$2,640,000
Net Income from Operations	$1,700,000	$ 960,000
Gain on Sale of Land	—	120,000
Dividends from Shaft	144,000	—
Net Income for Year	1,844,000	1,080,000
Retained Earnings, January 1, 20X8	1,616,000	1,250,000
	3,460,000	2,330,000
Dividends Paid (December 10)	800,000	240,000
Retained Earnings, December 31, 20X8	$2,660,000	$2,090,000

---

† The solution is provided in Appendix B to this text.

BALANCE SHEETS	Pivot	Shaft
Current Assets	$2,202,000	$1,740,000
Investment in Shaft	2,438,000	—
Plant and Equipment (Net)	4,200,000	2,770,000
	$8,840,000	$4,510,000
Accounts Payable	$1,180,000	$ 220,000
Common Stock	5,000,000	2,200,000
Retained Earnings	2,660,000	2,090,000
	$8,840,000	$4,510,000

You are also informed that:

1. During 20X7, Shaft had earned net income of $800,000 and paid a dividend on November 10 of $200,000.
2. Goodwill was written down by $5,000 for impairment in October 20X7 and by a further $3,000 in June 20X8.
3. The gain on sale of land relates to the sale of land with a book value of $300,000 held by Shaft to Pivot for $420,000 on November 1, 20X8.

REQUIRED

Prepare the consolidated income and retained earnings statement and consolidated balance sheet of Pivot for 20X8.

PROBLEM 12B†   You are informed that:

(a) Protect Inc. had acquired a 75% interest in Shield Inc. in two purchases. On July 1, 20X4 it purchased 30,000 shares for $28.00 each (i.e., $840,000). An additional 120,000 shares were purchased on April 1, 20X5 for $26.00 each (i.e., $3,120,000).

(b) Financial statements were not prepared at the dates on which the shares were purchased but at January 1, 20X4, Shield had retained earnings of $1.4-million. On April 1, 20X5, the assets of Shield were considered to be fairly valued except for an item of plant having a five-year remaining life and no residual value that was undervalued by $320,000.

(c) During 20X4, Shield had earned net income of $1.2-million and it had paid an interim dividend of $160,000 on March 12 and a final dividend of $240,000 on December 7.

(d) Goodwill was written down for impairment by $34,000 in October 20X5.

The abbreviated combined income and retained earnings statements and balance sheets of Protect and Shield at December 31, 20X5 were as follows:

COMBINED INCOME AND RETAINED EARNINGS STATEMENTS	Protect	Shield
Sales	$ 6,200,000	$5,200,000
Cost of Goods Sold	$ 2,200,000	$1,700,000
Administration and Other Expenses	1,600,000	1,900,000
Total Operating Expenses	$ 3,800,000	$3,600,000
Net Income from Operations	$ 2,400,000	$1,600,000
Dividends from Shield Inc.	270,000	—
Net Income for Year	2,670,000	1,600,000
Retained Earnings at January 1, 20X5	3,600,000	2,200,000
	6,270,000	3,800,000
Dividends Declared and Paid:		
Interim on March 10	—	(200,000)
Final on December 3	720,000	(320,000)
Retained Earnings at December 31, 20X5	$ 5,550,000	$3,280,000

---

† The solution is provided in Appendix B to this text.

BALANCE SHEETS	Protect	Shield
Current Assets	$ 2,540,000	$1,640,000
Investment in Shield	3,960,000	—
Plant and Equipment	4,290,000	4,280,000
	$10,790,000	$5,920,000
Current Liabilities	1,240,000	640,000
Common Stock:		
8,000,000 shares of no par value issued at 50 cents each	4,000,000	—
200,000 shares of no par value issued at $10 each	—	2,000,000
Retained Earnings	5,550,000	3,280,000
	$10,790,000	$5,920,000

REQUIRED

Prepare the combined consolidated income statement and statement of retained earnings of Protect for 20X5.

REVIEW QUESTIONS

1. Explain what you understand by the term, "insider trading".
2. What is the "early warning requirement" and why is it required by the various provincial securities commissions?
3. Differentiate between friendly and hostile takeovers.
4. What do you understand by the term "a leveraged buyout"?
5. What is the basic rule covering the recognition of income from a subsidiary where the controlling interest has been acquired in two separate transactions in the same year?
6. How is goodwill affected by the disposal of a part interest in a subsidiary?
7. Explain how fair market value adjustments are treated in step acquisitions of interests in subsidiaries where the original investment **did not** allow the investor company to exert significant influence over the affairs of the investee company.
8. On the date that an 80% interest in a subsidiary was acquired, the plant and equipment having a 10-year life was undervalued by $40,000. What adjustment to the investment account in respect of the undervalued plant and equipment would be necessary if the interest in the subsidiary was reduced to 60% exactly two years after acquisition of the 80% interest?
9. Income is only recognized from the date of each acquisition in the case of step acquisitions of interests in a subsidiary. Why then should the parent company's share of net income from a subsidiary be calculated for the entire year on its interest at the end of the year in the case of a disposal of a part of its interest in a subsidiary?
10. Why is it necessary in the case of a disposal of a part interest in a subsidiary, to break the cost of the equity sold down into its various elements?
11. Explain how the sale of a part interest in a subsidiary some years after acquisition is disclosed in the consolidated financial statements in the year of disposal.
12. Explain what adjustments, if any, are necessary where the disposal of a part interest in an investee company makes a change from the equity to the cost method obligatory.

EXERCISES

EXERCISE 12–1   On April 1, 20X2, Pitch Inc. purchased a 20% interest in Sway Inc. for $52,000. On that date, the fair market value of the depreciable assets of Sway having an 8 year remaining life were considered to be undervalued by $40,000. At January 1, 20X2, the equity of Sway consisted of common stock of $100,000 and retained earnings of $25,000.

Six months later, Pitch purchased another 40% interest in Sway for $95,000. The assets that had been undervalued at April 1, 20X2 were now undervalued by $37,500 and had a useful expected life of 7½ years. No other changes were necessary.

The net incomes of Pitch and Sway for the year ended December 31, 20X2, before making any adjustment for the purchase of the controlling interest in Sway, were $400,000 and $80,000 respectively.

REQUIRED

Calculate the consolidated net income for 20X2 of Pitch on the assumption that Pitch could exert significant influence over the affairs of Sway after the purchase of the 20% interest on April 1, 20X2, and that goodwill was written down for impairment by $1,000 in December 20X2. Ignore income tax effects.

EXERCISE 12–2   You are provided with the following extracts from the balance sheets of Postage Inc. and Stamp Inc. at December 31, 20X5:

	Postage	Stamp
Common Stock (shares of no par value issued at $10 each)	$500,000	$100,000
Retained Earnings:		
Balance at January 1, 20X5	210,000	30,000
Net Trading Income for 20X5	88,000	24,000
Dividends from Stamp	3,000	—
Dividends Declared and Paid (August 20X5)	(48,000)	(10,000)
	$753,000	$144,000

During the calendar year ended December 31, 20X5, Postage's dealings in the stock of Stamp were as follows:

1.   Three-thousand shares were purchased on January 1, 20X5 for $15 each; and
2.   Five-thousand shares were purchased on September 1, 20X5 for $16 each.

The assets and liabilities of Stamp were considered to be fairly valued throughout 20X5. Goodwill was written down for impairment by $1,000 in June 20X5 and a further $1,500 in November 20X5.

REQUIRED

Prepare the combined consolidated income and retained earnings statement of Postage for the year ended December 31, 20X5. Ignore income tax effects.

EXERCISE 12–3   On October 1, 20X2, Pilchard Inc. purchased a 10% interest in Sardine Inc. for $100,000. At January 1, 20X2, the equity of Sardine consisted of common stock of $400,000 and retained earnings of $300,000.

Nine months later on June 30, 20X3, Pilchard purchased another 60% interest in Sardine for $550,000. At that date, it was determined that certain plant and equipment of Sardine having a 10-year remaining life was undervalued by $60,000.

Information relating to the trading activities and dividends paid by Pilchard and Sardine for the two years ended December 31, 20X3 were as follows:

	Pilchard		Sardine	
	20X2	**20X3**	**20X2**	**20X3**
Net Trading Income	$400,000	$440,000	$120,000	$160,000
Dividends Declared and Paid:				
Interim on May 31	—	—	10,000	30,000
Final on November 30	140,000	150,000	20,000	40,000

REQUIRED

Calculate the consolidated net income for Pilchard for 20X2 and 20X3 if goodwill was written down for impairment by $1,000 in December 20X3. Ignore income tax effects.

EXERCISE 12–4

On April 1, 20X2, Province Inc. purchased a 30% interest in State Inc. for $600,000 that **did not** allow it to exert significant influence over the affairs of State. At January 1, 20X2, the equity of State had consisted of common stock of $1-million and retained earnings of $300,000.

Six months later, on October 1, 20X2, Province purchased another 30% interest in State for $660,000. After this purchase, Province **could** exert control over the affairs of State. On that date, a revaluation of all assets and liabilities of State was carried out and it was determined that certain assets having a 10-year remaining useful life (with no residual value) were undervalued by $400,000.

You are also informed that:

(a) The net incomes of Province and State for the year ended December 31, 20X2, before making any adjustment for the purchase of the controlling interest in State, were $4-million and $800,000 respectively.

(b) During 20X2, State declared and paid an interim dividend of $160,000 on September 1 and a final dividend of another $160,000 on December 15.

(c) Goodwill was written down for impairment by $4,000 in December 20X2.

REQUIRED

Give the consolidated net income of Province for 20X2, including all income from State to which it is entitled. Ignore income tax effects.

EXERCISE 12–5

On January 1, 20X4, Play Inc. purchased a 10% interest in Serve Inc. for $32,500 when Serve had common stock of $200,000 and retained earnings of $60,000.

Play purchased an additional 50% interest in Serve on July 1, 20X5 for $270,000. At that date, the net assets of Serve were considered to be fairly valued except for certain plant having a 10-year life, which was undervalued by $40,000. Goodwill was written down for impairment by $5,000 in December 20X5.

The net incomes (excluding any share of the net income from longterm investments in subsidiaries) and dividends paid by the two companies for the years ended December 31, 20X4 and 20X5 were as follows:

		Play	Serve
20X4:	Net Income from Operations	$200,000	$120,000
	Dividends Declared and Paid (October)	80,000	40,000
20X5:	Net Income	240,000	150,000
	Dividends Declared and Paid (November)	100,000	50,000

REQUIRED

Ignoring income tax effects, give answers **with suitable explanations** to the following questions:

1. What goodwill, if any, arose as a result of the first acquisition? The second acquisition?
2. What income from Serve was included in the consolidated income statement in 20X4? In 20X5?
3. What adjustment for the excess depreciation on the fair market value of assets was recognized by Play in 20X4? In 20X5?
4. What was Play's net income in 20X4?
5. What was the consolidated net income for 20X5?

EXERCISE 12–6 On January 1, 20X4, Plaice Inc. had purchased a 75% interest in Sole Inc. The investment was recorded using the equity method, and the ledger account at December 31, 20X4 was as follows:

Investment in Sole

20X4				
Jan. 1	Purchase Consideration	220,000		220,000
Dec. 10	Dividends Received		60,000	160,000
Dec. 31	Net Income	120,000		
	Goodwill Impairment		4,000	
	FMV Adjustment		3,000	273,000

The adjustments to the fair market values of the net assets were being amortized on a straight-line basis over 10 years.

On July 1, 20X5, Plaice sold 20% of its interest in Sole for $80,000. Financial statements were not prepared at July 1, 20X5 but the net income of Sole for the year ended December 31, 20X5 amounted to $240,000, which was assumed to have accrued evenly throughout the year.

REQUIRED

From the information given above:

1. Calculate the gain on the sale of part of the investment in Sole; and
2. Complete the Investment in Sole account as it would appear in the ledger of Plaice immediately after the sale of part of the investment in Sole (ignore income tax effects).

EXERCISE 12–7 On August 31, 20X3, Plow Inc. purchased a 75% interest in Share Inc. for $750,000. At January 1, 20X3, Share had common stock of $500,000 and retained earnings of $240,000. At the date of acquisition, certain plant having a five-year remaining life was undervalued by $40,000. Net income for 20X3 was $90,000. Goodwill was written down for impairment by $5,000 in November 20X3.

On December 31, 20X3, Plow sold 20% of its interest in Share for $160,000.

REQUIRED

1. Give the "Investment in Share" account as it would appear in the ledger of Plow at December 31, 20X3 after the sale of the investment if the equity method was used.
2. Give the journal entry recording the sale of part of the investment.
3. Explain what adjustment is necessary on the balance sheet to record the fair market value adjustment at December 31, 20X3.
4. Give the adjustment to the goodwill figure appearing on the consolidated balance sheet at December 31, 20X3.

EXERCISE 12–8 On June 30, 20X3, Pike Inc. purchased a 75% interest in Salmon Inc. for $300,000. At January 1, 20X3, Salmon had common stock of $200,000 and retained earnings of $100,000. Net income for 20X3 was $40,000. On June 30, 20X3, the assets and liabilities of Salmon were considered to be fairly valued except for plant and equipment having a five-year remaining life that was undervalued by $40,000. Goodwill was written down by $5,000 for impairment in November 20X3.

On December 31, 20X3, Pike sold 20% of its interest in Salmon for $65,000.

REQUIRED

Ignoring income tax effects:

1. Give the "Investment in Salmon" account as it would appear in the ledger of Pike on January 1, 20X4 on the assumption that the full equity method of accounting for the investment was used.

2. Calculate the gain or loss on the disposal of the part interest in Salmon.
3. What adjustment to the goodwill arising on consolidation is required in view of the sale of part of the investment?
4. How would the fair market value adjustments be reflected on the consolidated balance sheet after the disposal of the part interest?

PROBLEMS

PROBLEM 12–1

On July 1, 20X4, Pilfer Inc. purchased a 40% interest in Steal Inc. for $108,000 which allowed Pilfer to exert significant influence over the affairs of Steal. On the date of acquisition, the fair market value of the depreciable assets of Steal having a five-year remaining life were considered to be undervalued by $40,000. At January 1, 20X4 the equity of Steal consisted of common stock of $100,000 and retained earnings of $30,000. Goodwill was written down for impairment by $2,000 in August 20X4 and a further $3,000 in December 20X4.

Three months later, Pilfer purchased another 20% interest in Steal for $53,000. The assets that had been undervalued at July 1, 20X4 were now undervalued by $36,000 and their useful life had been revised at six years. No other changes were necessary.

The trading activities of Pilfer and Steal for the year ended December 31, 20X4, **excluding** any adjustment for the purchase of the controlling interest in Steal, were as follows:

	Pilfer	**Steal**
Sales	$900,000	$320,000
Expenses	400,000	220,000
Net Income for Year	$500,000	$100,000

You are also informed that at January 1, 20X4, Pilfer had retained earnings of $420,000.

REQUIRED

Prepare the combined consolidated statement of income and retained earnings for the year ended December 31, 20X4.

PROBLEM 12–2

On January 1, 20X6, Peter Inc. purchased a 40% interest in Simon Inc. for $72,000 when Simon had common stock of $100,000 and retained earnings of $40,000. At the date of acquisition, the assets and liabilities of Simon were considered to be fairly valued. All revenues and expenses accrued evenly throughout the year. Goodwill was written down for impairment by $2,000 in May 20X6 and by a further $3,000 in November 20X8.

The trading activities of Simon for 20X6 and 20X7 were such that it had earned net income of $160,000 and paid dividends of $145,000.

The abbreviated financial statements of the two companies at December 31, 20X8 were as follows:

BALANCE SHEETS	**Peter**	**Simon**
Current Assets	$170,500	$ 75,000
Investment in Simon	117,000	—
Plant and Equipment (Net)	300,000	155,000
	$587,500	$230,000
Current Liabilities	$ 65,000	$ 35,000
Common Stock	300,000	100,000
Retained Earnings	222,500	95,000
	$587,500	$230,000

COMBINED INCOME AND RETAINED EARNINGS STATEMENTS	Peter	Simon
Sales	$600,000	$300,000
Cost of Goods Sold	$300,000	$200,000
Operating Expenses	120,000	40,000
	$420,000	$240,000
Net Operating Income	$180,000	$60,000
Dividends from Simon	12,000	—
Net Income	192,000	60,000
Retained Earnings at January 1, 20X8	90,500	55,000
	282,500	115,000
Dividends Declared and Paid (December 10)	60,000	20,000
Retained Earnings at December 31, 20X8	$222,500	$ 95,000

REQUIRED

Prepare the consolidated balance sheet and combined income and retained earnings statement for 20X8 on the assumption that on June 30, 20X8, Peter purchased a further 20% interest in Simon for $45,000 and there was no change in the value of the net assets.

PROBLEM 12–3 The equity section of the balance sheet of Strong Inc. at January 1, 20X4 was as follows:

Common Stock: 20,000 shares of no par value	$600,000
Retained Earnings	100,000
	$700,000

During the two years ended December 31, 20X5, the trading results and dividends paid by Strong were as follows:

Year	Net Income	Dividends Declared and Paid
20X4	$240,000	$80,000 — August 25
20X5	320,000	$80,000 — October 30

Pungent Inc.'s dealings in the stock of Strong were as follows:

(a) Purchased 5,000 shares in Strong on July 1, 20X4 for $50 each. This purchase allowed Pungent to exert significant influence over the affairs of Strong.

(b) Purchased another 6,000 shares in Strong on October 1, 20X5 for $60 each.

On July 1, 20X4, the assets of Strong were considered to be fairly valued except for an item of equipment having a five-year remaining life that was considered to be undervalued by $40,000. The value of the same piece of equipment on September 30, 20X5 was unchanged (i.e., undervalued by $40,000), but on that date it was estimated that it only had a four-year remaining useful life. Goodwill was written down for impairment by $3,000 in December 20X4 and by a further $4,000 in November 20X5.

Additional relevant information relating to Pungent was as follows:

Net Operating Income for 20X4	$400,000
Dividends Declared and Paid in 20X4	180,000
Net Operating Net Income for 20X5	420,000
Dividends Declared and Paid in 20X5	200,000
Retained Earnings at December 31, 20X4 determined using the full equity method	810,000

REQUIRED

From the information given above, calculate:

1. The goodwill appearing on the consolidated balance sheet at December 31, 20X5

2. The consolidated net income for 20X4
3. The consolidated net income for 20X5
4. The consolidated retained earnings at December 31, 20X5
5. The net adjustment to the equipment appearing on the consolidated balance sheet at December 31, 20X5

PROBLEM 12–4

On July 1, 20X3, Plate Inc. purchased a 30% interest in Spoon Inc. for $75,000 that allowed it to exercise significant influence over the affairs of Spoon. At January 1, 20X3, Spoon had retained earnings of $40,000. On that date, it was also established that on acquisition date the depreciable plant and equipment of Spoon was undervalued by $60,000 and that the assets to which these values applied would last 10 years from that date. Goodwill was written down for impairment by $5,000 in December 20X4.

On June 30, 20X8, Plate purchased a further 35% interest in Spoon for $81,500. At that date, other than the decrease in value as a result of depreciation, the fair market value of the depreciable assets referred to above had not changed; these assets were, therefore, now undervalued by $30,000 and had a remaining useful life of five years.

The abbreviated financial statements of the two companies at December 31, 20X8 were as follows:

COMBINED INCOME AND RETAINED EARNINGS STATEMENTS	Plate	Spoon
Sales	$980,000	$400,000
Cost of Goods Sold	$500,000	$250,000
Operating Expenses	300,000	100,000
	$800,000	$350,000
Net Operating Income	$180,000	$ 50,000
Dividends from Spoon	13,000	—
Net Income	193,000	50,000
Retained Earnings at January 1, 20X8	89,500	55,000
	282,500	105,000
Less: Dividends (Paid December 10)	60,000	20,000
Retained Earnings at December 31, 20X8	$222,500	$ 85,000

BALANCE SHEETS		
Current Assets	$183,000	$110,000
Investment in Spoon	156,500	—
Plant and Equipment (Net)	420,000	135,000
	$759,500	$245,000
Current Liabilities	$137,000	$ 60,000
Common Stock	400,000	100,000
Retained Earnings	222,500	85,000
	$759,500	$245,000

You are also informed that the trading activities and dividends paid by Spoon during the period between January 1, 20X3 to December 31, 20X7 was as follows:

20X3:	Net Income	$ 60,000
	Dividends Paid (September 15)	(20,000)
20X4–7:	Net Income	140,000
	Dividends Paid	(165,000)

REQUIRED

Prepare the consolidated balance sheet and combined income and retained earnings statement of Plate for 20X8.

PROBLEM 12–5 The following information was extracted from the financial statements of Steer Inc. for the two years ended December 31, 20X4 and 20X5:

	20X4	20X5
Common Stock: 20,000 shares of no par value	$400,000	$400,000
Retained Earnings at January 1	200,000	320,000
Net Income from Operations for Year	200,000	240,000
Dividends Paid — August 20X4	80,000	—

You are also informed that:

(a) Pilot Inc.'s purchases of the shares of Steer were as follows:
  i.   Purchased 3,000 shares in Steer on January 1, 20X4 for $62 each. This purchase **did not** permit Pilot to exert significant influence over the affairs of Steer.
  ii. Purchased another 9,000 shares in Steer on July 1, 20X5 for $60 each.

(b) Goodwill was written down for impairment by $25,000 in December 20X5.

(c) In view of the economic conditions prevailing on July 1, 20X5, the net assets of Steer were considered to be fairly valued on that date.

REQUIRED

Provide answers to the following questions:

1.   What goodwill arose for consolidation purposes from the first acquisition of the shares in Steer on January 1, 20X4?
2.   What goodwill arose from the second acquisition of shares in Steer on July 1, 20X5?
3.   What income from Steer was recognized by Pilot for the Year Ended December 31, 20X4?
4.   What income would have been recognized by Pilot as having been contributed by Steer for the first six months of 20X5?
5.   What were the minority interests in Steer appearing on the consolidated balance sheet at December 31, 20X5?
6.   What would the consolidated net income of Pilot for 20X5 have been if the net income from operations of Pilot for 20X5 had amounted to $600,000?

PROBLEM 12–6 You are informed that:

1.   During 20X2, Perfume Inc. purchased a 100% interest in Scent Inc. in three purchases as follows:
  (a) A 20% interest, which **did not** allow it to exert significant influence over the affairs of Scent on January 1, 20X2 for $180,000;
  (b) An additional 20% interest on May 1, 20X2 for $258,000; and
  (c) The purchase of the entire 60% holdings of the minority interests from them on September 1, 20X2 for $706,000.

2.   On May 1, 20X2, the assets and liabilities of Scent were considered to be fairly valued except for an item of plant having a 10-year remaining life and no residual value, which was undervalued by $90,000. At September 1, 20X2, this same item of equipment was still considered to be undervalued, but now by $100,000, and to still have a remaining 10-year life from that date. Goodwill was written down for impairment by $4,000 in June 20X2 and by a further $6,000 in December 20X2. All revenues and expenses accrued evenly throughout the year.

The abbreviated financial statements of Perfume and Scent at December 31, 20X2 were as follows:

COMBINED INCOME AND RETAINED EARNINGS STATEMENTS	Perfume	Scent
Sales	$2,900,000	$1,500,000
Operating Expenses	2,200,000	1,200,000
Net Operating Income	700,000	300,000
Dividends from Scent	80,000	—
Net Income	780,000	300,000
Retained Earnings at January 1, 20X2	400,000	260,000
	1,180,000	560,000
Dividends Declared and Paid:		
First interim on March 31	—	(20,000)
Second Interim on July 15	(200,000)	(40,000)
Final on December 15	(250,000)	(60,000)
Retained Earnings at December 31, 20X2	$ 730,000	$ 440,000

BALANCE SHEETS		
Current Assets	$ 886,000	$ 440,000
Investment in Scent	1,144,000	—
Plant and Equipment (Net)	1,032,000	800,000
	$3,062,000	$1,240,000
Current Liabilities	$ 532,000	$ 200,000
Common Stock	1,800,000	600,000
Retained Earnings	730,000	440,000
	$3,062,000	$1,240,000

REQUIRED

Prepare the consolidated combined income and retained earnings statement and consolidated balance sheet of Perfume for the year ended December 31, 20X2.

PROBLEM 12-7 The equity section of the balance sheet of Stay Inc. at January 1, 20X4 was as follows:

Common Stock: 20,000 shares of no par value	$400,000
Retained Earnings	200,000
	$600,000

During the two years ended December 31, 20X5, the trading results and dividends paid by Stay were as follows:

Year	Net Income	Dividends Declared and Paid
20X4	$200,000	$80,000 — August
20X5	240,000	$60,000 — October

Park Inc.'s dealings in the stock of Stay were as follows:

(a) Purchased 3,000 shares in Stay on July 1, 20X4 for $40 each. This purchase did not permit Park to exert significant influence over the affairs of Stay.
(b) Purchased another 9,000 shares in Stay on September 1, 20X5 for $45 each.
(c) Sold 4,000 shares in Stay on January 1, 20X6 for $44 per share.

Goodwill was written down for impairment by $4,000 in December 20X5.

REQUIRED

Answers to the following questions:

1. What goodwill arose from the first acquisition of the shares in Stay on July 1, 20X4?

2. What goodwill arose from the second acquisition of shares in Stay on September 1, 20X5?
3. What income from Stay was recognized in 20X4 by Park for the Year Ended December 31, 20X4?
4. What income from Stay was recognized by Park for the year ended December 31, 20X5?
5. What were the minority interests in Stay appearing on the consolidated balance sheet at December 31, 20X5?
6. What was the gain or loss on the sale of the 4,000 shares in Stay on January 1, 20X6?

PROBLEM 12–8   The following information relates to Poor Inc. and Shabby Inc.:

(a) Poor had purchased a 60% interest in Shabby for $480,000 on January 1, 20X1 when Shabby had common stock of $500,000 (i.e., 500,000 common shares of no par value) and retained earnings of $200,000. At the date of acquisition, the net assets of Shabby were considered to be fairly valued. Goodwill arising on acquisition was written down for impairment by $6,000 in December 20X3 and by a further $3,000 in March 20X5.

(b) The increase in retained earnings of Shabby of $200,000 between the date of acquisition and January 1, 20X5 was made up of net income earned of $300,000 and dividends paid of $100,000.

(c) On July 1, 20X5, Poor sold 75,000 of its shares in Shabby for $200,000. The gain or loss arising from this transaction is of a capital nature and, consequently, it does not appear on the income statement of Poor for 20X5.

(d) The combined income and retained earnings statements of the two companies at December 31, 20X5 were as follows:

	Poor	**Shabby**
Sales	$4,000,000	$3,200,000
Cost of Goods Sold	$1,200,000	$1,800,000
Administration and Other Expenses	1,000,000	900,000
Total Operating Expenses	$2,200,000	$2,700,000
Net Income from Operations	$1,800,000	$ 500,000
Dividends from Shabby	120,000	—
Net Income for Year	1,920,000	500,000
Retained Earnings at January 1, 20X5	1,100,000	400,000
	3,020,000	900,000
Dividends Declared and Paid:		
Interim on May 10	—	(80,000)
Final on December 3	600,000	(120,000)
Retained Earnings at December 31, 20X5	$2,420,000	$ 700,000

REQUIRED

From the information provided above, give:

1. The combined consolidated income statement and statement of retained earnings of Poor for 20X5; and
2. The capital gain or loss from the sale of shares.

PROBLEM 12–9   Passage Inc. accounted for its investment in its 75%-owned subsidiary, Strait Inc., using the full equity method. Passage's interest in Strait had been acquired in two purchases. On July 1, 20X5, Passage sold 20% (i.e., one-fifth) of its investment in Strait for $785,000.

At June 30, 20X5, immediately after the preparation of the financial statements for the six months ended on that date, the investment account in the ledger of Passage was as follows:

Investment in Strait

20X3				
Jan. 1	Purchase Consideration	2,200,000		2,200,000
Dec. 10	Dividends Received — Revenue		320,000	
	Dividends Received — Pre-Acquisition		40,000	1,840,000
Dec. 31	Net Income	320,000		
	Goodwill Impairment		20,000	2,140,000
20X4				
Dec. 5	Dividends Received — Revenue		200,000	1,940,000
Dec. 31	Net Income	300,000		2,240,000
20X5				
Mar. 31	Purchase Consideration	1,280,000		3,520,000
June 24	Dividends Received — Revenue		300,000	3,250,000
June 30	Net Income	450,000		
	Goodwill Impairment		45,000	
	FMV Adjustment — Plant		25,000	3,600,000

Required

1. Give the gain or loss on the sale of shares in Strait.
2. Analyze the equity sold into the three categories of equity, retained earnings, and current net income.
3. Explain how the three amounts established in point 2 above would affect the consolidation of the consolidated financial statements of Strait at December 31, 20X5.

13 Consolidations: Effective Acquisitions and Disposals of Interests

LEARNING OBJECTIVES

After studying this chapter you should be able to:

1. Understand the nature of effective acquisitions and disposals of interests in subsidiaries; and
2. Be able to apply the techniques necessary to account for this aspect of the consolidation process.

EFFECTIVE ACQUISITIONS AND DISPOSALS OF INTERESTS IN SUBSIDIARIES

The extent of control exercised by a parent company over the affairs of a subsidiary may be reduced by either selling part of its interests in a subsidiary or through the issue by the subsidiary of additional shares to outside parties. It is also possible for a parent company to increase its interests in a subsidiary by either purchasing additional shares from the minority shareholders or taking up additional shares issued by the subsidiary.

Even though the purchase and sale of existing shares is commonplace, the position relating to changes in ownership arising from the issue of additional shares is somewhat rare and requires a different analysis. This is because such changes in ownership represent effective acquisitions or disposals of interests in subsidiary companies. It is also an area to which few specific rules apply. However, the basic principles relating to the accounting for these effective acquisitions and disposals of interests are examined in this chapter.

In view of the complexity of the material covered in this chapter, income tax considerations have been ignored. These would, of course, be taken into account in practice.

THE REQUIREMENTS FOR THE ISSUE OF SHARES

The issue of corporate securities is strictly controlled to avoid the possibility that corporate officers would misuse their positions of trust and issue shares to themselves, related parties, or other persons at prices below their current market value. This control is exercised either directly through the application of corporate law or by the regulation of the marketing of

324

corporate securities.[1] A detailed discussion of the ways in which control over the issue of securities is carried out is beyond the scope of this chapter, but for a full understanding of the material covered in this chapter it is necessary to briefly outline the conditions under which shares may be issued.

The most common way in which shares in companies are issued is on the formation of a company. In these cases, besides the issue of a certain number of shares to those persons who were the original applicants for incorporation of the company, the directors are empowered to issue shares to those persons who have subscribed and paid for shares in the company. These shares may be issued to a single company, an individual, or to a large number of individual shareholders. Any shares not taken up are usually controlled by the directors, who can issue them at their discretion to whomever they like. Very often, the sale of shares to the investing public is through an underwriter, who undertakes to sell the shares in the company in return for a fee or commission.

All **public issues** of shares must be preceded by the issuing of a prospectus. This is a document issued by the promoters of the company for the first issue of shares and, thereafter, by the company for each additional share issue.[2] It is a detailed document providing full information on the company and its activities, its management, the share issue, and other relevant information.

From time to time, companies issue additional shares. These additional shares may be offered either to the existing shareholders or to outside interests, depending upon the purpose of the issue. Normally, issues to shareholders are made to increase the share capital of the company concerned. Issues to outside interests may be made to acquire assets or control over other companies.

Where a company issues additional shares to **its existing shareholders**, these shares are usually offered to them in proportion to their existing shareholdings in the company. This practice is based on the principle that shareholders have a pre-emptive right to maintain their proportionate interest in the company and, consequently, they should be able to purchase additional shares in the company in proportion to their existing holdings. In Canada, this right is **not enshrined in law** and, even though many companies voluntarily follow this principle, it must be specifically included in the articles of incorporation to be enforceable. It also only applies to shares that are issued for cash.[3]

Where shares are offered to shareholders, they have the right to take up the shares themselves, waive their rights to these shares, or to sell their rights to someone else. Where the shareholders waive their rights to take up shares or fail to comply with the terms of the issue, the shares may be issued to anyone at the discretion of the directors. Other than any restrictions placed on the directors by the articles of incorporation relating to the shareholders' pre-emptive rights, any unanimous shareholder agreements, or other legal restrictions imposed through securities legislation, the only restriction placed on the directors is that the shares may not be issued for less than their fair market value.[4]

Where the shares are issued to a single company or individual **to acquire certain assets or control over another company**, the shares are issued following the passing of a special resolution at a special general meeting of the company called for that specific purpose. In most jurisdictions, the passing of a special resolution requires the approval of two-thirds majority of the shareholders having voting rights and who have exercised this right in person or by proxy.[5] Where a two-thirds majority is not obtained, the meeting is adjourned and, on re-convening, a simple majority usually suffices. After being passed by the special general meeting, the special

---

[1] For example, by the Securities Commissions in Alberta, British Columbia, Ontario and Quebec.
[2] For example, as required by the Ontario *Securities Act*, sections 52–53.
[3] *Canada Business Corporations Act*, section 28.
[4] *Ibid.*, section 25.
[5] *Ibid.*, section 133.

ILLUSTRATION 13–1

ESTABLISHING THE GAIN OR LOSS ON THE ISSUE OF SHARES BY A SUBSIDIARY TO OUTSIDE INTERESTS BEFORE AND AFTER THE SHARE ISSUE

Parent Inc. acquired a 90% interest in Subsidiary Inc. on January 1, 20X7 for $150,000 when Subsidiary had common stock of 100,000 shares of no par value which had been issued for $1.00 per share and retained earnings of $60,000. During the year ended December 31, 20X7, Subsidiary reported net income of $80,000 which included the write-off of goodwill of $300 for impairment.

On January 1, 20X8 Subsidiary issued another 20,000 shares of common stock to its minority shareholders at $1.25 per share.

The calculation of the gain or loss to Parent on the additional share issue by Subsidiary may be carried out by analyzing the equity before and after the share issue as follows:

	Total (100,000 shares)	Parent (90,000 shares)	Minority Interests (10,000 shares)
Analysis of Equity before Issue:			
Common Stock (100,000 shares)	$100,000	$ 90,000	$ 10,000
Retained Earnings	60,000	54,000	6,000
		144,000	16,000
Purchase Consideration		150,000	
Goodwill		$ 6,000	

Goodwill Impairment of $300

Net Income — 20X7	80,000	72,000	8,000
Minority Interests			$ 24,000

Analysis of Equity after Issue:

On the issue of 20,000 shares of no par value to the minority the interests of the parent company drops from 90% to 75% (90,000/120,000 shares) and that of the minority increases from 10% to 25% (30,000/120,000 shares).

		Total (120,000 shares)	Parent (90,000 shares)	Minority Interests (30,000 shares)
Common Stock (120,000 shares)		$125,000	$ 93,750	$ 31,250
Retained Earnings		60,000	45,000	15,000
			138,750	46,250
Purchase Consideration — Note 1				
Original Amount	$150,000			
Less: Goodwill Impairment	300			
	149,700			
Less: Effective Sale — Note 2	6,200		143,500	
Goodwill			$ 4,750	
Net Income — 20X7		80,000	60,000	20,000
Minority Interests				$ 66,250

Gain or Loss on Issue of Shares?

The issue of additional shares resulted in a loss of $18,200, which is calculated in the following manner:

Share of Equity **before** Issue	= 90% of $240,000 =	$216,000
Share of Equity **after** Issue	= 75% of $265,000 =	198,750
		17,250
Add: Effective sale of goodwill (15/90 × [$6,000 − $300])		950
Loss on Issue of Additional Shares		$ 18,200

ILLUSTRATION 13–1 (Continued)

The Detailed Analysis of the Loss is:

Difference in share of Retained Earnings capitalized at date of acquisition and after the additional share issue (i.e., $54,000 − $45,000)	$ 9,000
Less: Increase in Value of Common Stock (i.e., $93,750 − $90,000)	3,750
	5,250
Add: Effective Sale of 1/6th of Goodwill (i.e., [$6,000 − $300] × 15/90) on reduction in effective interest in equity from 90% to 75%, which is $5,700/6)	950
Add: Sale of Net Income since acquisition of (i.e., 90% of $80,000 − 75% of $80,000)	12,000
Loss on Issue of Additional Shares	$ 18,200

Recording of the Effective Loss:

Parent would record the effective loss by means of the following journal entry:

Loss on Issue of Shares in Subsidiary Company	18,200	
Investment in Subsidiary		18,200

Reduction of Investment account to $203,500
(i.e., $143,500 plus share of post-acquisition net income of $60,000)

Notes:

[1] The purchase consideration must be adjusted for any write-down of goodwill.

[2] The purchase consideration is reduced by $6,200 being the change in retained earnings of $9,000 (i.e., $54,000 − $45,000) as adjusted by the goodwill sold of $950 (i.e., 15/90 of $5,700 [$6,000 − $300]) less the increase in the share of the common stock of $3,750 (i.e., $93,750 − $90,000).

---

resolution must normally be approved by either the Supreme Court having jurisdiction in that area or the body having the authority to oversee share dealings in that area like, for example, the Ontario Securities Commission.

DISPOSAL OF AN INTEREST THROUGH THE ISSUE OF SHARES TO OUTSIDE PARTIES

In recent years, many large public companies have formed subsidiaries and then sold part of their interests in these subsidiaries to the general public. Reasons for this are that the parent company may wish to realize a gain on the appreciation in the value of its investments, reduce their risk and/or cash requirements in financing the activities of the subsidiaries, or draw the attention of investors to the subsidiaries rather than to the parent company itself. It may also do so to divest itself of control.[6]

As outlined earlier, when shares are issued by the subsidiary company to external parties, an effective disposal of interests occurs because there is a dilution of the extent of control exercised by the parent company. This dilution affects not only the actual degree of control but also the parent company's share of the retained earnings, the current earnings and any capital surpluses in existence prior to the issue of additional shares.

For example, if a parent company holds a 90% interest in a subsidiary having 100,000 common shares, the subsequent issue of an additional 20,000 shares to outside parties would

---

[6] For example, on February 5, 1993, *The Globe and Mail* reported that Quno Corporation, formerly the Quebec and Ontario Paper Company Ltd., had filed a $135-million initial public offering of shares. The move was designed to allow its parent company, Chicago-based Tribune Company, to relinquish voting control over Quno Corporation. The move would increase the general public's interest in the voting shares to 51%. Reasons given were that Tribune would be able to "deconsolidate" the money-losing newsprint maker from its financial statements and use the equity method of accounting so that it only needs to recognize its share of Quno's losses.

reduce the parent company's interest in the subsidiary from a 90% to a 75% interest (i.e., from 90,000/100,000 shares to 90,000/120,000 shares). This means that the parent company has given, lost, sold, or otherwise divested itself of a 15% interest in the subsidiary to minority interests.

The accounting for **effective disposals of interests in subsidiaries** involves a reduction in the carrying value of the investment in the books of the parent company and a recognition of a gain or loss arising from the issue of shares. From an accounting point of view, there is no difference whatsoever between any gains or losses arising from effective disposals or normal sales of shares. As a result, the CICA *Handbook*[7] requires that when a subsidiary company issues shares to interests outside the consolidated group, the effect of the change in the parent's interest as a result of the share issue should enter into the determination of consolidated net income. Whether or not the gain is of a revenue or capital nature is, however, not clear.

The most important aspect in accounting for these effective disposals of interests in subsidiaries is to establish the gain or loss arising from the share issue and any effective sale of net income earned subsequent to the original acquisition. This can be established **in two ways**. The one is to compare the situation "before and after" the share issue. The second, and more common method, is to analyze the "investment account" at the date of sale to establish the impact of the effective sale on the interest in the subsidiary. Irrespective of which method is used, it is important to note that, in addition to the gain or loss on the effective disposal of the interest, an adjustment to the net income earned since acquisition is also required.

An explanation of the establishment of the gain or loss arising from an effective disposal of interests in a subsidiary by comparing the position "before and after" the share issue is provided by Illustration 13–1. In this case, the actual effective loss on the share issue amounted to $18,200, made up of the forfeiture of capitalized retained earnings at the date of acquisition of $9,000, and goodwill of $950 that is only partly offset by an increase in the share of common stock of $3,750. There is also the effective sale of net income since acquisition of $12,000. These amounts are reflected in the "Investment in Subsidiary Inc." account in the ledger of Parent and would be adjusted in the consolidated income statement.

The alternative calculation of the effective gain or loss arising from the additional share issue is provided by Illustration 13–2 which uses the same information as Illustration 13–1. This method is based on the analysis of the investment account after the share issue.

In Illustration 13–2, the loss on the effective disposal of interests of $18,200 is established by determining the difference between the amounts of the share of the investment effectively sold of $36,950 and the Parent's share of the proceeds of the share issue of $18,750. This determination can be made using a four-step procedure or by analyzing the adjustments to the investment account.

The adjustments and disclosure of information relating to an effective disposal of interests are relatively simple. In the case of the position outlined in Illustrations 13–1 and 13–2, the adjustment is made up of two items. First, there is the effective sale of the part interest of the investment of $6,200 (i.e., the effective sale of pre-acquisition retained earnings of $9,000, plus part of the goodwill of $950, from which the adjustment to the common stock of $3,750 must be deducted). Second, there is the effective sale of the right to $12,000 of post-acquisition earnings from the subsidiary.

As far as the disclosure of these items is concerned, it would appear that the most suitable disclosure would be to reflect the $6,200 as a "loss on the sale of shares by a subsidiary company" on the consolidated income statement with a suitable explanation, and to deduct the effective sale of the rights to $12,000 of the post-acquisition retained earnings from the opening consolidated retained earnings. Alternatively, the two items could be grouped together but, with post-acquisition retained earnings, this would fail to satisfy the disclosure principle of deducting like items from one another.

---

[7]   Section 1600.

ILLUSTRATION 13–2
ESTABLISHING THE GAIN OR LOSS ON THE ISSUE OF SHARES BY A SUBSIDIARY TO OUTSIDE INTERESTS BY ANALYZING THE INVESTMENT ACCOUNT

Parent Inc. acquired a 90% interest in Subsidiary Inc. on January 1, 20X7 for $150,000 when Subsidiary had common stock of 100,000 shares of no par value that had been issued for $1.00 per share and retained earnings of $60,000. During the year ended December 31, 20X7, Subsidiary reported net income of $80,000, which included the write-off of goodwill of $300 for impairment.

On January 1, 20X8 Subsidiary issued another 20,000 shares of common stock to its minority shareholders at $1.25 per share. On that date, the investment account **after adjustments** for the additional share issue would have been as follows (refer to analysis of equity before additional issue of shares in Illustration 13–1):

Investment in Subsidiary

20X7				
Jan. 1	Purchase Consideration	150,000		150,000
Dec. 31	Share of Net Income	72,000		
	Goodwill Impairment		300	221,700
20X8				
Jan. 1	Loss on Sale of Investment — as detailed below		18,200	203,500

Establishing the Effective Loss:

The effective loss of $18,200, using the following four-step procedure, was determined by:

1. Calculating the change in Patent's ownership in Subsidiary as one-sixth or 16.666%. The interest in Subsidiary held by Parent before the issue of shares by was 90% (i.e., 90,000/100,000), which dropped to 75% (i.e., 90,000/120,000 shares) on the issue of shares.
2. Determining Parent's share of the fair market value of the subsidiary's equity effectively sold by the share issue. This was $36,950 calculated as one-sixth of the equity of $221,700 before the share issue (i.e., $221,700/6).
3. Calculating Parent's share of the new equity raised from the proceeds of the subsidiary's share issue. This was 75% × 20,000 shares × $1.25/share = $18,750.
4. Establishing the loss as the difference between the equity sold by the share issue and Parent's share of the proceeds of the share issue. This was a loss of $36,950 − $18,750 = $18,200.

Analysis of the Effective Loss:

The effective loss of $18,200 could also have been established from the analysis of the investment account and figures from the analysis of equity. This analysis would also have been required to be able to prepare the consolidated financial statements at December 31, 20X8. This analysis was:

Sale of Retained Earnings at Acquisition	
90% of $60,000 − 75% of $60,000 = $54,000 − $45,000 =	$ 9,000
Add: Sale of 1/6th of Goodwill Remaining	950
	9,950
Less: Adjustment to Purchase Consideration − 1/6th of Proceeds of	
the Additional Share issue (20,000 shares at $1.25 = $25,000)	3,750
Sale of 1/6th of Post-Acquisition Earnings − 1/6 × $72,000	6,200
Loss on Effective Sale	12,000
	$ 18,200

The disclosure of the effective loss in the consolidated income statement would have been to show a "loss on sale of shares in subsidiary company of $6,200" (i.e., $9,000 + $950 × $3,750) and to deduct $12,000 from the consolidated retained earnings at January 1, 20X8.

ACQUISITIONS THROUGH THE ISSUE OF SHARES BY A SUBSIDIARY TO ITS PARENT COMPANY

The possibility of encountering a situation where a subsidiary company issues shares to its parent company is somewhat remote. However, anything is possible and this could occur no matter how improbable it may appear to be. For example, it could occur where an offer to take up shares has been made to existing shareholders in terms of a pre-emptive right and none of the shareholders exercised their options, leaving the parent company in a position to take up all the shares itself. Such an issue could possibly also take place in cases where the parent company sells assets to its subsidiary and the selling price is to be settled by a share issue. However, no matter how well intentioned any such sale may be, it would be difficult to obtain approval of such action from a securities commission. However, these transactions represent effective acquisitions of interests in subsidiaries, and this section deals with the accounting for them.

ISSUING SHARES TO THE PARENT COMPANY

The Issue of Shares at Their Fair Value

The issue of additional shares by a subsidiary to its parent company is treated in the same way as step acquisitions. The value of the shares that must be issued at their fair market value is offset against the equity acquired to give the goodwill or negative goodwill arising on consolidation. This position is outlined in Illustration 13–3, which shows that the equity acquired as a result of the issue of shares to the parent company was greater than the purchase consideration and gave rise to negative goodwill of $2,000. In other respects, the adjustment to the equity at the date of acquisition and the net income from that date are calculated in exactly the same manner as that applying to normal acquisitions of additional interests in subsidiaries.

It is important to note that the negative goodwill in Illustration 13–3 arose from the reapportionment of the equity between the parent and the subsidiary. This represents an effective acquisition because additional interests of $2,000 (i.e., $4,000 + $4,000 – $6,000) were transferred from the minority to the parent company.

The Treatment of the Negative Goodwill

There are two schools of thought regarding the treatment of negative goodwill arising in these cases.

The first holds that the negative goodwill should be written off against the proportionate share of the nonmonetary assets acquired. The second school of thought holds that, as the negative goodwill applies to the acquisition of the controlling interest in the subsidiary, it should be deducted from any unamortized goodwill remaining from the first acquisition. The argument is that as the two amounts for goodwill arise from the acquisition of the same equity items of the subsidiary, they should be treated as a single amount. The issue has not been resolved, but the latter treatment appears the most logical and practical way to handle the matter.

Disclosure of Effective Acquisitions

The disclosure of information relating to effective acquisitions follows the same form as that applying to effective dispositions. In this respect, any adjustments must be reflected in the income statement. The change in the value of the investment would be reflected as a "gain arising from the issue of shares in a subsidiary" or some other appropriate description. Any additional rights to post-acquisition earnings should preferably be shown as a separate item where they occur.

ILLUSTRATION 13–3

ISSUE OF SHARES BY A SUBSIDIARY DIRECTLY TO ITS PARENT COMPANY

Parent Inc. acquired a 75% interest in Subsidiary Inc. on January 1, 20X4 for $200,000 when Subsidiary had issued 80,000 shares of common stock of no par value for $2 per share and retained earnings of $80,000. On December 31, 20X4 Subsidiary issued an additional 20,000 additional shares directly to Parent at $3.50 per share. At that date, the retained earnings of Subsidiary had increased by $80,000. In December 20X4, the goodwill arising on acquisition was written down for impairment by $4,000.

The analysis of the equity in this situation is as follows:

	Total	Original Acquisition (60,000/80,000 shares or 75% interest)	Additional Acquisition (+20,000 shares to give an 80% interest)	Minority Interests (Reduced from 25% to 20%)
Common Stock (80,000 shares of no par value)	$160,000	$120,000		$40,000
Retained Earnings	80,000	60,000		20,000
		180,000		
Purchase Consideration		200,000		
Goodwill		$ 20,000		

> Goodwill Impairment of $4,000

	Total	Original Acquisition	Additional Acquisition	Minority Interests
Additional Issue of 20,000 shares of Common Stock at $3.50/share	70,000		$ 70,000	—
Adjustment to Common Stock to give total interest of 80% of $160,000 + $70,000			(−6,000)	+6,000
Adjustment of Retained Earnings at the Date of Acquisition to correct proportions (i.e., $4,000 [i.e., 80% of $80,000] − $60,000)			+4,000	(4,000)
Net Income for Year	80,000	60,000	4,000	16,000
			72,000	
Purchase Consideration			70,000	
Negative Goodwill	_____		$ 2,000	

> The negative goodwill may be treated as an adjustment to the nonmonetary assets, or offset against the goodwill from the first acquisition.

	Total			Minority Interests
Total Equity	$390,000			
Minority Interests (20% of $390,000)				$78,000

The "Investment in Subsidiary" account in the ledger of Parent at December 31, 20X4 immediately after the recording of the increased investment in Subsidiary but before the adjustment for negative goodwill using the equity method is determined as follows:

Investment in Subsidiary

20X4				
Jan. 1	Purchase Consideration	200,000		
Dec. 31	Purchase Consideration	70,000		
	Net Income	60,000		
	Goodwill Impairment		4,000	326,000

SUMMARY

This chapter examines the position relating to effective acquisitions and disposals of interests in subsidiaries. In this respect, the issue of additional shares in a company to the minority interests results in the effective sale of any capital surplus and retained earnings by the parent to the minority. On the other hand, effective acquisitions occur where additional shares are issued by the subsidiary company to the parent. In these cases, the interest in the shares also entitles the purchasing company to an additional share of the capital surplus and retained earnings, and usually gives rise to negative goodwill. How this item should be treated has not been resolved. However, the possibility of encountering an effective acquisition in practice is somewhat remote.

REVIEW QUESTIONS

1. What adjustments to the investment account and income statement of the parent company are necessary in the case of effective disposals of interests in a subsidiary?
2. Is the goodwill arising on consolidation affected by a subsequent effective disposal of a part interest in a subsidiary? If so, how?
3. How are the effects of an effective disposal of a part interest in a subsidiary disclosed in the consolidated income statement in the year of occurrence? Does anything have to be disclosed on the consolidated balance sheet?
4. In what conditions can a company issue shares in itself to an individual in exchange for certain assets?
5. What adjustments to the equity acquired are necessary when additional shares are issued by a subsidiary to its parent company? Do these adjustments differ if the shares are issued to outside shareholders?
6. How is negative goodwill treated in the case of an effective acquisition of shares in a subsidiary?

EXERCISES

EXERCISE 13–1   Posh Inc. acquired 90% of the issued common stock of Shick Inc. on January 1, 20X5 for $470,000 when Shick had retained earnings of $120,000. During 20X8, however, Shick required additional capital for expansion purposes and, because Posh was unable to raise this capital, Shick issued an additional 100,000 shares of no par value for $200,000 to the general public on July 1, 20X8.

The equity section of the balance sheet of Shick on July 1, 20X8 immediately before and after the share issue was as follows:

	Before	After
Common Stock:		
200,000 shares of no par value	$300,000	
300,000 shares of no par value		$500,000
Retained Earnings	200,000	200,000
Net Income to July 1, 20X8	80,000	80,000
	$580,000	$780,000

Goodwill was written down for impairment by $14,000 in April 20X8.

REQUIRED

Calculate the gain or loss to Posh at July 1, 20X8 arising from the effective disposition of the part interest in Shick.

EXERCISE 13–2 Professor Inc. acquired an 80% interest in Student Inc. on July 1, 20X7 for $210,000. At January 1, 20X7, the equity section of the balance sheet of Student had consisted of common stock of $150,000 (100,000 shares of no par value) and retained earnings of $60,000.

On October 1, 20X7, Student issued 20,000 additional common shares to Professor for $40,000. Net income for 20X7 amounted to $72,000, made up of $30,000 for the six months ended June 30, 20X7, $18,000 for the next three months and $24,000 for the last three months. Goodwill is accounted for on an impairment basis and where negative goodwill arises, this amount is merely deducted from the balance of goodwill on that date. Goodwill was not adjusted for impairment in 20X7.

REQUIRED

Calculate:

1. The share of net income from Student recognized by Professor for 20X7; and
2. The minority interest appearing on the consolidated balance sheet of Professor at December 31, 20X7.
3. The goodwill appearing on the consolidated balance sheet of Professor at December 31, 20X7.

PROBLEMS

PROBLEM 13–1 On January 1, 20X4, Peer Inc. purchased a 25% interest in See Inc. for $50,000 when See had common stock of 80,000 shares of no par value that had been issued for $100,000 and retained earnings of $80,000. The net income for the financial year ended December 31, 20X4 amounted to $40,000.

On June 30, 20X5, Peer was issued an additional 70,000 common shares at $3.50 per share. At that date the assets of See were considered to have been fairly valued. Financial statements were not prepared at June 30, 20X5, but the net income for 20X5 of $120,000 was considered to have been earned evenly throughout the year. A dividend of $50,000 was declared and paid during November 20X5.

REQUIRED

1. Give the "Investment in See" account as it would appear in the ledger of Peer at December 31, 20X5 on the assumption that any goodwill arising on consolidation was not written down for impairment in 20X5.
2. Calculate the total minority interests at December 31, 20X5.

PROBLEM 13–2 Pun Inc.'s interest in Sun Inc. arose through the following transactions:

(a) On January 1, 20X1, Pun purchased 80% of the equity (i.e., 48,000 of 60,000 shares) of Sun for $140,000. At that date the common stock and retained earnings of Sun had amounted to $120,000 and $40,000 respectively.

(b) On July 1, 20X5, Sun had issued an additional 20,000 shares of common stock for $80,000 to outside interests. An income statement at July 1, 20X5 was not prepared but the net income for 20X5, which had accrued evenly throughout the year, amounted to $80,000 before taking the dividend of $20,000 paid on April 30, 20X5 into account.

At December 31, 20X5, the equity section of the balance sheet of Sun was as follows:

Common Stock — 80,000 shares		$200,000
Retained Earnings:		
Balance at January 1, 20X5	$100,000	
Net Income for Year	80,000	
	180,000	
Dividends Paid April 20X5	20,000	160,000
		$360,000

Additional Information:

(a)   Goodwill was written down for Impairment by $4,000 in December 20X1 and by a further $1,000 in December 20X5.

(b)   During the period January 1, 20X1 to December 31, 20X4, Sun had earned net income of $100,000 and paid dividends of $40,000.

REQUIRED

1.   Give the "Investment in Sun" account in the ledger of Pun at December 31, 20X5; and

2.   Determine the gain or loss on the effective disposal of the interest in Sun.

Consolidations: Joint Ventures, Complicated Groups, and Other Matters

14

LEARNING OBJECTIVES

After studying this chapter you should be able to:

1. Understand the nature of joint ventures and the accounting for these entities in Canada;
2. Apply consolidation techniques to complicated groups of companies; and
3. Recognize and eliminate the effects of joint and cross holdings of interests between companies on consolidation.

INTRODUCTION

There are four important aspects of the consolidation process that still have to be covered. These are the accounting for joint ventures, the consolidation of complicated groups of companies, joint holdings and the consolidation of financial statements where cross or reciprocal holdings of interests exist. These four areas are dealt with in this chapter.

A. JOINT VENTURES

Joint ventures are business activities in which two or more persons, enterprises or companies come together to undertake some business venture for their common gain. These ventures normally have relatively short lives, but this is not always the case. This type of venture dates back to the Middle Ages when individuals pooled their resources to finance voyages from Europe to the East for silks and spices. In fact, it was the regulation of ventures of this nature that gave rise to our present corporate form of organization. The use of the term "share" to refer to a partial investment in a company stems from the share of resources contributed to these early joint ventures.

The Nature of Joint Ventures

Today, the carrying on of business by means of joint ventures is quite common. Joint ventures take many forms and may have long or short lives depending upon their nature. For example, a longterm situation may exist where a company is jointly owned (i.e., on a 50:50

basis) by two companies. In many countries, like Australia, joint ventures are normally carried on as unincorporated associations. In Canada, however, joint ventures are carried on through both incorporated and unincorporated entities. They are not subsidiaries but are included in this chapter because they are treated for accounting purposes **as associated companies to which proportionate consolidation** applies.

A joint venture is defined by the CICA *Handbook*[1] as an economic activity resulting from a contractual arrangement by which two or more venturers jointly control the economic activity. They are associations that are based on a **contractual relationship between the venturers (i.e., legal or natural persons)** and not on the extent of investment in the venture. This is important because, if the association were based on the extent of an investment in a company, this would comprise an investment over which the investor could exert significant influence or control.

The major difference between joint ventures and other ventures in which there is shared control, like partnerships,[2] is that there must be **joint control** by the parties to the venture irrespective of the extent of their investment in the joint venture. In this respect, **joint control is defined** by the CICA *Handbook* as the **contractually agreed sharing** of the continuing power to determine its strategic operating, investing and financing policies. The essential feature of a joint venture is, therefore, that **no single party** to the joint venture can control it.

Types of Joint Ventures

The following three types of joint ventures are recognized:

(a) **Jointly controlled operations** in which the venturers each use their own assets to carry out one aspect/stage of the venture, as in a series of manufacturing operations over which there is joint control. These joint ventures are often used where production sharing takes place, where different parties produce different parts of a product.

(b) **Jointly controlled assets** in which jointly controlled assets are used to carry out the activities of the joint venture. These are popular in the extractive industries (i.e., mining and oil and gas), where some aspect of the venture, like the assaying of ore samples, is carried out by a jointly controlled laboratory.

(c) **Jointly controlled (accounting or economic) entities** in which each venturer has an interest in a company or trust. These are the most common forms of joint ventures and where the accounting requirements are more complicated.

The Use of Proportionate Consolidation

The CICA *Handbook* requires that interests in joint ventures should be recognized in the financial statements of each venturer using proportionate consolidation. This is because it is believed that consolidated financial statements prepared on a proportionate basis provide users with the most appropriate information about the resources, obligations, risks and operations of persons carrying on business through joint ventures.

The philosophy behind proportionate consolidation is that if a participant in the joint venture has contributed a set proportion of the resources to the venture, the participant owns the same proportion of the net assets of the venture and, consequently, these should be reflected on the consolidated balance sheet. This form of consolidation is, therefore, based on the proportionate ownership of assets and not control.

Proportionate consolidation combines the investor company's proportionate share of the assets, liabilities, revenues and expenses with those of the investor company to give **the same**

---

[1] Section 3055.

[2] In Canada, a partnership must be carried on with the intention of making a profit, whereas a joint venture can be carried on for any purpose (e.g., for charitable purposes).

results as the equity method. In such cases, the goodwill arising on consolidation is calculated in the normal manner. However, instead of determining the venturer's share of the net income from the joint venture, the venturer's proportionate share of the revenues and expenses of the joint venture are added to those of the venturer (i.e., the investor company). Similarly, instead of reflecting the amount of the investment in the joint venture as a single amount, the venturer's proportionate share of the assets and liabilities of the joint venture are added to those of the venturer.

For example, if a venturer is entitled to a one-third share in the joint venture, the venturer shares in the revenues and expenses of the joint venture to the extent of one-third. The consolidation is carried out by recognizing a one-third proportionate share of the assets, liabilities, revenues and expenses by adding them to the venturer's figures. The net result after adjusting for the amortization of goodwill is the same "consolidated" net income as if the equity method had been used. This situation is outlined in Illustration 14–1.

1. Accounting for Jointly Controlled Operations With jointly controlled operations, the venturers each use their own assets, incur their own liabilities, carry their own inventories and incur their own expenses. In such cases, participation in the joint venture is treated as an extension of each venturer's own operations.

On consolidation, the venturers each include in their financial statements the contractually agreed **proportionate share of the revenues and expenses arising directly from the sale of the goods and services of the joint venture**. Depending upon the arrangement amongst the venturers, the costs incurred by each venturer in using their individually owned assets are either absorbed by the venturer concerned or transferred to a combined joint venture income statement. With this latter arrangement, there would have to be an equitable sharing of revenues and costs and profits and losses.

2. Accounting for Jointly Controlled (or Jointly Owned) Assets With joint ventures covering the use of jointly controlled (or owned) assets, the venturers recognize in their individual financial statements their contractually agreed share of the assets, liabilities, expenses and revenues. Adjustments between the venturers relating to the value of assets contributed, liabilities and expenses incurred are, therefore, often necessary.

3. Accounting for Jointly Controlled Entities In the case of jointly controlled entities, the position is more complicated because each venturer has a direct interest in the entity involved. Joint ventures of this nature are similar to entities of the private sector in that they own their own assets, incur their own liabilities and expenses, and earn their own revenues. The only difference is that the contract between the parties establishes joint control and the extent to which the venturers share in the profits or losses of the joint venture.

Accounting for **jointly controlled entities** is more complicated because, besides the apportionment of revenues and expenses between the venturers, etc., it also involves the treatment of gains or losses arising from the transfer or sale of assets to, or by, the joint venture. The complications arise because the CICA[3] considers that, when assets are transferred by a venturer to a joint venture, the venturer gives up control of those assets and receives in return some degree of joint control over the venture. The venturer contributing the assets is, therefore, considered to have entered into an arm's length transaction (e.g., a sale) with the other venturers. The transfer of the assets to a joint venture is, therefore, at their fair market values. The recognition of gains or losses on the transfer of these assets must take place at the date of transfer and be treated as detailed below.

---

[3] CICA *Handbook*, section 3055.

Gains Arising from the Transfer of Assets to Jointly Controlled Entities

As the transfer of assets to a jointly controlled entity is considered to be a transaction at arm's length, any **gains** arising from the transfer must be **recognized in the financial statements** at the time of the transfer. The recognition of these gains is in two parts. First, that part of the gain applying to non-related venturers (i.e., those parties to the joint venture other than the venturer transferring the assets) is calculated so that it can be deferred and

---

ILLUSTRATION 14–1
PROPORTIONATE CONSOLIDATION OF A SINGLE JOINT VENTURE

Investor Inc. entered into a joint venture with four other parties. In terms of the agreement between them, Investor and the four other parties to the joint venture would each contribute assets to the value of $160,000 and share equally in profits and losses from the venture. Project Inc. was duly formed on January 1, 20X4 to carry on the business of the joint venture. On that date, Investor transferred assets having a fair market value of $160,000 and a book value of $140,000 to Project. At the date of transfer, these assets had a five-year remaining useful life after which time they were expected to have no residual value.

The abbreviated financial statements of Investor and Project at December 31, 20X4 were as follows:

COMBINED INCOME AND RETAINED EARNINGS STATEMENTS	Investor	Project
Sales	$4,000,000	$1,800,000
Gain on Sale of Assets	20,000	—

> The gain of $20,000 represents the difference between the fair market and book values of the assets transferred to Project apportioned as follows:
>
> | | |
> |---|---|
> | Gain relating to Non-Related Venturers | $16,000 |
> | Gain relating to Investor | 4,000 |
> | Total Gain | $20,000 |

	Investor	Project
Total Revenues	$4,020,000	$1,800,000
Cost of Goods Sold	$1,980,000	$ 760,000
Amortization of Capital Assets	220,000	160,000
Administration Expenses	1,354,000	470,000
	$3,554,000	$1,390,000
Net Operating Income	$ 466,000	$ 410,000
Dividends from Investee Company	24,000	—
Net Income	490,000	410,000
Retained Earnings at January 1, 20X4	600,000	—
	1,090,000	410,000
Dividends Paid	250,000	120,000
Retained Earnings at December 31, 20X4	$ 840,000	$ 290,000

BALANCE SHEETS	Investor	Project
Current Assets	$ 520,000	$ 650,000
Investment in Project	160,000	—
Capital Assets	2,100,000	800,000
Accumulated Amortization	(400,000)	(160,000)
	$2,380,000	$1,290,000
Current Liabilities	$ 340,000	$ 200,000
Common Stock	1,200,000	800,000
Retained Earnings	840,000	290,000
	$2,380,000	$1,290,000

ILLUSTRATION 14–1 (CONTINUED)

As the proportionate basis of consolidation recognizes a proportionate share of assets, liabilities, revenues and expenses, the consolidated process using this method would have been as follows:

COMBINED INCOME AND RETAINED EARNINGS STATEMENTS

	Consolidated	Workings Investor	Project 1/5th
Sales	$4,360,000	$4,000,000	$ 360,000
Gain on Sale of Assets — see Note 1	3,200	3,200	—
Total Consolidated Revenues	$4,363,200	$4,003,200	$ 360,000
Cost of Goods Sold	$2,132,000	$1,980,000	$ 152,000
Amortization of Capital Assets	251,200	220,000	32,000
Less: Amortization Adjustment — see Note 2			(800)
Administration Expenses	1,448,000	1,354,000	94,000
Total Consolidated Expenses	$3,831,200	$3,554,000	$ 277,200
Consolidated Net Income	$ 532,000	$ 449,200	$ 82,800
Retained Earnings at January 1, 20X4	600,000		
	1,132,000		
Dividends Paid	250,000		
Retained Earnings at December 31, 20X4	$ 882,000		

BALANCE SHEETS

	Consolidated	Workings
Current Assets	$ 650,000	(520,000 + 130,000)
Capital Assets	2,256,000	(2,100,000 + 160,000 – 4,000)
Less: Adjustment for Sale of Assets — see Note 2		
Accumulated Amortization — see Note 2	(431,200)	(400,000 + [32,000 – $800])
	$2,474,800	
Current Liabilities	$ 380,000	(340,000 + 40,000)
Deferred Gain on Sale of Assets — see Note 3	16,000	(80% of $20,000)
Less: Amortization for Year	(3,200)	
Common Stock	1,200,000	
Retained Earnings	882,000	
	$2,474,800	

Notes:

[1] The amortization of one-fifth of Investor's share of the gain on the sale of the plant of $20,000 of which $16,000 is attributable to the non-related venturers.

[2] The amount of $800 (i.e., 20% of $20,000/5 years) is the amortization of one-fifth of the $4,000 recognized for each year until the capital assets that were transferred to Project at $160,000 (but with a book value of $140,000) are fully amortized.

[3] The "Deferred Gain on the Sale of Assets" of $12,800 is the balance of the deferred gain relating to the non-related venturers. This is the amount of $16,000 less the amortization of $3,200 (i.e., one-fifth) for the year ended December 31, 20X4, and the $4,000 is the proportion of the gain attributable to Investor.

[4] Other than the adjustments explained in the above notes, the assets, liabilities, revenues and expenses are reflected at one-fifth, which is Investor's share of the joint venture.

amortized in a systematic manner against revenues over the life of the assets transferred. Second, the share of the gain attributable to the venturer transferring the assets is set aside to be offset against the proportionate share of the venturer's interest in the assets. This adjustment is then amortized over the life of the asset concerned.

A comprehensive example covering a situation where a gain arose on the transfer of assets to a joint venture is provided as Illustration 14–1. This illustration shows that:

(a) The revenues and expenses and assets and liabilities of the joint venture are proportionately allocated to the parent company (i.e., 20% of the sales of Project amounting to $360,000, 20% of the cost of goods sold, etc.).

(b) The gain on the sale of the assets by Investor to the joint venture is proportionately allocated between Investor and the other "non-related" venturers in the agreed proportion of 20% to each of the venturers. In this case, the apportionment is $4,000 to Investor (i.e., the related venturers' portion) and $16,000 to the non-related venturers.

(c) The $16,000 proportion of the gain on the sale of the assets applying to the non-related venturers is deferred and amortized as a revenue item of $3,200 per year over the five-year life of the assets. The remaining balance (i.e., $12,800 in 20X4) is reflected as a deferred gain on the balance sheet until fully amortized.

(d) The gain on sale apportioned to Investor of $4,000 is deducted from the 20% proportion of the capital assets from the joint venture of $32,000 (i.e., 1/5 × $160,000) to reduce it to $28,000 (i.e., 1/5 × $140,000). This has the effect of restoring the 20% proportion of capital assets (transferred at $160,000) to the cost of 20% of the book value of $140,000.

(e) The $4,000 referred to above is amortized over the five-year life (at $800/year) of the asset to eliminate the excess share of the amortization of $20,000 calculated on assets of $160,000 instead of an amount of $140,000. This is achieved by deducting it from both the amortization expense and accumulated amortization on the balance sheet.

Losses Arising from the Transfer of Assets to Jointly Controlled Operations

As with gains, losses arising from the transfer of assets to a joint venture must also be recognized. In these cases, the CICA *Handbook* takes a somewhat conservative approach by requiring that if the decline in the value of the assets is not considered to be temporary in nature, the share of the loss attributable to the non-related venturers should be immediately written off against revenues. The share of the loss applicable to the venturer who transferred the assets is, however, considered to be unrealized and is only recognized on the sale of the asset to an independent third party (i.e., someone totally unconnected to the joint venture). This amount is, therefore, deferred and used to increase the value of the venturer's share of the transferred assets to their original book value. An adjustment to the amount for amortization of the asset is also required.

The Disclosure of Interests in Joint Ventures

As outlined above, interests in joint ventures must be proportionately consolidated. Venturers are also required to disclose separately the total amounts of the major components of their interests in joint ventures. These disclosures would cover current and capital assets, current and longterm liabilities, revenues and expenses, cash flows, and their share of any contingencies and capital commitments of the joint ventures in which they had an interest.

B. ACCOUNTING FOR COMPLICATED GROUPS OF COMPANIES

Complicated Groups of Companies

Up to this point, the illustrations explaining the consolidation process have been limited to a parent company and its investment in a single subsidiary. Even though this does occur in practice, affiliated groups are normally considerably more complicated than a two-company situation.

There are a number of reasons for this. For example, "pyramiding" provides the means whereby a parent company can control a vast corporate empire by virtue of holding of, say a 51% interest, in a company that in turn, or *ad infinitum*, may control other companies by having a similar 51% interest in them. The corporate form of organization also lends itself to the divisionalization of business activities and it is common for companies to hold their fixed properties through wholly-owned subsidiaries. Furthermore, risky ventures and the carrying on of activities in foreign countries provide other additional reasons for trading through subsidiary companies rather than as branches of the parent company.

As a result, affiliated groups of companies usually consist of a number of companies arranged in both vertical and horizontal patterns. The accounting for these complicated groups of companies is outlined and explained in the following two subsections.

The Consolidation of Vertically Arranged Groups of Companies

The consolidation of vertically arranged groups of companies is somewhat difficult. This is because the tiered nature of these groups requires that the interests in the subsidiaries be adjusted as one moves up the tiered structure.

The importance of this is that the net income and retained earnings of the companies within the group are affected by the extent of ownership as one moves from one tier to the next. For example, assume that a parent company acquired a 75% interest in a subsidiary company that had, in turn, acquired an 80% interest in a sub-subsidiary on the same date. If the net income of the parent company was $200,000 and that of the subsidiary and sub-subsidiary were $80,000 and $50,000 respectively, the consolidated net income of the group would amount to $290,000 calculated as follows:

Recognition of Net Income in Vertically Arranged Groups of Companies

	Total	Sub-subsidiary 80%	Subsidiary 75%	Consolidated	Minority Interests
Sub-subsidiary	$ 50,000	$40,000			$10,000
Subsidiary		75% : 25%	$30,000		$10,000
	$ 80,000		60,000		$20,000
			$ 90,000	$ 90,000	—
Parent	$200,000			200,000	—
				$290,000	
Total Net Income	330,000				
Less Minority Interests	40,000				$40,000
Consolidated Net Income	$290,000				

An illustration of the consolidation of a vertically arranged group of companies consisting of the parent company, a subsidiary, and a sub-subsidiary is provided in Illustration 14–2. As far as possible, the figures used are the same as those used in Illustration 14–3, so that the differences between the consolidation of horizontally and vertically arranged groups can be clearly seen.

In Illustration 14–2, the net income of the group is determined by apportioning the amounts between the sub-subsidiary, the subsidiary, and the parent company on a tiered basis to give the consolidated net income of $317,000. The important issue is that it is not only the net income of the subsidiary that is apportioned but also that from the sub-subsidiary. This also applies to the retained earnings brought forward at the beginning of the year in which the consolidation is carried out. In other respects, however, the consolidation of vertical and horizontal groups of companies is the same.

The date on which the companies appearing in the various tiers (i.e., subsidiaries or sub-subsidiaries) were acquired is also important because it affects the amount of net income

---

ILLUSTRATION 14–2
CONSOLIDATION OF A VERTICAL GROUP OF COMPANIES IN WHICH THE INTERESTS
IN THE SUBSIDIARY AND SUB-SUBSIDIARY WERE ACQUIRED ON THE SAME DATE

The abbreviated financial statements of Parent Inc., Second Inc. and Third Inc. at December 31, 20X5 were as follows:

	Parent	Second	Third
BALANCE SHEETS			
Current Assets	$ 200,000	$250,000	$150,000
Investment in Subsidiary Companies	420,000	250,000	—
Capital Assets (Net)	500,000	350,000	240,000
	$1,120,000	$850,000	$390,000
Current Liabilities	$ 40,000	$ 57,500	$ 60,000
Common Stock	500,000	400,000	200,000
Retained Earnings	580,000	392,500	130,000
	$1,120,000	$850,000	$390,000
COMBINED INCOME AND RETAINED EARNINGS STATEMENTS			
Sales	$1,200,000	$980,000	$600,000
Cost of Goods Sold	$ 650,000	$530,000	$350,000
Expenses	350,000	300,000	190,000
	$1,000,000	$830,000	$540,000
Net Operating Income	$ 200,000	$150,000	$ 60,000
Dividends from Subsidiaries	36,000	15,000	—
Net Income	236,000	165,000	60,000
Retained Earnings at January 1, 20X5	444,000	287,500	90,000
	680,000	452,500	150,000
Dividends Paid	100,000	60,000	20,000
Retained Earnings at December 31, 20X5	$ 580,000	$392,500	$130,000

Notes:
[1] The retained earnings at January 1, 20X4 and the trading activities and dividends paid by the three companies in 20X4 were as follows:

	Parent	Second	Third
Retained Earnings at January 1, 20X4	$ 300,000	$200,000	$ 60,000
Net Income	200,000	120,000	40,000
Dividends from Subsidiaries	24,000	7,500	—
	524,000	327,500	100,000
Less: Dividends Paid (December)	80,000	40,000	10,000
Retained Earnings at December 31, 20X4	$ 444,000	$287,500	$ 90,000

ILLUSTRATION 14–2 (Continued)

[2] On July 1, 20X4, Parent acquired a 60% interest in Second for $420,000. On the same day, Second acquired a 75% interest in Third for $250,000. On the date of acquisition, all assets and liabilities were considered to be fairly valued. In December 20X4, goodwill arising on the acquisition of Second and Third was written down for impairment by $2,000 and $3,000.

Analysis of Equity of Second in Third

	Total	75%	Minority Interests
Common Stock	$200,000	$150,000	$ 50,000
Retained Earnings	60,000	45,000	15,000
Net Income 20X4 — 6 months	20,000	15,000	5,000
		210,000	
Purchase Consideration		250,000	
Goodwill		$ 40,000	

Goodwill Impairment of $3,000 in December 20X4

Net Income 20X4 — 6 months	20,000	15,000	5,000
Dividends Paid	(10,000)	(7,500)	(2,500)
Net Income 20X5	60,000	45,000	15,000
Dividends Paid	(20,000)	(15,000)	(5,000)
Minority Interests			$ 82,500

Analysis of Equity of Parent in Second

		60%	
Common Stock	$400,000	$240,000	$160,000
Retained Earnings	200,000	120,000	80,000
Net Income 20X4 — 6 months	60,000	36,000	24,000
		396,000	
Purchase Consideration		420,000	
Goodwill		$ 24,000	

Goodwill Impairment of $2,000 in December 20X4

Net Income 20X4 — 6 months	60,000	36,000	24,000
Dividends Paid	(40,000)	(24,000)	(16,000)
Net Income 20X5	150,000	90,000	60,000
Dividends Paid	(60,000)	(36,000)	(24,000)
Minority Interests			$308,000

Adjustment — Parent's Interest in Third through Second:			
	Total	60%	Minority Interests
Net Income from Third — 20X4	$ 15,000	$ 9,000	$ 6,000
Less: Goodwill Impairment	(3,000)	(1,800)	(1,200)
Additional Retained Earnings — 20X4		$ 7,200	—
Net Income from Third — 20X5	45,000	$ 27,000	18,000
Additional Minority Interests — 20X5			$ 22,800

ILLUSTRATION 14–2 (Continued)

CONSOLIDATED FINANCIAL STATEMENTS

Balance Sheet:

Current Assets ($200,000 + $250,000 + $150,000)	$ 600,000
Capital Assets ($500,000 + $350,000 + $240,000)	1,090,000
Goodwill ($24,000 + $40,000 − $2,000 − $3,000)	59,000
	$1,749,000
Current Liabilities ($40,000 + $57,500 + $60,000)	$ 157,500
Minority Interests ($82,500 + $308,000 + Additional Interest of $22,800)	413,300
Common Stock	500,000
Retained Earnings	678,200
	$1,749,000

Combined Income and Retained Earnings Statement:

	Consolidated	Parent	Second	Third
Sales	$2,780,000	$1,200,000	$980,000	$ 600,000
Cost of Goods Sold	$1,530,000	$ 650,000	$530,000	$ 350,000
Expenses	840,000	350,000	300,000	190,000
Net Income	$2,370,000	$1,000,000	$830,000	$ 540,000
Net Income from Third (75%)	$ 410,000	$ 200,000	$150,000	$ 60,000
			+45,000	−45,000
			195,000	15,000
Less: Minority Interests				
40% of $195,000* from Second	93,000		78,000	—
25% of $60,000 from Third	—	—	—	15,000
Consolidated Net Income	317,000	$ 200,000	$117,000	$ Nil
Retained Earnings at January 1, 20X5				
(i.e., [$444,000 − Dividends of $24,000] + [$36,000 − Goodwill of $2,000] + Additional $7,200 from Third for 20X4)	461,200			
	778,200			
Dividends Paid	100,000			
Retained Earnings at December 31, 20X5	$ 678,200			

* As the controlling interest in Third is held by Second, the minority interests deducted from the income of Second of $78,000 includes 40% of the $45,000 additional interests of the minority transferred from Third.

recognized by the parent company. In this respect, the normal rules relating to pre- and post-acquisition net income apply and, if a company acquires an interest in another company during the financial year, it only recognizes its share of net income from the date of acquisition. It should also be noted that with the consolidation of vertical groups of companies, the fair market values assigned to net assets and the net amounts for goodwill are merely aggregated as if the group was arranged in a horizontal pattern.

At one time, there was considerable support for the idea that fair market value adjustments and goodwill should be apportioned in relation to the interests in the companies calculated on a tiered basis along the lines of the 80% and 75% apportionment given in the above explanation of the recognition of net income. However, this results in a proportionate consolidation of certain assets that violates the principle of control. It also affects the values of assets transferred from one company to another in internal re-organizations of the group and is no longer considered an acceptable approach.

Consolidation of Horizontally Arranged Groups of Companies

The consolidation of companies arranged in a horizontal pattern is quite straightforward. The analysis of equity for each company is carried out in the normal manner and the assets and liabilities of these companies are aggregated to give the consolidated financial statements. In this respect, the consolidation process is virtually identical to that illustrated in the previous chapters except that, up to this point, there was only one subsidiary company.

The consolidation of a horizontally arranged group of companies consisting of the parent company and two partly owned subsidiaries is provided in Illustration 14–3. In this Illustration, the figures for each company to be consolidated are obtained independently of one another and entered on a columnar spreadsheet where they are aggregated with those of the parent company to give the consolidated financial statements. This is illustrated by the consolidated net income of the group of $335,000, which is obtained by merely adding the net income less minority interests of the two subsidiaries to that of the parent company. Similarly, the goodwill figure of $60,000 is arrived at by merely adding the goodwill from the two acquisitions to one another.

With horizontally arranged groups of companies, it makes little or no difference to the consolidation process if the dates on which the interests in the subsidiaries acquired are different. This is because the consolidation process is essentially one of aggregation of the interests in different companies with those of the parent company on an individual basis.

Consolidating Complicated Groups of Companies in Practice

In practice, groups of companies seldom consist of neatly arranged horizontal or vertical groups of companies. They usually consist of a combination of both forms of arrangements in which some companies are wholly-owned and others are not.

When consolidating these groups, it is necessary to work logically through the structure of the group. Normally, the consolidation process is broken down into various sub-groups that are then, in turn, consolidated with one another until the final stage of the consolidation is reached and the consolidation is with the parent company. What happens is that the companies forming the lowest tiers are consolidated first, and then the next tier, etc.

It is also possible to consolidate more than one tier at a time. In those cases where the companies making up a vertical arranged group are wholly owned, this poses no problems. However, where the companies are partly owned, a proportionate adjustment is necessary as one moves from tier to tier.

There are, however, no set rules and each situation should be examined on its own merits. One word of caution — always maintain proper working papers. Shortcuts can cause enormous headaches. Take some advice from someone who knows!

C. JOINT HOLDINGS OF INTERESTS IN SUBSIDIARIES

From time to time, joint holdings of interests in subsidiaries occur. For example, on the acquisition of a subsidiary, the parent company may find that the subsidiary owns shares in another company in the group.

As this type of situation complicates the consolidation process, these joint holdings should be eliminated as soon as possible through an internal re-organization. However, it is often not possible to eliminate these joint holdings immediately, and until such time that an internal re-organization is carried out, the consolidation process must take this situation into account.

Assume, for example, that immediately after the acquisition of a subsidiary, the parent company finds that it owns a 56% interest in it by virtue of a direct holding of 20% and an indirect holding of another 36% through another subsidiary (i.e., 60% of 60%). In these cases, it would be possible to treat the interest of the parent company as a 56% interest in the subsidiary for consolidation purposes. However, this would make the calculation of the goodwill, the elimination of gains or losses on intercompany transactions, etc., more difficult. The analysis of equity is, therefore, normally carried out as if it were a step acquisition. The different interests are, therefore, applied to the tiers to which they relate, as with the consolidation of vertical groups of companies.

ILLUSTRATION 14–3
CONSOLIDATION OF A HORIZONTAL GROUP OF COMPANIES IN WHICH THE INTERESTS IN THE SUBSIDIARY AND SUB-SUBSIDIARY WERE ACQUIRED ON THE SAME DATE

The abbreviated financial statements of Parent Inc., Second Inc. and Third Inc. at December 31, 20X5 were as follows:

	Parent	Second	Third
BALANCE SHEETS			
Current Assets	$ 200,000	$250,000	$150,000
Investments in Subsidiary Companies	670,000	—	—
Capital Assets (Net of Depreciation)	250,000	600,000	240,000
	$1,120,000	$850,000	$390,000
Current Liabilities	$ 17,500	$ 80,000	$ 60,000
Common Stock	500,000	400,000	200,000
Retained Earnings	602,500	370,000	130,000
	$1,120,000	$850,000	$390,000
COMBINED INCOME AND RETAINED EARNINGS STATEMENTS			
Sales	$1,200,000	$980,000	$600,000
Cost of Goods Sold	$ 650,000	$530,000	$350,000
Expenses	350,000	300,000	190,000
	$1,000,000	$830,000	$540,000
Net Operating Income	$ 200,000	$150,000	$ 60,000
Dividends from Subsidiaries	51,000	—	—
Net Income	251,000	150,000	60,000
Retained Earnings at January 1, 20X5	451,500	280,000	90,000
	702,500	430,000	150,000
Less: Dividends Paid	100,000	60,000	20,000
Retained Earnings at December 31, 20X5	$ 602,500	$370,000	$130,000

Notes:

[1] The retained earnings at January 1, 20X4 and the trading activities and dividends paid by the three companies in 20X4 were as follows:

	Parent	Second	Third
Retained Earnings at January 1, 20X4	$ 300,000	$200,000	$ 60,000
Net Income from Trading Operations	200,000	120,000	40,000
Dividends from Subsidiaries	31,500	—	—
	531,500	320,000	100,000
Less: Dividends Paid (December)	80,000	40,000	10,000
Retained Earnings at December 31, 20X4	$ 451,500	$280,000	$ 90,000

ILLUSTRATION 14–3 (Continued)

[2] On July 1, 20X4, Parent acquired a 60% interest in Second for $420,000 and a 75% interest in Third for $250,000. On the date of acquisition, all assets and liabilities were considered to be properly valued.

[3] Goodwill is accounted for on an impairment basis.

The Analysis of Equity is carried out for Third and Second as follows:

Analysis of Equity: Parent in Third

	Total	75%	Minority Interests
Common Stock	$200,000	$150,000	$ 50,000
Retained Earnings	60,000	45,000	15,000
Net Income 20X4 — 6 months	20,000	15,000	5,000
		210,000	
Purchase Consideration		250,000	
Goodwill		$ 40,000	

Goodwill Impairment of $3,000 in December 20X4

Net Income 20X4 — 6 months	20,000	$ 15,000	5,000
Dividends Paid	(10,000)	(7,500)	(2,500)
Net Income 20X5	60,000	45,000	15,000
Dividends Paid	(20,000)	(15,000)	(5,000)
Minority Interests			$ 82,500

Analysis of Equity: Parent in Second

		60%	
Common Stock	400,000	240,000	$ 160,000
Retained Earnings	200,000	120,000	80,000
Net Income 20X4 — 6 months	60,000	36,000	24,000
		396,000	
Purchase Consideration		420,000	
Goodwill		$ 24,000	

Goodwill Impairment of $1,000 in December 20X4

Net Income 20X4 — 6 months	60,000	36,000	24,000
Dividends Paid	(40,000)	(24,000)	(16,000)
Net Income 20X5	150,000	90,000	60,000
Dividends Paid	(60,000)	(36,000)	(24,000)
Minority Interests			$ 308,000

The consolidated balance sheet and consolidated combined income and retained earnings statement are prepared as follows:

Consolidated Balance Sheet:

Current Assets ($200,000 + $250,000 + $150,000)	$ 600,000
Capital Assets ($250,000 + $600,000 + $240,000)	1,090,000
Goodwill ($24,000 + $40,000 − $1,000 − $3,000)	60,000
	$1,750,000
Current Liabilities ($17,500 + $80,000 + $60,000)	$ 157,500
Minority Interests ($82,500 + $308,000)	390,500
Common Stock	500,000
Retained Earnings	702,000
	$1,750,000

ILLUSTRATION 14–3 (Continued)

Consolidated Combined Income and Retained Earnings Statement:

	Consolidated	Parent	Second	Third
Sales	$2,780,000	$1,200,000	$980,000	$600,000
Cost of Goods Sold	$1,530,000	$ 650,000	$530,000	$350,000
Expenses	840,000	350,000	300,000	190,000
Total Expenses	$2,370,000	$1,000,000	$830,000	$540,000
Total Net Income	$ 410,000	$ 200,000	$150,000	$ 60,000
Less: Minority Interests	75,000	—	60,000	15,000
Consolidated Net Income	335,000	$ 200,000	$ 90,000	$ 45,000
Retained Earnings at January 1, 20X5 — see note	467,000			
	802,000			
Dividends Paid	100,000			
Retained Earnings at December 31, 20X5	$ 702,000			

Note: The retained earnings at January 1, 20X5 was as follows:

Retained Earnings of Parent at January 1, 20X4 ($451,500 less dividends of $31,500 [i.e., $24,000 from Second and $7,500 from Third])	$420,000
Add: Share of Net Income from Subsidiaries for 20X4:	
Second (60% of $60,000)	36,000
Third (75% of $20,000)	15,000
	471,000
Less: Goodwill Impairment ($1,000 + $3,000)	4,000
Balance Attributable to Group at January 1, 20X5	$467,000

In practice, the easiest method of eliminating cross or joint holdings is to sell the shares to an outside party and then re-purchase them through another company in the group. These transactions can be carried out easily as cash transactions, which overcome the problems caused by intercompany transactions because any gains or losses are realized and do not have to be eliminated in the consolidation process.

D. CROSS HOLDINGS OF INTERESTS

The Nature of Cross Holdings

As with joint holdings, cross or reciprocal holdings of interests between affiliated companies sometimes occur. They can seriously complicate the consolidation process and should be eliminated as soon as possible by an internal re-organization or the sale of these interests. In fact, the *Canada Business Corporations Act*[4] requires that any subsidiary holding shares in its parent company must sell those shares within five years of becoming a subsidiary. Similar provisions apply in provincial corporate legislation.

Cross holdings occur where, for example, the parent company acquires an 80% interest in a subsidiary only to find that the subsidiary holds a 10% interest in the parent. A consolidation problem arises because where 80% of the net income of the subsidiary is recognized by the parent, 10% of this and other net income of the parent company accrues to the subsidiary.

---

[4] section 30.

A "to and fro" situation takes place because, as 80% of this adjustment is recognized by the parent, another 10% thereof accrues to the subsidiary. This continues until the amounts involved are immaterial.

The CICA *Handbook*[5] requires that where a subsidiary company holds shares issued by its parent company, these represent treasury shares. The cost of these shares held by the subsidiary must, therefore, be deducted from the share capital of the parent company in the consolidated financial statements.

As with joint holdings, the problem arising from cross holdings is how to apportion the net income between the parent and subsidiary companies. This can be achieved by mechanically apportioning each "to and fro" transfer of net income between the companies. However, as this is very time-consuming, the apportionment is normally carried out using one of two methods; one is the mathematical method of using simultaneous linear equations and the other is the more popular "treasury stock method".

The Mathematical Approach

This method can be used for all forms of cross holdings whether they apply to parent-subsidiary cross holdings or between any two companies within the group. All that is required is to determine the net income of the companies concerned on the **cost basis excluding any dividends** received.

Assume the unrealistic situation where a parent company holds a 90% interest in a subsidiary that, in turn, holds a 20% interest in the parent company. Assume further that the net income from operations of the parent company and the subsidiary were $200,000 and $60,000 respectively. Using simultaneous linear equations, the apportionment of the net income of the subsidiary between the treasury shares and the parent company may be carried out as follows:

Let P = the interest of the Parent; and
     S = the interest of the Subsidiary

Then:

$$P = 200,000 + 0.9S$$
$$S = 60,000 + 0.2P$$

Solving for P:

$$P = 200,000 + 0.9(60,000 + 0.2P)$$
$$= 200,000 + (54,000 + 0.18P)$$
$$P - 0.18P = 200,000 + 54,000$$
$$0.82P = 254,000$$
$$P = \$309,756$$

Solving for S:

$$S = 60,000 + 0.2(200,000 + 0.9S)$$
$$= 60,000 + (40,000 + 0.18S)$$
$$S - 0.18S = 60,000 + 40,000$$
$$0.82S = 100,000$$
$$S = \$121,951$$

Apportionment based on net income of P:

P's net income of	$309,756
Share of net income attributable to Treasury Shares (20%)	61,951
Consolidated net income	$247,805

Alternatively, using the net income of S:

Net Income of $200,000 from P + $60,000 from S is	$260,000
Less: 10% of net income of S of $121,951	12,951
Consolidated net income	$247,805

---

[5] Section 1600.

The "Treasury Stock Method"

The treasury stock method can only be used where the cross holdings occur between the parent company and a subsidiary, and only in cases where the amounts involved are not material.

This method is carried out by merely treating the interest in the parent company held by the subsidiary as the parent company's treasury stock. The justification for the use of this method is that the parent company would have used some of the resources of the subsidiary concerned to purchase its own stock. As a result, the cross holding of interests and the accrual of income on these shares is ignored.

The treasury stock method merely treats the interest of the subsidiary as treasury stock that is deducted from the consolidated equity in the normal manner. This is acceptable because the interest of the subsidiary in the parent would seldom, if ever, exceed 20% and would normally be accounted for using the cost method. Any dividends received from the parent company are merely deducted from the dividends paid on the consolidated statement of retained earnings.

SUMMARY

This chapter covers accounting for joint ventures, complicated groups of companies, and joint and cross holdings of interests.

Joint ventures are associations arising from contractual agreement amongst venturers in which no single party to the venture has control over it. These ventures can be carried out through companies or as unincorporated associations. Joint ventures may consist of those in which there are controlled operations, controlled assets, or as jointly controlled entities. No matter what form they take, they must be accounted for by the venturers concerned using proportionate consolidation.

With the consolidation of complicated groups of companies, the consolidation process differs depending upon whether the companies are arranged in horizontal or vertical arrangements or a combination of these arrangements. Horizontal arrangements merely require the aggregation of the companies being consolidated, whereas vertically arranged groups require a proportionate adjustment of profits and retained earnings as the consolidation process moves upwards from the sub-subsidiaries through the subsidiaries to the parent company.

Joint and cross holdings of interests complicate the consolidation process. Ideally, these investments should be eliminated as soon as possible but where they exist, their effects on the group must be eliminated in the consolidation process. Joint holdings are treated in the same manner as piecemeal acquisitions, while cross holdings are eliminated using either the mathematical approach or the "treasury stock" approach.

SELF-STUDY PROBLEM

(covering income tax effects on effective gains or losses on bonds)

PROBLEM 14A†   On January 1, 20X1, Investor Inc., a provider of venture capital, agreed to enter into a joint venture with three other venturers to recover the cargo of a sunken ship off the coast of Newfoundland. The joint-venture was to be carried out through a company, Recovery Inc., formed for that purpose. Each venturer was to take a 25% interest in the venture, which was expected to be carried on for a period of five years, after which the venture was to be wound up. Each venturer was to contribute $500,000 in cash plus equipment or materials to the value of $900,000 to the venture.

† The solution is provided in Appendix B to this text.

Investor's contribution of materials or equipment was diving and recovery equipment that had been acquired by it as a distribution of assets from a previous venture of a similar nature. This equipment had a carrying value of $600,000 at January 1, 20X1 and was not expected to have any value at the end of the five-year venture period.

The abbreviated financial statements of Investor and Recovery for the year ended December 31, 20X1 were as follows:

	Investor	Recovery
INCOME AND RETAINED EARNINGS STATEMENTS		
Dividends Received	$19,000,000	—
Interest Revenue	9,950,000	—
Sales of Salvaged Goods	—	$9,000,000
Gain on Equipment Contributed to Recovery	300,000	—
Total Revenues	$29,250,000	$9,000,000
Cost of Goods Sold, at Recovery Cost	—	$2,000,000
Administration Expenses	$17,700,000	1,100,000
Amortization of Equipment	—	720,000
Salvage Expenses	—	2,600,000
Total Expenses	$17,700,000	$6,420,000
Net Income for Year	$11,550,000	$2,580,000
Retained Earnings at January 1, 20X1	7,450,000	—
	19,000,000	2,580,000
Dividends Paid	8,000,000	400,000
Retained Earnings at December 31, 20X1	$11,000,000	$2,180,000
BALANCE SHEETS		
Cash at Bank	$1,600,000	$1,500,000
Inventory of Salvaged Goods	—	3,500,000
Investment in Recovery Inc.	1,400,000	—
Other Investments	24,600,000	—
Equipment, at cost	—	3,600,000
Accumulated Amortization	—	(720,000)
	$27,600,000	$7,880,000
Current Liabilities	$600,000	100,000
Common Shares	16,000,000	5,600,000
Retained Earnings	11,000,000	2,180,000
	$27,600,000	$7,880,000

REQUIRED

Prepare the consolidated balance sheet and Income and retained earnings statement of Investor for 20X1.

REVIEW QUESTIONS

1. How is a joint venture defined by the CICA? What is the essential feature of a joint venture?
2. What is the distinction between a partnership and a joint venture?
3. Describe and distinguish the three types of joint ventures.
4. What accounting problem arises from the transfer of assets at a profit (or loss) to joint ventures that are separate entities?
5. Describe what is meant by proportionate consolidation. Do you see any advantages in using this method?

6. How are horizontally arranged groups of companies consolidated with one another?
7. How does the consolidation of vertically arranged groups of companies differ from that of horizontally arranged groups of companies?
8. How is goodwill treated in the consolidation of vertical groups of companies?
9. What is a joint holding of interests? How are they accounted for in the consolidation process?
10. Describe what is meant by a cross holding of interests. How are they accounted for?
11. In what circumstances can the "treasury stock" method of accounting for cross holdings be used?

EXERCISES

EXERCISE 14–1
On January 1, 20X2, Peter Inc. entered into an agreement with Quinton Inc., Ralph Inc., Sam Inc. and Trevor Inc., whereby they would combine their resources and carry on the business of property developers through a newly formed company named PQRST Inc. Peter would be the major shareholder holding a 25% interest in the venture.

At December 31, 20X2, the abbreviated income statements of Peter and PQRST were as follows:

	Peter	PQRST
Net Trading Income	$700,000	$1,000,000
Dividends from PQRST	200,000	—
Net Income	900,000	1,000,000
Less: Dividends Paid	300,000	800,000
	600,000	200,000
Retained Earnings at January 1, 20X2	360,000	—
Retained Earnings at December 31, 20X2	$960,000	$ 200,000

REQUIRED

Prepare the abbreviated "consolidated" income and retained earnings statement of Peter for 20X2 using proportionate consolidation and then prove the correctness of the consolidated retained earnings using the equity method of recording the share of net income from PQRST.

EXERCISE 14–2
On April 1, 20X1, Pelican Inc. transferred plant with a book value of $1,180,000 and a six-year remaining useful life to a joint venture known as XYZ at $1.5-million. Pelican was to share in the joint venture to the extent of 15%.

XYZ had been established on April 1, 20X1 and its income statement for the nine months ended December 31, 20X1 reflected net income of $270,000. At December 31, 20X1, XYZ's balance sheet reflected total capital assets and total accumulated amortization thereon of $4,670,000 and $649,800 respectively.

REQUIRED

Answer the following questions:

1. What type of joint venture is XYZ?
2. How much of the gain on the sale of plant would Pelican recognize in its consolidated income statement for the year ended December 31, 20X1? December 31, 20X2?
3. How would Pelican account for the balance of the gain on sale of plant in 20X1 and 20X2?
4. How much of the plant of XYZ would Pelican include in its consolidated balance sheet at December 31, 20X1?
5. If Pelican had earned net income of $865,000 during the year ended December 31, 20X1, what consolidated net income would it report on its consolidated income statement for 20X1?

EXERCISE 14–3   Prefer Inc. and Choose Inc. were two unrelated companies. On January 1, 20X7, they decided to form a joint venture, Vantage Inc. On that date Prefer contributed plant with a book value of $24,000 and having a fair market value of $30,000 to the joint venture in exchange for a 30% interest in Vantage. At January 1, 20X7, the plant had a three-year remaining useful life. On the same date, Choose contributed cash of $40,000 and inventory with a book value of $20,000 but with a selling price of $30,000 to Vantage for a 70% interest in the joint venture.

The abbreviated balance sheets and income statements for Prefer and Vantage at December 31, 20X7 were as follows:

INCOME STATEMENTS	Prefer	Vantage
Sales	—	$ 20,000
Cost of Goods Sold	—	(20,000)
Amortization of Capital Assets	—	(10,000)
Gain on Transfer of Assets to Vantage	$ 6,000	—
Net Income (Loss)	$ 6,000	$ (10,000)

BALANCE SHEETS		
Cash	$ 3,000	$ 60,000
Inventory	—	20,000
Investment in Vantage	30,000	—
Plant	—	30,000
Accumulated Amortization	—	(10,000)
	$33,000	$ 100,000
Current Liabilities	—	$ 10,000
Common Stock	$27,000	100,000
Retained Earnings	6,000	(10,000)
	$33,000	$ 100,000

REQUIRED

Prepare the consolidated balance sheet and income statement of Prefer for 20X7.

EXERCISE 14–4   On January 1, 20X2, Pill Inc., acquired a 75% interest in Swallow Inc. and an 80% interest in Taste Inc. Goodwill of $40,000 and $120,000 arose from the acquisition of the interests in Swallow and Taste respectively. In December 20X2, the goodwill was written down by $24,000 for impairment.

The abbreviated statements of retained earnings of the three companies at December 31, 20X5 were as follows:

	Pill	Swallow	Taste
Net Income for Year	$100,000	$ 40,000	$320,000
Dividends Received	160,000	—	—
	260,000	40,000	320,000
Less: Dividends Paid	120,000	—	200,000
	140,000	40,000	120,000
Retained Earnings at January 1, 20X5	200,000	64,000	40,000
Retained Earnings at December 31, 20X5	$340,000	$104,000	$160,000

The net income earned and dividends paid by the three companies from January 1, 20X2 to December 31, 20X4, together with the retained earnings at January 1, 20X2, were as follows:

	Pill	Swallow	Taste
Net Income (20X2–20X4)	$400,000	$100,000	$ 20,000
Dividends Paid (20X2–20X4)	(320,000)	(60,000)	—
Retained Earnings at January 1, 20X2	120,000	24,000	20,000
Retained Earnings at December 31, 20X4	$200,000	$ 64,000	$ 40,000

REQUIRED

Prepare the consolidated income and retained earnings statement of Parent and its subsidiary companies for the year ended December 31, 20X5.

EXERCISE 14–5   On July 1, 20X4, Shoot Inc. purchased an 80% interest in Target Inc. for $196,000. At that date, Target had common stock of $200,000, retained earnings of $20,000, and assets and liabilities that were properly valued. Net income for the six months ended December 31, 20X4 was $40,000 and no dividends were paid.

Pistol Inc. acquired 100% control over Shoot on January 1, 20X5 on the payment of $800,000. At that date, the equity of Shoot consisted of common stock of $600,000 and retained earnings of $120,000. On acquisition, the net assets of Shoot were considered to be fairly valued.

The abbreviated financial statements of the three companies at December 31, 20X5 were as follows:

	Pistol	Shoot	Target
BALANCE SHEETS			
Investments in Subsidiaries	$ 800,000	$196,000	—
Other Assets	900,000	704,000	$400,000
	$1,700,000	$900,000	$400,000
Current Liabilities	$ 100,000	$ 48,000	$ 40,000
Common Stock	1,000,000	600,000	200,000
Retained Earnings	600,000	252,000	160,000
	$1,700,000	$900,000	$400,000
COMBINED INCOME AND RETAINED EARNINGS STATEMENTS			
Net Income from Operations	$ 240,000	$180,000	$140,000
Dividends Received	80,000	32,000	—
	320,000	212,000	140,000
Retained Earnings at January 1, 20X5	400,000	120,000	60,000
	720,000	332,000	200,000
Dividends Paid	120,000	80,000	40,000
Retained Earnings at December 31, 20X5	$ 600,000	$252,000	$160,000

REQUIRED

Prepare the consolidated balance sheet and combined income and retained earnings statement for 20X5 after the write-down of goodwill by $8,000 for impairment in November of that year.

PROBLEMS

PROBLEM 14–1   On January 1, 20X5, three mining companies, Lorna Inc., Martin Inc., and Nadine Inc. agreed to establish a joint venture to prospect for minerals in Labrador for a period of five years. Lorna contributed cash of $5-million; Martin contributed $4-million, consisting of cash of $1-million and equipment valued at $3-million; and Nadine contributed $1-million in equipment. In terms of the agreement, the profits or losses of the joint venture were to be distributed between Lorna, Martin, and Nadine in the ratio of 5:4:1.

The joint venture was incorporated as Lomana Exploration Inc. in January 20X5. Prospecting rights to a tract of land were obtained, and prospecting commenced immediately.

The venture was extremely successful and by the onset of winter, it had located one lead and two cobalt deposits. Fifty percent of the rights to mine these deposits had been sold at a gain of $20-million in September 20X5.

The abbreviated financial statements of Martin and Lomana at December 31, 20X5 were as follows:

CONSOLIDATED INCOME AND RETAINED EARNINGS STATEMENTS	Martin	Lomana
Sales and Production Revenues	$23,200,000	—
Royalty Revenues	14,400,000	—
Dividends Received from Lomana Exploration	1,920,000	—
Gain on Sale of Prospecting Equipment	600,000	—
Gain on Sale of Mining Rights	—	$20,000,000
Interest and Other Revenues	1,900,000	1,280,000
Total Revenues	$42,020,000	$21,280,000
Production Expenses	$12,600,000	—
Prospecting Expenses	—	$ 8,200,000
Administration and Other Expenses	11,700,000	3,640,000
Amortization of Capital Assets	6,200,000	1,960,000
Amortization of Mining Rights	1,200,000	240,000
Total Expenses	$31,700,000	$14,040,000
Net Income for Year	$10,320,000	$ 7,240,000
Retained Earnings at January 1, 20X5	18,560,000	—
	28,880,000	7,240,000
Less Dividends Paid	4,000,000	4,800,000
Retained Earnings at December 31, 20X5	$24,880,000	$ 2,440,000

BALANCE SHEETS		
Cash and Short-term Deposits	$ 2,040,000	$ 240,000
Inventory of Ore and Minerals	17,800,000	—
Investment in Lomana Exploration	4,000,000	—
Mining Properties	31,510,000	—
Mining Rights	5,800,000	12,400,000
Equipment (net)	16,470,000	8,050,000
	$77,620,000	$20,690,000
Accounts Payable	$ 2,740,000	$ 350,000
Bank Loan	10,000,000	7,900,000
Common Shares	40,000,000	10,000,000
Retained Earnings	24,880,000	2,440,000
	$77,620,000	$20,690,000

Additional Information:

(a) The gain on the sale of prospecting equipment arose from the transfer of this equipment to Lomana Exploration.

(b) In view of the short-term nature of the venture, the gain on sale of the mining rights was treated as a revenue gain.

(c) The prospecting equipment transferred by Martin to Lomana Exploration had a book value of $2.4-million and was expected to be valueless at the end of the five-year venture period.

REQUIRED

Prepare the consolidated income and retained earning statement and balance sheet of Martin at December 31, 20X5.

PROBLEM 14–2 Ready Inc., Willing Inc., and Able Inc. agreed to form a six-year joint venture called Clay Venture Inc. on January 1, 20X1 to exploit a deposit of potter's clay in the Oakville area. They were to share revenues and expenses at the rate of 45% for Ready, 25% for Willing and 30% for Able. To acquire the property and bring the venture to the stage of selling the clay required the contribution to the joint venture of assets worth $1.4-million in the agreed revenue and expense sharing ratio. As part of its contribution to the venture, Able transferred certain assets to Clay Venture at an amount in excess of their book values.

The abbreviated financial statements of Able Inc. incorporating its share of the joint venture, and that of Clay Venture at December 31, 20X1, together with the relevant workings, at the end of its first year of operations, were as follows:

	Able	Workings for Able	Clay Venture
INCOME STATEMENT			
Revenues	$3,360,000	($3,000,000 + $360,000)	$1,200,000
Gain on Sale of Plant	21,000	([70% × $180,000]/6)	—
	3,381,000		1,200,000
Expenses	2,331,000	($2,100,000 + $240,000 − $9,000)	(800,000)
Net Income from Operations	$1,050,000		$ 400,000
BALANCE SHEET			
Current Assets	$1,125,000	($900,000 + $225,000)	$ 750,000
Capital Assets, at cost	1,841,000	($1,310,000 + $585,000 − $54,000)	
Amortization of Capital Assets	(331,000)	($250,000 + $90,000 − $9,000)	(300,000)
	$2,635,000		$2,400,000
Current Liabilities	$ 480,000	($300,000 + $180,000)	$ 600,000
Deferred Gain on Sale of Assets	105,000	([70% × $180,000] − $21,000)	—
Share Capital	1,000,000		1,400,000
Retained Earnings	1,050,000		400,000
	$2,635,000		$2,400,000

REQUIRED

1. What was the unrealized profit on the assets transferred to Clay Venture by Able?
2. Over how many years were the assets transferred to Clay Venture being amortized?
3. Show how the expenses of $2,331,000 were established.
4. Show how the amount of $105,000 for deferred Gain on Sale was established.
5. Reconstruct the income statement and balance sheet of Able Inc. at December 31, 20X1, before the inclusion of its share of Clay Venture.

PROBLEM 14–3 On January 1, 20X1, Investor Inc. acquired a 40% interest in a joint venture, Venture Inc. Investor's contribution to the joint venture was equipment valued at $400,000. The equipment had a carrying value of $350,000 at January 1, 20X1, and at that date the equipment had an expected remaining useful life of five years.

In December 20X1, Venture sold goods to Investor for $500,000 that included a markup of $100,000 for cash. At December 31, 20X1, all these goods were still held by Investor as inventory. There were no other intercompany transactions and Venture did not declare any dividends in 20X1.

The abbreviated financial statements of Investor and Venture for the year ended December 31, 20X1 were as follows:

	Investor	Venture
INCOME AND RETAINED EARNINGS STATEMENTS		
Sales	$8,200,000	$3,000,000
Gain on Equipment Contributed to Venture	50,000	—
Total Revenues	$8,250,000	$3,000,000
Cost of Goods Sold	$5,400,000	$2,400,000
Administration Expenses	1,850,000	155,000
Amortization of Equipment	450,000	200,000
Total Expenses	$7,700,000	$2,755,000
Net Income for Year	$ 550,000	$ 245,000
Retained Earnings at January 1, 20X1	550,000	—
Retained Earnings at December 31, 20X1	$1,100,000	$ 245,000

BALANCE SHEETS

	Investor	Venture
Cash at Bank	$ 200,000	$ 45,000
Accounts Receivable	700,000	200,000
Inventory	800,000	600,000
Investment in Venture	400,000	—
Plant and Equipment, at cost	2,300,000	1,000,000
Less: Accumulated Amortization	(700,000)	(200,000)
	$3,700,000	$1,645,000
Accounts Payable	$ 900,000	$ 400,000
Common Shares	1,700,000	1,000,000
Retained Earnings	1,100,000	245,000
	$3,700,000	$1,645,000

REQUIRED

Prepare the consolidated balance sheet and income and retained earnings statement of Investor for 20X1

PROBLEM 14–4   You are informed that:

(a) Strain purchased an 80% interest in Tear on January 1, 20X7 for $300,000 when Tear had common Stock of $250,000 and retained earnings of $100,000. Net income earned by Tear in 20X7 amounted to $60,000 and dividends of $20,000 were paid.

(b) Push purchased a 60% interest in Strain on July 1, 20X8 for $700,000.

(c) On acquisition of the investments, all assets and liabilities were considered to be fairly valued.

(d) Goodwill was written down for by $3,800 impairment in December 20X8.

You are also provided with the following abbreviated balance sheets and income statements of Push Inc., Strain Inc. and Tear Inc. at December 31, 20X8:

BALANCE SHEETS

	Push	Strain	Tear
Current Assets	$ 560,000	$ 400,000	$200,000
Investment in Strain	700,000	—	—
Investment in Tear	—	300,000	—
Fixed Assets	800,000	500,000	320,000
	$2,060,000	$1,200,000	$520,000
Current Liabilities	$ 300,000	$ 84,000	$ 50,000
Common Stock	1,000,000	800,000	250,000
Retained Earnings	760,000	316,000	220,000
	$2,060,000	$1,200,000	$520,000

COMBINED INCOME AND RETAINED EARNINGS STATEMENTS

	Push	Strain	Tear
Net Operating Income	$ 500,000	$ 250,000	$100,000
Dividends Received	60,000	16,000	—
Net Income	560,000	266,000	100,000
Retained Earnings at January 1, 20X8	400,000	150,000	140,000
	960,000	416,000	240,000
Dividends Paid (December 1)	200,000	100,000	20,000
Retained Earnings at December 31, 20X8	$ 760,000	$ 316,000	$220,000

REQUIRED

Prepare the consolidated balance sheet and combined income and retained earnings statement for 20X8.

PROBLEM 14–5   You are furnished with the abbreviated balance sheets and income statements of Profess Inc., Show Inc. and Teach Inc. for 20X4:

	Profess	Show	Teach
BALANCE SHEETS			
Current Assets	$ 230,000	$100,000	$190,000
Investment in Show	130,000	—	—
Investment in Teach	180,000	—	—
Capital Assets (Net)	900,000	220,000	240,000
	$1,440,000	$320,000	$430,000
Current Liabilities	$ 160,000	$ 40,000	$ 30,000
Common Stock	600,000	250,000	100,000
Retained Earnings	680,000	30,000	300,000
	$1,440,000	$320,000	$430,000
RETAINED EARNINGS STATEMENTS			
Retained Earnings at January 1, 20X4	$ 480,000	$ 20,000	$160,000
Net Operating Income	200,000	10,000	140,000
Retained Earnings at December 31, 20X4	$ 680,000	$ 30,000	$300,000

Profess had acquired its investments as follows:

(a) A 60% interest in Show had been acquired by Profess on January 1, 20X3 when Show had an accumulated loss of $30,000. During 20X3, Show had earned net income of $50,000 and paid no dividends.

(b) Profess had acquired a 20% interest in Teach on its incorporation for $20,000. On July 1, 20X4, Profess had acquired an additional 40% interest in Teach for $160,000.

(c) In December 20X3, Profess had recognized an impairment in the value of goodwill of $4,000 arising on the acquisition of Teach.

REQUIRED

Prepare the consolidated balance sheet and combined income and retained earnings statement of Profess for 20X4.

Interim, Segment and Summary Reporting 15

LEARNING OBJECTIVES

After studying this chapter you should be able to:

1. Understand the objective of interim reporting;
2. Apply the requirements of the CICA for interim reporting;
3. Appreciate the need for segment reporting and prepare the disclosure of segment information; and
4. Understand why the Securities and Exchange Commission approved the use of summary reporting in the USA.

THE SCOPE OF THE CHAPTER

To meet the needs of modern corporate reporting, information must be provided to shareholders and other interested parties on a timely basis. The twelve-month reporting period is considered to be far too long to have to wait before assessments of the value, earnings and growth potential of a company can be carried out. Interim reporting by companies is, therefore, required. Similarly, the consolidation of financial statements leads to a situation where much of the information regarding the operations and activities of the group of companies is masked through the aggregation of information. Consequently, the information must be "deconsolidated" through segment reporting. And, the insatiable demand by the financial analyst community for information in financial reports has led to a situation where the basic purpose of financial reports has been overlooked. Finally, in an attempt to return to basics, a system of summary reporting applies in the USA. This chapter covers these three areas.

A. INTERIM REPORTING

The Requirement to Issue Interim Reports

The term "interim reporting" is used in accounting to refer to the provision of information by a company to its shareholders and other interested parties on a regular basis. The purpose of these reports is to provide investors and others with timely information as to the progress of the enterprise. Even though many other forms of special reports may be issued to shareholders, they are seldom issued at regular intervals and, consequently, are not considered to be interim reports.

Interim reporting was first carried out voluntarily by management about 1900 in both Britain and the USA in an attempt to better inform their shareholders of their operations and activities. It is believed that the first interim report issued in North America was by the US Steel Corporation in 1902. In 1910, the New York Stock Exchange included the requirement that all newly listed companies must issue quarterly information.[1] In 1973, generally accepted accounting principles for these reports were established in the USA by APB *Opinion No. 28: Interim Financial Reporting* issued in 1973. This was followed soon thereafter by the requirement of the Securities Exchange Commission that all companies whose securities were publicly traded on US security markets must file quarterly reports with it in a specified manner (i.e., as Form 10-Q). Today, interim reporting in the USA follows FASB standards.

In Canada, the issue of interim reports followed much the same pattern as that in the USA. Today, the form and contents of these reports are specified by the CICA *Handbook* and their issue is a requirement of securities legislation.[2] They are required to be issued three times a year at the end of the first, second and third quarters by companies whose securities are publicly traded. They must also present comparative information for the same periods from the previous year.

The Contents of Interim Reports

The CICA *Handbook*[3] specifies what information should be presented in interim reports. These reports are, essentially, abbreviated financial statements. They are issued three times a year on a quarterly basis, which is normally after three months, six months, and nine months after the financial year end. However, this could differ in cases where the financial year of the reporting entity has been changed or a new reporting entity had been formed. Their objective is to communicate information to users that will allow them **to predict the year-end results of operations and the financial position of the company**.

As interim reports are used by the same persons who use the annual financial statements, they should be prepared using the same generally accepted accounting principles as those used for the annual financial statements. This is necessary to ensure that the information provided is comparable with that presented in the annual financial statements, consistent from year-to-year, and relevant and reliable.

For many years the whole issue of interim reporting had been considered in need of review because interim reports could be prepared in three different ways. These were the integral approach using the actual results of operations for the period under review, the discrete approach using the actual figures to estimate the results of operations for the period under review in relation to the entire year, and a combination of the two approaches. There was also considerable concern regarding the quality of the information presented in interim reports. As a result, the CICA's Accounting Standards Board and the FASB undertook a joint review of the position in 1999. The following reporting requirements are the result of that review and apply to all interim period beginning on or after January 2001.

The Interim Reporting Requirements

Interim reports must be prepared by all profit-oriented enterprises that are required to do so. Essentially, this means that the companies must be those companies whose securities are

---

[1] *The Journal of Accountancy*, May 1910.
[2] For example, that required by the Ontario Securities Commission in terms of section 76 of the Ontario *Securities Act*.
[3] Section 1751.

publicly traded. However, any company may elect to prepare interim statements for the benefit of their shareholders.

The objective of interim reports is to communicate information to users and other interested parties to allow them to predict the results of operations of the reporting entity for the year under review and its financial position at the end of that year. Even though it is recognized that interim reports do not provide as much information as the annual financial statements, the reporting requirements are that **they should provide sufficient information to allow investors and other interested parties to be able to reach a decision on the performance and continued existence of the reporting entity**. To do so, the minimum reporting requirements are that they consist of a balance sheet, an income statement, a statement of retained earnings, and a cash flow statement.

The way in which they must be presented is as follows:

1. **An income statement** for the current interim period is required giving both the figures for the current interim period and the cumulative interim figures for the year-to-date, with comparable figures for the comparable interim periods (i.e., current and year-to-date) of the immediately preceding financial year. The information provided must be presented using the same headings, line items, and subtotals as those used in its most recent annual financial statements. In addition, the basic and fully diluted earnings per share must appear on the face of the income statement for those companies that are required to present such information.

2. **The statement of retained earnings** must be presented giving the cumulative figures for the interim period-to-date with comparative figures for the period-to-date for the preceding financial year.

3. **A balance sheet** at the end of the current interim period must be presented with comparative figures taken from the company's balance sheet at the end of the preceding financial year.

4. **The cash flow statement** for the interim period-to-date must be presented with comparative figures for the immediately preceding financial year.

For example, the interim income statement for the second quarter would be presented in a four-column format giving the actual and preceding years' figures for the second interim period plus the cumulative figures for the first and second quarters for the current year and the preceding financial year. The presentation is as follows:

	Three Months Ended June 30		Six Months Ended June 30	
	20X1	20X0	20X1	20X0
Financial information, as required				

As far as the other statements are concerned, the statement of retained earnings for the second quarter must be presented in a two-column format giving the figures for the six months to June 30 for the current year with the comparative figures for the preceding year covering the same period (i.e., to June 30, 20X0). The balance sheet, however, must give the financial position at June 30, 20X1 with the comparative figures for the full year ended December 31, 20X0. The cash flow statement must give the cash flows for the current six months with the comparative figures for the same six months for the preceding year.

To the extent that the interim financial statements do not include certain information, they are also required to include that information in the interim statements. The items specifically required are:

1. The disclosure of any departures from the generally accepted accounting principles used in preparing the annual financial statements, and that the interim financial statements must be read with the most recent annual financial statements;

ILLUSTRATION 15–1
INFORMATION TO BE DISCLOSED IN INTERIM STATEMENTS

The following information would be required to be presented in the interim financial statements for the third quarter of 20X2 by a company having a December 31 year end:

Balance Sheet at	September 30, 20X2	December 31, 20X1
Income Statements for:		
9 months ended	September 30, 20X2	September 30, 20X1
3 months ended	September 30, 20X2	September 30, 20X1
Statement of Retained Earnings for:		
9 months ended	September 30, 20X2	September 30, 20X1
Cash Flow Statement for:		
9 months ended	September 30, 20X2	September 30, 20X1
3 months ended	September 30, 20X2	September 30, 20X1

---

2. They must also include a statement that they follow the same accounting policies and methods as their most recent annual financial statements except those accounting policies or methods that have occurred since the last annual financial statements and that are clearly outlined in the interim financial statements;
3. A description of any cyclical nature of its operations;
4. The effects of any change in accounting estimates, to avoid misleading comparisons;
5. Segmented information relating to all reportable segments (see following section of this chapter);
6. Subsequent events relating to events since the last interim report;
7. Details of any business combinations, acquisitions or disposals of interests in subsidiaries, joint ventures, and any investments accounted for using the equity method;
8. Any restructuring of the company, discontinued operations, and extraordinary items;
9. The amount of any contingencies; and
10. Any other information required for the fair presentation of financial position, results of operations, or cash flows for the interim period.

Reporting requirements 4, 5, and 10 apply to both the current interim period and the current financial year to date, whereas the balance of the reporting requirements applies to the current financial year only. The application of these reporting requirements is reflected by Illustration 15–1 showing what information must be presented in its interim financial statements for a company having a December 31 year end for the third quarter ended September 30, 20X2.

Earnings per Share Data

Earnings per share data is also required to be presented on the face of the interim reports if this information is required to be disclosed: that is, to those public companies whose securities are publicly traded.

The Practical Difficulties in Preparing Interim Reports

It is recognized that detailed information relating to certain expenses, like annual bonuses and income taxes, is only available towards the year end. The interim reports should, therefore, include a reasonable estimate of the required amounts. In the case of annual bonuses, for example, an estimate of the amounts required should only be included if there is a legal requirement to pay such bonuses or past practice has set a precedent for the payment of these amounts. Income tax expense, on the other hand, should be calculated using the rate of tax that is expected to apply to total earnings.

The Quality of Information Provided by Interim Reports

The interim reporting requirements require extensive and comprehensive reporting. They are the result of serious concerns expressed by members of the financial analyst community and the investing public that companies were not complying with the interim reporting requirements; interim reports were not being issued on time, and that insufficient information was being disclosed particularly where the information was unfavourable. Whether the current reporting requirements, which are considerably more demanding, will rectify the situation, remains to be seen.

It should be borne in mind that part of the problem is that, unlike the position in the USA, the information provided by interim reports is not required to be audited and, consequently, these reports are not subject to the scrutiny and certification by the reporting company's auditors. To address the potential problem of the non-disclosure of relevant information, the Toronto Stock Exchange's Committee on Corporate Disclosure has recommended that fines be imposed on the directors and chief executives of delinquent companies along the lines imposed on those relating to incorrect statements in prospectuses and other statutory reports.

B. SEGMENT DISCLOSURES

The Need for Segmented Information

With the broadening of the activities of multinational corporations into different industries, foreign countries and markets during the 1960s, it soon became obvious that the consolidated results of operations and financial position presented in consolidated financial statements were not suitable for analyzing the profitability and earnings potential of these companies. Not only was the information relating to profitable and unprofitable operations grouped together, but details of the activities of the business were being withheld from investors. It, therefore, became clear that the information provided had to be broken down in some way or other. This was achieved in the USA by the requirement that segmented information be included in financial reports in terms of the FASB's *SFAS No. 14: Financial Reporting for Segments of a Business Enterprise* issued in 1976. However, pressure from the financial analyst community in both Canada and the USA resulted in the withdrawal of these reporting requirements in 1997 and their replacement with more detailed requirements that were developed jointly by the CICA and the FASB.

In effect, **the provision of segmented information is the de-consolidation or disaggregation of the information provided in the consolidated financial statements of diversified corporate enterprises.** The provision of this information has been mandatory in Canada since June 1979 for companies to which the requirements of section 1700 of the CICA *Handbook* apply. This chapter explains and presents the requirements for segment reporting.

The Segment Disclosure Requirements

The objective of segment disclosures as defined by the CICA *Handbook*[4] **is to provide information about the different types of business activities in which an enterprise engages and the different economic environments in which it operates.** This information is provided to

---

4 Section 1701.

help users of financial statements better understand the enterprise's performance, to assess its prospects for future cash flows, and to make more informed judgments about the enterprise as a whole.

The requirement to provide segment disclosures applies to those companies whose securities are publicly traded on recognized stock exchanges or traded on over-the-counter markets (e.g., for bonds), co-operative business enterprises,[5] deposit-taking institutions, and life insurance enterprises. Private and closely held companies are exempted from this requirement.

The requirements are that the financial statements of qualifying reporting entities should include selected information **for each reportable segment based on the way management assesses the performance of these segments, and how the entity organizes the operations and activities of these segments**. These reporting requirements are referred to as representing **a management approach** because the requirements are based on the disclosure of information relating to the reporting entity's profit or operating centres.

Reporting in this manner requires that the entity discloses additional information on **each of its operating segments**. These segments are broadly defined as those separate components of the reporting entity's activities that earn revenues, incur expenses, and their results are reviewed periodically by management.

The requirements stress that the review by management (or the chief operating officer) should be for the purpose of allocating resources. This includes those reportable segments that are at the start-up stage and that have no earned revenues. However, **those segments that do not earn revenues, like the corporate headquarters, its computing services, etc., are not considered to be reportable segments**. Operating segments displaying similar longterm financial performance may be aggregated, provided that they produce similar products and services, or where the nature of the production process is comparable.

Reporting Operating Segments

As outlined above, qualifying reporting entities are first required to disclose information on their operating segments. The criteria for reporting such segments are based on the following three quantitative tests and an affirmative answer to **any of these three tests** requires disclosure of that segment. The three tests are:

The 10% Revenues Test: To be a reportable segment, the reported revenues of the operating segment from sales to both its external customers and its intersegment sales (or transfers) must be at least 10% of the total revenues for all operating segments.

The 10% Profits Test: Similarly, the profits (or losses) must be at least 10% of the absolute amount of the combined profit from all operating segments that did not report a loss of 10% or 10% of the combined loss of all operating segments that reported losses.

The 10% Assets Test: As with the two previous tests, the assets of the operating segment must be at least 10% of the combined assets of all operating segments.

The application of the three tests is relatively straightforward. The **10% revenues and 10% operational assets tests** pose no problems because they involve nothing more than simple calculations. With the **10% operational profits test**, however, problems may arise where some segments are profitable and others are not. This problem is recognized by the CICA *Handbook*, which specifies that in these cases, the determination of the total operating profits and losses must be determined on an "absolute basis". What this means is that the operating

---

[5]   Co-operative enterprises are formed to benefit their members and are used extensively in Ontario for co-operative housing projects. In certain cases, they carry on business activities, but this form of business venture is rare in Canada.

profits and operating losses **are aggregated** separately to give the **absolute operating profits** and the **absolute operating losses,** and the 10% rule is applied against the greater of the two.

For example, assume that a company had five operating segments, three of which operated at a profit and two had operated at a loss. To determine the reportable segments would involve the following analysis:

Segment	Operating Profit/Loss		Absolute Profits	Absolute Losses
A	Profit of	$ 100,000	$ 100,000	—
B	Loss of	(240,000)	—	$ (240,000)
C	Profit of	1,400,000	1,400,000	—
D	Profit of	700,000	700,000	—
E	Loss of	(700,000)	—	(700,000)
	Total	$1,260,000	$2,200,000	$ (940,000)

In this case, the reportable segments would be B, C, D, and E because they are greater than 10% of the absolute amount of profits of $2.2-million. Segment A would be aggregated and presented under the heading of "other items".

The extent to which segmented information should be provided is that **at least 75%** of the reporting company's **total external revenues** from affiliated and non-affiliated customers by operating segment should be disaggregated into separate operating segments. Where the operating segments identified using the 10% test are less than 75% of the reporting entity's total external revenues, the next largest operating segment (or segments) should be included as a reportable operating segment until the total revenues of the reported segments meets the 75% criterion. The balance of the disaggregated information should then be combined and reported under the heading of "other segments", so that the total revenue figure agrees with the amount shown in the financial statements. The same procedure must be repeated for the profits and operating assets. If the business activities of the reporting entity are such that a considerable number of operating segments qualify for separate disclosure, then from a practical point of view, these should be **restricted to a maximum of ten** unless there is a specific reason for disclosing segments in excess of 10.

The 75% rule does not specifically apply to profits and assets. However, if the disclosable segments do not cover 75% of the revenues, profits or assets, it would be advisable to add additional segments until at least a level of 75% is reached by all three categories.

Where the reporting entity's operations **involve only one activity**, like the mining of phosphate deposits, then it should report on that activity as a single segment unless it carries out similar activities in different locations. In these cases, the reporting would be on the basis of the reporting entity's activities in different geographic locations (see subsequent section, entitled Enterprise-Wide Disclosures).

An example of the determination of operating segments using the three tests is provided in Illustration 15–2. In this illustration, there are only two reportable operating segments (i.e., shoes and travel goods) because they are the only two segments that are identified by the three tests as reportable segments and because they jointly exceed the 75% requirement.

The Disclosure of Reportable Operating Segments

The disclosure requirements for operating segments are extensive. **First, the basis of identifying the entity's reportable segments and the basis of its internal organization must be disclosed. Second, the entity must disclose the types of products and services applying to each reportable segment. And, third, the entity must report on how the profit or loss for each reportable segment was determined in considerable detail.**

ILLUSTRATION 15–2
DETERMINING REPORTABLE OPERATING SEGMENTS

Reporting Inc. manufactures shoes, leatherwear, travel goods and a range of leather handbags and other fashion products. Operations are divisionalized but transfers of goods between the different divisions are fairly commonplace. During the year ended December 31, 20X5, the company reported consolidated net income of $200-million and at December 31, 20X5, the capital assets and goodwill of the company amounted to $320-million. The breakdown of these figures into operating statements based on the management reporting system together with intersegment transfers during the year and other relevant information is provided below:

	Total	Shoes	Outwear	Travel	Fashion
			(000s)		
Operating Profit:					
Sales to Outside Parties	$2,300,000	$1,100,000	$200,000	$900,000	$100,000
Materials and Expenses	1,900,000	830,000	164,000	830,000	76,000
Operating Profit	400,000	270,000	36,000	70,000	24,000
Administration Expenses	(80,000)	(49,000)	(11,000)	(9,000)	(11,000)
Amortization of Capital Assets	(20,000)	(8,500)	(5,000)	(4,000)	(2,500)
Income Taxes	(40,000)	(22,000)	(7,000)	(4,500)	(6,500)
Total Net Income	260,000	190,500	13,000	52,500	4,000
Less: Minority Interests	60,000	48,000	—	12,000	—
Consolidated Net Income	$ 200,000	$ 142,500	$ 13,000	$ 40,500	$ 4,000
Intersegment Sales:	$ 420,000	$ 120,000	$ 20,000	$200,000	$ 80,000
Capital Assets and Goodwill:					
At January 1, 20X5	$ 280,000	$ 192,000	$ 38,000	$ 40,000	$ 10,000
Acquisitions/Disposals	40,000	30,000	(8,000)	10,000	8,000
Total Assets	$ 320,000	$ 222,000	$ 30,000	$ 50,000	$ 18,000

The determination of reportable segments is carried out by applying the three 10% tests.

With The 10% Revenue Test we get:

Shoes	($1,100,000 + $120,000)/$2,720,000	=	44.85%	—	Include
Outwear	($200,000 + $20,000)/$$2,720,000	=	8.09%	—	Exclude
Travel	($900,000 + $200,000)/$2,720,000	=	40.44%	—	Include
Fashion	($100,000 + $80,000)/$2,720,000	=	6.62%	—	Exclude

On the basis of this test, only shoes and travel goods are reportable segments because the total revenues from these segments exceed 75% (i.e., 44.85% + 40.44% = 85.29%).

Similarly, with The 10% Profits Test we get:

Shoes	$270,000/$400,000	=	67.50%	—	Include
Outwear	$36,000/$400,000	=	9.00%	—	Exclude
Travel	$70,000/$400,000	=	17.50%	—	Include
Fashion	$24,000/$400,000	=	6.00%	—	Exclude

Once again, only shoes and travel are reportable segments because they exceed the 75% total (i.e., 67.50% + 17.50% = 85.00%).

And, finally with The 10% Operational Assets Test we get:

Shoes	$222,000/$320,000	=	69.37%	—	Include
Outwear	$30,000/$320,000	=	9.38%	—	Exclude
Travel	$50,000/$320,000	=	15.62%	—	Include
Fashion	$18,000/$320,000	=	5.63%	—	Exclude

Therefore, on the basis of the three tests, shoes and travel are the only reportable segments because with each test they exceed 75%. Outwear and fashion are then grouped together as "Other Segments".

The information on the determination of the profit or loss for each segment is essentially the same as the CICA *Handbook's* disclosure requirements for the income statement (i.e., section 1520). It does not, however, include earnings per share, the results of discontinued operations, reporting accounting changes, and extraordinary items. Notwithstanding these exclusions, the list of required disclosures is formidable. **Each reportable segment** requires disclosure of revenues from external customers, revenues from intersegment transactions, interest revenues, interest expense, amortization of capital assets and the impairment of goodwill, any other revenues or expenses of unusual magnitude, the proportionate share of net income from investee companies,[6] income tax expenses or benefits, and any other significant noncash items other than the amortization of capital assets and the write down of goodwill. Comparative figures for the previous year, as adjusted for any changes in the groupings of segments, are also required.

In addition, if management considers an operating segment reported in the previous period but not in the current period as being of continued significance, information on that segment should be included in the current period, even though it may not satisfy the requirements of the 10% tests. Where this occurs, the comparative figures for the previous year should be restated to reflect the nature of the current period's reportable segments.

These reporting requirements are extensive. An objective assessment suggests that the interests of both preparers and users may perhaps have been better served by a detailed columnar income statement covering all aspects of the trading activities of the business, instead of the requirements of this section. The stated objective of these detailed income statement type disclosures is to provide an indication of "... the measure reported to the chief operating decision maker for the purposes of making decisions about allocating resources to the segment and assessing its performance."[7] Whether these requirements will provide readers with the desired additional information remains to be seen.

Reactions to these reporting requirements have been varied. Generally speaking, they have been welcomed by the financial analyst community, but criticized by others as requiring too much detailed information and making compliance expensive.

An example of segmented disclosure is provided in abbreviated form as Illustration 15–3, which is a continuation of Illustration 15–2. This illustration shows how the trading activities are described, how segment profits and losses and segment assets are measured, how management identifies reportable segments, and how segment profits or losses and segment assets are reported.

The Interim Reporting Requirements

Section 1751 of the CICA *Handbook* requires that segment information must be included in interim statements. The requirements are the same as those required for reportable segments: revenues from external customers, intersegment revenues, and profit or loss for each segment. In addition, segment information should also include any material change in the total assets from that disclosed in the previous annual report, any change in the make-up of the different segments from the previous year, and a reconciliation of the net segment profit or loss with that of the reporting entity before discontinued operations and extraordinary items. Where the reporting entity has been subject to an internal reconstruction, information on the composition of the restated segment for prior periods is also required. As with the disclosure requirements for interim reports, this information should be provided for the current interim period and cumulatively to date in comparative form.

---

[6] In addition to the share of net income, it also requires information on the effects of the investment in the assets of the investee company on the determination of the profit or loss for each segment, as well as any changes in these assets during the current year.

[7] CICA *Handbook*, paragraph 1701.32.

ILLUSTRATION 15-3
REPORTING OPERATING SEGMENTS

Using the same information provided in Illustration 15–2, the presentation of the segmented information is by note disclosure along the following lines:

Note 11
The company has two operating segments, shoes and leather goods. The shoe segment manufactures the Emily & Edgar line of shoes for sale to footwear retailers. The travel segment produces Kumfy Travel Goods for sale to the distributors of leather products.

The accounting policies of the segments are the same as those described in Note 1, *Summary of Significant Accounting Policies*. Segment performance is evaluated based on consolidated net income. Intersegment sales are made at current market prices.

The company's reportable segments are separately managed business units that manufacture, sell and distribute the different products. An analysis of these activities by segment is given below:

	Consolidated	Shoes	Travel	Other Segments	Eliminations
			(000s)		
Sales:					
To Outside Parties	$2,300,000	$1,100,000	$ 900,000	$300,000	
Intersegment Sales		120,000	200,000	100,000	$(420,000)
Total Sales	$2,300,000	$1,220,000	$1,100,000	$400,000	$(420,000)
Net Operating Income	$ 400,000	$ 270,000	$ 70,000	$ 60,000	
Administration Expenses	(80,000)	(49,000)	(9,000)	(22,000)	
Amortization of Capital Assets	(20,000)	(8,500)	(4,000)	(7,500)	
Income Taxes	(40,000)	(22,000)	(4,500)	(13,500)	
Total Net Income	260,000	190,500	52,500	17,000	
Minority Interests	60,000	48,000	12,000	—	
Consolidated Net Income	$ 200,000	$ 142,500	$ 40,500	$ 17,000	
Capital Assets and Goodwill	$ 320,000	$ 222,000	$ 50,000	$ 48,000	
Capital Expenditures during Year	$ 48,000	$ 30,000	$ 10,000	$ 8,000	
Disposals during Year	(8,000)			(8,000)	
	$ 40,000	$ 30,000	$ 10,000	—	

1. The information provided in the covering note (i.e., Note 11) is required in terms of paragraphs 1791.29(a), 1791.29(b) and 1701.34 of the CICA *Handbook*.
2. As the consolidated net income of $200-million reflected above is the same as that for the year from operations, it does not require reconciliation with the figure appearing on the consolidated income statement.
3. A reconciliation of the segment assets with those appearing on the balance sheet would also be required.

Restatement of Previously Disclosed Information

If a reporting entity changes the structure of its internal organization in a manner that changes the composition of its reportable segments, the corresponding information for earlier periods should be provided and restated unless it is impracticable to do so. If restatement does not occur, then the entity should disclose, in the year in which the change occurred, segment information on both the old and the new bases, unless it is impractical to do so.

Enterprise-wide Disclosures

In addition to the segment reporting requirements considered earlier in this section, information on three additional matters must be disclosed, if not disclosed elsewhere by the reporting entity. These are:

ILLUSTRATION 15–4
REPORTING GEOGRAPHIC INFORMATION AND INFORMATION ABOUT MAJOR CUSTOMERS

The revenues and utilization of assets attributable to the countries in which the company carries on business:

	Revenues from External Customers	Capital Assets and Goodwill
	(000s)	
Canada	$ 754,220	$257,600
United States — see note below	1,088,450	45,325
Mexico	210,405	17,075
Japan	125,605	—
Other foreign countries	121,320	—
Total Sales to External Customers	$2,300,000	$320,000

Note: Revenues of $322,715,000 arose from a contract to supply a range of shoes to the Smart Suzy chain of retail shoe stores operating on the American west coast. Other revenues from the USA, like those from Mexico, Japan, and other foreign countries, were to smaller retail outlets.

1. **Products and Services**
   The reporting entity should disclose the **revenues** from its external customers for each of **its products and services or each group of products and services**.

2. **Geographic Disclosures**
   The reporting entity should disclose the **total revenues** from external customers **in the entity's country of domicile and from all the foreign countries** in which it carried on business. Where the revenues from one or more external foreign customers are material (considered to be 5% or more), these should be reported separately. Similarly, it must also report on the total capital assets and goodwill situated in its country of domicile and all foreign countries with the proviso that where the assets held in a particular foreign country are material, then these assets must be disclosed separately. It should also be noted that either one of the **revenues** or **capital assets plus goodwill** would satisfy the need to disclose the country as a separate geographic segment. Materiality in relation to geographic disclosures is not defined and it is a matter of professional judgment.

   An example of how this information should be disclosed is provided as Illustration 15–4 that is, once again, a continuation of Illustrations 15–2 and 15–3.

3. **Major Customers**
   The reporting entity is also required to disclose information on the extent of **its reliance on major customers**. The reporting criterion is 10% or more of the **total revenues from transactions** with its customers in a foreign country. If the reporting entity has major customers of this nature, it must disclose this fact as well as the revenues from each such customer, and the segments reporting those revenues. An example of this type of disclosure is presented in Illustration 15–4.

C. SUMMARY REPORTING

In 1987, the Securities and Exchange Commission in the USA approved the use of "summary financial reporting".[8] This approval was granted following a request by General Motors Corporation that it be allowed to report to its shareholders in summary form rather than

---

[8] See John C.C. Macintosh, "The SEC Approves the Use of Differential Reporting", *Akron Business and Economic Review*, Spring 1989, pp. 38–45, for a full review of the situation.

through the traditional annual report. The approval was granted on condition that General Motors would continue to provide all information required by the SEC for annual report filing purposes (i.e., Form 10-K), and that this information would be included as an appendix to the proxy statement for the election of directors that is mailed to all shareholders prior to the annual general meeting of a company.

The significance of this ruling is that it drew attention to the fact that there was, in the USA, no requirement that companies whose shares are publicly traded must report to their shareholders through the traditional annual report.[9] Provided shareholders are furnished with all the information they are required to receive, companies are free to report to their shareholders in any form they wish provided the financial statements and auditor's report are presented to shareholders.

The move by General Motors Corporation was the result of a series of changes to the SEC's reporting requirements that, since 1980, have resulted in the information being presented to shareholders in the annual reports of companies becoming almost identical with the detailed information required by the SEC in its filing requirements (i.e., Form 10-K). There was, consequently, no need for two sets of financial reports providing the same information. Concern was also expressed that the original purpose of financial reports, which is the communication of information to interested parties, had been overlooked because the information provided was, largely, too complicated for the average investor[10] to understand.

In 1981, the Financial Executives Institute, together with Deloitte Haskins and Sells (now Deloitte and Touche), investigated the possibility of providing shareholders with summary reports. Nineteen major US corporations were invited to rewrite their annual reports in a more simplified manner without regard for FASB and SEC requirements other than those relating to the inclusion of misleading information and the omission of material facts. They were also asked to stress that Form 10-K was available to shareholders on request.

The summary reports produced differed considerably from one another. Some replaced the non-financial sections with an expanded letter to shareholders, others significantly reduced or eliminated the information provided in the annual report. Generally speaking, the reports tended to condense the information provided and, as a result, they were referred to as summary annual reports. What emerged from the exercise were annual reports that were considerably shorter (an average of 11 rather than 24 pages in length) and easy to read and understand. There was also a consensus amongst the participating companies that it would be practical and suitable to issue summary reports to their shareholders.

The reaction of the financial analyst community to the move was adequately predictable. In a survey carried out in May 1987,[11] 64% of financial analysts surveyed (16 out of 25) opposed the idea, with two analysts going so far as to state that they would stop covering the activities of companies issuing summary reports to their shareholders. This did not, however, deter a number of companies, like the McKesson Corporation of San Francisco and ExxonMobil[12] of Irving, Texas, from going ahead and issuing summary reports.

---

9 The position in Canada is that the issue of an annual report to shareholders is voluntary except in Quebec where it is required in terms of that province's securities legislation.

10 Figures produced by the New York Stock Exchange show that roughly one out of every four adults in the USA own stocks traded on US security markets either in their own right or indirectly through investing in mutual funds. A large number (i.e., in the region of 40%) are retired persons or nonemployed adults like housewives.

11 *Investment Analysts' Attitudes Towards Summary Annual Reports*, A Survey by Hill and Knowlton, Inc., New York, May 1987.

12 The audit report of the 2003 Summary Annual Report of ExxonMobil issued by PricewaterhouseCoopers L.L.P. on February 25, 2004, included, *inter alia*, the following statement: "In our opinion, the information set forth in the accompanying summary balance sheets as of December 31, 2003 and 2002, and the related summary statement of income and cash flows for each of the three years in the period ended December 31, 2003, is fairly stated, in all material aspects, in relation to the consolidated financial statements from which it has been derived."

To what extent this form of reporting will continue to be used is not clear but a considerable number of companies in the USA are issuing them to their shareholders. To date, there has been no similar movement in Canada.

SUMMARY

Interim reporting refers to the issue of quarterly reports by companies. In Canada, companies whose securities are publicly traded are required to issue these reports to their shareholders at the end of the first, second and third quarters of their financial year. The objective of interim reports is to communicate information to investors and other interested parties to allow them to predict the results of operations of the reporting entity for the year under review and its financial position at the end of the year. They are essentially abbreviated financial statements and consist of a balance sheet, an income statement, a statement of retained earnings and a cash flow statement. The information contained in these statements is similar to that presented in the annual financial report. In order to ensure that they serve their stated purpose, comprehensive reporting requirements are prescribed by the CICA *Handbook*.

Segment reporting is also outlined. This form of reporting requires that public enterprises and certain other enterprises disclose specific information about operating segments, their products and services, their geographic areas of operations, and their major customers.

Finally, this chapter briefly describes summary reporting. This method of reporting has, since 1987, been approved as a means by which companies in the USA can report to their shareholders. Where it is used, companies still have to provide shareholders with the required information and to file the necessary reports with the Securities and Exchange Commission.

REVIEW QUESTIONS

1. What is meant by the term "interim reporting"?
2. What is the objective of interim reporting?
3. What does interim reporting consist of?
4. What is the purpose of reporting segmented information? Why is it considered important?
5. What is an operating segment? What are the criteria for reporting an operating segment?
6. Are generally accepted accounting principles applied to segment reporting? Does the reporting of segmented information vary from the principles normally applied to consolidated financial statements?
7. What is a dominant operating segment?
8. If 90% of a company's activities relate to one operating segment but operational assets are spread equally over two operating segments, should segmented information be provided? If so, why?
9. How are export sales reflected in the financial statements?
10. What conditions led to the request that summary reporting be allowed in the USA, and what does summary reporting mean?

EXERCISES

EXERCISE 15–3 The Priscilla Tire Company Inc. produces radial-ply tires for the local and export market. During the year ended December 31, 20X5, its sales of tires and assets were as follows:

Country	Sales to Unaffiliated Customers	Transfers to Affiliated Customers	Capital Assets and Goodwill
Canada	$4,000,000	$ 600,000	$10,000,000
USA	2,400,000	—	8,100,000
Mexico	550,000	2,000,000	500,000
Brazil	200,000	—	1,400,000
Peru	65,000	—	600,000
Nigeria	920,000	250,000	3,350,000
Ghana	120,000	—	600,000
	$8,255,000	$2,850,000	$24,550,000

REQUIRED

Using the information provided, determine which countries represent reportable geographic segments.

EXERCISE 15–2   The following information relates to the activities of Jackson Peters Inc., a Canadian multinational company, for the year ended December 31, 20X5:

Segment	Revenue from Unaffiliated Customers	Revenue from Affiliated Customers	Operating Profit	Identifiable Assets
A	$3,000,000	$1,000,000	$300,000	$ 7,000,000
B	800,000	—	60,000	200,000
C	1,500,000	—	(100,000)	3,000,000
D	700,000	—	50,000	80,000
E	1,600,000	—	220,000	1,240,000
F	1,000,000	—	80,000	400,000
G	500,000	300,000	(20,000)	120,000
	$9,100,000	$1,300,000	$590,000	$12,040,000

REQUIRED

Determine the reportable operating segments for Jackson Peters from the above information.

EXERCISE 15–3   Diversified Enterprises Inc. is a corporation having its head office in Toronto but that also carries on substantial trading activities in the USA, Mexico, Brazil and Argentina.

Details of its trading activities were as follows:

	Canada	USA	Mexico	Brazil	Argentina	Consolidated
			000s			
Sales to Unaffiliated Customers						
Single Customers	$ 80,000	$210,000	$ 4,000	$ 7,000	$ 9,000	$ 310,000
General Sales	280,000	30,000	76,000	78,000	46,000	510,000
Total Sales	$360,000	$240,000	$ 80,000	$ 85,000	$ 55,000	$ 820,000
Capital Assets and Goodwill	$670,000	$105,000	$100,000	$115,000	$210,000	$1,200,000

REQUIRED

From the analysis of the trading activities of the company for the year ended December 31, 20X5 given above:

1. Determine which geographic segments (if any) are reportable in terms of section 1701 of the CICA *Handbook* using:
   i. The revenue test;
   ii. The capital assets and goodwill test.

2. Give the required disclosures for major customers on the assumption that the sales to single customers were to individual buyers only.

3. If Diversified Enterprises wanted to report on the basis of two geographic segments, North America (i.e., Canada and the USA) and Latin America (i.e., Argentina, Brazil and Mexico), could it do so? Explain why or why not.

16

Foreign Exchange Transactions and Foreign Operations

LEARNING OBJECTIVES

After studying this chapter you should be able to:

1. Understand the nature of international trade, currencies, and the rates of exchange between currencies;
2. Translate transactions carried out in foreign currencies into Canadian dollars;
3. Distinguish between fully integrated and self-sustaining foreign operations and be able to translate the financial statements of foreign operations into Canadian dollars using Canadian generally accepted accounting principles; and
4. Consolidate foreign subsidiaries.

INTERNATIONAL TRADE AND FOREIGN OPERATIONS

Since time immemorial, communities have traded with one another. For example, the trading in olive oil in the Mediterranean region dates back thousands of years. In those early times, certain commodities were also only available in certain areas and, to obtain these goods, other goods had to be given up in exchange. As a result, a system of barter developed. As trade developed, barter gave way to the settlement of transactions in gold which, in earlier times, was the only real means of exchange. Today, most international trade is conducted in US dollars, Swiss Francs, British Pounds and Japanese Yen. On January 1, 2001, the Euro, the common currency of 12 of the 15-nation European Union, was used for the first time as an international currency[1] and the currencies of member countries of participating countries (e.g., Belgium, France, Germany, and the Netherlands) were no longer used. Up to that time, the Euro had only been used to settle amounts between governments in the EU. Prices of goods in the EU are now quoted in both Euros and the local currency to prepare the population for the issue of Euro coins and banknotes on January 1, 2002.

---

[1] Other than the countries that joined the EU on May 1, 2004 (i.e., Cyprus, the Czech Republic, Estonia, Hungary, Latvia, Lithuania, Malta, Poland, the Slovak Republic, and Slovenia), the three member countries not having adopted the Euro are the United Kingdom, Denmark and Sweden. Reasons for this are the international role of the British Pound and the fear by these three countries that the adoption of the common currency would lead to the loss of their separate cultures and identities.

International trade developed rapidly in the 18th century following the Industrial Revolution. As communications between countries improved, the industrial countries of Europe and America found ready markets for their products and lucrative investment opportunities in various parts of the world. This continued into recent times, and the 1960s were characterized by the development of the multinational corporation. Today, with the emergence of Japan as a major trading nation and other potential industrial giants like Brazil, China, and Korea, the pattern of international trade has changed. The production of goods has also moved to "third world" countries, like Mexico and Malaysia, where labour and other costs of production are considerably lower than in developed countries. In addition, the provision of services as an international activity has also increased dramatically. With a general increase in the prosperity of the world's nations, international trade will continue to grow in importance. For Canada, even though the majority of its trade is with the USA, international trade is still a very important part of its economic activity. Originally, the Canadian economy was resource-based but it now ranks in the 10 most important industrial nations,[2] and many Canadian companies have expanded their operations through branches or subsidiaries in the USA and in foreign countries.

This chapter is concerned with the accounting for transactions carried out in a foreign currency and the translation of the financial statements of foreign operations into Canadian dollars.

CURRENCIES AND RATES OF EXCHANGE

Money is generally accepted as a means of exchange, the means of paying for goods and services, and the settlement of debt. It also acts as a common denominator so that the value of various goods and services can be related or compared with one another. The money used in any country is referred to as the currency of that country.

The currencies of different countries are traded on foreign exchange markets by dealers in foreign exchange. The price payable for foreign currency is known as the **rate of exchange** and refers to the amount of foreign or local currency that would be received for a unit of the currency exchanged.

Rates of exchange are normally expressed in terms of the unit of local currency, but this is not necessarily the case. For example, even though Canadian rates of exchange are normally expressed as Canadian $1.00 = US $0.73, it could also be expressed in terms of the US dollar as US $1.00 = Canadian $1.37. Irrespective of how the rates are expressed, in this case one dollar of Canadian currency would be exchanged for 73 American cents, or one US dollar would purchase $1.37 in Canadian currency.

These rates of exchange can fluctuate widely and depend on the confidence buyers and sellers place on the value and stability of the currencies concerned. If, for example, the rate of exchange between the Canadian dollar and the US dollar increases from Canadian $1.00 = US $0.73 to Canadian $1.00 = US $0.75, we would say that the Canadian dollar has strengthened in relation to the US dollar. If, however, the rate of exchange dropped to Canadian $1.00 = US $0.71, we would say that the Canadian dollar had weakened or declined in value in relation to the US dollar.

Exchange rates also vary depending on when the foreign currency is to be delivered. If the foreign currency is purchased for immediate delivery, the rate of exchange is called the **spot rate**. However, if the foreign currency is only to be delivered at some future date, the rate of exchange is called the **forward rate of exchange**. Dealers in foreign exchange also quote different rates for the purchase or sale of foreign currency. These aspects of exchange rates are further examined in a later chapter.

---

[2] Canada's position as being in the top 10 industrialized nations has been threatened by India, Korea, and Spain, whose economies have grown substantially over the past decade.

THE TRANSLATION OF FOREIGN CURRENCY TRANSACTIONS

All transactions carried out by Canadian companies (or individual traders) in a foreign currency should be translated into Canadian dollars at the rate of exchange in effect on that day. The objective is to reflect the transaction in such a way as to portray economic reality. For example, the purchase of goods for resale for US $10,000 when the exchange rate between the US dollar and the Canadian dollar was Can $1.00 = US $0.74 would be translated as Canadian $ = US $10,000 – 1.00/0.74 = $13,513.

If the purchase of goods for US $10,000 was on credit, the amount recorded as a liability would have been recorded on the date of purchase at $13,513. Any change in the rate of exchange between the date of the purchase and the date on which the liability is discharged would give rise to an exchange gain or loss. For example, if the liability of US $10,000 was discharged when the rate of exchange between the Canadian and US dollar was quoted at Can $1.00 = US $0.75, the amount owing would have been reduced to $13,333. On discharge of the liability, it would have given rise to a "Gain on Foreign Exchange" of $180. The entries relating to these transactions are illustrated hereunder in journal entry form.

On Purchase of the Inventory:		
Inventory	13,513	
Accounts Payable		13,513
On Settlement of the Amount Owing:		
Accounts Payable	13,513	
Cash (US $10,000 × 1.00/0.75)		13,333
Gain on Foreign Currency Transaction		180

The gain on the foreign exchange transaction is credited to the income statement and not against the cost of the goods purchased **because, once established, the cost of the goods is left unchanged**. This is because it was only the exchange rate between the currencies that changed and not the cost of the goods themselves. If the purchase had been for cash, the amount would have been recorded at the amount paid out in cash on that date.

If, in the above case, the amounts owing in a foreign currency are unpaid at the balance sheet date, the liability must be adjusted at that date by using the prevailing rate of exchange. Any gain or loss arising from the adjustment would be included in the income statement for that period. Similarly, if amounts are owed to the reporting entity at the balance sheet date, they must also be adjusted to reflect the correct amount owing to it on that date. This would also apply to any nonmonetary items arising from foreign transactions that are carried on the balance sheet at their fair market value. This is necessary to ensure that all assets and liabilities are reflected on the balance sheet of the reporting entity at their correct amounts and that the net income (or loss) for the period is correctly stated.

It should be noted that gains or losses on foreign exchange transactions represent economic events. If the amounts owing or receivable have changed in value because the rates of exchange between currencies have changed, they must be recognized and adjusted accordingly. The only exception to the immediate write-off of foreign exchange gains and losses applies to regulated industries (e.g., cable television companies) where the regulator (e.g., the Canadian Radio and Television Commission) has ruled that these exchange gains or losses may be deferred and included in the determination of the future rates charged to customers.

TRANSACTING BUSINESS IN FOREIGN COUNTRIES

Unless a business enterprise carries on business through a branch office or subsidiary in the foreign country from which it imports goods, the transacting of business in foreign currencies is seldom carried out on credit. This is because orders for the supply of goods placed in foreign countries normally involve substantial amounts of money, and few traders would be prepared to take the risk of extending credit to their foreign customers. The reason for this is that, in case of non-payment, there are only limited means of recovering their debts. Governmental agencies and the local Chambers of Commerce can exert significant pressure on delinquent traders but, despite what our politicians tell us, there is no such thing as international law. For example, recourse to the International Court of Justice (in The Hague in the Netherlands) is only possible if the parties to the dispute have agreed to take the matter to the Court and abide by its decision.

Foreign transactions are, therefore, normally settled in cash on completion of the contract on a f.o.b. (free on board) or similar type basis. For example, a contract for the supply of goods may require payment on the delivery of goods to the Air Canada Cargo Depot at Hong Kong International Airport or on being loaded on to a ship in Rotterdam bound for Canada. Similarly, the export of goods from Canada may require settlement of the amount owing before the goods are removed from the country.

As outlined earlier, foreign transactions are carried out in one of the so-called "hard currencies" consisting of US Dollars, Swiss Francs, the Euro, British Pounds, Japanese Yen, or the currency of the foreign country concerned. Foreign countries may also insist on payment in one or other of these "hard currencies" because they may also need the foreign currency to pay for imported goods. Where considerable reciprocal trade between countries takes place, transactions between the countries may be carried out in the currency of either country.

Where **risk exists**, payment is usually on a "cash with order" basis. Normally, however, settlement of the amounts owing is either **by the electronic transfer of funds to the supplier or by using "letters of credit"**. Electronic transfers are made by the purchaser's bank directly to the supplier's bank account in the foreign country or through an associated bank. "Letters of credit", on the other hand, are guaranteed lines of credit arranged by the purchaser with his own bank against which cheques can be drawn in virtually any currency. In these latter cases, the cheques are issued by the purchaser's agent in the foreign country on being satisfied that the supplier has complied with the terms of the contract.

THE USE OF A SINGLE CURRENCY BY CANADA AND THE USA?

The settlement of transactions conducted in foreign currencies is time consuming and an expensive exercise for those businesses involved in foreign trade. The benefit of having a single currency, like the Euro, is that it eliminates this problem for transactions between countries using different currency.

Economists are predicting an increased move towards the use of a single currency between countries. This could be achieved by adopting the currency of another country as the local currency as, for example, Panama, which uses the US dollar as its currency. It could also be achieved by adopting a set rate of exchange between currencies.

Such arrangements could yield considerable benefits. However, the adoption of the currency of another country means that the adopting country loses its ability to control its economy through the setting of local interest rates and by being unable to control the supply of money in circulation. Any suggestion that Canada should adopt the US dollar as its currency has, therefore, been viewed with disfavour by successive federal governments. The linking of the Canadian dollar to the US dollar has similarly been looked upon unfavourably for the same reason. However, as trade between Canada and the USA increases (it already exceeds Canadian $1-billion per day), the federal government may be unable to ignore the situation.[3]

---

[3] In fact, Canadian Nobel Prize-winning economist Robert Mundell has expressed the viewpoint that the world is headed towards a small group of dominant currencies that would include the US dollar, the Japanese yen, [presumably the Swiss franc], and the Euro (*The Globe and Mail*, May 30, 2000). He stated that in such an environment, it

In fact, an increasing number of Canadian companies are already using the US dollar for internal and external reporting purposes.

The free trade agreement between Canada, Mexico and the USA may, in fact, have set the stage for the eventual use of a single currency in North America. This is because the EU started off as an economic union in which tariffs between the member countries were eliminated. Today, it is an economic and political union with its own parliament in Brussels and with a single currency in use by 12 of its 15 member states. The same could easily occur in North America between Canada, the USA, and Mexico.

For the foreseeable future, however, the adoption of the US dollar by Canada is highly unlikely. No matter how beneficial it would be for trade between the USA and Canada, the view of the federal government is that it would not allow Canada to pursue its own economic policies. Like the setting of accounting standards, the maintenance of a separate currency is also a matter of national pride.

TRANSLATING FOREIGN OPERATIONS

Where foreign operations have been carried on, it is necessary to restate the foreign entity's financial statements in such a manner that they reflect the results of operations and the financial position of the entity concerned as if they were expressed in Canadian dollars. This means that they should, as far as is possible, be restated using Canadian generally accepted accounting principles.

The need to restate the translated financial statements in Canadian GAAP is important because accounting principles and reporting practices are largely dependent upon the political, economic and legal system in operation in the countries in which they operate. Generally accepted accounting principles in foreign countries are often different from those in Canada. For example, the systematic amortization of goodwill only applies to relatively few countries. Similarly, differences in accounting principles apply to the creation of reserves, the revaluation of assets, and the recording of income taxes in different countries. The translation process should, therefore, be carried out in a manner designed to provide information like that presented in Canada. If this were not the case, it would be difficult to assess the results of operations and economic viability of the foreign operation. It is also necessary to restate the financial statements of foreign operations so that they can be combined or consolidated with those of the parent company. In the language of the day, the restatement should be carried out in a way that best reflects the extent to which the foreign operation has been **exposed** to changes in the rates of exchange.

Foreign operations may be carried out on either a **fully integrated** or **self-sustaining basis.** In this respect, a foreign operation is carried on through a subsidiary company, a division, branch, joint venture, or similar type of entity that normally undertakes and/or records its economic activities in a currency other than that used by the reporting entity. As outlined above, more and more Canadian companies are, however, using a single currency (like US dollars) to account for their local and foreign operations. In this respect, it should be noted that, provided companies use Canadian GAAP, there is no legal or other requirement that Canadian companies must prepare and present their financial statements in Canadian dollars.

Fully integrated foreign operations are defined as those operations that are financially or operationally interdependent with those of the reporting entity. This would occur, for example, with a branch office of a transport business in Buffalo, NY, which is so completely integrated with those of its Head Office in St. Catharines, Ontario, that fluctuations in the exchange rates would affect the St. Catharines Head Office as if it had carried on the trading operations itself.

---

would be inevitable that Canada would, in time, have to link its exchange rate for the Canadian dollar to that of the USA.

On the other hand, **self-sustaining foreign operations** are defined as those operations that are so financially and operationally independent of the reporting entity that exposure to changes in exchange rates is limited to reporting the reporting entity's net investment in the foreign operation: for example, the case of a Canadian meat-packing company that owns a cattle ranch in Brazil where contact with the Brazilian company is limited to the attendance at board meetings and at relatively few other times. In such cases, fluctuations between the Canadian dollar and the Brazilian Real would only affect the value of the investment in the books of the Canadian parent company.

It is sometimes difficult to establish whether a foreign operation is a fully integrated or a self-sustaining operation. Even where the operations are carried on many thousands of kilometres away from each other through a company, it does not necessarily mean that the operations are self-sustaining. This depends largely on the system of control over its operations and the extent to which it operates independently from its parent company.

To further complicate the issue, foreign operations may be carried out through branch operations or through foreign subsidiaries. Branch operations are often used to assess the business opportunities in a foreign country and it is only when it becomes apparent that a permanent or semi-permanent foreign operation should be established that a company is formed. At times, a controlling interest is purchased in an existing business but, in most cases, companies are formed to carry on business in the foreign country. In this chapter, for convenience all references to foreign operations should be construed as being carried out through subsidiary companies.

THE TRANSLATION OF THE FINANCIAL STATEMENTS OF FULLY INTEGRATED FOREIGN OPERATIONS

The Translation Process

As the operations of fully integrated subsidiaries are interdependent with those of the parent company, the translation of the financial statements should be consistent with those prepared by the parent company. The translation process should, therefore, be carried out in a way that reflects the operations and activities of the subsidiary as if it were merely an extension of the parent company. To achieve this objective, section 1650 of the CICA *Handbook* recommends that for integrated foreign operations, the **temporal method** of translation must be used.

Before the issue of the current section 1650 of the CICA *Handbook* in 1983, the financial statements of foreign subsidiaries were translated using the **current/noncurrent method**. Current assets and current liabilities were translated at their current values, whereas capital assets, longterm liabilities and capital were translated at cost. The **current/noncurrent method** was subsequently replaced by the **monetary/nonmonetary method** of translation in which monetary items were translated at their current value while nonmonetary items were left unchanged at their historical cost.

Following the issue of section 1650 of the CICA *Handbook*, however, the **temporal method** was recommended as the only acceptable method of translating the financial statements of foreign subsidiaries. This method is essentially the same as the monetary/nonmonetary method, except that the translation of the items on the balance sheet follows the same method as that used by its parent company. As liabilities are normally expressed in monetary terms, a valuation problem seldom arises. If it does, the same treatment as that used by the parent company should be used because the operations of the subsidiary company are considered part of those of the parent company.

The effect of this is that, although the basic monetary/nonmonetary distinction still applies, the translation of items is no longer based on the simple rule of whether they were monetary or nonmonetary in nature, but how they are treated by the parent company. For example, temporary investments would be translated at their market (or current) rate on the balance sheet of a subsidiary if this is the way they are recorded by the parent company.

An important feature of the temporal method is that every transaction of the foreign subsidiary is considered a transaction of the parent company itself. This means that each transaction should, in theory, be translated at the rate of exchange on the date on which the transaction took place. The income statement is, therefore, translated into Canadian dollars as if the transactions had been carried out in the currency of the parent company. **For practical purposes**, however, average rates of exchange may be used for the normal trading operations of the subsidiary. It is only with those transactions involving major items like the payment of dividends and the purchase and sale of assets that the actual rates of exchange are used.

The translation process also requires that there is an immediate recognition of exchange gains or losses. This is because, had the parent company entered into the transactions itself, it would have recognized exchange gains or losses when they occurred. Where a company uses a single currency to account for its worldwide operations, foreign currency gains and losses are recognized with every foreign currency transaction.

The need to consider all transactions of fully integrated foreign subsidiaries as an extension of the activities of the parent company complicates the position in other areas. For example, in many countries goodwill is not subject to the rules applicable in Canada and the United States. In these circumstances, one would have to treat goodwill according to the requirements of the CICA *Handbook*. As these adjustments could affect many years, substantial adjustments to the financial statements of the foreign operation may be necessary.

The Mechanics of the Translation Process

The actual procedures to be followed in using the temporal method are outlined as follows:

(a) Monetary items are translated at the rate of exchange at the balance sheet date.

(b) Nonmonetary items are normally translated at the historical rates of exchange on the date they were acquired. The only exception is where the items are recorded at their market price, in which case they are translated at the rate of exchange at the balance sheet date.

(c) Amortization expenses are translated at the same historical rates of exchange as the assets to which they relate.

(d) Revenues and expenses are translated at the rates of exchange in effect when they occur. It is, however, acceptable to use the average rate of exchange or other methods of approximation where necessary.

(e) Any gains or losses arising from the translation process should be included in net income in the period in which they occur. This applies equally to gains and losses arising from the translation of intercompany loans, bonds, longterm loans and mortgages.

(f) Dividends paid are recorded at the rate of exchange on the date of payment or receipt.

(g) Common stock is translated at the rate applicable at the date of acquisition so that, on consolidation, the amount can be reconciled with the investment account of the parent company.

To summarize the position, the translation of financial statements using the temporal method maintains the historical cost accounting model. It translates nonmonetary assets at the rates in effect when they were acquired and monetary assets at the rates in effect on the balance sheet date. The retained earnings figure brought forward from the **previous year** is the same as the closing figure in Canadian dollars at the end of the previous year. Net income is determined using the actual or average rates of exchange for revenues and expenses except amortization, which are based on the historical rates applicable to those assets. Finally, any differences arising from the translation of items are written-off to net income in the year in which they occur. An example of the use of the temporal method is outlined in Illustration 16–1.

The translation of the financial statements effected in Illustration 16–1 commences with the balance sheet. Monetary items are translated at the rate of exchange of US $1.00 = Can $1.44, while the nonmonetary assets, including any amortization thereon, are translated at the rates of exchange applicable on the dates on which they were acquired. In this illustration, this only applies to the motor trucks and the amortization thereon, and the fuel and sundry supplies. The fuel and sundry supplies have been translated at the rate of US $1.00 = Can $1.43, which is the average rate of exchange between September 30 and December 31, 20X4 (i.e., US $1.00 = [Can $1.42 + Can $1.44]/2).

As outlined above, common stock is similarly translated at the rate of exchange applying at the date on which the interest in the subsidiary was acquired (i.e., at US $1.00 = Can $1.32). This is important because if this were not the case, it would be difficult to reconcile the "investment in subsidiary account" in the ledger with the parent company's interest in the equity of the subsidiary for consolidation purposes.

Finally, the assets and liabilities sides of the balance sheet are balanced with one another by using the retained earnings figure as the balancing or "plug" figure. This retained earnings figure is then used as the balance of retained earnings at December 31, 20X4 on the combined income and retained earnings statement.

The translation of the income statement has been carried out by using the average rates of exchange for sales, purchases, administrative expenses, interest, and the like, which have been assumed to have accrued evenly throughout the year. Where cyclical trading patterns exist, more realistic adjustments of sales, purchases, and other items may be required. And, as capital assets are recorded at the rate of exchange applicable on their purchase date, amortization is based on the historical rate of exchange. The net income for the year is then determined by working backwards from the retained earnings figure established from the balance sheet. The gain or loss on exchange for the year is established, once again, as the balancing or "plug" figure and reflected as a revenue or expense item.

The loss on translation of $173,500 reflected on the income statement is a composite figure. It represents the net changes in the translation of the monetary and other nonmonetary items (e.g., like inventory) on the balance sheet that have arisen from the translation process. It may be broken down into its individual components but, in practice, this is seldom carried out. This is because it represents the balancing figure on the income statement, and no specific disclosures of translation gains or losses are required by the CICA *Handbook*.

Adjustments for Cyclical Trading Patterns

Where cyclical trading patterns exist or exchange rates do not change evenly throughout the year, purchases and other items must be adjusted on a basis that reflects this position. The normal manner in which this is carried out is to adjust the figures using average quarterly or monthly rates of exchange. For example, if the purchases of goods to the value of FCU 1,000,000 (i.e., 1,000,000 Foreign Currency Units) took place over the four quarters of the year in quantities of FCU 100,000, FCU 200,000, FCU 300,000 and FCU 400,000 when the average rates of exchange for the four quarters were 4.0, 4.1, 4.2, and 4.4 FCUs to the Canadian dollar, the purchases' figure would be calculated as follows:

First Quarter	FCU 100,000/4.0	=	Can $ 25,000
Second Quarter	FCU 200,000/4.1	=	48,780
Third Quarter	FCU 300,000/4.2	=	71,429
Fourth Quarter	FCU 400,000/4.4	=	90,909
			Can $236,118

ILLUSTRATION 16–1
THE TRANSLATION OF THE FINANCIAL STATEMENTS OF AN INTEGRATED FOREIGN OPERATION

The abbreviated financial statements of Niagara Transport (USA) Inc., a fully integrated foreign subsidiary company of Niagara Transport Inc. of St. Catharines, Ontario, for the financial year ended December 31, 20X4 were as follows:

INCOME STATEMENT

Transport Revenue	US $1,800,000
Less:	
Administrative Expenses	US $ 170,000
Amortization of Capital Assets	350,000
Fuel and Oil	320,000
Interest Expense	130,000
Salaries and Wages	600,000
Income Tax Expense	110,000
	US $1,680,000
Net Income for Year	US $ 120,000

STATEMENT OF RETAINED EARNINGS

Retained Earnings at January 1, 20X4	US $ 160,000
Net Income for Year	120,000
	280,000
Less: Dividends Paid (September 30, 20X4)	40,000
Retained Earnings at December 31, 20X4	US $ 240,000

BALANCE SHEET

Cash	US $ 60,000
Accounts Receivable	260,000
Fuel and Sundry Supplies on hand	90,000
Motor Trucks	2,800,000
Less Accumulated Amortization	(1,200,000)
	US $2,010,000
Accounts Payable	US $ 70,000
Longterm Loan (10%)	1,300,000
Common Stock	400,000
Retained Earnings	240,000
	US $2,010,000

Additional Information:

[1] Niagara Transport (USA) was formed and commenced business on January 2, 20X3 and on that date it purchased the motor trucks.

[2] The fuel and sundry supplies were all purchased evenly during the last three months of 20X4.

[3] At December 31, 20X3, the balance of Retained Earnings of Niagara Transport (USA) in Canadian dollars amounted to $235,000.

[4] The relevant rates of exchange between the US and Canadian dollar were as follows:

January 1, 20X3	US $1.00	=	Can $1.32
June 30, 20X3			Can $1.34
December 31, 20X3			Can $1.38
Average for 20X3			Can $1.36
June 30, 20X4			Can $1.41
September 30, 20X4			Can $1.42
December 31, 20X4			Can $1.44
Average for 20X4			Can $1.40

ILLUSTRATION 16–1 (Continued)

The translation of the financial statements of Niagara Transport (USA) into Canadian dollars at December 31, 20X4 would be carried out as follows:

	US Dollars	Conversion	Can Dollars
BALANCE SHEET			
Cash	$ 60,000	1.44/1.00	$ 86,400
Accounts Receivable	260,000	1.44/1.00	374,400
Fuel and Sundry Supplies on hand	90,000	Note 1	128,700
Motor Trucks	2,800,000	1.32/1.00	3,696,000
Less Accumulated Amortization	(1,200,000)	1.32/1.00	(1,584,000)
	$ 2,010,000		$ 2,701,500
Accounts Payable	$ 70,000	1.44/1.00	$ 100,800
Longterm Loans (10%)	1,300,000	1.44/1.00	1,872,000
Common Stock	400,000	1.32/1.00	528,000
Retained Earnings	240,000	balancing	200,700
	$ 2,010,000	figure	$ 2,701,500
STATEMENT OF RETAINED EARNINGS			
Retained Earn. at January 1, 20X4	$ 160,000	given	$ 235,000
Net Income for Year	120,000	balancing	22,500
	280,000	figure	257,500
Less: Dividends Paid	40,000	1.42/1.00	56,800
Retained Earnings at December 31, 20X4	$ 240,000		$ 200,700
INCOME STATEMENT			
Transport Revenue	$ 1,800,000	1.40/1.00	$ 2,520,000
Less:			
Administrative Expenses	$ 170,000	1.40/1.00	$ 238,000
Amortization of Vehicles	350,000	1.32/1.00	462,000
Fuel and Oil Expense	320,000	1.40/1.00	448,000
Interest Expense	130,000	1.40/1.00	182,000
Salaries and Wages Expense	600,000	1.40/1.00	840,000
Income Tax Expense	110,000	1.40/1.00	154,000
Loss on Exchange — Notes 2 and 3	—	balancing	173,500
	$ 1,680,000	figure	$ 2,497,500
Net Income for Year	$ 120,000		$ 22,500

Notes:

[1] The rate of exchange in this case is 1.43/1.00 calculated by taking the average of the rates on September 30, 20X4 and December 31, 20X4 (i.e., [(1.42 + 1.44)/2]/1.00).

[2] No specific disclosure requirements relating to gains or losses on foreign currency translations are required by the CICA *Handbook* for the translation of integrated foreign operations. Its inclusion in the income statement as a separate item is, however, considered desirable.

[3] The gain or loss is merely the result of the inclusion of a series of balancing or "plug" figures. In this case, the retained earnings of $200,700 for the foreign company were determined as the difference between the translated assets and liabilities after deducting the amount included as common stock. This figure of $200,700 then provided the balance on the Statement of Retained Earnings which, in turn, was balanced by the inclusion of the net income figure of $22,500. Finally, to arrive at the figure of $22,500 for net income on the income statement, it was necessary to include the "loss on translation" of $173,500.

THE TRANSLATION OF THE FINANCIAL STATEMENTS OF SELF-SUSTAINING FOREIGN OPERATIONS

The Current Rate Method

With self-sustaining foreign operations, the interest of the Canadian company is on the determination of the value of its investment at the end of the reporting period and the income from operations for the period covered by the financial statements. It is, therefore, necessary to translate all the assets and liabilities of self-sustaining operations into Canadian dollars at the rate of exchange at the balance sheet date. This is also necessary to reflect the results of operations for the period involved in a realistic manner.

The translation is carried out using the "current rate method". It was introduced through the revision of section 1650 of the CICA *Handbook* following the issue of *Statement of Financial Accounting Standards No. 52: Foreign Currency Translation* by the Financial Accounting Standards Board in 1981. Before the issue of this *SFAS No. 52*, the translation of self-sustaining operations in the USA and in Canada was by using the temporal method.

The basic objective of the current rate method is, within the limitations of using historical cost accounting, to reflect the value of the investment in the foreign operation at an amount approximating its actual value. It, therefore, attempts to reflect the economic reality of the holding of a foreign investment. For example, assume that a Canadian company formed a foreign subsidiary having common stock of 9,000,000 foreign currency units when the rate of exchange between the Canadian dollar and the foreign currency unit was Can $1.00 = FCU 22. In this case, the Canadian parent company would have reflected its investment in the foreign operation at Can $409,090 (i.e., FCU 9,000,000/22). Assume that after two years, the foreign subsidiary had earned FCU 2,000,000 to give a total investment of FCU 11,000,000. If at that date the rate of exchange had dropped to Can $1.00 = FCU 32, the investment would only be worth Can $343,750 (i.e., FCU 11,000,000/32) and would have to be reflected at that amount in the books and the balance sheet of the Canadian parent company. On the other hand, if the foreign currency unit had increased in relation to the Canadian dollar, the increased value of the investment would have been recognized at the current rate of exchange.

It is, however, necessary to retain a link between the value of the foreign investment in the ledger of the parent company and the amount reflected as the equity of the foreign subsidiary. The common stock of the foreign subsidiary is, therefore, translated at the rate of exchange on the date on which the investment in the subsidiary was acquired. Adjustments to the equity (i.e., the common stock, any capital surpluses and the retained earnings) of a self-sustaining foreign subsidiary to reflect its current value are effected by accumulating the translation gains or losses in a ledger account that is deducted from the equity of the company concerned.

The objective of reflecting economic reality while retaining the link between the original cost of the investment is achieved by deferring the translation gains and losses and deducting them from the total equity on the translated balance sheet. Using the above example, if the retained earnings of FCU 2,000,000 amounted to Can $71,430, the difference in value would have been entirely due to a weakening of the FCU in relation to the Canadian dollar. This would, therefore, have been disclosed on the translated balance sheet using the current rate method to give the amount of $343,750. The way this would be reflected is:

	Foreign Currency Units	Canadian Dollars
Common Stock	FCU 9,000,000	$409,090
Retained Earnings	2,000,000	71,430
	11,000,000	480,520
Less: Deferred Losses on Translation	—	136,770
Balance of Investment	FCU 11,000,000	$343,750

Where there is a sale of part of the interests of the parent company in a self-sustaining operation, there would also be a proportionate reduction in the share in the deferred gains or losses on translation. For example, if the parent company reduced its interest in the foreign subsidiary by one-fifth, the net investment would be reduced by $68,750 (i.e., $343,750/5), made up of a 20% reduction in the common stock, and the deferred losses on translation. In cases where the dividends paid in any year exceeded the net income for that year, part of the cumulative translation gain could be taken into income.

The Mechanics of the Current Rate Translation Process

Translation using the current rate method is straightforward. The mechanics of the translation process are that:

(a) Assets and liabilities including intercompany loans of the foreign operation are translated into the currency of the reporting entity at the rate of exchange at balance sheet date;

(b) Revenues and expenses (including amortization) are translated at the rates of exchange on the dates on which they occur. However, it is also acceptable to use the average rate of exchange for the year or other methods of approximation where necessary.

(c) Dividends received or paid are recorded at the rates of exchange in operation on the dates the dividends were received or paid.

(d) Any gains or losses arising from the translation of the financial statements, including those from intercompany loans, should be deferred and included in a separate component of shareholders' equity. In the event of a reduction in the net investment in the foreign operation, an appropriate proportion of these deferred gains or losses should be included in net income.[4]

(e) As with the temporal method, the figure for retained earnings brought forward from the previous year is the same figure as the closing retained earnings as translated into Canadian dollars at the previous reporting period.

(f) As outlined above, the common stock and other capital surplus accounts are, however, recorded at the original exchange rate so that they can be offset on consolidation against the amounts recorded by the parent company.

(g) The exchange gains or losses for the current year are added to the balance of the deferred gains or losses brought forward from the previous year.

The operation of the current rate method in translating the financial statements of a self-sustaining foreign subsidiary is outlined in Illustration 16–2. It shows that where the rates of exchange changed evenly throughout the year, all revenue and expense items are translated at the average rate of exchange for the year including any amounts calculated for amortization. Any interest payments on longterm loans and items, like legal fees or other extraordinary payments, that are material in amount are translated at the rates of exchange applicable when the payments were made. The net income using the current method is then added to the retained earnings brought forward from the beginning of the year. Any dividends paid are translated at the rate of exchange applicable on the date on which they are paid.

The assets and liabilities are translated at the rates of exchange on the last day of the financial year to give the total equity. The total equity consists of the common stock as translated at the date of acquisition and the retained earnings at the end of the current year as adjusted by the accumulated gains or losses on the translation of the assets and liabilities. As far as the parent company is concerned, economic reality is provided in that the total equity of the self-sustaining subsidiary is $623,000 (i.e., $643,000 + $292,000 − $312,000), which is the same as the equity of F2,370,000 translated at a rate of exchange of Can $100 = F3.8.

---

[4] CICA *Handbook*, section 1650.

The Disclosure Requirements Relating to the Changes in the Accumulated Gains or Losses on Translation

Section 1650 of the CICA *Handbook* specifically requires disclosure of those "significant elements" that gave rise to changes in the accumulated gains and losses on foreign exchange translation reflected as part of shareholders' equity.

The **operational words** of the relevant section are **significant elements**. This indicates that it is only those important changes and the reasons for such changes that must be disclosed. Details of individual changes in the values of the net assets would not be necessary except where they are unusual in magnitude or nature or where they have arisen through the sale by

---

ILLUSTRATION 16–2
TRANSLATION OF THE FINANCIAL STATEMENTS OF A SELF-SUSTAINING FOREIGN OPERATION

The abbreviated financial statements of Emmsaz SN, the completely self-sustaining foreign subsidiary of EMM Inc., at December 31, 20X3 are as follows:

INCOME STATEMENT

Sales	F 3,500,000
Cost of Goods Sold	1,800,000
Administrative Expenses	800,000
Amortization of Capital Assets	500,000
Income Tax Expense	150,000
	F 3,250,000
Net Income	F 250,000

STATEMENT OF RETAINED EARNINGS

Retained Earnings at January 1, 20X3	F 320,000
Net Income for Year	250,000
Retained Earnings at December 31, 20X3	F 570,000

BALANCE SHEET

Cash	F 120,000
Accounts Receivable	900,000
Inventory	750,000
Equipment (Net)	1,100,000
	F 2,870,000
Accounts Payable	F 500,000
Common Stock	1,800,000
Retained Earnings	570,000
	F 2,870,000

Additional Information:

[1] At December 31, 20X2, the balance of retained earnings of Emmsaz SN in Canadian dollars amounted to $218,000.

[2] The accumulated losses on foreign exchange translation at December 31, 20X2 amounted to $270,000 and were reflected as a deduction from shareholders' equity on the translated balance sheet at that date.

[3] The rates of exchange between the foreign currency unit (F) and the Canadian dollar were as follows:

At date of formation of Emmsaz SN	Can $1.00 =	F 2.8
For the currency year:		
January 1, 20X3	Can $1.00 =	F 3.0
June 30, 20X3		F 3.4
December 31, 20X3		F 3.8
Average for 20X3		F 3.4

ILLUSTRATION 16–2 (Continued)

The translation of the financial statements of Emmsaz SN into Canadian dollars (to the nearest thousand) at December 31, 20X3 would be carried out as follows:

INCOME STATEMENT

		Conversion	
Sales	F 3,500,000	1/3.4	$1,029,000
Less:			
Cost of Goods Sold	F 1,800,000	1/3.4	$ 529,000
Administration Expenses	800,000	1/3.4	235,000
Amortization of Capital Assets	500,000	1/3.4	147,000
Income Tax Expense	150,000	1/3.4	44,000
	F 3,250,000		$ 955,000
Net Income for Year	F 250,000		$ 74,000

STATEMENT OF RETAINED EARNINGS

Retained Earnings, January 1, 20X3	F 320,000	given Income	$ 218,000
Net Income for Year	250,000	St.	74,000
Retained Earnings, December 31, 20X3	F 570,000		$ 292,000

BALANCE SHEET

Cash	F 120,000	1/3.8	$ 32,000
Accounts Receivable	900,000	1/3.8	237,000
Inventory	750,000	1/3.8	197,000
Equipment (Net)	1,100,000	1/3.8	289,000
	F 2,870,000		$ 755,000
Accounts Payable	F 500,000	1/3.8	$ 132,000
Common Stock	1,800,000	1/2.8	643,000
Retained Earnings	570,000	Income St.	292,000
Accumulated Exchange Losses		see Note 1	(312,000)
	F 2,870,000		$ 755,000

Notes:
[1] The exchange loss for the current year amounted to Can $42,000 because the total deferred exchange losses are now Can $312,000, up $42,000 from the balance at the beginning of the year of $270,000.
[2] Dividends paid would have been translated at the rate of exchange in operation on the date they were paid.

the investor company of part of its interest in the foreign entity. As a result, compliance with this requirement would probably only require note disclosure of the reason for the change, the total increase or decrease in the accumulated gains or losses, and how this amount was made up.

TRANSLATION OF FINANCIAL STATEMENTS OF SELF-SUSTAINING FOREIGN OPERATIONS WHERE THE ECONOMIC ENVIRONMENT IS HIGHLY INFLATIONARY

Section 1650 of the CICA *Handbook* requires that where foreign operations are carried out in an economic environment that is highly inflationary in nature in relation to that of the reporting entity, the foreign currency may not be a reliable measure of value. In these cases, the temporal method should be used to translate the operations of foreign subsidiaries.

ILLUSTRATION 16–3

TRANSLATING THE "COST OF GOODS SOLD" OF INTEGRATED FOREIGN OPERATIONS

The translation of the cost of goods sold of a fully integrated foreign subsidiary in FCUs (Foreign Currency Units) for the financial year ended December 31, 20X3 is illustrated below. Here, the rates of exchange to the Canadian dollar were 4.0 FCUs = Canadian $1.00 at the date of acquisition of beginning inventory and at the beginning of the year, 4.4 FCUs at the end of the year with an average of 4.2 FCUs for the year. Purchases took place evenly throughout the year and the ending inventory was all acquired on October 1, 20X3 when the rate of exchange was 4.4 FCUs = Can $1.00.

The translation of the cost of goods sold is carried out as follows:

	FCUs	Conversion	Canadian $
Beginning Inventory	FCU 1,600,000	1/4.0	$ 400,000
Purchases	4,800,000	1/4.2	1,142,857
Freight Inwards	800,000	1/4.2	190,476
	FCU 7,200,000		1,733,333
Less: Ending Inventory	1,200,000	1/4.4	272,727
Cost of Goods Sold	FCU 6,000,000		$1,460,606

THE TRANSLATION OF TRADING OPERATIONS

The translation of trading operations of foreign subsidiaries requires the translation of the beginning and ending inventory as well as the purchases, freight charges, etc., to arrive at a realistic gross profit figure.

With fully integrated foreign operations, this translation is carried out using the rates of exchange in effect on the date on which the inventory was acquired. It is also subject to any adjustments relating to the application of the "lower-of-cost-and-market" rule. Purchases and other components of the cost of goods are adjusted using the average rate of exchange for the period unless the purchases took place on some cyclical pattern. An example of the translation of the cost of goods sold of a fully integrated foreign subsidiary where the purchase of goods took place evenly throughout the year is provided in Illustration 16–3. This shows that with this foreign subsidiary, the cost of goods sold amounted to $1,460,606.

The translation of the cost of goods sold with self-sustaining operations is carried out by merely translating every item at the average rate for the year or by merely translating the cost of goods sold at the average rate. This is the same as the adjustment of other income statement items. Using the figures provided in Illustration 16–3, the cost of goods sold with self-sustaining operations translated, using the current rate method, would be $1,428,571 (i.e., FCU 6,000,000/4.2).

TRANSLATING THE STATEMENT OF CASH FLOWS

The following rules apply to the translation of the statement of cash flows:

(a) Those items relating to cash flows from operations are translated at the rates of exchange used for the income statement.
(b) Other items are translated at the rate of exchange in operation at the date on which they occurred.
(c) The effects of translation gains or losses on cash flows must be disclosed separately so that the balances of cash and cash equivalents at the end of the period agree with the balances appearing on the balance sheet of the reporting entity.

CONSOLIDATING FOREIGN SUBSIDIARIES

The Actual Consolidation

As explained under consolidations, the financial statements of foreign subsidiaries must be consolidated with those of the parent company if control as defined by the CICA *Handbook* exists. In this respect, the parent company must have the continuing power to determine the strategic operating, investing and financing activities of the subsidiary without the co-operation of others.[5]

The actual consolidation procedure is quite straightforward and is carried out using the financial statements of the subsidiary that have been translated, as far as possible, into Canadian GAAP. As outlined earlier, the translation would have followed with the procedures for either fully integrated or self-sustaining foreign operations.

As outlined earlier in this chapter, the common stock of the foreign subsidiary is translated into Canadian dollars using the rate of exchange at the date on which the interest in the subsidiary was acquired. This is necessary to reconcile the parent company's investment in the subsidiary with its share of the subsidiary's equity at the date of acquisition. It also allows the goodwill arising on acquisition and any fair market value adjustments at that date to be carried forward at their original amounts and amortized in the normal manner. The net income earned and dividends paid after acquisition are detailed in the analysis of equity using the translated amounts.

With fully integrated foreign subsidiaries, the consolidation procedure is no different from that applying to domestic subsidiaries. The only possible difference arises from the inclusion of exchange gains and losses in the income statement which may be treated as disclosable items on the income statement.

The position with self-sustaining foreign operations is, however, slightly different. This is because any "deferred gains or losses arising on translation" are treated as part of the post-acquisition equity of the foreign subsidiary and these amounts must, therefore, be allocated between the parent company and the minority interests on consolidation. As these amounts are included as post-acquisition adjustments to the translated equity of the foreign subsidiary, they are disclosed as capital adjustments on the consolidated balance sheet of the parent company as an addition or deduction to the consolidated equity. The treatment of these amounts in the analysis of equity is outlined in Illustration 16–4 using the information presented in Illustration 16–2.

Illustration 16–4 shows that the "accumulated exchange gains or losses" are apportioned in the analysis of equity between the parent company and the minority interests. As far as the parent company is concerned, its portion of the "accumulated exchange gains or losses" are capital items and must, therefore, be reflected as part of its consolidated equity. The aggregation of assets and liabilities and the preparation of the consolidated income statement are, however, carried out in the normal manner.

It should be borne in mind that the temporal method treats an integrated foreign operation as a continuation of the parent company's activities. Therefore, the accounting for the subsidiary follows that of the parent company and is at historical cost. With self-sustaining operations, however, the parent company's total interest in the subsidiary is reflected at the current rate of exchange. The differences between the original cost and its present value are adjusted through the retained earnings and the accumulated exchange gains or losses.

In these cases, the consolidation process is carried out by analyzing the equity of the subsidiary in the normal manner, except that the accumulated gains and losses are analyzed separately in the year in which the consolidation is being carried out. They are then added to or deducted from the consolidated retained earnings and the minority interests, as the case may be.

---

5   Para. 1590.03.

ILLUSTRATION 16–4
THE ANALYSIS OF EQUITY OF A SELF-SUSTAINING FOREIGN SUBSIDIARY

This illustration uses the information provided in Illustration 16–2. However, to show how the equity of the company is analyzed on consolidation at December 31, 20X3, it is necessary to assume that Parent Inc. had acquired an 80% interest in Emmsaz SN on January 1, 20X2 for an amount totalling $778,400 when the retained earnings of Emmsaz SN amounted to $180,000 when translated into Canadian dollars.

It is also necessary to assume that at the date of acquisition the rate of exchange between the Canadian dollar and foreign currency unit (F) was Can $1 = F2.8. Furthermore, during 20X2, Emmsaz SN earned net income of $58,000 and paid a dividend of $20,000. Net income of $74,000 was earned in 20X3 but no dividends were declared in that year. During 20X3 the Accumulated Exchange Loss increased by $42,000 to $312,000.

On December 31, 20X2, the translated equity of Emmsaz SN was as follows as determined when the rate of exchange was Can $1 = F2.9:

Common Stock (F1,800,000/2.8)	$643,000
Retained Earnings ($180,000 + $58,000 − $20,000)	218,000
Less: Accumulated Exchange Loss	(270,000)
Total Equity	$591,000

The "analysis of equity" of Emmsaz SN would, therefore, be as follows:

	Total	80%	Minority Interests
At Acquisition:			
Common Stock	$643,000	$514,400	$128,600
Retained Earnings	180,000	144,000	36,000
		658,400	
Purchase Consideration		778,400	
Goodwill		$120,000	
Since Acquisition:			
Net Income — 20X2	58,000	$ 40,800	11,600
Dividends Declared and Paid	(20,000)	(16,000)	(4,000)
Accumulated Exchange Loss	(270,000)	(216,000)	(54,000)
Net Income — 20X3	74,000	59,200	14,800
Accumulated Exchange Loss	(42,000)	(33,600)	(8,400)
Total Minority Interests (20% × $623,000)			$124,600

Notes:
[1] Parent's share of the Accumulated Exchange Loss would be $249,666 (i.e., $216,000 from 20X2 and $33,600 from 20X3) and would be reflected as part of its consolidated equity.

[2] The balance of the Accumulated Exchange Losses would form part of the minority interests and amount to 20% of the equity of Emmsaz SN at December 31, 20X3 of $124,600 (i.e., 20% × [$643,000 + $292,000 − $312,000]).

Where the Equity Method Applies to Foreign Companies

Where control over the financing and investing activities of the subsidiary does not exist but the investor company still exercises significant influence over it, the equity method should be used. The financial statements of the foreign company should, first, be translated according to the requirements for either integrated or self-sustaining foreign operations into Canadian dollars using Canadian GAAP. Second, the equity method should be applied to those figures and the investor company's share of the net income from the "foreign subsidiary" reflected in the normal manner. However, a separate entry recording its share of the "accumulated exchange gains or losses" would be required to adjust the investment account with self-sustaining foreign operations. Using the figures from Illustration 16–4, this would amount to $33,600 in 20X3 and be recorded as follows:

Accumulated Exchange Losses	33,600	
Investment in Emmsaz SN		33,600
Equity Adjustment Arising from Recognition of Exchange Losses for year (i.e., 80% × $42,000)		

In those cases where it is felt that there is no significant influence, the investment must be carried at cost. This would not require an immediate write-down of the investment because section 3050 of the CICA *Handbook* specifically states that the investment should be carried at its value at the date on which the equity method ceased to apply. No retroactive adjustments would be required and, from that time onwards, only dividend income would be recognized. However, where the value of the investment has declined and this is considered to be permanent, the investment should be written down accordingly.

SUMMARY

This chapter outlines the procedures to be followed in translating the operations of fully integrated and self-sustaining foreign subsidiaries.

The temporal method is used to translate the operations of subsidiary companies that are fully integrated with those of their parent company. The philosophy underlying the use of the temporal method is that the operations of fully integrated foreign subsidiaries are an extension of operations of the parent company. Consequently, the translation of items should be carried out in a way that reflects that position. This applies equally to gains or losses on translation that are expensed through the income statement when they occur.

On the other hand, self-sustaining foreign operations are translated using the current method. Revenues and expenses are translated at the average rate for the year except where the rate of exchange did not change evenly throughout the year or where the amounts involved are material. In this latter case, they are translated at the rates of exchange on the dates on which they occurred. Gains or losses arising on translation are not expensed immediately but are deferred and added to or deducted from the shareholders' equity.

The current method requires that assets and liabilities are translated at the rate of exchange applicable on the last day of the financial year. The difference between the values of the translated assets and liabilities gives the total equity which, as far as the parent company is concerned, reflects the current value of the investment. To maintain continuity from year to year the common stock is, however, translated at the rate of exchange applicable when the investment was acquired.

SELF-STUDY PROBLEMS
(Covering the translation of foreign operations)

PROBLEM 16A† Forbes Fasteners (USA) Inc. of Seattle, WA, is a wholly-owned subsidiary of Forbes Lock & Key Ltd. of Vancouver. At December 31, 20X3, its balance sheet and combined income and retained earnings statements were as follows:

BALANCE SHEET

Cash at Bank	$ 233,700
Accounts Receivable	748,200
Inventory	442,600
Capital Assets	1,489,200
Less Accumulated Amortization	(324,100)
	$2,589,600

† The solution is provided in Appendix B to this text.

Accounts Payable	$ 88,200
Income Taxes Payable	97,100
Longterm Loan (8%)	600,000
Common Stock	1,000,000
Retained Earnings	804,300
	$2,589,600

INCOME AND RETAINED EARNINGS STATEMENT

Sales		$5,532,700
Opening Inventory		$ 471,800
Purchases		2,177,400
Freight and Transportation Expenses		432,100
		3,081,300
Closing Inventory		442,600
Cost of Goods Sold		2,638,700
Administration Expenses	1,189,300	
Amortization of Capital Assets	166,800	
Interest Expense	60,000	
Selling Expenses	680,100	
Income Tax Expense	166,200	2,262,400
Total Expenses		$4,901,100
Net Income		$ 631,600
Retained Earnings at January 1, 20X3		422,700
		1,054,300
Dividends Paid (September 30)		250,000
Retained Earnings at December 31, 20X3		$ 804,300

Additional Information:

(a) Forbes Fasteners (USA) Inc. was formed on July 1, 20X1 and commenced operations immediately.

(b) The capital assets were purchased in two stages on July 1, 20X1 and March 31, 20X2. Relevant details are as follows:

	Cost	Amortization to December 31, 20X2	Amortization for 20X3	Balance at December 31, 20X3
Purchases July 1, 20X1	$ 922,500	$ 92,350	$ 81,300	$ 748,850
Purchases March 31, 20X2	566,700	64,950	85,500	416,250
Balances	$1,489,200	$157,300	$166,800	$1,165,100

(c) Interest on the longterm loan was payable at the rate of eight percent per year on March 31 and September 30 in each year.

(d) All revenues and expenses accrued evenly throughout the year.

(e) Inventory, based on FIFO valuation basis, was all purchased on September 30 in both 20X2 and 20X3.

(f) The policy of the company is to treat income taxes payable as a monetary liability.

(g) At December 31, 20X2, the retained earnings of the company were Canadian $868,100.

(h) Relevant rates of exchange were as follows:

January 1, 20X1	Can $1.00	=	US $0.78
July 1, 20X1			0.80
January 1, 20X2			0.82
June 30, 20X2			0.84
December 31, 20X2			0.78
June 30, 20X3			0.76
December 31, 20X3			0.74

REQUIRED

Restate the above financial statements of Forbes Fasteners (USA) on the assumption that its operations were fully integrated with those of Forbes Lock & Key.

PROBLEM 16B† On January 1, 20X1, the Canada Drug Company Inc. acquired a controlling interest in Kentdrug PLC of Canterbury, England, by a share exchange. At the date of acquisition, the rate of exchange between the Canadian dollar and the British pound was Can $1.00 = £0.48. Kentdrug PLC has a December 31 year end. No goodwill arose on acquisition.

Additional information:

(a) All purchases, sales, administrative expenses and income taxes occurred evenly throughout the year.

(b) At January 1, 20X4, the retained earnings of Kentdrug adjusted for the amortization of goodwill up to the end of 20X3 amounted to Canadian $1,954,232.

(c) Relevant rates of exchange between the Canadian dollar and the British pound were as follows:

January 1, 20X4	Can $1 =	£0.48
September 30, 20X4		£0.47
December 31, 20X4		£0.49
20X4 Average		£0.46

The abbreviated balance sheet and combined income and retained earnings statements of Kentdrug at December 31, 20X4 were as follows:

BALANCE SHEET

Cash	£ 450,000
Inventory	840,000
Accounts Receivable	1,420,000
Plant and Equipment, cost	2,450,000
Accumulated Amortization	(910,000)
	£4,250,000
Accounts Payable	£1,040,000
Common Stock	2,000,000
Retained Earnings	1,210,000
	£4,250,000

COMBINED INCOME AND RETAINED EARNINGS STATEMENT

Sales		£7,780,000
Cost of Goods Sold:		
Opening Inventory	£ 690,000	
Purchases	5,220,000	
Ending Inventory	(840,000)	5,070,000
Gross Profit		2,710,000
Administrative Expenses	1,540,000	
Amortization of Capital Assets	460,000	
Income Taxes	270,000	2,270,000
Net Income		440,000
Retained Earnings at January 1, 20X4		1,270,000
		1,710,000
Dividends (paid September 30, 20X4)		500,000
Retained Earnings at December 31, 20X4		£1,210,000

---

† The solution is provided in Appendix B to this text.

REQUIRED

Translate the balance sheet and combined income and retained earnings statement of Kentdrug PLC into Canadian dollars on the assumption that its operations were completely self-sustaining.

REVIEW QUESTIONS

1. What is the basic rule relating to the translation of transactions carried out in a foreign currency?
2. How do gains or losses on foreign exchange transactions arise? When are these gains or losses determined and how are they reflected in the financial statements of the companies concerned?
3. What is the basic objective of the translation of the results of operations and financial position of foreign subsidiaries?
4. To what extent, if any, does the translation of foreign operations follow the use of Canadian generally accepted accounting principles?
5. Define "fully integrated" and "self-sustaining" foreign operations.
6. What makes "fully integrated" and "self-sustaining" foreign operations so different that they are accounted for using different methods?
7. How does the "temporal method" of translating the operations of foreign subsidiaries differ from the "monetary/nonmonetary method"?
8. How are gains and losses on the translation of the operations of foreign subsidiaries accounted for using the "temporal method"? Why are they treated in this way?
9. Why is it necessary to start with the balance sheet when translating the operations of a foreign operation using the "temporal method"?
10. Why is common stock translated at the rate of exchange applying at the date on which the interest in the subsidiary was acquired?
11. Describe the "current rate method" of translating foreign operations.
12. What is the basic consideration of translation using the "current rate method"?
13. If someone states that "the objective of using the current rate method is to reflect economic reality," what do they mean?
14. How are gains or losses arising on the translation of foreign operations using the "current rate method" treated? Why is this the case?

CASES

CASE 16–1   **Diamond Endearment Inc.**

Diamond Endearment Inc. is a Toronto-based importer of gemstone diamonds and other precious stones. It was formed by Isak Greenbaum on his immigration to Canada from Eastern Europe in the 1930s. In 1950, to expand its operations, the company went public and 60% of the company was owned by the general public and its shares were actively traded on the Toronto Stock Exchange. Besides retaining his seat on the board of directors, Isak Greenbaum recently retired from active participation in the management of the company, and the business is now run by his eldest son David, aged 42 years.

The company operates as a direct importer of both cut and uncut stones. The cut diamonds are mainly imported from Amsterdam in the Netherlands, whereas the uncut stones are obtained from Namibia, Botswana and Tanzania. It operates a number of jewellery outlets in Toronto and other major Canadian cities. A considerable number of diamonds are set by the jewellery outlets, but most of its business is from the sale of cut diamonds to the jewellery trade in both Canada and the USA. Other precious and semi-precious stones are imported from various parts of the world.

Some five years ago, at the insistence of Bernard Greenbaum, Isak's youngest son (aged 35 years), an office was opened in New York City. On the advice of the company's auditors, the New York City venture was conducted through Diamonds Galore Inc., a company registered under the laws of the State of New York.

Bernard relocated to New York and the venture proved extremely successful. Not only was the US business re-directed through the New York office, but the move coincided with an upsurge in diamond buying by the American public.

Two years ago, following an approach by Tinkley's, an American chain of retail jewellery outlets, Diamonds Galore had entered into an association by which 20% of the shares in Diamonds Galore was exchanged for a 10% interest in Tinkley's. In terms of the agreement, Diamonds Galore would supply cut diamonds to Tinkley's jewellery outlets, and both parties were guaranteed a seat on the board of directors of the other's company.

The association with Tinkley's proved highly beneficial to both parties. Business in diamonds had increased threefold and, to meet the needs of the American market, Bernard was beginning to negotiate directly with suppliers in Amsterdam to fulfill his contracts with Tinkley's and other New York-based jewellery manufacturers. During the current year direct imports from the Netherlands had amounted to almost 25% of its cut diamond sales — up 11% from the previous year.

Sales by Diamonds Galore had increased from a little over US $900,000 in the first year of operations to almost US $2-million before entering into the association with Tinkley's. The upward trend was continuing and Bernard estimated that for the current year it was expected to reach $9-million and overtake the Toronto operation, which had sales of over $12-million, within two years. David had jokingly suggested at the last board meeting that perhaps he would also relocate to New York City.

The board of directors of Diamonds Galore was made up of four members and, on average, one out of every two meetings of the board was held in Toronto. Of the directors, three (i.e., Isak, David and Bernard Greenbaum) were also directors of Diamond Endearment and, although Bernard was responsible for the running of the New York office, all policy matters were referred to the full board of directors. Cash in excess of its day-to-day requirements had always been remitted by the New York office to Toronto to pay for the gemstones supplied. As Diamonds Galore extended its operations, more and more money was required to pay for its own purchases of gemstones. At the present time, however, Diamonds Galore still obtained the majority of its stones from Toronto. Since its formation, Diamonds Galore had been treated as an integrated foreign operation for accounting purposes.

REQUIRED

1. Consider the correctness or otherwise of the present treatment of Diamonds Galore as a fully integrated operation of Diamond Endearment from a financial reporting point of view.
2. Identify the factors that could, now or in the future, cause Diamonds Galore to be treated as a self-sustaining operation.
3. Explain how a change in the accounting for Diamonds Galore from an integrated to a self-sustaining operation could be effected.
4. Consider how, in the event of the business moving its head office/holding company to the USA, the re-organization could be effected.

CASE 16–2   ### Mark Taylor Consulting Inc.

Mark Taylor Consulting Inc. is a Hamilton, Ontario, consulting company to the steel industry. It operates offices in the USA (i.e., in Chicago, Philadelphia and Atlanta) as well as in Europe. The centre for its European operations is Sheffield, England, where operates through Mark Taylor and Associates PLC. It has branch offices in the Czech Republic, Germany, Hungary, Poland and Italy. The company has a worldwide reputation as mineralogists and, in particular, its expertise in relation to the production and behaviour of specialized steel alloys under various conditions.

Its offices in the USA are operated on a fully integrated basis with those of its head office. Due to the proximity of its operations, projects are undertaken together and, for all intensive purposes, the US operations are an extension of the Hamilton office. However, the Sheffield office operates as a fully self-sustaining operation in its relationship with the Hamilton office, but its branch offices are, as far as is possible across national borders, fully integrated with it. The reason for this was that most of its recent consulting work had been in Eastern Europe and, to expand its operations, it had been necessary to recruit additional staff from Eastern European countries. Far more flexibility is required because the North American style of management has, in the past, not proved successful with its Eastern European employees.

There is considerable contact between the North American and European operations and, from time to time, personnel are drawn from one operation to assist the other. In this respect, the North American operation has greater expertise in the area of thermo-physics, whereas the European operation is recognized as the leader in the fields of elasticity and extrusion.

The company has been very profitable in recent years and, to adequately encourage and reward its employees, it has decided to introduce a bonus system. It has been suggested that because of the interchange of expertise, ideas and personnel between the two operations, 40% of the total profits on **a worldwide basis** would be set aside for the payment of bonuses. The problem is how to arrive at an equitable allocation of profits between the North American and European offices. In this respect, the allocation would be based on the results of operations as reflected by the financial statements of Mark Taylor Consulting prepared following Canadian generally accepted accounting principles. Once this issue was resolved, the amounts payable to each employee would have to be determined on a similar basis across the North American and European operations.

The following alternatives have been suggested:

(a)   The allocation should be based on the total fee income. To smooth the accrual of fees from year to year, this could be based on the average fee income over, say, three years.

(b)   Alternatively, the amounts could be allocated on the basis of net income adjusted, as necessary, to eliminate fluctuations from year to year.

REQUIRED

Consider and analyze the two suggestions in the light of the problems arising from accounting for the North American and European operations on a self-sustaining basis, whereas each operation accounted for its individual operations on an integrated basis.

CASE 16–3   **The Beaver Equipment Corporation Inc.**

The Beaver Equipment Corporation Inc. is a Kitchener-based manufacturer of sophisticated sprayers, electronic timers, shut-off valves and other high-tech agricultural equipment. Over the past few years it has developed a market for its products in Chile, Peru and certain other South American countries. At present, sales of new equipment to these countries amounted to over $10-million a year. The trade in parts had also grown tremendously over the past few years.

Attempts to use local business organizations to service its customer needs had proved unsuccessful and for some time it had become obvious that the company would have to open a branch office in one of these countries. The need was mainly to train sufficient people to service their equipment but, in view of the growing demand for their products, it was also good policy to establish a central distribution point.

The matter had been fully investigated and the company had decided that Santiago, Chile, would be the best place to open such an office. The Chilean share of the US and Canadian winter deciduous fruit market had increased dramatically over the past few years and was expected to grow even further in importance. Santiago was also well placed to serve the Peruvians and other South American countries. From an investment point of view, the country was enjoying stable government; there was almost full employment and the inflation rate, though high by North American standards, had been kept under control and seemed to have stabilized.

The problems, which are inherent in doing business in any South American country, were:

(a) There was a general lack of suitably trained professional accounting and managerial personnel.
(b) The accounting systems had evolved from those used in Spain and Portugal in the mid-1700s and, even though there was some application of international accounting standards, the accounting systems were different from those used in Canada.
(c) Government regulations required that any foreign business company carrying on business in these countries had to have a certain percentage of local nationals serving in key capacities or on the board of directors. It was, therefore, not possible to use the services of more than a handful of Canadian citizens.
(d) The risk that unstable political conditions would return.

Besides the inflationary problem and the distance from Kitchener, the only area of real concern was satisfying the government regulations relating to the employment of foreign nationals. Managerial and accounting staff could be familiarized with Canadian requirements in Canada and an accounting system could be designed to meet the company's requirements. If necessary, persons could be appointed to key positions on the understanding that they would only act as figureheads. The risk factor could also be eliminated through the use of transfer pricing.

REQUIRED

Consider and advise the management of Beaver Equipment Corporation whether to run its Chilean operation as a self-sustaining or a fully integrated operation.

EXERCISES

EXERCISE 16–1   ABC Trading Company Inc., which has a December 31 year end, carries on the business of importer of textiles. During December 20X2, it imported goods as follows:

Source	Currency	Total Purchases in Country of Origin	Exchange Rates	
			On Purchase	On December 31
Australia	Dollar	1,400,000	Can $1 = 1.12486	Can $1 = 1.13674
Brazil	Real	30,000	Can $1 = 1.375	Can $1 = 1.401
Hong Kong	Dollar	8,500,000	Can $1 = 160.112	Can $1 = 156.032
Japan	Yen	6,400,000	Can $1 = 800.240	Can $1 = 802.352
USA	Dollar	1,800,000	Can $1 = 0.78455	Can $1 = 0.76124

REQUIRED

1. Give the entries required to record the above purchases in the journal of ABC Trading Company.
2. Calculate the outstanding liabilities relating to these purchases at December 31, 20X2.

EXERCISE 16–2   On October 20, 20X4, Jacob Inc. purchased 10,000 VCRs from a German manufacturer for €200 each. The terms of the contract were that the goods would be shipped freight on board immediately and that payment would be effected by a banker's draft drawn on the Deutsche Bank on February 28, 20X5. The VCRs were shipped f.o.b. Hamburg on November 1, 20X4 and were delivered to Jacob on November 15, 20X4. The rates of exchange between the Canadian dollar and the Euro on the relevant dates were as follows:

October 20, 20X4	Can $1 = € 0.73
November 1, 20X4	Can $1 = € 0.74
November 15, 20X4	Can $1 = € 0.75
December 31, 20X4	Can $1 = € 0.73
February 28, 20X5	Can $1 = € 0.72

REQUIRED

Prepare the journal entries to record the above purchase, the balance outstanding at December 31, 20X4, and settlement of the liability on the assumption that Jacob has a December 31 year-end. (Note: Risk passes to the purchaser on the goods being loaded f.o.b. the carrier.)

EXERCISE 16–3   REQUIRED

Answer the following questions:

1. TNT Inc., a Toronto-based company, purchased equipment from BOM of Taipai, Taiwan, on November 1, 20X5 for 400,000 Taiwanese dollars when the rate of exchange was Can $1.00 = T $1.65. At December 31, 20X5, the financial year end of TNT Inc., the rate of exchange was Can $1.00 = T $1.69. On January 28, 20X6, when the rate of exchange was Can $1.00 = T $1.63, TNT Inc. paid the amount owing to BOM. If this was the only foreign transaction of TNT, what amount would it reflect as a gain or loss on foreign exchange transactions for both 20X5 and 20X6?

2. On January 1, 20X4, Cayman Industries Inc. formed a British subsidiary, Cayman PLC. On February 1, 20X4, Cayman PLC purchased inventory for British £100,000. At December 31, 20X4, the financial year end of both Cayman Industries Inc. and Cayman PLC, 40% of these purchases were still on hand. The rate of exchange between the British pound and the Canadian dollar were British £1.00 = Can. $2.10 for the period January 1 to June 30, 20X4, and British £1.00 = Can. $2.20 from July 1 to December 31, 20X4. At what amount would this inventory be restated in Canadian dollars at December 31, 20X4, if Cayman PLC was a fully integrated foreign subsidiary?

3. Gleam (Pty) Ltd. is an Auckland, New Zealand-based self-sustaining subsidiary of Munro Electronics Inc. of Toronto. Its balance sheet at December 31, 20X6 reflected equipment at cost of 10,230,000 New Zealand dollars (i.e., before accumulated amortization) made up of purchases of NZ$ 9,860,000 on January 1, 20X5 when the rate of exchange was Can $1.00 = NZ$ 1.44 and additional purchases of NZ$ 370,000 on July 1, 20X6 when the Can $1.00 = NZ$ 1.32. Amortization is charged on these amounts at 10% per year on the straight line basis. What would the net book value of the equipment be in Canadian dollars at December 31, 20X6 if the rate of exchange on that date was Can $1.00 = NZ$ 1.35?

EXERCISE 16–4   The income statement of Peter Inc. of Detroit, MI, for the year ended December 31, 20X4 was as follows:

Sales		$7,400,000
Beginning Inventory	$ 840,000	
Purchases	4,800,000	
Cost of Goods Available for Sale	5,640,000	
Less: Ending Inventory	760,000	4,880,000
Gross Profit		2,520,000
Less: Administration Expenses	834,000	
Amortization Expense	325,000	
Selling Expenses	232,000	1,391,000
Net Income		$1,129,000

Additional Information:

1. The operations of Peter are fully integrated with those of its parent company, Paul Inc. of Windsor, Ontario.
2. The amortization expense relates to plant purchased in 20X1 when the rate of exchange between the Canadian and US Dollar was Can $1.00 = US $0.70.
3. The inventory held by Peter at January 1 and December 31, 20X4 was all purchased when the rate of exchange was Can $1.00 = US $0.72 and Can $1.00 = US $0.80 respectively.

4. Sales and expenses all occurred evenly throughout the year.
5. The rate of exchange between the Canadian and US dollar increased evenly from Can $1.00 = US $0.74 at January 1, 20X4 to Can $1.00 = US $0.82 on December 31, 20X4.
6. The translation of assets and liabilities of Peter into Canadian dollars at December 31, 20X4 resulted in a loss on exchange of Can $87,000.

REQUIRED

Prepare the income statement of Peter at December 31, 20X4 translated into Canadian dollars using the temporal method.

EXERCISE 16–5 The following abbreviated balance sheet and income statement apply to Sana PS for 20X4:

BALANCE SHEET

Current Assets	D 8,000,000
Plant (Net)	12,000,000
	D 20,000,000
Current Liabilities	D 3,000,000
Common Stock	10,000,000
Retained Earnings	7,000,000
	D 20,000,000

INCOME STATEMENT

Sales	D 32,000,000
Cost of Goods Sold	D 18,000,000
Administration and Other Expenses	7,000,000
Depreciation Expense	3,000,000
	D 28,000,000
Net Income	D 4,000,000

STATEMENT OF RETAINED EARNINGS

Retained Earnings at January 1, 20X4	D 3,000,000
Net Income for Year	4,000,000
Retained Earnings at December 31, 20X4	D 7,000,000

Additional Information:

1. Sana PS is an 80%-owned foreign subsidiary of Percival Enterprises Inc. of Toronto, which has a December 31 year end.
2. The rates of exchange between the Canadian dollar and the Dinor (the local currency in which Sana PS operates) on the relevant dates were as follows:

January 1, 20X4	Can $1.00 = 32 Dinors
December 31, 20X4	Can $1.00 = 36 Dinors
Average for 20X4	Can $1.00 = 34 Dinors

3. The investment in Sana was made on January 1, 20X1 when there were 40 Dinors to the Canadian dollar.
4. The plant was all purchased when the rate of exchange was Can $1.00 = 42 Dinors.
5. Revenues and expenses, other than amortization, all accrued evenly throughout the year.
6. The operations of Sana PS were completely self-sustaining.

REQUIRED

From the above information, calculate:

1. The net income of Sana PS in Canadian dollars for 20X4.
2. The equity of Sana PS in Canadian dollars at December 31, 20X3.

3. The accumulated translation adjustment at December 31, 20X4 in Canadian dollars if the retained earnings of Sana PS at December 31, 20X3 amounted to Can $93,750.

EXERCISE 16–6 On January 1, 20X1, Pelt Inc. of Niagara Falls (Canada) acquired an 80% interest in Stone Inc. of Omaha, Nebraska, for Can $500,000 when Stone had common stock of US $400,000 and retained earnings of US $150,000. At the date of acquisition, the assets and liabilities of Stone were considered fairly valued. Goodwill was written down for impairment by $1,000 on December 31, 20X1.

The operations of Stone were completely self-sustaining and during the year ended December 31, 20X1, it paid a dividend of $60,000 (on December 1) and reported net income of $200,000 which had accrued evenly throughout the year.

Relevant rates of exchange between the two currencies were as follows:

January 1, 20X1	Can $1.00 = US $0.90
December 1, 20X1	Can $1.00 = US $0.85
December 31, 20X1	Can $1.00 = US $0.84
Average for 20X1	Can $1.00 = US $0.88

REQUIRED

Prepare the ledger account recording the investment in Stone in the ledger of Pelt to reflect the investment in Stone at December 31, 20X1.

PROBLEMS

PROBLEM 16–1 Katrina's Inc. of Calgary is an exclusive dress shop having a December 31 financial year-end. On November 10, 20X4, it placed an order with Leonard Fashions of California for 200 dresses a month for the three months of March, April and May 20X5.

The cost of the dresses was US $15,000, which would be due and payable on March 1, 20X5 on the first delivery of dresses. However, before proceeding with the order, Leonard Fashions asked for a deposit of US $3,000. This deposit was paid on December 1, 20X4. The amount outstanding was paid in three equal instalments of $4,000 each on March 31, April 30, and May 31, 20X5.

The rates of exchange between the Canadian and US dollar on the following dates were:

November 10, 20X4	Can $1.00 = US $0.74
December 1, 20X4	Can $1.00 = US $0.72
December 31, 20X4	Can $1.00 = US $0.73
March 1, 20X5	Can $1.00 = US $0.75
March 31, 20X5	Can $1.00 = US $0.76
April 30, 20X5	Can $1.00 = US $0.78
May 31, 20X5	Can $1.00 = US $0.77

REQUIRED

Give:

1. The journal entries to record the purchase of the dresses;
2. The outstanding liability to Leonard Fashions on December 31, 20X4; and
3. The average purchase cost per dress to Katrina's Fashions.

PROBLEM 16–2 Juliana Inc. of Rochester, N.Y. is a wholly owned subsidiary of Nederlander Inc. of Hamilton, Ontario. Its operations are fully integrated with those of its parent company.

The abbreviated combined income and retained earnings statement for the year ended December 31, 20X4 is given below.

Sales		$10,500,000
Beginning Inventory	1,200,000	
Purchases	5,292,000	
Cost of Goods Available for Sale	6,492,000	
Less: Ending Inventory	1,468,000	5,024,000
Gross Profit		5,476,000
Less: Expenses		
Administration Expenses	1,366,000	
Amortization of Capital Assets	725,000	
Selling Expenses	823,000	
Income Taxes	920,000	3,834,000
Net Income for Year		1,642,000
Less: Dividends Paid (October 1)		500,000
		1,142,000
Retained Earnings at January 1, 20X4		3,500,000
Retained Earnings at December 31, 20X4		$ 4,642,000

You are also provided with the following additional information:

1. The amortization expense relates to plant purchased in 20X1 when the rate of exchange between the Canadian and US dollar was Can $1.00 = US $0.72.
2. The retained earnings of Juliana in Canadian dollars at December 31, 20X3 was $4,510,000.
3. The inventory held by Juliana was all purchased on October 1 in each year.
4. Sales and Expenditures all occurred evenly throughout the year.
5. The retained earnings of Juliana at December 31, 20X4 established from the revaluation of the assets and liabilities sides of the balance sheet amounted to $5,750,000.
6. The rate of exchange between the Canadian and US dollar increased evenly and the rates of exchange between the Canadian and US dollar were:

October 1, 20X2	Can $1.00 = US $0.74
January 1, 20X3	Can $1.00 = US $0.76
June 30, 20X3	Can $1.00 = US $0.78
December 31, 20X3	Can $1.00 = US $0.80
June 30, 20X4	Can $1.00 = US $0.82
December 31, 20X4	Can $1.00 = US $0.84

REQUIRED

Translate and present the combined income and retained earnings statement of Juliana at December 31, 20X4 in Canadian dollars.

PROBLEM 16–3 Eighty percent of the shares of common stock of Jonas Holdings Inc. of Albany, N.Y., are held by Easop Inc. of Toronto. The operations of Jonas are fully integrated with those of Easop Inc.

The abbreviated balance sheet of Jonas at December 31, 20X5 was as follows:

Cash		$ 200,000
Inventory		850,000
Accounts Receivable		1,650,000
Plant	2,400,000	
Less: Accumulated Amortization	640,000	1,760,000
		$4,460,000
Accounts Payable		$1,120,000
Common Stock		2,400,000
Retained Earnings		940,000
		$4,460,000

Additional Information:

1. Easop acquired its interest in Jonas on the formation of Jonas when the rate of exchange between the Canadian and US dollar was Can $1.00 = US $0.88.
2. At December 31, 20X4, the retained earnings of Jonas was Can $1,182,933.
3. The after tax net income of Jonas for 20X5 was translated to Can $490,000, and a dividend from Jonas that translated into Can $124,000 was received by Easop on December 4, 20X5.
4. The plant was acquired in two purchases. The first consisted of plant having a 10-year life purchased for $800,000 on January 1, 20X3 when the rate of exchange was Can $1.00 = US $0.74. The second was for plant having an eight-year life which cost $1.6-million on January 3, 20X4 when the Canadian dollar was worth US $0.80. Jonas amortizes its plant using the straight-line method.
5. The inventory on hand at December 31, 20X5 was acquired evenly over the last six months of 20X5.
6. The rates of exchange between the Canadian and US dollar for 20X5 were as follows:

January 1, 20X5	Can $1.00 = US $0.76
December 31, 20X5	Can $1.00 = US $0.80
Average for 20X5	Can $1.00 = US $0.78

REQUIRED

Translate the balance sheet of Jonas at December 31, 20X5 into Canadian dollars using the temporal method.

PROBLEM 16–4 Relish Inc. had extended its operations to Argentina in 20X1 by forming Salsa Enterprises S.A. as a wholly owned subsidiary with common stock of 2,000,000 Argentinian Pesos.

Information relating to the company is as follows:

1. At the date of formation of Salsa Enterprises, the rate of exchange between the Canadian dollar and the Argentinian Peso was Can $1.00 = Peso 2.16. Plant having an expected useful life of 30 years was acquired on January 1, 20X1 for P 1,800,000, and trading operations commenced immediately. No additional plant has been acquired.
2. The retained earnings of Salsa Enterprises at December 31, 20X5, expressed in Canadian dollars, amounted to $468,000.
3. The relevant rates of exchange between the Canadian dollar and the Peso were as follows:

January 1, 20X6	Can $1.00 = P 1.47
August 31, 20X6	Can $1.00 = P 1.39
December 31, 20X6	Can $1.00 = P 1.31
Average for 20X6	Can $1.00 = P 1.41

4. At December 31, 20X6, the balance sheet of Salsa Enterprises and the income statement for the company for the year ended on that date were as follows:

BALANCE SHEET

Cash		P 600,000
Inventory		1,300,000
Accounts Receivable		800,000
Plant, at cost	1,800,000	
Less: Accumulated Amortization	360,000	1,440,000
		P 4,140,000
Accounts Payable		P 400,000
Common Stock		2,000,000
Retained Earnings		1,740,000
		P 4,140,000

**COMBINED INCOME AND
RETAINED EARNINGS STATEMENT**

Sales	P 10,000,000
Cost of Goods Sold	P 7,000,000
Administrative and Selling Expenses	1,600,000
Amortization of Capital Assets	60,000
	P 8,660,000
Net Income	P 1,340,000
Dividends Paid (August 31)	300,000
	P 1,040,000
Retained Earnings at January 1, 20X6	700,000
Retained Earnings at December 31, 20X6	P 1,740,000

REQUIRED

Translate the above balance sheet and income statement of Salsa Enterprises into Canadian dollars on the assumption that the operations of Salsa Enterprises are completely self-sustaining.

PROBLEM 16–5 Canadian Software Limited (CSL) is a Markham, Ontario multinational computer software company. On January 1, 20X4, it formed Nova Dias Software SN (NDS) as a wholly-owned foreign subsidiary in a South American country. Financing was provided by the infusion of share capital of Canadian $160-million when the rate of exchange between the Canadian dollar and the local Peso was Can $0.40 = P 1.00 and by the raising of a four-year longterm loan of P 200-million.

At December 31, 20X4, the abbreviated balance sheet of NDS was as follows:

Cash	P 63,600,000
Accounts Receivable	230,400,000
Inventory, at cost	175,200,000
Prepaid Expenses	18,400,000
Plant and Equipment, at cost	398,400,000
Less: Accumulated Amortization	(39,840,000)
	P 846,160,000
Accounts Payable	P 84,160,000
Longterm Debt (Repayable on December 31, 20X8)	200,000,000
Common Stock	400,000,000
Retained earnings	162,000,000
	P 846,160,000

You are also informed that:

(a) Inventories were purchased when one P 1 = Can $0.30.
(b) Prepaid expenses were paid when P 1 = Can $0.25.
(c) Capital assets were purchased shortly after the date of NDS's formation, at a time when P 1 = Can $0.40
(d) All current liabilities were incurred at a time when P 1 = Can $0.25.
(e) Exchange rates were as follows:

January 1, 20X4	P =	Can $0.40
December 31, 20X4		Can $0.20
Average for Year		Can $0.30

(f) No dividends were paid in 20X4.

During 20X4, the South American country experienced severe financial problems. The rate of inflation exceeded 100% accompanied by substantial increases in interest rates. Despite these conditions, NDS still earned net income of P 162,000,000 in 20X4.

REQUIRED

1. Discuss which method of translation of NDS's financial statements is required in terms of section 1650 of the CICA *Handbook*; and
2. Translate NDS's balance sheet into Canadian dollars at December 31, 20X4 using **both** the temporal and current rate methods on the assumption that the translated income statement of NDS at December 31, 20X4, using the **current rate method**, reflected net income of Can $15.2-million.

PROBLEM 16–6 Midar Ltd., an American company, is a wholly-owned subsidiary of Cancar Ltd. of Halifax, NS. The financial statements of Midar for the year ended December 31, 20X6 were as follows:

BALANCE SHEET

Cash	$ 300,000
Accounts Receivable	500,000
Inventory	400,000
Land	800,000
Plant and Equipment	2,200,000
Accumulated Amortization	(350,000)
	$3,850,000
Accounts Payable	$ 600,000
Mortgage Payable	2,400,000
Common Stock	300,000
Retained Earnings	550,000
	$3,850,000

INCOME STATEMENT

Sales		$5,000,000
Cost of Sales:		
Opening Inventory	$ 600,000	
Purchases	4,000,000	
	4,600,000	
Closing Inventory	400,000	4,200,000
Gross Profit		800,000
Expenses:		
Administration	300,000	
Amortization of Capital Assets	50,000	
Selling	80,000	
Income Taxes	120,000	550,000
Net Income for the Year		250,000
Retained Earnings at January 1, 20X6		400,000
		650,000
Dividends Paid (June 30, 20X6)		100,000
Retained Earnings at December 31, 20X6		$ 550,000

Additional information:

(a) Midar was incorporated on January 1, 20X2. At that time Cancar invested cash of US $200,000 in Midar.

(b) The land and plant and equipment were purchased on January 1, 20X3 for US $3-million. The plant is being amortized on a straight-line basis over its estimated useful life of 40 years. In order to help fund the purchase of the plant, Cancar invested an additional US $100,000 on January 1, 20X3. Midar also contributed cash of $300,000 that it had on hand at the time. The remainder of the purchase price (i.e., US $2.6-million) was borrowed from a mortgage company on January 1, 20X3. The balance of the mortgage outstanding at December 31, 20X6 was $2.4-million.

(c) All of the inventory on hand at year end was purchased evenly throughout 20X6.

(d)　All inventory on hand at the beginning of the year was purchased on September 30, 20X5.

(e)　On January 1, 20X6, the retained earnings of Midar, in Canadian dollars, amounted to $540,000.

(f)　All sales, purchases and expenses occurred evenly throughout the year.

(g)　The rates of exchange were as follows:

January 1, 20X2	US $1.00	=	Can $ 1.35
January 1, 20X3			1.45
September 30, 20X5			1.37
December 31, 20X5			1.39
Average for 20X5			1.38
June 30, 20X6			1.43
December 31, 20X6			1.40
Average for 20X6			1.42

REQUIRED

Translate the financial statements of Midar into Canadian dollars on the assumption that:

1.　Its operations are fully integrated with those of Cancar; and
2.　It is a completely self-sustaining subsidiary of Cancar.

17 Financial Instruments and the Hedging of Currency Risk

(contributed by Ian P.N. Hague[1])

LEARNING OBJECTIVES

After studying this chapter you should:

1. Understand the nature of financial instruments and be able to classify them into their various categories.
2. Understand how financial instruments are recognized, measured, presented and disclosed.
3. Understand how to account for hedges of currency risk using forward contracts, options and swaps.

INTRODUCTION

Over the past decade, the operation of capital and financial markets has changed dramatically. They have been deregulated to reduce governmental intervention and have become considerably more sophisticated as the financing of business operations has become more complex. As a result, many new financial instruments have been developed to raise capital, minimize financial risks, provide off-balance sheet financing,[2] and for many other purposes. Financial instruments such as forward contracts, futures, options and swaps are now commonly encountered by accountants.

To respond to these developments, the Accounting Standards Board (AcSB) entered into a joint venture with the International Accounting Standards Committee (IASC) to develop appropriate accounting standards for financial instruments. As a result of that cooperation, the AcSB issued recommendations on the disclosure and presentation of financial instruments in 1995 as section 3860 of the CICA *Handbook*. The IASC issued virtually identical requirements at the same time. Since then, the AcSB has focused its attention on the recognition and measurement of financial instruments and hedge accounting.

Proposals to measure all financial instruments at fair value, with no hedge accounting, developed by representatives of the AcSB jointly with representatives of the IASC and eight

---

[1] Principal of the Accounting Standards Board, Toronto.

[2] Off-balance sheet financing refers to the financing activities over and above the amounts reflected as assets and liabilities on the balance sheet of the reporting entity.

other national accounting standard-setters (the Joint Working Group on Financial Instruments) were considered too radical. Therefore, the AcSB has recently focused its attention on developing standards that bring Canadian accounting to a par with the best standards internationally. As a result, the AcSB issued three Exposure Drafts in March 2003 dealing with the recognition and measurement of financial instruments, hedges and the accounting for hedges, and comprehensive income. When finalized, these exposure drafts will operate in harmony with the accounting standards of the FASB and those of the newly constituted International Accounting Standards Board (IASB).

Even though the exposure draft recommendations have already been broadly accepted by the AcSB, certain aspects are to be re-exposed in 2004. They are expected to be finally approved by the end of 2004 and apply to interim and annual financial statements relating to financial years commencing on or after October 1, 2005.

It should be noted that the accounting proposals on financial instruments do not apply to certain financial instruments dealt with elsewhere in the CICA *Handbook*. In this respect, they specifically exclude interests in subsidiary companies (section 1590); longterm investments over which the reporting entity can exert significant influence (section 3050); investments in joint ventures (section 3055); life insurance contracts (section 4210) and employer's obligations under employee stock option and stock purchase schemes (section 3870).

In addition to financial instruments, the proposals apply to certain commodity contracts that are used in the same way as financial instruments (i.e., they are actively traded, or are capable of being settled other than by delivery of the commodity itself), but do not apply to commodity contracts that can result only in the future delivery of items like crude oil, minerals, and wheat, etc.

Before examining the various aspects of accounting for financial instruments, it should be noted that the proposed standards cover a broad group of financial assets, financial liabilities, contracts, hedges, and other aspects of national and international financial dealings. A detailed treatment of all the complexities would require a detailed and separate study and is, consequently, beyond the scope of this text. What this chapter attempts to do is present the basic theoretical issues relating to the accounting for financial instruments and the hedging of foreign currency risk.

A. THE NATURE OF FINANCIAL INSTRUMENTS

A financial instrument is **defined** as **any contract that gives rise to both a financial asset of one party and a corresponding financial liability or equity instrument of another entity**. A financial instrument, therefore, requires a matching of financial assets and liabilities across different entities. For example, a mortgage of $500,000 would be a financial asset in one entity and an equal financial liability of $500,000 in another entity.

To be classified as a **financial instrument** is largely dependent upon the extent to which a contract complies with the normal characteristics of assets, liabilities, and equities. This means that financial assets, financial liabilities and equity instruments represent, respectively, future economic benefits, future sacrifices of economic benefits, or the residual interest in an entity. **Financial assets** comprise cash, a contractual right to receive cash or another financial asset, the right to exchange a financial instrument with another entity under conditions (or terms) that are potentially favourable, or an equity instrument of another entity.

A **financial liability** is similarly defined as a contractual obligation to deliver cash, or to exchange financial instruments with another entity under terms that are potentially unfavourable. The definition of an **equity instrument** is any contract that evidences a residual interest in the assets of an entity after deducting all of its liabilities.

What is important is that these definitions envisage a series of contractual rights or obligations that **are discharged** on the **receipt or payment of cash**, or **the exchange of financial assets, financial liabilities, or equities**. And, as the name implies, financial instruments do not involve the transfer of physical (or non-financial) assets. They can, therefore, only be settled by the receipt or delivery of cash, financial assets, or another financial (or equity) instrument.

Financial instruments may be broadly classified as primary or secondary. **Primary financial instruments** consist of many financial instruments with which accountants are familiar. They may be as simple as a banknote that represents an asset to the holder and a liability of the Bank of Canada, accounts payable and accounts receivable (including loans), or instruments relating to the issue of corporate debt and equity securities like bonds, shares and debentures. **Secondary financial instruments** are commonly referred to as **derivatives**. They are so named because their value is derived from other sources, including changes in fair values and cash flows of primary financial instruments. Their value often depends on changes in foreign currency rates, interest rates, commodity prices, or similar variables. Their importance in current financial dealings is because even though they may be exposed to substantial risk, they offer the potential for huge profits, often with minimal relative amounts of investment.[3]

Derivatives are defined by the AcSB as financial instruments that **have all of the following characteristics**:

(a) The value of the instrument changes in response to changes in a specified interest rate, financial instrument price, commodity price, foreign exchange rate, index of prices or rates, credit rating or credit index, or other variable;

(b) They require an initial investment that is considerably lower than that required for other types of contracts that would be expected to have similar responses to market factors; and

(c) They are settled at a future date.

Companies enter into **derivative contracts** to reduce the risk arising from changes in cash flows and fair values that may, in turn, affect their earnings. These risks may result from changes in the purchase or selling prices of goods and commodities, from changes in values of assets and liabilities on the company's balance sheet, or from changes in cash flows from items such as variable-rate debt. Typical forms of derivative instruments are option contracts, forward contracts, futures contracts, currency or interest-rate swaps, and guarantees.

An **embedded derivative** is a derivative which is embedded in another contract. These are complicated financial instruments from that the derivative portion may or may not be separated from the host contract. In general, where the embedded derivative has economic characteristics or risks that differ from the host contract, and that are similar to other derivatives, then it must be treated as a separate derivative. If such an embedded derivative cannot be so separated, the contract containing the embedded derivative and the host contract must be accounted for in its entirety at fair value.

Physical assets are not financial instruments because, even though they may be converted into cash, they do not create obligations to deliver cash or any other financial assets. Similarly, prepaid expenses and deferred revenues may create obligations to receive or deliver goods and services but are not financial instruments because they do not represent cash or other financial assets. However, the proposed standards would include certain contracts to manage financial risks associated with physical assets, such as exchange-traded commodity contracts entered into to manage the price at which a physical asset is to be acquired. For example, a company may enter into commodity futures contracts through the Chicago Board of Trade in commodities such as corn, soybeans or wheat to "fix" the price at which it will acquire such commodities. Such contracts would be accounted for in accordance with the proposed standards.

---

[3] The importance of trading in derivatives is provided by a report in *The Globe and Mail* of December 19, 1995, which stated that Canadian financial institutions held almost US $2-trillion in financial derivatives on their books in April 1995. This amount far exceeded their equity. The relative importance of the various types of derivatives was that daily trading in foreign exchange derivatives was $19-billion a day followed by interest rate derivatives of $15-billion a day.

Liabilities that are noncontractual in nature, like income taxes, are also not financial instruments because they are created by law and do not provide a corresponding asset in another entity in the sense contemplated by the definition of a financial instrument.

B. FORWARD CONTRACTS, OPTIONS, SWAPS

Forward Contracts

A forward exchange contract is an agreement by which one party enters into a contract with a dealer in foreign currency (usually an investment or merchant bank) to purchase (or sell) in advance a required amount of foreign currency. They are called **forward purchase contracts** if they involve the purchase of foreign currency or **forward sales contracts** if they relate to the sale of foreign currency. They are classified as financial instruments because they create contractual rights and obligations for the delivery of foreign currency from one entity to another.

When a business enterprise enters into a contract for the purchase of goods from a foreign supplier and the rates of exchange between the currencies are expected to change, the transaction may be hedged by entering into a **forward purchase contract**. The objective of entering into such a contract is to limit the amount payable on foreign currency transactions to a fixed amount.

For example, assume that a Canadian trader decides to hedge an amount of Australian $100,000 payable in 90 days time by entering into a **forward purchase contract**. If the current rate of exchange is Canadian $0.95 = Australian $1.00, the foreign exchange dealer may quote a 90-day rate of Canadian $0.98 = Australian $1.00. The rate quoted is called the forward exchange rate which, in effect, means that the cost of the hedge is Canadian $3,000 (i.e., the difference between the amount of Canadian $95,000 [the amount of $100,000 × 95/100]) at the date on which the liability was incurred and the amount of Canadian $98,000 (100,000 × 98/100) required to settle the known liability 90 days later. Any subsequent changes in the rate of exchange between the Canadian and Australian dollars would not affect the amount payable by the Canadian company.

This means that in 90 days, on payment of the amount due to the foreign exchange dealer, the trader who hedged the transaction would receive either Australian $100,000 in cash, a draft for Australian $100,000, or evidence that Australian $100,000 has been deposited by electronic transfer to the Australian supplier's bank account in Sydney. The amount payable for the currency or draft by the Canadian trader would be Canadian $98,000 irrespective of the actual exchange rate between the Canadian and Australian dollars on the date of settlement. Depending on the actual exchange rate in 90 days, this contract may be beneficial or detrimental to the entity (i.e., it might cost less, or it might cost more). However, whichever is the eventual result, the entity may have been more comfortable knowing that it had "locked-in" a pre-determined rate.

Traders who export goods may also wish to enter into a **forward sales contract** to hedge an amount receivable in a foreign currency. These contracts are, like forward purchase contracts, normally entered into with the trader's commercial bank. Here, the trader enters into an agreement to **sell** to the bank a certain amount of foreign currency at a set rate of exchange on a future date. For example, if a trader has exported goods to Brazil for which it is to receive 10,000,000 Reals in 60 days and the trader is concerned that the Brazilian Real will weaken in relation to the Canadian dollar, the trader can enter into a forward sales contract to sell this currency to his bank at the bank's forward exchange rate. An expected loss on exchange can, therefore, be limited to a known amount.

When traders borrow or lend money, they may also wish to hedge the amounts involved to reduce the risk of incurring losses. In these cases too, the traders may use forward purchase or forward sales contracts.

Futures contracts are very similar to forward contracts, with the primary difference being the right of the holder to sell the contract. Originally, futures contracts were only used for commodities. They were introduced in the 1860s by the Chicago Board of Trade, which allowed farmers to sell their crops in advance by using "corn futures". Over the years, the use of futures contracts has spread to all types of commodities. In the 1970s, their use was extended to financial instruments. Today, they are widely used for trading in securities (i.e., bonds, debentures, and equities), debt instruments (i.e., treasury bills, municipal bonds, certificates of deposit, and mortgages), and foreign currencies. They are traded on a futures exchange, like the Toronto Futures Exchange, which is operated along the lines of a stock exchange. All transactions in futures contracts are handled by futures brokers.

Futures contracts also consist of **index futures**, which are based on parcels of shares in publicly traded companies on the Toronto Stock Exchange, like the "Toronto 35" index. With the Toronto 35 Index, the share prices of 35 publicly traded shares are calculated daily and when compared with the index on the previous day, provide an indication of the movement in the general price of securities traded on the Toronto Stock Exchange. Units of these parcels of shares may be bought and sold like any other financial futures contract.

Futures contracts can be used for both **hedging and speculative purpose**s. They are useful as hedges because currency futures can be purchased for later delivery at a specified rate. When they are used for speculative purposes, **speculators** buy and sell futures contracts with the objective of making a profit from correctly anticipating movements in the prices at which they are traded. They are often used in conjunction with other financial instruments and, in the terminology of the futures market, include "forward rate agreements" for currency rate futures, and "straddles" or "spreads" covering more than one futures contract.

The first accounting standard covering futures contracts was the FASB's *Statement of Financial Accounting Standards No. 80: Accounting for Futures Contracts* (1980). This standard only applied to commodity futures because financial futures were to be covered by *SFAS No. 52: Foreign Currency Translation* (1981).[4] However, *SFAS No. 80*[5] is important because it **defined** a futures contract as:

(a) A legal agreement between a buyer and a seller and a futures exchange;
(b) That obligates the purchaser to accept, and the seller to deliver, a standardized quantity of a commodity or financial instrument at a specified date (or period);
(c) Which can be effectively **closed out** (i.e., cancelled or replaced) before the delivery date by entering into an **offsetting contract** for the same commodity or financial instrument **or** by making a cash settlement; and
(d) Requires settlement of all changes in value on open contracts on a regular, usually daily, basis.

Futures contracts are, therefore, entered into with a futures exchange broker and not the individual buyers and sellers, and they require either delivery of the items covered or a cash settlement. All changes in value must be settled by the brokers in cash on a daily basis after offsetting assets and liabilities against one another. Despite these requirements, only **very few** futures contracts result in actual delivery because the majority are **closed out** before the specified settlement date. In fact, index futures do not even provide for the delivery of the shares covered by the index.

Forward exchange contracts and futures contracts are **executory contracts**.[6] The contract between the person entering into the contract and the foreign exchange dealer is not

---

4 Paras. 17–19.
5 Para. 15. SFAS No. 80 has since been superseded by SFAS No. 133, *Accounting for Derivative Instruments and Hedging Activities*.
6 For an excellent explanation of executory contracts, see "A Note on Accounting and Executory Contracts," by Henderson, Scott, and Graham Peirson, *Abacus*, Vol. 20, No. 1, 1983.

recognized until it is executed or carried out by the two parties. In this respect, an executory contract is one in which the right to receive services is exactly offset by an equal duty to render those services. Neither leg of the contract is capable of being settled independently. As a result, the only asset or liability that can be considered to exist before such time as the contract has been completed by both parties is the net exposure. For example, a forward exchange contract to acquire £100,000 at an exchange rate of Canadian $2 = £1 on March 31, 20X1 does not result in any right or obligation to foreign currency until March 31, 20X1. Prior to that date, the only right of the person entering into the contract is to be able to receive £100,000 in exchange for Canadian $200,000 on March 31, 20X1, and the only obligation of the foreign exchange dealer is to deliver £100,000 in exchange for Canadian $200,000 on March 31, 20X1. Neither the £100,000 nor the Canadian $200,000 is a separate asset or liability until March 31, 20X1.

Of course, the forward exchange contract in the previous paragraph has a fair value prior to March 31, 20X1, determined based on the difference between the contracted exchange rate and the prevailing market rate at the valuation date for a forward contract for settlement on March 31, 20X1. Thus, if three months after entering into the forward exchange contract the forward exchange rate for March 31, 20X1 is Canadian $2.1 = £1, the person entering into the contract has a valuable right, since they have a contract entitling them to acquire £100,000 for $200,000, whereas another market participant entering into a contract at the valuation date to acquire £100,000 on March 31, 20X1 would be required to deliver Canadian $210,000. Thus, the contract has a fair value at the valuation date of Canadian $10,000, being equal to the amount that another party would be willing to pay the contract holder, and the amount that the contract holder would be willing to receive, in exchange for the original contract.

Options

An option is a contract that allows, but does not require, the holder to buy (or call) or sell (or put) a specific or standard commodity, an equity security, or other financial instrument at a specified price (i.e., the exercise or strike price) during a specified period, or on a specific date.[7] Options lapse if they are not exercised. The normal period is for 60-, 90-, or 120-days, but longterm options may run for two or three years. Like forward contracts, options apply to commodities as well as financial instruments.

The major difference between options and forward contracts is that a holder of an option need not exercise the option and, therefore, will lose only the amount paid to purchase the option. A forward contract, however, requires delivery of the items covered by the contract. They also differ from forward contracts in that a fee, known as a **premium**, is charged by the seller of the option. This premium applies to all options and is designed, in the event of the option not being exercised, to compensate the party granting the option for the risk involved. As a result, options are usually significantly more expensive than forward contracts.

Options take the form of **call (purchase) options** that give the purchaser the right to buy shares (or commodities, currencies, or other financial instruments) at what is called the **strike (or exercise) price**, irrespective of their market prices on the specified option date. Similarly, the holder of a **put (or sale) option** has the right to sell shares (or other commodities, currencies, etc.) at the strike price without regard for the prevailing market prices. When the **market price** (also called the **spot price**) of a call is lower than the option price,

---

[7] Options were first traded by the Chicago Board of Trade on the Chicago Options Exchange in 1973. Today, they are traded on futures markets in all major financial markets and the trading in options in Canada is handled, primarily, by the Montreal Exchange.

the option is described as being **out-of-the-money** (i.e., the relationship between the option price and the market price is unfavourable to the holder). On the other hand, **if the market price of a call is lower than the option price** (i.e., the relationship between the option price and the market price is favourable to the holder, making it profitable to exercise the option), the option is referred to as being **in-the-money**. The term **at-the-money** refers to the position where the market price and the exercise price are exactly the same. The **cost of the option** is the **premium**, which is generally payable by the purchaser in full when granted the option.

The premium is **not included** in **out-of-the-money** and **in-the-money calculations**. This is because even the smallest decrease in the market price to below the option price would make it profitable for the holder to exercise the option, as any such decrease would, at the very least, offset a portion of the premium.

The **decision to exercise an option** depends upon the existing conditions. For example, an investor may hold an option to purchase shares at a strike price of $80 each. If the market price of the shares rises above the strike price, the investor would probably exercise his option. If not, the investor would not bother to do so because it would serve no purpose. In this case, the cost to the investor would be the full amount of the premium paid for the option.

Even though there are two parties to an option contract, options are always described from the viewpoint of the buyer or owner of the contract. For example, a buyer may purchase the following option — 1 Northern Mining March $70 Put at a premium of $2. This option contract allows the **buyer to sell** (i.e., to put) 100 Northern Mining shares for $7,000 at any time up to the end of the month of March, for which the seller receives a premium of $200.

The **buyer** of an option always purchases a contract. However, the **seller** could act in one of two ways, by either **selling long** (i.e., selling securities actually owned) or **selling short** (i.e., selling securities not owned by the seller).

While the buyer of an option has purchased a contract, the seller of the contract can be acting in one of **two capacities**, namely, **selling long or selling short**. For example, a trader sells 1 Polycom Oct $50 Call — Premium $5 that had been previously purchased by the trader at a premium of $2. The original cost of the option (i.e., $200) is now worth $500. The trader, therefore, makes a profit of $300 (less expenses) by **selling long**. On the other hand, suppose the trader sold the 1 Polycom Oct $50 Call — Premium $5 without owning the option. This is called **selling short**, and the option is actually created through the short sale.

Selling long means the seller actually owns the securities to which the option applies. If the seller does not own the shares/securities to which the option applies, the option could still be **sold short** in anticipation of profiting from a decline in the market price of the shares/securities. In these cases, the trader can sell the option by borrowing the securities from someone else so that they can be delivered to the purchaser if the option is exercised.

Calculating the Value of Options

The value of an option is the sum of its **intrinsic (or actual) and its time value**. The intrinsic value of an option is the amount by which the **strike price** differs from the current **market price** of the financial instrument to which the option applies. An option can, therefore, **only** have an intrinsic value if it is in-the-money. The **time value** is the amount by which the option's market value exceeds its intrinsic value and represents the cost of bearing the risk of loss over the exercise period. The time value is proportionately decreased as the option moves towards its expiry date, at which date it has no value.

For example, assume an investor purchased a 120-day call option to buy 1,000 $100 BCF 8% bonds at $99 each at a premium of 12% on July 1, 19X1, when the market price of the bonds was $102. As the option is **in-the-money** (market price is higher than the buying price because the buying price is \$99,000 and the market price is \$102,000), its value on July 1 would have been:

Intrinsic Value of Option of (\$102 – \$99) × 1,000	\$ 3,000
Time Value of Option (plug figure)	9,000
Premium (i.e., cost of the option of 12% of \$100,000)	\$12,000

However, if the bonds were selling at \$101 each on September 30, 19X1 (i.e., on the expiry of 90 days), the option would be valued at only \$4,250 because the intrinsic value would have changed and its time value eroded by the passing of 75% of the time over which it could be exercised. This is outlined as follows:

Intrinsic Value of Option of (\$10 – \$99) × 1,000	\$2,000
Time Value of Option ([120 – 90]/120 × \$9,000)	2,250
Sum of Intrinsic and Time Values	\$4,250

It should be remembered that if the option is **out-of-the-money**, it has no intrinsic value, although it may still have a time value. In this case, the option is really only worth what someone else would be prepared to pay for it. But, **for accounting purposes**, it is always considered to have a time value until such time that the option lapses: that is, the option has a market value. The treatment of options recorded at market value is provided in Illustration 17–1, which shows that the overall effect of purchasing the option was a gain of \$20,000.

ILLUSTRATION 17–1
ACCOUNTING FOR OPTIONS RECORDED AT MARKET VALUE

On November 1, 20X2, Cataldo Enterprises Ltd. purchased 10,000 January 31, 20X3, \$100 6% Debentures in the New Brunswick Power Corporation Call Option market at \$9 — premium \$8. At purchase date of the options, the debentures were trading at \$101. At December 31, 20X2, the debentures had increased to \$102 in value. On January 31, 20X3, Cataldo Enterprises exercised its option when the debentures were trading at \$103.

If Cataldo Enterprises had a December 31 year-end, accounted for options at fair value, and adjusted option values at year-end and at the date of exercising its options, the position would be as follows:

Journal Entries

20X2
Nov. 1	Options NB Power Corp: Intrinsic Value (10,000 × [\$10 – \$99])	20,000	
	Time Value ([8% × \$1,000,000] – \$20,000)	60,000	
	Cash (\$8 × 10,000)		80,000
	Recording Premium on NB Power Corporation on purchase of option		
Dec. 31	Options — NB Power Corporation	10,000	
	Gain on Options Trading		10,000
	Recognition of Fair Value Adjustment from \$101 to \$102		
Dec. 31	Options Expense — Proportionate write-off of Time Value	40,000	
	Option — NB Power Corporation		40,000
	Write-off of 60/90 days × \$60,000 of option's time value		
20X3			
Jan. 31	Options — NB Power Corporation	10,000	
	Gain on Options Trading (10,000 × [\$103 – \$102])		10,000
	Recognition of Fair Value Adjustment from \$102 to \$103.		
Jan. 31	Options Expense — Proportionate write-off of Time Value	20,000	
	Options — NB Power Corporation		20,000
	Write-off of 30/90 days × \$60,000 of option's time value		

ILLUSTRATION 17–1 (Continued)

Jan. 31	Investment Account	990,000	
	Cash		990,000
	Exercise of call option — 10,000 $100 6% Debentures in NB Power Corporation at $99		
Jan. 31	Investment Account	40,000	
	Options — NB Power Corporation		40,000
	Write-off of balance on options account on exercising of option (i.e., balance of intrinsic value of $20,000, plus fair value adjustments of $10,000 + $10,000)		

Ledger Accounts

Option — 10,000 NB Power Corporation $100 6% Debentures Call — Premium $8

20X2				
Nov. 1	Premium — Intrinsic Value	20,000		
	Time Value	60,000		80,000
Dec. 31	Marking to Market Adjustment (10,000 × [$101 − $100])	10,000		90,000
	Options Trading Expense (60/90 days × $60,000)		40,000	50,000
20X3				
Jan. 31	Marking to Market Adjustment ([10,000 × [$103 − $102])	10,000		60,000
	Options Trading Expense (30/90 days × $60,000)		20,000	40,000
	Investment Account		40,000	Nil

Investment Account — NB Power Corporation 8% Debentures

20X3				
Jan. 31	Cash — Exercise of Option 10,000 $100 Debentures at $99	990,000		990,000
	Options Adjustment	40,000		1,030,000

Notes

[1] The overall position is that by purchasing the option for $80,000, Cataldo Enterprises was able to purchase the debentures for $40,000 less than their market value (i.e., $1,030,000 − $990,000).

[2] The debentures are recorded at fair value of $1,030,000.

Swaps

A swap is **an agreement to exchange (or swap) a series of cash flows**. In this respect, a **currency swap** is a variation of a forward exchange contract in which the parties agree to exchange specified amounts of two different currencies on future dates. They may also be used to eliminate fluctuations in foreign currencies if the parties swap liabilities denominated in their own individual currencies. For example, a Canadian trader exposed to foreign currency risk arising from debt denominated in Euros may swap the cash flows from that liability with cash flows from a liability in Canadian dollars held by a trader in Europe.

An **interest rate swap** is a contract to exchange a fixed interest obligation for a specific floating interest rate on debt denominated in the same currency (or vice-versa). For example, a party wishing to avoid the risk of being exposed to rising interest rates may swap a floating (or variable) rate obligation for a fixed rate obligation. In view of the risk involved, swaps are seldom used in isolation and are normally linked to other financial instruments. For example, **caps** and **floors** are contracts intended to protect holders against interest rate moves above and below stated levels. **Swaptions** are options to enter into swaps having the right to exchange a floating interest rate cash flow for a fixed rate cash flow in a future period.

Some swap contracts might involve an exchange of currency and interest rates — **a cross-currency interest rate swap**.

There is no exchange of assets or liabilities with swaps, because they are purely an exchange of a series of payments. They allow the parties to alter the terms of their financial agreements and when combined with external financing, provide useful and flexible forms of financing. They are also simple to use and are, therefore, very useful for hedging purposes. They may also be used for speculative purposes.

C. CLASSIFICATION, RECOGNITION AND MEASUREMENT OF FINANCIAL INSTRUMENTS

The AcSB requires that for the **recognition and measurement of financial instruments**, the following four basic principles must be satisfied:

1. When they meet the definitions of assets or liabilities, they are recognized on the balance sheet.
2. Only items that meet the definitions of assets or liabilities should be reported in the financial statements.
3. Fair value is the most relevant measure (although there are some significant exceptions to this principle).
4. Special accounting for items designated as part of a hedging relationship applies only in clearly delineated circumstances (see later).

Since financial instruments are established by contract and **contract establishes rights and obligations** for the entity, which satisfy the definitions of assets or liabilities, **all financial instruments are recognized on the balance sheet**. Furthermore, gains and losses do not establish rights and obligations. There is no right associated with a loss, or obligation associated with a gain. Therefore, gains and losses do not meet the definitions of assets or liabilities and, therefore, are not generally recognized on the balance sheet. (Such gains and losses may however, be deferred elsewhere; see later).

The valuation of many financial instruments at their fair values reflects the relevance of fair value for many financial instruments (consider, for example, what information is most relevant to you about your own investments — the price you paid for them, or their current value?) and the increasing reliability of such values.

The AcSB standard requires that **when financial instruments or derivatives are initially recognized**, they must all be recorded at their fair value. Thereafter, they **must continue to be valued at their fair value at the end of each and every financial period,** except for (a) loans and receivables, (b) debt instruments that the company has the intent and ability to hold to maturity, and (c) most financial liabilities, which must be valued at their amortized cost (i.e., cost less any write-downs, with amortization of discounts or premiums). Equity investments that do not have a quoted market price are valued at cost.

The issues relating to hedging relationships are examined later in this chapter.

Recognition and Derecognition

A reporting entity must **recognize** a financial asset or financial liability only when it becomes a party to the contractual agreement giving rise to the financial instrument. For example, a forward exchange contract is recognized as an asset or liability on the commitment date. Similarly, option contracts become assets or liabilities when the holder or writer becomes a party to the contract.

Derecognition is the term given to the removal of an asset or liability from the balance sheet. For a financial liability, this occurs when it is extinguished through being discharged, settled, or cancelled. For a financial asset, this generally occurs when the asset is sold, transferred, or otherwise disposed of. However, in some circumstances an entity may dispose part of a financial asset while retaining other parts: for example, in separating rights to interest payments from rights to principal, or in transfers of accounts receivable while retaining an interest in the accounts transferred. The accounting for these more complex derecognition transactions is beyond the scope of this chapter.

The Four Types of Financial Instruments and Their Measurement

The essential starting point from which to determine the measurement of particular financial instruments is their classification. Four types (or categories) of financial instruments are recognized:

(a) **Financial assets or financial liabilities held for trading** are those financial instruments held as part of an investment portfolio that is subject to short-term profit-taking through buying and selling. The major criterion in being classified as financial instruments falling into this category is that there should be active and frequent trading with the objective of generating a profit. In addition, **all derivatives must be classified in this category**. The AcSB also proposes that any other financial instrument may be classified as held for trading, by election on initial recognition. These financial instruments are measured at fair value.

(b) **Held-to-maturity investments** are financial assets with fixed or determinable maturity values and payments that an entity has the ability and intent to hold to maturity. These will be debt instruments, such as investments in government and corporate bonds. There are strict penalties for classifying a financial asset in this category and changing one's mind about the intent to hold the asset to maturity. Instruments in this category do not include investments that were, when acquired, designated as being held for trading, or that meet the definition of loans and receivables. These financial instruments are measured at amortized cost.

(c) **Loans and receivables** are financial assets resulting from the delivery of cash or other assets by a lender to a borrower in return for a promise to pay on demand, or on a specified date, a set amount, usually with interest. The major criterion with these financial instruments is that the loans and receivables must have a finite life and a definite repayment date. They exclude loans and receivables that are quoted in an active market (i.e., debt securities and indefinite period preferred shares) or are designated as being held for trading. These financial instruments are measured at amortized cost.

(d) **Available-for-sale financial assets** are those that are not classified as loans and receivables, or held-to-maturity investments, or held for trading. This category covers those financial instruments that do not fit any of the above three categories. Typically, many equity investments will be classified here. These financial instruments are measured at fair value, except for equity investments with no quoted market value, which are measured at cost.

The AcSB requires that financial instruments should generally not be reclassified into different categories while they are held. However, there are two exceptions. First, if there has been **a change in intention or ability** and it is no longer appropriate to carry a held-to-maturity investment at amortized cost, it should be reclassified into the available-for-sale category and revalued at fair value. Any difference between its carrying value and fair value should be treated as a gain or loss as outlined below. Second, **when a quoted market price becomes available** for a financial asset for which a price was not previously available, it should be revalued at fair value and the difference between the carrying value and the fair value should be recognized in income as a gain or loss. In those cases where a **quoted market price is no longer available**, and it becomes appropriate to value the financial asset at cost or amortized cost, the most recent fair value becomes its new cost.

The Treatment of Gains and Losses

Comprehensive Income   The issue of reporting comprehensive income is covered in Chapter One. However, in view of the importance of this aspect of current financial reporting in accounting for financial instruments, it is necessary to cover its operation before examining gains and losses on financial instruments.

As outlined earlier, it was in 2003 that the AcSB issued, as part of the revision of the CICA *Handbook* requirements on financial instruments, an *Exposure Draft* in which it is proposed that companies should present certain gains and losses in **other comprehensive income**, rather than directly in the income statement. Gains and losses presented in other comprehensive income include such items as unrealized gains and losses on translating financial statements of self-sustaining foreign operations, gains and losses on hedges of unrealized foreign currency translation losses and gains, gains and losses on financial assets classified as available-for-sale, and gains or losses on derivatives designated as cash flow hedges. Other comprehensive income is to be displayed with the same prominence as other financial statements as part of the annual financial statements.

Details of how this statement of comprehensive income is to be presented appear in Chapter One. Readers are, therefore, referred to this section regarding the disclosure of gains and losses from hedging transactions and available-for-sale financial assets, which are covered in this chapter.

Gains and Losses on Financial Instruments   Gains or losses on financial instruments arise from changes in value, as well as from interest and dividend income or expense during the time that the instrument is recognized. The requirements are that:

1. Gains or losses arising from changes in value of **financial assets or liabilities held for trading** must be recognized in the income statement in the period in which they arise.
2. A gain or loss arising from changes in value, other than an impairment loss, on **an available-for-sale asset** must be recognized in **other comprehensive income** until such time that the financial instrument is derecognized. At that time, the cumulative gain or loss must be recognized in net income for the period (see Illustration 17–2). Any premium or discount included in other comprehensive income relating to a debt instrument, classified as available for sale, with a fixed maturity date should be written off to net income over the remaining life of the debt instrument.
3. For **financial assets or liabilities carried at amortized cost**, a gain or loss is recognized in net income when the financial asset or liability is derecognized or impaired. Any amortization of the asset or liability is recognized in net income when it occurs.
4. When financial assets or liabilities form part of a **hedging relationship**, gains and losses are accounted for in accordance with the requirements relating to hedges (see later).

Gains or losses may also arise on derecognition of a financial instrument. The difference between the carrying amount **of a liability** and the amount paid to extinguish that liability is **a gain or loss relating to that financial instrument** and must be included in the income statement. Similarly, on outright disposition of a financial asset any difference between the proceeds received and the carrying amount is a gain or loss for immediate inclusion in the income statement. As noted earlier, more complex, partial derecognition of a financial asset and the consequential gain or loss recognition is beyond the scope of this chapter.

ILLUSTRATION 17–2
ACCOUNTING FOR AN AVAILABLE-FOR-SALE FINANCIAL ASSET

On November 30, 20X1, Investco purchases 300 equity shares of ABC Technologies, a company listed on the Stock Exchange, for $20 per share. Investco decides to classify the equity shares as available-for-sale financial assets. At December 31, 20X1, Investco's fiscal year end, the quoted price of ABC Technologies equity shares on the Stock Exchange is $23.50 per share. On April 15, 20X2, Investco sells 200 of the equity shares at the Stock Exchange quoted price of $24.50 per share.

Journal entries to record these events are as follows (transaction costs are ignored).

20X1				
Nov. 30	Available-for-sale financial assets (300 × $20)		6,000	
	Cash			6,000
	Purchase of 300 equity shares of ABC Technologies, classified as available-for-sale financial assets			
Dec. 31	Available-for-sale financial assets (300 × $3.50)		1,050	
	Other comprehensive income			1,050
	Gain on ABC Technologies shares recognized in other comprehensive income			
20X2				
Apr. 15	Cash (200 × $24.50)		4,900	
	Other comprehensive income		700	
	Income (700 [200 × $3.50] from other comprehensive income + $200			
	[200 × ($24.50 – $23.50)] additional gain since last reporting date on shares sold)			900
	Available-for-Sale Financial Assets — see Note			4,700
	Sale of 200 ABC Technologies shares and associated recognition of gain in income			

Note that the remaining 100 shares are worth $2,450, rather than the $2,350 at the previous reporting date. Thus, if there were no further changes in prices there would be a further $100 to be recognized in available-for-sale financial assets and other comprehensive income at the next reporting date, giving a fair value of the remaining shares of $2,450 and an accumulated balance in other comprehensive income of $450 (representing 100 shares times the difference between the original purchase price of $20 and the current fair value of $24.50).

Interest Income and Interest Expense Interest income and interest expense from financial instruments should be recognized and measured in a way that reflects the **effective yield** on the instrument (see Illustration 17–3). Any fees relating to the cost or issue of financial instrument should be capitalized in determining the effective yield.

These requirements may have widespread effects. For example, when borrowing costs are capitalized (i.e., with construction projects), the total interest expense must first be calculated by including the borrowing costs as part of the interest expense and then be deducted and capitalized separately. Similarly, where bonds have been purchased at a premium or discount, these amounts must be amortized over the tenure of the bonds as adjustments to the interest to give the effective yield of interest. In cases where interest-bearing financial instruments may be redeemed before their maturity date, the effective yield must be calculated on the assumption that they will be redeemed at the earliest possible date. For financial instruments classified as liabilities, but which have the legal form of shares or other equity instruments (i.e., like redeemable preference shares), interest includes dividends and similar distributions.

D. PRESENTATION AND DISCLOSURE

Balance Sheet Classification

The **balance sheet classification** of a financial instrument, or its component parts, should reflect the substance of the contractual arrangement and not its legal form. For example, when a financial instrument like a preferred share specifies a definite settlement or redemption date,

ILLUSTRATION 17–3
CALCULATING INTEREST INCOME USING THE EFFECTIVE YIELD METHOD

On January 1, 20X4, Investors Inc. acquires a debt instrument that matures on June 30, 20X6. The debt instrument has a principal amount of $1,000 and pays fixed interest of 5 percent annually. Investors Inc. acquires the debt instrument for its fair value of $934.14, representing an annual yield of 8 percent.

Year	Opening Amortized Cost	Interest Income	Cash	Closing Amortized Cost
20X4	$934.14	$74.73	$50.00	$958.87
20X5	958.87	76.71	50.00	985.58
20X6	985.58	$39.42	$1,000.00 + $25.00	0.00

The total gains and losses recognized in net income in each of the three years are $124.73 in 20X4, $126.71 in 20X5 and $64.42 in 20X6.

or provides the right to require settlement or redemption, it meets the definition of a **financial liability** and should be classified as such. Preferred shares not conferring such rights are classified as **equities**.

In most cases, the legal form of a financial instrument is consistent with its substance. However, some innovative financial instruments may sometimes result in financial instruments that combine features frequently associated with equities and liabilities (for example, debt that is convertible to equity). A financial instrument may also contain many features that are common to both liabilities and equities. Where this occurs, reference to the definitions of assets, liabilities and equities in section 1000 of the CICA *Handbook* may be necessary to ensure that they are properly classified.[8]

Offsetting Financial Assets and Financial Liabilities

A financial asset and a financial liability should be offset against one another and presented as the net amount on the balance sheet only when the entity has a **legally enforceable right to set off** and settlement is intended to take place through such right. The right to set off is a debtor's legal right to settle all or part of an obligation by applying one amount against the other owed to the debtor.

Disclosure Requirements

The **disclosure requirements** for financial instruments include any significant terms and conditions that may affect the amount, timing, and certainty of future cash flows as well as information about the manner in which financial instruments have been classified, where they are recorded on the balance sheet and where associated gains and losses are recognized.

It is important to note that, even though some financial instruments are not measured at fair value, because they are not required to be so measured or because they fall outside the scope of the recognition and measurement standard (for example, insurance contracts that are not recognized as financial instruments), fair value disclosures are required for all financial instruments.

---

[8] As outlined in section 1000 of the CICA *Handbook*, **assets** are economic resources that are controlled by an entity as a result of past transactions or events from which economic benefits may be obtained. To be classified as an asset, they must (1) provide future benefits or cash flows; (2) the entity must be able to control the assets; and (3) the transaction giving rise to the benefits or cash flows has already occurred.

The **extent of disclosure** is a matter of professional judgment. However, full disclosure would probably require the disclosure of such information as the principal, stated or face value of the instrument; the maturity, execution or expiry date of the instruments; any redemption or conversion options; the conditions and the date and price at which the options are exercisable; scheduled future cash receipts or payments of the principal; the amount of interest, dividends or any other return on the principal; any collateral security held or pledged; and details of any instrument that provides for an exchange of one instrument for another. Additional detailed disclosures (which represent detailed information that is beyond the scope of this chapter) apply in cases when the reporting entity is exposed to interest rate and credit risk. Disclosures should group like items together and present information in a manner that is most likely to result in a user of the financial statements understanding the extent to which the entity uses financial instruments to manage risks, and the manner in which financial instruments are accounted for.

E. HEDGING RELATIONSHIPS

What Is a Hedge?

The term "hedge" may be used in a general way to describe the actions taken to reduce risk arising from changes in prices. For example, it is generally recognized that the investment in the shares of companies whose securities are publicly traded is **a hedge against inflation** because share prices normally increase in times of inflation and lessen the effects of a decrease in the purchasing power of the dollar. Hedging may be a conscious activity of an entity, such as when an entity acquires financial instruments (often derivatives) specifically to manage particular risks, or may be more passive, such as when an entity has foreign currency debt that naturally offsets foreign currency risk associated with sales in the same foreign currency.

To meet the requirements of a hedge, any **changes in the value or cash flows** of the hedging instrument and the net market value of the position being hedged should be **the same or closely correlated** with one another. A trader may, for example, enter into a forward exchange contract with his commercial bank to hedge a known future liability by **purchasing** foreign currency to be delivered at the future date of the liability. From that point onwards, any gain (or loss) in the value of the foreign currency purchased would exactly offset any increase (or decrease) in the hedged liability.

The existence of a hedge may be merely implied by, for example, the investment in some asset (like gold or marketable securities) to offset the effects of an expected fluctuation in price. It may also exist through the arrangement of investments or affairs in such a way as to provide an **effective hedge** against foreign currency fluctuations or any other form of risk. For example, the investment in foreign interest-bearing securities to offset the effects of price fluctuations on obligations payable in the same foreign currency may be an effective hedge.

Various choices in constructing a hedging relationship are possible. For example, a Canadian company contracts to purchase goods in Spain for €500,000 on February 1, 20X3. The goods were to be shipped from Barcelona on May 1, 20X3, the date on which €500,000 is payable. On February 1, 20X3, the exchange rate is €1.00 = $1.40, resulting in a Canadian dollar liability of $700,000. The company wishes to ensure that changes in the exchange rate movements during the period February 1, 20X3 to May 1, 20X3 do not result in exchange gains or losses on this liability. This transaction could be hedged by, say:

(a) Investing an amount on February 1, 20X3 that would amount to €500,000 on May 1, 20X3.
(b) Purchasing €500,000 in currency on, say, February 1, 20X3, and holding it until May 1, 20X3.

(c) Entering into an option contract to purchase €500,000 at a specified rate of exchange to be settled on May 1, 20X3.

(d) Entering into a forward exchange contract with a dealer in foreign exchange so that €500,000 would be available on May 1, 20X3 to settle the amount outstanding.

The nature of the hedging instrument may not be obvious from its form because to be classified as a hedge, for accounting purposes, is dependent on the intention of management. Hedges can take a number of forms, depending on their operation. For example,

1. The hedge of the exposure to variability in a cash flow of a recognized asset or liability, or a forecasted (or anticipated) transaction, that is attributable to a particular risk. These are referred to as **cash flow hedges**. A common example is a hedge of future cash flows from sales or purchases denominated in a foreign currency.

2. A hedge of the exposure to changes in the fair value of a recognized asset or liability, or of an unrecognized firm commitment, that is attributable to a particular risk. Such a hedge is referred to as **a fair value hedge**. These hedges may be entered into to hedge the amount owing after the receipt of goods. In such a case, the hedge is of **an actual liability** incurred sometime in the period between the incurring of the liability and the settlement of that liability. They may also be used to hedge an exposed foreign currency asset or liability, or to hedge a firm commitment.

3. A hedge of a **net investment** in a self-sustaining foreign operation. These are hedges of the foreign currency exposure arising from having invested in a self-sustaining foreign operation.

Accounting for Hedges

Hedge accounting must be distinguished from hedging. Hedge accounting is the process by which normal accounting (as discussed so far in this chapter) is modified so that the income statement effect of risk exposures in a **hedged item** and the **hedging instruments** managing those exposures are reflected in the same accounting period. The circumstances in which hedge accounting is permitted require that there be a hedging relationship. However, not all hedging relationships will qualify for hedge accounting and since hedge accounting is optional, an entity will not always elect to apply hedge accounting to all hedging relationships. For example, since there are costs of documentation and record-keeping associated with hedge accounting, an entity may choose not to apply hedge accounting to exposures that would result in little income statement volatility.

The accounting for hedges depends upon whether the relationship is considered a hedging relationship. If it is so designated, then to apply hedge accounting, **three conditions must be satisfied**. First, the entity must have identified, at the inception of the hedging relationship, **the nature of the specific risk exposure** being hedged in accordance with its risk management objective and strategy. Second, it must have **formal documentation** of the risk management objective and strategy, the nature of the hedging relationship, and the method of accounting for it, and how the effectiveness of the hedging relationship is to be established. And, third, throughout the term of the hedging relationship, the entity should have **reasonable assurance** that the relationship will be effective.

Hedge accounting is applied only when gains, losses, revenues and expenses **relating to a hedging item** would otherwise be recognized in net income in **a different period from those relating to the hedged item**. This is because hedge accounting modifies the normal basis for recognizing the gains, losses, revenues and expenses associated with a hedged item or a hedging item in an entity's income statement. The application of hedge accounting is optional and an entity should, therefore, only apply hedge accounting under conditions that justify its use.

Understanding of the accounting for hedged transactions is relatively straightforward once the jargon involved with hedged transactions is understood. This jargon becomes understandable when it is viewed in the form presented in Illustration 17–4. This shows that where a

ILLUSTRATION 17–4
DIAGRAMMATICAL EXPRESSION OF CONDITIONS IN WHICH THE HEDGE OF A PURCHASE TRANSACTION TAKES PLACE

When a trader enters into a contract to purchase goods, the day on which the order is placed is known as the commitment date or trade date. The date on which the goods are received is known as the goods received date and the liability date, or settlement date, is the date on which the amount payable is to be settled. Diagrammatically, this is as follows:

Sequence of Events

Commitment (Trade) Date   Goods Received Date   Liability (Settlement) Date
(i.e., Order Placed)   (i.e., Amount Payable)

Hedge of an Anticipated Foreign Currency Commitment (Cash Flow Hedge)

Commitment Period†
Hedge Entered Into   Exposed Liability Period

Hedge of a Foreign Monetary Liability (Fair Value Hedge):

Exposed Liability Period
Hedge Entered Into

† Note that the proposed standard permits a hedge of a foreign currency firm commitment to be accounted for as either a cash flow hedge or a fair value hedge.

---

trader enters into a contract to purchase goods from a supplier, the trader incurs a commitment to settle the amount owing on a certain date. The date on which the contract of purchase is entered into is known as the **commitment date or trade date**, the date on which the goods are received (or the risk of ownership passes) is the **goods received date**, and the date on which the liability is to be settled is the **liability date or settlement date**. With the hedge of an expected cash flow, the hedge is entered into before the goods are actually received and the hedge is of the amount expected to be paid for the goods. Such a hedge is referred to as **a cash flow hedge**. When, however, the hedge is entered into after the receipt of goods, the hedge may be of an existing liability and, when the liability to which it applies has been revalued, it is known as **a fair value hedge**.

Fair Value Hedges An entity may designate a derivative instrument[9] as a hedge of the changes in the fair value of an asset or a liability attributable to a particular risk. This may be carried out provided that at the inception of the hedge, there is formal documentation of the hedging relationship and the entity's risk management objective and the strategy for undertaking the hedge, and how the hedging instrument's effectiveness is to be assessed, including a method of determining the gain or loss resulting from the hedge.

---

[9] Or, for a hedge of foreign currency risk only, a non-derivative financial instrument.

ILLUSTRATION 17–5
A FAIR VALUE HEDGE OF A PURCHASE COMMITMENT

On November 1, 20X4, a Canadian company, having a December 31 year end, contracts (a firm commitment) to purchase US $100,000 of inventory for delivery on January 15, 20X5. Fearing that the Canadian dollar will weaken relative to the US dollar, the company enters into a forward exchange contract on November 1, 20X4 with its bankers to purchase US $100,000 on January 5, 20X5 for Canadian $125,000 and designates it as a hedge of the US/Canadian foreign currency exposure relating to the purchase commitment.

The Canadian equivalent value of a forward contract to acquire US $100,000 on January 15, 20X5 at other relevant dates is as follows:

December 31, 20X4	$128,000
January 15, 20X5	$131,000

The journal entries recording the forward contract and the hedge accounting would be as follows:

20X4

Nov. 1	No entry on placing of purchase order		
Nov. 1	No entry on entering into the forward contract (transaction costs are ignored)		
Dec. 31	Forward exchange contract	3,000	
	Gain (income statement)		3,000
	Change in value of forward contract from November 1 to December 313,000		
Dec. 31	Loss (income statement)	3,000	
	Purchase commitment		3,000
	Hedge accounting entry to reflect change in value of purchase commitment due to foreign currency risk.		
Jan. 15	Inventory	125,000	
	Purchase commitment	3,000	
	Forward exchange contract		3,000
	Cash (Canadian $)		125,000
	Purchase of inventory and settlement of forward exchange contract. Note that the inventory is recognized at the amount 'locked-in' by the forward exchange contract and that the net income statement effect is zero. Without hedge accounting, a gain on the forward contract would have been recognized in income in 20X4 and a corresponding loss in 20X5.		

Gains or losses on a fair value hedging instrument must be recognized in current period net income. To ensure that gains and losses on the hedged item are recognized in net income at the same time, the carrying amount of the hedged item is adjusted for the gain or loss attributable to the risk hedged, and is also recognized in current earnings.

An illustration of the nature and operation of a fair value hedge using a forward exchange contract is presented in Illustration 17–5.

Cash Flow Hedges As outlined above, a **cash flow hedge** is a hedge of the exposure to changes in a cash flow of a recognized asset or liability, or a **forecasted (or anticipated) transaction**, that is attributable to a particular risk. They are entered into to limit a company's exposure to fluctuations in, and expected future liability arising from, price changes or fluctuations in foreign exchange rates (or other risks). To ensure that gains and losses on the hedged item are recognized in net income at the same time, gains and losses on the hedging instrument attributable to the risk being hedged are recognized in other comprehensive income until such time as the corresponding losses or gains on the hedged item affect net income.

An illustration of the operation of a cash flow hedge using a currency option to hedge foreign currency risk in an anticipated transaction is provided in Illustration 17–6.

ILLUSTRATION 17–6
ACCOUNTING FOR CASH FLOW HEDGES ARISING FROM THE EXERCISE OF AN OPTION

On May 15, 20X2, a trader who has a June 30 year end entered into a contract to purchase goods from a German supplier to the value of 1-million Euros. The goods were to be loaded on a ship bound for Montreal on August 1, 20X2. Payment for the goods was to be on August 1, 20X2, by electronic transfer to the supplier's bank account.

To hedge the amount payable, the trader entered into an option contract on June 1, 20X2 to purchase €1-million at €1.00 = $1.70 to be delivered on August 1, 20X2. The cost of the option was $20,000, reflecting its fair value at that date (the spot rate is €1.00 = $1.70 and the two-month forward rate is €1.00 = $1.72).

Case 1: On June 30, 20X2, the one-month forward rate of exchange was €1.00 = $1.73.

The decision to exercise the option would depend upon the rate of exchange between the Euro and the dollar on August 1, 20X2. If the rate of exchange between the Euro and the Canadian dollar was €1.00 = $1.76, the trader would exercise his option because the cost of purchasing the Euros would be $60,000 more than the hedged cost of $1,700,000.

The journal entries recording the transaction would have been as follows:

20X2			
May 15	No entry		
June 1	Option contract	20,000	
	Cash		20,000
	Purchase of option contract		
June 30	Option contract	10,000	
	Other comprehensive income		10,000
	Adjustment for increase in value of option		
Aug. 1	Purchases (€1-million × 1.76/1.00)	1,760,000	
	Cash to Supplier		1,760,000
	Payment of amount due		
	Option contract	30,000	
	Other comprehensive income		30,000
	Increase of value of option contract to August 1		
	Cash (from Option Giver of 1-million × [$1.76 – $1.70])	60,000	
	Option contract		60,000
	Other comprehensive income	40,000	
	Purchases		40,000
	Receipt of cash from options giver (i.e., $1,760,000 – $1,700,000), write-off of options contract and transfer of gains and losses from other comprehensive income to net income (purchases)		

Note that the net cost of the purchases in this case is $1,720,000 — being the 'locked-in' rate of $1,700,000, plus the cost of the option of $20,000 (a better result than the unhedged cost of $1,760,000 would have been).

Case 2: If the rate of exchange between the Euro and the Canadian dollar on August 1, 20X2 had been €1.00 = $1.65, the trader would let the option lapse as it would be cheaper to purchase the goods for $1,650,000. In such a case, the cost of the hedge would be written off as an expense. The journal entries for June 1 and June 30, 20X2 would be unchanged from that given above, but on August 1, 20X2, the position would have been as follows:

Aug. 1	Purchases (€1-million × 1.65/1.00)	1,650,000	
	Cash to Supplier		1,650,000
	Payment of amount due		
	Option contract	30,000	
	Other comprehensive income		30,000
	Decrease in value of option contract to August 1		
	Purchases	20,000	
	Other comprehensive income		20,000
	Release of balance from other comprehensive income. The total costs of the purchases is $1,670,000, being the cash cost plus the cost of the option.		

Cash flow hedging requires careful record-keeping to track the amounts in other comprehensive income relating to each designated hedge and to be in a position to transfer those amounts from other comprehensive income to net income at the time that the hedged item affects net income. In many cases it will be clear when the hedged item affects net income. For example, in Illustration 17–6 the payment occurs immediately and thus the expense affects net income at that time. In other cases, however, the hedged item may not affect net income until sometime after the expiry of the hedge. For example, if a piece of plant or machinery is acquired and designated as the hedged item, that plant or machinery will only affect net income as it is depreciated. Therefore, it is over the course of the depreciation of the plant or machinery that any amounts in other comprehensive income would be transferred to net income. Luckily, in this instance, to save record-keeping, the AcSB proposes that on acquisition of the plant or machinery an entity may elect an accounting policy of adjusting the initial carrying amount of the plant and machinery by the amount in other comprehensive income and depreciated the net (or gross) amount.

Discontinuing Hedge Accounting Hedge accounting may be discontinued in a number of circumstances, voluntarily and mandatory. Hedge accounting is discontinued prospectively if any of the following events occur:

(a) The hedging instrument no longer exists — it has matured, expired, been sold, terminated, cancelled or exercised.
(b) The hedged item no longer exists — it has matured, expired, been sold, terminated, cancelled or exercised.
(c) The forecast transaction is no longer expected to occur.
(d) The hedging relationship no longer meets qualifying requirements — either the hedging relationship is no longer effective or the company voluntarily chooses to terminate its designation of the hedging relationship.

Prospective discontinuance means that hedge accounting continues to apply up to the date of the event leading to the discontinuance, but ceases from that date. The effects of previous hedge accounting are not reversed. For example, if a hedging relationship no longer meets qualifying requirements, any adjustment to the carrying amount of a hedged item that is measured at amortized cost, made as a result of a fair value hedge, continues to be amortized to net income. Any cumulative gains or losses related to the hedged item previously recognized in other comprehensive income in a cash flow hedge are carried forward to be recognized in net income when the anticipated transaction occurs, at which time they are accounted for in the same manner as if the hedge had remained effective. If the anticipated transaction is no longer expected to occur, any cumulative gains or losses related to the anticipated transaction previously recognized in other comprehensive income are recognised in net income.

Effectiveness Testing Effectiveness testing is a key aspect of hedge accounting, with the effects of any ineffectiveness being required to be recognized immediately in net income. If there is no longer sufficient probability of effectiveness in the future then hedge accounting is required to be discontinued, but a new hedge may be designated going forward. The methods of effectiveness testing are beyond the scope of this chapter.

SUMMARY

This chapter outlines the nature of financial instruments and explains three fundamental financial instruments — forward contracts, options and swaps. It also explains the basic classification, recognition, measurement, presentation and disclosure requirements for financial instruments, as well as introducing a basic explanation of when hedge accounting is applied and the two primary types of hedge accounting — fair value and cash flow hedges — as they apply to hedges of currency risk.

More information on accounting for financial instruments can be obtained by studying the CICA *Handbook* Sections 3855, Financial Instruments — Recognition and Measurement, 3865, hedges, and 3860, Financial Instruments — Disclosure and Presentation. The AcSB is also in the course of developing implementation guidance to further explain the application of these *Handbook* Sections.

REVIEW QUESTIONS

1. What are financial instruments? How are they defined?
2. What is a forward exchange contract? How does it differ from a futures contract?
3. What is an options contract? What is the essential difference between the manner in which an options contract would be used to manage risk, rather than a forward contract?
4. Explain what is an option contract that is "in-the-money" versus "out-of-the-money".
5. Explain the terms "intrinsic value" and "time value".
6. How is the value of an option calculated?
7. What is a currency swap? An interest rate swap?
8. What are the four basic principles underlying AcSB proposals for recognition and measurement of financial instruments?
9. What do you understand by the term "derecognition"?
10. What are the four types of financial assets for accounting purposes? How is each type measured?
11. How are gains and losses on each types of financial assets identified in question 10 accounted for?
12. How are interest income and expense on financial instruments recognized and measured?
13. Distinguish between "hedging" and "hedge accounting".
14. What is the purpose of hedge accounting?
15. What modification is made to normal accounting when accounting for a fair value hedge?
16. What modification is made to normal accounting when accounting for a cash flow hedge?
17. When is hedge accounting discontinued?

CASE

CASE 17–1   Ruston-Wheeler Ltd.

Ruston-Wheeler Ltd. is a Winnipeg-based manufacturer of snowblowing equipment. It produces equipment used for the clearing of snow from airport runways, parking lots, and city streets where conventional snowploughs are unsuitable.

At a meeting of the board of directors of the company held in March, the company had approved a plan to manufacture a range of small but highly effective snowblowers for homeowners, small businesses, and municipalities for clearing sidewalks. The snowblowers were to be marketed under the name of "Snow Tempest". Prototypes of two models had been extensively tested and, as the result of a positive marketing survey, production was to commence immediately to take advantage of the upcoming winter weather. Contracts had already been signed with two hardware warehouse chains, and a number of retailers had agreed to sell the snowblowers on consignment. Prospects for the venture looked good.

The snowblowers were powered by a gasoline engine imported from Great Britain. Orders had been placed for the delivery of 10,000 units a month for the three-month period September through November at a cost of British £70 each. Payment was to be effected on loading on the carrier in Liverpool harbour. Shipping dates had already been arranged and payments of £700,000 were due on September 4, October 3, and November 6.

You, as chief financial officer of the company have been asked to advise the board on the best possible method of handling the payment of the amounts due. There are four possibilities:

1. The company could instruct its bankers to transfer the money on each payment date directly to the supplier. Charges were approximately one and one-half percent of the amount transferred.

2. It could enter into a series of forward exchange contracts so that the British pounds would be available when required. Past experience had shown that the premiums on forward exchange contracts were in the region of four percent.

3. British pounds could be purchased "forward" by purchasing three different futures contracts. The costs involved amounted to a premium of about six percent per year plus a commission of one-quarter of one percent on the total amounts involved.

4. It could enter into a currency swap agreement with the Manitoba Wheat Exchange to swap American dollars obtained from sales of snowblowing equipment to the United States for British pounds paid for wheat. Unfortunately, the amount of American dollars available varied depending upon sales to the USA, which normally only occurred in December and January. There was, however, a possibility of purchasing British pounds directly from the Wheat Exchange.

The rates of exchange between the Canadian dollar and the British pound had remained relatively stable over the years at Canadian $1.00 = British £0.47 to 0.51. Nothing seemed to indicate that this would differ much in the immediate future.

REQUIRED

Consider the advantages and disadvantages of each possibility with a view to arriving at a broad policy on which method to use.

EXERCISES

EXERCISE 17–1   On June 15, 20X2, the city of Tecumseh entered into a contract with an American supplier to supply it with three fire engines at a cost of US $120,000 each. Payment was to be made on delivery of the fire engines on September 15, 20X2.

As the City of Tecumseh was concerned that the US dollar would strengthen in relation to the Canadian dollar, it hedged the transaction on July 15, 20X2. The relevant rates of exchange between the Canadian and US dollar and the 60-day forward exchange rate were as follows:

June 15, 20X2	Can $1.00 = US $0.80
July 15, 20X2	0.76
September 15, 20X2	0.75
60-day Forward Exchange Rate at July 15, 20X2	0.72

REQUIRED

Answer the following questions:

1. Is this a hedge of an anticipated foreign currency commitment or a hedge of a future monetary liability?

2. Was the hedge entered into at a premium or a discount?

3. How should the transaction be treated to comply with the proposed requirements of the CICA *Handbook*?

4. What is the cost of each fire engine to the City of Tecumseh? Provide journal entries in support of your answer.

5 Would the cost of the fire engines have been any different if the transaction had not been hedged?

EXERCISE 17–2 On November 1, 20X4, Local Trader Inc. placed an order with a supplier to purchase 4,000 computer keyboards at 400 Foreign Currency Units (FCU) each. The terms of the order were that the keyboards were to be airlifted to Toronto on December 1, 20X4. Payment was to be effected on March 1, 20X5. The keyboards were duly delivered on December 1, 20X4.

Rates of exchange between the Canadian dollar and the FCU were as follows:

November 1, 20X4	Can $1.00 = FCU	400
December 1, 20X4		410
December 31, 20X4		390
January 1, 20X5		380
February 1, 20X5		375
March 1, 20X5		385

REQUIRED

1. From the information provided above, give the journal entries (without explanations) to record the above transactions in the ledger of Local Trader on the assumption that Local Trader had a December 31 year end.
2. If Local Trader entered into a hedge on November 1, 20X4, would the hedge be a hedge of a forward purchase contract or a hedge of a forward sales contract?
3. If Local Trader decided to hedge the amount payable on December 2, 20X4, would the hedge be a hedge of an anticipated foreign currency commitment or a hedge of a foreign monetary liability?

EXERCISE 17–3 On September 1, 20X6, the Chancery Mutual Fund anticipating an increase in interest rates, placed an order with its options broker to buy 100,000 February five-year 8% $100 Province of Manitoba bonds call options at $102.50 and at a premium of $12.

The value of the bonds on the date of purchasing the option was $103. By December 31, 20X6, the bonds had increased in value to $104 but by February 28, 20X7, they had fallen in value to $102.00 and Chancery allowed the option to lapse.

REQUIRED

Prepare the journal entries recording the trade in the option by the Chancery Mutual Fund on the assumptions that:

1. The fund recorded its investments at market value;
2. Marking to market adjustments were only made on December 31, and February 28; and
3. The year-end of the fund was December 31.

PROBLEMS

PROBLEM 17–1 Maxwell Jones Inc. is a Canadian manufacturer of extrusion moulds for the non-ferrous metal industry. On September 15, 20X6, it entered into a contract to purchase special alloys from the Klaus Steel Company of Zurich for 400,000 Swiss francs when the spot rate was SF 1.33 = Canadian $1.00. The amount was payable in full on February 1, 20X7. The alloys were dispatched and loaded f.o.b. on a ship in Hamburg bound for Canada on October 1, 20X6 when the rate of exchange was SF1.35 = Canadian $1.00. On the following day (i.e., October 2, 20X6), Maxwell Jones hedged the liability by entering into a contract to receive 400,000 Swiss Francs on February 1, 20X7, at the 120-day forward rate of SF 1.37 = Canadian $1.00, but did not designate the hedging relationship as such for accounting purposes.

The financial year end of Maxwell Jones was December 31 and on that date the spot rate of exchange between the Canadian dollar and the Swiss Franc was SF 1.34 = Canadian $1.00 and the 30-day forward rate was SF 1.35. The spot rate of exchange between the Canadian dollar and the Swiss Franc on February 1, 20X7 was SF 1.36 = Canadian $ 1.00.

REQUIRED

Prepare the journal entries to record the above transactions, the amounts outstanding at December 31, and the collection of the receivable and payment of the amount outstanding on due date.

PROBLEM 17–2   Bryan, the proprietor of OddjobCo Ltd., has had a successful year and on January 1, 20X5 invests $40,815 surplus cash in a zero coupon corporate bond, which will pay OddjobCo Ltd. $50,000 when the bond matures on December 31, 20X7 (representing an effective interest rate of 7%). OddjobCo Ltd. prepares financial statements annually at December 31, and is about to adopt the new requirements for recognition and measurement issued by the Accounting Standards Board.

REQUIRED

Advise Bryan as to the alternative methods of classification and accounting for the corporate bond and demonstrate the accounting effects, using journal entries, of each alternative. (Show all workings.) Explain the circumstances in which each classification may be used assuming that the fair value of the corporate bond is $81.63 per 100 at January 1, 20X5, $89.00 per 100 at December 31, 2005, and $95.00 per 100 at December 31, 20X6.

18

The Nature and Control of Government and Nonprofit Organizations

Note: Chapters 18, 19, and 20 are connected. Chapter 18 discusses and presents the general accounting features of nonbusiness organizations (i.e., the nonprofit and governmental sectors) as they apply throughout the world and in the Canadian political environment. Chapter 19 presents the accounting requirements of the CICA's Public Sector Accounting Board for the public sector in Canada. The specific accounting requirements of the Accounting Standards Board of the CICA for Canadian nonprofit organizations are presented in Chapter 20.

LEARNING OBJECTIVES

After studying this chapter you should be able to:

1. Understand the nature and importance of the government and nonprofit sector in Canada;
2. Identify the basic characteristics of government and nonprofit organizations, the areas in which they differ from profit-oriented enterprises of the private sector, and their general accounting requirements;
3. Recognize the need to control the operations and activities of these organizations and the application of fund accounting; and
4. Appreciate the difficulties in measuring the performance of government and nonprofit organizations.

NONBUSINESS ORGANIZATIONS AND THEIR PLACE IN THE ECONOMY AND SOCIETY

Throughout time communities have established organizations to satisfy their various social and other needs. Even though these organizations varied considerably in nature from one another and from community to community, they consisted of governing bodies and other organizations concerned with the well-being of the communities in which they operated.

The position is no different today. Virtually every country in the Western world is characterized by a significant governmental sector and the existence of numerous organizations providing services to the community. These latter organizations are known as nonprofit organizations (NPOs) which, as their description implies, are operated without the intention of making a profit. These two groups of organizations are referred to as nonbusiness organizations (NBOs)[1] and, for convenience, this description is used throughout the chapter.

Nonbusiness organizations account for a significant segment of the economy. Even though estimates vary, it is believed that together they account for approximately 30% of the total economic activity in Canada.

The Government (or Public) Sector

In Canada, the government sector consists of a three-tiered federal system made up of the federal, provincial and local government units. The federal government exercises overall control over the country in such matters as defence and foreign affairs, while the day-to-day operation of government in the provinces is handled by the provincial governments. The running of the smaller communities, like cities and towns, is under the control of the local governments. At each level of government, certain operations are delegated to smaller bodies more suited to the control of specific functions. These bodies are either fully or partly financed by the level of government concerned.

The purpose of the three levels of government is to serve the communities over which they have jurisdiction. This sector is referred to as the public sector because it is concerned with public issues. Its responsibility is to provide "good government". This means that the government should actively pursue courses of action designed to promote the welfare and general well-being of those over which it exercises its authority. In doing so, it should operate in an efficient and effective manner and restrict its levels of expenditures to the amounts required without imposing excessive taxes on its citizens or the excessive use of borrowed money.

The federal government also operates certain **crown corporations** that are business-type organizations in which the government is the sole shareholder and which are exempted from the payment of income taxes. Crown corporations are normally formed to carry on the various activities of the government through independently run corporations (like the Royal Canadian Mint and Canada Post Corporation) for control and other purposes, much along the lines of the divisionalization of enterprises in the private sector.

Nonprofit Organizations[2]

NPOs consist of bodies created to cater for the specific needs and activities of the communities in which they operate. They may consist of government-sponsored bodies like educational institutions and welfare organizations that operate as **an extension of the government sector**.[3] Many NPOs are also formed to satisfy the cultural, religious, social, recreational, psychological, and other needs of society.

---

[1] This term was first used by the Financial Accounting Standards Board in their *Statement of Financial Accounting Concepts No. 4: Objectives of Financial Reporting by Nonbusiness Organizations* (Stamford, CN, 1980) because it covered both governmental and nonprofit organizations.

[2] The Canadian Centre for Philanthropy (*A Provincial Portrait of Canada's Charities*, Research Bulletin, Spring/Summer 1997) reported that in 1994 NPOs in Canada received 60% of their revenues from the three levels of government. Of this amount, about 93% (i.e., 56% of 60%) went to hospitals and teaching institutions (i.e., universities and colleges).

[3] The importance of the nonprofit sector as an extension of the government was confirmed by the then Canadian Federal Minister of Finance, the Hon. Paul Martin, where he stated in an address to the National Volunteer Association that the charitable sector was poised to have a growing impact on social and economic policy because it offered the greatest hope for maintaining social programs and job creation in an era of governmental financial restraint (*The Globe and Mail*, October 6, 1997). The nonprofit sector is also used by the government for other purposes. Mr. John Bryden, former MP for Hamilton-Wentworth (*Canada's Charities: A Need for Reform*, MP's Report, October 1996), suggests that many NPOs, like the Canadian Non-Smokers' Rights Association, which in 1997 received government grants of $522,568 (representing 97.3% of its total revenues) and only $23,156 in membership fees, are little more than lobby groups for the federal government. In others, like Wildlife Habitat Canada, they are used to by-pass

There is, consequently, considerable diversity amongst NPOs. They can operate as trusts (for scholarships and charities), unincorporated associations (for "voluntary associations" like nonprofit clubs and interest groups), corporations without a share capital formed under the provisions of federal and provincial legislation (for the provision of health-care, education and training, child care services, nonprofit housing, and community economic development), and in Ontario, as co-operatives without share capital (for the distribution of goods, the provision of housing, and other specialized services to their members).

They are normally classified into three groups. These are:

1. **Public institutions** consisting of airport authorities, co-operative housing corporations, hospitals, schools, colleges and universities, etc., that are formed by specific legislation. Their activities are usually monitored by the level of government by which they have been formed.

2. **Charities** that solicit tax deductible donations from the public. To be classified as a charity, an NPO must be registered with the Canada Revenue Agency and receive a registration number. To qualify for a registration number, the NPO must have been formed for the purposes of promoting social welfare, civic improvement, pleasure or recreation, or any other purpose except profit.[4] Classification as a charity is relatively easy and, once registered, charities are exempt from federal income taxes on their income and may issue tax deductible receipts for donations.

3. **Other NPOs** that are not public institutions and that do not carry out charitable work. These consist of clubs, interest groups, professional associations, etc., and only enjoy income tax exemption on their revenues.

In Canada, the distinction between public institutions and charities has not generally been recognized. However, the federal Department of Finance has now acknowledged that ignoring the distinction between them is incorrect for income tax purposes.[5]

The Differences between Governmental Entities and NPOs

The major difference between governmental bodies and NPOs is that the three levels of government have the right to pass legislation and to levy taxes on the community.[6] As a general rule, NPOs do not have that authority[7] and must rely on either the government or the public for the funds required to operate. In other respects they are quite similar and, from both an operational and philosophical point of view, it is often difficult to differentiate between them.

Their Similarities

NPOs are also grouped with the government sector because the services they provide and their economic activities are similar (see later). For example, the provision of resources

---

parliament because they raise revenues through the levying of taxes, an activity that should only be exercised by the government itself.

[4] As revised by the Canada Revenue Agency in 2003 by RC 4106(E) 1204. Certain operational criteria also apply. In order to be classified as a charity by the Income Tax Act, the organization must operate in a manner that satisfies a "disbursement quota" of spending a minimum of 80% of the amounts for which it issued income tax donation receipts on expenditures in furthering its charitable activities. Charities may also award scholarships and grant assistance to persons in need, and pay amounts of up to 50% of their income tax exempt donations to other Canadian charities.

[5] Department of Finance, *Position Paper: Measures to Simplify and Improve the Fairness of the Federal Sales Tax*, Ottawa: Government of Canada, April 1996.

[6] A by-law of a town or city council has the same effect in its jurisdiction as a provincial or federal law. Similarly, towns and cities raise their operating revenues through the levying of property taxes.

[7] In certain jurisdictions, school boards have limited taxing powers.

to an NPO for the retraining of unemployed workers is really no different from a grant to a governmentally sponsored educational institution. Similarly, they both require the inflow of public resources to operate. In many cases, the only distinguishing feature is that governmental bodies may be directly run by governmental employees or appointees, whereas NPOs usually employ their own staff and are run by elected representatives of the public.

Accounting for NBOs has, until the 1970s, been largely ignored by standard setting bodies. It is, therefore, understandable that accountants seeking guidance on accounting procedures for these organizations looked to associations like the National Committee on Governmental Accounting in the USA and similar bodies in Britain and Canada. As a result, NPOs have tended to follow the accounting procedures used by governmental bodies.

THE SCOPE OF THIS CHAPTER

The accounting requirements of the three levels of government with their various departments, ministries, agencies and divisions are a complex area of accounting. The procedures used are also often specific to the area of concern and level of government involved, and have traditionally been based on the need to control the inflows and outflows of public resources. The primary concern of this chapter is to describe and outline **in a general manner** the nature and control of NPOs and similar governmental bodies. The specific accounting requirements for the public sector and NPOs are covered in the following two chapters.

THE BASIC CHARACTERISTICS OF NBOs[8]

The Lack of a Profit Motive

The most important characteristic of NBOs is that there is a general lack of a profit motive. This is because, irrespective of whether they are governmental bodies or NPOs, their purpose is to provide services to the communities over which they have jurisdiction or in which they operate, and not to make a profit.

The **lack of a profit motive** refers to the overall objective of their activities. This does not mean that they must be run at a loss, but that their operations over a period of time should be such that they break even; any profits earned in one period should be used to offset losses in another. Furthermore, losses incurred in certain areas may be offset by profits in others. They may also carry on certain activities at a profit in order to subsidize the provision of certain services.

The size or extent of the operations of NPOs is of no consequence. All that is required is that they serve the interests of the community and are not operated with the intention of making a profit. For example, an association promoting the appreciation of art or music may be relatively inactive and only have a few members, but it is an NPO.

The Lack of Defined Ownership Interests

There are no defined ownership interests with NBOs as there are in the private sector. This is because their operations are controlled by the representatives of the members of the organization. These representatives are either elected to these positions in terms of the constitution/charter of the NPO concerned or, in the case of governmental bodies, by being appointed by a higher level of government to these positions.

As there are no defined ownership interests, the assets of these organizations are either owned by the community or held in trust for their members by the elected representatives.

---

[8] See the FASB's *Statement of Financial Accounting Concepts No. 4: Objectives of Financial Reporting by Nonbusiness Organizations*, *op cit*., where these characteristics are fully discussed.

In the event of the cessation of activities by NPOs, the assets are realized and the proceeds applied in accordance with the constitution/charter of the NPO concerned. If the constitution/charter of the NBO is silent on the matter or the NPO is a government entity, the assets revert to the state.

There Is No Expectation of a Proportionate Return on the Resources Provided

Significant resources are provided to NBOs by **resource providers** who do so without the expectation of receiving a return proportionate to the amount of resources provided. For example, publicly sponsored radio stations in Canada (e.g., CRJT in Toronto) and the sponsors of public television (e.g., PBS) in the USA do not expect to receive benefits from the sponsored bodies commensurate with the extent of their donations or contributions to the NBO.

The description "resource provider" is normally used to refer to persons, corporations, or institutions rather than taxpayers. This is because resources that are for charitable, humanitarian, religious or other nonprofit purposes are normally provided over and above the payment of taxes. As a result, those who benefit from the provision of these resources are usually different from those who actually provide the resources.

THE NATURE OF NBO GOODS AND SERVICES

NBOs provide numerous services to the society in which they operate. No matter how different these services may appear to be, they may be classified into two groups of activities. These are trading (or enterprise) activities and, for convenience, are referred to as social services. These social services are usually not saleable because they are those services that business enterprises are unable or unwilling to supply. Where they are saleable, the proceeds from their sale seldom result in sufficient inflows of resources to make the activity viable. As a result, they must receive inflows of public resources to be able to operate.

On the other hand, the trading activities of NPOs are those activities that are essentially "business like" in nature and provide services to the community on a user-charge basis (e.g., the provision of utilities, health care, gift shops and restaurants at hospitals, souvenir shops at sporting "halls of fame", and the like). The social services, on the other hand, represent all those other activities of NPOs of a social nature, like the provision of recreational, religious and welfare facilities.

The distinction is not always clear-cut or mutually exclusive. Where recreational facilities and social activities are provided, these may fall into either group depending upon the nature of the activities and the extent to which they are financed from user fees. For example, a lakeside marina may be heavily subsidized by a city as a service to its residents, or be completely self-financing and run purely for the benefit of its fee-paying members. The former may form part of the sponsoring city's "parks and recreation department", while the latter would be a completely independent NPO financed entirely from membership fees. Each case must, therefore, be closely examined to determine how the NBO should be treated for accounting purposes.

MAJOR DIFFERENCES BETWEEN NBOs AND PROFIT-ORIENTED ENTERPRISES

The Economic Activity of NBOs

The major difference between NBOs and profit-oriented enterprises of the private sector is their economic activity. In this respect, the economic activity of NBOs providing social services differs from that of "profit-oriented" organizations in that the bulk of their financial

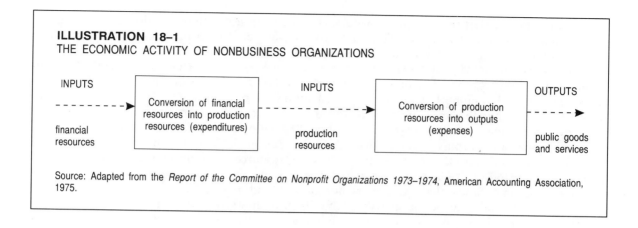

ILLUSTRATION 18-1
THE ECONOMIC ACTIVITY OF NONBUSINESS ORGANIZATIONS

INPUTS

financial resources

Conversion of financial resources into production resources (expenditures)

INPUTS

production resources

Conversion of production resources into outputs (expenses)

OUTPUTS

public goods and services

Source: Adapted from the *Report of the Committee on Nonprofit Organizations 1973–1974*, American Accounting Association, 1975.

resources is obtained from public donations, subsidies, or government grants. As these sources of revenues are not self-generated, the economic activity of these organizations may be represented by a straight line. This is reflected by Illustration 18–1 that shows that the flow of resources is a conversion process in which all inputs are converted into final goods or services.

With profit-oriented enterprises, however, the outputs of the enterprise are in the form of goods or services that are saleable and give rise to significant inflows of financial resources into the entity. They are, therefore, to a large extent self-financing, and the economic model can be regarded as a continuous activity — outflows are converted into inflows that in turn become outflows in a continuous operation.[9] Inputs can be matched against expenditures and, for this type of activity, the measurement focus is on determination of **net income, financial position, and changes in financial position**.[10]

As far as the economic activity of NBOs is concerned, the outflow-inflow relationship or loop of the economic activity does not exist because the goods or services produced are either not saleable or result in insignificant inflows of resources. And if, for some reason or other, the flow of goods is interrupted, the transformation process comes to an end. These organizations must, therefore, continually receive new inflows of resources to finance their operations. If not, they cease to operate.

The accounting significance of this is that the **measurement focus** for NBOs should be on the determination of **financial position and changes in financial position and not on net income determination**.[11]

The implication of this difference in economic activity is that applying generally accepted accounting principles developed for profit-oriented enterprises to NPOs providing social services is **not appropriate**. It also suggests that where the revenues from NBOs and NPO trading activities consist of inflows of a significant proportion of their resources from user fees, and these inflows can be matched against expenditures, their operations are comparable to those

---

[9]   The difference in economic activity between profit-oriented enterprises of the private sector and NBOs providing social services was first recognized by the American Accounting Association (*Report of the Committee on Nonprofit Organizations, 1973–74*, 1975) and by Robert N. Anthony (*Financial Accounting in Nonbusiness Organizations*, Research Report for the Financial Accounting Standards Board, 1978). However, the FASB only gave this major aspect of NBO accounting footnote recognition in *SFAC No. 4*. The CICA also recognized this in the introduction to section 4400 of the CICA *Handbook*.

[10]   American Accounting Association, *Report of the Committee on Nonprofit Organizations, 1973–74*, Supplement to *The Accounting Review*, April 1975.

[11]   *Ibid.*

of profit-oriented enterprises of the private sector, and the accounting should be based on net income determination. The application of GAAP developed for profit-oriented enterprises to NPO trading activities is, therefore, appropriate.[12]

The economic activity of NBOs also dictates, to a very large extent, their level of operations. In this respect, the plan of operations of any NBO is based on that level of expenditures that would be supported by the expected inflow of resources. The higher the inflow of resources, the higher the level of services provided. For example, if an NBO wished to operate at a level requiring expenditures of $2.8-million, it would have to ensure that the inflow of resources (plus any surplus carried forward from operations from the previous year) would not exceed $2.8-million. If, however, the inflow of resources is only expected to amount to $2.6-million, the NBO would either have to reduce its planned level of operations by $200,000 or raise additional funds through borrowings or by fund raising.

This model of the economic activity of NBOs also shows why the emphasis of accounting for these organizations has traditionally been on a cash flow basis. In the normal course of events, outflows of cash should not exceed inflows. Consequently, NBO accounting systems are essentially designed to reflect this situation and show how well the NBO has matched outflows with inflows. This also explains why accrual accounting has, in the past, only enjoyed limited support by these organizations. Today, however, a full accrual system of accounting is required.

The Use of Fund Accounting

Funds are defined in NBO accounting as **separate fiscal and accounting entities having their own set of self-balancing accounting records**. The word "fiscal" is used rather than "financial" to draw attention to the public nature of the resources and the restrictions that are placed on their use.

The use of **fund accounting** should form the basis of all governmental and NPO accounting.[13] Its purpose is to ensure that the resources provided, donated, endowed or otherwise set aside for specific purposes are used as required. This is achieved through a system of accounting where the amounts involved are accounted for in **separate funds** in accordance with the restrictions placed on their use by the donor or provider of resources, or the legal provisions governing the operation of the NBO concerned. The necessary revenue and expense accounts are opened and used as required by each fund.

Fund accounting is also sometimes **used for administrative convenience** when it is desirable to account for some or other activity separately from the other activities of the NBO. The accounting records of NBOs, therefore, normally consist of a number of separate but interrelated funds.

Depending upon the complexity of the NBO and its resources, a fund may consist of anything from as little as two ledger accounts to the completely self-balancing set of books and records. The **main fund** is the **operating fund** which accounts for all activities of the NBO that are not accounted for in its other funds. They come into existence in two ways. First, where there is a budget appropriation for a specific activity that warrants separate treatment. Second, they come into existence when resources are received that must be kept separate from the other resources of the NBO and applied for specific purposes.

---

[12] See *Governmental Accounting, Auditing and Financial Reporting*, Second Edition, Chicago: Municipal Finance Officers Association, 1980, for a full discussion of this point.

[13] As outlined in the chapter on the CICA's accounting requirements for NPOs, the CICA also allows these organizations to use the deferral method of accounting. It is a method whereby resources are deferred on receipt and withdrawn as and when required. It is based on the assumption that an NBO will use its resources in accordance with the conditions attached to them. Its critics feel that it will lead to even less disclosure in a segment of the economy that is already plagued by a lack of disclosure.

An example of the former is where the NBO appropriates or designates resources for, say, the purchase of equipment or for some specific purpose like the awarding of a scholarship. When this occurs, the appropriated funds should be withdrawn from the NBO concerned and held in a separate account until required. As far as the latter is concerned, a separate fund would be created as soon as funds are received to fund the scholarship.

For example, assume that a university received an amount of $2-million from Jones & Barrow, Chartered Accountants, to endow a chair of accounting. In this latter case, the journal entries required to create as would be:

On receipt of the cash:		
Cash	2,000,000	
The Jones & Barrow Endowment Fund		2,000,000
On investment of the scholarship funds:		
Investment — Jones & Barrow Endowment Fund	2,000,000	
Cash		2,000,000

It is important to note that a fund always consists of two basic elements: the **net assets** of the fund and the **fund balance**. In this respect, the net assets of the fund are represented by the fund balance which is the "capital or equity" of the fund; and in the above example the net assets would be the investment of $2-million represented by the fund balance of $2-million.

There is, however, no specific requirement that NBOs must use separate funds. As a result, many **smaller** NBOs account for their activities through a single fund that specifies that certain amounts are restricted for certain purposes, and those amounts that are not so restricted. In these cases, the cash or other resources provided, donated, or appropriated for specific purposes are not kept separate from each other but are combined in single banking, investment and asset accounts. The fund balance of the entity is, however, segregated for accounting and reporting purposes. Where the use of resources is restricted for certain purposes, these are referred to as **restricted funds.** The resources available for the normal operations of the entity are referred to as **unrestricted funds** and may be used by the NBO as it sees fit. Full details of the restricted and unrestricted fund balances must, of course, be provided. Such a situation is reflected by a nonprofit organization in Illustration 18–2.

With **unrestricted funds**, the only restriction on their use is that the purpose for which they are used falls within its jurisdiction and is connected with its main objective and activities. For example, a sporting association may subsidize the running of a sporting clinic but may not make a donation to a political party unless its constitution/charter specifically provides for the use of its resources for political purposes — which is, of course, highly unlikely.

Illustration 18–2 shows that the operating fund is the main fund of the Maxville Athletic Club. It also shows that an internally restricted fund-building fund, created by the club to account for the funds raised for that purpose, has been conveniently incorporated into its balance sheet. Here the fund-raising activities for the building fund are shown as part of the restricted building fund balance and that the investments apply to the building fund.

With the larger and more **complicated NBOs**, it is usually necessary to use separate funds to account for those resources that are **restricted**. Where this occurs, it is referred to as a **restricted fund accounting** system. This aspect of accounting for NPOs is examined in detail in a later chapter.

Transfers between funds are common. They occur mainly where resources are set aside for specific purposes (e.g., for scholarships by a university) or for capital projects like the purchase of equipment. Where they occur, **they require equal but opposite entries in the funds concerned.** In the case of cash transfers, money is withdrawn from the bank account of one fund and paid into the bank account of the other fund. For example, if a charity transfers $50,000 from its operating fund to its special projects fund, the transfers in journal entry form would be recorded in each fund as follows:

ILLUSTRATION 18–2
THE FINANCIAL STATEMENTS OF A SMALL UNCOMPLICATED NONPROFIT ORGANIZATION
USING RESTRICTED FUNDS

THE MAXVILLE ATHLETIC CLUB
STATEMENT OF OPERATIONS FOR THE YEAR ENDED DECEMBER 31, 20X4

		20X4	20X3
Receipts			
Membership Fees		$ 4,300	$ 3,800
Operating Grant from the City of Maxville		13,500	11,800
		17,800	15,600
Expenses			
Athletic Meetings	$10,340		8,340
Affiliation Fees — Canadian Athletic Association	900		868
Trophies and Prizes	235		195
Operating Expenses	5,108		4,900
Amortization of Equipment	1,065	17,648	980
Excess of Revenues over Expenses		$ 152	$ 317

BALANCE SHEET AT DECEMBER 31, 20X4

		20X4	20X3
Assets			
Cash on Hand		$ 1,430	$ 805
Equipment (detailed as required)		8,954	9,455
		10,384	10,260
Building Fund Investments		4,435	3,200
Total Assets		$14,819	$13,460
Represented by:			
Liabilities and Fund Balances			
Current Liabilities		$ 652	$ 680
Accumulated Funds (Unrestricted):			
Balance at January 1, 20X4	9,580		9,263
Add: Surplus for Year	152	9,732	317
Building Fund (Restricted):			
Balance at January 1, 20X4	3,200		2,942
Fund Raising Activities	1,210		236
Interest on Investments	25	4,435	22
		$14,819	$13,460

STATEMENT OF CASH FLOWS FOR YEAR ENDED DECEMBER 31, 20X4

Cash from Operations		
Excess of Revenues over Expenses		$ 152
Add: Amortization of Equipment not Expended in Cash		1,065
		1,217
Cash from Financing Operations		
Cash Received from Fund-Raising Activities and Interest	1,235	
Investment in Building Fund	(1,235)	
Purchase Equipment	(592)	(592)
Increase in Cash		625
Cash at January 1, 20X4		805
Cash at December 31, 20X4		$ 1,430

In the Operating Fund:
Interfund Transfer — Special Projects Fund   50,000
   Cash at Bank   50,000

In the Special Projects Fund:
Cash at Bank   50,000
   Interfund Transfer — Operational Fund   50,000

Trusts Administered by NBOs

From time to time, NBOs are required to administer trusts for the benefit of the persons under their jurisdiction or members or the general public. A trust is merely a contract whereby a donor transfers property to trustees for the benefit of third parties. In these cases, the NBO would act as trustee for the beneficiaries of the trust. The difference between a donation and the transfer of property to a trust is that the legal ownership of the property is vested in the trustees and not the beneficiaries. In certain cases, the failure to administer the trust in accordance with the trust deed could result in the property covered by the trust reverting to another party. Where NBOs administer trusts, they are treated as separate funds of the NBO.

THE SEPARATE FUNDS USED BY NBOs

The funds used by NBOs fall into three categories. These are the **operating or general funds**, the **proprietary, trading or enterprise funds**, and the **endowment and restricted funds**. Within this framework, many other funds can be created for specific purposes. However, NBOs should always restrict the number of funds to those that are really necessary because accountants should not increase the complexity of the administration of these entities.

The Operating Funds

All NBOs have some main activity that is accounted for in the **operating or general fund** of the organization concerned. For example, the purpose of a university is to provide higher education and to create the conditions in which research can be carried out.[14] These activities should, therefore, be accounted for in its operating or general fund. Such a fund would reflect revenues from student tuition fees, governmental operating and research grants, gifts, contributions and donations towards its operations, income from endowments and any other unrestricted revenues. Expenditures would include the salaries and allowances paid to its faculty members, administrators and support staff, academic instruction expenses, the funding of general research, administrative and operational expenses, student services, and student support expenses funded from general revenues like scholarships, teaching assistantships, and fellowships.

Depending upon the specific needs of the NBO, additional ancillary funds may be required to improve administration. Examples of these additional funds are **capital projects funds,** which account for major capital expenditures. These funds are normally closed on the completion of the project and the capital assets to which they relate are transferred to the relevant fund. And, **debt service funds** may be used to service longterm debt (i.e., the repayment of principal and interest) and to receive and disburse loan funds to the various other funds of the NBO concerned.[15]

---

[14] Unfortunately, there is a tendency amongst certain academics to consider research as the main activity of these institutions.

[15] For example, *The Globe and Mail* (March 18, 1996) reported that Nav Canada, a nonprofit organization to be operated by the major Canadian airlines, air-traffic controllers and business-jet owners, is to raise between $2.5-billion and $3-billion through a debt issue to finance the operation of the world's first privately run air-traffic systems. A debt of such magnitude would, no doubt, be serviced through a debt service fund.

The Proprietary, Trading or Enterprise Funds

The proprietary, trading or enterprise funds represent that group of funds operated by the NPO concerned with providing goods and services to itself, its membership or the general public for a fee. They are referred to by many names. For example, as **enterprise funds** if they operate like enterprises of the public sector, like cafeterias at hospitals or a lakeside marina. They are also referred to as **internal service funds** if they provide services, like general maintenance or "transport pools", to the operating fund.

These funds are operated with the intention of being entirely or predominantly self-supporting. In this respect, they provide services for which they charge an amount at least sufficient to cover their costs. They are also often run with the objective of making a profit that may be used to subsidize other activities of the NBO. For example, the profits derived from a bookstore at a sporting "Hall of Fame" that sells books, souvenirs, T-shirts and the like may be used to subsidize the general maintenance and upkeep of the "Hall of Fame".[16]

These funds are similar to enterprises of the private sector. Their economic activity is such that the sale of their goods and services give rise to inflows of resources that allow the activity to be self-financing or relatively self-financing. If their inflows of resources are sufficient to cover their costs, they can continue to operate without the need to receive additional revenues in the form of grants or public donations. The measurement of the performance of these funds should, therefore, be on net income determination along the lines applicable to business enterprises.

It is, however, fully recognized that the decision to classify the provision of certain services as enterprise or trading activities is often difficult. This is because a conflict may rise between the necessity of having to maintain control over their activities and the fact that they may not be "entirely or predominantly self-sufficient". Here, the solution is that NBOs should establish and maintain those funds that are required for **sound financial administration**.

The Endowment and Restricted Funds

These funds are used by NBOs when it is acting as a trustee or agent for other parties. This group of funds consists of endowment funds, trust funds, special assessment funds, special revenue funds and agency funds. The common feature of all these funds is that the use of the resources to which they apply are all restricted to be used for some specific purpose.

Endowment funds are those funds that administer funds received with the express condition that the principal must be retained intact and only the earnings may be spent. For example, an amount may be received from a donor to fund a scholarship or to endow a chair of, say, accounting at a university. In these cases, it is only the interest or other earnings on the principal that may be expended.

Restricted funds are those funds established to administer donations or contributions received that are required to be used for some specific purpose like the like the funding of research on some specific topic, the purchase of equipment, the dispensing of food to needy families and the like. They are referred to as **expendable funds** if they cease to exist once the amounts received have been spent. An example of an expendable trust fund is where a fund is created to control the purchase of equipment from a federal government grant.

At times, **special assessment funds** are required to account for specific levies against a segment of persons. For example, where students are charged a special fee to cover breakages of laboratory equipment that is refundable if not depleted at the end of the semester.

Finally, **agency funds** are used to account for funds raised for some specific purpose. For example, the employees of an NBO may raise money to be used for famine relief in Africa,

---

16   As with the *Basketball Hall of Fame* in Springfield, Massachusetts.

Asia or South America by having amounts deducted from their salaries. In these cases, the NPO would act as an agent for the employees by collecting the amounts donated and its payment to the relief organization concerned.

THE SEARCH FOR OBJECTIVES AND STANDARDS OF NBO ACCOUNTING

Since the early 1970s, considerable attention has been paid to establishing the objectives of accounting and generally accepted accounting principles for governmental bodies and NPOs. Even though the majority of the work on the topic was carried out in the USA, attempts to improve NBO accounting were carried out elsewhere. For example, in 1975, the Chartered Institute of Public Finance and Accountancy (CIPFA) in Britain recommended that the accounting standards of the International Accounting Standards Committee should be adopted for the trading activities of governmental organizations and their general activities where they were compatible with NBO accounting.

Significant steps in the USA were that, in 1970, the American Accounting Association appointed two research committees to consider the basic accounting objectives of these bodies. In 1974, the American Institute of Certified Public Accountants (AICPA) recognized the need to formulate financial reporting objectives and issue statements and audit guides to their members. In 1979, the Financial Accounting Standards Board (FASB) also became concerned with the issue. Shortly thereafter, in 1984, the Governmental Accounting Standards Board (GASB) was formed under the sponsorship of the Financial Accounting Foundation as the body that would henceforth be responsible for setting accounting standards for governmental bodies in the USA.

A major development occurred in 1980 when the FASB issued *Statement of Financial Accounting Concepts No 4: Objectives of Financial Reporting by Nonbusiness Organizations* as part of its "conceptual framework of accounting". In this *SFAC*, the FASB stated that it had concluded that it was not necessary to develop an independent conceptual framework for any particular category of entities. It had, therefore, formulated objectives of financial reporting for NBOs based on its objectives of financial reporting for business enterprises[17] to meet the informational needs of the external users of their financial statements. In particular, it stated that these objectives had been designed to allow those who provide resources to determine whether the NBOs would be able to continue to provide the services for which they were formed. To fully satisfy these requirements, it also amended *SFAC No. 2* and *SFAC No. 3* (as reissued as *SFAC No. 6*) to cover both NBOs and business enterprises.

The approach adopted by the FASB was based on its belief that the emphasis of the financial reporting by NPOs should be on the balance sheet rather than the operating statement (i.e., the equivalent of the income statement). This approach is referred to as the "net assets" approach and represented a **major change in accepted reporting philosophy** for NBOs in the USA. Until this time, the reporting philosophy was based on the principle of accountability. In this regard, those persons entrusted with the use of public resources were required to report on the faithful discharge of their duties.

Accountability or stewardship accounting had been under attack in the USA for many years for failing to provide the type of information required for the efficient operation of security markets. This led to the adoption of the decision usefulness approach to financial

---

[17] The FASB restated the objectives contained in *SFAC No. 1: Objectives of Financial Reporting by Business Enterprises* in *SFAC No. 4* (1980) by replacing the terms "present and potential investors and creditors" with "resource providers," and "making rational investment, credit and similar decisions" with "making decisions about the allocation of resources". In doing so, it effectively adapted the objectives of financial reporting by business enterprises to NBOs. Similarly, changes to their *SFAC No. 2* (and its re-issue as *SFAC No. 6*) also narrowed the perceived differences of accounting for NBOs and business enterprises.

reporting in the early 1960s by the AICPA and later by the FASB which, for no apparent reason, had decided to develop accounting principles for NPOs. Having "staked out its turf", a decision usefulness reporting philosophy was applied by the FASB to nonbusiness entities. Even the research study carried out by Robert N. Anthony for the FASB in 1978[18] was, as the researcher stated, based on the premise that the financial accounting principles developed for profit-oriented enterprises of the private sector "... should apply to financial reporting in nonbusiness organizations unless the circumstances or the information needs in nonbusiness organizations require a different treatment of the transaction in question."

This approach by the FASB led to the viewpoint that there is little or no reporting differences between NBOs and business enterprises. Therefore, generally accepted accounting principles developed for profit-oriented enterprises should apply equally to NBOs.

As a first step in this direction, the FASB issued its highly contentious *SFAS No. 93: Recognition of Depreciation by Not-for-Profit Organizations* (1988) that required all NPOs in the USA other than those that are governmentally sponsored, to amortize their capital assets (other than works of art or historic treasures) in the same manner as business enterprises. This requirement was based on the grounds that this was necessary to determine the cost at which NPOs provide their services and whether the NPOs concerned had maintained their capital.

Reaction to this requirement was negative. Many private colleges and universities in the USA stated that they would rather accept a qualified audit report than comply with *SFAS 93*. It also led to a jurisdictional dispute between the GASB and the FASB that was only resolved in 1990 when it was agreed that accounting standards of the FASB would only apply where a GASB pronouncement on the same topic had not been issued. The GASB reaffirmed that accountability was the primary objective of NBO reporting and to ensure that the amortization of capital assets need not apply to governmentally sponsored colleges and universities, the GASB issued its *Statement of Government Accounting Standards No 15: Governmental College and University Accounting and Reporting Models* (1991) to take precedence over *SFAS No. 93*. Since that time, the FASB has issued *SFAS No. 116* and a number of pronouncements dealing with various aspects of NBO accounting that have been considerably less contentious.

In 1999, however, the GASB issued *GAS No. 35: Basic Financial Statements — and Management's Discussion and Analysis — for Public Colleges and Universities* to extend its reporting requirements for state and local governments[19] to government-sponsored colleges and universities. This was a major change in approach because it required government-sponsored colleges and universities to **report on a dual basis** (i.e., on an organization-wide basis as well as a fund basis) **and to amortize their capital assets over their expected useful lives**. These reporting requirements were to be phased in over a three-year period for reporting periods commencing after June 15, 2001.

The stated reason for the change in the GASB's reporting philosophy was that the dual reporting model would preserve the nature of fund accounting while organization-wide reports would give aggregated information about the organization as a whole. The decision to amortize capital assets was based on the stated need to provide objective, consistent, and comparable information about operating costs and resource flows.

The CICA had also become involved with the topic and, in 1980, it issued a research report, *Financial Reporting by Non-Profit Organizations*, that reached conclusions relatively similar to those of the FASB. Since that time, it has been engaged in ongoing research on the topic of governmental accounting through its Public Sector Accounting Board (PSAB).

---

[18] *Research Report: Financial Reporting in Nonbusiness Organizations*, Financial Accounting Standards Board, 1978, p. 22. Reasons given were that (1) it was not necessary to "reinvent the wheel" because if the FASB had developed an accounting treatment to apply to one set of circumstances, it should be applied in other similar circumstances, and (2) there should only be one coherent and internally consistent body of generally accepted accounting principles.

[19] In terms of *GAS No. 34: Basic Financial Statements — and Management's Discussion and Analysis — for State and Local Governments*. Government Accounting Standards Board, Norwalk, CT, 1999.

More recently, the AcSB of the CICA has followed the lead of the FASB by amending section 1000 of the CICA *Handbook* to include NPOs. This was followed in 1989 by the issue of section 4230 of the CICA *Handbook* covering specific items like the need for adequate disclosure of their activities, the use of accrual accounting, and the accounting for donations by NPOs. The section was subsequently withdrawn. Up until this time, the CICA *Handbook* had not applied to NPOs. The CICA's PSAB has also issued a number of *Public Sector Accounting Statements* dealing with various aspects of governmental accounting.

The CICA followed the lead of the FASB by adopting a "net assets" approach towards financial reporting and moved towards applying GAAP developed for business enterprises to NPOs. Proposals similar to those of the FASB relating to the amortization of capital assets and other proposals relating to financial reporting, the recognition of contributions, etc., were made by the CICA's *Exposure Draft: Non-Profit Organizations* issued in January 1992. They were approved in December 1995. In proposing these accounting requirements, the CICA, like the FASB, stated that these requirements were designed to cater for the informational needs of externals users of NPO financial statements and, in particular, **to allow users to determine the cost at which NPO services were provided**.

As in the USA, the CICA's accounting requirements for NPOs were **not accepted** by certain governmental ministries/departments/entities. For example, **they were rejected** by the Ontario Ministry of Municipal Affairs and Housing and the Canada Mortgage and Housing Corporation because they did not meet their information needs or comply with their own legally prescribed accounting principles for capital assets and loan financing. To obviate the need for auditors to issue qualified audit reports, the Institute of Chartered Accountants of Ontario ruled[20] that auditors of noncomplying entities may certify the financial statements of the affected entities with the statement that the financial statements were prepared in accordance with regulatory legislation.[21]

The CICA's accounting requirements for NPOs are examined separately in a later chapter.

To many accountants and accounting academics, the application of GAAP developed for profit-oriented enterprises of the private sector to NBOs is a matter of great concern.[22] The most important concern is that **the economic activity of NBOs providing social services is unique to NPOs and governmental entities**, and that different accounting and reporting criteria should apply to them. The FASB and the CICA have, however, not been receptive to change.

Whether the American and Canadian accounting requirements for NPOs will satisfy their reporting requirements and those of the users of their financial statements remains to be seen. Reaction to them to date has generally not been positive.[23]

---

[20] *Memorandum* from Technical Services of the Institute of Chartered Accountants of Ontario to "All Practising Units" dated April 1998.

[21] In terms of sections 5100 or 5701 of the CICA *Handbook*.

[22] See, for example, R.K. Mautz, "Monuments, Mistakes and Opportunities", *Editorial Comment* in *Accounting Horizons*, June 1988, pp. 123–28 and "Not-for-Profit Reporting", *Journal of Accountancy*, August 1989, pp. 60–66; John Macintosh, "Finding the Right Fit: A Call to Recognize the Special Nature of Not-for-Profit Organizations", *CA Magazine*, March 1995, pp. 34–38. Robert N. Anthony, "The Nonprofit Accounting Mess", *Accounting Horizons*, June 1995, pp. 44–53, and the reply by Robert H. Northcutt, Chairman of the FASB's Task Force on Accounting Issues for Not-for-Profit Organizations, "Observations on Professor Anthony's Commentary", in the same issue of *Accounting Horizons*, pp. 54–55, and the reply by Anthony, "Reply: Nonprofit Accounting Standards", *Accounting Horizons*, September 1995, pp. 100–103.

[23] Mr. Robert H. Northcutt stated in his rebuttal of Anthony's criticisms of the FASB's standards (see previous footnote) that "... early reaction to financial statements prepared in accordance with the FASB's new standards, particularly from members of the boards of not-for-profit organizations, has been extremely favorable" (*op cit*.). Anthony ("Reply: Nonprofit Accounting Standards", *op cit*.), however, on examining the list of eleven "favorable responses" to the FASB's standards supplied by Mr. Northcutt, found that not one came from a not-for-profit board member, one was by a FASB board member, and another stated that her views on the standards were "neutral".

ACCOUNTABILITY BY NBOs

Accountability refers to the responsibility of persons who have control over the resources of others to report on the use of those resources to the providers of those resources. Traditionally, this merely covered the responsibility to report on the custodianship over resources. Today, accountability has a wider meaning and covers the achievement of the goals set by the organization as well as reporting on the efficiency and effectiveness of operations.

As NBO activities usually involve the use of public funds, they should be subject to strict legal and other controls. Public officials and elected representatives are also expected to carry out their duties **in the utmost good faith** and to give an account of their actions when called upon to do so. In this sense, they must **not only act in a manner that is above reproach, but they must also be seen as acting in such a manner**.[24] The accounting system should, therefore, provide the information necessary to allow those in control of these organizations to demonstrate that they have complied with the necessary legal requirements and the faithful discharge of their duties.[25]

Unfortunately, evidence suggests that many NPOs in Canada are not fully accountable for their actions. Other than where the activities of NPOs are controlled by specific legislation, there is **no effective monitoring of their activities** in Canada because control over these organizations is merely based on monitoring their compliance with income tax legislation covering their tax status. As there are no revenue consequences, the Canada Revenue Agency (CRA) attaches a low priority to this area. Consequently, few NPOs comply with these requirements.[26] The problem is so bad that Mr. John Bryden, Member of Parliament for Hamilton-Wentworth, concluded in 1996[27] that the lack of suitable disclosure of information to the public through the disclosures required by the Canada Revenue Agency was so widespread that **the noncompliance appeared to be deliberate**.

This situation is largely due to the lack of effective control over these organizations. Unlike the position in England and Wales where there is, for example, a *Charity Commissioner*, appointed by the State to "preserve the integrity of charity" by monitoring the activities of charities and their compliance with their *Charities Act*, 1993[28], there is no such person in Canada.

As far as the accounting requirements are concerned, much of this problem arises from **the assumption that more and better disclosure would provide sufficient transparency of NBO activities**. This was expected to resolve any problems arising from the actions of the directors or trustees of the NBOs concerned. In the absence of any effective control over these organizations, one would have presumed that the CICA would have required disclosure of the extent

---

[24] Unfortunately, this aspect of public office is apparently little understood in Canada and public officials at all levels seem to disregard this responsibility. For example, *The Hamilton Spectator* of August 6, 1991, reported that certain Members of the "Citizens' Forum on Canada's Future" (formed on November 1, 1990 by the federal government under the Chairmanship of Mr. Keith Spicer) refused to make their expense claims public until the completion of the Forum's work when requested to do so in April 1991 by a Parliamentary Sub-Committee. The Commission delivered its report in June 1991 but by August 6, 1991, only one of the twelve Commissioners, namely, Mr. Robert Normand, had complied with this request. No further disclosures were requested or made. Similar examples of this attitude by public officials are commonplace.

[25] In February 2004, in presenting her Report to Parliament, the Auditor General, Ms. Sheila Fraser, reported that $100-million spent as part of the federal government's sponsorship program to increase its visibility in the Province of Quebec went to advertising agencies, many of which had strong ties to the ruling Liberal Party. In presenting her Report, the Auditor General stated that she could find little evidence to show how the money had been spent properly by the federal Public Works Department. These revelations, now referred to as **the sponsorship scandal**, led to a political crisis and the appointment of both a Parliamentary Commission of Inquiry and a Judicial Inquiry to investigate the issue. None of these commissions has, as yet, completed its work.

[26] Basically, the requirements for charities are that they must use at least 80% of their revenues for promoting their objectives and that they must disclose the salaries paid to their top five executives.

[27] *Canada's Charities: A Need for Reform*, MP's Report, October 1996.

[28] *Charities and the Charities Commission*, London: The Charity Commissioners of England and Wales, June 1996.

to which they complied with the specific reporting requirements of the Canada Revenue Agency (see Chapter Twenty). **This is not the case**. Even where control is exercised by the CRA through its audit procedure, the findings are not disclosed, and the general public, that has a right to be informed of transgressions by NPOs, is left with little idea of what has occurred.

The public is becoming more and more concerned with the actions of those who control charities, and change is necessary. This disillusionment is rampant. In a poll conducted by the Angus Reid Group Inc.,[29] it was found that 46% of all respondents agreed with the statement that many charities and nonprofit organizations were run by disorganized amateurs. The same percentage also agreed with the statement that they had heard so many stories of corruption among charitable organizations that they were reluctant to donate to any such organization.

To counter the negative way in which the nonprofit sector was viewed in Canada, a study group under the Chairmanship of Dr. Ed Broadbent was set up by the Volunteer Sector Roundtable,[30] to re-examine accountability by the Canadian volunteer sector[31] (i.e., charitable and advocacy or lobby groups) and see how it could be improved. In February 1999, the study group presented its report[32] in which it recommended the creation of a Voluntary Sector Commission by the federal government along the lines of the Charities Commission in England and Wales which was created to monitor the activities of charities in that country.[33] The study group also recommended the development of a *Good Practice Guide* covering fiscal control and the improvement of the governance of these organizations through the training and selection of members of their boards of directors.[34] To date, no action on these matters has been reported.

MANAGEMENT CONTROL IN NBOs

Management control in NBOs covers the efficient management of resources and the use of modern management techniques. It requires a system of control designed to produce a formal plan of operations, accurate and timely operating results, a continuous review of operations and financial position. This control is closely connected with accountability because overall control must be exercised through a system whereby each official is responsible for his or her actions to others. **To be effective**, there must be a proper evaluation of programs, the choice of alternative courses of action, longterm planning, the increase in productivity, and a system of control in which the ultimate objective is efficiency and effectiveness of operations and the elimination of waste.

---

[29] *The Globe and Mail,* October 17, 1997.

[30] Consisting of Canadian Centre for Philanthropy, Canadian Conference of the Arts, Canadian Council for International Co-operation, Canadian Council on Social Development, Canadian Environmental Network, Canadian Parks/Recreation Association, Community Foundation of Canada, Representative for the Faith Communities, National Voluntary Health Agencies, National Voluntary Organizations, United Way of Canada-Centraide Canada, and Volunteer Canada.

[31] The stated reason for the use of the term "voluntary sector" rather than "nonprofit" or "charitable" is that these organizations all rely on the work of volunteers as directors.

[32] Panel on Accountability and Governance in the Voluntary Sector, *Building on Strength: Improving Governance and Accountability in Canada's Voluntary Sector*, Ottawa, February 1999.

[33] *Charity Accounts: The New Framework*, London: Charities Commissioners in England and Wales, 1995.

[34] It also suggested, following the classification of the Charities Commission in England and Wales, that NPOs should be split into two groups: those with annual operating budgets of $200,000 and those with operating budgets of more than $200,000. The reporting requirements of the "smaller NPOs" would be less stringent than those for the "larger NPOs" and essentially allow them to present unaudited financial statements with less disclosures relating to their governance practices. In presenting these recommendations, it acknowledged that much of the information it suggested was already required by the Canada Revenue Agency's Form T3010; but, as this Form was considered "user unfriendly", it should be reviewed with the objective of making the reporting more relevant and easier to complete.

Unfortunately, **management control is difficult to achieve in NBOs because the competitive profit regulator of the marketplace is absent**. In government, the size of the budget allocation and the number of employees is often used as a measure of importance and/or the success of the operation. Furthermore, decision making, particularly in government bodies, is often based on **short-term considerations** and is frequently based on **the line of least resistance**. Evidence of mismanagement, waste and overspending in government are commonplace and, no doubt, this also applies to many NPOs. Management control in these bodies is, therefore, often little more of an academic concept than an established practice.

FINANCIAL REPORTING OBJECTIVES

In 1980 the FASB issued *SFAC No. 4* in which it listed seven objectives of financial reporting by NBOs. It stated that these objectives stemmed from the common interests of those who provide resources to these organizations to determine whether or not they would be able to continue to provide the services for which they were formed. As a result, the first three objectives stated that financial reporting by these organizations should help **present and future resource providers** in making resource allocation decisions and in assessing the services provided and the ability of the NBO to continue to provide those services, and to provide the information required to assess how management had discharged its stewardship responsibilities. The balance of the objectives covered the provision of information about the economic resources, performance, and cash flows of the NBO as well as the explanations and interpretation of the information provided.

As outlined earlier, the CICA did not formulate separate accounting concepts or financial reporting objectives for NPOs. What it did was expand section 1000 of the CICA *Handbook* to include NPOs. As before, the CICA's PSAB would continue issuing accounting and auditing statements and standards for the public sector.

Section 1000 was expanded by incorporating those areas where the nature of NPOs and profit-oriented enterprises differed substantially from one another: for example, the use of a statement of revenues and expenses or an operating statement instead of an income statement, drawing attention to the fact that the focus of the financial statements of NPOs was on the needs of members and contributors of resources and not investors and loan creditors, and by stressing the added importance of being able to assess management's stewardship. The objective of financial statements, however, remained unchanged. Therefore, the objectives of the financial statements of NPOs in Canada, like those of profit-oriented enterprises, are to **communicate** information useful to users in making **resource allocation decisions** and **assessing management's stewardship**.

THE CONTROL OVER NBO ACTIVITIES

The Use of the Budget as a Means of Control

The principal control measure of NBOs is what is referred to as the budgetary procedure. The function of the budget is to regulate or control the operations of the NBO by determining in advance the level of financial activity and, through the careful monitoring of expenditures, to ensure that these levels are not exceeded without prior approval. In cases where additional expenditures have been underestimated or where expenditures are to be incurred because of unforeseen circumstances, prior authorization of the expected increases in spending must be authorized by the NBO concerned.

Ideally, t**he budget procedure should consist of four stages**: preparation, authorization, execution and review. First, the budget should be **prepared** by detailing the expected expenditures and revenues so that it reflects a realistic projection of the financial activities for the period concerned. The second stage is the **authorization** stage where the budget is approved by the NBO concerned. Approval is normally by the board of directors who may, if they feel so inclined, present the plan of operations to the membership at its annual general meeting. Third, the expenditures and revenues must be closely monitored during the **execution** stage to ensure that expenditures are in accordance with the amounts authorized and that the expected revenues have been collected. Finally, the budget should be **reviewed** to determined the reasons for the differences between actual and expected levels of revenues and expenditures. Such reviews establish the reasons for the failure to meet expected levels of activity or expenditures and how the budgetary procedure could be improved to rectify the position in future years.

The budgetary system can lead to excessive expenditures unless it is properly controlled. This is because **budgets are normally prepared on an incremental basis.** For example, if the rate of inflation were eight percent during the year, the amounts budgeted are increased by eight percent across the board irrespective of whether that amount would actually be required. And, because budgeted amounts that are unused at the financial year-end may normally not be carried forward to the next year, departmental heads make sure that nothing remains unspent at the year-end. There is, consequently, usually a flurry of activity in the weeks preceding the year-end as all unused budgeted amounts are spent.

Budgets are also often prepared in a manner that builds into the expenditures, a reserve to cover additional unexpected items that may arise. This is known as **budget slack** and is usually evidenced by a consistent surplus from operations that is referred to as "coming in below budget". The only real way this practice can be controlled is to ensure that amounts requested are realistic estimates of required expenditures and to carefully monitor the amounts spent as they occur. From time to time, it is also useful to use **zero-based budgeting** that starts with a zero base and requires that all expenditures must be justified in their entirety. The problem is that it is very time consuming and, as employees soon develop ways of justifying expenditures, its effectiveness is only short-lived. However, it is always a worthwhile exercise.[35]

Some NBOs have also used program budgeting that ties all expenditures and revenues to individual programs rather than departments or activities. However, this form of budgeting does not enjoy much support because it complicates the accounting system.

The **budget appropriations are normally incorporated into the accounting records.** There are a number of ways in which this may be carried out. A frequently used method is to record the budget in reverse form. For example, if an NBO having a December 31 year end had budgeted an amount of $4,000 for building maintenance for 20X5, the budgeted amount of $4,000 would be recorded in the records of the NBO by crediting the building maintenance expense account with $4,000 and by debiting a "budget controlling account" with $4,000. If, building maintenance expenses of $2,000 were paid out on the last day of March, $600 in June 10, and $1,250 was incurred in November, the building maintenance expense account at December 31 would appear as follows:

Building Maintenance Expense Account

20X5				
Jan. 1	Budgeted Amount		4,000	4,000 Cr
Mar. 31	Materials and Labour Expense	2,000		2,000 Cr
June 10	Paint Expense	600		1,400 Cr
Nov. 30	Sundry Materials Expense	1,250		150 Cr
Dec. 31	Reversal of Budgeted Amount	4,000		3,850 Dr

What this shows is that at January 1, 20X5, an amount of $4,000 was budgeted for building maintenance expense. As the actual building maintenance expenses are incurred, they reduce the amount available to be spent on this item until such time as the entire amount of

---

[35] For an actual example of how zero-based budgeting was used at McMaster University in Hamilton, Ontario, see John A. McFarlane, "There's Nothing to It; Zero Base Budgeting in Action", *CA Magazine*, December 1976, pp. 28–32.

$4,000 has been spent. In this particular example, the building maintenance expenses amounted to $3,850 were being debited against the budgeted amount, showing only $150 was still available at the end of November. At December 31, when the budget amounts are reversed to restore the ledger to a record of receipts and expenses and assets and liabilities, it shows an amount of $3,850 as having been spent on building maintenance during the year. The advantage of this procedure is that it provides a continuous record of the status of the amounts budgeted for expenditures. It also shows whether revenues are being received or collected as planned.

An example of how the budget may be incorporated into an integrated NBO accounting system is provided as part of Illustration 18–3. In that case, an amount of $2,500 for office stationery expenses has been budgeted for the year as part of the total budget expenses of $459,765.

ILLUSTRATION 18–3
EXAMPLE OF A LEDGER ACCOUNT USING AN INTEGRATED BUDGET AND ENCUMBRANCE SYSTEM

A typical Office Stationery ledger account would appear as follows:

Operating Fund							Account # 126
Office Stationery Expense							
		Encumbrances			Expenditures		
Date	Details	Dr.	Cr.	Balance	Dr.	Cr.	Balance
20X3							
Jan. 1	Budget					2,500.00	2,500.00
Feb. 24	Purch. Order #311	300.00		300.00			2,200.00
Mar. 10	Adjust. P/O #311		300.00	Nil	300.00		2,200.00
May 23	Purch. Order #654	400.00		400.00			1,800.00
June 6	Reversal P/O #654		400.00	Nil			2,200.00
	Paper P/O #654				415.00		1,785.00

The Encumbrance Reserve and Accounts Payable ledger accounts recording the above information would be as reflected hereunder:

Operating Fund				Account # 47
Encumbrance Reserve				
20X3				
Feb. 24	Purchase Order #311		300.00	300.00
Mar. 10	Transfer P/O #311 to Payables	300.00		Nil
May 23	Purchase Order #654		400.00	400.00
June 6	Reversal P/O #654	400.00		Nil

Operating Fund				Account # 49
Accounts Payable				
20X3				
Mar. 10	P/O #311 — Ajax Stationery		300.00	300.00
30	Cash	300.00		Nil
June 6	P/O #654 — GTD Printers		415.00	415.00
28	Cash	415.00		Nil

ILLUSTRATION 18–3 (Continued)

The journal entries recording the office stationary expenses in 20X3 in the three ledger accounts given above were as follows:

Recording the Budget in Reverse Form:

Jan. 1	Budget Account (say)	459,765.00	
	Office Stationery		2,500.00
	Sundry Other Expense Accounts		457,265.00

Placing of Purchase Order # 311:

Feb. 24	Office Stationery Encumbrance	300.00	
	Encumbrance Reserve		300.00
	Placing of order for stationery with Ajax Suppliers per Purchase Order #311		

Receipt of Stationery per Purchase Order #311

Mar. 10	Office Stationery Expense	300.00	
	Office Stationery Encumbrance		300.00
	Transfer from encumbrance to expense		
	Encumbrance Reserve	300.00	
	Accounts Payable		300.00
	Transfer of encumbrance for Purchase Order #311 for Ajax Stationery to Accounts Payable		
May 30	Accounts Payable	300.00	
	Cash		300.00
	Settlement of amount owing to Ajax Stationery		

Placing of Purchase Order # 654:

May 23	Office Stationery Encumbrance	400.00	
	Encumbrance Reserve		400.00
	Placing of order for stationery with GTD Printers per Purchase Order #654		

Receipt of Stationery per Purchase Order #654:

June 6	Encumbrance Reserve	400.00	
	Office Stationery Encumbrance		400.00
	Reversal entry of May 23 — incorrect cost of stationery from GTD Printers		
	Office Stationery Expense	415.00	
	Accounts Payable		415.00
	Recording of amount owing to GTD Printers		
June 28	Accounts Payable	415.00	
	Cash		415.00
	Settlement of amount owing to GTD Printers		

Control over Capital Expenditures

To control capital expenditures, most NBOs use a **tender system**. This means that once the NBO has decided to spend money on capital projects, it calls upon suppliers of capital goods, contracting companies and consultants to "tender" for the contract to carry out this expenditure. In this respect, a tender is an offer by a supplier or contractor to supply goods and services at a certain price and quality by a certain date. The tender system is used to ensure that contracts over a certain amount are not awarded to friends or associates and that the NBO receives value for its money by having a competitive bidding system. Unfortunately, like accountability, this aspect of NBO control is often disregarded. This is a matter of great concern.[36,37]

Tenders are called for by advertising in newspapers or trade journals. Full details of the goods or services to be supplied are given and contractors have to submit sealed tender documents to the NBO by a certain date. On that date, the tenders are opened in the presence of a senior official and the NBO decides on which tender to accept. They are under no obligation to accept the lowest tender and the decision to accept a tender often includes consideration of other factors like reliability and quality of workmanship.

It should also be noted that the budgetary procedure applies equally to capital expenditures. In this respect, the estimated capital expenditures for the year must be approved in advance in the form of the **capital budget** together with the manner in which they are to be financed. These should be carefully monitored and be subjected to the review procedure.

The Use of Encumbrance Accounting

As part of the system to ensure that the amounts budgeted for goods or services are not overspent, NBOs use a system of encumbrance accounting. Amounts to be spent are **encumbered** or set aside to meet expected obligations in an **encumbrance reserve** and against **the expense account** as soon as a purchase order for goods or services is made out to ensure that the budgeted amounts are not overspent. On receipt of the goods or services, the entry recording the encumbrance is reversed by debiting the encumbrance reserve and crediting accounts payable and the invoice is processed in the normal manner. Encumbrance accounting only applies to transactions carried out on credit.

At year-end, the outstanding purchase orders are **not cancelled** because they are legal commitments and treated as expenditures for goods that have not as yet been received. In order not to understate the liabilities at the year-end, the encumbrance reserve account is left intact and reflected together with accounts payable on the balance sheet. As the encumbrances do not represent actual expenditures for the year in which they were recorded, they are removed from the expense accounts to which they have been charged by crediting the expense accounts accordingly and debiting an **Adjustment for Outstanding Encumbrances** account that is **deducted from the unrestricted fund balance** on the balance sheet at the year end. At the beginning of the following year, the purchase orders are reversed by debiting the expense accounts with these amounts and crediting the Adjustment for Outstanding Encumbrances accordingly. This procedure is called **allowing the outstanding encumbrances to lapse**.

An encumbrance system should always be used and an example of the operation of such a system is provided by Illustration 18–3. In this case, the ledger account provides columns for both encumbrances and actual expenditures that show that the NBO has budgeted $2,500 for office stationery for the year ended December 31, 20X3. On placing an order for duplicating paper of $300 on February 24, the purchase order was treated as an encumbrance of $300 by debiting the encumbrances columns in the office stationery expense account with this amount and crediting the encumbrances reserve account accordingly. On receipt of the stationery and the invoice for $300, the encumbrance was reversed and entered as a credit purchase on that date. A second order for paper was placed on May 23 but, in this case, the invoiced amount

---

[36] For example, *The Globe and Mail* of May 3, 2000, reported that the Auditor-General at that time, Mr. Denis Desautels, in examining a sample of 50 sole-sourced (i.e., contracts placed with a single supplier without calling for tenders) contracts of the federal Department of Public Works in November 1999, stated that the awarding of these contracts did "not pass the test of public scrutiny". The problem is ongoing because *The Globe and Mail* of December 4, 2000, reported that an audit of Natural Resources Canada had revealed that $90-million worth of contracts had been awarded without bothering to get competitive bids.

[37] The problem of by-passing the tender process is ongoing. For example, the *The Globe and Mail* of April 12, 2002, reported that the Prime Minister rushed through a decision to spend $101-million on two new Challenger executive jets despite objections from senior officials in three departments (justice, defence, and public works) that the government was not following proper procedures by not putting the purchase of the jets out to public tender.

differed from the encumbered amount by $15. The encumbered amount of $400 was, therefore, reversed and the correct amount of $415 owing was entered as a purchase on credit. The ledger account in this illustration also shows that on June 30, after recording of the relevant entries relating the purchase of paper, an amount of $1,785.00 was still available for the purchase of office stationery.

The Use of Accrual Accounting

Originally, all governmental bodies and NPOs used a system of cash accounting to monitor their inflows and outflows of resources. This changed some twenty odd years ago when it was recognized that for the proper reporting of the results of operations, it was necessary to accrue all outstanding revenues and expenses. Today, a full accrual method of accounting is recommended for use by NPOs. Regrettably, many NPOs still use a cash-based accounting system.

Control over Borrowings

NBOs have, in the past, tended to finance a substantial portion of their capital expenditures from longterm loans. The rationale behind this was because their operations are ongoing and moneys are borrowed on a basis, and over a period of time, that spread the burden of carrying the debt over those who were to benefit from the facilities. Today, however, governments are increasingly moving activities previously handled by them to the nonbusiness sector (e.g., the Toronto Airport Authority). As a result, borrowings to finance their activities are similar to those in the business sector, which have repayment periods that are considerably shorter than the period over which the benefits are expected to continue.

The raising of loans must, however, be subject to control to ensure that the NPOs do not overextend themselves through excess borrowings. Strict control over their borrowings is, therefore, usually imposed by the level of government having overall control over their activities.

Accounting for the Capital Assets of NBOs

The accounting for capital assets and, particularly, the issue of whether these assets should be amortized is a controversial area in NBO accounting. Two schools of thought exist. The one adopted by the CICA and FASB is that to determine the costs of providing goods and services, a full accrual basis of accounting and the amortization of capital assets is required. Arguments in support of this viewpoint are that the amortization of capital assets on a cost allocation basis provides some measure of the amount by which the service potential of the asset has decreased. Furthermore, from a capital maintenance point of view, an organization is seen as having **failed** to maintain its financial capital unless it recovers all of its expenditures (including amortization of capital assets) from revenues.

The alternative and traditional viewpoint is that amortization is an expense required for net income determination purposes but is not necessarily an item that is required to determine whether or not the services of NBOs are being provided at a reasonable cost. Arguments supporting this position are that all cost allocations are arbitrary in nature and it is difficult to estimate the useful lives of capital assets within any real degree of accuracy. For example, the rate of amortization on buildings used for educational purposes is difficult to determine because certain buildings that are still in daily use at Cambridge University in England are at least 600 years old.

The issue is now largely only of academic interest. This is because the accounting requirements of the CICA, the FASB, and those of the GASB for state- and government-sponsored colleges and universities all require that the capital assets of NBOs, other than historical treasures and works of art (and in the case of the GASB, assets forming part of the infrastructure of the USA), must be amortized on a rational and systematic basis over their expected useful lives. However, certain NBOs in Canada have not accepted the CICA accounting requirement of amortizing capital assets and certain NPOs (e.g., universities) write off assets financed from current revenues as an expense. The three methods of accounting for the capital assets of NBOs are given below:

The Immediate or Later Expensing of Assets With this method, NBOs expense their assets either as soon as they are acquired or some time thereafter. In these cases, the assets are expensed through the statement of operations or by being debited against the fund balances. To be able to do so, the assets must be of relatively little value, or the NBO should be operating at a surplus.

Defer and Depreciate The costs of the NBO assets are deferred and amortized over their expected useful lives as a cost of providing services, as with profit-oriented enterprises of the private sector. Notwithstanding the fact that it is now required, this method does not enjoy widespread acceptance by NBOs because it is felt that, other than with enterprise or trading activities, the amortization of capital assets plays little part in the accounting for the activities of NBOs providing social services.

The Linking of Asset Lives with Their Sources of Finance The linking of the lives of assets to amortization period or repayment period of the loans from which the assets were financed is still widely used by housing corporations (e.g., the Canada Housing and Mortgage Corporation), local government units, and those NBOs established by this level of government. With this method, fixed assets are initially carried at cost and the amortization of the loan (i.e., the interest and capital repayment) is charged against revenues instead of the amortization charge.

This method is based on the philosophy that underlies most governmental capital expenditures: if the financing of the assets is spread over the useful lives of the asset concerned, the linking of asset lives to the repayment period **spreads the burden of financing the asset over the period and among the persons benefiting from the expenditures**. And, over the period of the loan, the amortization of the loan against revenues achieves the same result as amortizing the asset.

FINANCIAL REPORTING BY NBOs

The financial reports of NBOs should be documents prepared **primarily for accountability purposes**. This is particularly important in the case of NPOs because, as outlined earlier, they are generally considered to be an extension of the government sector. To achieve this objective, they should be drawn up in such a way that they show that the resources provided have been used as required and that the NBO has complied with any legislative requirements governing its activities. The reporting is, therefore, directed mainly at the elected representatives, the controlling bodies (e.g., the provincial government in the case of health care facilities), other resource providers, and their members. Additional information may also be provided to satisfy the specific needs of the government, its statistical and economic agencies, employees and the general public.

Today, following the **change in reporting emphasis by the FASB and the CICA**, the stated objective of these financial reports is to reflect **the costs at which the NBO has provided its services**. The accounting requirements have been developed to standardize financial reports so that the activities and operations of similar NBOs are comparable with one another. To meet the decision usefulness objective of financial reports, they are now supposed to be directed at resource providers and creditors for economic decision making purposes.

The financial reports of NBOs are prepared as general purpose statements covering the entity as a whole. However, as they are often used by management for internal purposes, they may include additional detailed schedules of such items as their capital expenditures, loan indebtedness and details of various funds. The form in which NBOs report is detailed in the next two chapters.

THE TERMINOLOGY OF NBO ACCOUNTING

Over the years, governmental and NPO accounting have developed a different terminology to describe their activities. Even though active steps have been taken to reduce the use of specific terminology by these organizations, certain activities and aspects of the accounting system are so different from profit-oriented accounting that a distinct terminology is used. In others, the same terminology is used as in profit-oriented organizations.

This situation is not problematical because the terminology used by NBOs is readily understood by accountants and is, in many cases, self-explanatory. In this respect, a **balance sheet** is often referred to as a **statement of financial position** because it may more correctly describe the nature of the statement. There is no income statement, but a **statement of operations**. Here, as the objective of NBO accounting is not on net income determination, the term provides a more correct description of what the statement is presenting. As a result, we have a **surplus (or deficit) from operations** and **not profits (or losses)**. And, finally, the **equity** or **capital** of the fund is the **fund balance** that reflects the balance of inflows less outflows into the fund.

PERFORMANCE MEASUREMENT OF NBOs

It is generally recognized that the major problem facing NBO accounting is the measurement of the performance of these organizations. Their operations are not profit-oriented and, consequently, **the normal measures of performance** of net income determination or the return on investment **are not appropriate**. There is also widespread confusion among the non-profit sector, accounting academics, and many practising accountants as to where the extent of compliance with the budget is considered to be an indication of NBO performance. This is because those persons trained in profit-oriented or business accounting find it difficult to appreciate that a surplus or deficit from operations by an NBO is not a surrogate for net income or a net loss.

The performance of these organizations must, therefore, be based on some other measure. For example, how does one measure the performance of a religious body? Is it based on the number of members who attend services regularly? Or is it based on the extent of the monetary contributions of its members? Or is there some other way? Literature on the topic indicates that the only way in which the performance of NBOs can be measured is to compare their actual operations and activities with those planned for the short-, medium- and longterm.

To be effective, planning requires a **longterm objective or mission statement** to set the goals or purposes of the planned activity. This objective is usually based on a period in excess of five years. Once this longterm objective has been set, the policies and strategies to achieve it may be decided upon and implemented over the medium-term of from two to five years. The year-to-year monitoring of the success of implementing these policies or strategies is carried out by comparing the actual levels of expenditures on these programs (and, where applicable, the collection of revenues) with those estimated in the annual budget.

For example, assume that the Federal Department of Health delegates the curbing of the use of drugs by Canadian youths to an NBO formed for that specific purpose. Assume also that the longterm objective of this NBO was to effect a significant reduction in the use of drugs by teenagers and those in their early twenties over a 10-year period by bringing about a change in the attitude towards drug-taking along the lines of that used to recognize the health consequences and anti-social nature of smoking tobacco.

If the policies and strategies designed to achieve this objective are to mount an educational campaign to alert pre-primary, primary and junior high school students to the dangers of drug-taking, it would probably involve the making of videotape for school viewing, the issue of pamphlets, the mounting of a series of lectures at schools, and advertisements during prime-time television. The monitoring of the carrying out of these programs from year to year would be achieved through a comparison of actual expenditures on these activities with those budgeted.

ILLUSTRATION 18–4
THE LINK BETWEEN PLANNING AND THE MEASUREMENT OF PERFORMANCE
WITH NONBUSINESS ORGANIZATIONS

Planning:

Longterm (Objectives)	Medium-term (Strategies)	Short-term (Operations)

Measurement:

Social Changes	Program Indicators	Operational Success

Quantification: ◄ -

Difficulty in Quantification

Adapted from the *Report of the Committee on Accounting in the Public Sector 1974–76*, American Accounting Association, 1977, p. 37.

The measurement process that is presented diagrammatically in Illustration 18–4 indicates that it is only over the longterm that any success or failure of the program can be measured. The year-to-year control of the resources provided in developing the videotapes, the printing of pamphlets, and their distribution to schools can easily be measured through comparing actual levels of expenditure with the budgeted amounts. This comparison is by itself, however, totally **inadequate** as a measure of performance. This is because the apparent success or otherwise of the program could only be gauged by monitoring the number of drug-related incidences or court appearances by youths in the age group at which the program is directed. Finally, however, the success of the program could only be measured many years later, on establishing that a reduction in drug-taking by this group has actually occurred. This would require statistically valid proof that there had been a definite decline in drug abuse and drug-taking supported by, say, a report by the Royal Canadian Mounted Police on a reduction in the use of drugs by this age group, the demand for drugs and a decline in the flow of drugs into Canada.

What Illustration 18–4 also shows is that there is an increase in the level of difficulty in quantifying or establishing the success or otherwise of the program as one moves from the short-term to the medium- and longterm aspects of the program. In this respect, it is easy enough to see whether the development of videotape and pamphlets has been carried out according to plan. However, to establish how successful they have been in curbing the use of drugs in the medium-term is not that easy. Finally, to determine whether a social change has actually occurred is even more difficult to establish. Social indicators do, however, exist.

Unfortunately, the complexity of measuring NBO performance is not appreciated, and resolving of this issue represents one of the major challenges facing accountants.

SUMMARY

This chapter examines the nature, control and accounting procedures used by nonbusiness organizations. In this respect, the term "nonbusiness" refers to both nonprofit organizations and organizations of the government sector. These two types of organization are grouped together because, from both an operational and philosophical point of view, they are similar, and it is often difficult to distinguish between the two.

NBOs differ considerably from one another. The most important feature is that they are service-oriented and there is, consequently, a general lack of a profit motive. There is also a lack of defined ownership interests, and the providers of resources to the NBOs do not expect to receive a return proportionate to the resources provided.

They also differ from enterprises of the private sector insofar as their economic activity is concerned. In this respect, the economic activity of NBOs is represented by a straight line because resources are converted into goods and services for only so long as resources flow into the NBO. Consequently, these organizations must continually receive inflows of resources from resource providers in order to continue to operate. To control the use of resources, the accounting system is also characterized by strict control procedures like the budget procedure, the tender system for capital expenditures, fund accounting and encumbrance accounting.

As NBO activities involve the use of public funds, they should be subject to strict legal and other controls, and be accountable to the public for their actions. This means that public officials and elected representatives are expected to carry out their duties in the utmost good faith and give an account of their actions when called upon to do so. As a result, the accounting system should provide the information necessary to allow those in control of these organizations to demonstrate that they have complied with the necessary legal requirements and the faithful discharge of their duties.

Unfortunately, evidence suggests that many NBOs in Canada are not fully accountable for their actions. Other than where the activities of NPOs are controlled by specific legislation, there is no effective monitoring of their activities in Canada because control over these organizations is merely based on the monitoring of their compliance with income tax legislation covering their tax status. Much of the blame for this situation also lies with the accounting requirements that are based on the assumption that more and better disclosure would provide sufficient transparency to resolve any problems arising from the actions of the directors or trustees of the NBOs concerned. This is, however, not the case.

Determination of performance of NBOs is the most important area of accounting for NBOs. Here, the only real way in which the performance of these organizations can be established is by comparing the results of operations with the longterm objectives and the effectiveness of the policies and strategies used in the medium-term to achieve their objectives. Short-term monitoring of operations through compliance with the budget is, by itself, insufficient as a measure of their performance.

REVIEW QUESTIONS

1. What is the basic difference among the three levels of government and other NBOs?
2. Into which three groups are nonprofit organizations normally grouped?
3. What are the requirements for registration with the Canada Revenue Agency as a charity?
4. Define a nonprofit organization, a governmental body and a crown corporation.
5. At times it is difficult to distinguish between NPOs and similar governmental bodies. What single distinguishing feature shows whether they are NPOs or governmental bodies?
6. What three characteristics distinguish NBOs from enterprises of the private sector?
7. What is the CICA's objective of NPO accounting?
8. Distinguish between the economic activity of NBOs and that of enterprises of the private sector.
9. From an operational point of view, what is the importance of the difference between the economic activity of NBOs and that of enterprises of the private sector?
10. What is the purpose of the budget? List and explain the four stages of the budget procedure.
11. Describe how the budgeted amounts are incorporated into the accounting records.

12. Distinguish between incremental and zero-based budgeting. Why does incremental budgeting often lead to the unnecessary waste of resources?
13. What is the objective of the "tender" system?
14. What is meant by the term "encumbrance accounting"? Is it used for all expenditures of the NBO?
15. Define a fund in NBO accounting. What are the two basic elements of a fund?
16. What are the arguments for and against the amortization of the capital assets of NBOs?
17. Explain why the measurement of performance of NBOs is so difficult.
18. How can the performance of an NBO be measured?

CASES

CASE 18–1   The Dundas Symphony Orchestra

The Dundas Symphony Orchestra had enjoyed both federal and provincial government financial support since its formation in the late 1920s. It also had a membership of some four hundred sponsors and patrons who contributed various amounts to the orchestra in return for reduced prices for attending its concerts.

It had, since 1936, operated out of the MacNeal Theatre, which had been donated to it by Mrs. Margaret MacNeal in memory of her late husband. It was run by a nine-member board of advisors consisting of two members appointed by the Federal Department of Arts and Culture, two members appointed by the Provincial Ministry of Education, and five members elected by its members. The day-to-day administration was handled by a full-time musical director who was also its conductor. With the general decline in attendance at its concerts over the years, it no longer maintained a full-time complement of musicians but drew the majority of its members from the large groups of European immigrant residents in the surrounding areas. To date it had been very successful in assembling the various sections of the orchestra but, over the past few years, it had begun to experience difficulty in attracting a full woodwind section. Accounting and administrative services were provided by a local firm of accountants.

The orchestra provided evening open-air concerts during the summer months. Its main activity was, however, to present concerts at various schools in southern Ontario in co-operation with the Department of Education as a means of stimulating an interest in music. In December of every year, it presented Handel's *Messiah* and other, similar works.

The board of advisors had just received a letter from the Federal Department of Arts and Culture informing them that, in view of the prevailing economic position, its budget had been cut by 10% and it would have to revise its expenditures on all of its activities and, in particular, on its sponsorship of musical and theatrical groups. To assist it in deciding what action to take, the Department was asking all recipients of grants or subsidies to furnish it with a detailed breakdown of their activities and what benefits flowed to the community from these activities.

At the meeting of the board of advisors called to consider this letter, the chairperson, Dorothy Parkinson, set the tone of the discussions by stating: "This orchestra has contributed to the cultural well-being of this area for over fifty years. It cannot cease to be a pillar of our society."

Similar sentiments were expressed by all. However, the reality of the situation soon became apparent. Classical music was really only enjoyed by relatively few people, and the local population was too small to support a "Boston Pops" type program. The base of sponsors was also too small to make up the difference, and without continued governmental funding, the orchestra could not afford to operate. Previous discussions with the provincial government, which provided funding for equipment, had provided little comfort because they were also cutting back on their expenditures. The only hope was to be able to convince the Ministry of Arts and Culture that its activities were, in fact, worthwhile and of benefit to the community.

An analysis of the activities of the orchestra showed that during the previous year it had given a total of six open-air concerts during the previous summer, 24 concerts to schools and three festive concerts in mid-December. Expenditures had exceeded receipts from concerts and the rental of the MacNeal Theatre by an amount of $420,000. However, it had received an operating grant from the Department of Arts and Culture of $350,000, replacement equipment costing $40,000 from the provincial government, and public donations of $28,000. Subscriptions and sponsorships brought in an additional $32,000, allowing it to show a surplus of about $20,000, some $3,000 over its budgeted surplus for the year.

You have been retained by the board of advisors to recommend how it could best present its case to the Department of Arts and Culture for a continuing operating grant.

REQUIRED

Prepare a report to the board of advisors on the possibility of convincing the Department of Arts and Culture to continue their grant. In preparing your report you must consider whether or not:

1. The performance of the Dundas Symphony Orchestra could be measured in a way that would reflect its contribution to the community; and
2. The past funding of the orchestra had, in fact, been an effective and efficient means of stimulating an interest in classical music.

CASE 18–2 **Research Funding Blues**

Over the past 10 years, the Bernard Brenner Trust had contributed a little over $1-million to the University of Southern Ontario to be used specifically for sociological and other related research.

During February 20X1, the Trustees approved a grant of $200,000 to a researcher to investigate the effect of rent control on the provision of affordable housing in the City of Lakeview to be carried out over a 12-month period commencing on April 1, 20X1. The grant was to be paid in four equal instalments on receipt of a quarterly report on the progress of the research and details of the expenses incurred. The first cheque for $50,000 was forwarded to the university by the Trust in March 20X1.

In late June, the Trust received a request for the second instalment of $50,000 as the research grant was already overspent. No progress report or details of expenditures were provided.

On receipt of the request, the Trustees wrote to the university asking for a report on the research project and its funding. They received a reply thanking them for their interest in the project but indicating that the policy of the university had been changed and it would no longer provide such information. The Trustees replied that as this was a requirement under which the grant was made and, as the university had agreed to this condition, such a report was required.

Eventually, after further correspondence on the matter, the Trustees received a statement of expenses, many of which were of concern. On investigation, it transpired that expenditures of about $36,000 had been charged against the account that were apparently not related to the research; sixteen-thousand dollars had been spent on furniture for the researcher's office, three monthly payments of $3,000 each had been paid to his daughter who was in Europe at the time, and the balance had been spent on a trip for himself and his wife to a health spa in New Jersey.

On expressing their concern, the Trustees were informed by the university that it did not require proper vouchers for disbursements from research grants as they relied upon the honesty and integrity of the researchers concerned. The university would, however, ask the researcher to refund the amount spent on the health spa. So far as the purchase of the furniture was concerned, it felt that it could be argued that it provided the proper atmosphere in which to carry out the research and that no action would be taken in this connection. Furthermore, the payment to the researcher's daughter was in order because she had carried out certain research on the topic for her father while she was in Switzerland.

Being dissatisfied with this response, the Trustees informed the university that it would not honour its commitment for the current research and was suspending the granting of any further research funding until it was satisfied that the university would ensure that research grants were properly used.

REQUIRED

Discuss:

1. How donations to a university, like the one mentioned above, would probably have been recorded and disclosed in its annual financial statements; and
2. Whether or not the **accounting** and **reporting** system could be designed to ensure that donations are applied in accordance with the wishes of the donors of those resources.

CASE 18–3   **The Sandtown Board of Education**

In reply to a question by a reporter for *The Sandtown Review*, Mr. Albert Chen, director of education, admitted that the board's procedures relating to the use of the tender system had not been followed by its maintenance department; a cost-overrun of $110,000 had not been approved by the board before it was incurred. This amount had subsequently been approved but, according to Mr. Chen, a full investigation into the matter was to be undertaken because there was concern that the public's contributions to the board were not being properly controlled. "The tender system is supposed to protect the public from unnecessary expenditures and here we have an overrun of over 25%," he added.

On being questioned further, Mr. Chen explained that three tenders had been received from engineering companies to overhaul and, if necessary, replace the heating systems at 20 of its school buildings during the 20X3 summer school recess. After due inspection of the equipment by prospective tenderers, three tenders amounting to $350,000, $380,000 and $445,000 were received.

The tender for $350,000 was rejected because the company involved was new in the area and concern regarding its reliability had been expressed, while the one for $445,000 was rejected as being too expensive. The tender for $380,000 by ZFP Heating and Engineering Company Ltd. had, therefore, been accepted.

Some two weeks before schools were to re-open, the engineering company had informed the maintenance department that extensive repairs to four furnaces were required. The furnaces could be patched up so that they would last another two or three years, but they were loath to do so as they could become dangerous. A spokesman for ZFP Heating admitted that they should have expected some of the furnaces to be in this position, but it must have been overlooked in submitting the tender.

The manager of the maintenance department had approved the additional expenditure because, as he said, "The furnaces had to be in proper working order. I did not know how much it would cost. In retrospect, I know I should have obtained prior approval from the board."

REQUIRED

Discuss:

1. Explain the purpose of the tender system and how cost overruns can be used, intentionally or otherwise, to by-pass the objective of the entire tender system;
2. In this case, the board recommended approval of the cost overrun payment. What would have occurred if it had refused to do so?

EXERCISES

EXERCISE 18–1   **REQUIRED**

In each of the following unrelated cases, describe what type of fund would be used to record and account for the activities being carried on.

1. The funding of Professorial Chair of Accounting endowed by a firm of accountants.
2. A marina, situated in and operated by the Town of Bayside on Lake Erie, that charges a fee for the provision of moorings, berths and the storage of boats.
3. Repayment of a loan by a nonprofit housing scheme.
4. The purchase of computers by a retraining centre from a provincial grant.
5. A transport pool operated by an Elizabethan Order of Nurses.
6. The building of a theatre by a performing arts group.
7. The recording of the receipts and disbursements of a family planning clinic.
8. The payment of a scholarship by a university.

EXERCISE 18–2 Provide suitable answers to the following questions relating to the Mountjoy Retirement Home:

1. The retirement home incorporates its budget into the accounting records using the "recording of the budget in reverse form". During the fiscal year ended December 31, 20X2, the board of directors approved a budget for the year that included advertising expense of $3,500 and building maintenance expense of $6,000. On September 15, after $5,430 had been spent on maintenance of the building, the board of directors approved a supplementary budget amount of $4,200 to cover repairs to the leaking roof. By December 31, 20X2, additional amounts of $3,320 and $4,350 had been spent on advertising and building maintenance respectively.

REQUIRED

Present three-column ledger accounts to record the above amounts in the ledger (including closing transfers) of the retirement home.

2. On November 2, 20X2, the operating fund paid $10,000 into the bank account of its capital development fund to be used specifically for the purchase of a new heating system. All capital expenditures are accounted for in the capital development fund until completed, at which stage they are transferred to the relevant fund of the home. After calling for tenders, an amount of $9,426 was approved by the board of directors on November 20, 20X2 for the new heating plant. The heating plant was duly installed by December 15 and the amount outstanding was paid on that date. The financial year end of the retirement home was December 31 and the heating plant was to be shown as an asset of the operating fund at December 31, 20X2.

REQUIRED

Give the journal entry/entries (without explanations) required to account for the payment for the heating plant in the two relevant funds, distinguishing clearly between the two funds.

EXERCISE 18–3 At December 31, 20X2, the financial year end of the Clarendon Institute for the Mentally Challenged, the encumbrance reserve account reflected a balance of $4,268. An analysis of this balance brought to light the following items:

(a) A purchase order for the supply of cutlery for $1,300.00 was issued on December 4, 20X2 but the cutlery had as yet not been received. On contacting the supplier, you were informed that the goods were on order and would be delivered in January 20X3.
(b) The entry recording a purchase order for cleaning materials amounting to $490 was duplicated in error. When the invoice relating to the purchase order was received, it reflected an amount of $478.33.
(c) Invoices totalling $2,021 were received on December 30–31, 20X2 but had not been processed. On comparing the invoices with the relative purchase orders, the following position had emerged:

Purchase Order #	Amount	Invoice Amount	Account Debited
1233	$ 412.00	$ 433.00	Office Furniture
1256	114.00	114.00	Cleaning Expenses
1257	816.00	844.00	Motor Vehicle Repairs
1259	88.00	88.00	Subscription Expense
1261	558.00	542.00	Stationery Supplies
	$1,988.00	$2,021.00	

REQUIRED

Prepare the journal entries to record/adjust the above amounts at December 31, 20X2 on the assumption that all encumbrances lapse at the end of the financial year.

EXERCISE 18–4

You are the accountant of Yorkdale University. On June 26, 20X2, you received a cheque for $100,000 from Mr. Alistair Cameron, a graduate of the university and a successful chartered accountant in public practice. The cheque had been forwarded on the understanding that it would be used to create a scholarship in memory of his late father, Mr. Falquar Cameron, to be awarded to the student obtaining the highest grades in the third year accounting courses at your university.

The scholarship was to be known as the "Falquar Cameron Scholarship" and was to be awarded each year in August commencing in 20X3 and was initially to be $6,000. Thereafter, it was to be adjusted upwards by five percent a year in order to take inflation into account.

The capital sum was to be invested in fixed interest bearing securities and, to maintain the capital of the scholarship fund, no more than two-thirds of the interest could be paid out in any year. In the event of insufficient interest being available to pay the scholarship, awarding of the scholarship was to be suspended until the capital amount of the fund had been restored to the level where it could, once again, pay the scholarship.

The scholarship was accepted and the money was invested in a five-year general investment certificate bearing interest at 11%/year on July 1, 20X2 with the Yorkdale University Credit Union. Interest was payable annually and credited immediately to a savings account at the credit union earning interest at six percent per year.

On August 1, 20X3, the first award was made to Charlotte Jones.

REQUIRED

1. Give the journal entries (including closing entries) required to record the scholarship, its investment, interest earned and payment to the recipient of the scholarship for the two years ended December 31, 20X2 and 20X3.
2. Explain how the fund and its investment would be disclosed in the financial statements/report of Yorkdale University for the financial year ended December 31, 20X3.

EXERCISE 18–5

On July 1, 20X4, Markham College received a contribution/gift of $200,000 in cash from Markham Business Machines to upgrade the College's computer facilities. The terms of the contribution were that the money could only be used to purchase new computers and networking equipment. On receipt of the cash, the College opened an MBM Equipment Fund and a bank account in the name of the equipment fund at the Bank of Toronto.

On July 12, 20X4, the College placed orders for computers and networking equipment to the value of $122,000 for its computer centre. The computers were delivered on August 3, 20X4, together with the invoice for $120,500, which included an additional quantity discount of $1,500. On August 15, 20X4, after installation and testing, the invoice was paid and the computer equipment transferred to the Markham College Operating Fund.

REQUIRED

Prepare the journal entries to record the above transactions in the separate records of the MBM Equipment Fund using a full encumbrance accounting system. (Note: This exercise is designed to test your knowledge on the operation of encumbrance accounting and nothing else.)

PROBLEMS

PROBLEM 18-1   The following three scenarios apply to Steele's College, which was formed in 20X3 as a polytechnic institute by an Act of the provincial parliament.

1. Following the appointment of an interim Board of Governors, an initial amount of $4-million dollars was paid into the Steele's College bank account at the Bank of Western Canada on March 3, 20X3. This amount was to be held in a development fund known as the Steele's College Development Fund. Immediately following the receipt of the cash, an amount of $600,000 in cash was transferred to the operating fund of the College. On March 6, 20X3, cash of $180,000 was transferred from the operating fund to an equipment fund.

    An order for equipment costing $167,000 was placed with Markham Business Machines Inc. on March 22, 20X3. On April 17, 20X3, the equipment ordered from MBM was received together with the invoice for $169,700. The additional amount of $2,700 covered modifications of the original order. The equipment was immediately transferred to the operating fund.

REQUIRED

Give the journal entries to record the above transactions in the individual funds on the assumption that Steele's College uses a full encumbrance system for all its purchases. Pay particular attention to the transfer of amounts between the three funds.

2. On August 15, 20X5, the Board of Governors of Steele's College decided to set aside an amount of $500,000 from its unrestricted accumulated funds into a restricted internal bursary fund to provide assistance to students experiencing financial difficulties in meeting their tuition fees. The amount was not paid into a separate fund but was to be treated as a restricted fund for reporting purposes. On September 20, 20X5, following the call for bursary applications, the board approved bursaries for the 20X5/X6 academic year valued at $420,000. The bursaries were to be treated as "bursaries payable" in the same manner as accounts payable. Payment of the bursaries was to be made in two installments on November 1 and March 1 in any year.

    On November 15, 20X5, following discussions with its auditors, the college agreed to transfer the unallocated balance of $80,000 and the $210,000 due for payment on March 1, 20X6 to a separate bursary fund to be known as the "Board of Governors Bursary Fund", which would be treated as a separate endowment fund, with all moneys invested in interest bearing securities until required.

    On November 16, 20X6, the amounts received by the Bursary Fund were invested in seven percent General Investment Certificates with the Canada West Trust Company.

REQUIRED

Give the journal entries to record the above transactions in the records of both the Steele's College Operating Fund and the Bursary Fund. (Hint: You may find T-accounts useful for proving your entries.)

PROBLEM 18-2   The Benefit Blood Service (BBS) is a nonprofit organization that collects donations of blood from donors, and distributes it and blood products to hospitals throughout the country. It has a December 31 year end and uses three funds: an operating fund, an equipment fund, and a research fund. It also uses a full budgetary control procedure and encumbrance accounting.

The operating fund handles its normal day-to-day operations; the research fund finances and controls its research activities on blood and blood products; and the equipment fund finances the equipment required by both the operating and research funds.

REQUIRED

Provide answers or describe how the following non-related events would be treated by BBS during the year ended December 31, 20X4:

(a) In July 1, BBS received a grant of $70,000 in cash from the federal government to fund research into the extraction of blood platelets. The amount was paid into the bank account of the operating fund on July 2. On July 4, however, it was decided to transfer this amount to the research fund to be held in a blood clotting research account. Arrangements to carry out the research on blood platelets were made and the following expenses were paid:

July 31	$35,600
August 31	$32,700

On September 1, the research was considered completed and the balance of the grant was repaid to the operating fund. Give the journal entries to record these transactions in the relative funds.

(b) On August 14, 20X4, an order for a centrifuge (i.e., equipment) to be used for separating blood products was placed by the equipment fund with Ajax Medical Equipment Inc. BBS uses a full encumbrance accounting system for all purchases of this nature. The order specified a price of $320,000 but when the invoice was received on August 30, 20X4, the amount invoiced was $304,000 after granting of a discount. The amount owing was paid on September 4, 20X4. Give the journal entries **to record** this purchase.

(c) The journal entry/entries recording the transfer of the equipment purchased in point (b) to the operating fund.

(d) In appreciation of the business placed with it, Ajax Medical Equipment donated an autoclave (i.e., equipment sterilizer) valued at $40,000 to BBS in October for use in its daily blood collection activities. Give the journal entries recording this donation specifying clearly where and in which fund it would be recorded.

(e) At December 31, 20X4, on an analysis of the outstanding purchases, it was found that the goods covered by the three purchase orders listed below had not been delivered:

Date	Purchase Order	Amount	Covering
Nov. 29	#1136	$ 280.00	Stationery expense
Dec. 3	#1157	$1,400.00	Cleaning materials expense
Dec. 28	#1267	$ 67.45	Maintenance expense

Give the journal entries required to record the necessary adjustments at year end.

(f) Explain how, if at all, the amounts outstanding on December 31 in point (e) above would be disclosed in the financial statements of BBS at December 31, 20X4.

PROBLEM 18–3 You are provided with the following four **unrelated cases** applying to nonprofit organizations all having a December 31, 20X5 year end:

Case 1: The Bayside Re-Employment Centre was formed in November 20X4. It was created to provide basic job training and a placement service. The Centre used a full encumbrance accounting system.

Details of the transactions relating to the purchase of equipment for the re-employment centre for January 20X5 were as follows:

(a)   On January 4, 20X5, the Centre placed orders for furniture with Ajax Suppliers Ltd. for the immediate delivery of furniture and equipment for $109,000. Of this amount, $44,000 applied to the general fund and $65,000 to the training fund.

(b)   Acting on a quotation of $17,500, an order for the supply of training materials was placed with BIM Services Inc. on January 14 for immediate execution.

(c)   Received invoices on January 20 relating to the purchase of the furniture and equipment for the general fund of $48,000 and $66,000 for the training centre. (The centre had failed to put the order out to tender before placing the orders).

(d)   On receiving the invoice and statement from BIM Services Inc. on January 31, the training centre found that it had only been charged $16,000 for its purchases of training materials because BIM had given the Centre a discount.

REQUIRED

Give the journal entries required by the Centre to record the above events and transactions, including the use of the system of encumbrance accounting.

Case 2: On December 28, 20X5, the first payment of $10,000 was paid by the Operating Fund of the Oakville Retirement Home into the bank account of its Debt Service Fund. This transfer was the first of 100 monthly payments of $10,000 to cover the monthly charge for interest and capital repayment of the mortgage from which the building of its retirement home had been financed. The payment of $10,000 made on December 31, 20X5 included interest of $9,950.

REQUIRED

Give the journal entry/entries (without explanations) required to account for the payment of the mortgage in the relevant funds.

Case 3: At December 31, 20X5, the Welfare Fund of the Emma Bart Houses, which had enjoyed a tax-free status since its establishment in 1887, had a fund balance of $48,000 invested in interest bearing securities. The last surviving beneficiary had died on August 4, 20X5. At a meeting of the Board of Directors of the Fund held on September 14, 20X5, it was decided to wind up (i.e., liquidate) the Fund on December 1. The charter of the Fund did not specify what was to happen to the funds in the event of its liquidation.

REQUIRED

Explain what would happen to the resources of the Fund on the liquidation of the Fund **after** the investments had been realized in cash.

Case 4: On December 4, 20X5, the Members of the Mississauga Squash Club decided to appropriate (i.e., set aside) an amount of $10,000 from its Operating Fund Balance to be used specifically (and only) for funding sports clinics in the future.

REQUIRED

Explain how this amount would be reflected on the balance sheet of the Operating Fund of the Squash Racquets Club at December 31, 20X5.

19

Public Sector Accounting Requirements

LEARNING OBJECTIVES

After studying this chapter you should be able to:

1. Understand the nature, operation and control of the public sector; and
2. Identify and interpret the objectives of accounting and financial reporting for this sector.

THE NATURE OF THE PUBLIC SECTOR

The broad characteristics and accounting requirements of the government and nonprofit sectors were outlined in Chapter Eighteen. In that chapter it was pointed out that accountability applies equally to this sector and that their operations are also strictly controlled through the use of the budgetary procedure, and fund and encumbrance accounting. It was also pointed out that the major difference between governmental entities and NPOs is that the three levels of government, acting on their own or indirectly through their various agencies, have the power to levy taxes on the community and pass legislation, while NPOs do not enjoy those powers.

Governmental entities serve the entire community and the sector is, therefore, referred to as **the public sector**. It was defined by the Public Sector Accounting Board (PSAB) of the Canadian Institute of Chartered Accountants (CICA) as comprising the federal, provincial, territorial and local governments and governmental entities, such as governmental funds, agencies and corporations.[1] Their revenues consist of taxes (including such items as fishing or other licences), fees imposed by the government, and penalties for infractions of the law.

Public sector entities are run by elected representatives of the public. The electorate can, if it so desires, replace them through the democratic process. These elected representatives should be fully accountable to the public for their actions. Unfortunately, elected representatives are often chosen on the basis of their popularity and not for their managerial abilities. And, as these representatives are interested in being re-elected, they often pursue courses of action that are not necessarily consistent with the objectives of efficiency and effectiveness. It is within this framework that accounting for the public sector operates.

---

[1] Definition per the *Terms of Reference of the Public Sector Accounting and Auditing Board* as approved by the Board of Governors in the Introduction to PSAB Recommendations, *PSA Handbook*.

ACCOUNTING RECOMMENDATIONS FOR THE PUBLIC SECTOR

The Canadian accounting requirements for the public sector are those of the PSAB and their recommendations are contained in the *PSA Handbook*. They were developed to provide reporting standards for the public sector that would provide preparers and the auditors of the various entities with the guidelines required to report publicly.

There is no legal or other requirement that compels government entities to comply with the accounting requirements of the PSAB. This is because governments are **sovereign entities** and have the **"supreme power" to act on their own**. Compliance with the recommendations of the PSAB is, therefore, **purely voluntary**. However, at both the federal and provincial levels, the work of the PSAB has been supported and these governments have stated that they will do everything in their power to support these recommendations.

Notwithstanding the fact that the recommendations of the *PSA Handbook* are voluntary, they are intended to apply to all governments and government agencies, unless the reporting entities are public sector profit-oriented (or business-type) enterprises, public sector NPOs, or other governmentally sponsored entities that do not fit the recommendations of the *PSA Handbook* for government organizations. Where this is the case, the following applies:[2]

1. If the reporting entity is a governmental body	then	the accounting requirements of the PSAB apply.
2. If the reporting entity is a governmentally controlled business type activity in which the principal activity is the selling of goods and services	then	the accounting requirements of the CICA *Handbook* for profit-oriented enterprises apply.
3. If the reporting entity is a public sector or governmentally controlled NPO	then	the accounting requirements of the CICA *Handbook* for NPOs apply.
4. If the reporting entity is a government body that carries on multiple activities or does not fit any of the criteria required for reporting by the PSA *Handbook*, or does not fit the recommendations of the CICA *Handbook* for profit-oriented enterprises or NPOs	then	these reporting entities may follow whatever sets of accounting requirements that best meets their reporting needs.

Public sector business-type organizations are separate legal entities with the power to contract on their own behalf and that can sue or be sued by others. They must have been delegated the authority to operate by the level of government to which they are responsible. Their principal activity must involve the sale of goods and services to outside parties. The critical issue is that their economic activity should be such that they can maintain their operations and meet their liabilities from revenues obtained from the sale of their goods and services, as with profit-oriented enterprises of the private sector.

THE ORIGIN OF THE GOVERNMENTAL ACCOUNTING SYSTEM

The governmental accounting system in Canada is based on the British model, which arose from the separation of the crown from parliament in the Middle Ages. **This conferred upon parliament the sole right to raise taxes and to control the spending of those taxes.**

Originally, all taxes and expenditures had to be approved in advance by the legislature. Today, at the federal level, even though legislative approval of expenditures is still important, it can be bypassed by the use of the federal Treasury Board (which approves governmental spending), through the use of "Orders in Council" of the Privy Council, and the use of its

---

[2] See paragraphs 5–8 of the Introduction to the Public Sector Accounting *Handbook*.

regulatory powers. However, the principle of legislative approval still remains relatively untouched at the provincial and local government levels.

The legislative control over the financing of government in those areas that still support the principle operates in the following manner. Once a year, the Minister of Finance presents a budget in which the proposed expenditures for the year and how they are to be financed are outlined. After the proposals have been presented to the legislature, legislation in the form of the appropriation bills (for expenditures) and any bills changing the taxing acts (for revenues) are introduced, debated, and finally passed into legislation. Supplementary budgets may be presented if the needs arise.

THE DESIGN OF THE GOVERNMENTAL ACCOUNTING SYSTEM

The legislative control over government operations has resulted in the development of government accounting systems for the two main purposes of, first, providing information for the day-to-day control of operations and, second, allowing public officials to demonstrate that they have discharged their duties as required. Ancillary objectives include reporting on the scope of operations and the costs at which services are provided. Many of the principles adopted by the PSAB were the result of a joint project with the US government carried out in the late 1990s.

1. The Provision of Information Required for Day-to-day Control of Operations

The **day-to-day control** of governmental operations is through the application of the budget procedure (the approval of expenditures, restricting expenses to the amounts approved, and a review of activities), fund accounting (accounting for the approved expenses in sets of accounting records through separate funds), and encumbrance accounting (a method of ensuring that expenses on amounts approved are not exceeded). These activities should also be properly controlled through a system of management control involving **the efficient management of resources** and the use of modern management techniques.[3]

The financial reports that are presented are on a fund-by-fund basis. They are detailed statements of the activities and operations of the individual reporting entities to ensure that they have complied with the budget and any other statutory requirements presented in a fund-by-fund format. These financial reports are designed mainly for **internal use. The financial statements of the individual funds** are often summarized in aggregate form to present a summary of the total activities of the entity.

2. The Demonstration of Accountability

The requirements of the PSAB are to allow legislators and public officials to demonstrate accountability through the issue of financial statements in summary form for the government as a whole. These financial statements are required to be presented using the same accounting practices and procedures that apply to enterprises of the private sector except where the nature of government entities differs to such an extent that following private enterprise accounting principles would be inappropriate. It is recommended that they are presented in a

---

[3] Unfortunately, management control is difficult to achieve in government because the competitive profit regulator of the marketplace is absent. In government, the size of the budget allocation and the number of employees is often used as a measure of importance and/or the success of the operation. Furthermore, decision making, particularly in government bodies, is often based on **short-term considerations** and is frequently based on **the line of least resistance**. Evidence of mismanagement, waste and over-spending in government are commonplace, as reflected by the Annual Reports of the Auditor-General. Management control in these bodies is, therefore, often little more of an academic concept than an established practice.

consolidated form to provide an overall picture of the entity's activities rather than on a fund-by-fund basis. Interests in public sector business-type entities and joint ventures are also included in the financial statements.

Where a government entity administers a trust or number of trusts, the PSAB recommendation is that they should be excluded from the financial statements of the entity. However, a description of these trusts and the trust balances should be disclosed by way of a note to the government entity's own financial statements.

The extent to which private enterprise accounting procedures are required to be used is reflected by the requirement that the cost method of accounting for investments should be used for any investments in business-type entities over which the government entity **cannot exercise significant influence or control**. Portfolio investments whose values have declined below their market price must also be adjusted by writing them down to market value or by using an allowance account.

In those cases where the government entity **can exert significant influence or control** over the operations and activities of business-type entities in which it has invested, the PSAB recommendations specifically require governments to account for these investments using the **modified equity method**. This method is, in fact, exactly the same method as that used by profit-oriented enterprises of the private sector for accounting for longterm investments. The term "modified equity method", used to clarify in this context, refers to a business-type presentation of the results of operations and the valuation of the investment. Furthermore, it is used to show that it **does not** incorporate the financing of capital expenditures out of operating revenues and other accounting procedures that are peculiar to government entities (see later).

In essence, the PSAB financial reports are summaries of the operations of the government entity to provide readers with some idea of the scope of the entity's activities. The extent to which the operations are summarized **detracts significantly from their usefulness** because, even though the reports may provide details of the total assets, liabilities, revenues and expenses, they do not provide sufficient detail for any proper analysis of activities. They are, therefore, designed for use by legislators to provide some idea of the extent of the entity's operations.[4]

THE PURPOSE OF THE FINANCIAL STATEMENTS OF GOVERNMENT ENTITIES

As outlined earlier, the primary purpose of the financial statements of governmental entities is for **accountability purposes**, which is the need to demonstrate that those entrusted with the responsibility of exercising legislative control over the financial operations of the entity have carried out their duties as required. Consequently, the financial statements required by the PSAB are designed to present information that is useful in evaluating the government's

---

[4] The entire issue of the nature and content of the financial statements of government entities has recently been reviewed in the USA.

The most important change was that government entities were to use a "dual form" of reporting. Government entities would present two sets of financial statements consisting of a government-wide set of financial statements and a set of fund financial statements. The government-wide financial statements would present the overall position using separate columns for its government activities and business type activities. The fund financial statements would present **the same information** but on a fund basis displaying the major funds individually and the nonmajor funds and proprietary (i.e., business-type funds) in aggregate form in a columnar presentation.

This form of presenting its financial statements was designed to provide information on an entity-wide basis for those users who found it was difficult to obtain a clear picture of the overall activities of the government entity using fund accounting. The fund basis of reporting was to provide detailed information on the individual funds which are, as outlined in the previous chapter, the primary means of control and management of government entities.

financial condition at the end of the accounting period and its financial performance during the accounting period.[5]

Legislators, as elected representatives of the public, are considered the primary users of government financial statements because they are the persons who grant authority to the government to administer public resources and financial affairs and who, in turn, are accountable to the public for their actions. Government financial statements are, therefore, the means by which a government accounts for its administration of public financial affairs and resources. They are also expected to provide the means by which persons not involved in the government's financial administration may obtain the information about government operations they require.

GOVERNMENT REPORTING ENTITIES

In Canada, the responsibilities of the federal government and those of the provincial and territorial governments are set out in the Constitution of Canada. Those of the local governments, like cities and towns, are set out in the various legislation of the provincial governments and they must operate within the bounds of that legislation and its regulations.

The Introduction to the PSA *Handbook* states that for purposes of applying the PSAB's Recommendations, the term, public sector, refers to federal, provincial, territorial and local governments, government organizations, government partnerships, and school boards. Government reporting entities, in addition, comprise the organizations that are controlled by it.[6] For reporting purposes, this includes all reporting entities, whether owned or controlled by the level of government concerned.

Certain aspects of this position require clarification:

(a) **Government entities are required to account for their activities to the level of government to which they are responsible**. This follows the normal principle of accountability where the minister responsible reports on the activities of the reporting in the legislature. This means that a verbal report is presented to the legislature and financial statements or reports are made available for public scrutiny by placing them on the proverbial "table". **Local government entities are treated differently** because their operations are controlled by the provincial governments. They must, therefore, account for their activities to the provincial or territorial government to whom they are responsible.

(b) A government **owns an organization if it has created or acquired it.** If the organization's capital structure is in the form of shares carrying the right to appoint members to its board of directors, then ownership requires that the government must hold sufficient shares to be able to elect a majority of members to the board of directors. This applies in the case of "Crown Corporations" like the Royal Canadian Mint, Canada Post, etc. If, on the other hand, the government **owns the organization's net assets**, then the legislation that led to the formation of the organization gives the government the legal right to those assets.

(c) **Control over a government organization** exists when a government has the authority to determine the financing and operating policies of another entity without requiring the consent of others. A government may choose not to exercise its authority over the organization and allow it to operate as an independent organization. In these cases, the government still has the authority to exercise control should it wish to do so.

Government Accounting Standard *GAS No. 34* also required the amortization of capital assets of government entities (other than historical treasures, works of art, and those forming part of the infrastructure) over their estimated useful lives. Assets forming part of the infrastructure were not to be amortized.

[5] PSA *Handbook* section 1100.07.

[6] PSA *Handbook*, section 1300.

THE PSAB'S OBJECTIVES OF THE FINANCIAL STATEMENTS OF GOVERNMENTAL ENTITIES

The PSAB's objectives of government financial statements are based on the information needs of users, taking into account the limitations of financial statements as a reporting medium, the nature of government operations and legislative control.[7] These objectives are that:

1. *Financial statements should provide a full account of the nature and extent of the financial affairs and resources that the government controls.*

2. *Financial statements should present information to describe the government's financial position at the end of the accounting period.* This information should allow:
   (a) An evaluation of the government's ability to finance its activities and to meet its liabilities and commitments; and
   (b) Its abilities to provide future services.

3. *Financial statements should present information to describe the changes in a government's financial position in the accounting period.* This information should be useful in evaluating:
   (a) The sources, allocation and consumption of the government's recognized economic resources in the accounting period;
   (b) How the activities of the accounting period have affected the net debt of the government; and
   (c) How the government financed its activities in the accounting period and how it met its cash requirements.

4. *Financial statements should demonstrate the accountability of a government for the resources, obligations and financial affairs for which it is responsible.* This would be achieved by providing information useful in:
   (a) Evaluating the financial results of the government's management of its resources, obligations and financial affairs in the accounting period; and
   (b) Assessing whether resources were administered by the government in accordance with the limits established by the appropriate legislative authorities.

THE GENERAL STANDARDS OF FINANCIAL STATEMENT PRESENTATION FOR GOVERNMENT ENTITIES

The PSAB's accounting requirements are that all federal, provincial and territorial government entities should present, as a minimum, **a statement of financial position, a statement of operations, a statement of net debt, and a statement of changes in financial position.**[8] These should conform with the requirements of financial statements of enterprises of the private sector. They should, therefore, disclose the accounting policies used in their preparation, include all relevant information, be presented on a comparative basis, and use consistent valuation bases, etc.

Where these financial statements have been subjected to an independent external audit, the auditor's report should be attached to the financial statements. Where they have not been audited, this fact should be disclosed.

The financial statements of government entities are complex documents. They also vary considerably from entity to entity and, as a result, it is impossible to provide a detailed description of them in a chapter of this nature. Consequently, only a brief description of the type and nature of the information presented in these financial statements is provided hereunder:

---

[7] PSA *Handbook*, section 1100.
[8] Additional requirements apply to local governments.

The Statement of Financial Position (or Balance Sheet)

The purpose of the statement of financial position is to **present the difference between the governmental entity's liabilities and its financial assets to give the entity's net debt and its accumulated surplus/deficit at the end of the accounting period**. These two amounts are considered as the two indicators that together explain the financial position of the entity at the end of the accounting period. The statement should, therefore, highlight these two aspects for the period under review.

The specific reporting requirements are as follows:

Liabilities and Longterm Debt The **liabilities** must be listed by major categories. For example, liabilities would be classified as accounts payable, borrowings, pension liabilities, and loans and advances from other governmental entities.

In view of the significance and importance of the **longterm debt** of governmental entities, the financial statements must disclose the extent and nature of the entity's longterm debt and details of the existence of sinking fund[9] and redemption provisions. Foreign borrowings must be expressed in Canadian dollar equivalents and, where security for loans has been given, details of such security should be disclosed.

Financial and Tangible Assets The financial assets should be classified into cash and temporary investments, revenues receivable, inventories of goods for resale, loans and advances to other governments, investments, etc. The nature and terms of a government's temporary investments should be given together with any applicable valuation adjustments. For marketable securities, market values should be disclosed and, in those cases where the market value has declined to below carrying value, they should be carried at the market value.

In addition, governmental entities are required to provide information on their **tangible capital assets** that have economic lives extending beyond the end of the current accounting period. This includes those assets that are held for use in the production or supply of goods and services on a continuing basis. This is considered necessary to be able to present information about the entity's stock of tangible capital assets and their amortization in the summary financial statements. It also provides information on the cost of using these assets to deliver programs.

Works of art and historical treasures which have cultural, aesthetic, or historical value are not recognized as tangible capital assets in government financial statements because reasonable estimates of the future benefits associated with such property cannot be made. Nevertheless, the existence of such property should be disclosed.

Fund Balances It is customary for the financial statements of public sector entities to reflect **their fund balances** relating to their various activities and restrictions. These may consist of reserves relating to some or other activity, the amounts of capital outlays relating to the principal portion of the longterm debt that has not matured and that is to be recovered in future years, reserves for such items as capital expenditures or debt retirement, and reserves for future operations or contingencies. Details of the fund balances and changes therein should be disclosed in notes and schedules to the financial statements.

The Statement of Operations

The broad requirement for the statement of operations is that it should report the revenues in the accounting period, detailing those from taxes, non-tax sources and transfers from other governments. It should also show the expenses, including changes in valuation

---

9 A sinking fund comprises cash or other assets set aside to retire debt or redeem stock.

allowances, for the period under review by function or major program. The surplus or deficit from operations for the period, together with the accumulated surplus or deficit at the beginning of the period, must also be disclosed.

Statement of Changes in Net Debt

The purpose of the statement of changes in net debt is to **report on the extent to which the expenditures of the accounting period have been offset by the revenues recognized in the period**. This is reflected by differences between the surplus or deficit from operations and the resulting change in net debt for the period. In those cases where the entity's financial assets exceed its liabilities, this statement is to be described as the statement of changes in net financial resources.

The statement of change in net debt should disclose the acquisition of tangible capital assets in the accounting period as well as any other significant items contributing to the surplus or deficit for the accounting period and the change in net debt in the period. In addition, this statement should also provide a comparison of the actual amounts received or expended and those budgeted for the period. This latter requirement is designed to show the extent to which the entity has met its revenue and spending targets (i.e., its operational effectiveness).

The Statement of Changes in Financial Position

The stated reason for the statement of changes in financial position is to show how the entity met its cash requirements, changes in its cash and cash equivalents, and its total cash requirements. The disclosure format follows the same pattern as for enterprises of the private sector. In this respect, it requires the inclusion of significant noncash items and should be drawn up under the three headings of cash flows from operations, investing activities and financing activities.

THE GOVERNMENT REPORTING MODEL

The PSAB's accounting recommendations for financial reporting represent a major departure from the traditional reporting model.

The traditional approach was to present a balance sheet reflecting the "net debt" of the reporting entity comprising its liabilities less its financial assets (i.e., cash, cash equivalents, and other monetary assets). The entity's capital expenditures were written off directly against revenues in the operating statement when purchased out of cash or, where the capital expenditures were financed from loans, attention to the cost of such capital expenditures was reflected in the operating statement as debt service charges (i.e., interest and loan repayment costs). **Control over borrowings** was, therefore, effected by drawing attention to the costs of its capital expenditures and the ability to service the loans from which the capital expenditures were made. The surplus or deficit from operations reflected on the operating statement was taken as **an indication of the entity's operational effectiveness and not as a measure of performance.** This approach was referred to as being **a financial resources model.**[10]

With the current move towards adopting **the reporting model applying to the private sector**, the tangible assets of the reporting government entity appear on the balance sheet as net assets (i.e., assets less liabilities) and the difference between revenues and expenses reports the surplus or deficit from operations in the accounting period. This model is referred to as **an economic resources model** by the PSAB because it reflects the total economic resources of the reporting entity. This model may also be referred to as a **net assets model.**

---

[10] The descriptions for "financial resources model" and "economic resources model" are those used by Martha Jones Denning, "Governments are different", *CAMagazine*, December 2001, pp. 32–34.

The adoption of the net assets model represents **a major change in government accounting** because government entities have traditionally been concerned with expenditures and how they were financed. The justification for adopting this method is that it will provide information on the costs at which government services are provided.

The application of the economic resources model was subjected to considerable criticism and there was **considerable disagreement** amongst governmental entities regarding the extent to which the PSAB's accounting and reporting requirements would meet their reporting needs. In fact, the proposed reporting model apparently **enjoyed such little acceptance** amongst senior government reporting entities that in February 2002, the PSAB approved a new Exposure Draft revising the reporting standards for application from January 2003.[11] These recommendations were eventually approved in August 2003 and are to apply to fiscal years ending on or after April 1, 2005. The extent to which these recommendations will be accepted and applied by governmental entities remains to be seen.

ADDITIONAL REPORTING REQUIREMENTS

In July 2003, the PSAB issued the *Draft Statement of Recommended Practice* covering the inclusion of a **Financial Statement Discussion and Analysis** section in the financial reports of governmental entities. The purpose of the FSD&A is to explain and highlight information in the financial statements and changes in financial position. However, at the date of this edition of the text going to press, it has as yet not been finally approved by the PSAB.

The disclosure of **subsequent events** is specifically required. This applies regardless of whether these events relate to the conditions that existed at the date of the financial statements or events that arose subsequent to the date of the financial statements. Obviously, suitable evidence should exist to verify the existence of such events.

Subsequent events arising from **the intentions of the government entity** announced by elected officials need to be carefully evaluated to ensure that they are supported by sufficient evidence to indicate that they can and will be fulfilled. For a federal, provincial, or territorial government, the intention should be supported by the enactment of legislation or the exercising of an authority under existing legislation.

Where the subsequent events relate to events **existing at the date of the financial statements**, the financial statements should be adjusted to incorporate these events. However, where the events relate to ice storms, floods and other calamities, the issue of longterm debt, the commencement of litigation, or significant restructuring, the financial statements should not be adjusted, but full details of these events and their financial and other effects on the governmental entity should be disclosed.

TRANSACTIONS INVOLVING PHYSICAL ASSETS

The method of financing the purchase of physical (or capital) assets by governmental entities dictates what accounting treatment applies. This is because the objective of the government accounting system is based on the need to disclose to taxpayers the reasons why certain expenditures were made.

There are three ways these expenditures may be treated. These are as operational expenses, withdrawals from reserves, and purchases from borrowings. Each treatment is described below:

1. Physical assets may be purchased out of operational revenues. These purchases are treated as operational expenses.

---

[11] *Exposure Draft: Objectives of Financial Statements — Federal, Provincial and Territorial Governments*, CICA, 2002.

2. A government entity may set aside amounts from its revenues over a period of years to fund the purchase of a physical asset. Expenditures of this nature are treated as "set ups" and "draw downs" of reserves in the financial statements.

3. A government entity may fund the purchase of physical assets from borrowings. In these cases, the treatment differs depending on whether the borrowings are annuity loans or lump sum borrowings. With annuity loans, the annual payments are treated as the amortization of these assets. Longterm loans that are only payable on a set date are retained intact on the balance sheet until maturity, at which time they are discharged by moneys withdrawn from sinking funds. The sinking funds are accumulated over the tenure of the loan by investing annual contributions from revenues (i.e., as expenses) so that on maturity date, they total the amount of the loan to be repaid. Irrespective of how they are treated, the "debt servicing" charges of interest and principal are treated as operating expenses.

THE AUDIT FUNCTION IN THE PUBLIC SECTOR

Government entities other than local governments are subject to audit by the Auditor-General or the provincial auditors in each province. This is an important control function at the federal and provincial government levels. Local authorities are, however, usually audited by public accountants.

The Auditor-General is an officer of parliament and not the government, and is responsible only to parliament. The holder of this office is appointed for 10 years by the Governor General-in-Council in terms of the *Financial Administration Act*. The duties of the holder of this office are to ensure that the government has spent the moneys it raised properly, and should any improprieties come to light, the Auditor-General is duty bound to bring these to the attention of parliament.

The Provincial Auditors are similarly officers of the provincial legislatures and hold office in terms of the applicable provincial legislation. For example, in Ontario, the Provincial Auditor is appointed by the Lieutenant Governor-in-Council after consultation with the Chair of the Standing Committee on Public Accounts.[12] The incumbent holds office until age 65 but can be re-appointed to serve for additional one-year terms until age 70.

To be able to carry out their responsibilities, there is a continuous monitoring of the financial and accounting controls of these entities. The Auditor-General or Provincial Auditors can undertake a detailed audit of any area to ensure that it is operating effectively and efficiently and, to be able to do so, they have access to all the financial books and records of the government. Once a year, the Auditor-General, and each of the Provincial Auditors, report on their findings to the legislative body to which they are responsible (i.e., the House of Assembly or the provincial parliaments). These reports usually contain a list of inefficiencies, waste of the taxpayers money, and any other matters they feel are of importance and should be made public. The governments concerned are duty bound to take action to remedy the matters raised in these reports.

Such a case occurred when the Auditor-General, Ms. Sheila Fraser, submitted her report to Parliament in February 2004. This Report drew attention to the fact that $250-million set aside for sponsoring cultural and sporting events landed up providing $100-million in commissions and fees to a handful of advertising firms some of which had strong ties to the government of the day. Since the Report was tabled, the Royal Canadian Mounted Police (RCMP) has laid charges against the bureaucrat who managed the program and the heads of two advertising agencies.

---

12 *The Audit Act*, 1978. Chapter 35, R.S.O., 1990.

What is most disturbing is that certain Members of Parliament and a senior government official have attempted to downplay the importance of the Auditor-General's findings. These persons have suggested that the money was not misspent despite the fact that in 2002, a federal "quick response team" that examined 126 of the 712 contracts issued (i.e., 17.7%) in carrying out the program found staggering abuse by the advertising agencies. In one case the response team found "a systematic pattern of overbilling" and in another that the president of an advertising agency had billed the program for 3,673 hours in one year (at least 10 hours per day for the entire 365-day year).[13]

It cannot be overstressed that the position of Auditor-General, like that of the provincial counterparts, is very important. To ensure that persons holding these positions can carry out their duties without **political interference**, their positions are protected by the Constitution. In Canada, the Auditor-General can only be removed from office by a joint motion in both houses of parliament. Removal of the Provincial Auditors from office is "for cause", which means that a motion to remove the incumbent from office must be introduced in the legislative assembly (i.e., the provincial parliament) and passed by a simple majority of votes.

Local governments are, however, normally audited by external public accountants. Their activities are monitored by the Provincial and Territorial Auditors, but they report directly to the local government councils and taxpayers.

SUMMARY

This chapter examines the nature of the public sector and government accounting systems. It points out that detailed financial records are required for the day-to-day running of these organizations but, because these financial records are unsuitable for reporting to the general public, the PSAB has recommended consolidated financial statements that present the total operations and activities of the government entity in summary form based on the accounting practices of enterprises of the private sector. The two most important matters required by these financial statements are to present a comparison of actual operations with those planned for the period under review, and to present information that shows that the government entity had complied with its authorized borrowings, investments and expenditures.

The PSAB's specific accounting requirements for these entities are then examined. These cover the demonstration of accountability by those entrusted with the use and control of public resources and the provision of the required information in an understandable manner. It then looks at the manner in which the financial statements should be prepared, and re-examines the manner in which government entities account for the acquisition of their capital assets. Finally, it explains the importance of the office of the Auditor-General and the provincial counterparts.

REVIEW QUESTIONS

1. What do you understand by the term "public sector"? How is it defined by the PSAB?
2. Do governments have to comply with the PSAB accounting requirements? If not, why?
3. Briefly, outline how the PSAB envisages the accounting for government-owned business-type entities, public sector nonprofit organizations, government entities carrying on multiple activities, and government administered trusts should be treated?
4. Who are considered the primary users of government financial statements? Why are these persons considered so important?
5. What is meant by the term "modified equity method"? Why is this term used?

---

[13] For a full report on the sponsor scandal, see *The Globe and Mail* (May 15, 2004) F2.

6. Outline the two purposes of a governmental accounting system.
7. What are the two basic purposes of the financial statements of government entities?
8. How has the PSAB defined a government reporting entity? To whom are they accountable?
9. When does a government entity own another entity?
10. List the four specific PSAB objectives of government financial statements.
11. What four financial statements must governmental entities present?
12. Outline the three ways government entities treat their expenditures relating to the purchase of their capital assets.
13. Why are the office of Auditor-General and the provincial counterparts so important? How is the office protected, and in what way can the Auditor-General be removed from office?

20 The Reporting Requirements for Nonprofit Organizations[1]

LEARNING OBJECTIVES

After studying this chapter you should be able to:

1. Identify the CICA's objectives of financial reporting for NPOs;
2. Recognize the three types of funds used by nonprofit organizations; and
3. Prepare the financial statements of NPOs using the CICA's reporting requirements.
4. Be conversant with the control over charities by the Canada Revenue Agency.

THE SCOPE OF THE CHAPTER

In Chapter Eighteen, the nature, control and accounting practices of nonbusiness organizations (NBOs) were examined. This chapter examines the accounting and financial reporting requirements of the Canadian Institute of Chartered Accountants for nonprofit organizations (NPOs) as well as the control over charities imposed by the reporting requirements of the Canada Revenue Agency.

As outlined in Chapter Nineteen, the accounting and reporting requirements for the government sector and governmental bodies are either specified by law or fall under the jurisdiction of the CICA's Public Sector Accounting Board (PSAB). Accounting for NPOs of the private sector is the responsibility of the AcSB of the CICA.

It should be noted that the PSAB has undertaken a review of the accounting requirements of governmental entities to determine which of these entities should follow the accounting requirements for the private sector contained in the CICA *Handbook*. It concluded that those governmental bodies obtaining the majority of their resources from user fees should account for their activities in the same manner as that applying to profit-oriented enterprises of the private sector (POEs). This also applies to NPOs of the private sector carrying

---

1 The CICA has followed the lead of the Financial Accounting Standards Board by adopting the term "not-for-profit organizations" in place of "nonprofit organizations". The term "not-for-profit" was, according to Robert N. Anthony ("The Nonprofit Accounting Mess", *Accounting Horizons*, June 1995) the term used by the US Internal Revenue Service to describe an activity that is carried on as a hobby, like keeping a stable of racehorses. He correctly points out that the term "nonprofit" is more widely recognized and used.

on similar activities because the introduction to sections 4400–50 of the CICA *Handbook* makes it clear that these accounting requirements only apply to those NPOs that provide social services and require a different accounting treatment from that applying to POEs.

THE CICA's REPORTING REQUIREMENTS FOR NPOs

The CICA's accounting requirements for NPOs were reportedly the result of **a compromise** between those persons who wanted the CICA to develop a separate set of accounting requirements for NPOs and those persons who felt that generally accepted accounting principles (GAAP) developed for enterprises of the private sector (i.e., the business sector) should be applied to NPOs. The compromise resulted in the present system, which **applies private enterprise accounting principles to NPOs** except where this is impracticable or where the reality of the differences between NPOs and business enterprises makes this impossible.

In developing their accounting requirements for NPOs, the CICA continued to recognize the need for fund accounting and to report on **a fund-by-fund basis**. However, it also allowed those NPOs that wished to do so to report on their activities along the lines of that applying to business enterprises in what is referred to as **the deferral method** (see later). The deferral method involves the deferment of contributions and their amortization as revenues over the period to which the contributions apply. It also requires the restatement of fund balances.

The CICA *Handbook* sections covering these accounting requirements consist of an introduction that specifies which sections of the *Handbook* apply to NPOs and six other sections. These six sections are (1) financial statement presentation (section 4400); (2) contributions — revenue recognition (section 4410); (3) contributions receivable (section 4420); (4) capital assets held by NPOs (section 4430); (5) collections held by NPOs (section 4440); and (6) reporting controlled and related entities by NPOs (section 4450). Reference to these various sections shall not be given unless specifically required.

The **stated objectives** of these reporting requirements **are to standardize financial reporting by NPOs and allow users to determine the cost at which the services of NPOs are provided**. The financial reports are, consequently, designed to present the financial position and results of operations of the NPO in a manner that would allow users to determine whether the NPO **could continue providing its services, achieving its objectives and meeting its obligations**. To achieve these objectives, the reporting requirements are designed to show the **total assets and liabilities and resources** controlled by the NPO.

The CICA's definition of an NPO is broad and far-reaching. NPOs are defined as entities, normally without transferable ownership interests, organized and operated exclusively for social, educational, professional, religious, health, charitable or other nonprofit purposes.

It is specifically required that a **mission statement** be given as an integral part of its financial statements. This should provide a clear and concise description of the NPO's purpose and its intended service to the community. This statement should also **provide details of its status in terms of income tax legislation**.

The **basic reporting philosophy follows that of the FASB which holds that the balance sheet is the major statement of the reporting system and that it is the change in the net assets (i.e., assets less liabilities) that provides the best indication of the results of operations.**[2]

This represented a major change in reporting philosophy. This is because the traditional NPO statement of financial position (i.e., the balance sheet) reflected the net debt of the reporting entity as comprising its current liabilities less its financial assets (i.e., cash, cash equivalents, and other monetary assets).

---

2 See, for example, Saleha B. Khumawala and Teresa P. Gordon, "Bridging the Credibility of GAAP: Individual Donors and the New Accounting Standards for Nonprofit Organizations", *Accounting Horizons*, September 1997, pp. 45–68.

The CICA's accounting recommendations now apply a **"net assets" or "change in net assets" approach to performance measurement** in which the performance of the NPO is to be measured by the change in net assets from one period to another. **Up to this time, the emphasis of the reporting system had been on the operating statement and on the inflows and outflows of resources.** As a result of this change, the fund balances of NPOs and changes in the fund balances are now referred to as **net assets** and **changes in net assets** respectively.

FINANCIAL REPORTING BY NPOs

As outlined above, NPOs can report on their activities using either the restricted fund method or the deferral method. These two methods are described hereunder:

The Restricted Fund Method

The restricted fund method of accounting for NPOs involves the reporting of details of the financial statement elements for the various funds in such a way that the organization reports its total general funds, one or more restricted funds, and (if applicable) an endowment fund (see later), together in a single statement. The financial statements for the individual funds are usually presented on a fund-by-fund basis in columnar form with the totals reflected in a total column. With this method, the equity of the individual funds can also be referred to as the net assets or as the fund balance.

The Deferral Method

The CICA allows the use of the deferral method by NPOs to account for contributions received (i.e., donations, grants, or other revenues) without having to account for them in separate restricted funds. It operates by setting aside funds received for restricted purposes as deferred contributions on the balance sheet as liabilities until required. Thereafter, the amounts required to meet the related expenses are transferred to the operating statement as revenues in the period in which the related expenses are incurred. The method can be used on its own or together with fund accounting.

As the reporting is not on an individual fund basis, revenues and expenses of the NPO may be reported as **a single column** for the NPO as a whole to give the total surplus or deficit from all operations of the NPO **along the lines of the income statement of business enterprises** of the private sector.[3] The assets and liabilities of the reporting entity are also reflected as a single column in aggregate form to give the "total net assets" of the NPO based on the formula of Assets – Liabilities = Net Assets. To provide details of the nature of the funds employed by the NPO, a statement of changes in net assets (i.e., the fund balances) must be presented giving details of those financed from unrestricted resources, those invested in capital assets, and resources restricted for specific purposes. Details of the operation of this method are outlined later.

---

[3] Despite repeated statements that this was not the case, the CICA's decision to allow NPOs to use the deferral method was clearly the application of a business approach to financial reporting by NPOs. This was made clear by the statement by the Canadian Association of University Business Officers (*CAUBO Financial Reporting Guide*, 1997) that, despite their recognition that the "bottom line" is not normally a measure of the degree of financial success of a university, it was believed that a business-type single reporting format (i.e., the deferral method) was required because many business people on the board of governors who would normally be considered relatively sophisticated users of financial information would have trouble understanding NPO financial statements prepared in a multi-column fund basis. This statement was made even though the multi-column fund accounting presentation is easily understood by those who are prepared to spend a few minutes grasping the difference between restricted and unrestricted funding.

It is important to note is that even though NPOs may follow the CICA's reporting requirements in preparing their financial statements using the deferral method, **this does not mean that they no longer use fund accounting**. The control function of fund accounting is so important that an NPO would probably need to continue to use a restricted fund accounting system in its books. In such cases, the deferral method would only be used by an NPO for external reporting purposes.

FUNDS RECOGNIZED BY SECTIONS 4400–50 OF THE CICA *HANDBOOK*

Only three types of funds are recognized by the CICA *Handbook* **for financial reporting purposes**. These are endowment funds, restricted funds, and the general or operating funds. **Endowment funds** are defined as those self-balancing sets of accounts that report the **accumulation of endowment contributions** that result in direct increases in net assets during the current period. The **restricted funds** account for assets or resources that are restricted to be used for a specific purpose.

An **operating fund** is used to report on the main activity of the NPO as well as all those other activities not required to be accounted for in separate funds. This would include operations financed from its normal operating funds that can be used **without restriction** (i.e., **unrestricted funds**) and those operations financed from funds that have been **specifically restricted** for that purpose (i.e., its **restricted funds**). Where the NPO uses funds that have been specifically created to account for its restricted resources, the operating fund is usually referred to as the **general fund**.

THE CICA's REPORTING REQUIREMENTS

NPOs report to their members, resource providers and other interested parties using financial statements that consist of **four statements**. These are the operating statement, a statement of financial position, a statement of changes in net assets, and a statement of cash flows. All of that are presented with comparative figures for the previous year. The names of these financial statements are for descriptive purposes only and NPOs may use whatever titles they think are appropriate.[4] The four statements must be presented using **full accrual accounting**.

To understand the reporting by NPOs and the reporting requirements of the CICA, the various financial statements and their elements are examined hereunder:

The Operating Statement

The operating statement of an NPO is the equivalent of the income statement for POEs. It is prepared on the basis of revenues less expenses to give the **excess of revenues over expenses** or **surplus from operations** for the period concerned. If, however, expenses exceed revenues, it would give an **excess of expenses over revenues** or **deficit from operations**.

Considerable latitude exists in the presentation of the operating statements of NPOs because there is no equivalent of section 1520 of the CICA *Handbook* that specifies what information must be presented in the income statements of profit-oriented enterprises. The CICA *Handbook* **merely suggests** that NPOs should disclose their revenues and expenses by object, function or program.[5] The **only specific reporting requirements** are that NPOs should include a mission statement and that those NPOs using fund accounting in their financial statements should provide a brief description of the purpose of each fund.

---

[4] CICA *Handbook*, section 4400.
[5] Paragraph 4400.31

☐ The Revenue Section

The **revenue section** includes all contributions towards operating costs, government operating grants, membership fees, any investment income, and any other receipts of a revenue nature. Government operating grants are specifically included in the definition of contributions.[6] Revenues are also deemed to include transfers from deferred contributions. These amounts must be brought into account at their gross, and not net, amounts.

Contributions are the life blood of NPOs. They are defined by the CICA as transfers of cash or other assets to an NPO as non-reciprocal (or one-way) settlement or cancellation of its liabilities by the government or any other person.[7] Contributions other than government operating grants are, in fact, donations to the NPO, but this term is no longer used by the CICA. However, no matter how they are defined, they represent the inflows of resources required to operate.

Where the contributions of cash are restricted in that they can only be used for specific purposes, like covering the amortization of capital assets, these contributions may be treated in two different ways depending upon the accounting system used by the NPO. These are (1) where the contributions are credited to a **separate restricted fund** or treated in a single fund as restricted resources using the restricted fund method; or (2) where the contributions are credited to a **deferred contributions account** and amortized to the operating statement over the period to which the contributions apply with the deferral method. Unrestricted contributions are treated as general revenues when received. The treatment of contributions to be used for the purchase of capital assets is covered later in a separate sub-section.

An NPO may also recognize contributions of **materials and services** provided a **fair value** for these items can be determined, and the contributed items represent those materials and services that the NPO would otherwise have had to purchase in order to carry out its normal operations. They are debited to the accounts concerned and credited as contributions received in the revenue section of the operating statement. **Fair value** is defined as the value that would be agreed upon in an arm's length transaction by willing parties who are under no compulsion to act. Each case must be examined on its own because it may not be possible to place a fair value on contributions like the services of volunteers. Contributions must also be disclosed by major source.

Membership fees received by NPOs are considered to be contributions if they are **not fees** for services to be rendered. It is up to the NPO to determine whether the fees are contributions and account for them consistently from year to year. Where the fees are partly for services rendered and partly as contributions, they should be apportioned accordingly.

Contributions also often take the form of **pledges** whereby supporters or members of the NPO pledge to pay a certain amount over to the NPO over a certain period. Some amounts are pledged for specific purposes, while others are merely contributions for the day-to-day operations of the NPO and are treated as unrestricted resources.

☐ The Expenses Section

The **expenses section** of the NPO's operating statement includes all those expenses incurred in delivering its services (like salaries, benefits, and administration expenses), the expenses of any related activities like research, as well as the amortization of capital assets. Financing expenses like the payment of interest on borrowed moneys would likewise be included as an expense incurred in delivering its services.

The CICA requires that the **capital assets of NPOs must be amortized** over their useful lives. This applies to all NPOs except those **small NPOs** whose average revenues for the current and preceding years are less than $500,000. If, however, the capital assets are held as

---

6 *Ibid.*, section 4410.
7 *Ibid.*

part of a **collection of works of art or historical treasures**, they are also excluded from this requirement. This exemption requires the satisfying of the three criteria that these collections must (1) be held for public exhibition, education or research; (2) have been preserved, cared for and protected; and (3) be subject to a policy that requires any proceeds from their sale to be re-invested in the collection or used for the care of the collection.

The CICA's justification for requiring the amortization of capital assets[8] is that all assets have limited useful lives. Recognizing the amortization of these assets over their useful lives allocates the cost of these assets to the periods over which services are provided so that the costs at which these services are provided can be determined. It is also considered necessary to establish whether the NPO has maintained its capital at the level required to operate.

For the purposes of section 4430 of the *Handbook*, **capital assets** are defined as consisting of both tangible and intangible assets held and used for the provision of services, administrative purposes, the production of goods, and the maintenance, repair and development or construction of other capital assets. They may have been acquired, constructed, or developed with the intention of being used on a continuing basis and are not intended for sale in the ordinary course of business. Where this applies, the treatment of capital assets is the same as that for POEs except that there is **no maximum amortization period**. As a result, capital assets having limited lives are required to be recorded at cost, and amortized on a rational and systematic manner over their useful lives.

Where the reporting NPO has financed capital assets out of current revenues (e.g., the purchase of library books by a university), these amounts must be reflected as a separate expense item in the operating statement.

☐ Contributions for the Purchase of Capital Assets

From time to time **capital assets or the money to purchase such assets** are contributed to NPOs. For example, someone may contribute $4,000 to an old age home to purchase a stereo system. As outlined earlier, the amount contributed represents **a restricted contribution** because it can only be used to purchase the stereo system. When acquired, the asset is recognized at its cost or fair value if the asset was donated.

The treatment of this contribution differs depending upon the nature of the capital asset. If the contribution relates to an asset that will not be amortized, then the amount is debited directly to the capital asset account and credited to the statement of changes in net assets (or statement of changes in fund balances using the restricted fund method). If, however, the amount relates to a depreciable asset, then the contribution must be debited to the capital asset account and credited to a deferred contribution account. As the asset is amortized, **an amount equal to the amortization expense** charged in the operating statement would be transferred from the deferred contribution account to the operating statement as revenue to offset the amortization expense.

These transfers from the deferred contributions account would continue until the asset has been completely amortized and the deferred contribution account has a nil balance. Where the asset is written off before it is fully amortized, the balance on the deferred contribution account would be transferred to the operating statement to offset the loss on the scrapping of the asset to which it applies. Such a situation is provided as Illustration 20–1.

The Statement of Financial Position or Balance Sheet

☐ Current Assets and Current Liabilities

The presentation and classification of assets and liabilities are the same as that applying to POEs. In this respect, section 1510 of the CICA *Handbook* applies equally to the **current**

---

[8] CICA *Handbook*, section 4430.

ILLUSTRATION 20–1
ACCOUNTING FOR CONTRIBUTIONS FOR THE ACQUISITION OF CAPITAL ASSETS

On February 1, 20X3, the Greytown Memorial Hall was notified that $8,000 had been left to it in terms of the Will of the late Gerry Townsend for the purchase of an entertainment system. The Memorial Hall had a financial year-end of December 31.
The cash was received on March 20, 20X3 and on April 1, 20X3, the Hall purchased an entertainment system that was expected to last for 10 years for $8,000. The journal entries recording the contribution and for the year ended December 31, 20X3 would have been as follows:

20X3
Mar. 20	Cash	8,000	
	Deferred Contribution for Entertainment System		8,000
	Receipt of cash		
Apr. 1	Entertainment System	8,000	
	Cash		8,000
	Purchase of entertainment system		
Dec. 31	Amortization Expense — Entertainment System	600	
	Accumulated Amortization — Entertainment System		600
	Amortization of $8,000/10 × 9/12		
Dec. 31	Revenue Contribution	600	
	Deferred Contribution for Entertainment System		600
	Transfer of contribution to cover annual amortization charges on Entertainment System		

The transfers from the deferred contribution account would continue until the entertainment system was fully amortized. At that time, the accumulated amortization would amount to $8,000, leaving the entertainment centre with a nil balance.

assets and current liabilities of NPOs and the disclosure requirements for capital assets differ little from that applying to POEs: for example, the disclosure of the amounts and terms of any interfund loans outstanding at the reporting date.

☐ Capital Assets

Each major category of **capital assets** must be disclosed at cost less accumulated amortization and any write-downs. The amortization method used and the rate at which the assets are being amortized must be disclosed. Any donated or contributed capital assets must be brought into account at their fair value at the date received and treated as outlined above. In those cases where the fair value cannot be reasonably determined, the asset may be brought into account at a nominal value.

☐ Longterm Liabilities

Longterm liabilities are, similarly, presented and disclosed in exactly the same manner as those of POEs. Those NPOs not using restricted funds to account for restricted contributions must list and describe these contributions as deferred contributions.

☐ Deferred Contributions

Contributions of cash towards meeting the operating expenses, research, or the purchase of capital assets are common with NPOs. They are often made with the specific requirement that they can only be used for some or other purpose. Where this occurs and the NPO **does not use restricted funds** to account for these contributions, they must be treated as deferred contributions using the **deferral method** of accounting. Where contributions are received and credited to restricted funds, the need to defer these contributions does not arise because they are treated as restricted resources using the **restricted fund method**.

Section 4420 of the CICA *Handbook* also requires that NPOs must recognize **contributions receivable** as assets when the amounts to be received can be reasonably estimated and collection is reasonably assured. As a result, **pledges** must be recognized when they are made and either treated as restricted resources or treated as deferred contributions until received. Once the conditions under which the pledges were made have been satisfied, they are recognized as revenues in the operating statement.

The accounting entries to record deferred contributions in the form of pledges are outlined below. For example, assume that $300,000 was pledged over four years by the members of a church congregation to pay the salary of an assistant minister and, during the year, persons who had pledged $2,000 reneged on their pledges. In such a case the entries in the first year would be as follows:

On Recognition of the Deferred Contribution:

Accounts Receivable/Pledges Receivable	300,000	
Deferred Contributions		300,000
Pledges for salary of assistant minister		

On Receipt of the Contributions in Cash and Recognition in Operating Statement:

Cash	73,000	
Deferred Contributions	2,000	
Accounts Receivable/Pledges Receivable		75,000
Receipt of first year's pledges of $75,000 less amounts of $2,000 from those who reneged on their pledges		
Deferred Contributions (on Balance Sheet)	73,000	
Amortization of Deferred Contributions (Revenues)		73,000
Transfer of pledges for salary of assistant minister		

☐ The Fund Balance of the NPO

Traditionally, the equity of an NPO has been the fund balance. The method of presentation of the fund balance is to start with the opening balance at the beginning of the year, and to add to this the surplus (or deduct the deficit) from operations. Any capital assets contributed to the NPO are debited to capital assets and credited as increases in the fund balance. Any interfund transfers are also either added or deducted from the fund balance, as the case may be. An example of the presentation for a restricted fund would be as follows:

Fund Balance:

Surplus from Operations for Year		$37,564
Balance at January 1, 20X4	1,522	
Sale of Capital Assets	465	
	1,967	
Less: Transfer to Equipment Fund	2,000	(33)
Balance at December 31, 20X5		$37,531

This presentation is still used by small and uncomplicated NPOs (see page 486).

Interfund transfers must be reflected as changes in the fund balance, giving full details of the need for such transfers.[9] Even though there may be numerous transfers between funds during a reporting period, they are normally aggregated and shown as a single item for

---

[9] Paragraph 4400.13 of the CICA *Handbook* requires that the amount and purpose of interfund transfers during the reporting period be disclosed. The explanatory material (para. 4400.16) suggests that judgment should be exercised to determine the proper level of disclosure of these interfund transfers. However, as the financial position of NPOs can so easily be manipulated and misrepresented through transfers from one fund to another, there should be full disclosure of the reasons for the transfers and the authority on which they were made.

reporting purposes provided that full details of the need for such transfers are given in the notes to the financial statements. Interfund transfers are illustrated below in journal entry form using an example covering the transfer of equipment costing $40,000 from a restricted equipment fund to the operating fund:

In the Equipment Fund:

Interfund Transfers — Operating Fund	40,000	
Equipment		40,000
Transfer equipment consisting of ... to Operating Fund		

In the Operating Fund:

Equipment	40,000	
Interfund Transfers — Equipment Fund		40,000

Where the NPO is more complicated and uses either the restricted fund method or the deferral method, the presentation of the fund balance is considerably more complex. This is because with the net assets approach, the fund balance now reflects the net assets of the NPO as a residual balance based on the formula of Assets – Liabilities = Net Assets (where Net Assets = Fund Balance). The CICA does, however, recognize the traditional form of presentation and allows the term "fund balance" to be used with the restricted fund method.[10]

The Statement of Changes in Fund Balances (or Net Assets)

This statement is used to provide details of the changes in the fund balances or net assets of the individual funds for the period covered by the financial statements using both the restricted fund and deferral methods. **The purpose of the statement is to give the total net assets invested in capital assets, as well as those net assets that are subject to restrictions as endowments and any other restricted net assets.** This statement may be, and is often, combined with the statement of operations.

The presentation details the changes in the amounts invested in net assets, distinguishing between those that are restricted and those that are not, as well as the net assets at the beginning of the year (i.e., the fund balances), the excess of revenues over expenditures (i.e., the surplus or deficit) from operations for the year, any internally imposed restrictions, and the balance at the end of the year. If the reporting is not on an individual fund basis, this statement provides information on the changes in the individual fund balances relating to restricted and unrestricted funds that would, otherwise, not be presented to interested parties.

The Statement of Cash Flows

The statement of cash flows is prepared for the NPO as a whole. It is presented in basically the same form as that with POEs. In this respect, it must be presented in a manner that distinguishes at least between the cash from operations and the components of cash flows from financing and investing activities. It must also be reconciled with the balances of cash and term deposits appearing on the statement of financial position in the normal manner.

---

[10] CICA *Handbook*, paragraph 4400.42.

THE FINANCIAL STATEMENTS

The CICA's Financial Statement Requirements

The CICA's requirements for the financial statements of NPOs are based on the **manner in which the NPOs account for their contributions**. If they use the **restricted fund method**, then they must report on the basis of the various restricted funds used by the NPO. However, the use of **a deferral method** depends on the method selected. In effect, there are three ways an NPO can report on its operations and activities.

The Restricted Fund Method

With the **restricted fund method**, (1) the revenues and expenses, and (2) the assets, liabilities and fund balances must be disclosed in columnar form reflecting details of the individual funds and also the total amounts. The balance for each fund and any changes thereto during the reporting period must also be shown. The operating statement should be presented in a manner that shows whether the fund operated at a surplus or a deficit (i.e., an excess of revenues over expenses or excess expenses over revenues). The results of operations must be reflected in a reconciliation of the fund balance in the **statement of changes in fund balances**. This reconciliation includes interfund transfers. It can take the form of a continuation of the operating statement or be given as a separate statement. The suggested format of this reconciliation for each fund is:

Fund Balance at Beginning of Year	$x,xxx,xxx
Surplus (or Deficit) from Operations	xxx,xxx
Interfund Transfers	xxx,xxx
Fund Balance at End of Year	$x,xxx,xxx

A distinction must be made on the balance sheet between restricted and unrestricted fund balances. Full details of the restrictions must, of course, be provided. Examples of how the fund balances should be reflected on the balance sheet using the restricted fund method for complex NPOs using multiple funds are provided later.

The Deferral Methods

There are **two deferral methods**. First, a full deferral method that **completely dispenses with accounting for individual funds,** could be used. All activities are presented in **a single set of financial statements** as if it were a single entity.[11] As outlined earlier, reporting is based on the equation of assets – liabilities = net assets in which the term "net assets" replaces the fund balance. It is, however, specifically required that changes in the net assets during the year must be disclosed, detailing those that are restricted and those that are unrestricted.

The net assets section of the statement of financial position (i.e., the balance sheet) using the deferral method would be presented for each of its internal funds under the headings of net assets restricted for endowment purposes, net assets internally restricted for other purposes (detailed), and unrestricted net assets to give total net assets. The columns under each heading would be further detailed as reflected in the following presentation, after replacing the details under Net Assets with:

---

[11] This method is popular with hospitals and similar health care facilities. Where these facilities have "foundations" to receive donations for development, research or patient care, the resources of the foundation are not included as part of the assets of the health care facility on the questionable grounds that they represent completely different entities.

Statement of Changes in Net assets
for the Year Ended December 20X2

Net Assets	Total	Invested in Capital Assets	Restricted for ...	Restricted for ...	Unrestricted
Balance, beginning of year	xxxxx	xxxx	xxxx	xxxxx	xxxx
Excess (deficiency) of revenues over expenses	xxxxx	xxxxx	xxxxx	xxxx	xxxxx
Endowment contributions	xxxxx	xxxx	xxxxx	xxx	xxxxx
Investment in capital assets	xxxxx	xxxxx	xxx	xxxx	xxxxx
Internally imposed restriction	xxxxx	xxx	xxxxx	xxxxx	xxxxx
Balance, end of year	$xxxxx	$xxxxx	$xxxxx	$xxxxx	$xxxxx

Second, the **deferral method may be used in conjunction with the restricted fund method**. In these cases, there is a fund balance for each and every fund that should be presented in a manner similar to that used for the restricted fund method but using the same details as for the deferral method.

The Financial Statements of Small, Uncomplicated NPOs

Notwithstanding the detailed reporting requirements of NPOs given above, many NPOs like charities, sporting associations, interest clubs (e.g., chess and bridge playing clubs), and associations of persons (e.g., the New Brunswick Society of Professional Photographers) are relatively small, and accounting for their activities is straightforward. All that is required is that these NPOs account for the various items in accordance with the CICA *Handbook* using a statement of financial position (or balance sheet), an operating statement, and a statement of cash flows for each fund. These NPOs would reflect their fund balance using traditional presentation (given on page 483).

The Financial Statements of Larger and More Complex NPOs

Large NPOs like universities are complex organizations and, consequently, their financial statements are also more complicated. An example of such a situation is provided by Illustration 20–2 that presents the operating statement and balance sheet of an NPO that accounts for its activities through three restricted funds (i.e., using the restricted fund method). This shows the individual Fund Balances at the end of the year plus the adjustments to reflect the amounts invested in Capital Assets at December 31, 20X3. In all other respects, these financial statements are self-explanatory.

If the reporting had been by an NPO reporting on **the basis of separate funds using the deferral method**, the reporting would have differed from that presented in Illustration 20–2 in two ways. First, the NPO would have accounted for some, if not all, of its activities through funds that were used to separate activities for control and administrative convenience. Some of the funds would, therefore, have been used to account for items like its capital assets, capital expenditures, and the like. Second, the liabilities side of the balance sheet would have reflected the various **deferred contributions accounts** to keep track of those contributions or other resources that were subject to restrictions that have been deferred.

An example of the operating statement and balance sheet of NPO **reporting on the basis of separate funds using the deferral method** is presented in Illustration 20–3. Here, the NPO operates through three funds. The contributions for its normal operations have been deferred in the operating and capital assets funds. As with the previous illustration, the capital assets appearing on the balance sheet of $17,652 have been reduced by the mortgage loans used

ILLUSTRATION 20-2

THE OPERATING STATEMENT AND BALANCE SHEET OF AN NPO CONSISTING OF THREE FUNDS THAT REPORTS ON THE INDIVIDUAL FUND BASIS USING THE RESTRICTED FUND METHOD

The following financial statements of the Lakeview Retraining Centre for the year ended December 31, 20X3 are presented in abbreviated and summary form to illustrate the application of reporting on an individual fund basis using the restricted fund method:

	Operating Fund	Restricted Fund	Endowment Fund	Total
Operating Statement for 20X3		000s		
Revenues				
Government Grant	$ 12,000	$ 3,000	—	$15,000
Contributions	1,553	245	—	1,798
Investment Income	—	21	$ 650	671
	$ 13,553	$ 3,266	$ 650	$17,469
Less Expenses				
Administration	$ 14,823	$ 161	$ 7	$14,991
Amortization of Capital Assets	1,240	17	—	1,257
	$ 16,063	$ 178	$ 7	$16,248
Surplus/(Deficit) for Year	$ (2,510)	$ 3,088	$ 643	$ 1,221
Fund Balances at January 1, 20X3	4,226	2,139	10,236	16,601
Interfund Transfers	3,140	(2,500)	(640)	—
Endowment Fund Contributions	—	—	51	51
Fund Balance at December 31, 20X3 — Note 1	$ 4,856	$ 2,727	$10,290	$17,873
Balance Sheet at December 31, 20X3				
Current Assets				
Cash and Term Deposits	$ 129	$ 421	$ 1,128	$ 1,678
Accounts Receivable	431	—	—	431
Materials on Hand	21	—	—	21
Investments	—	2,221	9,162	11,383
Capital Assets (less Accumulated Amortization)	5,011	85	—	5,096
	$ 5,592	$ 2,727	$10,290	$18,609
Current Liabilities	$ 351	—	—	$ 351
Mortgage Loan	385	—	—	385
Fund Balances				
Invested in Capital Assets — Note 2	4,626	—	—	4,626
Restricted Funds	—	$ 2,727	$10,290	13,017
Unrestricted Funds	230	—	—	230
	$ 5,592	$ 2,727	$10,290	$18,609

Notes:

[1] The Fund Balance of $4,856,000 includes the amounts invested in Capital Assets of $4,626,000 and the Unrestricted Funds of $230,000 (i.e., $4,626,000 + $230,000 = $4,856,000).

[2] The Amount Invested in Capital Assets of $4,626,000 does not agree with the Capital Assets less Amortization of $5,011,000 given in the assets section of the balance sheet because it has been reduced by the mortgage loan of $385,000 used to purchase some of these assets (i.e., $5,011,000 − $385,000 = $4,626,000).

to finance them. The balances on the deferred contributions accounts are being amortized as required. The individual fund balances are disclosed, and in other respects, it is similar to the position presented in Illustration 20–2. Reporting in the multiple column method outlined in Illustration 20–3 gives financial statements for an NPO that reflect its total resources.

ILLUSTRATION 20–3
THE OPERATING STATEMENT AND BALANCE SHEET OF AN NPO CONSISTING OF THREE FUNDS
THAT REPORTS ON THE INDIVIDUAL FUND BASIS USING THE DEFERRAL METHOD

The following financial statements of the Brantford Quality Control Centre for the year ended December 31, 20X1 are presented in abbreviated and summary form to illustrate the application of reporting on an individual fund basis using the deferral method:

	Operating Fund	Capital Assets Fund	Endowment Fund	Total
Operating Statement for 20X1		— 000s —		
Revenues				
Government Grant	$17,000	$10,000	$ 78	$27,078
Amortization of Deferred Contributions	2,528	4,245	—	6,773
Investment Income	—	—	2	2
	$19,528	$14,245	$ 80	$33,853
Less Expenses				
Administration	$17,440	$ 316	$ 7	$17,763
Amortization of Capital Assets	—	14,542	—	14,542
	$17,440	$14,858	$ 7	$32,305
Surplus/(Deficit) for Year	$ 2,088	$ (613)	$ 73	$ 1,548
Fund Balances, Beginning of Year	7,022	24,136	87	31,245
Interfund Transfers	(1,556)	1,622	(66)	—
Fund Balances, End of Year	$ 7,554	$25,145	$ 94	$32,793
Balance Sheet at December 31, 20X1				
Current Assets				
Cash and Term Deposits	$ 311	$ 272	$ 3	$ 586
Accounts Receivable	5,998	—	—	5,998
Materials on Hand	1,245	—	—	1,245
Investments	—	7,221	91	7,312
Capital Assets	—	17,652	—	17,652
	$ 7,554	$25,145	$ 94	$32,793
Current Liabilities	$ 820	—	—	$ 820
Deferred Contributions (detailed as required):	5,600	$ 6,402	—	12,002
Mortgage Loans	—	8,907	—	8,907
Net Assets:				
Invested in Capital Assets — see Note below	—	8,745	—	8,745
Externally Restricted Funds	—	—	$ 94	94
Unrestricted Funds	1,134	1,091	—	2,225
	$ 7,554	$25,145	$ 94	$32,793

Note: The Amount invested in capital assets of $8,745 is the amount of Capital Assets (less Accumulated Amortization) of $17,652 less the Mortgage Loan used to finance some of these Capital Assets of $8,907 (i.e., $17,652 – $8,907 = $8,745).

Where the deferral method is used on its own without any reference to individual funds, the operating statement consists of a single column giving the surplus or deficit from operations for the NPO as a whole. As outlined earlier, the balance sheet is prepared on the basis of Assets – Liabilities = Net assets with a detailed Statement of Changes in Net Assets. An illustration of reporting in this manner is provided by Illustration 20–4.

ILLUSTRATION 20–4
THE OPERATING STATEMENT AND BALANCE SHEET OF AN NPO WITH THREE FUNDS THAT
REPORTS USING A SINGLE COLUMN DEFERRAL METHOD

The following financial statements of the Lakeview Retirement Homes for the year ended December 31, 20X2 are presented to illustrate the single column deferral method:

Operating Statement for 20X2 (000s)

Revenues:

Rentals and Accommodation Charges		$11,543
Government Grant		10,000
Amortization of Deferred Contributions		5,339
		$26,882

Less Expenses

Administration	14,435	
Amortization of Capital Assets	11,224	25,659
Surplus for Year		$ 1,223

Balance Sheet at December 31, 20X2

Current Assets

Cash and Term Deposits		$ 3,493
Accounts Receivable		5,178
Capital Assets (less Accumulated Amortization)		15,478
		$24,149
Current Liabilities		$ 1,221
Deferred Contributions (detailed as required)		4,600
Mortgage Loans		9,884

Net Assets:

Unrestricted	2,826	
Investments in Capital Assets — see Note	5,594	
Endowments	24	8,444
		$24,149

Statement of Changes in Net assets for the Year Ended December 20X2

	Total (000s)	Unrestricted (000s)	Invested in Capital Assets (000s)	Endowments (000s)
Opening Balance	$ 7,221	$ 2,744	$ 4,457	$ 20
Surplus from Operations	1,223	1,223	—	—
Changes During Year	—	(1,141)	1,137	4
Closing Balance	$ 8,444	$ 2,826	$ 5,594	$ 24

Note: The figure for Net Assets invested in Capital Assets of $5,594,000 is the amount reflected as Capital Assets on the Balance Sheet of $15,478,000 less the Mortgage Loans of $9,884,000 (i.e., $15,478,000 – $9,884,000 = $5,594,000).

Reporting on the Basis of Groups (or Families) of Funds

Complex NPOs often account for their activities through a considerable number of funds. As a result, funds that are similar are reported in aggregate form as "families of funds" in exactly the same way as that presented in Illustrations 20–2 and 20–3. The operating statement and balance sheet would present the totals of, say, all its restricted funds and its endowment funds in aggregate form. Details of the individual funds must, of course, be reflected in the notes to the financial statements.

REPORTING CONTROLLED AND RELATED ENTITIES

Section 4450 of the CICA *Handbook* details the accounting requirements for NPOs having control or joint control over, or being able to exert significant influence over, other entities. These entities can be other NPOs, joint ventures or POEs.

The reporting of controlled and related entities depends upon whether control or significant influence exists and whether the reporting NPO has an economic interest in another entity.

To Which Entities Do These Requirements Apply?

The requirements of section 4450 of the CICA *Handbook* apply to all controlled entities, joint ventures in which the reporting NPO has an interest, and all those other entities over which the reporting NPO can exert significant influence. This applies whether they are NPOs or profit-oriented enterprises.

ADDITIONAL REPORTING REQUIREMENTS

Where Control over Another NPO Exists

Control is defined, as with POEs, as the continuing power to determine the strategic operating and financing policies of an entity without the co-operation of others. However, as there are no defined ownership interests with NPOs, control is presumed to exist when the NPO has the ability to appoint the majority of members to the board of directors. When two NPOs have the same board of directors, control is presumed to exist unless there is evidence to the contrary. Dependence by one entity on another **for funding** may also indicate that control exists.

Where control over another entity exists, considerable latitude in reporting is allowed. NPOs controlling another NPO may account for them in three different ways.[12] First, the controlled NPO may be consolidated with that of the controlling NPO along the lines provided for the consolidation of financial statements of POEs of the private sector. Even though certain aspects of consolidations do not apply to NPOs, the operating statement and balance sheet can be easily aggregated with those of the controlling NPO.

Second, the total assets, liabilities, net assets (i.e., equity), revenues and expenses of the controlled entity must be disclosed if the entity is not consolidated. Here, full details of the restrictions applying to the major categories of resources of the controlled NPO must be given, as well as any significant differences in its accounting policies. And, third, the reporting entity need not consolidate or disclose the assets, etc., of a **group of controlled NPOs** if they are individually immaterial and the reporting NPO discloses why consolidation or the detailed disclosure of the assets, etc., has not been carried out.

Where the Reporting NPO Is a Party to a Joint Venture

Joint control of an economic activity is similarly defined as the contractually agreed sharing of the continuing power to determine its strategic operating and financing policies. It applies to joint ventures consisting of associations of persons in which no single party controls the entity.

Where joint control exists, the interests of the reporting entity in each joint venture must be accounted for by using either proportionate consolidation or the equity method of accounting for longterm investments. The policy of accounting for joint ventures must be disclosed together with details of its relationship with the joint venture. In those cases where the equity

---

12 CICA *Handbook*, section 4450.

method is used, details of the total assets, liabilities, and net assets or shareholders' equity must be disclosed together with its revenues, expenses and cash flows for the period covered by the financial statements. It is also required to draw attention to any significant differences in accounting policies followed by the joint venture.

Where Significant Influence Exists

Significant influence is the ability to affect the strategic operating and financing policies of an entity. This applies where control is absent but, because of some factor or another, the entity can still influence the activities and operations of another entity.

The exercising of significant influence over another NPO requires that the relationship between the reporting entity and the significantly influenced entity must be disclosed, together with details of the significantly influenced NPO's purpose, intended community service, its income tax status and legal form. The nature and extent of the reporting NPO's economic interest in the significantly influenced NPO must also be given.

The Existence of Economic Interest

An NPO is considered to have an **economic interest** in another entity if the other entity holds resources for the reporting entity or if it is responsible for the liabilities of that entity. An economic interest may be assumed if the other entity solicits resources for the reporting entity or receives substantial resources from it. Similarly, such an interest exists if the other organization performs certain operations that assist, facilitate, or allow the reporting entity to achieve its objectives.

In those cases where an NPO has an economic interest in another entity, the nature and extent of this interest must be disclosed.

The Position with Profit-Oriented Enterprises

Controlled POEs must be either consolidated or accounted for using the equity method. Disclosure requirements are the same as those applying to controlled NPOs. Those NPOs over which significant influence is exercisable must be accounted for using the equity method in exactly the same manner as that applying to POEs of the private sector.

ADDITIONAL DISCLOSURES

The CICA's reporting requirements also require the following of the general reporting standards (section 1500) and the disclosure of accounting policies, any capital commitments, contingencies, subsequent events, foreign currency translation, etc.

THE CONTROL OVER CHARITIES BY THE CANADA REVENUE AGENCY

There is virtually no control over the activities and operations of NPOs in Canada. This is because the only control over NPOs are those that apply to public institutions that are required to report to their controlling government ministries or departments, and those that apply to registered charities in terms of the federal *Income Tax Act* (i.e., those that are allowed to issue tax deductible receipts for donations). Other NPOs and unregistered charities are only responsible to their members.

The reporting requirements of the Canada Revenue Agency (CRA) specify that every registered charity is required to file a copy of their financial statements and a completed Form T3010 with the CRA every year. If they do not do so, they could lose their registered status and the right to issue tax deductible receipts for donations. Charities have the right to specify that their financial statements remain confidential, but the information provided in Form T3010 is available to the general public. Other NPOs are required to complete another form, but these forms are not available for public scrutiny.

The financial statements filed by charities must consist of, at least, a statement of receipts and disbursements and a statement of assets and liabilities. If their gross revenues from all sources is more than $250,000 then it is recommended that they file audited financial statements. If they have not been audited, they must be signed by the charity's treasurer.

Form T3010 requires extensive financial disclosures. Where a charity's gross revenues from all sources exceeds $30,000, it must detail the type of activity for which it received fees and disclose the net revenue from these sources. It must also show the amounts spent on charitable programs, gifts to qualified donees (e.g., other charities), general administration, fund-raising, political advocacy activities (i.e., lobbying activities), any other disbursements, and any amounts that the charity has been allowed to accumulate for special purposes. This total amount must then be used to determine compliance with what is referred to as the "**80 percent rule**".

The "80 percent rule" or disbursement quota requires that the charity must detail the amounts spent in order to determine whether it has spent at least 80% of the amounts for which it issued tax-deductible receipts on its charitable activities. If, on assessment, the charity has spent more than the required 80%, the excess can be carried forward to be offset against any shortfall in the future. In order to comply with this requirement, the statement of receipts and disbursements must detail the revenues for which tax deductible receipts were issued, the total gifts and government grants received, and all other amounts according to their nature (e.g., membership fees, interest and dividends, any net realized capital gains, and any other income).

Charities must also explain how they have carried out their charitable services in sufficient detail to give readers a good understanding of what they actually did and whether their programs were carried on locally or outside Canada. They must also give the approximate percentage of its resources spent on its four most important fields of activity. If the charity carried on any political activities as an advocacy group or non-partisan interest group, they must provide details of these activities and the extent of gifts to qualified donees (i.e., other NPOs) to assist the recipient organization in carrying on its political activities.

Details of their fund-raising activities **that do not qualify as expenses for the "80 percent rule"** are also required. In this respect, they must disclose whether they used professional fund-raisers and the basis on which these fund-raisers were retained, and the total amounts paid to them. Details of their main fund-raising activity must be provided together with details on the number of times the activity was carried out, how many people were involved in the activity, and the net proceeds from the fund-raising activity. It must also disclose details of any income or assets transferred to its founders, directors/trustees, employees, or members and whether the relationship between the charities and these persons were at arm's length. And, finally, a charity must also disclose the number of persons in paid positions and the amounts paid to its five "most highly compensated managers" during the year.

Regrettably, the threat of losing their income tax exemption status has only been partially successful in monitoring the activities of charities because of staffing shortages and the low revenue priority attached to this area. Where the audit procedure of the CRA has been used to determine compliance with its rules and regulations, this has had little effect because the audit findings are not made public. Of the greatest concern is that a 1996 MP's Report[13] painted a disturbing picture of a widespread lack of accountability by registered charities

---

[13] *Canada's Charities: A Need for Reform*, by Mr. John Bryden, the Honourable Member of Parliament for Hamilton-Wentworth, 1996.

because the information contained in Form T3010 tended to be incomplete. This Report also concluded that the extent of these omissions suggested that they were deliberately made.

In an attempt to rectify this position, the federal Minister of Finance, Mr. Ralph Goodale, stated, in the delivery of the federal budget on March 23, 2004, that considerable amendments to the *Income Tax Act* were to be made to ensure that charities in Canada are properly controlled. These amendments would include the imposition of fines for the non-disclosure of information, the suspension of tax-free status on donations for non-compliance with the requirements, etc., and would apply to charities from March 22, 2005.

THE PERCEIVED SHORTCOMINGS OF THE CICA's REPORTING REQUIREMENTS

There are a number of perceived shortcomings in the CICA's reporting requirements. These are:

1. The major shortcoming is that they represent an attempt to apply the accounting principles developed over many years for profit-oriented enterprises of the private sector for the efficient operation of capital markets, to NPOs without any recognition of the differences in economic activity. Any suggestion of this was vehemently denied by the CICA, but it is **an undeniable fact** that the economic activity of NPOs differs considerably from that of POEs and, consequently, to many accountants, the reporting criteria should be different. The same accounting requirements also apply to the multi-million dollar trading-type enterprises distributing electric power (like Ontario's Hydro One or the B.C. Power Corporation) and those organizations involved with social activities like the distribution of food parcels to the poor.

2. The reporting requirements are largely based on those of the FASB which adapted its decision usefulness approach to financial reporting by POEs to apply to NPOs.[14] This approach relegates accountability, a reporting objective of considerable importance to NPOs, to a relatively minor role.

3. The "net assets" approach to the statement of financial position of NPOs is nothing more than the application of Hick's {1939}[15] concept of income as measured by the change in wealth as measured by the change in asset values from one period to another (see Chapter Three). The adoption of this approach raises the question of whether the emphasis on the "bottom line", which is merely an indication of the short-term operational effectiveness in the three-stage sequence of measuring NPO performance, is now to be considered a measure of NPO performance.

4. There is no specification of what type of information should be provided in the operating statements of NPOs along the lines of section 1520 of the CICA *Handbook* for business enterprises. In view of the lack of control over NPOs in Canada, one would have thought that the CICA would have required these organizations to, at least, provide details of the amounts spent on their main activities, the salaries paid to their, say, five most highly paid employees, the amounts spent on fund raising, and the overall effectiveness of their programs (i.e., the portion of every dollar received spent on satisfying their main objective). The fact that these are required by the Canada Revenue Agency for charities is not sufficient.

---

[14] In its *Statement of Financial Accounting Concepts No. 4: Objectives of Financial Reporting by Nonbusiness Organizations* (1980).

[15] John R. Hicks, *Value and Capital*, Oxford: Clarendon Press, 1939.

SUMMARY

This chapter examines, summarizes and presents the CICA's reporting requirements for NPOs. It commences with an examination of fund accounting and the deferral method of accounting for NPOs. It then outlines the various types of funds used by NPOs. It explains that there are three groups of funds; operating (or general) funds to account for the main activity of the NPO, proprietary or trading funds to account for those activities of NPOs that are similar to those carried on by POEs, and the fiduciary or trust funds to account for amounts received for specific purposes. The nature and operation of these various funds are outlined and explained.

The chapter then examines the CICA's accounting requirements for revenues, expenses, assets, liabilities and the fund balances of NPOs. It then covers the manner in which NPOs are required to report on their operations and activities. It explains that financial reporting by NPOs is based on the way in which contributions and other resources are treated by the reporting NPO. This may follow either the restricted fund or deferral method. With the restricted fund method, the reporting is on the basis of the restrictions placed on the resources of the NPO. The emphasis of the deferral method is on deferred contributions and how they have been used. Reporting using the deferral method may be on all funds or on the basis of total assets and liabilities plus details of the resources invested in net assets and any restrictions on resources.

It also outlines the reporting for controlled entities, interests in joint ventures, and those entities over which significant influence can be exercised. Even though considerable flexibility exists, the reporting for these interests largely follows that applying to profit-oriented enterprises of the private sector.

The chapter concludes with an examination of the reporting requirements of the Canada Revenue Agency for registered charities. Other than those applying to public institutions, these represent the only control over NPOs in Canada.

REVIEW QUESTIONS

1. What information **about** an NPO is required to be disclosed in the financial statements of NPOs?
2. What is the CICA's basic reporting philosophy for NPOs?
3. Must fund accounting be used by NPOs in terms of the CICA's reporting requirements for these organizations?
4. Describe the deferral method of accounting for the contributions received by NPOs.
5. What is the purpose of the operating fund?
6. What is the purpose of an endowment fund? A restricted fund?
7. How are contributions or donations of materials and services treated?
8. What reporting requirements apply to the capital assets of NPOs? What exemptions are available?
9. How are pledges receivable treated by NPOs? Why are they treated in this way?
10. Where are interfund transfers reflected in the financial statements of NPOs?
11. What is meant by the phrase "reporting on the basis of groups of funds"?
12. What are the accounting requirements for controlled NPOs? Joint ventures? Entities over which significant influence can be exercised?
13. Do the same reporting requirements apply to both controlled NPOs and profit-oriented enterprises?
14. To what category of NPOs do the reporting requirements of the Canada Revenue Agency apply? What do they require?
15. Explain what is meant by the "80% rule".
16. What are the perceived shortcomings of the CICA's reporting requirements for NPOs?

CASES

CASE 20–1 **The Mountainview Entertainment Park**

Even though the City of Mountainview was precluded from operating an entertainment park by provincial law, it investigated the possibility of transferring the City Zoological Park to an entertainment park to be situated on land purchased by the City two years before. The reason for doing so was because the City zoo was currently operating at a loss of about $600,000 a year and the buildings occupied by it were in need of extensive repairs. Unless the zoo could be transferred or taken over, the City would probably have to close it down.

The proposed entertainment park would operate as a zoological park interspaced with various entertainment facilities, which could remain open during the entire year as the area enjoyed a relatively mild climate. To attract visitors, it would provide entertainment in the form of waterslides and "white water" rafting, performing dolphin and other animal shows, skill-related entertainment, an open-air theatre, and a number of good restaurants. Some of these facilities would be provided and run by the Park itself while others would be run on a concessionary basis. To establish the park, it would be prepared to offer considerable incentives to outside interests, like the operators of theme parks in the USA, if they were prepared to participate in the venture.

A firm of marketing consultants had carried a feasibility study of the project and had come up with the conclusion that such an entertainment park would be a viable proposition, provided that:

(a) It continued to be a zoological park because the majority of the visitors to the zoo over the past five years had been families with young children;

(b) It catered for the needs of the balance of the residents of the city by providing recreational facilities; and

(c) It was easily accessible to the public.

The proposed entertainment park would be run as a nonprofit organization formed for that specific purpose. In terms of the proposal, the City would donate the animals and zoological equipment to the park, sell it the land at cost, and stand security for the additional $10-million required to establish the park, which was to be repaid over a period of 20 years.

The Faculty of Biology and Veterinary Science of the University of Western Canada, situated in Mountainview, would continue to assist with the care of the animals, while the Department of Dramatic Arts would perform a series of plays in the open-air theatre during the summer months. Adequate parking facilities would also be provided, and the City undertook to extend municipal transport to the park.

Reaction of the provincial government and the business community to the proposal were extremely positive and it was not long before the proposal was approved. By the time the Mountainview Entertainment Park had been formed, it had received a number of firm offers from fast-food restaurants, the local business community and others, including the operator of a theme park in California, to participate in the venture.

Following negotiations with the various parties, the entertainment park was scheduled to open on May 1 of the following year. It was to operate essentially as a zoological park with a petting zoo as well as having individual pens for dangerous animals. An entrance fee would be charged. Performing dolphins and other animal shows were also subject to an entrance charge and provided in partnership with a California theme park. All water-related entertainment and the parking facilities were to be provided at a fee sufficient to cover their costs and to provide a profit sufficient to cover the other entertainment provided by the park, like the theatre performances, at no charge. Restaurants were to be operated on a concessionary basis.

REQUIRED

As consultant to the Mountainview Entertainment Park, you are to advise its board of directors on the various funds and accounting procedures that would have to be implemented to properly account for its various activities.

CASE 20–2

The Atlantic Retirement Village

In response to the need to provide housing for senior citizens, representatives of the three major Christian churches in Atlantic Canada had met and agreed to sponsor the building of the Atlantic Retirement Village situated in Fairfax in two phases. Phase One was to be built immediately and run as a nonprofit organization by the Atlantic Christian Foundation. It would be inter-denominational and open to all. Phase Two would be built when the Foundation had repaid the loan required to build Phase One.

There were three categories of housing: one-bedroom cottages for married couples, apartments for single persons, and individual rooms for those requiring constant attention. The cottages were purchased by the couples concerned for $65,000 on the condition that on the death of one spouse, the surviving spouse would move to an apartment, and on the death of the surviving spouse, ownership of the cottage reverted to the foundation to be resold to another couple. Those requiring constant attention were moved to individual rooms. Single persons could also purchase apartments from the foundation for $35,000 on the condition that on their deaths, ownership of the apartment also reverted to the foundation. Cottages and apartments not sold were rented at $600 per person per month on the condition that if sold, tenants would vacate the apartments on three months notice.

An amount of $120 per month was charged to all occupants of the cottages and apartments to cover utilities and operating and maintenance charges. Those in the individual rooms were charged $400 per month. Any temporary shortfall in revenues for operations was loaned to the Village by the foundation.

Phase One of the Village consisted of 80 cottages, 200 apartments and 32 individual rooms. It was run by a manager who was supported by two clerical assistants, two cooks, two housekeepers, a maintenance staff of three and the seven members required to look after those in the individual rooms. There was also a chapel, a hospital, a dining hall, an office block, a maintenance building, staff accommodation, a gymnasium and swimming pool, and an entertainment centre. Residents were charged $5 per month for use of the gymnasium and swimming pool, and $10 for entertainment, which took the form of lectures, film shows, craft classes, dancing, and similar activities. Transportation to and from the City of Fairfax was provided by the Village at a charge of $2 per person per round-trip.

The hospital consisted of five private and five semi-private wards and was staffed by three full-time registered nurses and four nursing aides. Local physicians were available for emergency medical attention and consultation. The cost of operating the hospital was covered by a daily patient-charge recoverable from the Provincial Health Plan.

The accounting system in operation was designed to keep capital transaction relating to the purchase and sale of cottages separate from that received for maintenance, transport, the use of the gymnasium and entertainment. All capital receipts were to be applied in discharging the loan from the provincial government required to build Phase One and interest thereon. The loan from the provincial government was "fully open" and could be repaid in varying amounts at any time.

REQUIRED

Outline what accounting system and funds you would expect to be in operation at the Atlantic Retirement Village.

EXERCISES

EXERCISE 20–1

The Central American Relief Fund is a Canadian registered charity formed to provide poverty relief in Nicaragua using a restricted fund accounting system and full encumbrance accounting. It uses a relief fund to account for its relief operations, and an operating fund to account for all other activities. Each fund has its own bank account and interfund transactions are settled immediately in cash.

CARF receives cash funds from public donations, pledges from Canadian citizens, and grants from the Canadian government for humanitarian work and relief. It also receives noncash donations of food and clothing, and the assistance of volunteers for fund-raising activities and for carrying out relief programs. Aeros Nicaragua routinely provides free flights for volunteers travelling to Nicaragua and the free transportation of relief supplies to Nicaragua.

During the month of May 20X3, the following transactions took place:

May 1   Transfer of $10,000 from the operating fund bank account to the relief fund banking account.

May 2   The receipt of a donation of two used trucks from Markham Trucking Inc., an Ontario transportation firm, to be used to transport relief supplies in Nicaragua. The original cost of the trucks was $240,000, but at the time of donation their approximate market value was $150,000. The donor also offered to pay for the transportation of the trucks by sea to Nicaragua.

May 3   The receipt of donations of clothing valued at $8,000. The clothing was immediately packed for transfer to Nicaragua.

May 8   The receipt of unrestricted pledges for general CARF activities amounting to $18,000, to be spread over the 18 months commencing on June 1.

May 9   Receipt from Aeros Nicaragua of free return air tickets to Nicaragua valued at $1,100 each for four relief workers, and free air cargo space valued at $2,000 for the clothing received on May 3.

May 10   An invoice for $9,000 for shipping costs from Red Funnel Shipping Lines for the transportation of two trucks to Nicaragua. The amount was paid immediately by the relief fund and treated as being recoverable from the donor of the trucks, Markham Trucking Inc.

May 15   Receipt of the time of six volunteers who canvassed the public for cash donations. A total of 42 hours was involved. CARF recognizes these contributions at the minimum wage of $6/hour. Unrestricted cash donations received as a result of their efforts brought in $2,720.

May 17   Receipt of a contribution towards general operating expenses of $25,000 from the Luis de Campos Perreira Trust.

May 25   Salaries of $34,000 paid to employees from the operating fund bank account. Of this amount, $18,000 was for relief workers. This amount was immediately transferred to Nicaragua.

May 30   A verification of outstanding unrestricted pledges for the past twelve months showed that pledgors had reneged on pledges of $458. The amount was written off immediately.

REQUIRED

Provide the journal entries required to account for each of the above transactions in accordance with the CICA's accounting requirements for NPOs. The journal entries (including cash transactions) must specify the journal of the fund (or funds) concerned and give a full explanation of why the transaction has been treated in that way.

EXERCISE 20–2   You are provided with the following trial balances of the Winnipeg Chapter of the Daughters of Manitoba for the year ended December 31, 20X4:

Scholarship Fund (Restricted)	Dr.	Cr.
Scholarship Awarded	$ 2,400	
Cash Donations Received		$ 1,150
Interest Revenue		286
Transfer from General Fund		1,000
Cash on Hand	55	
Fund Balance at January 1, 20X4		3,067
Investments at Bank of Manitoba:		
General Investment Certificate	3,000	
Savings Account	48	
	$ 5,503	$ 5,503

Operating Fund	**Dr.**	**Cr.**
Annual Dinner Expenses	$ 2,400	
Administration Expenses	53,145	
Donations Made: National Council of Women	3,000	
Sundry Donations	440	
Honorarium Paid to Auditors	800	
President's Allowance	1,000	
Transfer to Scholarship Fund	1,000	
Annual Dinner Receipts		$ 2,040
Cash Donations Received		6,235
Interest Revenue		132
Membership Fees		40,000
Subscription Revenue		12,600
Cash at Bank	1,610	
Office Furniture and Equipment, at cost	8,300	
Accumulated Amortization — Furniture and Equipment		1,480
Fund Balance at January 1, 20X4		11,208
Investment — Bank of Manitoba	2,000	
	$73,695	$73,695

REQUIRED

Prepare the operating statement and balance sheet of the Winnipeg Chapter of the Daughters of Manitoba for 20X4 in a multi-column format using the restricted fund method on the assumption that the office furniture and equipment is amortized at the rate of 10 per year on the straight-line basis. (Note: When preparing the balance sheet, ensure that your Fund Balance is broken down into the appropriate components. Note also that the amortization has not yet been recorded for 20X4.)

EXERCISE 20–3   The following trial balance was extracted from the ledger of the Tiny Toes Co-operative Nursery School Inc. at December 31, 20X2:

	Dr.	Cr.
Accounts Payable		$ 4,690
Amount **due** from Provincial Government	$ 26,000	
Administration Expenses	16,718	
Cash	958	
Fees In Advance		1,560
Fee Revenues		48,000
Furniture and Equipment at January 1, 20X2	26,900	
Less: Accumulated Amortization at January 1, 20X2		8,600
Fund Balances at January 1, 20X2:		
Restricted		654
Unrestricted		16,950
Fund-raising Activities		29,728
Interest on Longterm Loan	996	
Longterm Loan Secured over Equipment — Balance at December 31, 20X2		11,200
Operating Grant from Provincial Government		128,000
Purchases Teaching Materials	10,600	
Rent Expense	24,000	
Salaries Expense	142,000	
Teaching Materials on Hand at January 1, 20X2	1,210	
	$249,382	$249,382

The board of directors of the nursery school consisted of seven members and had an enrolment of some 60 pre-school children. It employed four persons: the principal, at an annual salary of $46,000, who was responsible for the entire program, and three qualified teachers who worked five hours a day and were paid $32,000 each. One parent from each family was required to assist the teachers in the daily operation of the school and supervise "free time" for a pre-determined number of hours every month.

For provincial funding purposes, this assistance was considered to be equal to the services of one teacher.

The school operated out of rented premises. In 20X0, the board of directors had agreed to set aside one-quarter of all moneys raised from fund-raising activities in a building fund. A separate fund had not been established, and this amount was treated as **internally** restricted funds.

You are also informed that:

1. All **contributions** of goods and services are recognized **at fair value**.
2. **Contributions** of teaching materials by parents, local merchants, and other benefactors **were** valued at $4,300 for the year.
3. The inventory of teaching materials at December 31, 20X2 amounted to $1,470.
4. On July 1, 20X2, the school was donated a lawn mower costing $400 that was expected to last 10 years with no residual value.
5. **Amortization** was charged on all furniture and equipment at the rate of 10% per year. There were no purchases of furniture or equipment during the year.

REQUIRED

Prepare the **operating statement and balance sheet** of Tiny Toes Co-Operative Nursery School, Inc. for 20X2 on the assumption that the net assets invested in unrestricted funds at December 31, 20X5 was $4,916.

EXERCISE 20-4 At December 31, 20X2, the trial balance of North Finch Training Centre including most adjustments was as follows:

	Dr.	Cr.
Administration Expenses	$119,000	
Consumable Stores Expense	116,000	
Amortization of Capital Assets:		
Computer Equipment	14,000	
Training Equipment	38,000	
Rent Expense	120,000	
Salaries Expense	187,000	
Grant — Federal Government		$260,000
Grant — City of North Finch		75,000
Contribution — United Way Forward		150,000
Contributions (unrestricted)		194,000
Interfund Transfer	14,000	
Interfund Transfer		14,000
Cash at Bank	9,000	
Consumable Stores on Hand	12,000	
Training Equipment	170,000	
Accumulated Amortization — Training Equipment		72,000
Computer Equipment	60,000	
Accumulated Depreciation — Computer Equipment		14,000
Accounts Payable		17,000
General Fund Balance at January 1, 20X2		92,000
Investment — North Finch Credit Union	29,000	
	$888,000	$888,000

The North Finch Training Centre is a nonprofit organization that was formed to assist middle-aged persons who have been laid off or otherwise have lost their jobs, with the basic skills required to re-enter the workforce. In 20X2, a grant of $260,000 was received from the federal government to fund courses in carpentry, bricklaying and other building related skills. The United Way Forward also contributed another $150,000 to cover the salaries of two clerical assistants and running expenses. In addition, $194,000 was received from donations from business organizations and the general public.

During 20X2, the City of North Finch provided a special grant of $75,000 to be used specifically for the funding of computer equipment for a program to provide computer keyboarding and other basic computer knowledge. The terms of the grant were that the amount could only be used for the purchase of computer equipment and that all moneys held in the fund must be invested in the North Finch Credit Union.

During 20X2, computer equipment costing $60,000 was purchased from the grant from the City of North Finch.

REQUIRED

Prepare the operating statement and balance sheet of the North Finch Training Centre for the year ended December 31, 20X2 using a single restricted fund format.

EXERCISE 20–5   The following statement of changes in net assets applies to the Richmond Clinic for the year ended December 31, 20X4.

STATEMENT OF CHANGES IN NET ASSETS
for the year ended December 31, 20X4

	Invested in Capital Assets	Restricted	Unrestricted	20X4 Total
Balance, Beginning of Year	$185,000	$ 80,000	$125,000	$390,000
Excess of Revenues over Expenses	5,000	—	—	5,000
Endowment Contributions	—	50,000	—	50,000
Investment in Capital Assets	60,000	—	(60,000)	—
Internally Imposed Restriction	—	35,000	(35,000)	—
Balance, End of Year	$250,000	$165,000	$30,000	$445,000

REQUIRED

1. Explain what you understand by the following amounts:
   (a) The amount invested in capital assets;
   (b) The excess of revenues over expenses;
   (c) The investment in capital assets of $60,000 and the reduction in the unrestricted assets of $60,000.
   (d) The increase in the restricted net assets of $35,000 and the reduction in the unrestricted net assets of the same amount.

2. Give the net assets section of the statement of financial position (i.e., the balance sheet) of the Richmond Clinic at December 31, 20X4

PROBLEMS

PROBLEM 20–1   At November 30, 20X4, the following trial balance was extracted from the ledger of the Wembley District Family Support Group, a registered charitable organization that distributed food and clothing to needy families for the City of Wembley:

	Dr.	Cr.
Cleaning Materials Expense	$ 689	
Motor Vehicle Operating Expenses	4,008	
Purchases for Needy Families:		
Clothing	12,823	
Food	40,661	
Rent Expense	13,200	
Repairs and Maintenance Expense	328	
Salary Expense	75,432	
Sundry Operating Expenses	1,295	

	Dr.	Cr.
Donations of Cash		$ 45,461
Operating Grant from City of Wembley		120,000
Cash at Bank	17,514	
Furniture and Equipment, at cost	6,780	
Accumulated Amortization — Furniture and Equipment		2,680
Inventory at January 1, 20X4 at fair value:		
Clothing	8,080	
Food	3,429	
Motor Vehicles, at cost	26,390	
Accumulated Amortization — Motor Vehicles		7,450
Accounts Payable		4,200
Encumbrance Reserve		3,546
Fund Balance — January 1, 20X4		27,292
	$210,629	$210,629

During the month of December 20X4 the Support Group:

(a) Received invoices totalling $3,823 relating to the encumbrance reserve. The difference of $277 was due to a single purchase order for clothing **that was that** amount less than the invoiced amount.

(b) Issued purchase orders for clothing and food amounting to $3,071 and $4,560 respectively. Invoices amounting to $2,790 and $3,389 that agreed with the purchase orders were received by December 31, 20X4 and recorded in the books. The balance of the purchase orders in the Encumbrances Reserve had not been invoiced or received by that date.

(c) Paid the following amounts:

Accounts Payable	$5,423
Salaries	7,890
Rent	1,200

(d) Received donations of cash of $6,200, clothing of $1,008 and food of $2,770.

(e) Recorded depreciation for the year using the straight-line method on the furniture and equipment at 10% and motor vehicles at 20%.

You are also informed that:

1. During the eleven months ended November 30, 20X4, the Support Group received donations of clothing and food **from local merchants with a fair value of** $24,522 and $31,982 respectively.

2. At December 31, 20X4, the Support Group had clothes valued at $3,100 on hand and food worth $2,370.

3. The financial year end of the Support Group is December 31.

4. A single restricted fund is used to account for the activities of the Support Group.

REQUIRED

Prepare the statement of revenues and expenses and balance sheet of the Wembley Family Support Group for 20X4. (Hint: Use T-accounts.) Any balance on the Encumbrance Reserve is to be deducted from the Fund Balance.

PROBLEM 20–2 The Bassetville Memorial Hospital Foundation ("the foundation") is a nonprofit corporation that has been classified as a registered charity under the *Income Tax Act*. The objectives of the foundation are to receive and maintain funds for the benefit of the Bassetville Memorial Hospital through the enhancement and improvement of the facilities and services provided by the hospital. These objectives specifically exclude disbursement of the funds towards operating costs or expenses associated with the hospital.

The adjusted trial balance of the foundation for the year ended December 31, 20X2 was as follows:

	Dr.	Cr.
Cash on Hand:		
Operating Fund	$ 52,400	
Research Fund	22,100	
Inventory of toys, games, etc.	4,200	
Accounts Receivable	5,900	
Longterm Investments:		
Operating Fund	600,600	
Research Fund	191,100	
Contributions to Hospital	214,100	
Research Grants Approved	72,000	
Research Grants Disbursed	72,000	
Fund-raising Expenses	59,400	
Administration Expenses:		
Operating Fund	25,600	
Research Fund	5,300	
Administering Research Grants	9,100	
Accounts Payable		$ 6,600
Due to Bassetville Memorial Hospital		93,300
Fund Balances at January 1, 20X1:		
Operating Fund		445,900
Research Fund		199,200
Transfer from Research Fund to Operating Fund		72,000
Contributions Received:		
For Research Purposes		66,700
For Non-Research Purposes		267,200
Bequests for Non-Research Purposes		32,200
Proceed from fund-raising Events		89,400
Interest Revenues:		
Operating Fund		33,800
Research Fund		24,600
Miscellaneous Receipts		2,900
	$1,333,800	$1,333,800

The foundation operates two funds: an operating fund and a research fund.

The operating fund is the main fund of the foundation. Its purpose is to collect contributions for non-research purposes, bequests, and the net revenues from fund-raising activities that are applied for the improvement of the facilities or services provided by the hospital. It also contributes recreational and other equipment to the hospital that is accumulated in a ledger account entitled "Contributions to Hospital".

The research fund receives and administers the accumulated balances of contributions received for specific or other research projects. When a specific project is approved by the board of directors, an amount equal to the approved budget is transferred from the research fund to the operating fund, which then administers the research grants. Expenditures on account of research projects are charged directly to the operating fund on the submission of approved invoices for payment by the researchers.

During 20X2, $72,000 for research grants was approved by the board of directors.

REQUIRED

Prepare the operating statement and balance sheet of the foundation for 20X2 using a multi-column restricted fund format.

PROBLEM 20–3   You are provided with the following information on two unrelated situations:

1. Alberta College is a School for the Deaf and is operated as a nonprofit organization. During 20X3, the school received a $600,000 donation from the family of a student tragically killed in a motor accident. The terms of the donation

were that the principal amount of the fund must be invested in AA-rated or better securities, and the interest on the fund must be used to provide scholarships to students. For the year ended December 31, 20X3, the fund earned interest of $24,000, and scholarships amounting to $17,000 were awarded to deserving students.

REQUIRED

Give the journal entries without explanations for the scholarship fund on the following assumptions:

(a) The school uses the deferral method of recognizing contributions, and records all entries in the general fund because it does not maintain a separate endowment fund for the scholarship.

(b) The school uses the restricted fund method and records all entries in a separate endowment fund for the scholarship.

2. On January 1, 20X2, a local computer software company donated several computers outfitted with specialized audio equipment to the school. The equipment is worth approximately $35,000 and has an estimated useful life of five years, with no salvage value. The school uses a straight line amortization policy.

REQUIRED

Give the journal entries related to the computer equipment for 20X3. Assume the school treats the donation as a restricted contribution, uses the deferral method of recognizing contributions, and does not maintain a separate fund for the donated equipment.

PROBLEM 20–4   The adjusted trial balances of the Society of Artists of Western Canada at December 31, 20X4 were as follows:

	Operating Fund	Benevolent Fund	Studio Eighteen
Administration Expenses	$ 183,520	$ 16,000	$123,880
Amortization of Capital Assets	56,800	3,540	21,200
Benefits Paid	—	73,000	—
Cost of Goods Sold	—	—	215,900
Salaries Expense	218,600	5,360	90,700
Rent	16,860	—	18,000
Cash at Bank	4,012	5,010	10,300
Term Deposits	28,028	20,000	—
Members Subscriptions Outstanding	80,860	—	—
Transfer to Benevolent Fund	40,000	—	—
Accounts Receivable	—	—	121,060
Inventory	—	—	52,100
Investment in *Studio Eighteen*	421,935	—	—
Investments	80,000	242,800	—
Furniture and Equipment	696,240	—	337,760
	$1,826,855	$365,710	$990,900
Members Subscriptions	$ 633,600	$ 70,400	—
Investment Income	5,040	18,570	—
Sales of Supplies, Books, Posters, etc.	—	—	$301,900
Commissions on Art Sales	—	—	127,500
Sundry Revenues	12,715	1,110	4,765
Accounts Payable	4,900	—	16,600
Accumulated Amortization	413,800	—	118,200
Loan Outstanding — Bank of Alberta	40,000	—	—
Transfer from Operating Fund	—	40,000	—
Fund Balances at January 1, 20X4	716,800	235,630	421,935
	$1,826,855	$365,710	$990,900

The Society has its headquarters in Calgary and has as its mission statement the promotion of Western art and, in particular, that of its members. It arranged exhibitions of the art of its members and received commissions on any art sold at those exhibitions. Many of its members are young, struggling artists. Some years back, it started a Benevolent Fund to ease the problems faced by its members who had fallen on hard times. It was financed by the transfer of 10% of members subscriptions to the Fund and from interest earned on its investments. The day-to-day running of the Society was through an operating fund.

The Society also runs an art shop called *Studio Eighteen* in which it originally sold art supplies. However, as the venture proved successful, it expanded its range of goods to include books, posters and stationery directed at the "upper market". It also held art on consignment for its members on a rotating basis. *Studio Eighteen* was operated and treated for accounting purposes as a profit-oriented enterprise of the private sector. *Studio Eighteen* is consolidated with the operating fund for financial reporting purposes.

REQUIRED

Prepare the consolidated operating statement and balance sheet of the Society of Artists of Western Canada in columnar form using the restricted fund method.

PROBLEM 20–5   The following trial balance was extracted from the books of the National Scanning and Testing Laboratory at December 31, 20X5:

	Dr.	**Cr.**
Administration and Operating Expenses	$ 594,300	
Salaries Expense	5,426,400	
Materials Expense	629,030	
Amortization of Capital Assets	185,065	
Mortgage Interest	204,000	
Cash and Term Deposits	954,000	
Accounts Receivable	56,000	
Materials on Hand	210,400	
Grants Receivable	1,800,000	
Land	752,000	
Buildings	1,848,000	
Laboratory Furniture and Equipment	2,792,000	
Operating Grant — Federal Government		$ 5,000,000
General Contributions		210,000
Fee Revenues		465,100
Amortization of Deferred Contributions for Year		1,460,000
Contributed of Materials at fair value		302,000
Contributions of Capital Assets at fair value		254,000
Accumulated Amortization — Buildings		217,000
Accumulated Amortization — Laboratory Equipment		652,000
Accounts Payable		809,000
Mortgage Payable — Current Portion		159,000
Mortgage Payable — Longterm Liability		1,426,000
Deferred Contributions Relating to:		
Purchase of Capital Assets		806,000
Research Activities		200,000
Unrestricted		65,400
Fund Balance at January 1, 20X5		3,425,695
	$15,451,195	$15,451,195

The laboratory was formed for the purpose of the screening of imported foodstuffs, clothing, furniture and children's toys to ensure that the preservatives, dyes, fillings, etc., did not pose a health hazard to consumers. All importers of these items were required to submit samples for scanning purposes before they were allowed to be sold.

The laboratories used a single operating fund in which contributions towards operating and other expenses were deferred using the deferral method of accounting for contributions.

REQUIRED

Prepare the operating statement and balance sheet of the National Scanning and Testing Laboratory for 20X5, using the deferral method and on the assumption that the net assets invested in unrestricted funds at December 31, 20X5 was $1,140,000.

PROBLEM 20–6 The following trial balances apply to the three funds of The Generous Hand at December 31, 20X4:

Trial Balance of The Generous Hand at December 31, 20X4

	Operating Fund	Endowment Fund	Building Fund (Restricted)
	Debits	**Debits**	**Debits**
Administration Expenses	$181,400	$12,400	$ 1,400
Amortization of Capital Assets	2,145	—	—
Relief Work	—	55,000	—
Interfund Transfer to Building Fund	4,000	—	—
Current Assets	3,698	3,375	4,877
Investments	6,000	—	7,000
Office Equipment, at cost	18,720	800	—
	$215,963	$71,575	$13,277
	Credits	**Credits**	**Credit**
Government Grants	$160,000	$68,000	—
Donations/Contributions Received	22,112	—	$ 5,980
Amortization of Deferred Contributions	2,310	—	—
Interest Revenue	165	—	230
Accumulated Amortization — Office Equipment	2,860	451	—
Interfund Transfer from Operating Fund	—	—	4,000
Current Liabilities	1,290		
Deferred Contributions	4,540	—	—
Longterm Liabilities	6,478	—	—
Fund Balance, Beginning of Year	16,208	3,124	3,067
	$215,963	$71,575	$13,277

You are also informed that:

(a) The Accumulated Amortization of Office Equipment of $2,860 includes the amount applicable to 20X4.

(b) Details relating to the investments in capital assets, and restricted and unrestricted fund balances for the three funds were as follows:

Fund Balances:	Operating Fund	Endowment Fund	Building Fund
Invested in Capital Assets	$8,600	—	—
Externally Restricted	—	$3,724	$11,877
Unrestricted	4,650	—	—

REQUIRED

Prepare the operating statement and balance sheet (i.e., the statement of financial position) of The Generous Hand for 20X4 on a multiple fund basis of reporting using the deferral method.

21 *Unincorporated Businesses*

LEARNING OBJECTIVES

After studying this chapter you should be able to:

1. Recognize the importance of the sole proprietorship and partnership form of business ownership; and
2. Account for the activities of these two forms of unincorporated business entities.

WHAT ARE UNINCORPORATED BUSINESS ENTITIES?

The term "unincorporated business entities" refers to two forms of business ownership, namely, the sole proprietorship and the partnership. These two types of entities represent an important sector of the economy and very often provide the seeds from which larger businesses develop. Many contemporary, large businesses were once small, "one-person" businesses.[1]

Partnerships are extensively used to carry on professional practices such as accountancy, dentistry, law and medicine. This is because corporations cannot normally hold professional qualifications. However, some professions, like architecture and engineering, do allow their members to incorporate. Where they do, the shareholders in these "professional companies" are strictly controlled by the legislation regulating the professional association concerned.[2]

The problem that arises in accounting for unincorporated businesses is that, from a legal perspective, these entities are not considered to be separate from their owners. Consequently, the individual assets and liabilities of the entities legally belong to the owners and, in the event of bankruptcy, they are subject to the claims of creditors of the owners. The question that arises is whether it is proper to present the financial position and results of the unincorporated business without taking into account the assets and liabilities held by the owners

---

[1] It is a rocky road for many new businesses. A report by Statistics Canada in *The Globe and Mail* of February 17, 2000 reported that about 23% of new businesses don't make it to their first birthday, 40% have exited before their second birthday, and 75% have ceased to exist by their eighth birthday.

[2] For example, in Ontario, section 3 of the Ontario *Business Corporations Act* states: "Where the practice of a profession is governed by an Act, a corporation may practise the profession only if that Act expressly permits the practice of a profession by a corporation and [is] subject to the provisions of such Act."

outside the business.[3] As a result, the CICA *Handbook* states that the limitations of such financial statements must be clearly stated, and that where the owners engage in other business or investment activities not included in the financial statements, it may be necessary to include sufficient details of the nature of the business to distinguish it from the other activities of its owners.

A. ACCOUNTING FOR SOLE PROPRIETORSHIPS

The Nature of Sole Proprietorships

Sole proprietorships (or single person businesses) represent the simplest form of business. They may vary from the local convenience store to the practice of a medical practitioner, optometrist, orthodontist, or the developer of computer software. In many cases, they are family-run businesses with only one member of the family representing the legal owner.

Although sole proprietorships may take many forms, they often had the following characteristics:

1. The owner is not financially-oriented and relies on accountants and other outside parties for financial advice.
2. In the start-up period, they rely heavily on borrowed funding to finance the venture. However, these persons are often highly innovative and, if their initial venture is successful, the business is a sole proprietorship for a limited time.
3. From an economic and social point of view, the sole proprietorship form of business ventures is extremely important, as this type of entity is often the driving force behind new industries and job creation. This form of entity also allows people laid-off from regular employment through, for example, downsizing or restructuring to continue to be economically active.

An individual can start an unincorporated business at any time. There are no legal formalities, other than to obtain the necessary licences to carry on business. In the case of the professions or regulated industries like, for example, the travel industry, registration with the regulatory body is required. The Canada Revenue Agency now insists that all sole proprietorships must have December 31 year ends. Prior to this, sole proprietorships could choose any year end.

The Objectives of the Accounting System

From an accounting perspective, sole proprietorships need an accounting system that facilitates the day-to-day operations of the business. It should provide a record of cash inflows and outflows, show amounts owing to creditors, give amounts due from customers or clients, track inventory levels, maintain adequate records for income tax purposes, and supply other relevant information.

Financial statements are also required for income tax and credit purposes. Unless the owner can produce a set of financial statements prepared by a professional accountant, it would be almost impossible to borrow money from a bank. Where the business is regulated, reporting to the regulatory or controlling body is also required.

---

[3] CICA *Handbook*, section 1800.

The Financial Statements of Sole Proprietorships

The financial statements of sole proprietorships should be prepared in accordance with generally accepted accounting principles. They should consist of, at least, a balance sheet and an income statement. The proprietary ownership theory applies to the financial statements of sole proprietorships[4] and, consequently, the balance sheet is drawn up using the equation of assets – liabilities = owner's equity.

To ensure that there is no doubt as to the nature of the business, the financial statements should clearly state the name under which the business is conducted and also the name of the owner. It should also be clear that the business is unincorporated and that the financial statements do not include all the assets and liabilities of the owner. An example of the manner in which the balance sheet of a sole trader would be headed follows:

Joseph P. Barnes
trading as
OAKVILLE PAINTING CONTRACTORS
Balance Sheet at December 31, 20X1

The capital of the owner should be presented by giving details of the opening balance, additional capital contributions, income or losses for the period, and **withdrawals** (known as **drawings**) by the owner. Salaries, interest or similar items paid or accrued to the owner should be disclosed separately in the income statement. These amounts may be disclosed by means of a note to the income statement. An illustration of the manner in which the capital of the owner could be presented is as follows:

Capital Account — Joseph P. Barnes		
Balance at January 1, 20X1		$262,342
Additional Contribution of Capital		23,675
		286,017
Net Income from Operations	92,456	
Less: Drawings	75,312	17,144
Balance at December 31, 20X1		$303,161

As sole proprietorships are not liable for income taxes in their own right because the owners are personally taxed on the taxable profits of the business, the CICA *Handbook*[5] specifically requires that no provision for income taxes be made in the financial statements. To avoid any possible misunderstanding on this point, the *Handbook* requires that specific reference to this should be made in a note to the financial statements or by expanding the description of the net income or loss to indicate that this amount has been established without providing for income taxes.

B. ACCOUNTING FOR PARTNERSHIPS

A partnership may be defined as an association of two or more persons who carry on, as co-owners, a business for profit. In this context, a person may be an individual, a business corporation, or any other entity having the same rights, privileges and responsibilities as an individual. The term "partnership" refers exclusively to associations formed for the purpose of carrying on business with **the intention of making a profit**. If this feature of the association is absent, it is not a partnership.

---

[4] See Chapter One.
[5] Section 1800.

A partnership must, therefore, have the three characteristics of having (1) **an agreement**, explicit or implied, between two or more persons; (2) **a profit motive**; and (3) the recognition that the parties to the agreement must be **co-owners**, meaning that each partner has the right to share in business profits, participate in the management of the business, and to hold an interest in the assets of the partnership. These latter rights are shared equally, unless the partnership agreement specifies otherwise.

The use of partnerships dates back to very early times. It was particularly important in Britain, because until the middle of the 19th century, the formation of companies was restricted to those formed for special purposes.[6] The onset of the Industrial Revolution in Britain in the mid-1700s brought about an increase in the number of businesses using this form of association and in 1890, the British *Partnership Act* was passed to clarify the law applying to partnerships which had become clouded as a result of numerous legal decisions.

All provinces in Canada, other than Quebec, have passed partnership acts based on the British *Partnership Act* (1890).[7] Partnerships in many other countries are covered by partnership acts, such as the *Uniform Partnership Act* in the USA. In countries with no partnership act, the parties rely on the law of contract to govern their activities.

Accounting for partnerships essentially follows the same pattern as that for sole proprietorships, except that there are multiple owners. But, because of the obvious importance of the individual share of profits, greater significance is given to the preparation of financial statements.

THE NATURE OF PARTNERSHIPS

The partnership form of entity ownership has many advantages. Partnerships allow an association of persons to pool their resources, expertise, and/or knowledge for their common benefit. However, they also have certain disadvantages in comparison to carrying on business as a corporate entity. The most important of these is that there is no limitation of the liability of partners. These aspects of partnerships are listed and discussed below.

1. The **liability of partners** in a **general partnership is unlimited**. The partners are, therefore, "jointly and severally" liable for the debts and obligations of the partnership. This means that in the event of a partner being found guilty of failing to satisfy a contractual obligation, the commission of a tort,[8] or the misappropriation of trust funds, the aggrieved party may seize the assets of the partnership and the assets of any partner or partners to satisfy their claim. For example, if a partnership had defaulted on the repayment of a loan, the creditor could take action against any partner to recover the loan.

   In the case of **limited partnerships**, the liability of the partners is limited to their contributions of capital to the partnership. With **limited liability partnerships**, the liability for certain acts is restricted to individual partners. These two specific forms of partnerships are dealt with later in the chapter.
2. Partnerships **have limited or uncertain life spans**. This means that a partnership terminates in the event of the death or retirement of a partner, the admission of a new partner, or the bankruptcy of an individual partner.
3. There is **joint control over the assets** of the partnership — all assets belong to the partnership.

---

[6] The development of the private company as we know it today only occurred in the early 1900s.
[7] 1890, 53 and 54 *Victoria* Ch. 39.
[8] That branch of the law concerned with the harm suffered by persons resulting from the activities of others.

4. There is **mutual agency**, which means that every partner is an agent for both the partnership and every other partner. One partner can, therefore, bind the other partners to a contract if he or she is acting within the apparent scope of the business.
5. **Partnerships are easier to form than companies.** All that is required to form a partnership is an agreement between the partners to do so. Once formed, partnerships have to be registered in most provinces. This involves registering the name under which the partnership will operate with the provincial registry office, providing the names and addresses of all the partners, and declaring that only those persons so named are partners. Penalties are imposed on partnerships that have not been registered.

DOES A PARTNERSHIP HAVE A SEPARATE IDENTITY?

In law, a partnership is not considered to have a separate identity, because it is viewed as a collection of persons, with each having their own rights and obligations. However, **in practice**, partnerships do have some sort of separate identity.

In certain cases, a partnership can sue and be sued in its own name without naming the individual partners. The creditors of a partnership are also entitled to have their claims settled from the proceeds of the partnership assets before looking to the assets of the individual partners. There is, therefore, some move towards recognizing a partnership as a separate legal entity.

In accounting, as with all forms of entity ownership, a partnership is recognized as an entity separate from its owners. Even though a change in the persons making up the partnership means that one partnership terminates and a new partnership begins, partnerships normally continue using the same partnership books, operate out of the same premises, etc.

THE PARTNERSHIP AGREEMENT

It is not necessary for the partners to draw up a formal contract because the normal principles of the law of contract apply. In fact, in the absence of a partnership agreement, it is the actions of the partners in relation to one another that determines whether a partnership exists. But, in the interests of the partnership and sound business practice, it is **highly desirable** that the relationship between the partners be included in a written partnership agreement. It is also important that every partner understands the conditions under which the business is to be carried out, as well as their individual duties and rights. The objective is to reduce the possibility of future disputes among the partners and to keep their relationship as amicable as possible by reducing friction between them.

The main purpose of the agreement is to set out clearly the objectives of the partnership and the responsibilities of each partner, particularly the extent to which they can enter into contracts on behalf of the partnership. The agreement should also specify the capital contribution of each partner, the ratio in which profits and losses will be apportioned between the partners, each partner's expected contribution in time and effort, how disputes are to be settled (e.g., by arbitration), what is to occur in the event of the death or retirement of a partner, procedures for admitting new partners, life insurance provisions for surviving partners to acquire the interest of a deceased partner, and procedures for the withdrawal of assets by partners.

PARTNERSHIP FORMATION

Once agreement between the partners has been reached, and each partner has carried out their obligations to one another, the partnership comes into existence. The initial obligations normally involve the payment of each partner's share of the capital into the partnership's bank account or, where the contribution is in the form of assets, the transfer of these assets to the partnership. From that point onwards, the partners' obligations involve carrying out their duties for their common benefit.

THE PARTNERS' CAPITAL AND LOAN ACCOUNTS

Accounting for the Partners' Capital

Partners usually contribute **capital** to the partnership in their profit-sharing ratio, but there is no requirement that they do so. Capital contributions are determined entirely by agreement between the partners and the basis should be specified in the partnership agreement.

Partners' **capital accounts** are created when partners contribute cash or other assets to the partnership. Contributions of noncash assets should be recorded at values agreed upon by the partners. Intangible assets, such as goodwill, could also be contributed. The **capital accounts** usually remain unchanged until the partnership comes to an end, or the partners are required to increase their contributed capital, in which case all partners would increase their capital amounts by a set percentage, to keep their capital balances at levels reflecting the profit-sharing ratio.

Assume, for example, that the partnership of Andrew, Barry and Charles required $450,000 in capital. If the profit-sharing ratio was 6:5:4 and this was also the capital contribution ratio between the partners, then $180,000 would have been contributed by Andrew, $150,000 by Barry, and $120,000 by Charles. If, some years later, an additional $90,000 was required and the partners are, by agreement, required to keep their capital accounts in the profit-sharing ratio, Andrew would contribute another $36,000, Barry, $30,000 and Charles, $24,000. The capital of $540,000 would be shown as $216,000, $180,000 and $144,000 in the respective capital accounts: that is, in proportion to the profit-sharing ratio.

In cases where a partnership needs additional capital for the day-to-day running of the business, like the need to finance accounts receivable, partners may be encouraged to leave part of their share of profits in the firm. These amounts are credited to **separate partners' current accounts** and the partners are compensated for doing so by the payment of interest on these balances at an agreed rate on, for example, the daily balances. Interest on partners' current accounts is treated as a business expense, based on the argument that the partnership would have had to borrow funds externally, resulting in interest on the loan (a business expense) if profits had not been re-invested in the business.

Partners' Loan Accounts

Partners may make loans to the partnership that are in excess of their capital contributions. Interest on partners' loans should be treated as an interest expense on the income statement and credited to the individual partners' current accounts. Interest on a loan does not constitute a distribution of profits to the partner but must be recognized as interest revenue by the recipient. Likewise, if a partnership lends money to a partner, the interest should be recorded as "interest revenue" on the income statement.

Drawings by Partners

Partners draw money out of the partnership every month or at set periods to cover their living expenses. These withdrawals are known as **drawings** and are considered to be **advances against their share of profits**. The amounts withdrawn are based on agreement among the partners and are usually based on the amount required by the partner receiving the smallest share of profits. And, as drawings are considered to be advances of profits, the partners' drawings accounts are closed off to the partners' current accounts at the end of the accounting period, together with their share of profits.

DETERMINING AND DISTRIBUTING PROFITS AND LOSSES

The establishment of the profit or loss of a partnership is carried out at set intervals (e.g., every three months) in exactly the same manner as for a sole proprietorship. The preparation of financial statements is, therefore, of great importance. Like sole proprietorships, the Canada Revenue Agency requires all partnerships formed since 1995 to have December 31 year ends.

The major difference between the financial statements of sole proprietorships and partnerships is that the profits or losses must be apportioned between the partners in their agreed profit-sharing ratio. For example, as Andrew, Barry and Charles had agreed to share profits in the ratio of 6:5:4, the allocation of profits of $300,000 would be $120,000 to Andrew, $100,000 to Barry and $80,000 to Charles. On apportionment, these amounts are transferred to the partners' current accounts.

A partner may be guaranteed a **minimum share of profits** in terms of the partnership agreement. Where this occurs, the agreed minimum share of profits is first allocated to the partner concerned, and then the balance of the profits is allocated to the remaining partners in the profit-sharing ratio. If in the example given above, Charles had been guaranteed profits of, at least, $90,000, the sharing of profits of $300,000 would be $114,545 to Andrew (i.e., 6/11 × $210,000), $95,455 to Barry (i.e., 5/11 × $210,000), and $90,000 to Charles.

In certain circumstances, the partnership agreement may, for example, provide for the allocation of a **salary or bonus** to a particular partner to compensate the person for taking on added responsibilities or to recognize outstanding performance. It may also be used to adjust for profit sharing in cases where a partner brings considerable expertise into the partnership, instead of capital. Regardless of the reason, such allocations are considered to be distributions of profits that should be reflected as an expense on the income statement and credited to the partners' current accounts. The remaining profits are then allocated to the partners in the profit-sharing ratio.

An example of the financial statements of a typical partnership is provided as Illustration 21–1. It illustrates the partners' share of profits in the ratio of 3:3:2, partners' salaries, interest payable on partners' current accounts, a loan from a partner, and the payment of the interest on this loan.

CHANGES IN OWNERSHIP OF THE PARTNERSHIP

Any alteration to the ownership composition (admission or retirement of a partner) automatically results in a legal dissolution of the partnership. In most instances, this does not result in the termination of the business activities of the partnership. It merely means a dissolution of a specific relationship between existing partners, a routine occurrence in larger partnerships. Various methods could be used to record changes in partnership composition. These are discussed below.

ADMISSION OF NEW PARTNERS

General Considerations

On the admission of a new partner, a new partnership comes into existence. It represents a new legal relationship; but whether a change in the number of partners represents a change in the nature of the entity from an economic point of view is not clear.

The problem arises if the continuing partners want to revalue the assets to more correctly reflect the current value of the partnership. The mechanics of this practice pose no problems because the asset values are changed and the differences are credited (or debited) to the continuing partners' capital or current accounts in their profit-sharing ratio. The question that remains unanswered is whether the partnership now represents a new economic entity. If it does, then any upwards revaluation of the assets should be viewed as an unrealized capital

ILLUSTRATION 21–1
THE FINANCIAL STATEMENTS OF A PARTNERSHIP

A typical set of financial statements, showing the allocation of partnership earnings, is shown below:

PULLEN, TUGSON & REMOVSKY
Dental Surgeons
INCOME STATEMENT FOR THE YEAR ENDED DECEMBER 31, 20X4

Revenues

Fees				$1,262,270

Expenses

Accounting Fees	6,000	
Amortization of Capital Assets	12,560	
Association Fees and Subscriptions	32,452	
Anaesthetics, Materials and Supplies	274,481	
Insurance	6,400	
Interest on Partners' Loan	2,373	
Interest on Partners' Current Accounts	3,971	
Salaries and Benefits	177,276	
Rent — Consulting Rooms	27,000	
Telephone and Utilities	12,925	555,438
Net Income for Year		$ 706,832

	Pullen	Tugson	Removsky	
Allocation of net income:				
Partners' salaries	$100,000	$ 90,000	$ 90,000	$ 280,000
Share of remaining profits (3:3:2)	160,062	160,062	106,708	426,832
	$260,062	$250,062	$196,708	$ 706,832

BALANCE SHEET AT DECEMBER 31, 20X4

Current Assets		
Cash		$ 47,321
Accounts Receivable		189,456
Inventory of Anaesthetics and Supplies		30,704
		267,481
Capital Assets		
Furniture and Equipment	91,218	
Less: Accumulated Amortization	23,566	67,652
		$ 335,133
Less: **Current Liabilities**		
Accounts Payable	34,309	
Loan from Pullen	50,000	$ 84,309
		$ 250,824

	Pullen	Tugson	Removsky	
Partners' Capital:				
Capital Accounts	$ 75,000	$ 75,000	$ 50,000	$ 200,000
Current Accounts:				
Balance at January 1, 20X4	$ 12,050	$ 11,446	$ 16,212	
Partner salaries	100,000	90,000	90,000	
Interest on Current Accounts	1,205	1,145	1,621	
Interest on Loan	2,373			
Share of profits	160,062	160,062	106,708	
	275,690	262,653	214,541	
Less: Drawings	261,432	254,312	186,316	
Balance at December 31, 20X4	$ 14,258	$ 8,341	$ 28,225	$ 50,824
TOTAL PARTNERS' CAPITAL				$ 250,824

gain. If not, it is merely a change in asset values that represents a departure from historical cost accounting. In such cases, the amortization charges for income tax purposes should be adjusted accordingly.

Changes in the Partners

One partner may, with the consent of the other partners, sell his interest in the partnership to another person. The transaction is merely one between the partners and, besides the adjustments to the partnership books, there is no other effect. All that happens is that the existing partnership comes to an end and a new partnership comes into being.

Recognition of Goodwill on Admitting a New Partner

It is common in the smaller partnerships to recognize the goodwill created by the continuing partners on admitting a new partner. The philosophy behind this practice is that the continuing partners have created goodwill (i.e., a good name and reputation, special skills and knowledge, etc.) that have all contributed to the making of profits and, consequently, a new partner should, at least, compensate them in part for doing so.

It is generally accepted amongst accountants that self-created goodwill is not reflected on the balance sheet. As a result, if goodwill is recognized, it is recognized as a contribution by the continuing partners and then eliminated by removing it in the profit-sharing ratio from **all the partners' capital accounts**. Such a situation is presented in Illustration 21–2, which shows that the capital accounts of Rhoda and Sheila at January 1, 20X4 were $72,000 and $48,000 respectively and that Terri was required to pay $60,000 into the partnership to pay for her share of the goodwill of $22,500 and her capital of $37,500 (i.e., 3/12 of $150,000). Illustration 21–2 also shows that Rhoda and Sheila withdraw surplus cash from the practice to reduce their capital accounts to the required amounts.

Adjustments between Partners

An alternative way of recognizing goodwill on the admission of a partner is for the incoming partner to pay the existing partners for their share of the goodwill in the old profit-sharing ratio. In the case given in Illustration 21–2, Terri would pay $13,500 (i.e., 3/5 of $22,500) to Rhoda, $9,000 (i.e., 2/5 of $22,500) to Sheila, and $37,500 into the partnership for her interest in the business. Adjustments to Rhoda's and Sheila's capital accounts would be by the withdrawal of cash from the partnership.

Adjustments in Larger Partnerships

In the larger partnerships of accountants and lawyers, the adjustments described in Illustration 21–2 may not be considered suitable. In these cases, the partners view the partnership as a continuing entity (i.e., applying economic substance over legal form because changes in ownership composition occur frequently) and new partners may be admitted in a number of ways.

The existing partners may, for example, share in the equivalent of goodwill by specifying that **the new partner only receives a salary** for the first two years of being a partner. On the distribution of profits, the difference between the new partner's salary and the share of profits he or she would have received is distributed to the other partners in the old profit-sharing ratio.

Alternatively, **new partners do not pay an initial contribution**. In return, they agree that while they are partners, they will retain all retiring partners as consultants for a specified fee (i.e., a "pension") of, say, 10% of his or her last share of profits, for a specified time period after retirement. The agreement would normally also provide for the payment of a set amount to the partner's spouse or children in the event of death before the expiry of the specified

ILLUSTRATION 21-2
RECOGNITION OF GOODWILL ON ADMISSION OF NEW PARTNER

Rhoda and Sheila had successfully practised as physiotherapists in partnership for many years, sharing profits and losses in the ratio of 3:2. On January 1, 20X4, they agreed to admit Terri to the partnership. The relevant terms of the partnership agreement were that:

1. For the purposes of admitting Terri to the partnership, the goodwill of the partnership would be valued at $90,000.
2. The goodwill would not appear as an asset in the balance sheet of the partnership.
3. The new profit-sharing ratio would be 5:4:3.
4. The capital of the partnership would be fixed and increased by $30,000 to $150,000, from the current figure of $120,000.

If the adjustments for goodwill are **reflected in the books** of the partnership, the capital accounts of Rhoda, Sheila and Terri before and after admitting Terri to the partnership would be as follows:

Capital Account — Rhoda

20X4				
Jan. 1	Balance (3/5)		72,000	(72,00)
	Recognition of Goodwill (3/5)		54,000	(126,000)
	Goodwill Adjustment (5/12)	37,500		(88,500)
	Cash	26,000		(62,500)

Capital Account — Sheila

20X4				
Jan. 1	Balance (2/5)		48,000	(48,000)
	Recognition of Goodwill (2/5)		36,000	(84,000)
	Goodwill Adjustment (4/12)	30,000		(54,000)
	Cash	4,000		(50,000)

Capital Account — Terri

20X4				
Jan. 1	Goodwill Adjustment (3/12)	22,500		22,500
	Cash		60,000	(37,500)

The journal entries recording the above transactions are as follows:

Recognition of goodwill

20X4			
Jan. 1	Goodwill	90,000	
	Capital Account — Rhoda (3/5)		54,000
	Capital Account — Sheila (2/5)		36,000

Write-off of goodwill

20X4			
Jan. 1	Capital Account — Rhoda (5/12)	37,500	
	Capital Account — Sheila (4/12)	30,000	
	Capital Account — Terri (3/12)	22,500	
	Goodwill		90,000

Cash adjustments to capital accounts

20X4			
Jan. 1	Capital Account — Rhoda	26,000	
	Capital Account — Sheila	4,000	
	Cash Payments		30,000
	Cash Deposit	60,000	
	Capital Account — Terri		60,000

"pension" period. This arrangement is popular because it does not place a financial burden on the younger new partners at a time when they can often least afford it, and it provides for a limited pension for retiring partners.

RETIREMENT OR DEATH OF A PARTNER

When a partner **retires** from the partnership, the partnership legally ceases to exist. The partner's capital account balance and amounts remaining on the current account are paid out to the retiring partner. The remaining partners then form a new partnership, with or without admitting a new partner or partners. If there is an agreement among the partners to retain the retiring partner as a consultant, it must be honoured, because failure to do so would be a breach of contract.

The **death of a partner** also terminates the partnership from a legal perspective. Financial statements must be prepared up to the date of death and profits distributed in the normal manner. The balance on the deceased partner's capital account must then be paid over to the estate. Many partnership agreements contain provisions designed to ease the lot of the deceased partner's spouse and children: for example, the immediate payment of an amount of $50,000 in cash to the spouse to tide the family over until the deceased partner's estate has been wound up.

Most partnership agreements contain provisions for the withdrawal of a partner from the partnership. This is important because it determines the amount to be paid out to the partner or the estate and, consequently, the agreement may specify that assets be revalued at their fair market value, record goodwill, or both.

DISSOLUTION OF A PARTNERSHIP

The Normal Dissolution of a Partnership

Where a partnership comes to an end, it is referred to as the dissolution or liquidation of a partnership. In such cases, the assets of the partnership are either sold or taken over.

The way a dissolution takes place is to realize the assets, pay off any liabilities, and repay the capital and current account balances to the partners. This is normally achieved through the use of a realization account in the ledger, to which all balances on the asset accounts are transferred until sold or disposed of otherwise. The proceeds from the realization of the assets should be applied in the following sequence:

1. The liabilities of the partnership to outside parties must first be settled;
2. Any loans from the partners and the balances on their current accounts are then repaid; and
3. Finally, the capital accounts are repaid after adjustment for any gains or losses arising from the sale of the partnership assets.

The "Garner vs. Murray" Rule

The dissolution of a partnership normally poses no problems. From time to time, however, the capital and current accounts of a partner may be in debit.

In the event of the partnership agreement being silent on the matter, the dissolution of the partnership follows the rule laid down by the British case of *Garner vs. Murray*.[9] This rule relates to the interpretation of Section 47 of the British *Partnership Act*, 1890, which states that, in the event of the dissolution of a partnership, the residue after the payment of the

---

[9] 1904, 1 Ch. 57.

ILLUSTRATION 21–3
APPLICATION OF THE "GARNER *VS.* MURRAY" RULE

The partnership of Frank, George & Harry was dissolved following the bankruptcy of Harry on September 4, 20X2. Unbeknown to Frank and George, Harry had lost $200,000 by trading in derivatives and, in trying to recoup some of his losses, he had withdrawn all the cash in the partnership's bank account. Upon discovery, the misappropriated amount was debited to Harry's current and capital accounts, leaving a debit balance of $25,000. At that point, the capital accounts of Frank and George reflected $60,000 and $40,000 respectively. Profits and losses were shared between the partners in the ratio of 3:2:2.

On November 30, 20X2, the partnership assets had been realized. After the payment of amounts due to outside parties, the realization account reflected as loss (debit balance) of $17,500. On that date, the balance in the partnership banking account was $57,500.

Closing off of the capital accounts of the three partners would, in terms of the "Garner vs. Murray" rule, be carried out as follows:

	Total	Frank	George	Harry
Balance on November 30, 20X2	$75,000	$60,000	$40,000	$(25,000)
Loss on Realization of Assets	(17,500)	(7,500)	(5,000)	(5,000)
	57,500	52,500	35,000	(30,000)
Apportionment of Harry's loss (3:2)	—	(18,000)	(12,000)	30,000
	$57,500	$34,500	$23,000	$ Nil
Cash Paid Out	$57,500	$34,500	$23,000	$ Nil

---

amounts owing to outside parties must be divided among the remaining partners in the proportion in which the profits were divisible (i.e., the debts of any partners are absorbed by the remaining partners in their profit-sharing ratio). In the case of *Garner vs. Murray*, the court held that unless another method was specified by the partnership agreement, this also applied to deficiencies in the partner's capital accounts. An example of the application of this ruling is given in Illustration 21–3.

Piecemeal Dissolution of a Partnership

At times, the dissolution of a partnership may be spread over a considerable period to enable the partnership to realize the assets at higher prices than those that would be realized from a liquidation sale. The partners may, however, not wish to wait until all the assets have been realized before distributing the cash available from the sale of assets. This is known as the piecemeal dissolution or installment liquidation of a partnership.

The problem is that it is not possible to determine the realization price of the assets in advance. Therefore, to ensure that too much money is not distributed, the payments to the partners must be limited to an amount that would not require them to pay money into the partnership should there be losses on realization of the remaining assets. The main objective in making a preliminary distribution in this manner is, therefore, to ensure that adequate capital is maintained by the partnership to absorb all possible future realization losses.

The above objective can be achieved by assuming the worst possible position: that any unsold partnership assets are worthless at the date of a preliminary distribution of cash to partners. The asset values are, therefore, debited to the partners' capital accounts in the profit-sharing ratio, thereby reducing the capital balances to a value equalling the available cash. Thereafter, whenever remaining assets are sold, the proceeds are distributed in cash to the partners in their former profit-sharing ratios. For example, assume that a partnership consisted of three partners sharing profits and losses in the ratio of 4:4:2 and the capital accounts reflected a total of $300,000 after the payment of amounts owing to outside parties and current accounts. If this $300,000 was represented by cash of $20,000 and assets of $280,000, all that is required is to debit the capital accounts with $280,000 and to credit the asset accounts accordingly. The $20,000 can then be paid out in cash in the profit-sharing ratio, bringing the capital accounts to zero. On the subsequent sale of any assets, the proceeds are, once again, paid out to the partners in their former profit-sharing ratios. This process is repeated until all the assets have been realized. Adequate records must, however, be maintained to calculate profits or losses on the sale of assets for tax purposes.

THE INCORPORATION OF A PARTNERSHIP

As part of the progression from a small to a large business, many business ventures commenced as sole proprietorships, then became partnerships and, finally, they were incorporated. There are numerous reasons why sole proprietorships become partnerships. However, the change from a partnership to a company occurs when the owner may want to (1) separate the ownership and management of the business, (2) streamline the management of the business by limiting those who can contract on its behalf, (3) limit the liability of the partners, (4) give the business a continuity of existence, and/or (5) broaden its capital base. The decision to form a private or public company is usually based on the need for capital and the ease with which it can be raised.

The first requirement is to form a company. Once the company has been formed, the assets are transferred from the partnership to the company at their fair market value in return for shares in the company. The issue of shares is in the same ratio and at approximately the same value as the partner's capital accounts. Where the share capital is to be less than the total of the fixed partnership capital, the differences would be treated as loans to the company by the shareholders.

The accounting procedures for the sale of the partnership assets are facilitated by the use of a realization account in the manner described in the earlier chapter on business combinations. Similarly, the adjusting entries in the company are exactly the same as those relating to the acquisition of a business.

LIMITED PARTNERSHIPS

The provinces, other than Nova Scotia and Prince Edward Island, allow certain partnerships to carry on business under restricted conditions with limited liability known as **limited partnerships**. Their formation is covered either in the individual partnership acts or by special legislation. In these limited partnerships, **there are general partners and limited partners**. The **general partners** carry on the partnership's business and have unlimited personal liability, while the **limited partners** have complete protection from liability provided they do not take an active part in the running of the partnership.

The objective of having a limited partnership is to allow outside parties to contribute capital to a partnership in the expectation of sharing in profits. These are often large ventures and are normally only available to persons with considerable capital resources. Although they may take many forms, they are usually established by a single person (or organization), called the general partner, who has considerable expertise in the type of activities to be carried out. The general partner divides the investment into smaller units and sells these to the limited partners who are prohibited from taking an active part in the running of the partnership. These units are traded like shares on the various stock exchanges and their trading results are reported in the financial press.

LIMITED LIABILITY PARTNERSHIPS

In 1998, the law relating to partnerships in Ontario and Alberta was amended to allow partnerships of persons to form limited liability partnerships (LLPs). Similar changes in other provinces are expected.

The objective of the changes was to allow **the formation of a legal entity in which the individual partners in a partnership are not personally liable for the negligent acts of a single partner or an employee supervised by a negligent partner**. In other respects, however, the partners in the partnership remain jointly and severally liable for the acts and debts of the partnership including those liabilities arising from contracts or fraud.

There are two types of LLPs, namely, **provincial LLPs** and **extra-provincial LLPs**. Provincial LLPs are those that are registered in the province in which the partnership carries on business and extra-provincial LLPs are those that are registered in another province or other jurisdiction (e.g., in Alberta or the state of Illinois). These partnerships must, of course, be **distinguished from limited partnerships**.

The **formation of an LLP** occurs when the partners sign an agreement designating the partnership as such. An **existing partnership** can be converted into a limited liability partnership if all the existing partners sign an amendment to the partnership agreement. At present, extra-provincial LLPs may not carry on business in Ontario but can do so in Alberta provided the LLP meets the requirements of the Alberta *Partnership Act*.[10]

An LLP may carry on business for the sole purpose of practising a profession provided **all** the following conditions are satisfied:

(a) The Act governing the profession must expressly permit those persons who are licensed to practise a profession (e.g., Chartered Accountants) to form LLPs;
(b) The professional governing body must establish minimum insurance requirements for partnerships;
(c) The partnership agreement must designate the partnership as an LLP;
(d) The LLP must register its name under the relevant provincial legislation;[11] and
(e) In all cases, an LLP must include the words "limited liability partnership" or the abbreviation "LLP" as part of its name (or the French equivalents "Société en nom collectif" or "SNC").

SUMMARY

This chapter presents and explains the accounting requirements for sole proprietorships and partnerships. Sole proprietorships are the simplest form of business, and the accounting process is designed to provide the owner with information required for the day-to-day management of the business. Even though the financial statements are prepared to provide the owner with the results of operations and financial position of the business, they are, in practice, mainly required for income tax and credit purposes.

Partnerships are more complicated, and business operations are based on the rights, duties and relationships between the partners who pool their knowledge and resources for their common benefit. The liability of the partners for the debts and obligations of the partnership is unlimited.

Accounting for partnerships follows the same pattern as for any other business. The major differences are that the capital of the partnership is contributed in set amounts, and this usually dictates the sharing of profits. Partnerships legally terminate on the admission or retirement of partners requiring adjustments that vary, depending on whether they relate to small or large partnerships. Specific accounting requirements also apply to the dissolution of partnerships. The chapter concludes with the adjustments that are necessary when a partnership is incorporated as a company and a brief look at limited partnerships and limited liability partnerships.

---

10 The Amendments to the Ontario *Partnership Act* received Royal Assent on June 11, 1998, while that amending the Alberta *Partnership Act* received Royal Assent on May 19, 1999.
11 Under the Ontario *Business Names Act* or the Alberta *Partnerships Act*.

REVIEW QUESTIONS

1. What accounting equation applies to sole proprietorships? What does it show?
2. What are the main uses of the financial statements of sole proprietorships?
3. What aspects of a partnership are important?
4. What is normally included in a partnership agreement?
5. What are the partners' drawings and what do they represent?
6. Why is goodwill sometimes brought into account on the admission of a new partner? What alternatives are there?
7. What is the "Garner *vs.* Murray rule", and when is it applied?
8. What problem may arise with a piecemeal dissolution of a partnership?
9. Sally, Terri and Ursula carry on business together in partnership. The capital, which is fixed, is $100,000 for Sally, $80,000 for Terri and $70,000 for Ursula. The net income for the year ended December 31, 20X2 is $150,000. How would the profits be shared among the partners if the partnership agreement: (a) does not specify how profits are to be shared; (b) specifies that Ursula be paid a salary of $60,000 and the remaining profits be shared in accordance with the capital accounts?
10. Distinguish between limited partnerships and limited liability partnerships.

EXERCISES

EXERCISE 21-1 **REQUIRED**

Provide journal entries to record the following three related events in the records of changes to the partnership between Ralph and Simon:

(a) Ralph and Simon are in partnership, sharing profits and losses equally. Their capital accounts are $120,000 each. Tim privately purchases Simon's interest in the partnership for $140,000 and joins Ralph as an equal partner.

(b) Ursula is admitted as a junior partner to share in 25% of the profits. Ursula's capital account is to be $70,000 and the capital accounts of Ralph and Simon are to be adjusted to reflect the profit-sharing ratio.

(c) Vera is admitted to the partnership with a 20% share of the profits. Her capital account is to be $80,000 and the capital accounts are to be proportionate to the profit-sharing ratio of 3:3:2:2. For purposes of the change in partnership, goodwill is valued at $120,000 and is not to be reflected on the balance sheet of the new partnership.

EXERCISE 21-2 Rodney, Stuart and Thelma are in partnership and share profits in the ratio 3:2:1. The abbreviated balance sheet of the partnership at December 31, 20X3 is as follows:

ASSETS		CAPITAL ACCOUNTS	
Cash	$110,000	Rodney	$140,000
Sundry Assets (net of amortization)	220,000	Stuart	100,000
	330,000	Thelma	60,000
Less: LIABILITIES			
Accounts Payable	30,000		
	$300,000		$300,000

You are further informed that:

(a) Thelma decided to retire on December 31, 20X3. She agreed to accept $80,000 in cash for her interest in the partnership, **including** her share of the goodwill. This amount was paid to Thelma by Rodney and Stuart on December 31, 20X3, in proportion to the profit-sharing ratio between them. After Thelma's retirement, the capital accounts of the remaining two partners were to reflect the existing profit-sharing ratio between them.

(b) Immediately after the retirement of Thelma, Unity was admitted as a partner. For the purposes of the admission of Unity to the partnership, the goodwill was valued at $120,000. It was decided that once the admission of Unity had been effected, the goodwill would not appear as an asset on the balance sheet of the new partnership.

(c) In terms of the agreement between the partners, the capital accounts of the partnership were to total $360,000 and that Unity was to share in the profits to the extent of one-sixth. The sharing of the remaining five-sixths of the profit between Rodney and Stuart was to remain unchanged.

REQUIRED

Prepare:

1. A schedule giving the balances on the partners' capital accounts after the retirement of Thelma; and
2. A schedule giving the partners' capital accounts after the admission of Unity to the partnership. Regardless of your determination in part (1) above, use the amount of $300,000 as the total capital of Rodney and Stuart after the retirement of Thelma.

EXERCISE 21–3 Aaron and Beatrice were in partnership, sharing profits and losses equally. It was agreed that Aaron would retire from the partnership on December 31, 20X3 and that his son, Caleb, would join Beatrice in the partnership with effect from January 1, 20X4. In terms of the agreement between Beatrice and Caleb, Caleb was to receive a one-third share of the profits.

At December 31, 20X3, the abbreviated balance sheet of the partnership was as follows:

Cash at Bank	$ 86,000
Accounts Receivable	206,600
Inventory	139,400
	432,000
Less: Accounts Payable	58,800
	$373,200
Capital Accounts:	
Aaron	$204,000
Beatrice	169,200
	$373,200

It was agreed that, for both the dissolution of the partnership and the admission of Caleb to the partnership, goodwill should be valued at $132,000. Beatrice and Caleb further agreed that goodwill would not be shown on the balance sheet of the new partnership.

Beatrice and Caleb also agreed that:

(a) Aaron would transfer $80,000 to Caleb's capital account from his capital account on his retirement as a gift;
(b) Sufficient money would be paid into the partnership to enable Aaron to take his interest in the partnership out in cash; and
(c) Beatrice and Caleb would pay enough cash into the partnership to ensure that the capital of the partnership at January 1, 20X4 was $300,000.

All cash transfers were made on January 1, 20X4, as planned.

REQUIRED

1. Provide a schedule showing the adjustments to the partners' capital accounts at December 31, 20X3 and January 1, 20X4; and
2. Prepare the balance sheet of the partnership on January 1, 20X4.

EXERCISE 21–4   You are provided with the following abbreviated balance sheet of Tom, Dick and Harry, manufacturing jewellers, at December 31, 20X4. The three partners share profits and losses in the ratio of 3:2:2.

Cash at Bank	$ 2,000	Accounts Payable	$ 37,000
Accounts Receivable	95,000	Capital Accounts:	
Inventory	140,000	Tom	153,000
Work in Process	72,000	Dick	102,000
Capital Assets (net)	85,000	Harry	102,000
	$394,000		$394,000

On November 10, 20X4, the partners received a firm offer from Isakov Jewellery Brokers Inc. (IJB) to purchase the assets of the partnership. The purchase consideration was:

(a)   21,000 shares in IJB with a fair market value of $18 per share; and
(b)   An amount of $42,000 in cash.

The offer was accepted by the partners, who decided to hold their shares in IJB.

REQUIRED

Give the journal entries required to close the books of the partnership on January 1, 20X5.

EXERCISE 21–5   Leon, who had carried on a partnership with Matthew and Nathan, decided to retire on December 31, 20X1. The three partners shared profits and losses in the ratio of 6:5:4 and kept their fixed capital accounts at a total of $225,000. Profits not withdrawn from the partnership were credited to the partners' current accounts. Any adjustments to the fixed capital accounts not covered by balances in the current accounts were to be settled in cash. For purposes of the retirement, the partners agreed that goodwill would be valued at $180,000.

Matthew and Nathan decided not to admit another partner but continued to operate the partnership on their own effective January 1, 20X2. They agreed that:

(a)   The fixed capital of the partnership was to be $200,000;
(b)   Profits and losses between the two partners would be shared in the ratio of 3:2;
(c)   Goodwill would not appear on the balance sheet of the partnership;
(d)   Profits not withdrawn from the partnership were to be credited to the partners' current accounts; and
(e)   Adjustments to the fixed capital accounts were to be settled in cash.

To encourage partners to retain profits in the partnership, interest at the rate of 10% per year was to be paid on the current account balances, if any, at the **beginning** of each year.

The following information applied to the three years ended December 31, 20X3:

	20X1	20X2	20X3
Net Trading Profits after charging Interest on Current Accounts	$255,000	$220,000	$185,000
Current Accounts at January 1, 20X1:			
— Leon	14,000	??	??
— Matthew	18,000	??	??
— Nathan	8,000	??	??
Drawings — Leon	110,000	—	—
— Matthew	72,000	96,000	92,000
— Nathan	74,000	72,000	75,000

REQUIRED

Give the capital accounts for 20X3 **and** current accounts of the partners for 20X1 through 20X3, in columnar form.

EXERCISE 21–6   On July 1, 20X2, Louis and Mary entered into partnership sharing profits equally. The year end of the partnership would be December 31 in each year.

You are also informed that:

(a)   They agreed that they would each contribute $120,000 to the partnership as capital and that profits were to be determined on a six-monthly basis.

(b)   Drawings would be kept to a minimum. To compensate the partners for leaving their profits in the partnership, interest would be credited against the partners' current accounts and charged as an expense against the partnership revenues.

(c)   Profits and withdrawals from the partnership were as follows:

	Drawings/Interest		Profits
	Louis	Mary	Partnership
Drawings to December 31, 20X2	$42,000	$48,000	
Interest on Current Accounts to December 31	340	380	$ (720)
Profits to December 31 before interest on partners' current accounts			178,000

On January 1, 20X3, Louis and Mary admitted Nora to the partnership on the following terms and conditions:

1.   The partners would share profits in the ratio of 3:3:2, and the capital of the partnership after admitting Nora was to be $300,000.
2.   Nora was to be guaranteed a minimum share of profits of $100,000 in any year.
3.   Goodwill was to be valued on January 1, 20X3 at $80,000, but this amount would not appear on the balance sheet of the partnership.
4.   Profits and withdrawals from the partnership in 20X3 were as follows:

	Drawings/Interest			Profits
	Louis	Mary	Nora	Partnership
Drawings to December 31, 20X3	$132,000	$124,000	$76,000	
Interest on current accounts to December 31	2,600	2,400	1,400	$ (6,400)
Profits to December 31 before interest on partners' current accounts				372,000

REQUIRED

Give the partners' capital and current accounts for the period July 1, 20X2 to December 31, 20X3, in columnar form.

PROBLEMS

PROBLEM 21–1   On January 1, 20X2, Luke, who had maintained his capital account at a set amount of $240,000, admitted his two sons, Adam and Seth, into partnership. The partnership agreement stipulated that profits would be shared among the three partners in the ratio of 9:4:3 but that Adam and Seth would not withdraw profits of more than $32,000 and $24,000 respectively until they had accumulated capital balances of $72,000 and $54,000. At that stage, Luke would withdraw sufficient cash from the partnership so that the total capital of the partnership would be maintained at a fixed amount of $288,000, and would be in the same ratio as the share of profits. Profits not withdrawn from the partnership were to be credited to the partners' current accounts, before any transfers to the capital accounts were effected.

Interest at the rate of 10% per year was to be paid on current account balances at the beginning of each year. The financial year-end of the partnership was December 31, and at January 1, 20X2 Luke's current account reflected a credit balance of $14,000.

The following information applied to the three years ended December 31, 20X4:

	20X2	20X3	20X4
Net Trading Profits before Interest on Current Accounts	$225,400	$283,340	$299,224
Drawings — Luke	108,000	162,000	198,000
— Adam	32,000	32,000	56,000
— Seth	24,000	24,000	46,000

REQUIRED

Give the capital and current accounts of the three partners for 20X2 through 20X4, in columnar form.

PROBLEM 21–2   Andrews, Baker and Chan carried on a partnership writing software programs for the medical profession, sharing profits and losses in the ratio of 4:3:3. Effective January 1, 20X4, the partners agreed to amalgamate with Davis, who carried on a similar type of business. The abbreviated balance sheets of the two partnerships at January 1, 20X4 were as follows:

Andrews, Baker and Chan

Cash	$ 40,000	Accounts Payable	$ 54,000
Accounts Receivable	180,000	Bank Loan	120,000
Work-in-Process	310,000	Capital Accounts:	
Land and Buildings	200,000	Andrews	360,000
Equipment	260,000	Baker	270,000
Motor Vehicles	84,000	Chan	270,000
	$1,074,000		$1,074,000

Davis

Cash at Bank	$ 12,000	Accounts Payable	$ 22,000
Accounts Receivable	140,000	Capital Account	170,000
Work-in-Process	16,000		
Equipment	24,000		
	$ 192,000		$ 192,000

The terms of the amalgamation were as follows:

(a) Andrews was to retire from the partnership on December 31, 20X3 and was to leave $250,000 on loan to the new partnership. Any shortfall in cash to meet the repayment of Andrews' capital was to be borrowed from the bank.

(b) Baker was to take over one of the partnership cars for $54,000. At December 31, 20X3, the book value of this car was $48,000.

(c) Profits and losses in the new partnership of Baker, Chan and Davis were to be shared in the ratio of 3:3:2.

(d) Goodwill at June 30, 20X3 was to be $120,000 for Andrews, Baker and Chan and $30,000 for Davis. Goodwill was not to be reflected on the balance sheet of the new partnership.

(e) The new partnership was to take over all assets owned by the two partnerships. However, the land and buildings were to be revalued at $240,000 and Davis's work-in-process was to be revalued downwards by $4,000.

(f) The capital of the new partnership was to be $1-million.

(g) Any surpluses or deficiencies in the partners' capital accounts were to be transferred to their current accounts.

REQUIRED

1. Give the capital accounts of Andrews, Baker, Chan and Davis at December 31, 20X3, recording the above transactions in columnar form; and

2. Prepare the balance sheet of the new partnership at January 1, 20X4.

PROBLEM 21-3 Janice, Ken and Lawrence were each in practice as town planners. During December 20X4, they agreed to consolidate their practices with effect from January 1, 20X5.

The partnership agreement included the following matters:

(a) Each partner's capital contributions were to be the net assets of their individual practices at December 31, 20X4. These were as follows:

	Janice	Ken	Lawrence
Cash at Bank	$ 30,000	$ 12,000	$ 3,000
Accounts Receivable	102,000	88,000	108,000
Sundry Capital Assets	24,000	15,000	40,000
Less Accumulated Amortization	(3,000)	(9,000)	(27,000)
	153,000	106,000	124,000
Accounts Payable	3,000	16,000	4,000
	$150,000	$ 90,000	$120,000

(b) Each partner was to receive 20% of the gross fees charged to their respective clients during the first year of the partnership, after deducting a proportionate amount of expenses, in recognition of the business brought into the partnership. The proportionate expenses amounted to $120,000.

(c) The balance of the partnership profits was to be credited to the partners in the ratio of 5:3:4 for Janice, Ken and Lawrence respectively.

(d) On April 1, 20X5, Michael was admitted to the partnership. He contributed $90,000 in cash and was to share in the 20X5 profits equally with Ken calculated after the adjustment for fees in point (b) above (i.e., from April 1).

(e) During 20X5, the following billings for fees by the individual partners were as follows:

Janice	$360,000
Ken	150,000
Lawrence	210,000
New Business	418,000

(f) Total expenses for the year amounted to $403,000 (including the proportionate amount of expenses of $120,000).

(g) At the end of the year, the partners' capital accounts were to be fixed at a total of $450,000 and were to reflect their profit-sharing ratios. Excess amounts were to be paid out in cash.

REQUIRED

Prepare a statement in columnar form giving the capital accounts of the partners for the year ended December 31, 20X5.

PROBLEM 21-4 At December 31, 20X4, the following trial balance was extracted from the books of Johnston & Peters, a partnership of four persons carrying on the business of investment consultants and portfolio managers:

	Dr.
Administration Expenses	$1,053,883
Cash and Term Deposits	124,122
Accounts Receivable	298,040
Prepaid Expenses	31,422
Equipment, at cost	310,488
Partners Drawings:	
David Johnston	226,662
Jeremy McLean	225,432
Sandra Davidson	180,130
Martin La Salle	115,090
	$2,565,269

	Cr.
Revenues	$1,843,241
Allowance for Doubtful Debts at January 1, 20X4	25,000
Accumulated Amortization of Equipment at January 1, 20X4	85,717
Accounts Payable	169,612
Accrued Insurances	22,496
Partners' Capital Accounts at January 1, 20X4:	
David Johnston	120,000
Jeremy McLean	120,000
Sandra Davidson	100,000
Martin La Salle	60,000
Partners' Current Accounts at January 1, 20X4:	
David Johnston	2,010
Jeremy McLean	4,677
Sandra Davidson	5,694
Martin La Salle	6,822
	$2,565,269

Additional Information:

1. The partnership consisted of David Johnston, Jeremy McLean, Sandra Davidson, and Martin La Salle who shared profits and losses in the ratio of 6:6:5:3.
2. Amounts not included in trial balance:
   (a) Amortization of capital assets for the year amounted to $29,883
   (b) Increase in the Allowance for doubtful debts of $3,000
   (c) Interest on the partners' current accounts were as follows:

David Johnston	$ 602
Jeremy McLean	778
Sandra Davidson	673
Martin La Salle	1,902
	$3,955

REQUIRED

Prepare the income statement and balance sheet of the partnership for 20X4, giving a detailed breakdown of the capital and current accounts of the four partners.

Bankruptcy and Insolvency: An Overview

22

LEARNING OBJECTIVES

After studying this chapter you should be able to:

1. Know what legislation covers bankruptcy and insolvency in Canada;
2. Distinguish between receivership and bankruptcy; and
3. Understand the nature and operation of proposals.

BASIC CONSIDERATIONS

Up to this point, our examination of accounting topics has been based on situations where the going concern assumption applies. There are occasions, however, where this assumption cannot be made because the business entity is in receivership, facing bankruptcy charges, or being reorganized in an attempt to stave off bankruptcy or liquidation. In these cases, the business entity is usually in an insolvent position, which means that, for some reason or other, it is unable to pay its debts.

Where individuals become insolvent, they can voluntarily enter into **a formal or informal arrangement** with their creditors to **restructure their debt**. Alternatively, they can **file for bankruptcy**.

Bankruptcy is a **legal status** imposed upon the insolvent person by law. It is a legal process designed to provide **relief** for the insolvents to surrender their estate to a trustee. If the debtors are unable to reach agreement with their creditors on the restructuring of their debt, the trustee realizes the debtors' assets and settles the **claims of the creditors** in whole or in part (i.e., by, say, paying 20 cents in the dollar). The bankrupts can then apply to be **discharged from further liability** and may resume a normal life without the burden of former debts.

Professional accountants, like anybody else, can be declared bankrupt. When this occurs, their professional status and right to practise are suspended until such time as the bankruptcy is discharged. At that time, they can re-apply for membership of their controlling body. For example, former members of the Institute of Chartered Accountants of Ontario must re-apply for membership and, after their position has been considered and the application for re-admittance has been approved by an **Applications Committee**, they may resume practising as a Chartered Accountant.

With **companies**, the situation is similar. Any company may voluntarily reorganize itself if it finds itself in financial difficulties. If it is unable to restructure itself in a manner that would allow it to continue to operate, it is placed in bankruptcy and liquidated. Voluntary arrangements of this sort may be carried out with the protection of the courts. Where the restructuring is carried out **involuntarily** as the result of the action of its creditors, the reorganization or dissolution of the business must be effected with the protection of the courts.

The entire area of bankruptcy and insolvency is strictly controlled by legislation and has important accounting considerations. For example, the valuation of assets at their historical cost may no longer be suitable, and it may be impossible to report in a manner consistent with that of the previous period. Auditors are also required to qualify their audit reports if they are uncertain the entity can continue as a going concern.[1]

The administration of bankrupt estates and the reorganization or restructuring of companies is a highly specialized area and is carried out by **licensed trustees in bankruptcy**. The objective of this chapter is, therefore, not to provide a detailed presentation of these accounting requirements, but to outline the legal position relating to the administration of bankrupt estates and the reorganization of companies.

THE LEGISLATION APPLYING TO BANKRUPTCY AND INSOLVENCY

The legislation applying to bankruptcy and insolvency consists of two federal statutes, namely, the *Companies' Creditors Arrangement Act* (CCAA), 1933, and the *Bankruptcy and Insolvency Act* (BIA), 1985.

The CCAA permits a company that finds itself in financial difficulties to remain in possession of its assets while it presents a restructuring arrangement to its creditors. The objective is to provide the company with the time necessary to reorganize itself in a manner that will allow it to continue operating. During this time, the creditors cannot force the company into liquidation.[2] The only requirement is that a company seeking protection under the CCAA must have an outstanding issue of debentures or trust bonds: nothing a clever lawyer cannot arrange.

Very little is known about the **actual operation of the CCAA**.[3] It does not provide any guidelines, so that any proposal is limited only by the imagination and creativity of the accountants or lawyers involved. What is known is that protection afforded by the CCAA is expensive, somewhat difficult to obtain, essentially concerned with the rights of creditors, and designed to cater for the problems faced by large companies.[4] It can also be used by companies in addition to the BIA.

The most important statute is the **BIA**, which was substantially revised and amended in 1992. This act regulates the procedures relating to receivership, insolvency and bankruptcy of both companies and individuals. It was formerly known as the *Bankruptcy Act*, and its amendment in 1992 expanded the existing legislation to cover insolvency and receivership. As a result of these revisions, insolvency now takes on a wider meaning than the accounting definition of insolvency, where insolvent persons' liabilities exceed their assets. In this respect, insolvents are described as persons who are unable to pay their debts.

The objective of the BIA is to **shift** the previous emphasis of bankruptcy proceedings away **from bankruptcy towards the continued operation** of the business through reorganization. As with the CCAA, it is designed to provide individuals and companies struggling under crippling debt with protection from their creditors while they draw up plans to remain in operation. For individuals, its purpose is to allow debtors to reorganize their affairs rather than force them into bankruptcy.

---

[1]   Paras. 5510.51–53 of the CICA *Handbook*.
[2]   This protection is the same as that provided by Chapter 11 of the US Bankruptcy Code.
[3]   See *The Bottom Line*, May 1991, for a commentary on its revival as a means of protecting companies against its creditors.
[4]   As with the current attempts to restructure Air Canada to prevent it being liquidated.

THE ADMINISTRATION OF THE CCAA AND BIA

The CCAA and the BIA are administered by the **Superintendent of Bankruptcy** as part of the federal Department of Consumer and Corporate Affairs. The superintendent is given wide powers to supervise the administration of these Acts, including the right to engage persons to undertake investigations for the purpose of tracing or recovering the property of a bankrupt estate.

For the purposes of the BIA, each province is a bankruptcy district that can, if considered necessary, be divided into two or more bankruptcy divisions. The BIA designates various courts as having jurisdiction in bankruptcy in each province. For example, in British Columbia and Nova Scotia it is the Supreme Court, while the Ontario Court (General Division) is the designated court in that province. The presiding judge in bankruptcy matters is referred to as the bankruptcy judge.

Official receivers are appointed in each bankruptcy division. They are required to maintain public records relating to proposals and bankruptcies, and report to the Superintendent on every bankruptcy originating in his or her division.

Much of the day-to-day administration of the BIA is carried out by the **registrars in bankruptcy**. They are empowered by the court to act on behalf of the official receivers to hear bankruptcy petitions, approve the accounts of the trustees, grant orders for the discharge of bankrupts and other, similar duties. They may also make receiving orders and approve proposals for the settlement of the bankrupt's debts when they are not opposed by the creditors.

The actual day-to-day administration of bankrupt estates and the reorganization or liquidation of companies is carried out by **licensed trustees in bankruptcy**. These are suitably qualified natural persons who are licensed by the Superintendent of Bankruptcy to administer either the CCAA or the BIA. They are given broad powers and are required to carry out certain duties in carrying out the administration of these estates, which involve such matters as:

(a) Taking possession of a bankrupt's property, books, and any other relevant records.
(b) Taking steps to conserve the bankrupt's property.
(c) Carrying out the wishes of the creditors.
(d) Ensuring that any property of the bankrupt held by any other person is delivered to the trustee.
(e) If necessary, to institute legal proceedings as authorized by the creditors against any person believed to have committed a criminal offence.
(f) Keep proper books of account for the estate, report to every creditor on the status of the estate, and prepare whatever documentation is required.
(g) Report to the court before applying for a discharge as trustee.
(h) Apply to the court to be discharged from their duties.

The creditors may, at any meeting by special resolution, appoint or substitute another licensed trustee named in an assignment, receiving order or proposal. However, until relieved of their duties, the trustees continue to administer the debtor's affairs.

THE DIFFERENCE BETWEEN RECEIVERSHIP AND BANKRUPTCY

Where a person has borrowed money on the security of some or other asset (e.g., land and buildings, accounts receivable and inventory[5]) and has **defaulted** on the payment of interest, or in some other way failed to comply with the terms of the loan (or debt covenant), the holder of the security may petition the court having jurisdiction in that bankruptcy division to issue a

5 Banks normally require borrowers to give them a general lien over their accounts receivable and inventory.

receiving order against the debtor. In these cases, the creditor is known as a **secured creditor** and where a receiving order is made, the court appoints a **licensed trustee** in bankruptcy to take possession of the assets used as security. Unless the debtor can reach agreement with the creditor for the settlement of the claim, the trustee sells the assets on behalf of the secured creditor. The proceeds from the sale are then used to repay the amount owing to the creditor.

In the event of the property being sold for more than the amount owing, the excess is paid to the debtor. Where the property realizes an amount insufficient to settle the amount owing, the outstanding balance still owed is known as an **unsecured debt**. In these cases, the creditor has **an unsecured claim** against the debtor for this amount.

One or more **unsecured creditors** may petition the court to issue a receiving order against a debtor. If the petition is granted, the court then appoints a trustee to take possession of all the assets of the debtor on behalf of the creditors. In these cases, the petition is known as a **bankruptcy petition** because it normally results in the bankruptcy of the debtor.

Persons who have had receiving orders issued against them are referred to as **being in receivership**, while a bankrupt is a person who has been declared bankrupt by the court. In this respect, a person is **declared bankrupt** by the court on being recognized as having committed an act of bankruptcy.

THE CONDITIONS FOR BANKRUPTCY

The conditions for a bankruptcy petition are that the debtor has debts of at least $1,000 and during the past six months prior to the petition has committed at least one of the following **"acts of bankruptcy"**:

(a) Assigned his or her property to a trustee acting on behalf of his or her creditors.
(b) Fraudulently donated, transferred or disposed of his or her property or has attempted to do so.
(c) Left the country in an attempt to delay or defeat any action by his or her creditors.
(d) Not contested a petition for having a receiving order issued against him/her.
(e) Exhibited a statement of assets and liabilities to his or her creditors showing that he or she is insolvent.
(f) Notified his or her creditors that he or she is about to suspend payment of his or her debts.
(g) Ceased to meet his or her liabilities as they become due.

Insolvent persons can, with the approval of the court, make an **assignment** of all their property for the general benefit of their creditors. This means that insolvent persons voluntarily surrender their assets to a trustee so that the assets can be realized on behalf of their creditors. When the insolvent is deceased, an assignment of property is made by his or her legal representative. An insolvent person may not, however, make an assignment of his or her property to any one creditor.

It is important to note that the BIA's definition of a person includes partnerships, unincorporated associations, corporations, and their heirs, executors, administrators or other legal representatives of a deceased person. All references to insolvent persons or debtors must, therefore, be construed as applying equally to natural persons and companies except where specific requirements apply.

OBTAINING PROTECTION UNDER THE BIA

Individuals who are **contemplating declaring bankruptcy** or are seeking the protection of the BIA normally consult a licensed trustee in bankruptcy. The licensed trustee must provide them with two counselling sessions for a nominal fee.

To proceed further, the debtors must detail in a proposal how they wish to reorganize their affairs. This proposal is then filed with the official receiver by the trustee. If, however, the debtors do not have sufficient time to file a proposal, all they need to do is to file a **notice of intention** directly with the official receiver that they intend to make a proposal. Thereafter, they are allowed 30 days to submit a proposal to their creditors.

The lodging of a proposal or notice of intention with the official receiver automatically places the debtors in receivership and under the protection of the BIA. A trustee must be named in either the proposal or notice to file a proposal and must, within five days, forward copies of either the proposal or the notice of intention to every known creditor. This automatically stays the rights of both the secured and unsecured creditors to take action against the debtor. The making of a proposal is, by itself, not an act of bankruptcy because it can be made by anyone who finds themselves in a position where they cannot pay their debts.

The debtors must, within 10 days of lodging a proposal or notice of intention, lodge a projected cash flow statement with the trustee. They are also allowed another 21 days for the creditors to meet and vote on the proposal. The court has the power to add increments of 45 days up to a maximum of five months, provided it believes that the debtor is acting in good faith, the debtor is likely to make a viable proposal, and no creditor would be materially prejudiced by the extension of time. In total, with notices of intention the rights of creditors can be stayed for up to seven months.

On application by one or more creditors, the court may appoint an **interim trustee** to take control of the assets of the debtor. The interim trustee holds office during the period between the application for a receiving order and its issue or between the filing of a proposal or notice of intention and its acceptance by the creditors.

The BIA provides **debtor companies** with considerably more leverage in dealing with banks, landlords and suppliers. This is because, while the stay of proceedings of creditors is in effect, debtors may continue to operate their business. This is designed to ensure that banks negotiate with debtor companies before forcing them into bankruptcy. For example, a bank or other financial institution must give 10 days' notice that it is calling in its loan to a company. The debtor, immediately after receiving such notice, can file a notice of intention with the official receiver. This gives the debtors an automatic 30-day stay against all creditors. The debtors can also apply for extensions of 45 days each for protection, to a maximum of six months, in which time they must work out a reorganization plan. Throughout the process, there are specific requirements relating to the presentation of cash-flow statements, etc.

The objective of the **stay of proceedings** is to allow individuals or companies to reorganize or restructure themselves in such a way that they can continue to operate. In many cases it takes the form of the conversion of debt into equity.[6] In others, it requires some forgiveness of the amounts owing.

To assist them in restructuring the business, the stay of proceedings provides the following safeguards:

(a) The debtor may continue to deal with any assets, like inventory and accounts receivable, that have been pledged as collateral security for any loans.
(b) The landlord cannot pursue the debtors for any amounts outstanding, provided they continue to pay rent.
(c) Changes to any agreement relating to payments cannot be modified as a result of the insolvency of the debtor.
(d) Similarly, utilities must be provided as long as the debtor continues to pay for them.

---

6 For example, *The Globe and Mail* (December 11, 1992) reported that 89.5% of the debenture holders of Bramalea Ltd., the troubled Toronto property developer, approved a plan to restructure $545-million in debt that would give them a 52.7% controlling interest in the company. The proposal to restructure the company took place outside the bankruptcy court. It was also reported that if the company had been forced into bankruptcy, the debenture holders would have received a maximum of 39 cents on the dollar.

(e) Licence agreements cannot be cancelled on the grounds of insolvency or the failure to remit royalties prior to the lodging of the notice of intent. The debtor is also allowed to terminate a rental agreement irrespective of any clause to the contrary on the payment of no more than six months rental.

The BIA also provides **creditors** with some additional powers. For example, it allows them to repossess goods from a debtor if they were shipped within the 30 days prior to the buyer declaring bankruptcy or going into receivership. To be repossessed, the goods must be identifiable, unchanged, unsold, and in the hands of the debtor. This right must, however, be exercised within 10 days of being notified of the bankruptcy or receivership.

It is, however, feared that these new proposals could act in a detrimental manner towards some retailers. This is because banks have traditionally lent them up to 50% of the value of their inventories but, now, some are only prepared to lend up to 25%. This means that retailers will have to either borrow money at higher rates or provide additional collateral security to maintain present credit lines.

In 1998, the *Bankruptcy and Insolvency Act* was changed to prohibit the **holders of student loans** from declaring bankruptcy until the expiry of 10 years from their graduation dates. This follows the common practice of declaring personal bankruptcy by certain students to avoid having to repay their student loans. Avoidance of liability in this way was costing the government about $70-million a year. Additional changes were also made to ensure that **felons** (i.e., those convicted of a serious criminal offence) cannot declare bankruptcy to avoid the payment of their fines for a period of 10 years after conviction. Declaring bankruptcy to discharge the payment of credit card debt is only allowed after the amounts have been outstanding for nine months.

PROPOSALS

The Nature of Proposals

A **proposal** is a scheme of arrangement to save the business of an insolvent or bankrupt by restructuring it or its debt in a manner that allows it to continue to operate or to make a fresh start. In effect, it is an **outline of how the debtor intends to proceed** from that time onwards and may be made by the debtor without declaring bankruptcy.

Companies normally seek the advice of professional advisors to develop a reorganization plan and assist with any negotiations with creditors before lodging the notice of intention with the Official Receiver. Again, a trustee must be named in the proposal.

In making a proposal, the debtors place the creditors in a position where they must make a decision on which course of action to follow. In these circumstances, the acceptance of the proposal may give them the opportunity of receiving some payment from the debtors (like, say 40 cents in the dollar), which may be better than risking losing everything by forcing the debtors into bankruptcy and liquidating their estate. This is because bankrupt estates seldom pay more than a nominal amount (like five cents in the dollar) to unsecured creditors.

If the debtors have not already filed a proposal with the official receiver, they must work out a proposal with the trustee named in the notice of intention. To do so they must cooperate with the trustee by providing a statement of their affairs detailing their debts, their earnings, and personal possessions, and how they intend to meet their commitments. If the debtors fail to file a projected cash flow statement in 10 days or a proposal in the 30-day period following the lodging of a notice of intention, they are deemed to have assigned their property to the trustee.

Once the proposal has been completed, the trustee is required to submit it to the official receiver. If the receiver decides that the proposal is worthwhile and can be carried out successfully, the trustee sends notices to the creditors listed by the debtor advising them of the position of the debtor. It also invites them to prove their claims against the debtor. It also notifies creditors of the date of the first "meeting of creditors", at which time the proposal is either accepted or rejected by the creditors. If the proposal is rejected by the creditors or a single major creditor, the debtor is immediately forced into bankruptcy. A **creditor** is a person who has proved a claim against the debtor's or bankrupt's estate.

A proposal can take a **number of forms**. It could be a request for an extension of time or the forgiveness of debt or even a reduction in the amounts owing. The requirements are that the proposal must be made to the creditors in general or to a specific group or class of secured or unsecured creditors. To be able to vote on the proposal at the first "meeting of creditors", creditors must prove their claims with the trustee. At this meeting, the creditors also appoint inspectors to oversee the trustee's administration of the estate.

At the **first meeting of creditors**, the proposal is voted on by the two classes of creditors. These are the secured and unsecured creditors. For approval, the proposal must be approved by a majority of creditors representing at least two-thirds in value of the claims. Further meetings of creditors are called to deal with different aspects of administering the proposal.

The proposal is normally presented personally to the creditors by the debtor at the first "meeting of creditors" called for that purpose. However, it may also be presented by the receiver of an insolvent's property, the liquidator of the debtor's insolvent estate or the trustee of the bankrupt's estate if any of these persons believe that the debtor is not utilizing the remedies available. If creditors who have proved claims do not respond, it is assumed that they have accepted the proposal. At this point, the creditors are required to stop charging interest and refrain from taking legal action against the debtor.

Consumer Proposals

There are also **consumer proposals.** These are arrangements designed to allow those persons who are burdened with heavy debt to arrange with their creditors to pay a reduced amount or to extend payments over a five-year period. The requirements are that the debtors must have liabilities of less than $75,000 not including any debts secured over their principal residence. Consumer proposals apply to persons who have a steady job and who are capable of repaying what they owe. However, if the debtors default on their payments for three months or more, the proposal is cancelled. The debtors are not automatically declared bankrupt because they can work out a new arrangement with their creditors.

Where the creditors of a company have accepted a proposal for its reorganization, the proposal is submitted to the court for approval. Normally, this results in the write-down of assets and the elimination of the accumulated losses against the share capital or capital reserves of the company. If, however, either the court or the creditors do not accept the proposal, the company is liquidated.

SETTLEMENT OF CLAIMS

On realizing the assets, the trustee settles the claims of those creditors who have filed proof of their claims with him/her. The **claims of the secured creditors** are settled out of the proceeds from the sale of the assets over which the amounts owing were secured. Any remaining proceeds go towards settling the claims of the **unsecured creditors**. As pointed out earlier, if the amount realized on the sale of the assets is insufficient to settle the claims of the individual secured creditors, they have an unsecured claim for the balance against the bankrupt estate.

There are, however, **priorities** in relation to unsecured claims against the estate. The persons to whom these priorities apply are also sometimes referred to as **preferred creditors**. In this respect, the BIA lists the priorities of claims in the following order:

(a) Funeral expenses and any expenses incurred by the legal representative of the deceased in administering the estate of a deceased bankrupt.
(b) The costs of administration of the bankrupt estate.

(c) Government levies for supervision of the estate.

(d) Wages, salaries and commissions due to employees for the six months preceding the bankruptcy.

(e) Amounts owing for municipal taxes.

(f) Arrears in rent for the three months prior to the bankruptcy.

(g) Any fees relating to receiverships and assignments.

(h) Any amounts owing for workers' compensation or for income taxes deducted on behalf of employees.

(i) Claims for workers' compensation to which workmen's compensation does not apply.

(j) Any other claims by the government incurred prior to the coming force of the amended BIA.

The claims of the unsecured creditors are settled from the balance remaining on a *pro rata* basis: that is, in proportion to the amount owing. For example, if the amount remaining after the payment of secured creditors and priority claims amounts to $24,000 and the total unsecured claims are $200,000, the settlement would be 12 cents in the dollar.

It is interesting to note that in terms of the previous Act, the Canada Revenue Agency was treated as a preferred creditor. Now, however, the Canada Revenue Agency is treated like any other unsecured creditor. It is also interesting to note that there are no priorities or preferences of creditors in terms of the CCAA.

COSTS OF ADMINISTERING A COMMERCIAL BANKRUPTCY

A report in *The Globe and Mail* (October 11, 1995) made it quite clear that it is the trustees and legal experts in bankruptcies who are the greatest beneficiaries. Quoting statistics drawn from a random sample of 417 bankruptcies in Montreal and Toronto for the period between 1977 and 1987, it was found that the average payout to unsecured creditors was 2.53 cents in the dollar and 23.18 cents in the dollar to secured creditors. Of the most interest is that administration costs accounted for more than 50% of the value of the assets liquidated. The information provided in the report is given below in Illustration 22–1.

ILLUSTRATION 22–1
STATISTICS ON BANKRUPTCIES

	On Average
Payoff Rates to:	
Unsecured Creditors	2.53 cents
Secured Creditors	23.18 cents
Days in Bankruptcy	818 days
Total Administration Costs	$5,892.00 *
As a Percentage of:	
Total Assets	44.0 %
Total Liabilities	5.0 %
Trustee's Fees	$3,949.00 *
As a Percentage of:	
Total Assets	80.0 %
Total Liabilities	35.2 %

* As re-stated in 1993 dollars

Source: *Canadian Business Economics*, Summer 1995

DISCHARGE OF THE BANKRUPT AND TRUSTEE

Once the distribution of the assets of a bankrupt estate has been completed, the trustees petition the court for the discharge of the bankrupt. When this discharge is granted, the trustees apply to the court for their own discharge. The same applies on completion of the liquidation or reorganization of a company. The former bankrupt can then return to normal life.

SUMMARY

The chapter outlines the provisions of the two statutes covering bankruptcy and insolvency in Canada. These are the *Companies' Creditors Arrangement Act* (CCAA), 1933 and the *Bankruptcy and Insolvency Act* (BIA), 1985.

The CCAA is designed for use by large companies. The BIA, on the other hand, is the most important of the two. It was substantially revised and amended in 1992. These revisions and amendments were made to change the previous emphasis of bankruptcy law from the bankruptcy of the debtor to one of reorganization in a manner where the business can continue to operate. The operation of the BIA is essentially the same for both individuals and companies.

The chapter outlines how the BIA is administered, the difference between bankruptcy and receivership, the conditions for bankruptcy and how debtors can obtain protection from their creditors. It also details the making of proposals and the procedures necessary for the settlement of claims, the duties of trustees and the procedures for obtaining the discharge of bankrupts and trustees.

REVIEW QUESTIONS

1. What is meant by the terms "bankruptcy" and "insolvency"?
2. What legislation covers "bankruptcy" in Canada?
3. How is bankruptcy administered in Canada?
4. Outline the basic duties of licensed trustees in bankruptcy.
5. What is the difference between receivership and bankruptcy?
6. List the seven "acts of bankruptcy".
7. How does someone go about declaring bankruptcy?
8. Explain what you understand by "a proposal" and a "notice of intention" to file a proposal in relation to bankruptcy?
9. What is the most important effect of filing a proposal or "notice of intention"?
10. What happens when a proposal of an individual trader or company is rejected by creditors?
11. Outline the way the claims of secured and unsecured creditors are settled.
12. How do bankrupts and trustees obtain their discharge?

Appendices

Appendix A:
The Case Method of Instruction

THE OBJECTIVE OF USING THE CASE METHOD

It is believed that the case method of instruction was developed by the Harvard Business School shortly after its establishment in 1908. It has proved so successful that it is now recognized as one of the principal methods of instruction in the various business schools throughout the world. This is because it exposes students to authentic situations in which the student must sort fact from fiction, relevant from irrelevant information, and reach a conclusion based on an assessment of the position.

From an education point of view, the case study method falls into the broad category of simulation. It simulates real life situations and takes the student out of the role of spectator and gives them the role of player. It also changes the classroom relationship between instructor and student because it provides the student with a chance to formulate and voice opinions in a sanction-free environment encouraged specifically for that purpose. Its overall objective is to teach cognitive and analytical skills: the ability to recognize issues of importance and how to resolve them.

Generally speaking, simulation is not new to accounting. Virtually all accounting exercises, problems and other assignments are simulations in which the student is placed in a position where he or she is called upon to resolve an issue, determine a result, or establish a set of figures. And, provided these exercises, problems, and assignments have been properly drawn up, they provide simulated exposure to the type of situation the student can expect to find in practice. What is new, however, is to place students in a position where they must use their cognitive and analytical skills and, consequently, it fits well into the modern approach to teaching accounting.

THE DIFFERENCE BETWEEN
A CASE AND AN EXERCISE OR PROBLEM

The difference between a case and an exercise or problem is that with an exercise or problem, it is always possible to come up with an acceptable solution to the issue of concern. With a case, however, this is not necessarily the position. The situation may be such that a number of possible solutions may exist, all of which are perfectly valid. The objective is to consider the available facts and analyze the situation in such a manner that you arrive at the best possible alternative course of action.

THE SUGGESTED APPROACH TO ANALYZING A CASE

It is desirable to analyze and present the findings of the case in a logical manner. The following three-step procedure is one that is generally used for analyzing business cases:

Step One — The Reading of the Case

Read the case making notes of any points that appear to be of importance. Here, the use of pencilled notes in the margin is useful. With long cases (i.e., over 10 pages in length), it is desirable to number these notes for later easy reference.

Step Two — The Analysis of the Case

Once the case has been read an annotated, the points should be grouped by issue and ranked in order of importance. At this stage, the objective of the case should become apparent and this analysis and ranking procedure should then provide you with the information on which to base your conclusion, recommendation, or decision. If, at this stage, the objective of the case has not become apparent, you should re-read the case and, if necessary, annotate it once again and re-do Step Two.

Step Three — The Writing of the Case Analysis/Report

The writing of the case analysis or report is the most important step and, to do yourself justice, it should be presented in a systematic and logical manner. The following three-step method is recommended:

1. State, up front, what you believe to be the problem, issue or objective of the case.
2. Give your conclusion, recommendation or decision reached.
3. Support your conclusions by presenting an analysis of the issues that led to your conclusion. Where these cover more than one issue, they should be segregated and analyzed separately. You should also explain how you reached your conclusion by discussing the issues considered in the analysis. In doing so, you should consider and draw attention to the advantages and disadvantages of any alternative courses of action.

With accounting cases, the procedure needs to be modified because, as with the majority of cases provided in this text, knowledge of and the application of a particular accounting recommendation/standard is required. The analysis should, therefore, cover the following pattern:

(a) Identify all possible accounting approaches.
(b) Give and explain which CICA *Handbook* sections apply. The applicable *Handbook* sections are presented in the **Topical Index**.
(c) Provide reasons for recommending the use of any particular choice by considering the individual advantages and disadvantages of each possibility.

Your analysis should, therefore, be presented in a form that shows that it consists of three elements as follows:

> Problem/Issue/Objective
> Conclusion
> Analysis and Discussion

For **greater impact**, use the above three elements as headings in your case analysis.

The required presentation is what occurs in practice. If, for example, you are requested to investigate an issue or course of action to be presented to the board of directors of your employer company you would, in the course of your presentation, identify the issue or course of action, give your conclusion on how it should be resolved, and then provide them with the reasons you arrived at that conclusion. You would not bore the board with a long discussion before you told them what conclusion you have reached. In those cases where the case requirements request that you write a memorandum or letter, the basic three-point analysis must still be used, as adapted to suit the individual case requirements.

FINAL COMMENT

The cases used in this text are designed specifically to complement the material covered in the chapters to which they relate. As a result, they are often specific to the material covered whereas, in others, they may draw on your entire accounting, business and other knowledge. The method of presentation outlined in the section "The Suggested Approach to Analyzing a Case" may, therefore, not always apply. However, it (hopefully) provides the "right frame of mind" and a useful guide for analyzing cases.

Appendix B:
Solutions to Self-Study Problems

CHAPTER THREE

SELF-STUDY PROBLEM 3A

	Historical Cost	Adjustment	Price-Level Adjusted
INCOME STATEMENT			
Sales: February 28 — 50,000 units at $6 each	$ 300,000	115/104	$ 331,731
April 30 — 20,000 units at $7 each	140,000	115/102	157,843
November 30 — 75,000 units at $8 each	600,000	115/112	616,071
	$1,040,000		$1,105,645
Cost of Goods Sold:			
Opening Inventory — 12,500 units at $4 each	$ 50,000	115/96	$ 59,896
Purchases: January 31 — 60,000 units at $5 each	300,000	115/101	341,584
March 31 — 50,000 units at $4 each	200,000	115/103	223,301
October 31 — 32,500 units at $6 each	195,000	115/109	205,734
	745,000		830,515
Closing Inventory — 10,000 units at $4 each	40,000	115/108	42,592
Cost of Goods Sold	$ 705,000		$ 787,923
Gross Profit	$ 335,000		$ 317,722
Less: Administration Expenses	(175,000)	115/108	(186,343)
Amortization of Capital Assets	(10,000)	115/80	(14,375)
Income Tax Expense	(80,000)	115/108	(85,185)
Net Income Before Monetary Gain	70,000		31,819
Net Monetary Gain	—	Plug	38,145
Net Income for Year	70,00		69,964
Retained Earnings at January 1, 20X7	30,000	Given	26,334
	100,000		96,298
Dividends Paid (November 30, 20X7)	10,000	115/112	(10,268)
Retained Earnings at December 31, 20X7	$ 90,000	B/Sheet	$ 86,030

SELF-STUDY PROBLEM 3A (CONTINUED)

	Historical Cost	Adjustment	Price-Level Adjusted
BALANCE SHEET			
Cash	$ 35,000	N/A	$ 35,000
Accounts Receivable	95,000	N/A	95,000
Inventory	40,000	115/108	42,592
Equipment	100,000	115/80	143,750
Accumulated Amortization	(30,000)	115/80	(43,125)
	$ 240,000		$ 273,217
Accounts Payable	$ 25,000	N/A	$ 25,000
Bank Loan Payable	40,000	N/A	40,000
Common Stock	85,000	115/80	122,187
Retained Earnings	90,000	Plug	86,030
	$ 240,000		$ 273,217

SELF-STUDY PROBLEM 3B

1. Current Cost Accounting Using Financial Capital Maintenance

COMBINED INCOME AND RETAINED EARNINGS STATEMENT			(000s)
Sales			$13,800
Cost of Goods Sold at replacement value (given)			8,010
Gross Profit			5,790
Expenses:			
Administration and Selling		2,870	
Amortization of Capital Assets ([$11,000,000 + $12,000,000]/2 × 1/10)[1]		1,150	4,020
Net Operating Net Income			1,770
Realized Holding Gains:			
Inventory:			
3,000 units × ($260 − $220) =	$120,000		
5,000 units × ($260 − $250) =	50,000		
2,000 units × ($280 − $250) =	60,000		
6,000 units × ($300 − $250) =	300,000		
2,000 units × ($300 − $280) =	40,000		
9,000 units × ($330 − $280) =	450,000	1,020	
Amortization ($1,150,000 − $1,000,000)		150	1,170
Net Realized Income (i.e., Historical Cost)			2,940
Unrealized Holding Gains:			
Inventory — 4,000 × ($340 − $280)		240	
Equipment — see note		600	840
Net Income with Financial Capital Maintenance			3,780
Retained Earnings at January 1, 20X8			1,920
			5,700
Dividends (October 15)			1,800
Retained Earnings at December 31, 20X8			$ 3,900

---

[1] The amortization adjustment is calculated using the 20X7 current cost value of the equipment.

SELF-STUDY PROBLEM 3B (CONTINUED)

BALANCE SHEET

Cash	$ 1,125
Accounts Receivable	5,360
Inventory (4,000 × $340)	1,360
Equipment	12,000
Accumulated Amortization	(3,600)
	$16,245
Accounts Payable	$ 2,345
Common Stock (10,000,000 shares of no par value)	10,000
Retained Earnings	3,900
	$16,245

Note: The unrealized holding gain on the equipment of $600,000 for 20X8 was made up of the Increase in the current cost of the equipment of $1-million (i.e., $12-million − $11-million) less the backlog amortization of $250,000 less the realized holding gain of $150,000. The determination of this amount is clarified by the following two ledger accounts reflecting the current cost of the equipment at December 31, 20X8, and the accumulated current cost amortization to that date.

Equipment at Current Cost

		Dr.	Cr.	Balance
20X6				
Jan. 1	Purchase of Equipment	10,000,000		10,000,000
Dec. 31	Adjustment	500,000		10,500,000
20X7				
Dec. 31	Adjustment	500,000		11,000,000
20X8				
Dec. 31	Adjustment	1,000,000		12,000,000

Accumulated Amortization at Current Cost

20X6				
Dec. 31	Amortization for Year[1]		1,025,000	1,025,000
	Backlog Amortization		25,000	1,050,000
20X7				
Dec. 31	Amortization for Year[2]		1,075,000	2,125,000
	Backlog Amortization		75,000	2,200,000
20X8				
Dec. 31	Amortization for Year[3]		1,150,000	3,350,000
	Backlog Amortization		250,000	3,600,000

[1] ($10,000,000 + $10,500,000)/2 × 1/10 = $1,025,000
[2] ($10,500,000 + $11,000,000)/2 × 1/10 = $1,075,000
[3] ($11,000,000 + $12,000,000)/2 × 1/10 = $1,150,000

2. Current Cost Accounting Using Productive Capacity Capital Maintenance

(000s)

Shareholders' Equity	
Common Stock	$10,000
Capital Surplus ($1,200,000 + $1,170,000 − $840,000)	3,210
Retained Earnings ($720,000 + $1,770,000 − $1,800,000)	690
	$13,900

CHAPTER FOUR

SELF-STUDY PROBLEM 4A

PURCHASE OF INTERESTS

Purchase by Andrew Inc.

Workings

Calculation of Goodwill on Acquisition:

Net Assets Acquired at Fair Market Value	$14,400,000
Purchase Consideration — 3-million × $5.20	15,600,000
Goodwill on Acquisition	$ 1,200,000

Solution:

Current Assets ($4,200,000 + $3,875,000)	$ 8,075,000
Property, Plant and Equipment (net) ($12,050,000 + $14,115,000)	26,165,000
Intangible Assets ($1,600,000 + $80,000 + $1,200,000)	2,880,000
	$37,120,000
Current Liabilities ($2,740,000 + $1,970,000)	$ 4,710,000
6% Bonds ($5,000,000 + $1,700,000)	6,700,000
Common Shares (6-million shares of no par value [$6,000,000 + $15,600,000])	21,600,000
Capital Surplus	1,200,000
Retained Earnings	2,910,000
	$37,120,000

CHAPTER SEVEN
SELF-STUDY PROBLEM 7A

WORKINGS

ANALYSIS OF EQUITY

At Acquisition:	Total	75%	Minority Interests
Common Stock	$1,000,000	$ 750,000	$ 250,000
Retained Earnings — January 1, 20X4	400,000	300,000	100,000
Net Income 20X4 — 9 months	360,000	270,000	90,000
Less: Interim Dividend Paid	(60,000)	(45,000)	(15,000)
FMV Adjustments — Plant	160,000	120,000	—
		1,395,000	—
Purchase Consideration		1,715,000	
Goodwill		$ 320,000	

> Goodwill Impairment of $20,000 in 20X5
> FMV Adjustments — Plant = $120,000/4 = $30,000/year

Since Acquisition:			
Net Income 20X4 — 3 months	120,000	90,000	30,000
Dividends Paid	(100,000)	(75,000)	(25,000)
Minority Interests at December 31, 20X4			430,000
Net Income 20X5	560,000	420,000	140,000
Dividends Paid	(200,000)	(150,000)	(50,000)
Minority Interests at December 31, 20X5			$ 520,000

Reconciliation of Share of Net Income from Serene

Net Income (75% of [3/12 × $480,000])			$ 90,000
Less: FMV Adjustment (3/12 × $30,000)			7,500
Share of Net Income for 20X4			$ 82,500
Net Income (75% of $560,000)			$ 420,000
Less: Goodwill Impairment		$ 20,000	
FMV Adjustment		30,000	50,000
Share of Net Income for 20X5			$ 370,000

Reconciliation of Investment in Serene

Purchase Consideration			$1,715,000
Share of Net Income — 20X4		$ 82,500	
Less Dividend		75,000	7,500
Balance at December 31, 20X4			$1,722,500
Share of Net Income — 20X5		$ 370,000	
Less Dividend		150,000	220,000
Balance at December 31, 20X5			$1,942,500

SELF-STUDY PROBLEM 7A (CONTINUED)

CONSOLIDATED INCOME AND RETAINED EARNINGS STATEMENTS

	Consol.	20X4 Placid	20X4 Serene (3/12)	Consol.	20X5 Placid	20X5 Serene
Sales	$5,350,000	$4,700,000	$650,000	$7,900,000	$4,900,000	$3,000,000
Cost of Goods Sold	$2,255,000	$1,980,000	$275,000	$3,420,000	$2,040,000	$1,380,000
Administration Expenses	1,615,000	1,360,000	255,000	2,510,000	1,450,000	1,060,000
FMV Adjustment — Plant	7,500	7,500	—	30,000	30,000	—
	$3,877,500	$3,347,500	$530,000	$5,960,000	$3,520,000	$2,440,000
Total Net Income	$1,472,500	$1,352,500	$120,000	$1,940,000	$1,380,000	$ 560,000
Minority Interests (25%)	30,000	—	30,000	140,000	—	140,000
Net Income before Goodwill Charges	1,442,500	$1,352,500	$ 90,000	1,800,000	$1,380,000	$ 420,000
Goodwill Impairment	—			20,000		
Consolidated Net Income	1,442,500			1,780,000		
Retained Earnings at January 1	1,400,000			2,342,500		
	2,842,500			4,122,500		
Dividends Paid	500,000			800,000		
Retained Earnings at December 31	$2,342,500			$3,322,500		

CONSOLIDATED BALANCE SHEETS

	20X4		20X5	
Cash	$ 395,000	($215,000 + $180,000)	$ 342,000	($192,000 + $150,000)
Accounts Receivable	2,305,000	($1,615,000 + $690,000)	2,340,000	($1,560,000 + $780,000)
Inventory	1,230,000	($840,000 + $390,000)	1,340,000	($920,000 + $420,000)
Plant and Equipment (Net)	2,712,500	($1,800,000 + $800,000 + [$120,000 − $7,500])	3,560,500	($2,498,000 + $980,000 + [$120,000 − {$7,500 + $30,000}])
Goodwill	320,000		300,000	($320,000 − $20,000)
	$6,962,500		$7,882,500	
Accounts Payable	$1,190,000	($850,000 + $340,000)	$1,040,000	($790,000 + $250,000)
Minority Interests	430,000	Analysis of Equity	520,000	Analysis of Equity
Common Stock	3,000,000		3,000,000	
Retained Earnings	2,342,500		3,322,500	
	$6,962,500		$7,882,500	

CHAPTER EIGHT

SELF-STUDY PROBLEM 8A

WORKINGS

ANALYSIS OF EQUITY

At Acquisition:	Total	75%	Minority Interests
Common Stock	$1,000,000	$ 750,000	$ 250,000
Retained Earnings at January 1, 20X5	500,000	375,000	125,000
Net Income for 20X4 — 3 months	100,000	75,000	25,000
FMV Adjustment — Plant	80,000	60,000	—
Lease	48,000	36,000	—
		1,296,000	
Purchase Consideration		1,380,000	
Goodwill		$ 84,000	

> Impairment of Goodwill of $8,000 in 20X4
> FMV Adjustment — Plant = $60,000/6 = $10,000/year
>   Lease = $36,000/2 = $18,000/year

Since Acquisition:			
Net Income for 20X4 — 9 months	300,000	$ 225,000	75,000
Dividends Paid	(80,000)	(60,000)	(20,000)
Net Income for 20X5	310,000	232,500	77,500
Extraordinary Item	100,000	75,000	25,000
Dividends Paid	(80,000)	(60,000)	(20,000)
Minority Interests			$ 537,500

Retained Earnings at January 1, 20X5

Retained Earnings of Piper at January 1, 20X5			$1,630,000
Less: Dividends from Scot in 20X4 (75% of $80,000)			60,000
			1,570,000
Add: Share of Net Income from Scot in 20X4		225,000	
Less: Goodwill Impairment	8,000		
FMV Adjustment — Plant (9/12 × $10,000)	7,500		
Lease (9/12 × $18,000)	13,500	29,000	196,000
Consolidated Balance at January 1, 20X5			$1,766,000

SELF-STUDY PROBLEM 8A (CONTINUED)

SOLUTION

CONSOLIDATED INCOME AND RETAINED EARNINGS STATEMENT

	Consolidated	Piper	Scot
Sales	$8,430,000	$5,560,000	$2,870,000
Cost of Goods Sold	$3,220,000	$1,830,000	$1,390,000
Operating Expenses	3,080,000	1,920,000	1,160,000
Interest Revenue/Expense	—	(10,000)	10,000
Fair Market Value Adjustments — Plant	10,000	10,000	—
Lease	18,000	18,000	—
Total Expenses	$6,328,000	$3,768,000	$2,560,000
Total Net Income	$2,102,000	$1,792,000	$ 310,000
Less: Minority Interests	77,500	—	77,500
Net Income before Goodwill Charges and Extraordinary Item	2,024,500	$1,792,000	$ 232,500
Goodwill Charges	2,000		
Net Income before Extraordinary Item	2,022,500		
Extraordinary Item	75,000		
Consolidated Net Income for Year	2,097,500		
Retained Earnings at January 1	1,766,000		
	3,863,500		
Less: Dividends Paid	500,000		
Retained Earnings at December 31	$3,363,500		

CONSOLIDATED BALANCE SHEET

Cash ($218,000 + $85,000)	$ 303,000
Accounts Receivable ($1,885,000 + $670,000)	2,555,000
Inventory ($955,000 + $490,000)	1,445,000
Capital Assets (net) ($2,592,000 + $1,350,000 + $60,000 − [$7,500 + $10,000])	3,984,500
Goodwill ($84,000 − [$8,000 + $2,000])	74,000
Lease ($36,000 − [$13,500 + $18,000])	4,500
	$8,366,000
Accounts Payable ($920,000 + $345,000)	$1,265,000
Minority Interests per Analysis of Equity	537,500
Common Stock	3,200,000
Retained Earnings	3,363,500
	$8,366,000

CHAPTER NINE

SELF-STUDY PROBLEM 9A

WORKINGS

ANALYSIS OF EQUITY

At Acquisition:	Total	Pension 75%	Minority Interests
Common Stock	$600,000	$450,000	$150,000
Retained Earnings	60,000	45,000	15,000
Net Income 20X4 — 6 months	20,000	15,000	5,000
FMV Adjustment — Plant	40,000	30,000	—
		540,000	
Purchase Consideration		620,000	
Goodwill		$ 80,000	

> Goodwill Impairment of $5,000 in 20X4 and $10,000 in 20X5
> FMV Adjustment — Plant = $30,000/3 = $10,000/year

Since Acquisition:			
Net Income — 20X4 (6 months)	20,000	15,000	5,000
Net Income 20X5	40,000	30,000	10,000
Dividends Paid	(8,000)	(6,000)	(2,000)
Minority Interests			$183,000

Unrealized Profit in Inventory:

Downstream 20X4: $10,000 × 25/125 = $2,000
Upstream   20X4: $20,000 × 25/125 = $4,000
            20X5: $30,000 × 25/125 = $6,000

Minority Interests:

Balance per Analysis of Equity	$183,000
Less: Adjustment for Unrealized Profit in Inventory (25% of $6,000)	1,500
Balance at December 31, 20X5	$181,500

Retained Earnings at January 1, 20X5:

Balance at January 1, 20X5		$ 47,000
Add: Net Income from Stipend (20X4)		15,000
		62,000
Less: Goodwill Impairment	5,000	
FMV Adjustment	5,000	10,000
		52,000
Less: Unrealized Profit Adjustments:		
Downstream	2,000	
Upstream (75% of $4,000)	3,000	5,000
Balance at December 31, 20X4		$ 47,000

SELF-STUDY PROBLEM 9A (CONTINUED)

SOLUTION

COMBINED INCOME AND RETAINED EARNINGS STATEMENT

	Consolidated	Pension	Stipend
Sales		$900,000	$ 180,000
Less: Intercompany Sales		50,000	—
Sales	$1,030,000	$850,000	$ 180,000
Cost of Goods Sold		$580,000	$ 110,000
Less: Intercompany Purchases		50,000	—
Cost of Goods Sold	$ 640,000	530,000	110,000
Unrealized Profit in Inventory:			
20X4	(−2,000)	(−2,000)	—
20X4	(−4,000)	—	(−4,000)
20X5	+6,000	—	+6,000
Operating Expenses	70,000	40,000	30,000
FMV Adjustment for Amortization	10,000	10,000	—
Total Expenses	$ 720,000	$578,000	$ 142,000
Total Net Income	$ 310,000	$272,000	$ 38,000
Less: Minority Interests (25%)	9,500	—	9,500
Net Income before Goodwill Charges	300,500	$272,000	$ 28,500
Goodwill Charges	10,000		
Consolidated Net Income	290,500		
Retained Earnings at January 1	47,000		
	337,500		
Dividends Declared and Paid	40,000		
Retained Earnings at December 31	$ 297,500		

CONSOLIDATED BALANCE SHEET

Cash ($150,000 + $10,000)	$ 160,000
Accounts Receivable ($210,000 + $590,000)	800,000
Inventory ($133,000 + $272,000 − $6,000)	399,000
Plant and Equipment (Net) ($590,000 + $110,000 + [$30,000 − $5,000 − $10,000])	715,000
Goodwill ($80,000 − [$5,000 + $10,000])	65,000
	$2,139,000
Current Liabilities ($410,000 + $250,000)	$ 660,000
Minority Interests	181,500
Common Stock	1,000,000
Retained Earnings	297,500
	$2,139,000

SELF-STUDY PROBLEM 9B

WORKINGS

ANALYSIS OF EQUITY

At Acquisition:	Total	80%	Minority Interests
Common Stock	$1,000,000	$ 800,000	$200,000
Retained Earnings	250,000	200,000	50,000
FMV Adjustment — Land	(20,000)	(16,000)	—
		984,000	
Purchase Consideration		1,080,000	
Goodwill		$ 96,000	

> Goodwill Impairment of $12,000 in 20X4
> Land — $16,000 overvaluation is adjusted on balance sheet in full

Since Acquisition:			
Net Income — 20X4	130,000	104,000	26,000
Dividends Paid — 20X4	(50,000)	(40,000)	(10,000)
Net Income — 20X5	220,000	176,000	44,000
Dividends Paid — 20X5	(80,000)	(64,000)	(16,000)
Minority Interests			$294,000

Adjustments to Minority Interests:

Balance per Analysis of Equity	$294,000
Less: Unrealized Profit in Inventory of (20% of [$12,000 − Income Tax of $6,000])	1,200
Minority Interests at December 31, 20X5	$292,800

Retained Earnings at January 1, 20X5:

Retained Earnings of Penn		$600,000
Less: Goodwill Impairment		12,000
		588,000
Add: Share of Net Income from Sylvania ($104,000 − $40,000)		64,000
		652,000
Less: Unrealized Profits Adjustments — 20X4:		
Downstream of ($30,000 − Income Tax of $15,000)	15,000	
Upstream of 80% of ($10,000 − Income Tax of $5,000)	4,000	19,000
Adjusted Balance at January 1, 20X5		$633,000

SELF-STUDY PROBLEM 9B (CONTINUED)

CONSOLIDATED INCOME AND RETAINED EARNINGS STATEMENT

	Consolidated	Penn	Sylvania
Sales		$6,000,000	$2,200,000
Intercompany Sales		300,000	—
	$7,900,000	$5,700,000	$2,200,000
Cost of Goods Sold		$3,600,000	$1,040,000
Intercompany Purchases		300,000	—
	$4,340,000	3,300,000	1,040,000
Unrealized Profit in Inventory			
20X4 (25/125 × 50% × $300,000)	(−30,000)	(−30,000)	
(25/125 × $50,000)	(−10,000)		(−10,000)
20X5 (25/125 × $60,000)	12,000		+12,000
Operating Expenses	2,032,000	1,312,000	720,000
Total Expenses	$6,344,000	$4,582,000	$1,762,000
Total Net Income before Income Taxes	$1,556,000	$1,118,000	$ 438,000
Income Tax Expense (50%)	778,000	559,000	219,000
Total Net Income after Income Taxes	778,000	559,000	219,000
Minority Interests	43,800	—	43,800
Consolidated Net Income	734,200	$ 559,000	$ 175,200
Retained Earnings at January 1	633,000		
	1,367,200		
Dividends Paid	240,000		
Retained Earnings at December 31	$1,127,200		

CONSOLIDATED BALANCE SHEET

Current Assets ($1,354,000 + $700,000 − $12,000)	$2,042,000
Land ($200,000 + $120,000 − $16,000)	304,000
Plant Assets ($876,000 + $980,000)	1,856,000
Goodwill ($96,000 − $12,000)	84,000
	$4,286,000
Current Liabilities ($922,000 + $290,000)	$1,212,000
Future Income Taxes ($120,000 + $40,000 − 50% of $12,000)	154,000
Minority Interests	292,800
Common Stock	1,500,000
Retained Earnings	1,127,200
	$4,286,000

Note:
The current increase in the future income taxes of $6,000 is 50% of the unrealized profit of $12,000.

CHAPTER TEN

SELF-STUDY PROBLEM 10A

WORKINGS

ANALYSIS OF EQUITY

At Acquisition:	Total	80%	Minority Interests
Common Stock	$300,000	$240,000	$ 60,000
Retained Earnings at Jan. 1, 20X4	50,000	40,000	10,000
Net Income — 20X4 (6 months) (i.e., 50% of [$90,000 − $50,000])	20,000	16,000	4,000
FMV Adjustment	45,000	36,000	—
		332,000	
Purchase Consideration		360,000	
Goodwill		$ 28,000	

> Goodwill Impairment of $4,000 in 20X4
> FMV Adjustment = $36,000/6 = $6,000/year

Since Acquisition:			
Net Income 20X4 — 6 months	20,000	$ 16,000	4,000
Net Income 20X5	200,000	160,000	40,000
Dividends Paid 20X5	(100,000)	(80,000)	(20,000)
Minority Interests			$ 98,000

Unrealized Profit on Plant Sales:

Plant Sold by Pal to Sal:	20X4 — $16,000/8 × 3/12	=	$ 500
	20X5 — $16,000/8	=	2,000
Plant Sold by Sal to Pal:	20X5 — $20,000/10 × 6/12	=	1,000

Reconciliation of Retained Earnings at December 31, 20X4:

Balance at January 1, 20X5		$520,000
Less: Goodwill Impairment	4,000	
FMV Adjustment	3,000	
Unrealized Profit on Sale of Equipment ($16,000 − $500)	15,500	22,500
		497,500
Add: Share of Net Income from Sal (i.e., 80% of $20,000)		16,000
Adjusted Balance		$513,500

Reconciliation of Minority Interests at December 31, 20X5:

Minority Interests per Analysis of Equity	$ 98,000
Profit on Sale of Equipment (20% of [$20,000 − $1,000])	3,800
Adjusted Balance	$ 94,200

SELF-STUDY PROBLEM 10A (CONTINUED)

SOLUTION

CONSOLIDATED COMBINED INCOME AND RETAINED EARNINGS STATEMENT

	Consolidated	Pal	Sal
Sales		$1,200,000	$ 800,000
Sale of Plant		—	60,000
	$1,940,000	$1,200,000	$ 740,000
Cost of Goods Sold		$ 600,000	$ 500,000
Intercompany Purchases		—	40,000
	$1,060,000	600,000	460,000
Operating Expenses	350,000	250,000	100,000
FMV Adjustment	6,000	+6,000	—
Excess Amortization Adjustments	(−3,000)	(−2,000)	(−1,000)
Total Expenses	$1,413,000	$ 854,000	$ 559,000
Total Net Income	$ 527,000	$ 346,000	$ 181,000
Less: Minority Interests (20%)	36,200	—	36,200
Consolidated Net Income	490,800	$ 346,000	$ 144,800
Retained Earnings at January 1, 20X5	513,500		
	1,004,300		
Dividends Declared and Paid	320,000		
Retained Earnings at December 31, 20X5	$ 684,300		

CONSOLIDATED BALANCE SHEET

Current Assets ($640,000 + $280,000)	$ 920,000
Plant ($800,000 + $400,000 + $36,000 − $16,000 − $20,000)	1,200,000
Accumulated Amortization ($250,000 + $80,000 + [$3,000 + $6,000] − [$500 + $2,000] − $1,000)	(335,500)
Goodwill ($28,000 − $4,000)	24,000
	$1,808,500
Accounts Payable ($120,000 + $110,000)	$ 230,000
Minority Interests	94,200
Common Stock	800,000
Retained Earnings	684,300
	$1,808,500

SELF-STUDY PROBLEM 10B

WORKINGS

ANALYSIS OF EQUITY

	Total	75%	Minority Interests
At Acquisition:			
Common Stock	$2,000,000	$1,500,000	$ 500,000
Retained Earnings	600,000	450,000	150,000
Net Income 20X4 — 6/12	200,000	150,000	50,000
FMV Adjustment — Plant	60,000	45,000	—
Future Income Taxes on Undervalued Plant			
([$200,000 + $60,0000 − $100,000] × 50%)	80,000	60,000	
		2,205,000	
Purchase Consideration		2,545,000	
Goodwill		$ 340,000	

> Goodwill Impairment of $20,000 in 20X4
> FMV Adjustments — Plant = $45,000/5 = $9,000/year
> Future Taxes = $60,000/5 = $12,000/year

	Total	75%	Minority Interests
Since Acquisition:			
Net Income 20X4 — 6/12	200,000	$ 150,000	50,000
Dividends Paid — December 20X4	(80,000)	(60,000)	(20,000)
Net Income 20X5	300,000	225,000	75,000
Dividends Paid — December 20X5	(100,000)	(75,000)	(25,000)
Total Minority Interests			$ 780,000

Adjustment for Unrealized Profit in Plant:

20X5 $60,000/5 = $12,000/year

Retained Earnings at January 1, 20X5:

Retained Earnings from Psychic		$1,495,000
Add: Share of Net Income from See Since Acquisition		90,000
		1,585,000
Less: Goodwill Impairment	20,000	
FMV Adjustment — Plant (6/12)	4,500	
Future Taxes of $60,000/5 (6/12)	6,000	30,500
		$1,554,500

Minority Interests at December 31, 20X5:

Balance per Analysis of Equity	$ 780,000
Gain on Upstream Sales of Plant	
20X5 — 25% × 50% of ($60,000 − $6,000)	6,750
Adjusted Balance	$ 773,250

SELF-STUDY PROBLEM 10B (CONTINUED)

CONSOLIDATED COMBINED INCOME AND RETAINED EARNINGS STATEMENT

	Consolidated	Psychic	See
Sales	$8,400,000	$5,110,000	$3,290,000
Cost of Goods Sold	$3,120,000	$1,700,000	$1,420,000
Operating Expenses	3,140,000	1,810,000	1,330,000
FMV Adjustment — Plant	9,000	9,000	—
UP on Plant — 20X5	(−6,000)	—	(−6,000)
Total Expenses	$6,263,000	$3,519,000	$2,744,000
Total Net Income before Income Taxes	$2,137,000	$1,591,000	$ 546,000
Less: Income Tax Expense (50%) — see Note	1,085,000	812,000	273,000
Total Net Income after Income Tax	1,052,000	779,000	273,000
Less: Minority Interest (20%)	68,250	—	68,250
Consolidated Net Income	983,750	$ 779,000	$ 204,750
Retained Earnings, January 1, 20X5	1,554,500		
	2,538,250		
Dividends Declared and Paid	200,000		
Retained Earnings, December 31, 20X5	$2,338,250		

CONSOLIDATED BALANCE SHEET

Cash ($130,000 + $220,000)	$ 350,000
Accounts Receivable ($365,000 + $940,000)	1,305,000
Inventory ($800,000 + $880,000)	1,680,000
Plant and Equipment (Net)	
($3,970,000 + $1,940,000 + [$45,000 − $4,500 − $9,000] − [$60,000 − $6,000])	5,887,500
Goodwill ($340,000 − $20,000)	320,000
	$9,542,500
Accounts Payable ($580,000 + $740,000)	$1,320,000
Future Income Taxes	
($60,000 + $120,000 − [50% of {$60,000 − $6,000} − [$60,000 − $6,000 − $12,000])	111,000
Minority Interests	773,250
Common Stock (100,000 shares of no par value)	5,000,000
Retained Earnings	2,338,250
	$9,542,500

Note: The income tax expense of Psychic is (50% × [net income of $1,591,000 + FMV Adjustment of $9,000])
        + Future Income Tax of $12,000 which has been adjusted for Income Taxes) = $812,000

CHAPTER ELEVEN

SELF-STUDY PROBLEM 11A

1. **Effective gain on income statement** (against Scold) of $3,000 calculated as follows:

Value of bonds at July 1, 20X4 of 1,000 × $1,000	$1,000,000
Less: Discount (i.e., issued at 98) of $20,000 − (5/20 × $20,000)	15,000
Balance at July 1, 20X4	$ 985,000
Ten percent thereof	$ 98,500
Purchase Price	95,500
Effective Gain of	$ 3,000

Amortization of Effective Gain of $3,000/15 interest payments = $200/interest payment

2. **Interest Expense** of $77,900 (i.e., [$80,000 + $2,000] − [$4,000 + $300] + $200).

$80,000 (i.e., interest expense of $1,000,000 × 8%) + $2,000 (i.e., discount write-off of $1,000 for two interest payments) − $4,000 (i.e., interest revenue of $100,000 × 8% × 6/12) − $300 (i.e., discount on bonds purchased of $4,500/15 interest payments) + $200 (i.e., amortization of effective gain for one interest payment)

	Consolidated	Punish	Scold
Interest Expense		(4,000)	80,000
Discount Amortization		(300)	2,000
			82,000
Effective Gain			200
Interest Expense	77,900	(4,300)	82,200

3. **Reflection of Effective Loss**

The effective gain would be reflected as revenue on the consolidated income statement in 20X4 described as "Gain on Extinguishment of Debt — $$3,000." Thereafter, it would be included in the consolidated retained earnings and proportionately reduced over the life of the bonds.

4. **Disclosure on the Consolidated Balance Sheet at December 31, 20X4:**

Bonds Payable (i.e., 90% × $1,000,000)	$900,000
Less: Discount on Bonds (i.e., 90% × [$20,000 − $6,000]	12,600
Bond Liability	$887,400
or 90% of ($1,000,000 − $20,000 − $6,000 [i.e., 3 years × $2,000]) =	$887,400

SELF-STUDY PROBLEM 11B

ANALYSIS OF EQUITY

At Acquisition	Total	80%	Minority Interests
Common Stock	$1,000,000	$ 800,000	$ 200,000
Retained Earnings	250,000	200,000	50,000
		1,000,000	
Purchase Consideration		1,200,000	
Goodwill		$ 200,000	

> Goodwill Impairment of $20,000 in 20X1

Since Acquisition:

	Total	80%	Minority Interests
Retained Earnings	175,000	$ 140,000	35,000
Net Income — 20X3	358,800	287,040	71,760
Dividends Paid	(250,000)	(200,000)	(50,000)
Minority Interests			$ 306,760

Effective Gain included in Net Income of Secondary arising from the Purchase of Bonds by Primary:

Value of Bonds Outstanding at July 1, 20X3:		
Face Value of		$2,000,000
Premium (i.e., 2% × $2,000,000)	40,000	
Less: Amortization since issue of (4/20 [i.e., two years later] × $40,000)	8,000	32,000
Balance at July 1, 20X3		$2,032,000
20% thereof		$ 406,400
Purchase Price		387,200
Effective Gain		$ 19,200

> Amortization of Effective Gain = $19,200/8 = $2,400/year = $1,200/interest payment

Consolidated Retained Earnings at January 1, 20X3:

Retained Earnings of Primary at January 1, 20X3	$ 920,000
Less: Goodwill Impairment in 20X1	20,000
	900,000
Add: Share of Net Income of Secondary since acquisition	140,000
Consolidated Retained Earnings for 20X4	$1,040,000

SELF-STUDY PROBLEM 11B (CONTINUED)

CONSOLIDATED INCOME AND RETAINED EARNINGS STATEMENT

	Consolidated	Primary	Secondary
Sales	$6,000,000	$3,600,000	$2,400,000
Gain on the Retirement of Debt	19,200	19,200	—
Total Revenues	$6,019,200	$3,619,200	$2,400,000
Cost of Goods Sold	$1,820,000	$1,020,000	$ 800,000
Administration and Operating Expenses	2,150,000	1,250,000	900,000
Interest Expense ([$160,000 − $4,000]) + $1,200 − [$16,000 + $800])	140,400	157,200	(16,800)
Total Expenses	$4,110,400	$2,427,200	$1,683,200
Total Net Income before Income Taxes	$1,908,800	$1,192,000	$ 716,800
Income Tax Expense (50%) — see note	956,000	598,000	358,000
Total Net Income after Income Taxes	952,800	594,000	358,800
Less Minority Interests (20%)	71,760	—	71,760
Consolidated Net Income	881,040	$ 594,000	$ 287,040
Retained Earnings at January 1, 20X3	1,040,000		
	1,921,040		
Dividends Paid	400,000		
Retained Earnings at December 31, 20X3	$1,521,040		

CONSOLIDATED BALANCE SHEET

Current Assets ($1,143,000 + $637,200)	$1,780,200
Capital Assets (Net) ($4,672,000 + $910,000)	5,582,000
Goodwill ($200,000 − $20,000])	180,000
	$7,542,200
Current Liabilities ($400,000 + $236,400)	$ 636,400
Future Income Taxes ($280,000 + $165,000 + $9,000)	454,000
8% Bonds (80% of $2,030,000)	1,624,000
Minority Interests	306,760
Common Stock	3,000,000
Retained Earnings	1,521,040
	$7,542,200

Note: The income tax expense for Primary of $598,000 is 50% of $1,192,000 plus the bond premium adjustment of $4,000 (included with interest expense).

CHAPTER TWELVE

SELF-STUDY PROBLEM 12A

ANALYSIS OF EQUITY

At First Acquisition:	Total	40%	20%	Minority Interests
Common Stock	$2,200,000	$ 880,000	$ 440,000	$ 880,000
Retained Earnings	650,000	260,000	130,000	260,000
Net Income 20X7 (6/12)	400,000	160,000	80,000	160,000
FMV Adjustment Plant	200,000	80,000	—	—
		1,380,000		
Purchase Consideration		1,460,000		
Goodwill		$ 80,000		

At Second Acquisition:				
Net Income 20X7 (6/12)	400,000	$ 160,000	80,000	160,000
Dividends Paid — 20X7	(200,000)	(80,000)	(40,000)	(80,000)
Net Income 20X8 (9/12)	720,000	288,000	144,000	288,000
FMV Adjustment	120,000	—	24,000	—
			858,000	
Purchase Consideration			978,000	
Goodwill			$ 120,000	

> *First Acquisition:*
> FMV Adjustment Plant = $80,000/5 = $16,000/year
>
> *Second Acquisition:*
> FMV Adjustment Plant = $24,000/3 = $8,000/year
>
> Goodwill Impairment of $5,000 in October 20X7 and a further $3,000 in June 20X8

After Second Acquisition

Net Income 20X8 (3/12)	240,000	96,000	$ 48,000	96,000
Dividends Paid (December 10)	(240,000)	(96,000)	(48,000)	(96,000)
Minority Interests				$1,668,000

Retained Earnings at January 1, 20X8:

Retained Earnings of Pivot		$1,616,000
Less: Dividends Received from Shaft — 20X7		80,000
		1,536,000
Net Income from Shaft since Acquisition:		160,000
		1,696,000
Less: Goodwill Impairment — October 20X7	5,000	
FMV Adjustment 20X7	8,000	13,000
Consolidated Retained Earnings at January 1, 20X8		$1,683,000

Share of Net Income from Shaft:

Share of Net Income (40% × $720,000)		$ 288,000
Less: Goodwill Impairment — June 20X8	$ 3,000	
FMV Adjustment (9/12 × $16,000)	12,000	15,000
Adjusted Balance		$ 273,000

SELF-STUDY PROBLEM 12A (CONTINUED)

CONSOLIDATED INCOME AND RETAINED EARNINGS STATEMENT FOR 20X8

	Consolidated	Pivot	Shaft (3/12)
Sales	$6,700,000	$5,800,000	$ 900,000
Cost of Goods Sold	$2,810,000	$2,500,000	310,000
Administration Expenses	1,950,000	1,600,000	350,000
FMV Adjustments — Plant (3/12 × $16,000)	4,000	4,000	—
Plant (3/12 × $8,000)	2,000	2,000	—
Total Expenses	$4,766,000	$4,106,000	$ 660,000
Total Net Income	$1,934,000	$1,694,000	$ 240,000
Less: Minority Interests (40%)	96,000	—	96,000
Net Operating Income	1,838,000	$1,694,000	$ 144,000
Share of Net Income from Shaft	273,000		
Consolidated Net Income	2,111,000		
Retained Earnings at January 1	1,683,000		
	3,794,000		
Dividends Declared and Paid	800,000		
Retained Earnings, December 31	$2,994,000		

CONSOLIDATED BALANCE SHEET AT DECEMBER 31, 20X8

Current Assets ($2,202,000 + $1,740,000)	$ 3,942,000
Plant and Equipment (Net) ($4,200,000 + $2,770,000 + [$80,000 − {$8,000 + $16,000] + [$24,000 − $2,000] − $120,000)	6,928,000
Goodwill ($80,000 + $120,000 − $5,000 − $3,000)	192,000
	$11,062,000
Accounts Payable ($1,180,000 + $220,000)	$ 1,400,000
Minority Interests	1,668,000
Common Stock	5,000,000
Retained Earnings	2,994,000
	$11,062,000

SELF-STUDY PROBLEM 12B

ANALYSIS OF EQUITY

	Total	First Acquisition (15%)	Second Acquisition (60%)	Minority Interests
Common Stock	$2,000,000	$300,000	$1,200,000	$ 500,000
Retained Earnings	1,400,000	210,000	840,000	350,000
Net Income — 20X4 (6/12)	600,000	90,000	360,000	150,000
Dividends Paid — March 12	(160,000)	(24,000)	(96,000)	(40,000)
		576,000		
Transfer to Second Acquisition		—	+576,000	
		576,000		
		$ Nil		
Net Income — 20X4 (6/12)	600,000	$ 90,000	360,000	150,000
Dividends Paid — December 7	(240,000)	(36,000)	(144,000)	(60,000)
Transfer to Minority Interests		$54,000		+54,000
Net Income — 20X5 (3/12)	400,000	$ 60,000	240,000	100,000
Dividends Paid — March 12	(200,000)	(30,000)	(120,000)	(50,000)
Transfer to Minority Interests		$ 30,000		+30,000
FMV Adjustment — Plant (75%)	320,000		240,000	—
			3,456,000	
Purchase Consideration ($840,000 + $3,120,000)			3,960,000	
Goodwill			$ 504,000	

> Goodwill Impairment of $34,000 in October 20X5
> FMV Adjustment = $240,000/5 = $48,000/year

	Total	First Acquisition (15%)	Second Acquisition (60%)	Minority Interests
Net Income — 20X5 (9/12)	1,200,000	180,000	720,000	300,000
Dividends Paid — December 3	(320,000)	(48,000)	(192,000)	(80,000)
Minority Interests				$1,404,000

SELF-STUDY PROBLEM 12B (CONTINUED)

CONSOLIDATED COMBINED INCOME AND RETAINED EARNINGS STATEMENT

	Total	Protect	Shield (9/12)
Sales	$10,100,000	$6,200,000	$ 3,900,000
Cost of Goods Sold	$ 3,625,000	$2,200,000	$ 1,425,000
Administration and Other Expenses	2,875,000	1,600,000	1,275,000
FMV Adjustment	36,000	36,000	—
Total Expenses	$ 6,536,000	$3,836,000	$ 2,700,000
Total Net Income	$ 3,564,000	$2,364,000	$ 1,200,000
Less: Minority Interests (25%)	300,000	—	300,000
Net Operating Income before Goodwill Charges	3,264,000	$2,364,000	$ 900,000
Goodwill Charges	34,000		
	3,230,000		
Dividends from Shield	30,000		
Consolidated Net Income for Year	3,260,000		
Retained Earnings at January 1	3,600,000		
	6,860,000		
Dividends Declared and Paid	720,000		
Retained Earnings at December 31	$ 6,140,000		

CONSOLIDATED BALANCE SHEET

Current Assets ($2,540,000 + $1,640,000)	$ 4,180,000
Plant and Equipment ($4,290,000 + $4,280,000 + [$240,000 − $36,000])	8,774,000
Goodwill ($504,000 − $34,000)	470,000
	$13,424,000
Current Liabilities ($1,240,000 + $640,000)	$ 1,880,000
Minority Interests	1,404,000
Common Stock (8,000,000 shares of no par value issued at 50 cents each)	4,000,000
Retained Earnings	6,140,000
	$13,424,000

CHAPTER 14
SELF-STUDY PROBLEM 14A

		Workings	
	Consolidated	**Investor**	**Recovery (25%)**
INCOME AND RETAINED EARNINGS STATEMENT			
Dividends Received — Note 1	$18,900,000	$19,000,000	$ (100,000)
Interest Revenue	9,950,000	9,950,000	
Sales of Salvaged Goods	2,250,000		2,250,000
Gain on Equipment — Note 2	45,000	45,000	
Total Revenues	$31,145,000		
Cost of Goods Sold, at Salvage Cost	$ 500,000		500,000
Administration Expenses	17,975,000	17,700,000	275,000
Amortization of Equipment — Note 3	165,000		165,000
Salvage Expenses	650,000		650,000
Total Expenses	$19,290,000		
Net Income for Year	$11,855,000		
Retained Earnings at January 1, 20X1	7,450,000		
	19,305,000		
Dividends Paid	8,000,000		
Retained Earnings at December 31, 20X1	$11,305,000		
CONSOLIDATED BALANCE SHEET			
Cash at Bank	$ 1,975,000	$ 1,600,000	$ 375,000
Inventory of Salvaged Goods	875,000		875,000
Investments	24,600,000	24,600,000	—
Plant and Equipment, at cost — Note 4	825,000		825,000
Accumulated Amortization — Note 3	(165,000)		(165,000)
	$28,110,000		
Current Liabilities	$ 625,000	600,000	25,000
Deferred Gain — Note 5	180,000		180,000
Common Shares	16,000,000	16,000,000	
Retained Earnings	11,305,000		
	$28,110,000		

Notes:
[1] $19,000,000 less dividend from Recovery of 25% × $400,000.
[2] One-fifth of the deferral of $225,000 (i.e., 1/5 of [75% of $300,000]).
[3] $180,000 (i.e., $720,000/5 years) minus $75,000/5 years = $165,000 (i.e., 1/5 of the adjusted cost of the equipment of $825,000)
[4] $900,000 (i.e., 25% of the equipment $3,600,000) as reduced by $75,000 (i.e., 25% of gain on sale of $300,000) = $825,000.
[5] $225,000 (i.e., 75% × $300,000) less amortization adjustment for year of $45,000 (i.e., $225,000/5 years) = $180,000

CHAPTER SIXTEEN
SELF-STUDY PROBLEM 16A

	US $	Conversion	Can $
BALANCE SHEET			
Cash at Bank	$ 233,700	1.00/0.74	$ 315,811
Accounts Receivable	748,200	1.00/0.74	1,011,081
Inventory	442,600	1.00/0.75	590,133
Capital Assets	1,489,200	Workings	1,852,755
Less Accumulated Amortization	(324,100)	Workings	(402,803)
	$2,589,600		$3,366,977
Accounts Payable	$ 88,200	1.00/0.74	$ 119,189
Income Taxes Payable	97,100	1.00/0.74	131,216
Longterm Loan (8%)	600,000	1.00/0.74	810,811
Common Stock	1,000,000	1.00/0.80	1,250,000
Retained Earnings	804,300	Plug	1,055,761
	$2,589,600		$3,366,977

INCOME AND RETAINED EARNINGS STATEMENT			
Sales	$5,532,700	1.00/0.76	$7,279,868
Opening Inventory	$ 471,800	1.00/0.81	582,469
Purchases	2,177,400	1.00/0.76	2,865,000
Freight and Transportation Expenses	432,100	1.00/0.76	568,553
	3,081,300		4,016,022
Closing Inventory	442,600	1.00/0.75	590,133
Cost of Goods Sold	2,638,700		3,425,889
Administration Expenses	1,189,300	1.00/0.76	1,564,868
Amortization of Capital Assets	166,800	Workings	207,180
Interest Expense	60,000	Workings	78,961
Selling Expenses	680,100	1.00/0.76	894,868
Income Tax Expense	166,200	1.00/0.76	218,684
Loss on Exchange	—	Plug	368,424
Total Expenses	$4,901,100		$6,758,874
Net Income	$ 631,600		$ 520,994
Retained Earnings at January 1, 20X3	422,700	Given	868,100
	1,054,300		1,389,094
Dividends Paid (September 30)	250,000	1.00/0.75	333,333
Retained Earnings at December 31, 20X3	$ 804,300		$1,055,761

Workings

Balance Sheet Figures for Capital Assets

Purchases	—	July 1, 20X1	$ 922,500	1.00/0.80	$1,153,125
		March 1, 20X2	566,700	1.00/0.81	699,630
			$1,489,200		$1,852,755
Less:	Amortization ($92,350 + $81,300)		$ 173,650	1.00/0.80	$ 217,062
	Amortization ($64,950 + $85,500)		150,450	1.00/0.81	185,741
			$ 324,100		$ 402,803

Amortization for 20X3 is ($81,300 × 1.00/0.80) + ($85,500 × 1.00/0.81) = $207,180
Interest Expense for 20X3 is ($30,000 × 1.00/77) + ($30,000 × 1.00/0.75) = $78,961

SELF-STUDY PROBLEM 16B

BALANCE SHEET	Historical Cost	Conversion	Can $
Cash	£ 450,000	1/0.49	$ 918,367
Inventory	840,000	1/0.49	1,714,285
Accounts Receivable	1,420,000	1/0.49	2,897,959
Plant and Equipment, cost	2,450,000	1/0.49	5,000,000
Accumulated Amortization	(910,000)	1/0.49	(1,867,143)
	£ 4,250,000		$ 8,673,468
Accounts payable	£ 1,040,000	1/0.49	$ 2,122,449
Common stock	2,000,000	1/0.48	4,166,667
Retained earnings	1,210,000	I/S	1,846,924
Accumulated Exchange Gains	—	Plug	537,428
	£ 4,250,000		$ 8,673,468

COMBINED INCOME AND RETAINED EARNINGS STATEMENT

	Historical Cost	Conversion	Can $
Sales	£ 7,780,000	1/0.46	$ 16,913,043
Opening inventory	£ 690,000	1/0.46	$ 1,500,000
Purchases	5,220,000	1/0.46	11,347,826
Ending Inventory	5,910,000		12,847,826
Cost goods sold	840,000	1/0.46	1,826,087
	£ 5,070,000		$ 11,021,739
Gross Profit	£ 2,710,000		$ 5,891,304
Administrative expenses	(1,540,000)	1/0.46	(3,347,826)
Amortization of Capital Assets	(460,000)	1/0.46	(1,000,000)
Income Taxes	(270,000)		(586,956)
Net Income	440,000	1/0.46	956,000
Retained Earnings at January 1, 20X4	1,270,000	Given	1,954,232
	1,710,000		2,910,754
Dividends (paid September 30, 20X4)	500,000	1/0.47	1,063,830
Retained Earnings at December 31, 20X4	£ 1,210,000		$ 1,846,924

Appendix C:
Key Figures to Exercises and Problems

The following key figures to the exercises and problems for each chapter are provided where they lend themselves to the provision of such figures.

CHAPTER THREE

Exercise 3–1 Restated net income for 20X2 and 20X3 are $3,656,228 and $3,742,737 respectively

Exercise 3–2 Restated retained earnings on opening balance sheet at December 31, 20X2 (i.e., step 1) of $23,494. Retained earnings for 20X2 and 20X3 as restated for comparative purposes at December 31, 20X3 (i.e., steps 2 and 3) of $24,253 and $43,857

Exercise 3–3 Amortization of capital assets of $154,518, monetary loss of $9,340, and retained earnings at December 31, 20X6 of $337,818

Exercise 3–4 Amortization of capital assets of $152,141, monetary loss of $3,810, and retained earnings at December 31, 20X6 of $338,006

Exercise 3–5 1. Realized holding gains of $8,400, unrealized holding gains of $13,200, and retained earnings at December 31 of $27,200

Exercise 3–6 Cost of goods sold adjustment of $23,586

Exercise 3–7 Cost of goods sold adjustment of $17,295

Exercise 3–8 1. Financing adjustment of $13,409
2. Capital surplus arising from revaluation of $254,591

Problem 3–1 Retained earnings of $47,876 after dividends paid of $20,645 and net monetary loss of $355 (i.e., $7,497 – $7,142)

Problem 3–2 Retained earnings of $44,572 after dividends of $19,355 and net monetary loss of $645 (i.e., $4,216 – $3,571)

Problem 3–3 Restated retained earnings of $64,671 and net loss before monetary gains of $8,080

Problem 3–4 1. Monetary loss of $275 and retained earnings of $13,668

2. Net operating income of $1,633, realized holding gains of $13,034, and unrealized holding gains of $4,933

Problem 3–5
1. Retained earnings of $191,000 at December 31, 20X9 and operating net income of $42,000, realized holding gains of $83,000 and net unrealized holding gains of $57,000 for 20X9
2. Capital surplus of $178,000 to give shareholders' equity of $491,000

Problem 3–6
1. Net operating profit of $80,000, realized holding gains of $230,000, unrealized holding gains of $155,000
2. Capital surplus at December 31, 20X6 of $450,000

CHAPTER FOUR

Exercise 4–2
Plant and equipment of $740,000

Exercise 4–3
Common stock of $2,750,000 (i.e., 137,500 shares of no par value issued at $20 each)

Exercise 4–4
Total goodwill charges for year of $1,780,000

Exercise 4–5
2. Purchase price of $1,500,000

Exercise 4–6
1. Capital assets of $6,500,000
2. Capital assets of $7,000,000

Exercise 4–7
2. Total of liabilities side of balance sheet of $13,240,000

Exercise 4–8
2. Land of $1,403,800

Problem 4–1
2. Capital assets of $222,200
3. Capital assets of $198,000

Problem 4–2
2. The total impairment loss or goodwill charges for 20X3 of $47,819

Problem 4–3
2 (ii) Purchase price of $1,080,000

Problem 4–4
2. Goodwill of $540,000 and total of liabilities side of balance sheet of $5,900,000 at January 1, 20X2

Problem 4–5
1. Total of liabilities side of balance sheet of $3,805,000
2. Liquidation dividend of $1,987,000 made up of common stock of $1,000,000 + capital surplus of $100,000 + retained earnings of $887,000

CHAPTER FIVE

Exercise 5–3
2. Net income of Pillow for 20X5 of $94,000
3. Balance on investment account of Sleep at December 31, 20X5 of $282,000

Exercise 5–4
3. Balance on investment account at December 31, 20X4 of $134,000

Exercise 5–5
1. Balance on investment account at December 31, 20X4 of $345,200

Exercise 5–6
3. Balance on investment account at December 31, 20X7 of $140,000

Exercise 5–7
Share of net income from investee company of $60 and retained earnings at December 31, 20X2 of $540,000

Problem 5–1
1. Retained earnings of Peach at December 31, 20X5 of $476,000
2. Retained earnings of Peach at December 31, 20X5 of $494,000

Problem 5–2
2. Retained earnings of Plant at December 31, 20X3 and 20X4 of $1,320,000 and $2,575,000 respectively

Problem 5–3
1. Balance on investment in Class A shares and Class B shares at December 31, 20X5 of $106,000 and $98,000 respectively

Problem 5–5
1. Balance on investment account of $876,500 at December 31, 20X5

CHAPTER SIX

Exercise 6–1   1.   Balance on investment account at December 31, 20X2 of $296,000

Exercise 6–2   1.   Goodwill on acquisition of $16,000 and total of liabilities side of consolidated balance sheet of $621,000

Exercise 6–4   2.   Balance on investment account at December 31, 20X4 of $192,500

Exercise 6–5   2.   Consolidated net income of $460,000

Exercise 6–6   Goodwill on acquisition of $60,000. Total of liabilities side of balance sheet of $1,772,000 including minority interests of $85,000 at December 31, 20X4

Exercise 6–7   Goodwill on acquisition of $220,000 and minority interests at December 31, 20X4 of $1,440,000

Exercise 6–8   Goodwill on acquisition of $40,000 and minority interests at December 31, 20X3 of $90,000

Problem 6–2   Goodwill on acquisition of $60,000. Minority interests of $180,000 and total of liabilities side of consolidated balance sheet of $2,857,000 at December 31, 20X5

Problem 6–3   Goodwill on acquisition of $800,000. Minority interests of $580,000 and total assets on consolidated balance sheet of $11,720,000 at December 31, 20X5

Problem 6–4   Goodwill on acquisition of $60,000. Minority interests of $255,000 and total of a liabilities side of consolidated balance sheet of $3,700,000 at December 31, 20X4

Problem 6–5   Goodwill on acquisition of $25,000. Minority interests of $183,000 and total assets on consolidated balance sheet of $1,997,500 at December 31, 20X5

Problem 6–6   2.   Goodwill on acquisition of $100,000. Minority interests of $725,000 and total of liabilities side of consolidated balance sheet of $8,490,000 at December 31, 20X4

Problem 6–7   Goodwill on acquisition of $120,000. Minority interests of $280,000 and total of liabilities side of consolidated balance sheet of $14,096,000 at December 31, 20X5

CHAPTER SEVEN

Exercise 7–1   Minority interest at December 31, 20X6 of $105,000
Consolidated net income of $215,000 in 20X4 and $290,000 in 20X5

Exercise 7–2   Consolidated net income in 20X4 of $2,090,000 and retained earnings at December 31, 20X4 of $3,930,000

Exercise 7–3   1.   Consolidated retained earnings at December 31, 20X4 of $331,200
              2.   Net Adjustment on consolidated balance sheet for equipment of $11,200

Exercise 7–4   Goodwill on acquisition of $18,000
Net plant and equipment on consolidated balance sheet of $805,500
Total of liabilities side of consolidated balance sheet of $1,463,500

Exercise 7–5   1.   Balance on investment account at December 31, 20X4 of $1,224,000
              2.   Consolidated retained earnings at December 31, 20X4 of $2,592,000

Exercise 7–6   Share of net income from Snare in 20X7 of $33,750
Consolidated retained earnings at December 31, 20X8 of $2,496,250

Exercise 7–7   Goodwill arising on acquisition of $136,000
Consolidated net income before goodwill charges of $289,600 and net plant and equipment on consolidated balance sheet of $975,600

Problem 7–1   2.   Consolidated net income of $245,600 for 20X6 and $258,400 for 20X7

Problem 7–2   1.   Goodwill arising on acquisition of $60,000
Consolidated net income of $442,000

2. Balance on investment account at December 31, 20X7 of $383,000

Problem 7–3 Goodwill arising on acquisition of $400,000
Net plant and equipment on consolidated balance sheet of $11,900,000

Problem 7–4 Net income before goodwill charges of $872,500 and goodwill on consolidated balance sheet at December 31, 20X2 of $212,000

Problem 7–5 Goodwill arising on acquisition of $25,000
Total of liabilities side of balance sheet of $2,117,600

Problem 7–6 Goodwill arising on acquisition of $60,000
Consolidated net plant and equipment on consolidated balance sheet of $1,438,000

Problem 7–7 Goodwill arising on acquisition of $120,000
Minority interests of $204,000 and net plant and equipment on consolidated balance sheet of $1,562,000

Problem 7–8 Goodwill arising on acquisition of $200,000
Minority interests on analysis of equity at December 31, 20X8 of $520,000
Total of liabilities side of consolidated balance sheet in 20X7 of $2,977,000 and $3,237,000 in 20X8

Problem 7–9 Minority interests on analysis of equity at December 31, 20X6 of $180,000
Total of liabilities side of consolidated balance sheet in 20X5 of $1,648,200 and $1,828,000 in 20X6

Problem 7–10 1. Cash receipts from customers of $2,335,000
2. Adjustments to convert figures to cash basis of $385,000

Problem 7–11 1. Cash receipts from customers of $1,353,000 and cash paid to suppliers of $820,000
2. Amounts not expended in cash of $112,000. Adjustments to convert to cash basis of $117,000

CHAPTER EIGHT

Exercise 8–2 Consolidated net income of $1,008,000 and consolidated retained earnings at January 1, 20X1 of $676,500

Exercise 8–3 Goodwill on acquisition of $340,000, consolidated net income of $836,000, and consolidated retained earnings at January 1, 20X3 of $742,000

Exercise 8–4 Minority interests on analysis of equity at December 31, 20X6 of $366,000
Consolidated retained earnings at January 1, 20X6 of $2,490,000
Total of liabilities side of balance sheet of $7,230,000

Exercise 8–5 1. Consolidated net income of $982,000
2. Consolidated retained earnings of $2,982,000
3. Balance on investment account at December 31, 20X4 of $1,485,000

Exercise 8–6 Share of net income from Soda of $76,000
Balance on investment account at December 31, 20X2 of $754,000

Exercise 8–7 Consolidated retained earnings of $588,000 at December 31, 20X4 and $937,000 at December 31, 20X5

Exercise 8–8 Consolidated retained earnings at December 31, 20X7 of $1,314,000 and $1,800,00 at December 31, 20X8

Problem 8–1 Consolidated retained earnings at December 31, 20X3 of $29,500
Consolidated net income of $28,000 and total of liabilities side of balance sheet at December 31, 20X4 of $214,500

Problem 8–2   Goodwill on acquisition of $1,200,000
Consolidated retained earnings at January 1, 20X7 of $7,230,000 and consolidated net income for 20X7 of $5,760,000

Problem 8–3   Goodwill on acquisition of $60,000
Consolidated retained earnings at January 1, 20X8 of $428,000
Consolidated net income for 20X8 of $513,000
Total of liabilities side of consolidated balance sheet at December 31, 20X8 of $2,976,000

Problem 8–4   Total minority interests on analysis of equity at December 31, 20X4 of $216,000
Consolidated retained earnings at January 1, 20X4 of $539,500
Consolidated net income for 20X4 of $650,000

Problem 8–5   Goodwill on acquisition of $80,000
Consolidated retained earnings at January 1, 20X6 of $967,000
Consolidated net income for 20X6 of $1,168,000
Total of liabilities side of consolidated balance sheet at December 31, 20X7 of $4,656,000

Problem 8–6   3. Consolidated retained earnings at January 1, 20X6 of $618,500 and consolidated net income for 20X6 of $527,000
Total of liabilities side of consolidated balance sheet at December 31, 20X6 of $2,430,500

Problem 8–7   2. Retained earnings of Plunge at December 31, 20X1 of $950,000

CHAPTER NINE

Exercise 9–1   3. Balance on investment account at December 31, 20X6 of $454,400 and $604,000 at December 31, 20X7

Exercise 9–2   1. Consolidated net income of $251,000
2. Consolidated retained earnings at January 1, 20X6 of $126,000

Exercise 9–3   Consolidated net income of $326,000 and retained earnings at January 1, 20X8 of $202,000

Exercise 9–4   Consolidated net income of $234,000 and retained earnings at January 1, 20X7 of $238,40

Exercise 9–5   1. After tax consolidated net income of $528,000 made up of $404,000 from Pay and $124,000 from Say
Retained earnings at January 1, 20X8 of $416,000
2. Minority Interests reduced by $2,000, and inventory reduced by $20,000

Exercise 9–6   Consolidated net income of $420,000 made up of $304,000 from Pseudo and $116,000 from Sham
Retained earnings at January 1, 20X7 of $730,400
Future income taxes would be reduced on balance sheet by $17,000

Problem 9–1   1. Consolidated net income of $292,000 and retained earnings at January 1, 20X5 of $107,000
2. Consolidated net income of $291,500 and retained earnings at January 1, 20X5 of $109,000

Problem 9–2   Consolidated net income from Peel and Skin of $293,000 and $217,500 respectively
Retained earnings at January 1, 20X8 of $422,000
Total of liabilities side of consolidated balance sheet of $2,965,000

Problem 9–3   Consolidated net income of $298,000 for Pizza and $204,000 from Salami
Consolidated retained earnings at January 1, 20X7 of $249,000

Problem 9–4   Goodwill on acquisition of $72,000. Consolidated net income of $274,000 and consolidated retained earnings at December 31, 20X6 of $213,000

Problem 9–5   Net income before goodwill charges from Power and Speed of $193,400 and $56,640 respectively
Consolidated retained earnings at January 1, 20X5 of $192,400
Adjusted minority interests at December 31, 20X5 of $73,760

Problem 9–6   Minority interests on analysis of equity at December 31, 20X8 of $200,000
Net income before goodwill charges for 20X8 of $744,000
Consolidated retained earnings at January 1, 20X8 of $654,400
Total of liabilities side of balance sheet of $3,780,000

Problem 9–7   Net income before goodwill charges for 20X5 of $610,000 and $567,600 for 20X6
Consolidated retained earnings at December 31, 20X6 of 1,022,600
Minority interests on consolidated balance sheet at December 31, 20X5 and 20X6 of $238,000 and $282,400

Problem 9–8   Goodwill on acquisition of $120,000
Net income before income taxes of $850,000
Consolidated retained earnings at January 1, 20X5 of $566,250
Minority interests on consolidated balance sheet of $197,500

Problem 9–9   Goodwill on acquisition of $180,000
Net income before income taxes of $1,610,000
Consolidated retained earnings at January 1, 20X8 of $654,400
Minority interests on consolidated balance sheet of $199,600
Total of liabilities side of balance sheet of $3,801,000

Problem 9–10   Goodwill on acquisition of $80,000
Net income before income taxes of $1,240,000 for 20X5 and $1,264,000 for 20X6
Minority interests on consolidated balance sheet of $238,000 for 20X5 and $282,400 for 20X6

CHAPTER TEN

Exercise 10–1   1. Consolidated net income of $329,200 and consolidated retained earnings at January 1, 20X9 of $396,000
2. Minority interests reduced by $3,700

Exercise 10–2   1. Total retained earnings from Page of $560,000 and share of retained earnings from Sage of $166,800 to give total consolidated retained earnings at December 31, 20X4 of $726,800
2. Reduction in minority interests of $8,800

Exercise 10–3   1. Consolidated net income for 20X7 of $1,449,200
2. Consolidated retained earnings at January 1, 20X7 of $698,400

Exercise 10–4   1. Consolidated net income of $345,200 and consolidated retained earnings at January 1, 20X3 of $53,600
2. Minority interests at December 31, 20X3 of $109,200
3. Net reduction in equipment of $14,000

Exercise 10–5   1. The plant and equipment would be increased at December 31, 20X2 by $4,500
2. Reduce capital assets by $15,000

Exercise 10–6   1. Consolidated net income of $738,000 and consolidated retained earnings at January 1, 20X5 of $89,500
2. Reduction in minority interests at December 31, 20X5 of $2,500
3. Net reduction in equipment of $10,000

Exercise 10–8   Total net income before income taxes, minority interests or goodwill charges of $601,000
Consolidated net income of $276,000 and consolidated retained earnings at January 1, 20X5 of $177,000
Minority interests on consolidated balance sheet of $66,500

Exercise 10–9

1. After tax consolidated net income before goodwill charges from Pan of $524,500 and Skillet of $226,500
    Consolidated retained earnings at January 1, 20X6 of $1,010,750
2. Net equipment at December 31, 20X6 of $2,503,000
3. Minority interests at December 31, 20X6 of $295,750
4. Consolidated future taxes at December 31, 20X6 of $335,50

Problem 10–1

1. Share of net income from Sin of $451,000.
2. Balance on investment account at December 31, 20X5 of $2,249,000 and $2,380,000 at December 31, 20X6.

Problem 10–2

Goodwill on acquisition of $36,000
Consolidated net income of $251,400 and consolidated retained earnings at January 1, 20X5 of $204,800
Minority interests and total of liabilities side of balance sheet at December 31, 20X5 of $68,000 and $1,444,200 respectively

Problem 10–3

Total expenses of $1,196,400 for Pisa and $913,000 for Sienna
Consolidated retained earnings at January 1, 20X7 and December 31, 20X7 of $329,000 and $762,200 respectively

Problem 10–4

Goodwill on acquisition of $72,000
Consolidated net income of $633,200 and consolidated retained earnings at January 1, 20X5 of $329,800
Minority interests and total of liabilities side of balance sheet at December 31, 20X5 of $271,500 and $3,824,500 respectively

Problem 10–5

Total expenses for Play and Shuffle of $1,194,000 and $1,034,000 respectively to give consolidated net income (after goodwill charges) of $847,600
Consolidated retained earnings at January 1, 20X5 of $585,200
Minority interests and total of liabilities side of balance sheet at December 31, 20X5 of $345,200 and $3,406,000 respectively

Problem 10–6

Consolidated net income in 20X5 and 20X6 of $302,650 and $576,900 respectively
Minority interests at December 31, 20X5 and 20X6 of $180,400 and $211,600 respectively
Total of liabilities side of consolidated balance sheet at December 31, 20X5 of $1,908,050

Problem 10–7

Consolidated net income of $533,500 and consolidated retained earnings at January 1, 20X6 of $1,142,750
Total of liabilities side of balance sheet at December 31, 20X5 of $4,500,750 respectively

Problem 10–8

Total expenses for Priest and Sermon of $7,400,000 and $2,984,500 respectively to give after tax consolidated net income (after goodwill charges) of $1,201,200
Consolidated retained earnings at January 1, 20X5 of $1,268,800
Minority interests and total of liabilities side of balance sheet at December 31, 20X5 of $703,750 and $7,927,500 respectively

Problem 10–9

Consolidated net income in 20X5 and 20X6 of $427,050 and $550,600 respectively
Future taxes for 20X5 and 20X6 were $686,900 and $659,700
Minority interests sheet at December 31, 20X5 and 20X6 of $465,100 and $518,800 respectively
Total of liabilities side of consolidated balance sheet at December 31, 20X5 of $6,525,050.

Problem 10–10

Income tax expense of Plate of $1,824
Consolidated net income of $2,690,000 and retained earnings at January 1, 20X3 of $2,820,000
Future Taxes on consolidated balance sheet of $234,000

CHAPTER ELEVEN

Exercise 11–1
1. Effective gain of $8,400
2. (iii) Interest expense on the consolidated income statement of $103,700

Exercise 11–2
1. Effective gain of $9,700
2. Bond interest on consolidated income statement of $48,240
4. Bonds on consolidated balance sheet of $299,640

Exercise 11–3
1. Consolidated net income for 20X7 and 20X8 of $136,300 and $169,950 respectively
3. Interest expense on consolidated income statement for 20X8 of $8,120

Exercise 11–4
1. Effective gain of $5,250
2. Interest expense on consolidated income statement for 20X5 of $110,700
3. Balance on investment account at December 31, 20X5 of $532,550

Exercise 11–5
1. Effective gain of $11,700
2. Consolidated interest expense of $15,300

Exercise 11–6
1. (i) Goodwill of $43,000
1. (ii) Minority interests of $183,000

Problem 11–1
1. Balance on the bond asset account in the ledger of Prove at December 31, 20X3 of $28,460
2. Effective gain on purchase of bonds of $800
3. Interest expense appearing on the consolidated income statement for 20X3 of $8,680

Problem 11–2
1. Consolidated net income for 20X4 of $441,400
   Consolidated retained earnings at December 31, 20X4 of $1,085,900

Problem 11–3
1. Purchase price of the bonds was $165,750
2. Effective loss was $27,000
5. The bond interest appearing on the consolidated income statement was $35,000

Problem 11–4   Consolidated net income of $114,885

CHAPTER TWELVE

Exercise 12–1   Goodwill arising from first and second acquisitions of $15,000 and $6,000 respectively
Share of net income from Sway of $7,500 and consolidated net income of $417,750

Exercise 12–2   Goodwill arising from first and second acquisitions of $6,000 and $12,000 respectively
Share of net income from Stamp of $3,800 and consolidated retained earnings at December 31, 20X5 of $258,700

Exercise 12–3   Goodwill on acquisition of controlling interest of $26,000
Consolidated net income for 20X3 of $495,900. Dividend revenue in 20X3 of $3,000

Exercise 12–4   Goodwill arising from acquisition of a controlling interest of $48,000
Dividend revenue of $48,000 and consolidated net income of $4,158,000

Exercise 12–5
4. Play's net income for 20X4 of $204,000
5. Share of net income from Serve of $45,000 and consolidated net income for 20X5 of $278,800

Exercise 12–6
1. Gain on sale of investment of $7,700
2. Balance of $289,200 at July 20X5

Exercise 12–7
1. Balance on investment account after sale of part of the investment of $612,400
2. Gain on sale of investment of $6,900
4. Adjustment to goodwill of $23,000

Exercise 12–8
1. Balance on investment account after sale of part of the investment of $245,600
2. Gain on sale of investment of $3,600
4. Fair market value adjustment on balance sheet of $21,600

Problem 12–1   Goodwill arising from first and second acquisitions of $20,000 and $4,800 respectively
Share of net income from Steal of $7,200 and consolidated net income of $520,480

Problem 12–2   Goodwill arising from first and second acquisitions of $16,000 and $8,000 respectively
Share of net income from Simon of $12,000 and consolidated net income of $207,000
Total of liabilities side of balance sheet of $719,500

Problem 12–3   1. Goodwill on consolidated balance sheet at December 31, 20X5 was $46,000
2. Consolidated net income for 20X4 was $426,000
3. Consolidated net income for 20X5 was $517,250
5. Adjustment to equipment at December 31, 20X5 of $18,250

Problem 12–4   Goodwill arising from first and second acquisitions of $6,000 and $8,000 respectively
Share of net income from Spoon for 20X8 of $6,600 and consolidated retained earnings at January 1, 20X8 of $71,900
Total of liabilities side of balance sheet of $874,550

Problem 12–5   2. Goodwill of $258,000
3. Income from Steer of $12,000 in 20X4
5. Minority interests at December 31, 20X5 of $420,000
6. Consolidated net income of $647,000

Problem 12–6   Goodwill arising on acquisition of controlling interest of $42,000 and on 100% holding of $30,000
Dividends received and share of net income from Scent for 20X4 of $4,000 and $34,800 respectively to give consolidated net income for year of $829,600
Total of liabilities side of balance sheet of $3,311,600

Problem 12–7   3. Income from Stay of $12,000 for 20X4
4. Income from Stay of $44,000 for 20X5
6. Loss on sale of $1,667

Problem 12–8   1. Goodwill on acquisition of $60,000. Minority interests deducted in consolidated income statement of $137,500
Share of net income from Shabby of $112,500 and consolidated net income of $2,022,000
2. Gain on sale of part of investment of $26,750

Problem 12–9   2. Equity sold of $670,000 and sale of retained earnings of $20,000

CHAPTER THIRTEEN

Exercise 13–1   Adjusted goodwill after sale was nil
1. Balance on investment account at December 31, 20X8 of $520,000

Exercise 13–2   1. Negative goodwill of $3,133 from additional issue of shares
Share of net income for 20X7 was $34,400
2. Minority interests of $53,667

Problem 13–1   Goodwill from first acquisition of $5,000
Goodwill from second acquisition was Nil
1. Balance on investment account at December 31, 20X5 of $326,000

Problem 13–2   Goodwill before issue of $12,000
Goodwill after issue of $6,000 (i.e., $8,000 – $2,000)
1. Balance on investment account at December 31, 20X5 of $221,000
2. Effective loss of $2,000

CHAPTER FOURTEEN

Exercise 14–1   1. Consolidated net income of $950,000
2. Share of net income from investee company of $250,000

Exercise 14–2	3.	Deferred gain at December 31, 20X1 and 20X2 of $238,000 and $192,667 respectively
	4.	Net plant after adjustment of $561,030
Exercise 14–3	3.	Amortization expense of $2,400 and gain on sale of plant of recognized in income statement of $1,400
		Plant on consolidated balance sheet of $7,200 less accumulated amortization of $2,400

Exercise 14–4 Contribution to consolidated net income from Swallow was $30,000
Consolidated net income was $386,000
Consolidated retained earnings at January 1, 20X5 was $222,000

Exercise 14–5 Goodwill arising from the analysis of equity of Pistol in Shoot was $48,000
Total consolidated assets of $2,064,000
Minority interests on consolidated balance sheet of $72,000
Consolidated net income of $524,000

Problem 14–1 Consolidated net income $10,816,000
Equipment on balance sheet at December 31, 20X5 of $19,498,000

Problem 14–2	1.	The unrealized profit on the assets transferred to Clay Venture by Able of $180,000
	5.	Operating net income of $1,080 and total net assets on balance sheet of $2,380,000

Problem 14–3 Consolidated total revenues of $9,206,000 and consolidated total expenses of $8,638,000 to give consolidated net income of $568,000
Total of liabilities side of consolidated balance sheet of $3,902,000

Problem 14–4 Goodwill arising from analysis of equity of Push in Strain was $11,800
Total goodwill on consolidated balance sheet was $28,000
Total consolidated assets were $2,808,000
Consolidated net income was $595,200

Problem 14–5 Negative goodwill of $2,000 arose on analysis of the equity of Profess in Show
Consolidated net income was $262,000
Retained earnings at January 1, 20X4 was $538,000
Total consolidated assets were $1,902,000

CHAPTER FIFTEEN

Exercise 15–2 Reportable segments are A, C E and F

CHAPTER SIXTEEN

Exercise 16–1	1.	Purchases from Australian Supplier of Can $1,244,599
	2.	Total loss on exchange for the year ended December 31, 20X2 of $58,208
Exercise 16–2		Loss on exchange at December 31, 20X4 of Canadian $37,023
Exercise 16–3	1.	Loss in 20X6 of $8,713
	3.	Cost of purchases and accumulated amortization of NZ$10,230,000 and NZ$1,990,500 respectively
Exercise 16–4		Net income of Canadian $1,198,714
Exercise 16–5	1.	Net income of Canadian $117,647
	3.	Accumulated translation gain of Canadian $10,825
Exercise 16–6		Balance at December 31, 20X1 of $667,857 after inclusion of net income of $181,818
Problem 16–1	1.	Loss on foreign exchange at December 31, 20X4 of $58
		Gain on foreign exchange at May 31, 20X5 of $305
	3.	Average purchase cost of $32.92 each

Problem 16–2   Cost of goods sold of $6,203,970
                 Gain on exchange of $39,908

Problem 16–3   Retained earnings at December 31, 20X5 of $1,517,933

Problem 16–4   Accumulated gain on translation at December 31, 20X6 of $726,509
                 Retained earnings at December 31, 20X6 of $1,202,527

Problem 16–5   2. Retained earnings at December 31, 20X4 using temporal method of $42,552
                     Total accumulated deferred exchange loss using current method of $62,800

Problem 16–6   Restated common stock of $415,000 and exchange gain of $133,500 with integrated
                 foreign operation
                 Cumulative exchange gain of $23,000 and retained earnings at December 31, 20X6
                 of $752,000 with self-sustaining operations

CHAPTER SEVENTEEN

Exercise 17–1   4. Total cost using cash flow hedge of $500,000

Exercise 17–3   Write-off of time value of bonds at December 31, 20X6 of $766,667
                 Deferred loss on options trading at February 28, 20X7 of $100,000

Problem 17–2   Transfer from comprehensive net income to net income at December 31, 20X6 of
                 $2,857 when classifying as available for sale

CHAPTER EIGHTEEN

Exercise 18–2   1. Transfer of $9,780 to income summary account

Exercise 18–4   2. Interest receivable at December 31, 20X3 of $5,680
                 3. Fund balance at December 31, 20X3 of $110,680

CHAPTER TWENTY

Exercise 20–2   Total receipts of $62,443
                 Total accumulated fund balances at December 31, 20X4 of $12,703

Exercise 20–3   Excess expenses over revenues of $448 for 20X2 and fund balance at December 31,
                 20X2 of $16,502
                 Net assets invested in capital assets of $2,790 (i.e., $13,990 – $11,200)

Exercise 20–4   Operating surplus of $10,000 and total fund balance at December 31, 20X2 of
                 $102,000
                 Net assets at December 31, 20X2 of $177,000

Problem 20–1   Deficit from operations for year of $4,316
                 Total assets at December 31, 20X4 of $31,755
                 Encumbrance reserve of $1,452

Problem 20–2   Total net assets at December 31, 20X2 of $776,400
                 Total surplus from operations for year of $131,300
                 Total fund balances at December 31, 20X2 of $676,400

Problem 20–4   Surplus for year of $132,240
                 Total fund balance at December 31, 20X4 of $1,084,670

Problem 20–5   Surplus from operations for year of $398,305
                 Fund balance at December 31, 20X5 of $3,824,000
                 Net assets invested in capital assets of $2,938,000

Problem 20–6   Fund balances at December 31, 20X4 of $13,250 for the operating fund, $3,724 for
                 the endowment fund, and $11,877 for the building fund
                 Total amount invested in capital assets for the operating fund of $8,600

CHAPTER TWENTY-ONE

Exercise 21–2
1. Goodwill of $120,000 recognized
2. Cash adjustment paid to Rodney of $12,000

Exercise 21–3
1. Cash paid in by Beatrice and Caleb of $52,800 and $64,000 respectively

Exercise 21–4
Shares valued at $162,000 allocated to Tom

Exercise 21–5
Cash paid into capital accounts by Matthew and Nathan of $60,200 and $41,200 respectively
Balances on Matthew's current account at December 31, 20X3 of $58,600

Exercise 21–6
Share of profits for Louis and Mary of $88,640 in 20X2 and $136,000 in 20X3

Problem 21–1
Cash paid into capital accounts by Adam and Seth in 20X3 were $38,000 and $28,500 respectively
Balances on current accounts at December 31, 20X4 were $3,964 for Luke, $8,000 for Adam, and $2,000 for Seth.

Problem 21–2
1. Adjustments to Chan's current account after write-off of goodwill of $111,450
2. Work-in-Process at January 1, 20X4 of $322,000 and total of liabilities side of balance sheet of $1,570,400

Problem 21–3
Net income for year of $615,000 after charging expenses of $379,000

Problem 21–4
Current account balances at December 31, 20X4 of $121,706 for David Johnston, $125,779 for Jeremy McLean, $114,367 for Sandra Davidson, and $66,512 for Martin La Salle

Appendix D:
Using the Computer Program

Software, in the form of worksheet files that use either Excel™ 97 or later to solve consolidation problems, is supplied with this textbook.

Download software from http://www.captus.com/information/afa0937.xls

In order to use this software, you must have Excel™ 97 or later already loaded on your computer. Before you start using this software, it is suggested that you save a copy of the consolid.xls onto a floppy disk for backup purpose and a copy to your hard drive for faster operation. When you are finished working, save your file under a different name (not consolid.xls) to preserve the original blank worksheet file for future use. (You may also copy it again from the floppy disk, if you overwrite the blank worksheet.)

To start using the consolidation software, open the Excel™ application in Windows. Select consolid.xls file by selecting **File | Open** from the pull-down menu bar. Then follow the instructions below.

1. The problems in the book for which you may use the software are marked by 🖳. Read the problem in the book carefully before entering the information into the spreadsheet. Additional problems, not in the textbook, may also be solved using the software if the structure of the problem and available information are similar to the ones in the textbook for which the software may be used.

2. Decide which **method (i.e., Equity Method, Cost Method or the Multiple Acquisition Cost Method** described in Chapter Twelve) is appropriate to the problem, and click on the worksheet tab which is labelled with the same name, or click on the **Menu** button to select one of the methods in that manner.

3. Read the questions in the consolidation software carefully, and respond by entering the appropriate information. Ensure that all the related questions are answered.

4. If a question in the software is not related to your problem or the information is not available, **do not enter anything** for that question. If information has already been entered from a previous problem and still appears, delete that information by selecting that cell and pressing the delete key on the keyboard.

5. Enter data in the shaded areas only.

6. Please note that the years (e.g., 20X4 or 20X5, etc.) must be entered as 2004 or 2005, etc., because the program does not recognize an "X".

7. Enter the date in days, months and years (e.g., 01-Jan-04 or 31-Dec-05, etc.).

8. Enter percentages as decimal numbers (e.g., 80% is entered as 0.8).

9. When the question asks you to provide consolidated statements for two years, these will have to be performed as two separate exercises. First, fill in the required information for the first year, including the individual income statements and balance sheets for that year. Once the consolidation for that year has been completed, fill in the information for the second year. This is necessary because the program will not generate financial statements for both years on one spreadsheet.

10. The program will not always be able to perform the consolidation solely from the information in the question. If certain information is not provided, some minor calculations may be required before all information can be inputted. For example, the retained earnings at acquisition may not always be given and will have to be determined off-line before entering any additional information.

Index